COBOL PROGRAMMING

ALSO FROM TATA McGRAW-HILL

COBOL
Programming
Including MS COBOL and COBOL-85

Second Edition

M K ROY
D GHOSH DASTIDAR
Jadavpur University
Calcutta

Tata McGraw-Hill Publishing Company Limited
NEW DELHI

McGraw-Hill Offices

New Delhi New York St Louis San Francisco Auckland Bogotá Guatemala
Hamburg Lisbon London Madrid Mexico Milan Montreal Panama
Paris San Juan São Paulo Singapore Sydney Tokyo Toronto

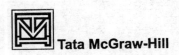
Tata McGraw-Hill

This edition can be exported from India only by the publishers,
Tata McGraw-Hill Publishing Company Limited

ISBN 0-07-460318-3

Published by Tata McGraw-Hill Publishing Company Limited,
7 West Patel Nagar, New Delhi 110 008 and printed at
A P Offset Pvt. Ltd., Zulfe Bengal, Dilshad Garden, Delhi – 110 095

To our Parents

PREFACE TO THIS EDITION

It is a pleasure to note that our "COBOL Programming" has received much
appreciation ever since its publication in 1982. The popularity of the
book is evident from the number of reprints that have run out within a
short span of time. We are grateful to numerous teachers who found the
book useful and recommended it to students.

In preparing this second edition some parts of the book have been
thoroughly revised keeping the overall organisation unchanged. Chapter 1
has been subjected to major revision to make the material up-to-date.
Chapter 11 which deals with table handling has been revised to provide
more explanations. In the case of other chapters only minor changes were
found necessary. A few mistakes which had inadvertently crept into the
previous edition have been corrected. The book has also been enlarged by
the inclusion of two new chapters, namely Chapters 21 and 22.

Chapter 21 primarily deals with MS-COBOL (MS is a trade mark of Microsoft Corporation, U.S.A.) which is generally used for personal computers.
In view of the growing popularity and extensive use of personal computers,
we decided to devote one full chapter on the subject. We believe users of
personal computers will find this chapter handy.

A general reader should read this chapter in the sequence in which it
appears within the book. However, a student who will use a personal
computer for programming practice may like to read at least a part of this
chapter much earlier. We take this opportunity to specify how the chapter
should be used by such a student.

Chapter 21 can be taken as divided into three parts. The first part
provides a general introduction to personal computer environment and
describes procedures for running a COBOL program. It is recommended that
this part be read having completed the first seven chapters of the book.
The second part of Chapter 21 deals with some limitations of MS-COBOL. A
student should use this part as a reference material as and when necessary.
It may also be mentioned in this connection that some of the limitations
listed in this part have been removed in later versions of MS-COBOL. The
third part of chapter 21 is most interesting. In order to enable interactive programming, the ACCEPT and DISPLAY verbs have been substantially
enhanced in MS-COBOL. A new section of data division known as SCREEN

SECTION has also been introduced for this purpose. The concept of interactive programming and the associated MS-COBOL features are introduced in
the third part with the help of several examples. Although these are
special features of MS-COBOL, many other COBOL compilers offer similar
facilities. As such, users working in a different environment may also
find the material useful. This part of Chapter 21 should be read after
having gone through the previous chapters.

COBOL-74 is no longer the latest standard. American National Standards
Institute (ANSI) has accepted a new standard COBOL in 1985. This new
standard known as COBOL-85, is a substantial revision of COBOL-74 and
incorporates many new features to enable improved programming. Although
most of the COBOL compilers being used today follow the guidelines of
COBOL-74, compilers incorporating COBOL-85 features have begun to appear.
All the significant enhancements of COBOL-85 have been discussed in Chapter
22. Many examples and three sample programs illustrating COBOL-85 features
have been included in this chapter.

Discussions on implementation differences had been one of the characteristic features of the book. However, modern COBOL compilers greatly
follow the guidelines of ANSI standard and thereby implementation differences among COBOL compilers have narrowed down substantially. Moreover,
now-a-days COBOL compilers are constructed and marketed by software houses
rather than computer manufacturers. As a result, an identical version of
COBOL is found to be implemented on different computers and some computers
may have different COBOL compilers offered by different software vendors.
Naturally, the materials presented under implementation differences have
lost their significance substantially. We, however, retain these portions
unchanged because they may still be of limited use.

While preparing this second edition we received various kinds of help
from our colleagues, friends and ex-students. We wish to put on record our
sincere thanks to Prof. D.K. Basu, Prof. R. Dattagupta, Dr. Subrata Roy,
Mr. Anirban Mukherjee and Mr. Kalyan K. Majumdar for their valuable sugges-
tions and help in the matter. We are also thankful to Mr. S. Sinha for
preparing the typescript and to Mr. Samaresh Bhattacharya for drawing the
diagrams.

M.K. Roy
D. Ghosh Dastidar

PREFACE

This book is intended for those who are interested in COBOL. It can well serve as a textbook at the undergraduate level where COBOL is included as a part of the curriculum. It can also be used by the participants of the COBOL courses offered under the Continuing Education Programme of the various Indian universities and institutions. Programmers and other computer professionals will also find the book helpful.

A knowledge of computers is not a prerequisite to follow the contents of the book. The various introductory concepts on computer systems and programming are discussed in the first two chapters. The basic aspects of the COBOL language have been introduced in the next five chapters. These have been presented in such a way that having gone through these five chapters, the reader would be able to write, at least, simple COBOL programs. Further details of the basic features as well as other essential features are covered in Chapters 8 to 14. The rest of the book deals with advanced topics.

We faced some difficulty in selecting the material for this book, because there exist different versions of COBOL. The 1974 American National Standard COBOL (called ANSI 74 or ANS 74 COBOL), which is the more recent version of COBOL, includes a number of incompatibilities with the previous version, namely, ANSI 68 COBOL. Most of the compilers that implemented ANSI 68 have been subsequently modified to incorporate some new features but they still retain some old features that are incompatible with ANSI 74 COBOL. Moreover, the ANSI standards leave many features to be defined and implemented by the implementors. As such, in this book, we have taken a middle course. We have assumed a typical implementation of our own and have described the features accordingly. In addition, at the end of each relevant chapter we have discussed the implementation differences of three COBOL compilers, namely, those for B-6700, DEC-10 and ICL-1900. This will help the reader in understanding the nature of differences that exist between one implementation and another. As regards the typical implementation of the text, the description has been based on carefully selected features of ANSI 74 and those of the said three implementations. Moreover, two other implementations, namely, IBM 370 COBOL and NCR VRX COBOL have also been taken into consideration for the said purpose. However, we have not included the implementation differences of these latter named versions, because information regarding IBM 370 COBOL is easily available elsewhere and most of the features as described here do not have much differences with the NCR VRX COBOL. In fact, we find that most of the ANSI 74 features have been faithfully implemented in NCR VRX COBOL.

To avoid any misinterpretation, we would like to spell out clearly the purpose of including implementation differences. The objective is to indicate to the reader where an implementation difference may exist and what its nature may be. The notes given under implementation differences, therefore, point out only some of the important and interesting differences. They certainly do not reveal all differences nor do they show the relative merits and demerits of the said compilers. Moreover, the information given under implementation differences are subject to change as the compilers are normally modified frequently. As such, the readers should not take these notes too seriously. In order to make use of implementation dependent features, one must consult the relevant manuals.

It will be wrong to assume that COBOL is an implementation dependent language. In fact, there are more similarities than differences. The differences arise only when one wants to make specific use of the language elements. A knowledge of implementation differences helps one to avoid writing the implementation dependent code. This makes a program portable so that it can be executed on different machines with minimum change.

COBOL is a powerful language and offers a lot of facilities. The power of COBOL cannot be fully exploited if one learns only a subset of COBOL that enables him to write an application program. This book, therefore, attempts to present the language features with as many details as may be useful. The book also covers a substantial part of ANSI 74. In fact, except for the debugging and communication modules of ANSI 74, all other language features have been included.

We thankfully acknowledge the help that we have obtained from the various published materials, a list of which is given in the bibliography. We are indebted to many of our friends and colleagues with whom we have had discussions regarding the contents and structure of this book. Notable among them are Mr. T.K. Basu of ICL (India) Pvt. Ltd., Mr. A. Banerjee, Mr. A.K. Majhi, Dr. Subrata Roy and Mr. D.P. Sinha. Our special thanks are to Sri Priyatosh Chakraborty for typing the manuscript and to Sri Samaresh Bhattacharya for drawing the figures.

Finally, we would like to include an apology to those readers who belong to the fair sex. In the text we have referred to the programmer or reader as "he". This may be taken to mean "he or she".

ACKNOWLEDGEMENTS

The following acknowledgement is reprinted from the American National Standard Programming Language COBOL, X3.23-1974 published by the American National Standards Institute, Inc.

The authors and copyright holders of the copyrighted material used herein

FLOW-MATIC (trademark of Sperry Rand Corporation), Programming for the UNIVAC I and II, Data Automation Systems Copyrighted 1958, 1959, by Sperry Rand Corporation; IBM Commercial Translator Form No. F 28-8013, copyrighted 1959 by IBM; FACT, DSI 27A5260-2760, copyrighted 1960 by Minneapolis-Honeywell have specifically authorized the use of this material in whole or in part, in the COBOL specifications. Such authorization extends to the reproduction and use of COBOL specifications in programming manuals or similar publications.

COBOL is an industry language and is not the property of any company or group of companies, or of any organization or group of organizations.

No warranty, expressed or implied, is made by any contributor or by the CODASYL Programming Language Committee as to the accuracy and functioning of the programming system and language. Moreover, no responsibility is assumed by any contributor, or by the Committee, in connection therewith.

M K Roy
D Ghosh Dastidar

CONTENTS

1
INTRODUCTION TO COMPUTER SYSTEMS

1.1 DATA PROCESSING

Modern computers can work at very high speeds and at the same time are very reliable. The work that is normally done by a computer is called data processing. Note that there are two words, data and processing. Data are entities that relate to a certain person, task or event. Processing means performing systematic operations upon the data to make them more useful. Such manipulations that a computer can perform on the data include calculation, comparison, reading and writing. Calculation refers to the execution of arithmetic operations, such as addition, subtraction, multiplication and division. Besides calculation, a computer can compare two data to determine which one is greater or to establish whether they are equal or not. Based on the result of the comparison it can also choose one of the two courses of action. Reading is the process of accepting data from some external medium and writing is the reverse process of reading. The results of calculations can be written by the computer onto some medium such as a sheet of paper.

The operations mentioned above are only elementary operations. By combining such elementary operations it is possible for the computer to perform processing that is complex in nature. However, the primary objective of data processing is to take the help of the computer to process some given data in a desired manner. Thus a computer can be called a data-processing equipment which accepts some data as its input and produces some "processed data" as its output. The processed data is often called information.

It is of importance to note that a computer cannot do anything on its own. It must be instructed to do a desired processing. That is why it is necessary to specify a sequence of operations that a computer must perform to solve a data processing problem. Such a sequence of operations written in a language that can be understood by a computer is called a program. It is the program that controls the activity of processing by the computer and the computer performs precisely what the program wants it to do. To enable a computer to execute a program automatically it is necessary that the program must be stored somewhere within the computer in advance. This pre-storing of the program is a fundamental requirement and this is why a computer is often referred to as a stored program computer.

1.2   COMPUTER ORGANIZATION

There are four basic units that constitute a computer.   These are:
    (i)   memory unit
    (ii) central processing unit (CPU)
  (iii) input unit
  (iv) output unit
    Memory or storage unit is the place where the program and data are
stored.   The memory is divided into a number of cells or words.   The
total number of words available in the memory determines the memory
capacity.   The unit that is normally used to express the memory capacity
is K (stands for kilo), which has a value of 1024 (1000 in some cases).
Thus a memory capacity 32K means that the memory consists of 32 × 1024 =
32,768 words.   To identify a particular word in the memory, a unique
number called the address is associated with each word.   Starting with 0,
the natural numbers are used for the purpose of addressing.   Thus if the
memory contains 32K words, the addresses vary from 0 to 32,767.   The
amount of information that can be accommodated in an individual word
depends on the size of the word.   Each word consists of a fixed number
of bits.   A bit can have a value of 0 or 1 and can be physically
represented in the memory as well as in other places of the computer by
means of two "states".   The number of bits in a word is called the
wordlength.   Computers having wordlengths of 8,16,24,32,48 or 64 are
very common.   The computer memory is often called random-access memory
(RAM) because the contents of any word can be accessed (for processing
or for other purposes) in the same amount of time regardless of the
position of the word within the memory.   In addition to the RAM, a
computer may have an additional memory known as read-only memory (ROM).
As implied by the name, the contents of ROM can be used but cannot be
altered by storing new information.   Normally, programs and data that
are essential for the basic functioning of the computer, are stored in
ROM.   The contents of ROM are not wiped even when the computer is switched off.   On the other hand, the contents of RAM get wiped when the
computer is switched off.   The central processing unit (CPU), which is
made entirely of electronic circuits, performs the tasks specified by
the program.   It brings the program instructions from the memory one at
a time and causes the internal circuits to execute the instruction. The
CPU begins the execution of a program with the first instruction.   Once
it has been executed, CPU takes the second instruction from the memory
and executes it.   In this way, instructions are executed by the CPU in
the order in which they appear in the program, until an instruction is
encountered that involves a change in this sequential order of execution.
Such instructions are known as control instructions.   A control instruction may specify alteration in the sequential order either unconditionally or only if certain conditions are satisfied. The input unit
consists of one or more input devices.   Data or program can be entered
into the computer through any one of these devices.   Similarly, the output unit consists of one or more output devices through which the
results of the processing can be obtained.   Some of the devices can be
used for input as well as for output.   Such a device is known as input-

output or I-O device. An input device, an output device, or an input-
output device, is also called a peripheral. More about these peripherals
has been discussed in Sec. 1.5.

In order to make the computer operational, the individual units must
be connected. Connection is necessary for transfer of information from
one unit to another. For example, before an instruction is executed, it
must be transferred from the memory to the CPU. Again, when a read
instruction is executed, data should be transferred from an input device
to the memory either through the CPU or directly. Connection of the
individual units can be done in a variety of ways. Figure 1.1 shows a
popular arrangement known as a unibus structure.

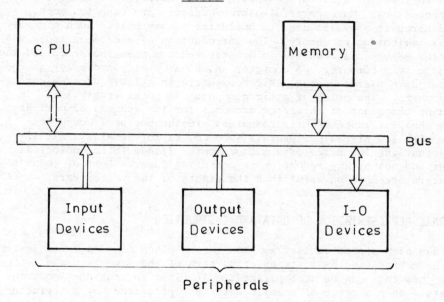

Fig. 1.1.   An Unibus Structure

Bus is something like a highway through which information flows
inside the computer. In reality, it is a set of parallel wires each of
which carries a bit of information. In addition to the wires that carry
data, there must be wires that carry control signals. Moreover, each
memory word is identified by an address. Similarly, each peripheral also
has an identifying address. Naturally, there must be wires to carry an
address as well. In short, a bus consists of data bus, address bus and
control lines. In a unibus structure, as shown in Fig.1.1, there is only
one bus and therefore, only two of the units can use the bus at the same
point of time — one of these units acts as a master and the other as a
slave. This results in a slower performance. Multibus structures are
used in larger computers. Again, there can be structures with more than

one CPU. However, a full discussion on these structures is beyond the scope of this book.

1.3 MICROPROCESSOR AND MICROCOMPUTER

The most spectacular advancement in the field of computer is the development of the microprocessor. A microprocessor is a chip of integrated circuit (IC) which has, within itself, the entire electronic circuits of a CPU. Development of microprocessors evolved with the introduction of 4 bit processors followed by 8 bit processors. Now we have 16 bit as well as 32 bit microprocessors. More powerful microprocessors are expected soon. Integrated circuits are also used to build the memory unit. Such a memory is known as semiconductor memory. The introduction of microprocessors and semiconductor memory has resulted in drastic reduction in the price and the physical size of a computer. A computer which has a microprocessor as the CPU is known as a microcomputer. Microcomputers invariably use semiconductor memory units. The price of a microcomputer is considerably low. In fact, a major component of the price accounts for the associated peripherals. The cheapest range of microcomputers are the personal computers which come with low priced peripherals (see Ch. 21 for details). It is noteworthy that the low price of a microcomputer is due to technological advancement and not by any reduction in computing power. Some of today's microcomputers are more powerful than the giants of the yesteryears.

1.4 INTERNAL REPRESENTATION OF DATA AND INSTRUCTION

From what has been stated earlier we know that a piece of data or an instruction must be represented by a string or pattern of the symbols 0 and 1. Let us now see how this can be accomplished. At first we consider only the numeric data. When a piece of numeric data is represented by a string of 0 and 1 it is called a binary number.

1.4.1 Binary Number System

The number system we normally use to denote numeric values is called the decimal system, which is characterized by the following:

    (i)   there are ten digits 0,1,2, ..., 9 and

    (ii) each digit position in a decimal number has a positional value, such as unit, ten, hundred, thousand, etc., apart from the intrinsic value of the digit in the said position.

Thus the decimal number 4315 consists of the digit 5 in the unit's position, 1 in the ten's position, 3 in the hundred's position and 4 in the thousand's position and its value can be written as

$$4 \times 1000 + 3 \times 100 + 1 \times 10 + 5 \times 1$$
$$\text{or} \quad 4 \times 10^3 + 3 \times 10^2 + 1 \times 10^1 + 5 \times 10^0$$

Note that the positional values are powers of 10 which is called the base or radix of the number system.

The binary number system is exactly like the decimal system except that the base is 2 instead of 10. We have only two digits 0 and 1 and the positional values are powers of 2. As such, in the binary number system, the rightmost position is the unit's position, the second position from the right is the 2's position and proceeding in this way we have the 4's position, 8's position, 16's position, and so on. Now, given a binary number we can very easily find its decimal equivalent in the following manner. Let 110101 be the given binary number. Its decimal equivalent is

$$1 \times 2^5 + 1 \times 2^4 + 0 \times 2^3 + 1 \times 2^2 + 0 \times 2^1 + 1 \times 2^0$$
or 53

"Binary digit" is often referred to by the common abbreviation "bit" which was informally introduced earlier during the discussion on the memory. A binary number consisting of n bits is called an n-bit number. Table 1.1 lists all the 3-bit numbers along with their decimal equivalents. With 3 bits, only 8 ($= 2 \times 2 \times 2$) different patterns of 0's and 1's are possible and from Table 1.1 it may be seen that a 3-bit number can have one of the 8 values in the range 0 to 7. In fact, it can be shown that any decimal number in the range 0 to $2^n - 1$ can be represented in the binary form as an n-bit number.

TABLE 1.1. 3-bit Numbers With Their Decimal Values

3-bit numbers	Corresponding decimal values
000	0
001	1
010	2
011	3
100	4
101	5
110	6
111	7

So far, we have tacitly confined the discussion to only positive integers. In order to include the negative numbers, one bit (usually the leftmost bit) is reserved to represent the sign. There are various ways in which the negative numbers are actually represented internally. The most popular of these is what is known as the 2's complement form. A detailed discussion of the 2's complement form is beyond the scope of the present book and is not necessary for our purpose. All that can be said about it is that in the 2's complement form, any integer in the range -2^{n-1} to $(2^{n-1} - 1)$ may be represented by n bits.

The numeric data need not always be integers, they may have fractional parts as well. Such a number is actually represented within the computer in two parts, the mantissa and the exponent. In fact, if n bits are used to represent a number, some of these represent the mantissa and the remaining bits represent the exponent. The value is determined by

$$\text{mantissa} \times 2^{\text{exponent}}$$

A number represented in this form is known as a floating point binary number. We shall not proceed further with floating point numbers as this again is beyond the scope of this book.

1.4.2 Binary Coding

Numeric data is not the only form of data that should be handled by a computer. Frequently, alphanumeric data are also used in the processing. An alphanumeric data is a string of symbols where a symbol may be one of the letters A B C ... Z or one of the digits 0 1 ... 9 or a special character, such as + - * / , . ( ) = (space or blank) etc. Sometimes the data may consist only of the letters ABC ... Z and the space character. Such data are often referred to as alphabetic data. However, any data must be represented internally by the bits 0 and 1. As such, the alphanumeric and alphabetic data are represented internally by means of what is known as binary coding. In binary coding every symbol that appears in the data is represented by a group of bits. There are quite a few standard sets of coding for the symbols. We shall mention only three of them. These are the 6-bit BCD (Binary Coded Decimal), the 7-bit ASCII (American Standard Code for Information Interchange) and the 8-bit EBCDIC (Extended Binary Coded Decimal Interchange Code). The representations of letters, digits and some special characters in these three codes are shown in Table 1.2.

The group of bits used to represent a symbol is called a byte. To indicate the number of bits in a group, sometimes a byte is referred to as "n-bit byte" where the group contains n bits. Thus a symbol in EBCDIC requires the representation of an 8-bit byte. However, the term byte is commonly used to mean a 8-bit byte and the term character is used to refer to a 6-bit byte. The term character is derived from the fact that in earlier computers 6-bit BCD codes were used to represent the symbols which are also called characters. Nowadays the EBCDIC code has become popular. In this book, the term character will be used to mean both the external symbol as well as the byte that represents it internally. Whether character means the symbol or byte will be apparent from the context and unless specifically mentioned otherwise, a character will mean a 8-bit byte.

The value of an alphanumeric or alphabetic data element is usually the name of some object. Obviously one would not like to perform any arithmetic on such data but one may like to compare them. Now, if we compare the alphabetic values A and B, which one should be greater? For an answer to such questions it is necessary to have some assigned ordering among the character set used by the computer. This ordering is known as the collating sequence. Table 1.2 shows the characters in their collating sequence (ascending order). This sequence may vary depending on the computer and the sequence given in Table 1.2 should be taken as a typical case. Of course, in most collating sequences the following rules are observed:

(i)   Letters are considered in alphabetic order (A < B < C < ... < Z).

(ii) Digits are considered in numeric order (0 < 1 < ... < 9).

(iii) In EBCDIC letters are taken to be smaller than the digits and the space character (Ƀ) is considered to be the smallest of all.

TABLE 1.2   BCD, ASCII, EBCDIC Codes for Different Symbols in EBCDIC Collating Sequence

Symbol	BCD (6-bit)	ASCII (7-bit)	EBCDIC (8-bit)
Ƀ (Blank/space)	01 0000	010 0000	0100 0000
	11 1011	010 1110	0100 1011

(Contd.)

TABLE 1.2   (Conta.)

Symbol	BCD (6-bit)		ASCII (7-bit)		EBCDIC (8-bit)	
<	11	1110	011	1100	0100	1100
(	11	1101	010	1000	0100	1101
$	10	1011	010	0100	0101	1011
*	10	1100	010	1010	0101	1100
)	10	1101	010	1001	0101	1101
;	10	1110	011	1011	0101	1110
,	01	1011	010	1100	0110	1011
>	00	1110	011	1110	0110	1110
=	01	1101	011	1101	0111	1110
"	01	1111	010	0010	0111	1111
+	11	1010	010	1011	1100	0000
A	11	0001	100	0001	1100	0001
B	11	0010	100	0010	1100	0010
C	11	0011	100	0011	1100	0011
D	11	0100	100	0100	1100	0100
E	11	0101	100	0101	1100	0101
F	11	0110	100	0110	1100	0110
G	11	0111	100	0111	1100	0111
H	11	1000	100	1000	1100	1000
I	11	1001	100	1001	1100	1001
-	10	0000	010	1101	1101	0000
J	10	0001	100	1010	1101	0001
K	10	0010	100	1011	1101	0010
L	10	0011	100	1100	1101	0011
M	10	0100	100	1101	1101	0100
N	10	0101	100	1110	1101	0101
O	10	0110	100	1111	1101	0110
P	10	0111	101	0000	1101	0111
Q	10	1000	101	0001	1101	1000
R	10	1001	101	0010	1101	1001
/	01	0001	010	1111	1110	0000
S	01	0010	101	0011	1110	0010
T	01	0011	101	0101	1110	0011
U	01	0100	101	0101	1110	0100
V	01	0101	101	0110	1110	0101
W	01	0110	101	0111	1110	0110
X	01	0111	101	1000	1110	0111
Y	01	1000	101	1001	1110	1000
Z	01	1001	101	1010	1110	1001
0	00	1010	011	0000	1111	0000
1	00	0001	011	0001	1111	0001
2	00	0010	011	0010	1111	0010
3	00	0011	011	0011	1111	0011
4	00	0100	011	0100	1111	0100
5	00	0101	011	0101	1111	0101
6	00	0110	011	0110	1111	0110
7	00	0111	011	0111	1111	0111
8	00	1000	011	1000	1111	1000
9	00	1001	011	1001	1111	1001

A few observations may be made from Table 1.2. If we look at the BCD and EBCDIC codes for the letters we find that the rightmost 4 bits are identical in every case. These 4 bits are called <u>numeric bits</u> and the left-most 2, or 4 bits (as the case may be) are called <u>zone bits</u>. It may also be noted that for the first nine letters A, B, ..., I, the numeric bits represent the values 1, 2, ..., 9 respectively. The same thing is repeated for the next nine characters, J, K, ..., R. For the remaining eight letters S, T, ..., Z, the numeric bits represent the values 2, 3, ..., 9. In all the three cases the zone bits are same for every letter in the group.

1.4.3 Coding for Numeric Data

A numeric data need not necessarily be represented in pure binary as describ-ed earlier. It may also be represented in the EBCDIC, ASCII or BCD as a string of digits. Essentially, such an internal representation retains the decimal form of the data and only the individual digits are coded. In the case of such decimal representation, the sign of the data is commonly repre-sented by the zone bits of the rightmost character. If the data is not an integer and has a fractional part, it is usually stored as an integer, ignoring the decimal point. The effect of the assumed decimal point is taken care of in the program at the time of operating on the data.

Thus we find that the numeric data may be represented internally in either of the two forms —binary and decimal. Therefore, it is worthwhile to make a comparison of these two forms to find out their advantages and disadvantages. Since we would like to input data and output results in decimal, the decimal form is preferable so far as the input-output is con-cerned. However, except a few, most of the computers cannot directly operate on decimal numbers. Therefore, the program should be written in such a way that before an arithmetic operation, the decimal numbers are converted from decimal to binary and after the operation the result is converted back from binary to decimal. Such conversions at every arithmetic operation has an adverse effect on the computation time required and also increases the complexity of programming. The complexity of programming may be decreased by providing ready-made programs for such conversion so that these may be included by the user in their programs. However, nothing can be done to reduce the computation time. Therefore, as a general rule, it may be suggested that external data be read in the decimal form. Then these may be converted to binary once for all. Having completed the operations, the final results may be converted from binary to decimal so that the output is in the decimal form. This would make the operations faster as conversion is not necessary at every stage. However, if the volume of arithmetic required is not much, the decimal representation may be used throughout the processing.

1.4.4 Operation Codes

We have so far discussed only the internal representation of data. However, as has been pointed out earlier, the entire program needs to be stored in the computer memory before the execution starts. For the purpose of storage and execution the instructions have to be coded as strings of the bits 0 and 1. For a given computer system, the codes for the various instructions are fixed. It is not necessary for our purpose to know the formats for the coded instructions and as such no further discussion is made on the subject. It is sufficient to know that the instructions or commands that constitute a program are also represented internally by strings of bits.

1.5 COMPUTER PERIPHERALS

Computer peripherals are the means of communication between the external world and the computer. Because of this important characteristic there have been very significant developments in peripheral devices. A wide range of peripherals with varying capabilities are now available in the market. The range is so large that it is not possible to include even a brief account of all of these within the framework of the present book. Only those peripherals that are commonly found with general purpose computers are described below.

1.5.1 Card Reader

At one point of time card readers were the most popular input devices. Today there are only handful of computer installations where cards are still used. The main reason for the card readers to become outdated is the availability of more convenient and low-cost alternatives. Data captured in the form of rectangular holes punched on a card can be fed into the computer through the card reader. The punched card, which is the medium in this case, is 19.3 cm in length, 9.5 cm in width and 0.018 cm in thickness. The card is divided into 80 columns marked by the numbers 1 to 80 from left to right. The card is again divided into 12 rows numbered 12,11,0,1,2,3,4, 5,6,7,8 and 9 from top to bottom. Only one character can be punched on one column. The digits are represented by punching just one hole in the corresponding row position. The alphabets are represented by codes requiring a combination of two holes in two of the row positions. The codes are as follows. For A to I the combination is 12, the respective row positions of which are 1 to 9. For J to R the combination is 11, the respective row positions of which are again 1 to 9. For S to Z the combination is 0, the row positions of which are 2 to 9 respectively. In the case of special characters a combination of two or three holes is used. The codes for the special characters are not universal and may vary depending on the computer. However, the representations of digits and letters are standard. The card codes are often called Hollerith codes after H. Hollerith who first used punched cards to handle the U.S. census data in 1880. Data can be captured on cards by punching them through a card punching machine.
   Although the data are supplied to the card reader in the form of a deck of cards, the card reader only reads the cards one after another. Thus the third card can be read only after the first two have been read. In other words, a card reader reads the cards in a sequential manner.
   The speed of a card reader can vary depending on the model. Usually, the speed ranges between 300 to 1200 cards per minute (cpm).

1.5.2 Printer

The purpose of a printer is to produce the results of processing on sheets of paper. There are many types of printers but they fall into one of the

two categories — impact printers and non-impact printers. In the case of
an impact printer, an inked ribbon exists between the print head and paper,
and characters are printed by the head striking the ribbon. Non-impact
printers use techniques other than the mechanical method of head striking
the ribbon. Thermal printers, electrostatic printers and laser printers
are examples of non-impact printers. Being able to eliminate mechanical
operations, these printers are very fast. However, these are not yet very
popular because of high cost and the requirement of a special kind of paper.
We shall, therefore, limit our discussion to impact printers only.

Impact printers can be classified into two categories — line printers
and serial printers. A line printer can print an entire line in a single
operation while a serial printer can print only one character at a time.
Line printers are much faster and costlier devices compared to serial
printers. Thus serial printers are generally used with small microcomputers
(especially personal computers) and line printers are used with larger
systems.

1.5.2.1   LINE PRINTER

The printing mechanism in a line printer may be different from that in
another model. In a chain printer several sets of type faces are fixed on
a horizontally-moving continuous chain. In a drum printer, a complete set
of type faces for each print position is embossed on a drum which rotates
on a horizontal axis. The ribbon lies in between the paper and the chain
or the drum. Behind the paper a set of hammers (one for each print position) are located. When the correct character moves past a print position,
the corresponding hammer strikes the paper from behind and this causes
printing.

A print line for most line printers consists of 132 print positions
although printers with a different number of print positions are also available. The output medium for a line printer is continuous stationery in fan-
fold form. At each fold, a line of perforations appears to make pages out
of the stationery. The width of each page is equal to the width of the
stationery and is in the range of 20 to 35 cm, with 30.5 cm being most
common. The length of a page is equal to the distance between two consecutive lines of perforations and is generally 25.4 cm but can have any other
value. Lines of small round holes appear on the two edges of the stationery
to enable its mounting and movement on the printer. Once a line is printed,
the paper is moved up so that the next line can be printed in the following
line position. It is possible to advance the paper by more than one line
by specifying the same in the program. The programmer can further specify
whether the line spacings should be given before or after the printing of
the current line. The facility for the total suppression of spacing is
also available. Further carriage control facilities can be obtained through
the carriage control tape. The carriage control tape is actually a piece
of paper tape whose length is equal to the length of the stationery used
for printing. In fact, while preparing the carriage control tape, a
slightly longer tape is taken so that when the two ends of this tape are
subsequently gummed together to make it an endless loop, the actual length
can be equal to the length of the stationery. The tape is divided into 12
channels numbered 1 to 12. By means of a small punching machine, it is
possible to punch a hole in a channel anywhere along the length of the tape.

Traditionally, a punching in channel 1 corresponds to the top of the page (the position where the first line in a page is to be printed). In a similar manner, channel 12 corresponds to the bottom of the page. Any intermediate position can be indicated by having punchings in other channels. When the endless carriage control tape is mounted on the line printer, a command like "advance to channel 2" advances the paper so that it is positioned corresponding to the punching in channel 2. Figure 1.2 shows a carriage control tape against a page of stationery.

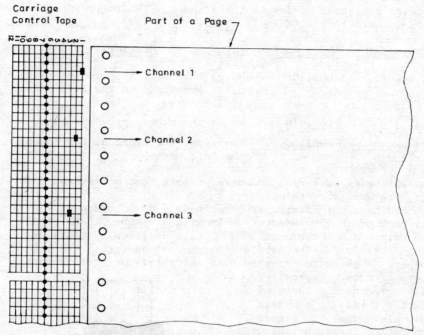

FIG. I.2. Carriage Control Tape with Continuous Stationery

Modern line printers include a microprocessor for the purpose of control. This microprocessor in addition to its other functions, eliminates the need of the carriage control tape described above. Codes equivalent to the punching in the carriage tape are kept in a store to meet the requirements of carriage control.

The speed of a line printer is measured by the number of lines it can print in a minute (line per minute [1pm]). Line printers in the range of 300 to 1400 1pm are very common.

1.5.2.2 SERIAL PRINTERS — DOT MATRIX AND DAISYWHEEL PRINTERS

The print head of a serial printer can print only one character at a time. The head moves along the line as the characters are printed. Depending on the width of the stationery used (25 to 35 cm), a serial printer can print a maximum of 74 to 132 characters in a line. The stationery can be either continuous stationery (as described in connection with line printers) or it can be a separate sheet of paper. The print head of a serial printer is generally capable of moving left to right as well as right to left so that bidirectional printing is possible. Control operations can be performed by sending special character codes to the printer. The following shows important control characters with ASCII codes.

Control character	ASCII Code	Meaning
Carriage Return	0001101	Moves the print head to the first print position on the left hand side.
Line Feed	0001010	Moves the paper up by one line.
Form Feed	0001100	Positions the paper at the top of the next page.

Two common varieties of serial printers, namely, dot matrix and daisy-wheel printers, are described below.

The print head of a dot matrix printer consists of a column of 7 or 9 small needles, each of which can move freely within a tube. Each needle can be used to print a dot corresponding to its position by means of "hammer" action that forces the needle to come out and press the ribbon against the paper. A character printed by a dot matrix printer appears as a matrix pattern of dots. Typically, a character is formed by 7 columns of dots. A character formed to a matrix of 7×5 dots is also popular. Figure 1.3 shows a character formed by selected dots in a 9×7 matrix. However, note that a character is printed column by column and not all at once. To start with, needles print the necessary dots of the first column. The head then moves to the next column position to print the required dots in the said column. In this way, seven head movements are required to print a character. The speed of a dot matrix printer lies in the range of 80 to 220 characters per second (cps). The quality of this type of printing is poor because the characters appear as patterns of dots. To improve the quality, a more dense matrix is used. Such dot matrix printers are known as near letter quality

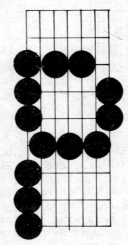

FIG. 1.3 Printed Image of a Character in 9×7 Matrix

<u>printers</u> and their print head contains 18 or more needles. The matrix patterns are usually 18×36 or more. Most near letter quality printers operate in one of the two modes — draft mode (9×7, for example) and letter quality mode (18×36, for example). In letter quality mode, the speed is usually 50 to 100 cps. Higher speed is achieved when the printer is used in draft mode.

The print head of a daisywheel printer is a daisy shaped flat disk of plastic or metal. Like the petals of a daisy, the disk has 96 spokes coming out of it in every direction. A character is embossed at the end of each spoke allowing the daisywheel to have 96 different characters. It is possible to replace one disk by another and thereby a varied choice of character fonts is possible. The disk is mounted on a carriage which can move horizontally. To print a character the carriage is first positioned. The disk is then rotated to bring the spoke containing the desired character in front of the ribbon and paper. An electro-mechanical hammer then strikes the spoke from behind; and the spoke bends and strikes the ribbon making the print of the character. The daisywheel printers are slower compared to dot matrix printers. The usual speed is in the range of 25 to 60 cps. However, the quality of printing is excellent. Figure 1.4 shows the disk of a daisy-wheel printer. Some printers use a golf ball instead of a daisywheel. In this case, type faces are embossed around the golf ball. Though expensive, the golf ball is more durable than the daisywheel.

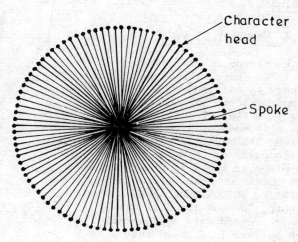

Fig. 1.4. Daisywheel

1.5.3 Keyboard and Visual Display Unit

The most common input device in modern computers is the keyboard. The keyboard of a computer is similar in appearance to that of a typewriter. There are a few additional keys for control purposes (see Ch. 21 for details). The keyboard contains a microprocessor within itself which controls the operations of the keyboard. Input is done by typing the characters on the keyboard.

The keyboard is normally accompanied by a visual display unit (VDU) which has a television-like screen. Characters can be displayed on this screen. A typical screen can hold 25 lines each of 80 characters. Some VDU can display in colour while others can display only in black and white. The latter type of displays are known as <u>monochrome</u> display units.

As the character keys are pressed on the keyboard, the characters are also displayed on the screen. This is known as an echo and it enables us to see the characters being passed to the computer as input. The screen always displays a special symbol known as the <u>cursor</u>. Its position on the screen denotes where the next character, when <u>typed</u>, will be displayed. As the characters are typed, the cursor automatically moves towards right ·always denoting the next input position. When the cursor reaches the end of a line or when the 'enter key' (see ch. 21) is pressed, the cursor is positioned at the beginning of the next line.

Figure 1.5 shows a VDU and keyboard. Note that the VDU can be used separately as an output device to display any output from the computer. A VDU and a keyboard are together called a <u>terminal</u>.

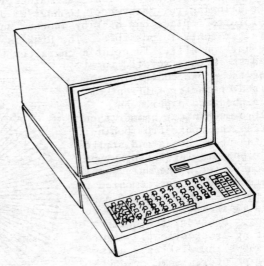

FIG. I.5, Visual Display Device Unit

1.5.4 Magnetic Disk

Unlike the peripheral devices described above, a disk drive can be used as an input as well as an output device. The medium in this case is a flat circular plate generally made of aluminium and coated with magnetic material like ferric oxide or chromium oxide. The plate is known as a disk which must rotate continuously within the drive at constant speed. One or both sides of the disk can be used to record data magnetically. Each surface is divided into a number of concentric <u>tracks</u> and each track is again <u>divided</u> into a number of <u>sectors</u>. Each sector has an identifying address. This address consists of the track number and sector number. Usually tracks are assigned consecutive numbers starting with 0 for the outermost track. If more than one surface is used, the surface number should also be included in the sector address. Figure 1.6 shows the layout of tracks and sectors on a disk surface. In some disks the 'sectoring' can be altered by a system software (discussed later). Such disks are known <u>soft-sectored disks</u>. Alteration in this context is limited to changes in the number and capacity of the sectors, keeping the total number of bytes unchanged. As opposed to the soft-sectored disks, there are <u>hard sector disks</u> where the sectors appears as slots on tracks and cannot be altered.

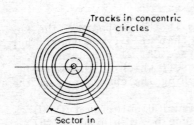

FIG. I.6. Tracks and Sectors on Magnetic Disks

Information to be stored on a disk by a single instruction must start from the beginning of a sector. If required, consecutive sectors can be used to store the information; but if the said information does not require an integral number of sectors, the remaining portion of the last sector is left unused.

The fact that each sector has an identifying address, is a major advantage of a disk drive as a peripheral device. In most peripheral devices, the information must be stored onto or retrieved from the medium in a sequential fashion. In the case of a disk, the information need not necessarily be accessed sequentially. This is why disk drives are often called random-access or direct-access devices.

The disk technology has been upgraded constantly and various kinds of disk drives are available in the market. In the following discussion, the conventional disk drives are described first. This is followed by a description of two very important developments.

1.5.4.1 *CONVENTIONAL DISK*

Generally, there is one read/write head for each surface of the disk. The head can move horizontally over the surface to any track position. It does not touch the surface but only floats on an arm. Sometimes, instead of a single disk, multiple disks are used. Such a stack of disks which provides more recording surfaces, is known as a disk pack (Fig. 1.7). It is important to note that all the heads move in unison, and as such, information can be accessed from the corresponding tracks (e.g., track 1) on all the surfaces without moving the arm. Such a group of corresponding tracks is known as a cylinder, and obviously there will be as many cylinders as there are tracks on each surface. As an example, let us consider the following specifications for a diskpack.

Number of surfaces	=	20
Number of tracks/surface	=	400
Number of sectors/track	=	60
Number of bytes/sector	=	180
Transfer rate	=	500 KB (kilo bytes)/s
Average seek time	=	30 ms
Average latency	=	10 ms

Obviously, there are 400 cylinders each consisting of 20 tracks. The total storage capacity is $20 \times 400 \times 60 \times 180 =$ 86.4 MB (megabytes = 10^6 bytes).

The term average seek time requires a little explanation. In order that read/ write can commence from a specified disk address, the head must move to the desired track. The amount of time required for the movement of a head is called seek time. Obviously seek time is not fixed, instead, it depends on the distance to be traversed by the head to reach the desired track. This is why seek time is quoted in terms of average value. When the read/write head has

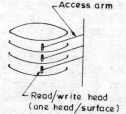

FIG. 1.7   Read/Write Heads in a Diskpack

moved to the correct track, there is a rotational delay in getting the specified sector beneath the head. This rotational delay is called latency. Average latency is taken to be half the time required for one revolution of the disk.

The above mentioned description relates to only one class of disks known as moving head disks. As opposed to these, there are fixed head disks where one head is provided for every track. This eliminates the requirement of head movement and thereby reduces the seek time to zero. However every head adds to the cost, thus making this drive an expensive device. Another disadvantage of fixed head drives is that the disk is not removable from the drive. In the case of moving head drives, the disk (or disk pack) can be removed and replaced by another disk (or disk pack).

The diameter of a disk is generally 35.6 cm (14 inches). Usually the storage capacity lies in the range of 20 to 1000 MB, and transfer rate lies in the range of 300 to 800 KB/s. The typical ranges for seek time and latenacy are 30 to 40 ms and 5 to 10 ms respectively.

1.5.4.2 WINCHESTER DISK

Winchester is the name of a disk technology that provides solutions to various problems in the conventional disks. For example, occasional contacts between the head and disk surface, during start and stop, is a major problem in conventional disks. In Winchester disks this contact has been properly planned. The head has been designed to provide a stable 'flight', with take off from the surface when the drive is turned on and landing on the surface when it is turned off. The disk surface is lubricated to prevent damage and an outside track is marked as a landing zone where the head rests when the disk is not in motion. The technology provides for greater precision, increase in the number of tracks per surface, as well as increase in the number of bytes per track.

A Winchester disk drive is a sealed unit that houses the disk pack as well as the heads. As such, the disk pack cannot be removed and replaced. While this is a disadvantage, its main advantage is its low price compared to the conventional disks. Moreover, being a sealed unit, it is almost free from any dirt and hardly requires any preventive maintenance. Common varieties of Winchester disks come in 13.3 cm ($5\frac{1}{4}$ in.), 20.3 cm (8 in.) or 35.6 cm (14 in.) in diameter. The storage capacity lies in the range of 20 to 1000 MB. It should, however, be noted that disk technology is being constantly upgraded and these figures are a subject to change.

1.5.4.3 FLOPPY DISK

Floppy disks are significantly different from conventional disks. These are made of mylar and are flexible. The size is also very compact. The most common varieties are 13.3 cm ($5\frac{1}{4}$ in.) in diameter. Floppies (also called diskettes) are often distinguished as single sided or double sided, depending on whether recording is done on one or both the sides. Floppies also differ in the amount of information that can be stored on one side. In this respect these are distinguished as single density or double density. A double sided double density (DSDD) floppy can hold about 1.2 MB of information.

The floppy drive is of a moving head variety, and therefore, the floppy can be removed and replaced by another. However, a number of differences with conventional moving head disks exist. First of all, a floppy is a single disk encased in a cardboard/plastic jacket. The floppy is inserted into the drive with the jacket on and the floppy rotates within the jacket. Another important difference is that the head actually contacts the surface during reading/writing, though in other times it is lifted up from the surface. In order that the head can contact the surface, there is a small oblong slot in the jacket. Fig. 1.8 shows a floppy disk.

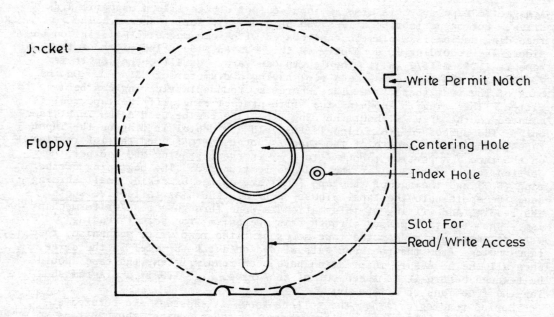

Fig. 1.8. Floppy Disk

The hole at the centre is to allow a spindle to lock the floppy so that it can rotate. The index hole is used to recognize the starting sector of any track. Imagine a line passing through the centre and the index hole. The line indicates the beginning of each track. (It may be noted that some kind of index mark is present in all varieties of disks.)

The purpose of the write permit notch is to protect valuable information recorded on the floppy from accidental damage. If this notch is covered with an opaque sticker, writing is not allowed on the floppy; only reading is possible. If the notch is not covered, reading as well as writing is possible. Floppy drives and floppies are inexpensive. At the same time, floppies offer a number of advantages. These are exchangeable. The storage capacity is high compared to its size and weight. Moreover, these are very portable. Because of these, floppy disks have found universal acceptance as cost effective and convenient alternative for cards. To capture basic input data onto floppies, an off-line (i.e., not connected with the computer) device called data-entry machine is available. This is a microprocessor-based machine with a keyboard, a floppy drive and a visual display unit. Data typed through the keyboard is recorded on the floppy. The display unit in most of the data entry devices provides a rolling display of only the last few characters entered through the keyboard. But this is quite sufficient for the purpose of seeing what data is being entered.

1.5.5 Magnetic Tape Drive

A magnetic tape drive is also an input-output device like a magnetic disk drive. But magnetic tape drives can provide only serial access. The recording medium is a plastic tape coated with some magnetic material on one side. The recording is done only on this coated side. The width of the tape is 1.27 cm (1/2 in.). The length can vary. Usually, the length is 731.5 m and the tape comes in a reel having a diameter of 25.4 cm. On the back of the reel there is a place where a round plastic ring can be fitted. This ring is known as the write-protect ring. If the tape reel is mounted on the drive without the ring, the tape can be used as an input tape only. The purpose of this ring is to avoid accidental writing on the input tapes. The entire length of the tape is not used to record the information on the tape. A portion (about 3 to 5 m) in the beginning and another portion (about 3 to 5 m) at the end are left unused. The beginning of the tape (BOT) and the end of the tape (EOT) are marked by fixing small shining adhesive spots onto the tape. These spots are known as reflective spots. The reading and writing of information is done through a read/write mechanism. When the tape passes through this mechanism, the actual reading/writing takes place. As the tape moves past the read/write mechanism, the tape unwinds from the reel and gets winded on a take-up reel in the drive. When all the necessary information have been read/written, the tape should be rewound before it is taken out of the drive. Fig. 1.9 is a diagram showing the functions of a tape drive.

During reading/writing, the rollers known as capstans are rotated at constant speed. The pinch rollers press the tapes against the capstans so that the tape also moves at constant speed. The purpose of the vacuum columns is to allow some slack in the tape and to isolate the reels from the capstan drives.

The magnetic tape is divided lengthwise into narrow strips called tracks. The number of tracks may be 7 or 9 depending on the tape drive. Actually 9-track tape drives have been introduced in recent times. Earlier tape drives used 7 tracks only. Data coded in the form of 7 or 9 bits are stored across the tracks to form a frame (Fig. 1.10). To detect and prevent possible errors only 8 (6 in the case of 7-track tapes) of the 9 tracks contain data.

The ninth/seventh track is called the parity track and contains a bit to make the total number of one bit in a frame odd or even. Some tape drives use even parity, some use odd parity, and some allow the choice of either even or odd parity by means of a switch. The density of the recorded information may vary from 80 to 2500 bytes per cm. Most common densities are 320 and 640 bytes per cm (800 and 1600 bytes per inch [bpi]). In the case of a 9-track tape, a byte can store a character in EBDIC, ASCII or BCD.

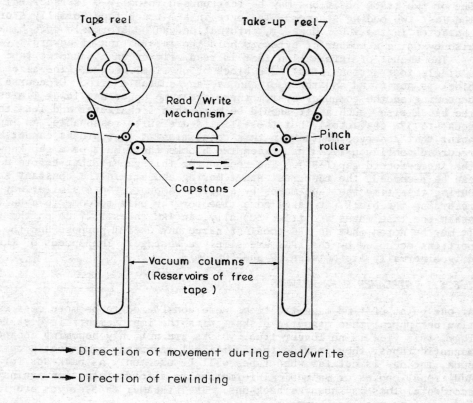

FIG. 1.3.   Magnetic-tape Unit

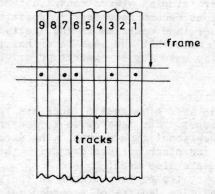

FIG. 1.10.   Magnetic-tape Frame

One or two track positions may be left unused (usually 0 is recorded) for the last two coding schemes. The byte in a 7-track tape normally stores a character in the BCD. However, information can be stored in pure binary also by using a number of bytes to hold the information of a word.

The amount of information that is read/written on a magnetic tape by a single instruction is called a block or physical record. The size of the block is not fixed and the user can use any suitable size. Of course, depending on the computer system there are some upper and lower limits on the block size (such as it should be more than 1 character and less than or equal to 32K character), but these limits are quite reasonable. An important point that deserves mention in this connection is that blocks cannot be recorded continuously. In between two blocks there must be a gap known as the inter-record gap (IRG). The reason for this gap is that before a block can be recorded, the tape must start moving and attain the constant speed. During this time the tape moves by a slight amount. In a similar way after recording the block, it takes some time for the unit to come to a halt and again the tape moves a little. Usually, an IRG takes 1.27 cm on the tape. It may be noted that an IRG does not serve any useful purpose and the portions occupied by the IRGs are simply a wastage. The speeds of the tape drives normally lie between 85 and 508 cm/s.

1.5.5.1 STREAMER TAPE DRIVE

At one point of time magnetic tapes were considered to be more cost effective peripheral than magnetic disks. With the improvements in disk technology, this view is no longer true. Disks are not only becoming cheaper than magnetic tapes, they provide the additional advantage of direct access. As such, the day is not far when tapes will be used only as back-ups for disks. Additional copies of valuable information to afford protection against accidental loss is known as back-ups. The streamer tape drives are ideal for creating such back-ups.

In traditional tape systems, inter-record gaps (IRG) are created because of start-stop in between recordings. In streamer tape drives, large volume of data (for example, from a disk) can be recorded without stopping the tape. This eliminates the gaps and thereby provides better utilization of tape space. If necessary, the streamer tape drive can be operated in a start-stop mode. However, stoping always causes a tape overrun, and slow reverse and forward motions become necessary to position the tape correctly. Therefore, when a streamer tape operates in the start-stop mode, the speed comes down drastically. Note that the same tape that is used for conventional tape drives is also used for streamer tape drives.

1.5.5.2 TAPE CARTRIDGE

A new introduction in the area of magnetic tapes are special digital cassettes, called cartridges. The tape drive for cartridges are much simpler compared to conventional tape drives. The vacuum columns are not required. The capstons and pinch rollers can drive the tape at constant speed. Other techniques are also used.

Usually, there are one, two or four tracks in the tape, which is either 0.38 or 0.64 cm in width. The density of recorded information lies in the range of 314 to 628 bits/m. The speeds lie between 7 to 100 cm/s. Commonly available cartridges can accommodate upto 65 MB of information. Cartridges are inexpensive and suitable for use with small computers.

1.6   COMPUTER SOFTWARE

The terms hardware and software are frequently mentioned in connection with computers. The physical devices that constitute a computer are collectively called the hardware. In fact, so far we have described only the hardware part of a computer. However, computers are also equipped with complementary products, collectively known as software. These products are nothing but programs and any program usable on a computer can be a part of the software.

Software can be broadly classified as application software and system software. Programs developed for solving specific problems through computer usage, come under the umbrella of application software. For example, a program that calculates the pay for individual employees of a business organization is an application software. System software refers to programs that provide the user with more facilities than those available in the bare machine. Compilers and operating systems are examples of system software. These will be described later. Today, system software plays as important a role as the hardware, and the two together constitute the computer system used for problem-solving.

It will be wrong to assume that a piece of software must always be in the form of a stand-alone program that can run independently. Instead, it can also be in the form of a routine. Like a program, a routine is also a sequence of instructions, but a routine cannot be executed alone. It must be executed in conjunction with other routines/programs. Generally, a routine is designed to accomplish a specific function that may be needed on several occasions.

An application software can be either a personal software or a software package. A personal software as indicated by the name, is a software designed and developed to meet requirements of a single user. For example, a software that has been developed for the management of the inventory of a particular industrial organization, is a personal software of that specific house. On the other hand, there can be a generalized software for inventory management which can be used by several industrial organizations. Such a software is known as a package. An essential characteristic of a package is that there should be multiple users. Naturally, a software package should include facilities so that it can be tuned to the requirements of a particular user. This is often done by providing additional data for the purpose of controlling the operations of the package.

The following is a brief account of some important constituents of system software.

1.6.1   Assemblers and Compilers

It was mentioned earlier that a program consists of a sequence of instructions. A specific computer has a specific set of instructions that are fixed during the design of the machine. This set of instructions constitutes what is commonly called the machine language and the instructions in a program must be drawn from the set. A machine language instruction normally consists of the operation code and the actual addresses of the operands in the memory. Both the operation code as well as the actual addresses should be given in binary. Obviously the writing of programs in a machine language is not convenient. Modern computer systems offer the facility of programming in more convenient languages which can be broadly classified into the two following groups:

    (i) assembly language
    (ii) high-level language

Assembly language is similar to machine language in the sense that in most of the cases there exists a one to one correspondence between the machine language instructions and the assembly language instructions. However, instead of binary codes one may use symbolic codes in the assembly language and obviously this is an advantage. For example, one might use the symbolic code ADD instead of a binary code, say 00011, to mean the operation of addition. In a similar manner, the programmer may also use symbolic names instead of actual addresses. However, like the machine language, the assembly language is very much dependent on the system and differs from machine to machine.

The high-level languages provide the user with the facility of writing programs more easily as these languages are designed precisely with this aim. FORTRAN, COBOL, ALGOL are some of the high-level languages. A program written in languages other than the machine language is called a source program. Whether it is an assembly-language program or a high-level language program, the program cannot be executed directly. The source program should be translated to a machine language program known as the object program. The translation of a source program to the object program is accomplished by means of a software which accepts the source program as its input and produces the object program as its output. The translator program is called an assembler if the source language is the assembly language. If the source is a high level language, the corresponding translator program is called a compiler.

Apart from the ease of program development, a high-level language has an advantage over the assembly language. While the assembly language is machine dependent, a high-level language is not so. A program written in a high-level language can be executed on any computer provided the compiler is available.

1.6.2 Linker and Loader

An object program produced by a language translator (compiler or assembler) may not be good for execution. To appreciate why this is so, let us think of a situation when a large program has been developed in parts so that the program is in the form of a number of routines. Let us also assume that each of these routines has been separately translated. Now, the object routines (known as object modules) must be combined together to form a load module (also known as run unit) which is finally executed. The software that accomplishes the job of linking the object routines into one load module, is known as linkage editor or simply linker.

Linking may also be necessary in a simple situation when the program is a single unit. This is due to the fact that certain complicated operations performed by a program are supported by routines provided within system software (IOCS routines described below, are examples of such routines). These routines are called <u>library routines</u>. Linking a program with the library routines is essential.

In some computer systems, the translator is versatile enough to accomplish translation as well as linking if the source program is a single unit or if all the source routines are given to the translator together as a single entity. In such a situation, the output of the translator is a load module rather than an object program.

The source program, the object program as well as the load module must be placed on some medium. Generally, a disk is preferred for the last two. The source program can appear on any medium from which input is possible (e.g., cards or disk). At the time of execution, the load module is loaded into the memory of the computer by means of a system software known as a <u>loader</u>. Note that unless the program is in the memory, it cannot be executed. Sometimes, linking and loading is done by a single software known as the <u>linking loader</u>.

1.6.3 Input Output Control System (IOCS)

All machine instructions do not require the same amount of time for their execution. The peripheral transfers are so slow compared to the other operations that several hundreds of computations may be performed within the time required for a single I/O operation. This mismatch in speed between the CPU and peripherals led to the introduction of <u>I/O channel</u> or <u>I/O processor</u>. I/O processors are processing units like CPU with a specialized set of instructions. An I/O processor is capable of controlling one or more peripheral devices and once an I/O instruction is initiated by the CPU, it can proceed with the instruction independently. This has made it possible to overlap I/O operations with computing. However, we must appreciate that it requires sophisticated programming to take advantage of the said overlapping. Moreover, there are several other considerations that make I/O programming fairly complex.

A software known as IOCS (input output control system) provides the necessary support to the programmer. Actually, IOCS is a set of routines that supervise the I/O operations at the machine language level. These routines greatly simplify the programmer's I/O instructions at the source language level. All the complexities associated with the simple-looking I/O instructions in a source program are taken over by the relevant IOCS routines that get linked with the program during the linking process.

1.6.4 Operating Systems

An operating system is a software program known as the supervisor, monitor or executive. This is the program that runs the system and it is a permanent resident of the computer memory. The other software programs are stored in an auxiliary memory (tape or disk) and are called into the memory whenever necessary. Sometimes, only a portion of the operating system is kept in the memory for all the time and the remaining portions are stored with other software programs in the auxiliary memory. The functions of an operating system include the control of I/O operations through the IOCS, calling of assemblers or compilers on demand, execution of the object program, etc. An operating system also arranges for the processing of one job to another without stopping the computer for human intervention. The principle is that whenever a STOP statement is encountered during the processing of a job, an entry is made into the operating system instead of stopping the computer. The operating system looks for the next job in sequence and hands over the control to this job. Thus all the jobs presented in a batch on an input device are processed one after another automatically. Such an operating system which can handle a batch of jobs without the operator's intervention is called a batch processing operating system. In order that the operating system can identify a new job and determine what action should be taken for the job, some control information is necessary. The control statements are written in a language known as the job-control language (JCL). Usually, every program and data sets are preceded and followed by JCL statements.

A batch-processing operating system is also known as monoprogramming operating system, because it handles only one program at a time. A mono-programming operating system need not necessarily operate in the batch mode described above. In many cases, the operating system works interactively. The job control commands in such cases are given through the terminal (keyboard and VDU). After completion of one job, the operating system looks for the next command from the user and works accordingly. The disk operating system (DOS) for personal computers is an example of such inter-active monoprogramming operating system (see ch. 21).

There are operating systems now in existence which permit a computer to operate on different programs simultaneously. The concept is that whenever one program is held up waiting for a peripheral transfer, another is able to use the processor. In such a system, known as the multiprogramming system, more than one program is stored in different portions of the memory. The operating system ensures that the memory area allocated to a particular program is not used by other programs and also allocates the necessary peripheral units to each program. The processor is allocated to the indivi-dual programs on the basis of a priority number assigned to it by the installation. A program is allowed to run either until it must wait for the completion of a peripheral transfer or until any transfer initiated by another program is completed. At such time, the operating system switches to the highest priority program that is ready to proceed. This technique attempts to maximize the utilization of various units of a computer. How-ever, the situation can only be exploited fully if a peripheral-limited (usually commercial) job is run with a processor limited (normally scienti-fic) job.

A variation of the process of running more than one program simulta-neously is known as time-sharing. In this system, the processor is shared between program on a timed basis so that each program gets in turn a certain time-slice. The system is attractive when the users have an access to the computer through remote interactive peripheral devices as terminals. As the jobs progress simultaneously, each user gets the impression that he has the computer all to himself.

It may be useful at this juncture to make a few remarks regarding the memory management of an operating system. In a time-sharing system all the programs which are running simultaneously are stored on an auxiliary memory (usually a magnetic disk). While a program is being executed, it is in the main memory. When its time-slice expires or when it requires an input-output operation, it is moved out of the memory and the next program is brought in. This process is known as swapping or roll-in - roll-out. In a multiprogramming environment, each of the programs that are running simultaneously is given space in the main memory. As such the operating system partitions the memory into a number of partitions and each program (including the resident part of the operating system) is allocated a partition. However, in order that the operating system can work satisfactorily, a large main memory is required. Some sophisticated operating systems work on the principle of virtual memory. In this case, the programs that are running simultaneously reside on some auxiliary store called the virtual memory. Each program is divided into a number of segments and the execution of a program starts by bringing only the essential segments (called the working set) into the main memory. As and when the other segments are required, the operating system brings them from the virtual memory. While bringing a segment, it may be required to send back some other segment (may be a segment of another program) to the virtual memory so that its space in the main memory can be overlayed by the incoming segment. In some operating systems the program is divided arbitrarily into some fixed-size segments. Such segments are called pages.

1.6.5 Utilities: Text Editor

In any computer installation, some standard jobs are frequently required. Printing of data stored on tape is an example of such a job. Arranging data stored on disk, in some desired order, is another example. To accomplish such standard jobs, some readymade programs/routines are provided as part of system software. These are known as utilities.

One utility that is of much interest, is the text editor. With the help of a text editor, it is possible to create and modify a "text" through the user terminal. The text in this case can be any document, program or data required by a program. Usually, the text gets stored on a disk in the form of a file (described in ch. 2) under a title. In ch. 22, a text editor called EDLIN has been described.

EXERCISES

1. What are the different units in a computer?

2. What do you understand by the size of the memory?

3. How does the CPU function?

4. What does the term "bit" stand for? How many different patterns of 0's and 1's are possible with (i) 5 bits and (ii) 8 bits?

5. Convert the following binary integers to their equivalent decimal integers:
   (i) 101, (ii) 11101, (iii) 10111, (iv) 11111, (v) 1011, (vi) 01101, and (vii) 10101101.

6. In how many ways can a numeric data be represented internally? State the merits and demerits of the different representations.

7. Assume that a processor can add two numbers on an average in 2 µs (1 µs (called microsecond) = 10^{-6}) and a card reader can read cards at a speed of 600 cpm. Find the number of additions that can be performed in the time required to read a card. Use this example to support the statement that there exists a considerable mismatch in speed between the peripheral devices and the processor.

8. Indicate whether the following peripheral devices can be used for input, output or both:
   (i) Card reader (ii) line printer, (iii) magnetic tape, (iv) magnetic disk, (v) console, (vi) floppy disk and (vii) streamer tape-drive.

9. Define the terms:
   (i) Inter-record gap (IRG), (ii) **sector** and (iii) **cylinder**

10. Can a COBOL program be directly executed on a computer? If not, state how such a program is executed.

11. Write short notes on:
    (i) Compiler, (ii) IOCS, (iii) multiprogramming, (iv) text editor, (v) linker and loader and (vi) time-sharing.

12. What are the two broad classifications of software? Discuss them.

2

FILE CONCEPTS AND PROGRAM LOGIC

2.1   FILE CONCEPTS

It was pointed out in the previous chapter that any data-processing job
consists of the reading of some input data and the writing of the desired
results, the results having been obtained by carrying out the necessary
processing on the input data. Naturally, any analysis of the problem should
begin with the organization of the input data as well as that of the output
results. Once this is settled, we can at least be clear about what data are
being provided to the program and what is to be obtained from it. As an
example, let us consider a simplified case of calculating the pay for the
employees of an organization. The input data in this case may consist of
the employee number, employee name, basic pay, dearness allowance, house-
rent allowance, provident fund deduction and income-tax deduction for every
employee. The output may consist of the gross pay, total deductions and net
pay for each employee. For the purpose of identification as well as better
presentation of the results, some of the input data, such as the employee
number, employee name, etc. may also be included in the results to be
obtained. Now, let us consider how the input data or the output results are
to be organized. We may think of presenting all the data items pertaining
to a particular employee together. This means that the entire input data is
considered as divided into groups—each group contains the data required
for the pay calculation of an individual employee. The advantage of such an
organization is that having read just one such group of data, the pay for
the corresponding employee can be calculated. The various items constituting
the result are also grouped—each group relates to an employee. Such a
group of related data items is commonly called a <u>record</u> and the entire data
which is nothing but a collection of records is called a <u>file</u>. It may be
noted that both the terms file and record are used in connection with the
input data as well as the output results. To make a distinction, they are
sometimes qualified as input file and input record or output file and output
record. It is not necessary that there should be just only one input and one
output file for a job. Depending on the requirement of a job and the convenience of design, there may be more than one input or output files.

The notion of file and record introduced above is very important and
will be used throughout the book. We may formally say that a file is a
collection of data relating to a class of entities. Logically, the information in a file is organized into records and a record is defined as an
ordered set of data items relating to an entity. The individual data items
in a record are also called <u>data fields</u> or simply <u>fields</u>. The number of

characters (or words if the data is represented in binary) used to represent a data field in a record is called the size of the field. The size of the record is the cumulative size of all the fields in it.

Generally, all records in a file should have the same structure. This means that the relative positions of the data fields within the record, size of the data fields and interrelationships of the data items should be identical. However, this may not always be the case. Sometimes, for convenience, records of different structures can be placed together in one file. Even in such cases it is usual to have only a finite number of different record types in a file. A special case of records with different structures is what is known as variable-length records. Sometimes in order to save storage space, records with different lengths are used. Such a situation usually arises when some of the data items are not relevant for all records and are dropped where they are not relevant. Such records are called variable-length records as opposed to fixed-length records which are used commonly.

2.2   RECORD LAYOUT

Before writing a program, it is necessary to finalize the arrangement of data in a file. This involves the design of arrangement or layout of data fields in a record. Methods for the preparation of record layouts are discussed below.

2.2.1   Card Layout

A record in the case of card files is a card of 80 columns. As such there can be only 80 characters in a card record. The card layout may be a table of data fields shown against the respective card columns as shown below.

Card columns	Data field	Data type
1 - 5	EMPLOYEE-NUMBER	Numeric (integer)
6 - 30	EMPLOYEE-NAME	Alphabetic
31 - 38	BASIC-PAY	Numeric (2 decimal places)
39 - 46	DEARNESS	-do-
47 - 54	HOUSE-RENT	-do-
55 - 60	PROVIDENT-FUND	-do-
61 - 66	INCOME-TAX	-do-

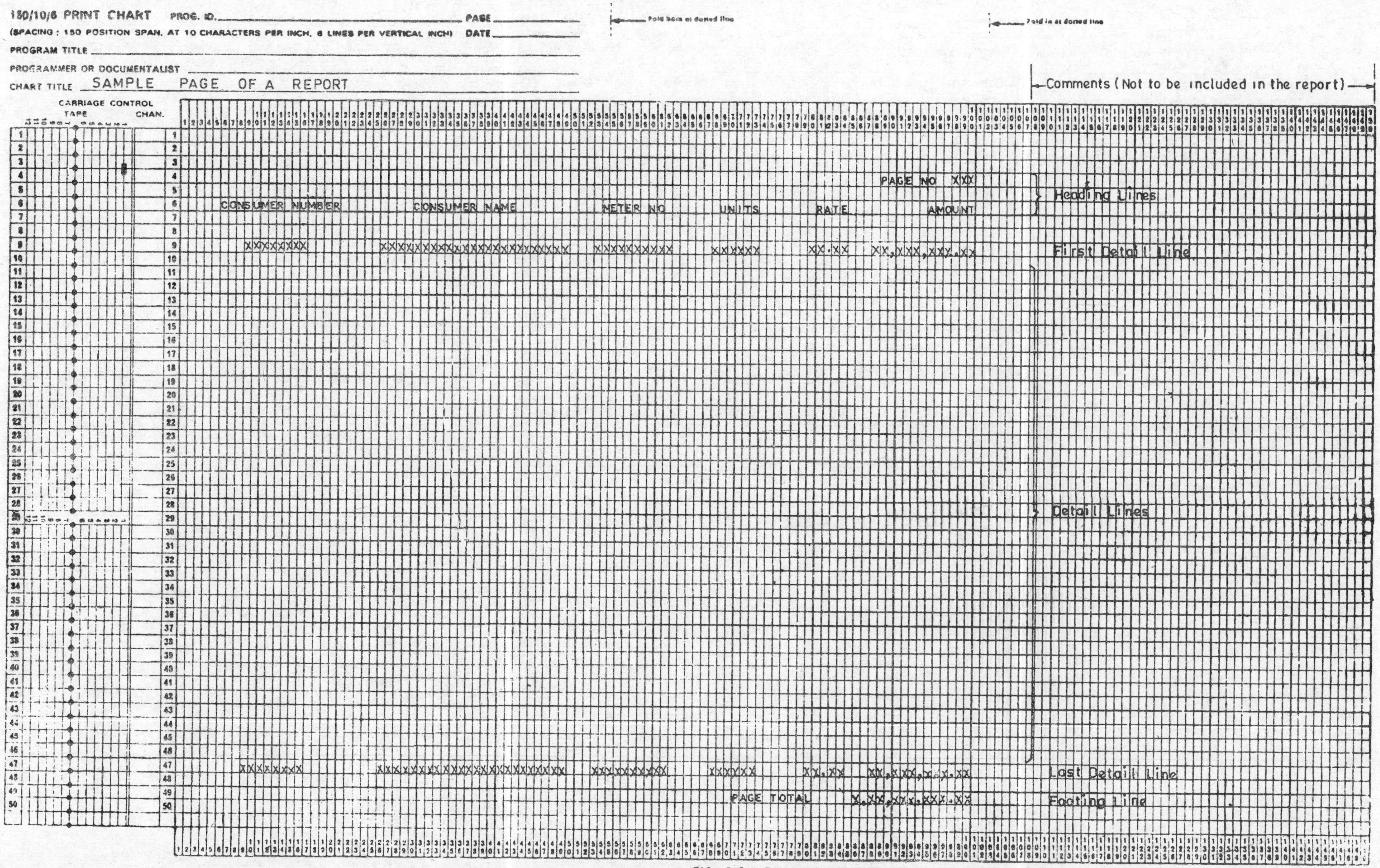

180/10/6 PRINT CHART PROG. NO. _____ PAGE _____

(SPACING : 150 POSITION SPAN. AT 10 CHARACTERS PER INCH. 6 LINES PER VERTICAL INCH) DATE _____

PROGRAM TITLE _____

PROGRAMMER OR DOCUMENTALIST _____

CHART TITLE SAMPLE PAGE OF A REPORT

CARRIAGE CONTROL
TAPE CHAN.

PAGE NO XXX

} Heading Lines

CONSUMER NUMBER   CONSUMER NAME   METER NO   UNITS   RATE   AMOUNT

First Detail Line

XXXXXXXXX   XXXXXXXXXXXXXXXXX   XXXXXX   XXXXXX   XX.XX   XX,XXX,XXX.XX

> Detail Lines

Last Detail Line

XXXXXXXXX   XXXXXXXXXXXXXXXXX   XXXXXX   XXXXXX   XX.XX   XX,XXX,XXX.XX

PAGE TOTAL   X,XXX,XXX,XXX.XX

Footing Line

Comments (Not to be included in the report)

FIG. 2.2. Print Chart

(i)   Heading   : It is printed at the top of every page of the
                         output. The heading itself may consist of more
                         than one line.

(ii)   Detail lines : These form the main body of the report. They
                         contain the results of processing and are
                         usually of the same format although there can
                         be exceptions.

(iii) Footing lines : These may contain the total of various fields
                         in a detail line. They usually appear at the
                         foot of every page and/or at end of the report.

Obviously, for every different line a layout is to be designed. These layouts are prepared on a standard chart known as the print chart. Figure 2.2
shows a print chart along with an illustration. The layouts are self-explanatory. It may be seen that the results are indicated on the print chart as
a group of X's; each X stands for a character. Fixed outputs such as headings
are shown in their exact forms. Editing characters, such as (.) and (,) in
the illustrations, that may be inserted within the results must also be in
their actual forms. The vertical spacings in between the various lines
should also be indicated on the print chart by keeping a suitable number of
vacant lines. In the case when a particular carriage control channel is to
be selected for a line, a note to that effect can be included in the place
shown in the print chart.

2.2.3 General Record Layout

Unlike the case of a card file or report file, the size of a record in a
magnetic tape or disk file is not fixed. The exact size of the record is
determined from the requirement of the job under consideration. Moreover,
a card reader and line printer are character peripherals as the data fields
must consist of data in the character form whereas this may not always be
the case for tape or disk records. A data field in such records can as well
be in binary (internal form). Normally, a layout table similar to the one
discussed in connection with card layout, is used. The leftmost column in
such cases obviously represents the character (word) positions instead of
card columns. In view of the fact that cards are becoming outdated, primary
data are being captured on floppy disks. However, same layout except for
the size of the record, can be used.

2.3 PROGRAM LOGIC — ALGORITHM

Having designed the record layouts for all the input and output files, the
next step is to finalize the computational steps that are necessary to
produce the output files starting from the input ones. This computational
procedure is called an algorithm. The term algorithm may be formally defined
as a sequence of instructions designed in such a way that if the instructions are executed in the specified sequence the desired results will be
obtained. The instructions, however, should be unambiguous and the result
should be obtained after a finite number of executional steps. The latter
condition actually states that an algorithm must terminate and should not

repeat one or more instructions infinitely. In other words, the algorithm
represents the logic of the processing to be performed.

There are various ways in which an algorithm can be expressed. When an
algorithm is expressed in a programming language, it becomes a program. Thus
any program is an algorithm although the reverse is not true. Besides
represented as programs, algorithms are often expressed in the form of what
is known as a flow chart.

A flow chart is a pictorial representation of an algorithm in which
boxes of different shapes are used to denote different types of operation.
The actual operations are stated within the boxes. The boxes are connected
by directed solid lines indicating the flow of operations. Usually, a flowchart is drawn before writing the program and the flow chart is then expressed in programming language to prepare the program. The advantage of this
two-tier operation in program writing is that while drawing a flow-chart
one is not concerned with the details of the elements of a programming
language. The main consideration is the logic of the procedure. Moreover,
since a flow-chart shows the flow of operations pictorially, any flaw in
the logic of the procedure can be detected more easily than in the case of
a program. Once the flow chart is drawn, the programmer can forget the logic
and concentrate on coding the operations in each box in terms of the statements of the programming language. Experienced programmers sometimes write
programs without drawing the flow chart. However, for a beginner, it is
recommended that a flow chart be drawn first in order to reduce the number
of errors and omissions in the program. Moreover, it is a good practice to
have a flow chart which may be of help during the testing of the program as
well as while incorporating further modifications in the program.

2.4 FLOW CHART SYMBOLS

Though the shapes of the boxes used in a flow chart are relatively standard,
many variations are also in existence. We shall use the following boxes:

     (i)   **Start-stop box**
    (ii)   Assignment box
   (iii)   Decision box
   (iv)   Input/output box, and
    (v)   Connectors.

(a) Start-stop box

The point at which an algorithm begins and the point where it terminates
are indicated by a circle.

(b) Assignment box

An assignment box is used to indicate the straightforward computation of
certain quantity. A rectangle is used to represent an assignment box.

The above layout is to a great extent self-explanatory but some points deserve mention. The columns 67-80 have not been mentioned in the table. This means that these columns are not used. Any suitable meaningful name can be used to identify a data field. However, we shall follow certain conventions for naming the data fields. The letters in a name should be written only in capitals. A digit will not be allowed as the starting character of a name. The different words in a name will be connected by a hyphen (-). No special character except a hyphen will be used in a name and the total number of characters will not exceed 30. The advantage of such a convention is that these rules conforms to the COBOL rules for a data name. The names used in a file layout can be carried in the program without any change. In the layout, note that under the entry "data type", the type of the data — numeric, alphabetic or alphanumeric, are mentioned. A note such as "2 decimal places" means that if the field consists of 8 digits, the first (leftmost) 6 digits represent the integral part of the data and the last (rightmost) 2 digits represent the fractional part.

The card layout table given above is of a general nature and does not require any special form. However, some standard card layout forms can also be used to design the said layout. A multiple-card layout form is shown in Fig. 2.1 along with the same layout illustrated above. Note that the fields on a layout form are separated by vertical lines drawn between the columns. The position of an assumed decimal point is shown by a short vertical line.

The card layout only shows the arrangement of data on a card, it does not contain the actual data. The data cards are to be punched from this layout. It will not be out of place to include something about card punching at this stage. A card can be punched with the help of a card-punching machine, the operation of which resembles that of a typewriter. Instead of feeding a blank stationery as in the case of a typewriter, here blank cards are fed through a hopper. The art of punching consists of registering a card by pressing the specific key on the key board. The card is then positioned at column 1. Characters can be punched by pressing the appropriate keys and as each column is punched, the card is shifted by one column. Once a card is finished, it can be released by pressing the release key and the next blank card can be registered. What is important for a programmer to know is how the data is punched within a field. When the data is shorter than the field defined, the numeric data should be shifted as far right as is possible within the field. This is what is known as right-justified punching. The left-hand unused columns may be left blank or may be filled with zeros. In the case of negative data a minus sign (—) can be overpunched on the rightmost digit position. The overpunching can be done by keeping the "multipunch" key pressed. If any character is punched with the multipunch key pressed then the card does not get shifted by a column after the punching. When the data is not numeric, it is usually punched left-justified which means that the data is shifted as much to the left as is possible within the field. The unused columns, if any, are left blank.

2.2.2 Report Layout

An output printed by a line printer is often called a report. Every line in a report is of 132 characters and forms what may be called a record of the report file or line-printer file. However, the contents of all the lines may not have an identical format. This is because a report often consists of:

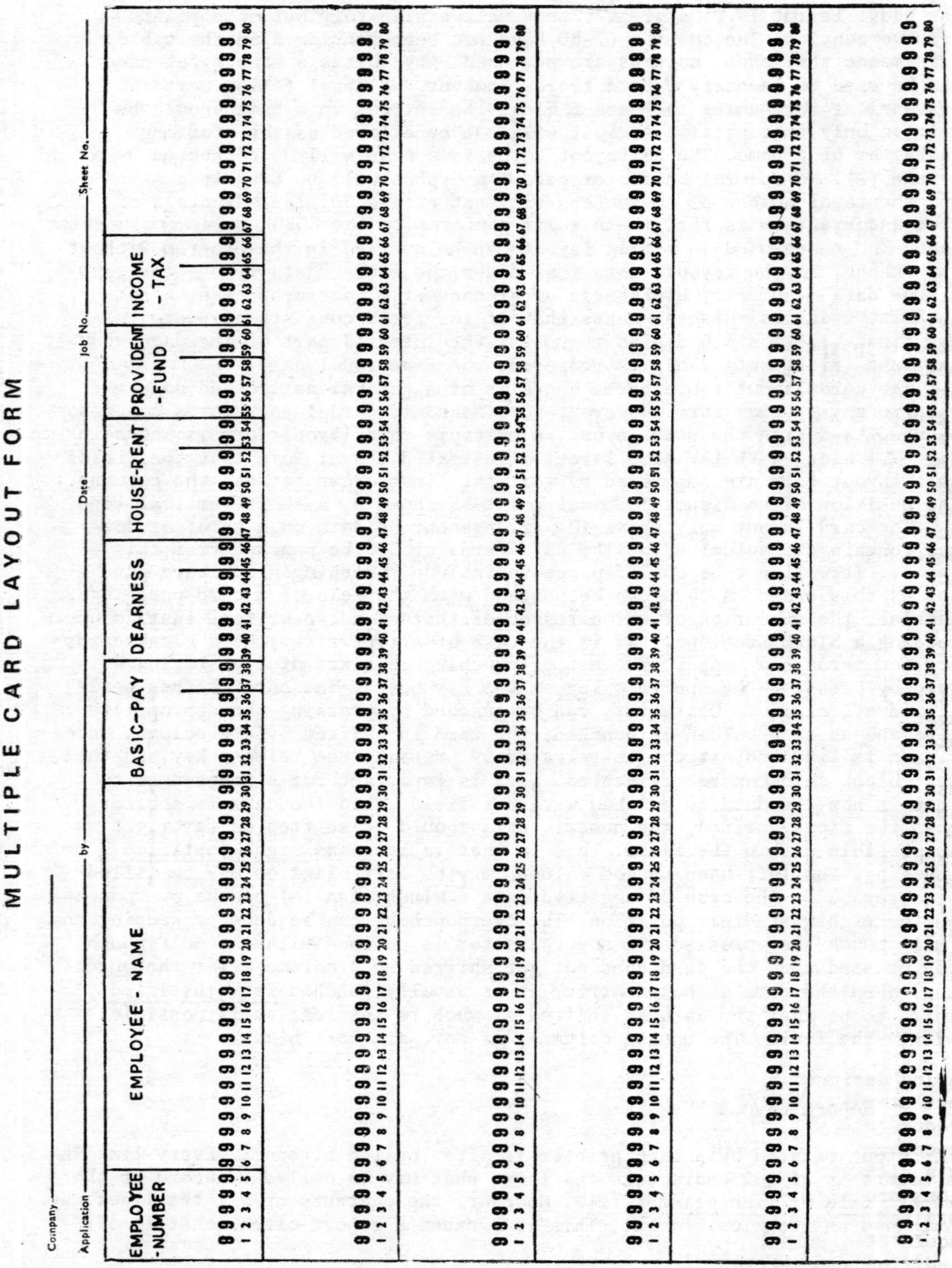

FIG. 2.1 Multiple-card Layout

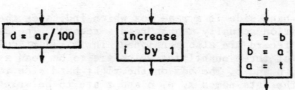

Note that the equality sign used in the assignment boxes shown above is not the equality sign used in mathematics. It simply stands for "replace by". As such the assignment in the first box means: compute ar/100 and replace the value of d by this result. The data name d may have a value before the control enters the box. However, after the assignment of the new value to d, the old value is lost. It may be noted that with this new meaning assigned to the equality sign, the computation indicated in the second box shown above can also be written as i = i + 1. The third box actually represents three assignments. These can also be represented by three boxes. However, when more than one assignment is placed in one box, they are assumed to be executed in their order of appearance. This means that t = b will be executed first followed by the execution of b = a and then the execution of a = t will be performed. The reader may notice that the operations shown in the third box means an interchange of the values of a and b.

(c) Decision box

The point at which a decision has to be made and the algorithm has to choose between two or three branches leading to other parts of the flow chart is indicated by a decision box. A diamond is used to represent such a box.

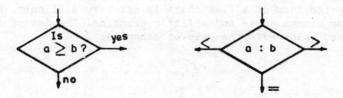

The use of the symbol colon (:) in the right-hand side box stands for a comparison: a : b means "compare a with b". There are three possibilities, viz., a < b, a = b and a > b. During execution the appropriate path is taken depending on the result of the comparison.

(d) Input/output box

The points at which the values of some data items have to be read or some results written are indicated by input/output boxes. Both the input and output boxes are represented by trapezoids, but in order to make a distinction between input and output, trapezoids of different shapes are used.

The box on the left-hand side is a read box which indicates the read operation. The read operation actually means "read a record". The data items
that constitute the record are also mentioned. In this particular example,
the record consists of three quantities which are to be read as the values
of the data names a, b and c. The box on the right-hand side is an output
box. The values of the data names x, p, q and z are to be written as a
record on the output file.

(e) Connectors

Frequently, a flow chart becomes too long to fit in a single page. Thus
when a flow chart spreads over more than one page, connector boxes are used
to serve as links among sections in different pages. A circle is used to
represent a connector and a letter or digit is placed with it to indicate
the link.

Connectors can also be used to establish links on the same page when it is
difficult to draw a flow line between two boxes. Obviously, the connectors
do not represent any operation and their use in a flow chart is only for the
sake of convenience.

2.5 SAMPLE FLOW CHARTS

A flow chart should be drawn using the symbols mentioned above. To describe
an algorithm in the form of a flow chart is not very difficult. What is
required is some common sense and a little practice. The art of flow chart-
ing is introduced below with the help of examples.

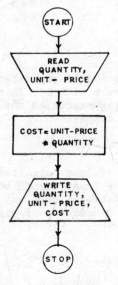

FIG. 2.3.   Sample Flow Chart I

Let us consider a very trivial problem. Given the quantity and unit price of a material, we want to compute its cost. Here the input file consists of just one record containing the fields QUANTITY and UNIT-PRICE. The output also consists of just one line, the fields being QUANTITY, UNIT-PRICE and COST. It may be noted that QUANTITY and UNIT-PRICE is being included in the output to make it more meaningful. The flow chart for this problem is shown in Fig. 2.3.

One would certainly not like to use a computer to solve a trivial problem such as this. However, if we have to compute the cost of 1000 different materials, we may like to take the help of a computer. What should be the flow chart in that case? Both the input and output files consist of 1000 records. The processing for a single record remains the same, but these steps should now be repeated 1000 times. The flow chart is shown in Fig.2.4.

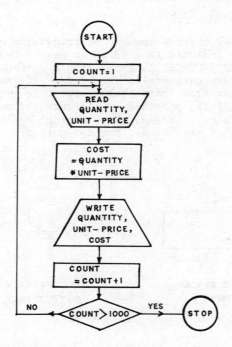

FIG. 2.4. Sample Flow Chart 2

There are a few things that should be noted from this flow chart. The data item COUNT is required to terminate the algorithm after the processing of 1000 records. To start with, COUNT is being assigned a value of 1. Every time a record is processed it is increased by 1 and then it is tested to see whether it has exceeded 1000 or not. Note that when 1000 records have been processed, the value of COUNT will be increased to 1001 and the control will go to the stop box. Such repetition of a portion of the flow chart is called a loop. It may be further noted that the flow chart for a given problem can never be unique. So long as it produces the correct output it is all right. For example, in this flow chart, COUNT has been increased before the test. It is also possible to increase the value of

COUNT after the test. In the latter case the test within the decision box should be COUNT $\geq$ 1000 or simply COUNT = 1000. Another point that deserves mention in this connection is that both the read and write operations have been assumed to be sequential. This means that the first time the read operation is executed, the values for QUANTITY and UNIT-PRICE will be assigned from the first record. The next read operation will assign these values from the second record, and so on. The same is also true for the write operation. The first execution of the write operation will write the first line of output. The next execution will write the second line, and so on. In most cases the read and write operations are sequential and for the time being we shall restrict ourselves to sequential reading and writing only.

2.6   ADDITIONAL FLOW-CHART SYMBOLS

In the above sample flow charts, the use of trapezoids as input/output boxes does not clearly indicate the medium or device being used. For example, when "Read QUANTITY, UNIT-PRICE" is shown within a trapezoid, we understand that the values for these data fields are being read from a file. However, it is not clear from the flow chart whether the file is a card file, magnetic tape or disk file. It is possible to indicate the medium/device if boxes of different shapes are used to indicate different mediums. Figure 2.5 shows the additional boxes that may be used for the purpose.

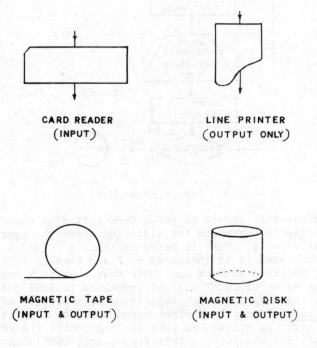

FIG. 2.5.   Additional Input/Output Boxes

Let us consider the sample flow chart shown in Fig. 2.4. We can replace the input/output boxes by the additional boxes to indicate that a card file is being read and a line-printer file is being produced. However, in this problem it is assumed that the card file contains 1000 cards. Suppose this information is not known and we want to continue the processing until all the cards have been processed. An easy solution to this problem would be to place an extra card at the end with a fictitious quantity. Usually a very high value (9 in all positions) is used for the purpose. In such a case, the loop in the flow chart can be controlled by keeping a test on QUANTITY immediately after the read box. As soon as the fictitious quantity is detected, the loop is terminated. However, such a technique may not be required as most programming languages provide a facility which detects whether the end of the input file has been reached or not. The facility is provided through the read operation. The read operation actually means "read a record if the end of the file has not been reached; otherwise take the action specified for end of file". Therefore, to be precise the input box is a combination of testing and reading. In the flow chart this can be indicated by having two outlets from the box one for the normal case, the other for the exceptional case when the end of file is reached. Such an input operation is called the input operation with a <u>trap for end of file</u>.

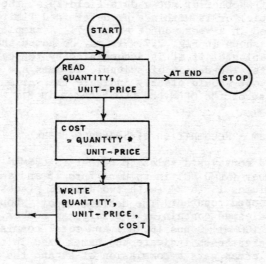

FIG. 2.6.   Sample Flow Chart 3

To illustrate the use of such boxes a flow chart for the same problem is shown in Fig. 2.6. It may be noted that the flow chart is valid for any number of cards in the deck.

Traps are usually used for the input operation. However, as we will see later, traps are occasionally used for output operations also.

2.7   MORE EXAMPLES OF FLOW CHARTS

Two sample flow charts are illustrated in this section. These flow charts use the additional input/output boxes introduced in the previous section. A careful study of these flow charts will give a good grasp of the flow-charting techniques.

2.7.1   Sample Problem — Card to Tape with Validation

Suppose that a card of a deck is either an issue card or a receipt card. The issue card contains the following fields: TRANSACTION-CODE, CUSTOMER-NUMBER, PRODUCT-NO-ISSUED, UNITS-SHIPPED, PRICE. The receipt card contains the following fields: TRANSACTION-CODE, PRODUCT-NO-RECEIVED, UNITS-RECEIVED and COST. The TRANSACTION-CODE can be either 1 or 2. If it is equal to 1, it is an issue card and if it is equal to 2, it is a receipt card. It is required to copy the valid transactions onto a magnetic-tape file. A transaction is invalid if the TRANSACTION-CODE is other than 1 or 2 or if the individual fields are not numeric. In case a transaction is not valid, appropriate error messages should be printed in the form of a report. In fact, such a job is often called a validation job. Validation usually means the determination of whether or not a data field is of the correct type (numeric or alphabetic) or is within a predetermined limit (such as the number of days worked in a week cannot exceed 7). A sample flow chart for the said problem is shown in Fig. 2.7. It may be noted that the flow chart will become more meaningful if it is accompanied by the card, report and magnetic-tape layouts. The design of suitable layouts are left as an exercise. The report layout should clearly indicate the various forms of error messages. The purpose of the OPEN and CLOSE boxes in Fig. 2.7 will be explained afterwards.

2.7.2   Sample Problem — Recognition of Sequence Break

Suppose a sales card contains a salesman number (SALESMAN-NO) in columns 1 to 6, cash memo number (MEMO-NO) in columns 7 to 13 and amount of sale (in rupees) (AMT) in columns 15 to 24 (with two decimal places). All cards for one salesman are grouped together. The desired report should consist of one line for each salesman containing the salesman number, total sales (TOTAL), commission (COMM), Bonus (BONUS) and total commission (TOT-COMM). (The names within parentheses indicate the names used in the flow chart in Fig. 2.8.) Each salesman gets a commission of 8% and the bonus is calculated according to the following table.

Total Sales	Rates for bonus
Less than Rs. 1000	nil
Rs. 1000 to Rs. 4000	2% of total sales
More than Rs. 4000	3% of total sales

The total commission is the sum of the commission and bonus.

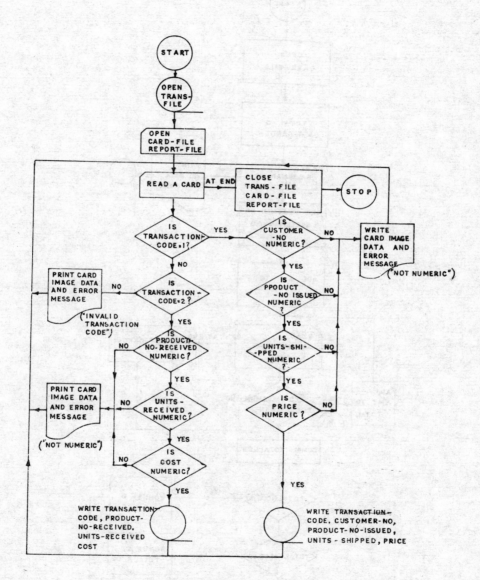

FIG. 2.7.   Sample Flow Chart—Card to Tape with Validation

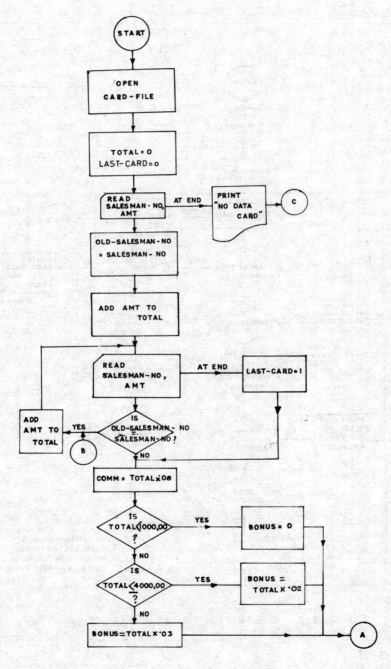

(contd,)

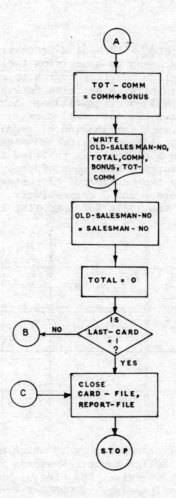

Fig. 2.8 Flow Chart showing Sequence Break

A flow chart for this problem is shown in Fig. 2.8. The important point here is the recognition of a break in the salesman number. Since the cards for a salesman number is grouped together, every time a card is read, it is checked to see whether the salesman number has changed or not. In case it is the same salesman, the only work to be done is to build up the TOTAL. A change in the salesman number indicates that the end of the previous salesman has been reached and it is time to calculate his figures and to print them. The reader should note how this logic has been given shape in the flow chart.

2.8 DECISION TABLES

Complex decision logic associated with a data-processing job is sometimes represented in a tabular form known as a <u>decision table</u>. In such cases the decision tables are used in place of flow charts to reveal the logic of an algorithm either in full or in part. A decision table summarizes the actions to be taken depending on the values of conditions that exist at the time the decision table is consulted. It lists all conditions to be tested and all actions to be taken with each combination of condition.

To make the concepts clear let us consider an example. The problem is to find out the rate at which a customer is entitled to get commission on purchases. The organization markets two types of products denoted by the numbers 1 and 2. Let there be two categories of customers — regular and casual — denoted by the numbers 1 and 2 respectively. Then the following decision table can represent the logic for computing the rate of commission.

PRODUCT-TYPE = 1	Y	Y	N	N
CUSTOMER-CATEGORY = 1	Y	N	Y	N
COMMISSION = 10%	X			
COMMISSION = 8%		X		X
COMMISSION = 12%			X	

In the above decision table Y stands for "yes" which means that the associated condition is true. In a similar manner, N stands for "no" indicating that the associated condition is false. Now, let us note the conditions listed in the decision table. These are: PRODUCT-TYPE=1 and CUSTOMER-CATEGORY=1. The conditions PRODUCT-TYPE=2 and CUSTOMER-CATEGORY=2 have not been used as these are not necessary. When the condition CUSTOMER-CATEGORY=1 is false, it is assumed that CUSTOMER-CATEGORY=2 is true. In a similar way when the condition PRODUCT-TYPE = 1 is false, the PRODUCT-TYPE=2 is assumed to be true. We can now try to find the meaning of this decision table. The first column after the double line indicates that if PRODUCT-TYPE=1 and CUSTOMER-CATEGORY=1, COMMISSION = 10%. X indicates the particular action to be taken. In a similar way, if PRODUCT-TYPE = 1 and CUSTOMER-CATEGORY = 2, COMMISSION = 8%, and so on.

From the above discussion, the following features of the decision table can be noted. A decision table consists of four sections as shown below.

Condition stub	Condition body
Action stub	Action body

The condition stub lists the various conditions and the condition body lists the various states of the conditions. The action stub lists the possible actions, whereas the action body indicates the actions that are to be carried out for each column of the condition body.

When the conditions in the condition stub are such that each condition has only two possible states — true or false — the decision table is called a limited entry decision table. The table in the above example is obviously a limited entry decision table. On the other hand, the stub can contain a condition which has more than two possible states. In such cases the decision table is called an extended entry decision table. To illustrate the use of an extended entry decision table, let us assume that the organization markets three types of products instead of two and these types are indicated by the numbers 1, 2 and 3. Then the following decision table will show the logic of determining the rate of commission.

PRODUCT-TYPE	1	1	2	2	3	3
CUSTOMER-CATEGORY	1	2	1	2	1	2
COMMISSION	10%	8%	12%	8%	10%	10%

In this form the conditions themselves have been carried into the condition body. The entry 1 against PRODUCT-TYPE indicates the case when PRODUCT-TYPE is equal to 1. The changes made in the action stub and action body, however, have nothing to do with the extended entry decision table. These changes have been made to show an alternative way of representing the action stub and action body.

The symbol dash (—) is sometimes used in a decision table to indicate that the particular state of the condition is irrelevant for the combination of conditions considered. This can help in reducing the columns of a decision table. In the above example when PRODUCT-TYPE is equal to 3, the rate for COMMISSION is 10% irrespective of the CUSTOMER-CATEGORY. Therefore, the above extended entry decision table can be abbreviated as follows:

PRODUCT-TYPE	1	1	2	2	3
CUSTOMER-CATEGORY	1	2	1	2	-
COMMISSION	10%	8%	12%	8%	10%

One of the advantages of a decision table layout is that it enables us to examine each possible combination of conditions called a <u>rule</u> to make sure that no possibility has been missed. If there are n conditions and if S_i denotes the number of possible states for the i-th condition, the total number of possible rules is given by $S_1 S_2 ... S_n$. It is, therefore, easy to verify whether the decision table covers all possible rules or not. For example, in the unabbreviated decision table above, we had two conditions. The number of states for these conditions were 3 and 2. Therefore, the decision table is a complete one as it covers all the $3 \times 2 = 6$ possible rules. Note that in the case of limited entry decision tables all $S_i = 2$. Therefore, the number of possible rules is given by 2^n where n is the number of conditions. However, an extensive use of dashes in a decision table makes the evaluation for completeness difficult and increases the risk of ambiguity (contradiction/redundancy) in the decision table. Sometimes, instead of a complete decision table only those rules which represent valid cases are shown in the decision table. Then to make the table complete, a dummy rule (usually written as ELSE) is written on the right of the table. This rule which represents "all other possibilities" is called the ELSE rule. To illustrate this we can consider the case of the extended entry decision table given above. In that case we assumed that PRODUCT-TYPE must be 1, 2 or 3 and the CUSTOMER-CATEGORY must be either 1 and 2. However, if there are chances of other values for these data items, an ELSE rule can be specified on the right of the condition body and a suitable action can be specified. What this action should be must arise from the context of the problem. For example, these exceptional cases represented by the ELSE rule may be treated as an error and the rate of COMMISSION may be replaced by zero. The decision table in this case will be as follows:

PRODUCT-TYPE	1	1	2	2	3	3	E L S E
CUSTOMER-CATEGORY	1	2	1	2	1	2	
COMMISSION	10%	8%	12%	8%	10%	10%	0

When the ELSE rule is used, the table is complete only by default and, therefore, must be carefully checked to see that no valid case is missed.

Besides completeness, the decision table has a parallel structure. This means that all the conditions to be considered are listed but the order in which these conditions are tested are irrelevant. In this respect decision tables differ substantially from flow charts. In flow charts, the conditions must be tested sequentially and, therefore, it is difficult to find out the combination of conditions that leads to a particular action. However, it is very easy in the case of decision tables.

2.9 DOCUMENTATION

The preparation of file layouts, flow charts and decision tables before writing a program helps one to commit less mistakes during program development. Moreover, the above-mentioned documents also help in incorporating future changes in the program. Since a program may need modifications from time to time, it is better to keep this need in view even at the program-development stage. The said documents should be prepared and retained for future references. It is not unlikely that a flow chart or any other document is found to contain mistakes during program testing. In such cases the relevant documents should also be modified along with the program. As we proceed, we shall see that the COBOL language also provides some features for better documentation of the program itself.

EXERCISES

1. Each card of a deck contains a tender paper number and the corresponding quotation. Draw a flow chart to print the amount of minimum quotation and the tender paper numbers with this quotation. Assume that there is only one tender quoting the minimum.

2. There is a disk file in which each record contains 5 data fields, namely, the examination roll number of a student, student's name, marks in mathematics, english and programming. The output should consist of the given items as well as the total marks for these three subjects. Prepare the file and report layouts and draw a flow chart.

3. The same as the previous exercise except that there is another field in the output called remarks. If any student secures less than 40 in any subject, the remark field will contain the word FAIL. On the other hand, if the average mark is greater than or equal to 40 but less than 50, the remarks will contain THIRD. If it is greater than or equal to 50 but less than 60, the contents of the remarks will be SECOND and in all other cases it will be FIRST.

4. The records of a disk file contain particulars about the shareholders of a company. For each shareholder there are two records. The first record contains the name and address and the second record contains the number of shares held, the total face value and type of share (1 digited field-0 means equity and 1 means preference). Besides these, both the

records contain the account number and a field called class of record. For the first record the class should be 1 and for the second it should be 2. The records are sorted and it may be assumed that for each snareholder the record of class 2 is preceded by the record of class 1. Draw a flow chart to create a magnetic-tape file where there is only one record for a shareholder. Design suitable file layouts.

5. Modify the flow chart of Exercise 4 to take into account the following errors in the input deck:

   (i)   The records of class 1 and 2 are interchanged.
  (ii)   One of the records for a shareholder are missing.
 (iii)   A record of class 1 is followed by a record of class 2 but the account numbers do not tally.
  (iv)   The class of record is other than 1 and 2.

All the above-mentioned cases should be considered as errors. In such cases, the information for that particular shareholder should not be placed on the magnetic-tape file. Instead, an edit list containing copies of such erroneous records with suitable error messages should be printed.

6. Draw a chart (actually part of a flow chart) showing the following logic. The mode of transport for despatching materials should be selected on the basis of the following rules:

 (a)   If the priority is not urgent and the weight is less than or equal to 5 kg, despatch by post.
 (b)   If the priority is not urgent and the weight is more than 5 kg, select a lorry if the distance is less than or equal to 250 km.
 (c)   If the priority is urgent, distance is less than 50 km and weight is less than 100 kg, select a van.
 (d)   In all other cases, use a train.

Assume suitable numerical values for the qualitative items, such as priority and transport mode.

7. Construct a decision table for Exercise 6.

3

INTRODUCTION TO COBOL

3.1 HISTORY OF COBOL

In the 1950s there was a growing need for a high-level programming language suitable for business data processing. To meet this demand the United States Department of Defence convened a conference on the 28th and 29th May 1958, which was attended by users from civil and governmental organizations, computer manufacturers and other interested groups. Out of this conference three groups were formed for the actual design of the language: one for short-term work, another for middle-term work and the third for long-term work.

In September 1959, the short-term committee submitted a report to the directorate. In the same year the directorate held a meeting and it was in this meeting that the new language was named COBOL (COmmon Business Oriented Language).

The short-term committee, having modified their earlier report, submitted a final report in December of the same year. The report was accepted and then published in April 1960. The board of directorate which is known as CODASYL (Conference on DATA System Language) COBOL programming language committee, established a COBOL maintenance committee to keep COBOL in step with the times.

On May 5, 1961, COBOL-61 was published with some revisions of the first accepted report and this provided the basis for later versions. The users started writing COBOL programs when the first COBOL compiler became available in early 1962. The next version with some new additions was published in 1965. But it was only in August 1968 that a standard version of the language was approved by the American National Standards Institute (ANSI). This version known as ANSI-68 COBOL or COBOL-68 is the first official standard of COBOL. The next revised official standard was introduced in 1974 and is known as ANSI-74 COBOL or COBOL-74 (the official name is American National Standard COBOL × 3.23 − 1974). This version is currently implemented in almost every machine. However, the revision process has been continuous and in 1985 a revised standard was introduced . This standard known as COBOL-85 is the latest version of COBOL.

3.2 CODING FORMAT FOR COBOL PROGRAMS

COBOL is a high-level language and therefore a COBOL source program must be written in a format acceptable to the COBOL compiler. Precisely for this reason, COBOL programs are written on COBOL coding sheets (see Fig. 3.1)

which use a standard format. There are 80 characters positions on each line
of the coding sheet and these positions are grouped into the following five
fields:

Positions	Field
1 - 6	Sequence
7	Indicator
8 - 11	Area A/Margin A
12 - 72	Area B/Margin B
72 - 80	Identification

Positions 8 to 72 actually contain the COBOL code. This area is divided
into two fields — area A and area B (also known as margin A and margin B).
COBOL requires that some of the entries must begin in area A and others
must be confined to area B only. Area A entries can be continued into area
B, if required.

The sequence field may be used to assign sequence numbers to the coding
lines. This field is optional and, if desired, may be left unused. When
used, the sequence number must be in the ascending order but need not be
consecutive. Usually, page number is written in the first three positions
(1 to 3) and line numbers are written in the remaining three positions (4
to 6).

The COBOL compiler, in addition to its normal work, can optionally
produce a printed copy of the source program being compiled. This copy is
known as source listing. Anything written in the identification field, will
be ignored by the compiler but will appear in the source listing.

The indicator field may contain an asterisk (*), a slash (/), or a
hyphen (-). An asterisk (*) or a slash (/) denotes that the line under
consideration is a comment line. The comment line is ignored by the compiler, but it appears in the source listing. The programmer is free to write
anything in a comment line, but generally notes indicating the intentions
of the programmer are included as comment lines. A comment line can appear
anywhere after the first line of the COBOL program. The difference between
an asterisk (*) and slash (/) is that in the case of the latter, the comment
line will be printed after page ejection (i.e., after skipping to the top of
the next page). No such page ejection will take place in the case of an
asterisk (*). The use of hyphen (-) will be discussed afterwards.

3.3   STRUCTURE OF A COBOL PROGRAM

For gaining familiarity with the basic structure of a COBOL program let us
take a close look of the program in Fig. 3.1. At this stage we are not
concerned with what the program does. Our interest is only to observe what
a COBOL program looks like.

The first thing to note is that there are four divisions in the
program. These are: IDENTIFICATION (sequence number 001010), ENVIRONMENT
(sequence number 001030), DATA (sequence number 001110), and PROCEDURE
(sequence number 002080) divisions. Every COBOL program must have these
four divisions.

Out of these divisions, the PROCEDURE DIVISION is the one where the
algorithm is described in terms of some elements of the COBOL language
called statements. For example, ADD COST TO TOTAL (sequence number 002180)

PROGRAM NO _____

CODED BY _____

DIVISION _____ SECTION _____

DATE _____

PAGE ____ OF ____

USER CODE _____ TASK NO. ____

COBOL CODING FORM

SEQUENCE		A	B	COBOL STATEMENT	IDENTIFICATION
PAGE NO. / LINE NO.		7 8 9 10 11	12 13 14 15 16 17 18 19 20 21 22 23 24 25 26 27 28 29 30 ...		73 74 75 76 77 78 79 80
0 0 1	0 1 0	IDE	NTIFICATION DIVISION.		
0 0 1	0 2 0	PROG	RAM-ID. SAMPLE.		
0 0 1	0 3 0	ENVI	RONMENT DIVISION.		
0 0 1	0 4 0	CONF	IGURATION SECTION.		
0 0 1	0 5 0	SOUR	CE-COMPUTER. B-6700.		
0 0 1	0 6 0	OBJE	CT-COMPUTER. B-6700.		
0 0 1	0 7 0	INPU	T-OUTPUT SECTION.		
0 0 1	0 8 0	FILE	-CONTROL.		
0 0 1	0 9 0		SELECT CARD-FILE ASSIGN TO READER.		
0 0 1	1 0 0		SELECT REPORT-FILE ASSIGN TO PRINTER.		
0 0 1	1 1 0	DATA	DIVISION.		
0 0 1	1 2 0	FILE	SECTION.		
0 0 1	1 3 0	F.D.	CARD-FILE.		
0 0 1	1 4 0	0 1	CARD-RECORD.		
0 0 1	1 5 0		0 2 ITEM-NO	PICTURE IS X(6).	
0 0 1	1 6 0		0 2 QUANTITY	PICTURE IS 9(6)V99.	
0 0 1	1 7 0		0 2 UNIT-PRICE	PICTURE IS 9(6)V99.	
0 0 1	1 8 0		0 2 FILLER	PICTURE IS X(5,8).	
0 0 1	1 9 0	F.D.	REPORT-FILE.		
0 0 1	2 0 0	0 1	REPORT-REC.		
0 0 1	2 1 0		0 2 FILLER	PICTURE IS X(4).	
0 0 1	2 2 0		0 2 R-ITEM-NO	PICTURE IS X(6).	
0 0 1	2 3 0	L	0 2 FILLER	PICTURE IS X(4).	
0 0 1	2 4 0		0 2 R-QUANTITY	PICTURE IS Z(5)9.99.	
0 0 1	2 5 0		0 2 FILLER	PICTURE IS X(6)	

NOTE WRITE NUMBERS 10, LETTERS I Ø U G Z C, SYMBOLS /

FIG. 3.1 An Example of a COBOL Program (cont'd.)

PROGRAM NO _____

CODED BY _____

DIVISION _____   SECTION _____

DATE _____

PAGE _____ OF _____

USER CODE _____   TASK NO. _____

COBOL CODING FORM

SEQUENCE PAGE NO.	LINE NO.	A	B	COBOL STATEMENT
0 0 2	0 1 0		02 R-UNIT-PRICE	PICTURE IS Z(5)9.99.
0 0 2	0 2 0		02 FILLER	PICTURE IS X(6).
0 0 2	0 3 0		02 AMOUNT	PICTURE IS Z(12)9.99.
0 0 2	0 4 0		02 FILLER	PICTURE IS X(72).
0 0 2	0 5 0		WORKING-STORAGE SECTION.	
0 0 2	0 6 0	77	COST	PICTURE IS 9(12)V99.
0 0 2	0 7 0	77	TOTAL	PICTURE IS 9(13)V99.
0 0 2	0 8 0		PROCEDURE DIVISION.	
0 0 2	0 9 0		START-THE-PROCESS.	
0 0 2	1 0 0		OPEN INPUT CARD-FILE, OUTPUT REPORT-FILE.	
0 0 2	1 1 0		MOVE O TO TOTAL.	
0 0 2	1 2 0		READ-AND-PRINT.	
0 0 2	1 3 0		READ CARD-FILE AT END GO TO PARA-LAST.	
0 0 2	1 4 0		MULTIPLY QUANTITY BY UNIT-PRICE GIVING COST.	
0 0 2	1 5 0		MOVE ITEM-NO TO R-ITEM-NO, MOVE UNIT-PRICE TO R-UNIT-PRICE	
0 0 2	1 6 0		MOVE QUANTITY TO R-QUANTITY, MOVE COST TO AMOUNT.	
0 0 2	1 7 0		WRITE REPORT-REC AFTER ADVANCING 2 LINES.	
0 0 2	1 8 0		ADD COST TO TOTAL.	
0 0 2	1 9 0		GO TO READ-AND-PRINT.	
0 0 2	2 0 0		PARA-LAST.	
0 0 2	2 1 0		MOVE SPACES TO REPORT-REC.	
0 0 2	2 2 0		MOVE TOTAL TO AMOUNT.	
0 0 2	2 3 0		WRITE REPORT-REC AFTER ADVANCING 3 LINES.	
0 0 2	2 4 0		CLOSE CARD-FILE, REPORT-FILE.	
0 0 2	2 5 0		STOP RUN.	

FIG. 3.1.   An Example of a COBOL Program

in the said program is a COBOL statement. Every statement begins with a verb (ADD in the example) which indicates the kind of operation that is to be performed during the execution of the statement. Usually a statement is terminated by a period (.). However, this is not mandatory. Two or more statements can also be separated by spaces or a comma (,) followed by a space. A group of such statements with the last one having a terminating period is called a sentence. In the said example, the statements starting with MOVE and terminating with AMOUNT followed by a period (.) (sequence number 002150 to 002160) are together a sentence. This sentence consists of four statements all beginning with the verb MOVE. To make the definition consistent, a single statement terminated by a period is also called a sentence.

Let us now consider the statement ADD COST TO TOTAL. COBOL being an English-like language, the meaning of this statement is quite apparent. The statement means that the present value of COST should be added to the present value of TOTAL and the result should be the new value of TOTAL. In fact, the data fields COST and TOTAL refer to some storage spaces in the memory. In COBOL such names for data fields are called data names. It is an essential requirement of the language that all data names which are used in the PROCEDURE DIVISION statements must be defined in the DATA DIVISION. While defining a data name in the DATA DIVISION, the size of the data item, its type, etc. must also be included in the definition. Since a data definition in the DATA DIVISION is merely a declaration and not an instruction to the computer, such a definition is called an entry and not a statement. Depending on the nature of a data item it has to be defined in different sections of the DATA DIVISION. Those data that belong to an input or output record should be defined in the FILE SECTION (sequence number 001120). Those data names that hold the results of intermediate computations should appear in the WORKING-STORAGE SECTION (sequence number 002050) of the DATA DIVISION. Any of these sections may or may not appear in the DATA DIVISION. However, the file section, when used, must be the first section followed by the WORKING-STORAGE SECTION. There can be other sections which will be introduced in due course.

The ENVIRONMENT DIVISION consists of two sections — the CONFIGURATION SECTION (sequence number 001040) and INPUT-OUTPUT SECTION (sequence number 001070). The CONFIGURATION SECTION describes the particular computer to be used to compile and execute the COBOL program. The various peripheral devices to be used by the program are specified in the INPUT-OUTPUT SECTION.

The IDENTIFICATION DIVISION consists of a number of standard paragraphs showing the name of the program, name of its author, date on which the program is compiled and similar information.

An entry or a statement of a COBOL program can be written in one or more coding lines (see Sec. 3.9 for further information).

3.4 CHARACTER SET

Since COBOL is a language, we must begin its study with the alphabet. The alphabet of COBOL is called the character set. There are 51 different characters in this set. These are shown below.

0-9	(10 numerals)
A-Z	(26 English letters - only capital letters)
	(Space or blank — sometimes denoted by ɓ)

-	(Minus sign or hyphen)
+	(Plus sign)
*	(Asterisk)
/	(Slash)
=	(Equal sign)
\$ or £	(Currency sign)
,	(Comma)
;	(Semi colon)
.	(Period or decimal point)
"	(Quotation mark)
(	(Left parenthesis)
)	(Right parenthesis)
>	(Greater than symbol)
<	(Less than symbol)

The above characters are often grouped for convenience of reference. The characters 0-9 are called numeric characters or digits. The characters A-Z are called letters and the remaining characters are called special characters. In some computers, small letters (a-z) are also included. Except in the case of non-numeric literals (discussed afterwards), small letters are treated at par with the corresponding capital letters.

3.5 COBOL WORDS

A COBOL word must be formed from the following characters:

                    0-9
                    A-Z and
                -   (hyphen)

A word must conform to the following rules:

(i) The total number of characters must not be greater than 30.

(ii) One of the characters must be a letter. Some compilers put the additional restriction that the first character must be a letter.

(iii) A word cannot begin or end with a hyphen.

(iv) A word must not contain a blank and any special character except a hyphen (-).

Examples

Valid Word	Invalid Word
GROSS-PAY	-GROSS- (as it starts and ends with a hyphen)
OVERTIME-HOURS	OVERTIME HOUR (There is a blank space between OVERTIME and HOUR hence these will be treated as two words)
A	
B12-4	
AGE-OF-THE-MAN	1-2-3 (No letter)
	QUALIFICATION-AND-EXPERIENCE-OF-THE-SENIOR-DIVISION-CLERK (Total number of characters is more than 30)

A COBOL word can be either a <u>user-defined word</u> or <u>reserved word</u>. A list of COBOL reserve words is given in Appendix B. These reserved words are used in COBOL statements and entries for specific purposes.

3.6 DATA NAMES AND IDENTIFIERS

A data name gives reference to the storage space in the memory where the actual value is stored. This value takes part in the operation when that particular data name is used in the PROCEDURE DIVISION. As we proceed we shall find that in certain cases a data name alone is not good enough for use in the PROCEDURE DIVISION. In such cases a data name has to be qualified by another data name or can be indexed or subscripted. At this stage it is difficult to explain the meanings of the terms qualified, indexed or subscripted data names which will be introduced in due course. The only important point is that a single data name or a data name qualified, indexed or subscripted is normally referred to by the general term <u>identifier</u>. Thus data names are only one form of identifiers. A data name must be a user-defined word and cannot be a reserved word.

Examples

Valid Data Names	Invalid Data Names
TOTAL-HOURS	DATA (Reserved word)
QUANTITY-REQUIRED	ADD (Reserved word)
A45	45 (No letter)
342B2	46+2A (+ is not allowed in a data-name)

3.7 LITERALS

Instead of a data name sometimes the actual values can also appear in the program. Such values are known as <u>literals</u>. For example, in Fig.3.1 the statement MOVE 0 TO TOTAL (sequence number 002110) indicates that the value zero will be moved to TOTAL. This constant 0 which is used in the body of the statement is a literal. A data name may have different values at different points of time whereas a literal means the specific value which remains unchanged throughout the execution of the program. For this reason a literal is often called a <u>constant</u>. Moreover the literal is not given a name; it represents itself and does not require to be defined in the DATA DIVISION. There are two types of literals —numeric and nonnumeric.

(a) Numeric

A numeric literal can be formed with the help of digits only. There may also be a sign (plus or minus) and/or a decimal point. If there is a sign, it must appear as the leftmost character of the literal and there must not be any blank space between the sign and the first digit. If a decimal point is used, it must not be the last character of a literal as a decimal point (or period) is also used to mark the end of a COBOL statement. If there is no decimal point, it is assumed to be an integer. If the sign is not mentioned, the literal is treated as positive. The maximum number of digits allowed in a numeric literal varies from compiler to compiler. For the purpose of this book we shall assume that a numeric literal can have a maximum of 18 digits.

(b)   Nonnumeric

In general, a nonnumeric literal is used to output messages or headings. A nonnumeric literal is composed of characters which are enclosed within quotation marks. The restriction on nonnumeric literal is that within two quotation marks there can be any character except another quotation mark. The maximum number of characters that are allowed within two quotation marks is again compiler dependent. Here we shall assume that the maximum number of characters may be 120. According to ANSI 74 specifications, a nonnumeric literal can also contain quotation mark within it. In that case, two contiguous quotation-mark characters must be written to specify a single quotation mark. However, before using this, the programmer must ensure that the facility is supported in the relevant compiler.

Examples

(i) Valid Numeric Literal	(ii) Invalid Numeric Literals
.725	''150'' (valid as nonnumeric literal but invalid as numeric literal)
12.5	- 46 (there is a blank space between the sign and the first digit 4)
—38.62	232467893456789.234568923 (the total number of digits is more than the acceptable number)

(iii) Valid Nonnumeric Literal

"SEVEN"
"DATA DIVISION"
"12.5"
"-24."
"HOUR/RATE"

(iv) Invalid Nonnumeric Literal

7	(valid as numeric literal but invalid as nonnumeric literal)
"EIGHT	(Invalid because there is no quotation mark on the right)
12.5"	(Invalid because there is no quotation mark on the left)

"BISHOP"S CANDLESTICKS"   (Invalid because only a single
                                 quotation mark has been used
                                 between P and S)

3.8 FIGURATIVE CONSTANTS

There is another type of literal in COBOL known as the <u>figurative constant</u>.
These are literals representing values that may be frequently used by most
programs. These are given some fixed names and when the compiler recognizes
these names it sets up the corresponding values in the object program. For
example, in Fig. 3.1 the statement MOVE SPACES TO REPORT-REC. (sequence
number 002210) uses the figurative constant SPACES. As a result the data
item REPORT-REC will be filled in with spaces. Also note that the statement
MOVE 0 TO TOTAL. (sequence number 002110) could have been written as MOVE
ZERO TO TOTAL. While the former uses a numeric literal 0, the latter makes
use of the figurative constant ZERO. The following is the list of figurative
constants and their meanings.

Figurative Constants	Meaning
ZERO ZEROS ZEROES	Represents the value 0, or one or more of the character 0, depending on the context.
SPACE SPACES	Represents one or more spaces or blanks.
HIGH-VALUE HIGH-VALUES	Represents the highest value in the collating sequence.
LOW-VALUE LOW-VALUES	Represents the lowest value in the collating sequence.
QUOTE QUOTES	Represents one or more of the single character ("). The word QUOTE may not be used to bound a nonnumeric literal.
ALL literal	Represents one or more of the string characters comprising the literal.

3.9 CONTINUATION OF LINES

A statement or an entry may be continued to the area B of the next line as
and when necessary. However, no COBOL word should be broken. Continuation
is also possible when a COBOL word is broken between lines, but in that
case a hyphen (-) is necessary in the indicator field of the next line.
Actually, a hyphen (-) in the indicator field means that the first non-blank
character in the area B of the current line is the character immediately
following the last non-blank character of the previous line. In case a non-

numeric literal is continued to the next line, the first non-blank character in area B of the continuation line must be a quotation mark (") and continuation is assumed to start from the character immediately following this quotation mark.

Example

The following shows how a non-numeric literal is to be continued. The dots denote those parts of the entry that are not shown here explicitly.

	Indicator field	Area A	Area B
Continued line		......	...."ABCDEFGHI
Continuation line			"JKLMNOPQRS".

The actual literal will be taken as "ABCDEFGHIJKLMNOPQRS".

3.10   LANGUAGE DESCRIPTION NOTATION

In the subsequent chapters the following notations will be followed to describe the syntax of COBOL statements.

(i)   All words written in capital letters are key words. They must be included when the entries of which they form a part are used. Key words are underlined. Words formed with capital letters and not underlined are called noise words which may be optionally included for better documentation. These words may be omitted without loss of meaning. Whenever any word is used, they must be spelled correctly.

(ii)   Operands to be provided by the programmer are shown in small letters.

(iii)   When a portion of a general format is enclosed in square, brackets [ ], the said portion can be included or omitted at the user's choice.

(iv)   The braces { } imply that a choice of one of the options has to be made from the two or more listed column-wise within these braces.

(v)   The punctuation marks , (comma) and ; (semi-colon) shown in the format can be used or omitted depending on the user's choice.

(vi)   The three consecutive periods (...) are used to convey the idea that the portion enclosed within the preceding brackets or braces can be repeated. Sometimes, braces with one possibility is used to delimit the said portion.

(vii)   The space character is used as a separator. Any number of consecutive spaces can also be used in place of a single space.

Example 1

The following is the syntax of a MOVE statement.

$$\text{\underline{MOVE}} \begin{Bmatrix} \text{identifier - 1} \\ \text{literal - 1} \end{Bmatrix} \text{\underline{TO} identifier - 2 [, identifier - 3]...}$$

Given the above syntax rule, let us examine whether the following MOVE statements are correct or not.

(i)   MOVE A B TO C
(ii)   MOVE 35 TO A B C
(iii) MOVE B TO C
(iv)   MOVE A TO 42

The answers are explained below.

(i)   This is not correct as the values of two identifiers are moved to one identifier whereas according to syntax the value of only one identifier may be moved to different identifiers.

(ii)   This is correct as either the value of an identifier or that of a literal may be moved to more than one identifier. In this case 35, a literal, is moved to three identifiers A, B and C.

(iii) This is also correct as the value of an identifier is moved to another identifier.

(iv)   This is not correct as the value of A, an identifier, is moved to 42 which is a literal. The syntax says that either an identifier or a literal may be moved to an identifier but not to a literal.

Example 2

The following is the syntax of a COBOL verb.

GO TO procedure-name-1 [, procedure-name-2]..., procedure-name-n

DEPENDING ON identifier

where a procedure name is a user defined word (like data name) but may also consist entirely of digits.

Let us now examine the validity of the following statements:

(i)   GO TO PROC-1 PROC-2 PROC-3 DEPENDING ON NODE-VALUE.

(ii)   GO TO NEW-PARA DEPENDING ON DATA-ONE.

(iii) GO 240 250 260 DEPENDING 200.

(iv)   GO 10 20 DEPENDING X.

The results of the examination are as follows:

(i)   The statement is correct provided PROC-1, PROC-2 and PROC-3 are valid procedure names and NODE-VALUE is a valid identifier. There is no violation of any rule.

(ii)   The statement is wrong because the syntax rule clearly shows that there must be at least two procedure names after GO TO (note that procedure-name-1 and procedure-name-n are shown as mandatory).

(iii) The statement is wrong because 200 cannot be a valid identifier.

(iv)   The statement does not contain any syntax error. Note that 10 and 20 may be valid procedure names.

The language description notation described above is equally applicable to entries as well as statements. The notation gives us clear idea about the grammatically correct forms for the concerned language element but it has nothing to do with the meaning of the said element.

3.11   IMPLEMENTATION DIFFERENCES

Since COBOL is a high-level language, it is natural to expect that the same COBOL program should run satisfactorily on different machines. Unfortunately, this is far from reality as there exist many differences among the elements of COBOL as implemented in the compilers of different computers. Even in the ANSI COBOL some elements are not standardized and these have been left for the implementor to specify. Moreover, according to ANSI standards, it is not necessary for an implementor to implement all the features. Various subsets of the language are also allowed.

It is important, therefore, to know about the implementation differences so that the programmer can choose the common features of COBOL and use them in the program. To meet this requirement, a short account of the implementation differences will be included at the end of each chapter. The discussions are based on three different implementations of COBOL and the following abbreviations will be used in the explanations.

DEC-10	DEC System 10 COBOL
ICL-1900	ICL 1900 Series COBOL
B-6700	Burroughs 6700/7700 COBOL

It may be noted that in B-6700 some ANSI 74 features have been implemented and can be used only if the source program is preceded by a compiler option card containing ∮ SET ANSI 74. ∮ is to be punched in column 7.

(a) Character Set

The character set listed in Sec. 3.4 conforms to ANSI-68 and ANSI-74. ICL-1900 also uses the same set. B-6700 uses three additional characters, viz., left square bracket ([ ), right square bracket ( ]) and colon ´(:). In a similar way, DEC-10 uses two additional characters, viz., the horizontal tab (⊣) and the exponentiation symbol (↑).

(b) Numeric Literals

Up to a maximum of 18 digits (excluding sign) can generally be used for a numeric literal. B-6700, however, can accept numeric literals up to a maximum of 23 digits.

(c) Nonnumeric Literals

A maximum of 120 characters is generally allowed for nonnumeric literals.
B-6700 allows nonnumeric literals up to a maximum of 256 characters.
Quotation mark character is not allowed within a nonnumeric literal in any
of the three compilers.

(d) Figurative Constants

B-6700 has two more figurative constants. These are:

UPPER-BOUND UPPER-BOUNDS	Represents the highest value allowable within the usage (see Chapter 8) of a data item.
LOWER-BOUND LOWER-BOUNDS	Represents the lowest value allowable within the usage (see Chapter 8) of a data item.

EXERCISES

1. How many divisions are there in a COBOL source program? Indicate
   whether all the divisions are necessary for a program. Indicate the
   order in which these divisions will appear in a program.

2. What is a data name? How is it different from a literal? Indicate
   whether a data name may be called an identifier.

3. What is the difference between a literal and figurative constant? How
   many different types of constants are there in COBOL?

4. Indicate whether each of the following is a data name, numeric literal,
   nonnumeric literal, figurative constant or none of these four.

   (i) NINE, (ii) 0, (iii) 19.8, (iv) 9.(, (v) 9, (vi) ZERO,
   (vii) "16.82", (viii) "THERE IS SOMETHING WRONG", (ix) "-46.7",
   (x) PROCEDURE, (xi) TAXABLE-INCOME, (xii) 16.82, (xiii) "TAKE HOME
   PAY =", (xiv) FIFTEEN, (xv) SPACES, (xvi) QUOTATION-MARK, (xvii) 9.,
   (xviii) -38.62A, (xix) 48.23A, (xx) RATE/HOUR.

5. A simplified syntax for the DIVIDE verb in COBOL is as follows:

$$\underline{DIVIDE} \left\{ \begin{array}{l} identifier\text{-}1 \\ literal\text{-}1 \end{array} \right\} \quad \underline{INTO} \quad \left\{ \begin{array}{l} identifier\text{-}2 \\ literal\text{-}2 \end{array} \right\} \quad \underline{GIVING} \ identifier\text{-}3$$

$$[\ ROUNDED \ ] [\ , \ identifier\text{-}4 \quad [\ ROUNDED \ ] \ ] \ ...$$

Identify the following statements as syntactically correct or not:

   (i)   DIVIDE 3 INTO CAKE GIVING MY-SHARE.
   (ii) DIVIDE 5 INTO 20 GIVING 4.
   (iii) DIVIDE 13 INTO I GIVING J K ROUNDED.
   (iv) DIVIDE I INTO J ROUNDED GIVING K.

4

IDENTIFICATION AND ENVIRONMENT DIVISION

The IDENTIFICATION DIVISION and ENVIRONMENT DIVISION are the two leading
divisions of any COBOL program. As indicated by their names, these divisions
contain entries that are required to either identify the program or describe
the computer system to be used for the compilation and execution of the
program. Except for a few, the entries in these divisions are used only for
documentation purposes and the writing of these entries in a COBOL program
is only a routine matter. However, what makes a general description of
these entries difficult is that these are not uniform for all computers and
compilers. The entries of the identification and environment divisions as
described below are to be considered as typical entries. These can vary
depending on the computer system used.

4.1 IDENTIFICATION DIVISION

The IDENTIFICATION DIVISION is the first division of every COBOL source
program. There may be several paragraphs in this division of which the
paragraph PROGRAM-ID is essential in most of the machines. The other paragraphs are optional and may be used mainly for documentation purposes. The
following shows the structure of this division.

IDENTIFICATION DIVISION.

PROGRAM-ID. entry.

[AUTHOR. entry.]
[INSTALLATION. entry.]
[DATE-WRITTEN. entry.]
[DATE-COMPILED. entry.]
[SECURITY. entry.]

The division heading and paragraph names should be coded as area A
entries. Each of the paragraph names must end with a period followed by at
least one blank space. The entries following the paragraph headings must
be terminated by a period. The entry in the PROGRAM-ID paragraph contains
the program name to be used to identify the object program. The program
name can consist of 1 to 30 characters and must contain at least one
letter located in any position within the name. However, these rules can
vary depending on the compiler to be used.

The entries in the other paragraphs are normally treated as comments and the programmer is free to write anything for these entries. However, it is recommended that only meaningful entries should be included in these places to provide better documentation. For example, the entry for the AUTHOR paragraph may include the name of the programmer. The entry of the DATE-COMPILED paragraph may contain the date of compilation. In most compilers if this entry is left blank, the compiler inserts the actual date in the source listing.

4.2   ENVIRONMENT DIVISION

The ENVIRONMENT DIVISION is the division that must follow the IDENTIFICATION DIVISION in a COBOL source program. Among all the four divisions this one is the most machine-dependent division. The computer and all peripheral devices required by the program are described in this division.

This division contains two sections — CONFIGURATION SECTION and INPUT-OUTPUT SECTION. Of these the CONFIGURATION SECTION appears first. The outline of the sections and paragraphs of this division is shown below.

```
ENVIRONMENT DIVISION.
CONFIGURATION SECTION.
SOURCE-COMPUTER. source-computer-entry.
OBJECT-COMPUTER. object-computer-entry.
[SPECIAL NAMES. special-names-entry].
[INPUT-OUTPUT SECTION.
FILE-CONTROL. {file-control-entry}... .
[I-O-CONTROL.  input-output-control-entry].]
```

For most compilers the COBOL source program must at least include the two section headings and the three paragraphs — SOURCE-COMPUTER, OBJECT-COMPUTER and FILE-CONTROL. The division headings, section headings and the paragraph headings should be coded as area A entries. The paragraph headings must be followed by a period and then a space. The entries in the paragraphs are area B entries and can start in the same line with the paragraph heading.

4.2.1   CONFIGURATION SECTION

This section contains an overall specification of the computer used for the purpose of compilation and execution of the program. There are in all three paragraphs in this section.

4.2.1.1   SOURCE-COMPUTER

This paragraph specifies the name of the computer used to compile the COBOL program. The following is the form of this paragraph.

```
SOURCE-COMPUTER. computer-name.
```

For example, if ICL 1901 is to be used for compiling the COBOL source program, this paragraph should be as follows:

SOURCE-COMPUTER. ICL-1901.

4.2.1.2 OBJECT-COMPUTER

The OBJECT-COMPUTER paragraph describes the computer on which the program is to be executed. The following shows the syntax for this paragraph.

OBJECT-COMPUTER. computer-name

[, MEMORY SIZE integer-1 $\begin{Bmatrix} \text{CHARACTERS} \\ \text{WORDS} \end{Bmatrix}$]

[, PROGRAM COLLATING SEQUENCE IS alphabet-name]

[, SEGMENT-LIMIT IS integer-2].

The computer name specifies a particular computer on which the object program is to be executed.

The MEMORY SIZE is used to indicate the amount of storage available to the object program. This clause is also used in conjunction with the SORT verb (see Chapter 14).

The PROGRAM COLLATING SEQUENCE clause specifies the collating sequence that is to be used to compare nonnumeric data items (see Sec. 10.1.1). The alphabet name in this clause should be defined in the SPECIAL-NAMES paragraph to specify a collating sequence. If this clause is absent, the machine's own collating sequence called NATIVE, is assumed.

The SEGMENT-LIMIT clause is used in most of the compilers to indicate that the sections having segment number less than the number specified in integer-2 should be held in the permanent area of storage and should not be transferred to and from the virtual memory. For further details see Chapter 20.

There should be a terminating period at the end of all the entries in this paragraph. The following is an example of the OBJECT-COMPUTER paragraph.

OBJECT-COMPUTER. ICL-1900

MEMORY SIZE 8000 WORDS.

4.2.1.3 SPECIAL-NAMES

This paragraph is used to relate some hardware names to user-specified mnemonic names. This paragraph is optional in all compilers. The following is the format of this paragraph.

SPECIAL-NAMES. [, CURRENCY SIGN IS literal-1]

[, DECIMAL-POINT IS COMMA]

[, CHANNEL integer IS mnemonic-names] ...

[, ALPHABET alphabet-name IS $\left\{\begin{array}{l} \text{STANDARD-1} \\ \text{NATIVE} \\ \text{implementor-name} \end{array}\right\}$]...

[, implementor-name IS mnemonic-name].

The first two clauses will be discussed later (see Sec. 5.6.4).

The CHANNEL clause is used to control the line spacing of line printers. This clause is used to associate a user-defined name called the mnemonic name with a channel in the printer carriage control. The range of integer depends on the particular line printer to be used. This mnemonic name can only be used in a WRITE statement.

The ALPHABET clause specifies a user-defined alphabet name that can be used to indicate a collating sequence in the PROGRAM COLLATING SEQUENCE clause discussed earlier or in the COLLATING SEQUENCE clause in the SORT verb. The word NATIVE stands for the computer's own collating sequence and STANDARD-1 stands for the ASCII collating sequence. The alphabet name is also used to define the external character set in which the data is record- ed on a file. For further discussion see Sec. 13.3.6.

The SPECIAL-NAMES paragraph can have other entries which are implemen- tor-dependent. These entries are not discussed here as they are not of general interest. In fact, the CHANNEL entry is also an implementor-defined clause. The entries can appear in the paragraph in any order.

As an example, let the SPECIAL-NAMES paragraph be as follows:

SPECIAL-NAMES. CHANNEL 1 IS PAGE-TOP.

We know that conventionally channel is associated with the top of the page. While instructing the computer to write a line on the line printer the programmer may like to specify that the line must be printed as the first line on a new page. This may be done by including the ADVANCING TO CHANNEL 1 clause in the write statement (the WRITE statement with the ADVANCING clause will be discussed later). The purpose of the special name clause illustrated above is to enable the programmer to replace CHANNEL 1 by PAGE-TOP in the ADVANCING clause. The idea is to provide better documen- tation. If one prefers to use CHANNEL 1 in the WRITE statement, the special name entry is not required.

4.2.2 INPUT-OUTPUT SECTION

This section contains information regarding files to be used in the program. There are two paragraphs in this section —FILE-CONTROL and I-O-CONTROL. Of these, the first one is used in almost every program. In the following some of the entries of the FILE-CONTROL paragraph will be discussed. The I-O- CONTROL paragraph and the other entries of this paragraph will be discussed later (see Sec. 13.9). The INPUT-OUTPUT SECTION as a whole is optional in many computers.

4.2.2.1 *FILE-CONTROL*

The FILE-CONTROL paragraph names each file and identifies the file medium through file control entries. The simplified format of a file control entry is given below.

<u>SELECT</u> [OPTIONAL] file-name   <u>ASSIGN</u>   TO   hardware-name.

In general, a COBOL source program uses some files. For each of these files, there must be a FILE-CONTROL entry. This entry names the file and assigns a peripheral device which holds that particular file. The file names that appear in the SELECT clauses must be unique and all these files must be described in DATA DIVISION. The file name should be formed according to the rules of data names.

The word OPTIONAL may be used only for input files. When the object program is executed, the optional files need not be present on every occasion. If the OPTIONAL clause is omitted for a particular file, the file must be present during the execution of the program. If the file is absent, an execution error will occur. On the other hand, if an optional file is absent, any attempt to open the file for reading will not result in an error, but the absent file will be considered to be an empty file which means that the file does not contain any record.

The ASSIGN clause assigns a particular physical peripheral device name to a file. The physical peripheral device names are machine-dependent. For the purpose of this book we shall use the device names <u>READER</u>, <u>PRINTER</u>, <u>TAPE</u> and <u>DISK</u> to mean card reader, line printer, magnetic tape and magnetic-disk device respectively.

An example of the FILE-CONTROL paragraph is given below.

```
FILE-CONTROL.
     SELECT CARD-DESIGN ASSIGN TO READER.
     SELECT PRINTER-FILE ASSIGN TO PRINTER.
```

This paragraph indicates that there are two files — CARD-DESIGN and PRINTER-FILE. The file named CARD-DESIGN is a card file while the other is a report file to be printed on a line printer.

4.3   IMPLEMENTATION DIFFERENCES

Both the IDENTIFICATION DIVISION and ENVIRONMENT DIVISION being greatly machine-dependent, only some of the important differences are mentioned below. For further details, the reader is advised to consult the relevant manuals.

(a) PROGRAM-ID Paragraph

In ICL 1900 series computers, this paragraph is compulsory and the entry must be of six characters in length with the first character strictly a letter and the last two strictly digits. The three characters in the middle can be either a letter or a digit. In the B-6700 and DEC-10 systems the entry is optional and treated as a comment. The entry can have more than one word. In DEC-10 it can also be used as a program name. In that case the name must consist of letters, digits or hyphens and should not use more than six such characters. Alternatively, the program name in DEC-10 may be enclosed in quotation marks.

(b) REMARKS Paragraph

This paragraph is not allowed in B-6700.

(c) ENVIRONMENT DIVISION

In ICL 1900 computers, SOURCE-COMPUTER, OBJECT-COMPUTER and the FILE-CONTROL paragraphs are mandatory. Moreover, the entry in the OBJECT-COMPUTER paragraph must contain MEMORY SIZE option besides the computer name. In DEC-10 all these entries are optional and treated as comment entries. In B-6700 MEMORY SIZE and DISK clauses are used with SORT verbs. There are default values. These are not comment entries.

(d) PROGRAM COLLATING SEQUENCE and ALPHABET Clauses

These clauses are additions in ANSI 74 COBOL and are available in B-6700, provided the compiler option ANSI 74 is set. Moreover, the ALPHABET clause, as shown in the text, is a simplified form of the ANSI 74 ALPHABET clause. There is no implementation difference with respect to PROGRAM COLLATING SEQUENCE clause. For ALPHABET clause, see Sec. 13.11.

EXERCISES

1. It is known that certain paragraphs in the IDENTIFICATION DIVISION are optional and other parts of the division are mandatory. Describe the mandatory portion.

2. Indicate which one of the following is correct:
    (i)   The SELECT clause appears in the I-O-CONTROL paragraph of DATA DIVISION.
    (ii) The SELECT clause appears in the I-O-CONTROL paragraph of FILE SECTION of DATA DIVISION.
    (iii) SELECT clause appears in the FILE SECTION of ENVIRONMENT DIVISION.
    (iv) SELECT clause appears in the FILE-CONTROL paragraph of the INPUT-OUTPUT section of the ENVIRONMENT DIVISION.
    (v)   SELECT clause appears in the CONFIGURATION SECTION of ENVIRONMENT DIVISION.

3. Write the IDENTIFICATION DIVISION and ENVIRONMENT DIVISION for the following.

   A program named BILL will be run on B-6700. This program uses one card file named OLD-MASTER and another file named NEW-MASTER which is attached to the printer.

4. Consider the following FILE-CONTROL paragraph and state which of the files must be available during the execution.

   FILE-CONTROL.

   ```
   SELECT OPTIONAL TAPE-FILE ASSIGN TO TAPE.
   SELECT OPTIONAL NEW-FILE ASSIGN TO TAPE.
   SELECT BASIC-FILE ASSIGN TO READER.
   SELECT RESULT-FILE ASSIGN TO PRINTER.
   ```

5. What is a mnemonic name? How would you associate the mnemonic name DETAIL-HEAD with carriage control channel 2? Why is this kind of association required?

5

FIRST LOOK AT DATA DIVISION

5.1 INTRODUCTION

The DATA DIVISION is that part of a COBOL program where every data item
processed by the program is described. It is important to note that unless a
data item is described in the DATA DIVISION, it cannot be used in the procedure division. The DATA DIVISION is divided into a number of sections and
depending on the use of a data item, it should be defined in the appropriate
section. For the time being only two of the sections of the DATA DIVISION
will be considered. These are as follows:

(a) FILE SECTION

The FILE SECTION includes the descriptions of all data items that should be
read from or written onto some external file.

(b) WORKING-STORAGE SECTION

The data items which are developed internally as intermediate results as
well as the constants are described in this section of the DATA DIVISION.
  The format of the DATA DIVISION is as follows:

```
        DATA DIVISION.
        [FILE SECTION.
        File section entries.
        ....
        ....]
        [WORKING-STORAGE SECTION.
        Working-storage entries.
        ....
        ....]
```

All the section names as well as the division name must be coded as margin
A entries.Each section of the DATA DIVISION is optional which means that a
section may be omitted if there is no data that may be described in a particular section. However, sections to be included must appear in the order
shown above.

5.2 LEVEL STRUCTURE

The data to be processed are internally stored in a specific area in the
memory of a computer. The area corresponding to a particular data item is
referenced by the data name used in the description of the said item. Data
names are user-created words. The rules for forming such names or words in
COBOL have been discussed earlier. However, it is important to note that
while the data name actually stands for a particular area in the memory, it
is the content of the area that takes part in the operation when referred
to by the said data name in the PROCEDURE DIVISION statements.

In COBOL a distinction is made between elementary and group data items.
A few elementary data may be combined to form a group. For example, DAY,
MONTH and YEAR may be three elementary data items. These may be combined to
form a group data named DATE. The organization may be shown pictorially as
follows:

DATE		
DAY	MONTH	YEAR

It may be noted that the memory space referred to by DATE is the combined
memory space for DAY, MONTH and YEAR. The advantage of such a grouping is
obvious. The programmer can now refer to the individual elementary items
DAY, MONTH, YEAR or to the group item DATE. An elementary data item is thus
the one which the programmer would always like to refer to as a whole and
not in parts.

To describe the hierarchical structure introduced above, the concept
of level number is employed in COBOL. A level number is a two-digit number
starting from 01. Single-digit numbers are written in a two-digit form with
a 0 or space preceding them. The most inclusive group must have the level
number 01. The first subdivisions can have any level number between 02 and
49. Further subdivisions should follow the same range with the restriction
that an item cannot have a level number less than or equal to the level
numbers of the group that may include it. Thus a group includes all elementary data or smaller groups beneath it until a level number equal to or less
than the level number of the said group is encountered. The following examples reveal the concept of the level numbers.

Example 1

```
01      DATE

    05      DAY

    05      MONTH

    05      YEAR
```

Example 2

```
01          PAY
     02          GROSS-PAY
          03   BASIC
          03   DEARNESS
          03   HOUSE-RENT
     02          DEDUCTIONS
          03   PF-DEDUCT
          03   IT-DEDUCT
     02          NET-PAY
```

The group DATE which was shown earlier in the pictorial form is illustrated in the first example. In the second example PAY is the most inclusive group which has three subdivisions, namely, GROSS-PAY, DEDUCTIONS and NET-PAY. GROSS-PAY is again subdivided into BASIC, DEARNESS and HOUSE-RENT. In a similar way DEDUCTIONS are further subdivided into PF-DEDUCT and IT-DEDUCT. It may also be noted that the elementary data items are BASIC, DEARNESS, HOUSE-RENT, PF-DEDUCT, IT-DEDUCT and NET-PAY. The structure can be pictorially shown as follows:

PAY

GROSS-PAY			DEDUCTIONS		NET-PAY
BASIC	DEARNESS	HOUSE-RENT	PF-DEDUCT	IT-DEDUCT	

Sometimes, in a hierarchical data structure such as this, the programmer may not require a data item to be referred to in the PROCEDURE DIVISION. Such a situation usually arises when a group and only some of its subdivisions are to be used in the program. The remaining subdivisions need not be used explicitly. In such situations the word FILLER may be used to name the elementary data to which the programmer does not wish to assign a specific name. FILLER can be used as many times as is required.

5.3 DATA DESCRIPTION ENTRIES

A data description entry describes a data item. It consists of a level number, data name (or FILLER) followed by a number of optional clauses terminated by a period. The purpose of an individual clause is to specify certain characteristics of the data item being described. In this chapter, we shall describe only two of these clauses — the PICTURE clause and the VALUE clause. Other clauses will be described gradually. It may be noted that these optional clauses may appear in any order within the data description entry (see Sec. 8.4 for exceptions). There must be at least one space between any two consecutive components of an entry. A component in this context is a level number, a data name or a clause. Except for the level number, no other component can appear in area A. In the case of level 01 entries, the level number must begin in area A and the rest must appear in area B. In the case of entries with other level numbers, the level number can begin anywhere within area A and B (column positions 8 to 72) but the other components following it must be in area B only. This last rule is also equally applicable to data division entries with special level numbers 66 and 88. These entries will be discussed in due course. The clauses in a data description entry can be optionally separated by a comma (,) or a semi-colon (;), but in that case the delimiter must have a space following it.

5.3.1 PICTURE Clause

The PICTURE clause describes the general characteristics of an elementary data item. These characteristics are described below.

(a) Class

In COBOL a data item may be one of the three classes — numeric, alphabetic or alphanumeric. As indicated by these names, the numeric items consist only of digits 0 to 9 and the alphabetic items consist only of the letters A to Z and the space (blank) character. The alphanumeric items may consist of digits, letters as well as special characters.

(b) Sign

A numeric data item can be signed or unsigned. Implicitly, a numeric data is considered as unsigned and during execution such unsigned data items are treated as positive quantities. However, an operational sign can be specified in the PICTURE clause to describe a signed data item. The way to specify the sign is described later but it is important to note that internally, the operational sign is not stored as a separate character. The operational sign is stored as the zone bits of the rightmost digit position of the data item. While preparing data for such an input-signed item, care should be taken to ensure that the data appears on the input medium in the same form. Thus an input data -1234 requires only 4 digit positions internally and must be captured on the input medium as 123M. In ANSI 74, however, facilities are available to have the operational sign as a separate character.

(c) Point Location

The position of the decimal point is another characteristic that can be specified in the case of numeric data items. If the said position is not specified, the item is considered to be an integer which means that the decimal point is positioned immediately after the rightmost digit. It may be noted that in COBOL the decimal point is not explicitly included in the data. The position of the decimal point is merely an assumed position. The compiler at the time of compilation only makes a note of this assumed decimal point. It generates the object code in such a way that the data items before taking part in the operations are aligned according to their assumed decimal points.

(d) Size

Size is another characteristic which specify the number of characters or digits required to store the data item in the memory.

   The four general characteristics described above can be specified through a PICTURE clause. This clause may also be used to describe other characteristics to be introduced later.
   The PICTURE clause is to be followed by a picture character string as shown below.

$$\left\{ \begin{array}{l} \underline{PICTURE} \\ \underline{PIC} \end{array} \right\} \quad IS \quad character\text{-}string$$

The character string can consist of 1 to 30 code characters that define the abovementioned attributes of the elementary item. The code characters and their interpretations are given below.

Code character	Meaning
9	Each occurrence of this code in the picture string indicates that the corresponding character position in the data item contains a numeral.
X	Each occurrence of this code indicates that the corresponding character position in the data item contains any allowable character from the COBOL character set.
A	Each occurrence of this code indicates that the corresponding character position in the data item contains only a letter or space character.
V	The occurrence of this in a picture string indicates the position of the assumed decimal point.
P	The occurrence of this indicates the position of the assumed decimal point when the point lies outside the data item.
S	The occurrence of this indicates that the data item is signed.

There is no special code to indicate the size. The total number of occur-rences of 9, X or A in the picture string indicates the size. The occurrences of V, P and S are not counted in determining the size of an item.

The allowable combinations are governed by the following rules:

(i)   In the case of an alphabetic item the picture may contain only the symbol A.

(ii) In the case of a numeric item the picture may contain only the symbols 9, V, P and S. These are called operational characters. It must contain at least one 9. The symbols V and S can appear only once and S, if it is included, must be the leftmost character of the picture string. The symbol P can be repeated on the right or on left (but not on the left of S) as many times as is required to indicate the position of the assumed decimal point.

(iii) In the case of an alphanumeric item, the picture may contain all Xs or a combination of 9, A and X (except all 9 or all A). In the latter case the item is considered as if the string consists of all Xs.

The PICTURE clause is only to be specified for elementary items; it cannot be used for a group item. The size of a group item is equal to the total of the sizes of all subordinate elementary items. The class of a group item is alphanumeric (see Sec. 5.7 for details).

The following examples illustrate the PICTURE specification.

Example 1

PICTURE IS S999V99

means that the data is a signed numeric with a size of 5 characters and the position of the assumed decimal point is before 2 places from the rightmost end.

Example 2

PIC IS PPP999

means that the numeric data is of 3 characters in size and there are 6 posi-tions after the assumed decimal point. Thus if the data in the memory is 375, the value will be taken as .000375. If, on the other hand, the picture were defined as 999PP, the value would have been 37500.

Example 3

PIC XXXXXX

means that the data is alphanumeric with a size of 6 characters.

Instead of repeating 9, X, A or P in the picture string, it is possible to write the number of occurrences of a character enclosed within parenthe-ses immediately after the said character. Thus

```
S9(3)V9(2)            is equivalent to S999V99.
X(7)                  is equivalent to XXXXXXX.
P(4)9(3)              is equivalent to PPPP999.
```

5.3.2 VALUE Clause

The VALUE clause defines the initial value of a data item. Normally the
initialization is done just before the first statement in the PROCEDURE
DIVISION is executed. The syntax of the VALUE clause in its most simple
form is

<u>VALUE</u>   IS   literal

The literal can be any numeric value, a nonnumeric string of characters
included within quote (") or any figurative constant. However, the class
of the literal must be compatible with that of the data item as specified
through the PICTURE clause.

<u>Examples</u>

```
VALUE IS 3.5.
VALUE IS "MY DATA".
VALUE ZERO.
```

The above examples illustrate how a numeric, nonnumeric or figurative
constant can be specified as a value. Note that the nonintegral numeric
literals must appear with a decimal point (.).
     Usually, the value clause is used in the WORKING-STORAGE SECTION to
define the initial value of a data item. If a VALUE clause is used at a
group level, it should not be used for any item within the group. Only
nonnumeric literals and figurative constants can be used to specify the
value of a group item. The VALUE clause must not be used for items defined
in the file section except in the case of condition names to be introduced
later.

<u>Example 1</u>

```
03   NUMBER-ONE   PIC  S9(3)V99   VALUE   -3.25.
```

The data item is a level 3 elementary item belonging to a group. The item
is signed and the initial value is -3.25.

<u>Example 2</u>

```
01   SOURCE-DATA      VALUE  IS  "243752".

     02 DATA-1        PIC 9(2).
     02 DATA-2        PIC 9(3).
     02 DATA-3        PIC 9(1).
```

Here the value has been specified at the group level. As a result, the item DATA-1, DATA-2 and DATA-3 will have respectively 24, 375 and 2 as their initial values. Although the value is specified as a nonnumeric string and the elementary items are numeric, there is no problem because the string consists only of digits. In fact, the value of a group data should be specified as a nonnumeric literal (see Sec. 5.7 for details).

5.4 FILE SECTION

The FILE SECTION must contain a file description entry followed by one or more record description entries for each of the files used in a program. The file description entry must begin with the level indicator FD followed by the file name. This file name must be identical with the file name specified in the select clause of the ENVIRONMENT DIVISION (see Sec. 4.2.2.1). A file description entry may have several clauses after the file name. All these clauses are optional except one (namely, the LABEL RECORDS clause). There must be a terminating period (.) at the end of a file description entry. Thus the format for a file description entry in its most simple form is

$$
\text{FD} \quad \text{file-name} \quad \underline{\text{LABEL}} \quad \left\{ \begin{array}{l} \underline{\text{RECORDS}} \text{ ARE} \\ \underline{\text{RECORD}} \text{ IS} \end{array} \right\} \quad \left\{ \begin{array}{l} \underline{\text{STANDARD}} \\ \underline{\text{OMITTED}} \end{array} \right\}
$$

The meaning of the LABEL RECORD clause will be explained in Sec. 13.3.3. As a general rule, STANDARD option should be specified for disk files, and OMITTED option should be specified for card reader and printer files. Though ANSI 74 standard specifies LABEL RECORD clauses as mandatory, many compilers treat it as optional. As such, for simplicity, we shall omit the LABEL RECORDS clause in the examples given in the initial part of this book. The coding rule for an FD entry is similar to that of level 01 entry. The label indicator FD must begin in area A and the rest of the file description entry must appear only in area B.

The record description entries that follow the file description entry, should describe the record types in the file. If different types of records appear in the same file, there should be one record description entry for each type of record. In the simplest case, a file will contain only one type of record (that is, all records having the same size and structure) and, therefore, only one record description entry will be needed.

A record description entry is a 01 level group item along with all its subdivisions. The data name that appears at level 01 is considered to be the record name. Even when the record should be defined as an elementary item (that is, the record is not subdivided into various fields), the record description entry must specify 01 as the level number.

Example

Each card of a card deck contains the following data fields in the columns
shown against them.

Card Columns	Date Field	Type
1-5	SALESMAN-NO	Numeric
11-15	QUANTITY	Numeric
21-30	UNIT-PRICE	Numeric (2 decimal places)
31-40	AMOUNT	Numeric (2 decimal places)

Let the file name be CARD-FILE. The entries for this file in the FILE
SECTION should be

```
FD    CARD-FILE.

01    CARD-RECORDS.

      02  SALESMAN-NO      PIC 9(5).
      02  FILLER           PIC X(5).
      02  QUANTITY         PIC 9(5).
      02  FILLER           PIC X(5).
      02  UNIT-PRICE       PIC 9(8)V99.
      02  AMOUNT           PIC 9(8)V99.
      02  FILLER           PIC X(40).
```

It may be noted that the name FILLER has been used for those fields on the
card which do not contain any data. Conventionally, such fields are described as alphanumeric items.

5.5 WORKING-STORAGE SECTION

The data in the working storage can be a group item containing all its
subdivisions as in the case of record description. There may also be elementary data items which do not belong to a group. Such data items should be
defined at a special level number 77. Level number 77 must begin in area A.

Example

```
WORKING-STORAGE SECTION.
77   ALPHA-STRING    PIC   X(20).
77   DATA-N          PIC   9(3) VALUE  ZERO.
01   DATE.
     05   DAY        PIC   99.
     05   FILLER     PIC   X VALUE  "/".
     05   MONTH      PIC   99.
     05   FILLER     PIC   X VALUE  "/".
     05   YEAR       PIC   99.
01   INTER-STRING    PIC   X(20).
```

It may be noted that an elementary item in the WORKING-STORAGE SECTION need not always be defined at the level 77. It can as well be defined at the level 01. This has been done in the case of INTER-STRING.

5.6 EDITING

The data to be printed in a report requires some editing before it can be printed. For example, it is desirable to print a numeric data item by suppressing the leading zeros. If necessary, the sign and decimal point can also be inserted in a numeric data. Editing is normally performed by moving a numeric data item to a field containing special editing characters in its PICTURE clause.

5.6.1 Edit Characters for Numeric Data

The following characters can be used in the PICTURE clause to indicate editing.

Z   * $ —   +   CR   DB   .   ,   B   0   /

The use of these edit characters are explained below.

Z (Zero Suppression)

The edit character Z has the same meaning as that of a 9 in the picture except that the leading zeros in the source data, if any, in the digit positions indicated by Z will be suppressed (replaced by space characters). It is obvious that Z cannot appear to the right of any 9. It may also be noted that after the decimal point either the digit positions are indicated by all Z or none at all.

Example

The following examples illustrate the use of Z editing characters. The character ⱡ is used to indicate a space character and the character ∧ is used to indicate the position of the decimal point.

Picture of the Field	Numeric Value Moved to the Field	Edited Value
ZZ999	04678	ⱡ4678
ZZ999	00052	ⱡⱡ052
ZZ999	1∧68	ⱡⱡ001
ZZZV99	38∧4	ⱡ3840
ZZZV99	0∧65	ⱡⱡⱡ65
ZZZZVZZ	0∧05	ⱡⱡⱡⱡ05
ZZZZVZZ	0	ⱡⱡⱡⱡⱡⱡ

(Asterisk)

The edit character * (asterisk) is identical to Z except that the leading zeros are replaced by asterisks instead of space characters.

Examples

Picture of the Field	Numeric Value Moved to the Field	Edited Value
**999	04678	*4678
**999	00052	**052
**999	1 ∧68	**001

$ (Currency Sign)

A single currency sign can appear at the leftmost position of a picture. In that case the $ character is inserted.

Examples

Picture of the Field	Numeric Value Moved to the Field	Edited Value
$99999	985	$00985
$99999	32264	$32264
$ZZ999	985	$ƀƀ985
$ZZ999	32264	$32264
$**999	985	$**985

— (Minus Sign)

A minus sign can appear either at the leftmost or rightmost position of a picture. If the value of an item is negative, a minus sign will be inserted in the said position. On the other hand, if the item is positive, a space character will be inserted.

Examples

Picture of the Field	Numeric Value Moved to the Field	Edited Value
− 9999	− 382	− 0382
− 9999	382	ⱡ0382
9999 −	− 382	0382 −
9999 −	382	0382ⱡ
− ZZZV99	− 46ᴧ52	− ⱡ4652
− ZZZV99	46ᴧ52	ⱡⱡ4652

+ (Plus Sign)

A plus sign has the same meaning as that of a minus sign except that when the item is positive a plus sign will be inserted instead of the space character. If the item happens to be negative, a minus sign will be inserted although there is a plus sign in the picture.

Examples

Picture of the Field	Numeric Value Moved to the Field	Edited Value
+ 9999	− 382	− 0382
+ 9999	382	+ 0382
9999 +	− 382	0382 −
9999 +	382	0382 +
+ ZZZV99	− 46ᴧ52	− ⱡ4652
+ ZZZV99	46ᴧ52	+ ⱡ4652

CR and DB (Credit and Debit Sign)

The two characters CR or DB symbol may appear only at the rightmost position of the picture. They are identical to the minus sign edit character. In other words, the symbols CR or DB will appear in the rightmost position only if the item is negative, otherwise they will be replaced by two space characters.

Examples

Picture of the Field	Numeric Value Moved to the Field	Edited Value
9999CR	−4562	4562CR
9999CR	4562	4562ƀƀ
ZZZCR	−42	ƀ42CR
ZZZ9V99DB	−152 ^ 25	ƀ15225DB
ZZZ9V99DB	152 ^ 25	ƀ15225ƀƀ

(Period or Decimal Point)

A period may be used to insert a decimal point and may not appear more than
once. Both the period and V cannot appear in the same picture. A period
must not also appear as the rightmost character in the picture. If the data
item to be edited has a V specified in its picture, then an alignment of
V with the said period takes place. As a result, zeros may be inserted in
the resultant edited data. If zero suppression is also specified, the period
stops zero suppression on its right. However, there is an important exception. If all the digits before and after the period happen to be zeros, the
period does not stop zero suppression and the entire field including the
period is space-filled (the period is not filled with space when an asterisk
(*) is used as a zero-suppression character).

Examples

Picture of the Field	Numeric Value Moved to the Field	Edited Value
9999.99	324 ^ 52	0324.52
ZZ99.99	45 ^ 25	ƀƀ45.25
ZZ99.99	245	ƀ245.00
ZZZZ.ZZ	0 ^ 05	ƀƀƀƀ.05
ZZZZ.ZZ	0	ƀƀƀƀƀƀƀ
****.**	0	****.**
$ZZZ9.99	0285	$ƀ285.00

, (Comma)

A comma, when used in a picture, is treated as an insertion character and
inserted wherever it appears. There can be more than one comma in a picture.
However, if zero suppression (including zero suppression by asterisk (*))

takes place to the right of any comma, the said comma will also be suppressed and a space character will take its position. A comma cannot appear either as the rightmost or leftmost character in a picture.

Examples

Picture of the Field	Numeric Value Moved to the Field	Edited Value
99,999	2456	02,456
99,999	37	00,037
ZZ,Z99	2456	ƀ2,456
,*	12	****12
*,***,**	246	****2,46
*,***,**	123456	1,234,56
ZZ,Z9.99	123 ∧ 45	ƀ1,23.45

B (Blank Insertion)

The appearance of a B anywhere in the picture will insert a space character in the edited data. There can be more than one B in a picture.

Examples

Picture of the Field	Numeric Value Moved to the Field	Edited Value
99B99B99	150182	15ƀ01ƀ82
99B99B99	46	00ƀ00ƀ46

0 (Zero Insertion)

A zero appearing in a picture will be treated in the same way as a B except that 0 will be inserted instead of a space character.

Examples

Picture of the Field	Numeric Value Moved to the Field	Edited Value
9900	12	1200
09990	456	04560

(Slash Insertion)

The edit character slash (/) also called virgule or stroke, may appear anywhere in the picture. If used, it will be inserted. There can be more than
one slash in the picture. However, this edit character being an ANSI 74
addition, may not be available at present in many compilers.

Examples

Picture of the Field	Numeric Value Moved to the Field	Edited Value
99/99/99	150681	15/06/81
999/999/99	3245	000/032/45

BLANK WHEN ZERO

BLANK WHEN ZERO is an editing clause which may be used along with a picture.
This will set the entire data item to blanks if its value is equal to zero.
However, the edit character asterisk (*) may not be used if BLANK WHEN ZERO
is specified. When this clause is used to describe a field whose picture
contains an asterisk, it is ignored by the compiler. The syntax of this
clause is as follows:

<u>BLANK</u>   <u>WHEN</u>   <u>ZERO</u>

Examples

Picture of the Field		Numeric Value Moved to the Field	Edited Value
ZZZ.99	BLANK WHEN ZERO	2$_\wedge$5	bb2.50
ZZZ.99	BLANK WHEN ZERO	0	bbbbbb
999.99	BLANK WHEN ZERO	0	bbbbbb

Floating Insertion

The currency symbol ($) can appear in multiples on the left-hand side of a
picture. In this case the character will be treated in the same way as the
Z character and only one currency symbol will be inserted immediately to
the left of the first non-zero digit of the data. Such a floating insertion
is also possible in the case of minus (−) and plus (+) signs. In the case

of the minus character, no sign will be inserted unless the data is negative.
The appearance of a period halts the floating insertion.

Examples

Picture of the Field	Numeric Value Moved to the Field	Edited Value
$$$$9.99	235 ∧ 25	℔$235.25
$$$$9.99	342	℔$342.00
++++.99	− 475 ∧ 25	− 475.25
++++.99	45	℔+45.00
----.99	− 3 ∧ 5	℔℔−3.50
----.99	3 ∧ 5	℔℔℔3.50
----.99	− 382	− 382.00

The edit characters can be used in combination, but the following rules
should be observed.

(i) Symbols + - CR DB and the operational character S are mutually
exclusive and only one of these may appear in a picture. These
symbols are known as report signs.

(ii) As floating-insertion characters, $ + - Z and * are mutually
exclusive. For example, if a (-) is used for floating insertion,
$ cannot be used in the same manner. However, $ may still occupy
the leftmost position (fixed insertion) with floating — signs on
its right.

(iii) In addition to the edit characters, the picture may contain the
operational characters 9 and V. However, both V and period (.)
should not appear in the same picture.

(iv) All edit characters and the operational character 9 specified in
a picture should be taken into consideration to determine the
size of the edited item.

5.6.2 Editing of Alphabetic and Alphanumeric Data

Although editing is primarily required for numeric data, limited editing is
also possible for alphabetic and alphanumeric data. An alphabetic data item
may contain only the B edit character. An alphanumeric data item may contain
only 0, B and / edit characters.

5.6.3 Examples of Editing

A few more examples of editing are given below.

Source Field		Receiving Field	
Picture	Source Data	Picture	Edited Data
9(5)	01234	ZZ999	ƀ1234
9(5)	00000	ZZZZZ	ƀƀƀƀƀ
9(5)	00357	*****	**357
S999V99	00793̄	+++9.99	ƀƀ−7.93
S999V99	00793·	+++9.99	ƀƀ+7.93
S999V99	01357̄	ZZ9.99CR	ƀ13.57CR
9(5)	00519	$$$$$9.99	ƀƀ$519.00
9(5)	00519	$ZZZZ9.99	$ƀƀ519.00
S9(5)	12345	−ZZ,ZZ9.99	ƀ12,345.00
9(5)	00045	ZZ,ZZ9.99	ƀƀƀƀ45.00
9(6)	011280	99B99B99	01ƀ12ƀ80
S9(4)V99	214680̄	Z(4).99DB	2146.80DB
9(4)	3182	999900	318200
V999	483	99.999	00.483
99V9	483	99.999	48.300
S9(5)	34215̄	9(5)+	34215−
S9(5)	34215̄	9(5) —	34215−
S9(5)	34215	9(5) —	34215ƀ

5.6.4 SPECIAL-NAMES Paragraph

If a currency symbol other than $ is required for editing, a one character symbol may be specified in the SPECIAL-NAMES paragraph of the ENVIRONMENT DIVISION. This character may not be a digit or letters A to D, L, P, R, S, V, X, Z or special characters blank * − , . ; ( ) + ' ' / = . The syntax is as follows:

> SPECIAL-NAMES.
>
> CURRENCY SIGN IS ''character''.

In order to edit a numeric data in the European manner it is possible to interchange the roles of comma (,) and period (.) as edit characters. This may be accomplished by the following entry in the SPECIAL-NAMES paragraph.

> DECIMAL-POINT IS COMMA.

5.7 CLASSES AND CATEGORIES OF DATA

In order that the class attribute of any data item in COBOL can be determined conclusively, all elementary data items are classified into the following five categories — alphabetic, numeric, numeric edited, alphanumeric and alphanumeric edited. The characters in the picture string determines the category of an elementary data item.

The following table shows the different categories and the corresponding symbols that may be used in the PICTURE character string.

Category	Symbols in PICTURE Character String
Alphabetic	A B
Numeric	9 P S V
Numeric Edited	9 P V and at least one of the editing symbols B / Z 0 + — * , . CR DB $
Alphanumeric	X 9 A (must contain at least one X or a combination of 9 and A)
Alphanumeric Edited	X 9 A B 0 / (must contain (i) at least one X with at least one of B 0 / or (ii) at least one A with at least one 0 or /)

These five categories of data are grouped into three classes — alphabetic, numeric and alphanumeric. The following table shows the relationship of a class and the corresponding categories.

Level of Data Item	Class	Category
Elementary	Alphabetic	Alphabetic
	Numeric	Numeric
	Alphanumeric	Numeric Edited Alphanumeric Alphanumeric Edited
Group	Alphanumeric	Elementary data within the group may belong to any category

The class of a data item indicates how the data is treated during execution. Thus a group item is treated as an alphanumeric data item regardless of the categories of the elementary items contained in it. For example, consider the following entries in the data division.

```
01 · THIS-GROUP.
      02  ELEMENTARY-ONE            PIC         9(5).
      02  ELEMENTARY-TWO            PIC         9(8).
```

The class and category for each of ELEMENTARY-ONE and ELEMENTARY-TWO are numeric. However, the class of the group item THIS-GROUP is alphanumeric.

Like the elementary data items, the literals and figurative constants can also be classified into appropriate categories. A numeric literal belongs to the numeric category and a nonnumeric literal belongs to the alphanumeric category. The figurative constant ZERO, ZEROS or ZEROES belongs to the numeric category and the figurative constant SPACE OR SPACES belongs to the alphabetic category. All other figurative constants belong to the alphanumeric category.

5.8 IMPLEMENTATION DIFFERENCES

(a) Single Digited Level Numbers

Single digited level numbers (1 to 9) can optionally be used in B-6700 and ICL-1900.

(b) Combination of V and P

Normally, the combination of V and P is not allowed in a PICTURE clause. However, DEC-10 and B-6700 will allow the use of V either at the left or at the right of all Ps. Since the use of such a V is superfluous, the said combination may not be used.

(c) Order of Data Definition in WORKING-STORAGE SECTION

Some systems require that the level 77 items must be defined before the level 01 items. According to ANS-74 it is not obligatory for the 77 level items to be defined first in the WORKING-STORAGE SECTION. Of the implementations considered here, B-6700 and ICL-1900 allow this flexibility.

(d) VALUE Clause

Some systems allow the abbreviation VA for VALUE. Of the three implementations, ICL-1900 does not allow this abbreviation.

(e) Editing

If editing is indicated only by a decimal-point (.) insertion with the zero suppression symbol * and the source data happens to be zero, then in B-6700 and DEC-10, the edited field will consist of asterisks and the decimal point. In ICL-1900 the decimal point too will be replaced by an asterisk.

In B-6700 and DEC-10 both a period (.) and V cannot appear in the same picture, whereas in ICL-1900 a decimal-point insertion should be indicated by a period followed by a V, e.g., 999.V99 is a valid picture in ICL-1900.

DEC-10 does not allow more than one period in a picture. In B-6700 and ICL-1900 additional periods are treated as insertion characters. The period can also be the last character in a picture string for B-6700. In such cases the entry must be terminated by a semi-colon which must immediately follow the said period and must be followed by a blank. In case the entry happens to be the last entry of the DATA DIVISION, a second period should be used in place of the semi-colon.

In ICL-1900 either £ or $ can be used as the currency symbol. In the other two only $ is to be used for the purpose.

The implementation of the symbol slash (/), though an approved editing character in ANSI 74, as an insertion character is yet to be done in all the three systems.

B-6700 provides two more editing characters — L and J. For their use the interested readers may consult the relevant manual. In B-6700 characters (appearing in an editing picture) other than the editing characters are considered as insertion characters.

(f) Special-names

The following characters are not allowed to replace the currency symbol $ in all the three systems considered by us.

> o   digits 0 to 9
> o   alphabets A - D, P, R, S, V, X-Z and space
> o   special characters * + — , . ; ( ) "

In addition to these, ICL-1900 does not allow the special character virgule (/) and B-6700 does not allow J and L for the said purpose.

(g) Numeric Data in Binary

In ICL-1900 the picture for a numeric data may contain 1 instead of 9. The character 1 indicates a binary digit. The symbol V may be used in combination with 1 to indicate the position of the assumed decimal point. This is a non-standard feature and is not available in the other systems.

EXERCISES

1. Indicate whether the following statements are true or false.
    (a) The symbol V in a PICTURE clause contributes to the field size.
    (b) The symbol V in a PICTURE clause indicates the assumed position of a decimal point.
    (c) The symbols S and P in a PICTURE clause contributes to the field size.

2. Find out the mistakes in the following DATA DIVISION entries.
    (a) FILE SECTION.
         FD   CARD-DESIGN.
         77   CARD-RECORD.
              03   NAME   PICTURE   IS   X(25).
              03   EARNING   PICTURE   IS   9(5)V99.

```
(b)  WORKING-STORAGE SECTION.
     FD   PRINTER-FILE.
     01   PRINT-REC          PICTURE   IS   X(39).
              02   NAME-1    PICTURE   IS   9(5)V99.
              02   E-1       PICTURE   IS   9(5)V99.
              02   TAX       PICTURE   IS   9(5)V99.

(c)  WORKING-STORAGE SECTION.
     01   GROUP-1
              02   A11      PIC   999.
              03   A12      PIC   X(20).
              03   A13      PIC   9(4)VXX.
     77   TEMP1            PIC   9(4)V99.
     77   TEMP2            PIC   9(4)V99.
```

3. Determine the sizes of the data items in each of the following cases.

    (a) SPPP9999.   (b) X(20).
    (c) 9(8)V9(4).   (d) SV9.
    (e) 9(5).   (f) 9(4)V99.
    (g) S9(4)V99.   (h) 99PPP.
    (i) −9(4).99   (j) $$$,$$$9.99.
    (k) $Z(5).99CR.   (l) 9(4)000.

4. Show the internal representations for the following data items.

	External Value	Picture
(a)	−12.38	S99V99
(b)	45000	99PPP
(c)	−.00123	SPP999
(d)	SYZ	A(3)

5. Rewrite Example 2 of Sec. 5.3.2 by specifying the value clause for the elementary items.

6. Describe the following group in the WORKING-STORAGE SECTION.

MASTER-REC

DATE-OF JOINING			DEPT	EMP-NO	EARNINGS				
DAY	MTH	YEAR			BASIC	ALLOWANCES			
						DA	HRA	OTHERS	
99	99	99	X(6)	9(5)	9(4)V99	999V99	999V99	999V99	

DEDUCTIONS		
PF	JT	LOAN
999V99	999V99	999V99

7. Define the following items with the initial values as specified.

Data Name	Description	Initial Value
TOTAL	Numeric, 9 digited with 2 decimal places	0 (zero)
HEADING	Alphabetic, 26 characters	THIS IS A SAMPLE PROGRAM
MAXIMUM	Numeric, 3 digited	highest value in collating sequence

8. A WORKING-STORAGE SECTION entry reads

        77   PRODUCT-RATE   PIC   99V99   VALUE   IS   20.5.

Indicate which one of the following is correct.

(a) The storage area allocated for PRODUCT-RATE is initialized to the value 20.5 just before the first statement in the PROCEDURE DIVISION is executed.

(b) At the time of compilation, the code for moving the value 20.5 to PRODUCT-RATE is generated whenever this symbol appears in the PROCEDURE DIVISION.

(c) During compilation, whenever the symbol PRODUCT-RATE appears in the PROCEDURE DIVISION, this will be replaced by the constant 20.5.

9. Indicate whether or not the following picture specifications are correct.

(a) $$Z(4).99   (b) $9(4)ZZ.99   (c) X(5)
(d) +9(5).99CR   (e) Z(5).Z9   (f) A(5)00

10. From the following find out the picture specifications that cannot be used in the record description of an input card file.

(a) 9999   (b) 9(5)V99   (c) 9(5).99   (d) $$$$9.99
(e) X(10)   (f) BB9(6).

6

PROCEDURE DIVISION AND BASIC VERBS

6.1 STRUCTURE OF THE PROCEDURE DIVISION

The PROCEDURE DIVISION contains statements which specify the operations to be performed by the computer. Each of these statements is formed with COBOL words and literals. A statement always starts with a COBOL verb. The following are examples of COBOL statements.

        ADD ALLOWANCE TO BASIC-PAY.
        IF TOTAL-PAY IS GREATER THAN 1000 GO TO PARA-TAX-CALCULATION.

The first statement begins with the COBOL verb ADD whereas the second starts with the COBOL verb IF. The second statement includes another statement within it which begins with the GO TO verb. When a statement is terminated by a period followed by a space, it is called a sentence. However, a COBOL sentence may not consist of one statement only. As in the second example, several statements can be combined to form one sentence. In such cases a space is sufficient to set apart each statement in a sentence. A semicolon (;) or comma (,) can optionally be used to delimit statements, but the semicolon or comma must be followed by a space. In earlier versions of COBOL it was also required that a period, comma or semicolon, when used to terminate or delimit a statement, must appear immediately after the last word of the statement. This punctuation rule has been relaxed in ANSI 74. However, it is better to observe the rule because some compilers may still retain it.

Sentences can be grouped together to form paragraphs and in turn paragraphs can be grouped to form sections. A paragraph or section must be headed by a name. The rules for forming a paragraph or section name are identical to those for data names. Moreover, some COBOL compilers also allow paragraph names consisting of numerical characters only. In order to indicate which one is a section name and which one is paragraph name, section names must be followed by the word SECTION with at least one space in between. The paragraph name or the word SECTION in the case of a section name should be terminated by a period. The need for grouping paragraphs into sections does not arise in most cases. As such the PROCEDURE DIVISION may not contain any section at all. However, in some special cases sections must be used. Even then the section names are user-defined and not fixed as in the case of the sections in DATA DIVISION and ENVIRONMENT DIVISION. The following format shows the simplified structure of the PROCEDURE DIVISION when it contains sections.

```
PROCEDURE DIVISION.
{section-name SECTION.
[paragraph-name.  [sentence]   ...  ]  ... } ...
```

The following format shows the simplified structure of the PROCEDURE DIVI-
SION when it does not contain sections.

```
PROCEDURE DIVISION.
[paragraph-name.  [sentence]   ...  ] ...
```

The paragraph name or section name must start in area A. The line
containing a section header must not contain anything else. However, any
statement may appear in the same line that contains the paragraph name with
the restriction that there must be at least one space between the terminating period of the paragraph name and statement. The statements and
sentences within a paragraph must be written in area B. There can be more
than one statement or sentence in a line. Alternatively, a statement or
sentence can be written in more than one line. In the latter case if a
word is broken in the middle and need to be continued to the next line, a
hyphen must be written in the column position 7 to indicate the continuation
(see Sec. 3.9).
  A paragraph can consist of one or more sentences that constitute its
body. The paragraph body is terminated by the appearance of another paragraph header or section header or the end of the PROCEDURE DIVISION. According to the ANSI 74 standard, a paragraph may not have any sentence at all.
Let us consider the following example.

```
PARA - ONE.
       MOVE  D-RATE  TO  RATE
       MULTIPLY  AMOUNT  BY  RATE  GIVING  DIVIDEND.
PARA - TWO.
PARA - THREE.
       .
       .
       .
```

The body of the paragraph named PARA-ONE consists of one sentence made
of two statements. The paragraph named PARA-TWO does not contain any sentence
(see Sec. 10.6 for the use of such null paragraphs).
  A section can consist of zero, one or more paragraphs constituting its
body. The section body is terminated by the appearance of another section
header or the end of the PROCEDURE DIVISION (see Sec. 13.10 for exceptions).
  In some COBOL statements it becomes necessary to make a reference to a
section name or paragraph name. When a section name is referred to, only its
name without the word SECTION must be used. To avoid any ambiguity, all
section names must be unique and must be different from paragraph names,
data names or any other names. All paragraphs within a section must have
unique names, but paragraph names need not be unique in the entire program.
In order to make a reference to a nonunique paragraph name, it should be
qualified as shown below.

$$\text{Paragraph-name} \left\{ \begin{array}{c} \underline{\text{OF}} \\ \underline{\text{IN}} \end{array} \right\} \text{section-name}$$

For example, suppose a section having the name FIRST-PART contains a paragraph named THIS-PARA. Let THIS-PARA be also the name of another paragraph in a different section. In such a case, the said paragraph should be referred to as THIS-PARA OF FIRST-PART. A qualification of a paragraph name is required only when it is referred to in a statement located in a different section. When referred to by statements located within the section where the nonunique paragraph name is defined, no qualification is necessary. Thus when THIS-PARA is referred to by some statement located within FIRST-PART, no qualification is necessary.

A paragraph name or section name is often referred to as a procedure name.

The COBOL verb which appears at the beginning of a statement designates the particular action that the statement will perform. There are several COBOL verbs to indicate different types of actions to be taken during execution. Some basic verbs in their simplest forms are introduced in the following Section.

6.2 DATA MOVEMENT VERB: MOVE

It frequently becomes necessary to move data from one place in the memory to another place. This is done with the help of the MOVE verb. The COBOL statement MOVE A TO B means that the value contained in the field named A should be transferred to the data field named B. Another example of a MOVE statement may be MOVE 3 TO COUNT. In this case the value 3 itself is moved to the field named COUNT. The general form of the MOVE verb is as follows:

$$\underline{\text{MOVE}} \left\{ \begin{array}{l} \text{identifier-1} \\ \text{literal-1} \end{array} \right\} \underline{\text{TO}} \text{ identifier-2 } [, \text{ identifier-3}] \ldots$$

Data movement is governed by the following rules.

(a) The contents of identifier-1 or the value of literal-1 is moved to identifier-2, identifier-3, etc. Note that there may be more than one receiving field whereas there must be only one sending field, the contents of all the receiving fields will be replaced by the value of the sending field. The contents of identifier-1 remain unaltered.

(b) When the sending field is numeric and the receiving field is numeric or numeric edited (i.e., picture contains edit symbols) the data movement is called numeric data transfer. In such cases the dominant factor in the movement is the alignment of the decimal points of the two fields. For the purpose of this alignment, the numeric fields for which the position of the decimal point is not explicitly indicated, the decimal point is assumed to be at the right of the rightmost digit. If the receiving field is not large enough to hold the data received, truncation can take place at either end depending on whether the integral part, fractional part or both can or cannot be accommodated (see examples given in this section for further clarification). However, if significant integral positions are likely to be lost, a warning to that effect is issued by the compiler. On the other hand, if the receiving field is larger than the sending field, zero-fill will take place in the unused positions to keep the numeric value unaltered.

(c) When both the sending and receiving fields are alphabetic, alphanumeric or alphanumeric edited, the data movement is called alphanumeric data transfer. In such cases the receiving area is filled from left to right and space fill occurs to the right if the receiving area is larger than the sending field. When the receiving area is smaller, truncation occurs from the right and the compiler gives a warning to that effect.

Ideally, both the sending and receiving fields should belong to the same category. However, quite often it becomes necessary to transfer a data to a field having a different category. The various rules for such moves are discussed in Chapter 9. Identifier-1, identifier-2, identifier-3, etc., can be group items. In such cases, the move is called a group move. Group move is also discussed in detail in Chapter 9. For the time being let us consider one particular type of group move that is very frequently used. This is when we wish to initialize a record area by spaces. For example, the statement MOVE SPACES TO REC-AREA will space-fill the entire area denoted by the group name REC-AREA.

Examples

(a) MOVE A TO B.

	Contents of A			Contents of B	
	Before execution	After execution		Before execution	After execution
(i)	PIC 9999			PIC 9999	
	1 2 3 4	1 2 3 4		4 6 8 0	1 2 3 4
(ii)	PIC 999			PIC 9999	
	3 8 2	3 8 2		7 8 4 5	0 3 8 2
					Zero fill on the left
(iii)	PIC 99V9			PIC 999V99	
	6 4 2	6 4 2		4 6 7 5 2	0 6 4 2 0
					Zero fill on left and right

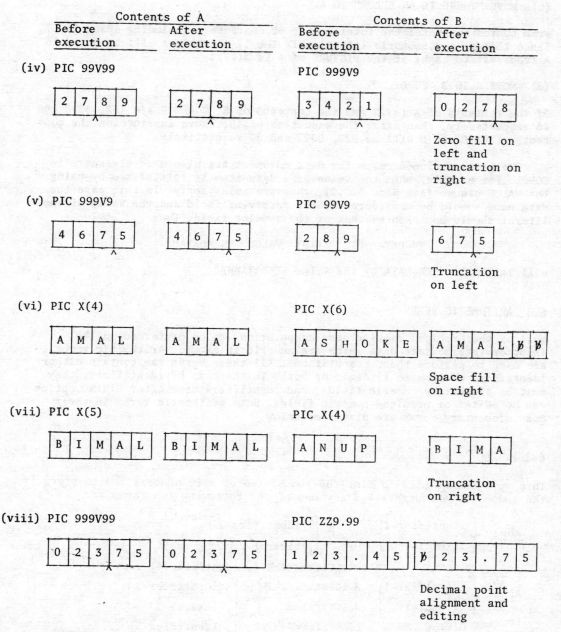

	Contents of A		Contents of B		
	Before execution	After execution	Before execution	After execution	
(iv)	PIC 99V99		PIC 999V9		
	2 7 ^ 8 9	2 7 ^ 8 9	3 4 2 ^ 1	0 2 7 ^ 8	Zero fill on left and truncation on right
(v)	PIC 999V9		PIC 99V9		
	4 6 7 ^ 5	4 6 7 ^ 5	2 8 ^ 9	6 7 ^ 5	Truncation on left
(vi)	PIC X(4)		PIC X(6)		
	A M A L	A M A L	A S H O K E	A M A L ␢ ␢	Space fill on right
(vii)	PIC X(5)		PIC X(4)		
	B I M A L	B I M A L	A N U P	B I M A	Truncation on right
(viii)	PIC 999V99		PIC ZZ9.99		
	0 2 3 ^ 7 5	0 2 3 ^ 7 5	1 2 3 . 4 5	␢ 2 3 . 7 5	Decimal point alignment and editing

(b) MOVE 15 to A.

In this case the number 15 will be moved to A and if the PICTURE of A is 999, then after the execution of the above statement A will contain 015.

(c) MOVE "THERE IS AN ERROR" TO A.

From quotes to quotes the total number of characters including space is 17. Since this is a nonnumeric literal, all the 17 characters will be moved to A from left to right if the PICTURE of A is X(17).

(d) MOVE A TO B, C, D.

If the contents of A is 22 and the contents of B, C and D are 452, 3892 and 46 respectively, then after the execution of the above instruction the contents of B, C and D will be 022, 0022 and 22 respectively.

The abovementioned rules for data movement are also used elsewhere in COBOL. For example, when the value of a data item is initialized by using the VALUE clause (see Sec. 5.3.2), the same rules apply. In this case the data name should be considered as the receiving field and the value of the literal should be taken as that of the sending field. Thus

77 NEW-DATA PIC X(10) VALUE "NEWDATA"

will initialize NEW-DATA by the value NEWDATAɓɓɓ.

6.3 ARITHMETIC VERBS

Most of the problems require some computations to be performed on the input or intermediate data which are numeric in nature. Arithmetic verbs are used to perform these computations. All these verbs can contain either identifiers or numeric literals or both. In the case of identifiers, they must be elementary numeric fields, and identifiers used after GIVING option can be edited or unedited numeric fields. Some arithmetic verbs in their most elementary forms are discussed below.

6.3.1 ADD

This verb can be used to find the sum of two or more numbers and to store the sum. The ADD verb takes any one of the following two forms.

$$\underline{\text{ADD}} \quad \begin{Bmatrix} \text{identifier-1} \\ \text{literal-1} \end{Bmatrix} \quad \begin{bmatrix} \text{identifier-2} \\ \text{, literal-2} \end{bmatrix} \quad \cdots$$

TO   identifier-3   [, identifier-4] ...

$$\underline{\text{ADD}} \quad \begin{Bmatrix} \text{identifier-1} \\ \text{literal-1} \end{Bmatrix} \quad \begin{Bmatrix} \text{identifier-2} \\ \text{literal-2} \end{Bmatrix} \quad \begin{bmatrix} \text{identifier-3} \\ \text{, literal-3} \end{bmatrix}$$

$$\underline{\text{GIVING}} \quad \text{identifier-4} \quad \text{[, identifier-5] ...}$$

Examples

(a) ADD A TO B

This example shows that the value of A will be added to the value of B and the result will be stored in B. The alignment of the decimal point is done automatically.

(b) ADD A B C TO D.

In this case the values of A, B and C will be added to the old value of D and the resultant sum will be the new value of D.

(c) ADD 15 A TO B.

This example shows that the number 15, the value of A and the value of B will be added and the resultant sum will be stored in B.

(d) ADD A, B GIVING C.

Here only the values of A and B will be added and the sum will be stored in C. The old value of C will be lost and that value will not take part in the summation.

(e) ADD A, B GIVING C, D, E.

In this case the value of A, B will be added and the sum will be stored in C, D and E. Hence after the execution of this statement, C, D and E will have the same value.

The above examples indicate that in the case of the TO option the previous value of the last named operand takes part in the summation and then this value is replaced by the result. However, this is not the case when the GIVING option is used. It should be mentioned here that the last named operand in both the cases can never be a literal as the resultant sum is always stored there. It is important to note that TO and GIVING cannot be used simultaneously. Thus ADD A TO B GIVING C would be wrong. The purpose is served by specifying the statement as ADD A B GIVING C. With GIVING option identifier-2/numeric-literal-2 is a must.

6.3.2 SUBTRACT

This verb is used to subtract one, or the sum of two or more numbers from one or more numbers and to store the result.
    The form of the SUBTRACT verb is as follows:

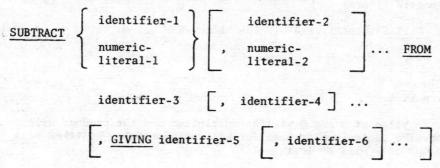

Examples

(a)   SUBTRACT A FROM B.

This statement means that the value of A will be subtracted from the value
of B and the subtracted result will be stored in B. The decimal point alignment will be done automatically.

(b)   SUBTRACT A, B FROM C.

This one shows that the value of B and A will be added and the resultant
sum will be subtracted from the value of C. After subtraction, the final
result will be stored in C. The old value of C will be lost.

(c)   SUBTRACT A, B FROM C GIVING D.

This indicates that the summation of the value of A and B will be subtracted
from the value of C and the final result will be stored in D. The old value
of D will be lost whereas in this case C will retain the old value.

(d)   SUBTRACT 15 FROM A B.

Here the number 15 will be subtracted from the values of A and B. A and B
will receive these new values.
    As in the case of the ADD statement, here also the last-named operand
must not be a literal as the final result will be stored there. If the
GIVING option is used, identifier-3, identifier-4 etc. can also be numeric
literals. For example, SUBTRACT A B FROM 50 GIVING C.

6.3.3   MULTIPLY

This statement causes one or more multiplicants to be multiplied by a multi-
plier and to store the products. The form of the MULTIPLY verb is as follows:

$$\underline{\text{MULTIPLY}} \quad \left\{ \begin{array}{l} \text{identifier-1} \\ \text{numeric-literal-1} \end{array} \right\} \quad \underline{\text{BY}} \quad \text{identifier-2} \quad \left[, \text{ identifier-3} \right] \ldots$$

$$\left[, \quad \underline{\text{GIVING}} \text{ identifier-4} \quad \left[, \text{ identifier-5} \right] \ldots \right]$$

Examples

(a)   MULTIPLY A BY B.

In this case the value of A and B will be multiplied and the product will
be stored in B. The decimal point position will automatically be taken care
of. The old value of B will be lost.

(b)   MULTIPLY A BY B GIVING C.

Here the value of A and B will be multiplied and the product will be stored
in C. The old value of C will be lost but B will contain its old value.

(c) MULTIPLY A BY B C D.

Here B will be multiplied by A and the result will be stored in B. Similarly, C will be multiplied by A and the product will be stored in C and the result of the multiplication of D and A will be stored in D.

(d) MULTIPLY A BY B C GIVING D E.

In this case the product of B and A will be stored in D, whereas the product of C and A will be stored in E.

In the case of the MULTIPLY statement also, literals cannot be used for identifier-2, identifier-3, etc. However, if the GIVING option is used, numeric literals are also permitted in place of identifier-2, identifier-3, etc. For example,

MULTIPLY TAX BY .05 GIVING TAX-BASE.

6.3.4 DIVIDE

The purpose of this verb is to divide one number by another and to store the result. There are several forms of this verb. One of its forms is as follows:

$$\underline{DIVIDE} \left\{ \begin{array}{l} \text{identifier-1} \\ \text{numeric-literal-1} \end{array} \right\} \underline{INTO} \ \text{identifier-2} \left[\text{, identifier-3} \right] \ldots$$

$$\left[\text{, } \underline{GIVING} \ \text{identifier-4} \left[\text{, identifier-5} \right] \ldots \right]$$

Examples

(a) DIVIDE 5 INTO A.

If the value of A is 20, then after the execution of this statement the value of A will be 4. The old value of A will be lost.

(b) DIVIDE 5 INTO A GIVING B.

If the value of A is 20, then after the execution of this statement the value of B will be 4. Here A will retain its old value.

(c) DIVIDE 3 INTO A GIVING B C.

Here the result of the division of A by 3 will be stored both in B and C.

(d) DIVIDE 2.5 INTO A B GIVING C D.

In this case A will be divided by 2.5 and the result will be stored in C, whereas the result of the division of B by 2.5 will be stored in D.

As in the case of the MULTIPLY statement, literals cannot be used for identifier-2, identifier-3, etc. Only when the GIVING option is used, are numeric literals also permitted in place of identifier-2, identifier-3, etc. For example, DIVIDE A INTO 25 GIVING V.

The second form of this verb is as follows:

$$\underline{\text{DIVIDE}} \left\{ \begin{array}{l} \text{identifier-1} \\ \text{numeric-literal-1} \end{array} \right\} \underline{\text{BY}} \left\{ \begin{array}{l} \text{identifier-2} \\ \text{numeric-literal-2} \end{array} \right\}$$

$$\underline{\text{GIVING}} \ \text{identifier-3} \ \left[\ , \ \text{identifier-4} \ \right] \dots$$

In this case identifier-1 or numeric-literal-1 will be divided by identifier-2 or numeric-literal-2, whatever may be the case. The result is stored in identifier-3, identifier-4, etc.

Examples

DIVIDE A BY 3 GIVING C.

If the value of A is 21 then after the execution of this statement C will contain 7.

There is another form of DIVIDE verb where there is a provision to store the remainder. Its form is

$$\underline{\text{DIVIDE}} \left\{ \begin{array}{l} \text{identifier-1} \\ \text{numeric-literal-1} \end{array} \right\} \left\{ \begin{array}{l} \underline{\text{INTO}} \\ \underline{\text{BY}} \end{array} \right\} \left\{ \begin{array}{l} \text{identifier-2} \\ \text{numeric-literal-2} \end{array} \right\}$$

$$\underline{\text{GIVING}} \ \text{identifier-3} \ \left[\ \underline{\text{REMAINDER}} \ \text{identifier-4.} \right]$$

Example

DIVIDE A INTO B GIVING C REMAINDER D.

If the identifier A, B, C and D are all two-digited numbers and if they contain 05, 37, 18 and 20 respectively before the execution of the statement, then after the execution of the statement, they will contain 05, 37, 07 and 02 respectively.

6.4   SEQUENCE CONTROL VERBS

Usually, the statements are executed sequentially one after another. This sequence can be altered with the help of a sequence control verb. There are several sequence control verbs in COBOL. In the present chapter we will discuss only two of these sequence control verbs.

6.4.1 GO TO

This verb is used to unconditionally transfer the control to elsewhere in
the program. Its form is as follows:

        GO   TO   procedure-name

As a result of the execution of this statement, the control is transferred
to the first statement of the paragraph or section mentioned in the procedure name.

Example

GO TO ERROR-ROUTINE

Suppose ERROR-ROUTINE is a paragraph name. The execution of this statement
will transfer the control to the first statement in ERROR-ROUTINE. On the
other hand, suppose ERROR-ROUTINE is a section name and FIRST-PARA is the
name of the first paragraph in this section. In this case control will be
transferred to the first statement in FIRST-PARA. It may be noted that GO
TO FIRST-PARA is identical to GO TO ERROR-ROUTINE.

6.4.2 STOP

This verb causes the termination of the execution of the object program.
Its form is

        STOP RUN

6.5   INPUT AND OUTPUT VERBS

Reading the data into the memory from some input medium (such as punched
cards) and writing the results from the memory onto some output medium
(such as continuous stationary) are of basic importance. The verbs OPEN,
READ, WRITE and CLOSE are available for such input-output operations.

6.5.1 OPEN

When a READ or a WRITE operation is performed on a file, it must be open.
The opening of a file may be done with the help of the OPEN verb. With the
OPEN verb it must also be indicated whether the file should be opened as an
input file or output file. If it is an input file, only reading is possible,
whereas in the case of an output file, only writing is possible. A file
once opened remains open until it is closed by a CLOSE statement. The OPEN
statement in its simple form is as follows:

$$\text{OPEN} \left\{ \begin{array}{llll} \text{INPUT} & \text{file-name-1} & [\,, \text{ file-name-2}\,] \ldots \\ \text{OUTPUT} & \text{file-name-3} & [\,, \text{ file-name-4}\,] \ldots \end{array} \right\} \ldots$$

Example 1

OPEN INPUT TRANSACTION, OLD-MASTER OUTPUT NEW-MASTER.

The example shows that there are two input files named TRANSACTION and OLD-MASTER and one output file called NEW-MASTER. All these files are opened and these are ready for reading or writing.

Example 2

OPEN INPUT KARD-FILE.
OPEN OUTPUT PRINT-FILE.

The first OPEN statement opens the KARD-FILE in input mode and the file is ready for reading. The next statement makes the PRINT-FILE ready for writing. There may be several OPEN statements in a program.

6.5.2   READ

The purpose of this verb is to make available the next logical record from an input file. It is important to note the meaning of "next" logical record in the above statement. The first time the READ statement is executed, the fitst record of the file will be read into the record area described in the FILE SECTION of the DATA DIVISION. The next time the READ statement is executed, the second record will be read in the same area. In this way each time a READ statement is executed the successive records will be read in the same area. Thus a time will come when there will be no more records in the file. In that case the statements following the AT END clause will be executed. The format of the READ statement is

READ   file-name   RECORD [INTO identifier-1]

AT END imperative-statement

It may be noted that each and every COBOL statement cannot appear after AT END; it must be an imperative statement or a sequence of imperative statements. We have not yet discussed which COBOL statements are imperative statements. We will discuss it later in this chapter. For the time being let us only note that the MOVE statement, GO TO statement and arithmetic statement (in the form presented earlier) are all imperative statements.

   The above syntax of READ requires that there must be a period to indicate the end of a READ statement. Note that for other verbs like MOVE ADD, SUB-TRACT,etc. discussed earlier, it is not necessary that the statements must be terminated by a period.

   The INTO option may be used first to read a record into the record area for the file and then to get it moved to the area indicated by identifier-1. Thus essentially, READ with the INTO option is a combination of a READ followed by a MOVE statement. However, when the INTO option is used, it is invalid to use the record name of the said file as identifier-1.

Example 1

READ OLD-MASTER AT END MOVE ZERO TO END-OF-RECORDS.

As a result of this statement, normally the next record from the OLD-MASTER file will be read. If there is no more record in OLD-MASTER, the value zero will be moved to the field named END-OF-RECORDS.

Example 2

READ TRANSACTION RECORD AT END GO TO PARA-END.

This example is similar to the earlier example. The next record from the TRANSACTION file will be read if it is available. If the file does not contain any more records, the control will be transferred to the paragraph named PARA-END.

Example 3

READ KARD-FILE INTO IN-REC AT END

              GO TO JOB-END.

This statement not only reads the next record into the record area of KARD-FILE but also moves the record into the area named IN-REC. When there is no more record in the KARD-FILE, the control is transferred to the paragraph named JOB-END. If the record area of the KARD-FILE has been named KARD-REC, the above statement is equivalent to

        READ KARD-FILE AT END GO TO JOB-END.

        MOVE KARD-REC TO IN-REC.

It may be noted that if the record has been successfully read, it is now available in KARD-REC as well as IN-REC.

6.5.3 WRITE

The WRITE verb releases a record onto an output file. The syntax of the WRITE statement can be different depending on the output device and medium used. The verb as described here can be used only to print results on a continuous stationery through a line printer. The form of the WRITE statement in such a case is

```
WRITE   record-name  [ FROM identifier-1 ]

         { BEFORE }                { integer-1    } [LINES]
        [{        }   ADVANCING    { identifier-2 } [LINES] ]
         { AFTER  }                { mnemonic-name }
                                   { hardware-name }
```

The first point to be noted is that in the case of the READ statement the file name is to be specified, whereas in the case of the WRITE statement it is required to mention the record name and not the file name. The ADVANCING phrase is used to control the vertical positioning of each record at the time of printing on the stationery placed on the printer. When the BEFORE phrase is used, the record is printed before the stationery is advanced, whereas the AFTER phrase may be used when the intention is to advance the stationery first and then to print the record. If integer-1 or identifier-1 is mentioned, the stationery is advanced by the number of lines equal to the value of integer-1 or to the current value of identifier-1.

If the mnemonic-name is specified, the printer will be advanced to the carriage control channel declared for the mnemonic-name in the SPECIAL-NAMES paragraph. This option is provided so that the hardware names which may be peculiar to a particular computer need not appear in the PROCEDURE DIVISION.

If the FROM option is used, the operation is identical to that of MOVE identifier-1 TO record-name followed by a WRITE record-name without the FROM clause. It is illegal to use the same storage area for both record-name and identifier-1.

It should be noted that after WRITE is executed, the record is no longer available.

Examples

(i)   WRITE TRANS-RECORD AFTER ADVANCING 3 LINES.

This WRITE statement indicates that TRANS-RECORD is a record name of a file that has been assigned to PRINTER. The current position of the stationery will be advanced by 3 lines, i.e., there will be 2 blank lines and the present record will be written on the third line.

(ii)   WRITE TRANS-RECORD BEFORE ADVANCING 3 LINES.

The record will be written first and then the page will be advanced by 3 lines. It may be mentioned here that if the ADVANCING phrase is not used, some compilers take the default value which is equivalent to "BEFORE ADVANCING 1 LINE". However, the ADVANCING phrase is mandatory for many compilers and it is therefore recommended that this phrase should be used even if it is required to print a line before advancing for 1 line.

6.5.4   CLOSE

When the processing of a file is over, the file may be closed. This is done with the help of the CLOSE-verb. The form of the CLOSE statement is

CLOSE   file-name-1   [, file-name-2]   ...

The file must be open when a close statement can be executed. Once a file is closed, it is no longer available to the program. It should be opened again if the file is required subsequently. It may be noted that unlike the OPEN statement, the nature of the use of the file (input or output) should not be mentioned in the CLOSE statement.

Example

CLOSE TRANSACTION, OLD-MASTER, NEW-MASTER, PRINT-FILE.

This statement will close all the four files — TRANSACTION, OLD-MASTER, NEW-MASTER and PRINT-FILE.

6.5.5 ACCEPT

The ACCEPT statement is used to read low-volume data from the operator's console, some other hardware device or from the operating system. The general format of the ACCEPT statement is as follows:

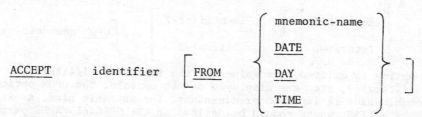

When the FROM option is omitted, the data is read into the identifier from the operator's console. At the time of execution, a message is displayed on the console (e.g., AWAITING COBOL INPUT) and the program is suspended until the operator enters the data through the console keyboard. Data entered by the operator will be left justified in the identifier. For example,

                    ACCEPT   FLAG-A

can be specified to read the value of FLAG-A from the console. It may be noted that no file definition is necessary.

The mnemonic-name option is implementor-dependent. The hardware device from which the data is to be read is to be equated to a mnemonic name in the SPECIAL-NAMES paragraph. For example, the following entry in the SPECIAL-NAMES paragraph

            TYPEWRITER-1   IS   CONTROL-DATA

may equate the mnemonic name CONTROL-DATA with the assumed implementor-name TYPEWRITER-1.   The

            ACCEPT FLAG-A   FROM   CONTROL-DATA

will read the value of FLAG-A from the hardware device indicated by TYPE-WRITER-1.

The DATE, DAY and TIME options are new features introduced in ANSI 74 COBOL. The DAY option returns the six-digit current date in the form YYMMDD where YY, MM and DD stand for year, month and day respectively. The DAY option returns a five-digit current date in the form YYDDD where YY stands for the year and DDD stands for the day of the year (001 to 365). The TIME option returns an eight-digit time in the form HHMMSSTT where HH, MM, SS, TT represent hour, minute, second and hundredths of a second respectively. For all the three options, the returned value is transferred to the identifier (in the ACCEPT statement) according to the rules of the MOVE statement. For example,

              ACCEPT   THIS-DAY   FROM   DATE

will transfer the value of the current date to THIS-DAY.

6.5.6 DISPLAY

The function of the DISPLAY statement is opposite to that of the ACCEPT statement. It is used to display low-volume results on the operator's console or some other hardware device. The general format of the DISPLAY statement is

$$\underline{\text{DISPLAY}} \quad \left\{ \begin{array}{l} \text{identifier-1} \\ \text{literal-1} \end{array} \right\} \left[\begin{array}{l} \text{, identifier-2} \\ \text{, literal-2} \end{array} \right] \dots \left[\underline{\text{UPON}} \text{ mnemonic-name} \right]$$

If the UPON option is omitted, the values of the identifier-1/literal-1, identifier-2/literal-2, etc. are displayed on the console. The UPON option with the mnemonic-name is implementor-dependent. The mnemonic name, as in the case of the ACCEPT verb, should be defined in the SPECIAL-NAMES paragraph. When more than one operand is specified, the values of the operands are displayed in the sequence they are specified. There will be no space between these values. The operands must be of the usage DISPLAY. (Usages will be discussed later.) The literals may be any literal or figurative constant except the ALL literal. If a figurative constant is specified, only one occurrence of the constant is displayed.

Example

Consider the following statement.

        DISPLAY   "RESULT IS",   **THE-RESULT**

and suppose that the picture and current value of THE-RESULT are 9(3) and 15 respectively. Upon execution of the statement, the following will be displayed on the console

        RESULT   IS   015

6.6 CONDITIONAL VERB: IF

Here we consider a simple form of the IF statements that enables us to make a comparison between two values. The form of the IF statement is

                IF   condition-1   statement-1

where the condition-1 may be one of the following

$$
\begin{Bmatrix} \text{identifier-1} \\ \text{literal-1} \end{Bmatrix}
\begin{Bmatrix}
\text{IS} \quad [\underline{\text{NOT}}] \quad \underline{\text{GREATER}} \quad \text{THAN} \\
\text{IS} \quad [\underline{\text{NOT}}] \quad \underline{>} \\
\text{IS} \quad [\underline{\text{NOT}}] \quad \underline{\text{LESS}} \quad \text{THAN} \\
\text{IS} \quad [\underline{\text{NOT}}] \quad \underline{<} \\
\text{IS} \quad [\underline{\text{NOT}}] \quad \underline{\text{EQUAL}} \quad \text{TO} \\
\text{IS} \quad [\underline{\text{NOT}}] \quad \underline{=}
\end{Bmatrix}
\begin{Bmatrix} \text{identifier-2} \\ \text{literal-2} \end{Bmatrix}
$$

Statement-I in the above format represents one or more COBOL statement. The IF statement is normally terminated by a period. This statement at first evaluates condition-1 which may be either true or false. If the condition is true, the statements following the condition are executed and the control is then passed to the next sentence after IF (provided that the statement before the period does not transfer the control to elsewhere in the program). If the condition is false, the control is transferred directly to the next sentence without executing the statements following condition-1. The condition-1 as shown above is known as a relational condition. The IF statement can also make use of other conditions which will be introduced later. For the time being we restrict ourselves to only relational conditions and further assume that identifier-1/literal-1 and identifier-2/literal-2 are numeric fields. The evaluation of condition-1 in this case is done algebraically. This means that the algebraic values (values considering sign) of the two fields are used to determine whether one is greater than, less than or equal to the other.

Examples

(i) IF A IS GREATER THAN B MOVE 3 TO X.

The nature of execution of this statement depends on the current values of A and B. For example, if A has a value 4 and B has a value 2, then 3 will be moved to X. Alternatively, if A has a value -4 and B has a value -2 then the move statement will not be executed and consequently the value of X will remain unchanged. In either case, after the execution of the IF statement, the control will reach the next sentence in sequence.

(ii) IF BASIC-PAY IS NOT GREATER THAN 500.00 GO TO LOWER-GROUP

In this case if BASIC-PAY is less than or equal to 500.00, the control will be transferred to the paragraph named LOWER-GROUP. Otherwise, the control will go to the next sentence in sequence.

More Examples

In the above, a few basic COBOL verbs have been introduced individually. However, while writing the program, one must choose the appropriate verbs and write the statements or sentences that should serve the purpose. We show below a few examples of COBOL statements used in combination to tackle particular situations.

(i) Suppose it is required to calculate the medical allowance that must be 20% of the basic pay or Rs. 250.00, whichever is greater. Further suppose that the basic pay is available in the data name BASIC-PAY which has been defined in the data division with the picture 9(5)V99. It is also assumed that the picture of MEDICAL-ALLOWANCE is also 9(5)V99. The required COBOL statements may be as follows:

```
MULTIPLY BASIC-PAY BY .2 GIVING MEDICAL-ALLOWANCE.
IF MEDICAL-ALLOWANCE IS LESS THAN 250.00
  MOVE 250.00 TO MEDICAL-ALLOWANCE.
```

Note that after the IF statement is executed, MEDICAL-ALLOWANCE will have the required value. Also note that the solution to a programming problem may not be unique. For example, the following COBOL statements will also do the same thing.

```
DIVIDE 5 INTO BASIC-PAY GIVING MEDICAL-ALLOWANCE.
IF MEDICAL-ALLOWANCE IS NOT LESS THAN 250.00
        GO TO END-OF-CALCULATION.
MOVE 250.00 TO MEDICAL-ALLOWANCE.

END-OF-CALCULATION.
  .
  .
  .
```

                              or,

```
IF BASIC-PAY NOT > 1250.00
    MOVE 250.00 TO MEDICAL-ALLOWANCE
    GO TO END-OF-CALCULATION.
MULTIPLY .2 BY BASIC-PAY GIVING MEDICAL-ALLOWANCE.

END-OF-CALCULATION.
  .
  .
  .
```

(ii) Suppose that the data name MESSAGE has been defined in the working storage section with the picture X(30). It is required to move the string "EXCEEDS CEILING" to MESSAGE if QUANTITY has a value greater than 1000. Alternatively, if QUANTITY is less than or equal to 125, MESSAGE should contain "REACHES DANGER LEVEL". In all other cases it should only have spaces. The COBOL statements for this should be

```
      MOVE    SPACES    TO    MESSAGE.
      IF   QUANTITY   IS  GREATER  THAN  1000
           MOVE  "EXCEEDS  CEILING"  TO  MESSAGE
           GO   TO   NEXT-CALCULATION.
      IF   QUANTITY  IS  NOT  GREATER THAN 125
           MOVE "REACHES DANGER LEVEL" TO MESSAGE.

   NEXT-CALCULATION.
             .
             .
             .
```

It may be noted that MESSAGE will contain spaces on the right.

   (iii)   A deck of cards is being read   as a file called EXAMINATION.
Each card contains, among other things, a field called TOTAL-MARKS which
contains the aggregate of all the marks obtained by a student. Write COBOL
statements to find the highest among the individual TOTAL-MARKS and to
store it in HIGHEST. Disregard ties and assume that TOTAL-MARKS contains
only positive numbers. When the reading of all the cards is over, the
control is transferred to the paragraph called NEXT-PROCESSING.

```
   MOVE ZEROS TO HIGHEST.

READ-PARA.

   READ EXAMINATION AT END GO TO NEXT-PROCESSING.
   IF TOTAL-MARKS IS GREATER THAN HIGHEST
   MOVE TOTAL-MARKS TO HIGHEST.
   GO TO READ-PARA.

NEXT-PROCESSING.
```

   (iv)   A deck of cards is being read   as a file called INCOME-TAX-FILE.
Each card contains, among other things, a field called EARNING. TAX is calculated from the following table.

EARNING	TAX
Less than or equal to 10000	0
Greater than 10000 but less than or equal to 15000	15% of the amount above 8000
Greater than 15000 but less than or equal to 20000	1050 + 18% of the amount above 15000
Greater than 20000	1950 + 25% of the amount above 20000

   Write COBOL statements to calculate TAX for each EARNING and after each
calculation, transfer the control to the paragraph named PRINT-PARA.

READ-PARA.

```
    READ INCOME-TAX-FILE AT END GO TO END-PARA.
    IF EARNING IS NOT GREATER THAN 10000
    MOVE ZERO TO TAX, GO TO PRINT-PARA.
    IF EARNING IS NOT GREATER THAN 15000
    SUBTRACT 8000 FROM EARNING, MULTIPLY
    0.15 BY EARNING GIVING TAX, GO TO PRINT-PARA.
    IF EARNING IS NOT GREATER THAN 20000
    SUBTRACT 15000 FROM EARNING, MULTIPLY 0.18 BY
    EARNING GIVING TAX, ADD 1050 TO TAX, GO TO PRINT-PARA.
    SUBTRACT 20000 FROM EARNING,
    MULTIPLY 0.25 BY EARNING GIVING TAX, ADD 1950 TO TAX.
```

PRINT-PARA.
```
    -

    -

    GO TO READ-PARA.
```

END-PARA.
```
    -
```

6.7 CATEGORIES OF COBOL STATEMENTS

Any COBOL statement falls into one of the three categories — imperative, conditional and compiler directing.

An imperative statement is one which directs the object program to take a specific action during execution. Except for the IF statement and READ statement, all other statements (in the form) discussed above, are imperative statements. A conditional statement is one which directs the object program to examine the truth value of a condition and to take subsequent action depending on the truth value. The IF statement is an example of a conditional statement. The compiler-directing statements are used to direct the COBOL compiler and no corresponding statement is generated for these in the object program. We have not yet seen any such statement. There are only two compiler-directing statements. These are the COPY and USE statements which will be discussed in due course.

It is important to be able to recognize an imperative statement. For example, the READ statement as shown in this chapter is not an imperative statement. This is because the AT END clause implicitly specifies a condition. If there are data cards to be read, the statement will read the next available card. If no more data cards are available, the READ statement does not read a card; instead, the statement after AT END is executed. However, we shall see afterwards that it is possible to specify the READ statement without the AT END clause. In that case the READ statement is considered to be an imperative statement. In fact, any statement which is not a compiler-directing statement or conditional statement must be an imperative statement. We give below a list of the conditional statements. These will be discussed in due course.

IF, SEARCH and RETURN statements.

ADD, SUBTRACT, MULTIPLY, DIVIDE and COMPUTE statements with SIZE ERROR option.

READ, WRITE, REWRITE and DELETE statements with INVALID KEY clause.

READ statement with AT END clause.

WRITE statement with END-OF-PAGE clause.

STRING, UNSTRING and CALL statements with ON OVERFLOW option.

When the term imperative statement appears in the format of a COBOL verb, it means either a single imperative statement or a sequence of consecutive imperative statements. Thus a READ statement can be written as follows:

```
READ  CARD-FILE RECORD AT END
          MOVE 1 TO ERROR-CODE
          GO TO END-OF-PROCESSING.
```

Here the imperative statement after AT END, consists of two imperative statements.

Another point that deserves mention in this connection is that some-times, a portion of a COBOL statement is called a phrase or clause for the purpose of reference. According to COBOL terminology, a portion of the PROCEDURE DIVISION statement should be called a phrase whereas a portion of an entry in the DATA or ENVIRONMENT DIVISION are to be called a clause. Thus, ideally, we should say SELECT clause and AT END phrase. Sometimes, portions of a clause can also be called a phrase. However, in this book we shall not observe any distinction between a clause and a phrase and they will be used interchangeably. Moreover, where a phrase or clause is optional, it will also be referred to as an option.

6.8   IMPLEMENTATION DIFFERENCES

(a)   ADD Statement

In ICL-1900 if the GIVING option is used, there can be just one field after GIVING whereas in the case of other computers there is no such restriction.

(b)   SUBTRACT Statement

When both FROM and GIVING options are used, ICL-1900 allows only one field after both FROM and GIVING whereas DEC-10 allows one field after FROM, but any number of fields after GIVING. For B-6700 the format is as given in the text.

(c)   MULTIPLY Statement

Except B-6700 all other computers allow only one field after both BY and GIVING. B-6700 allows only one field after BY when both BY and GIVING are used.

(d)   DIVIDE Statement

Except B-6700 all other computers allow just one field after INTO, BY and GIVING. B-6700 allows only one field after both INTO and BY when they are used with GIVING options. Only DEC-10 allows BY option without GIVING option. In this case the result will be stored in the first named operand and in that case this one must not be a literal.

(e)   GO TO Statement

The word TO is not optional in ICL-1900 and DEC-10.

(f)   READ Statement

In the case of the READ statement, AT is optional for DEC-10, B-6700 and ICL-1900.

(g)   WRITE Statement

In ICL-1900, line spacing does not take place if the ADVANCING option is not used. The maximum lines that can be advanced is limited to 31. If a mnemonic-name is used, it must be a name given to one of the hardware names CHANNEL-n (where n is an integer in the range 1 to 7, or in the case of the 2401 printer, 1 to 5). The hardware name is used as CHANNEL-n (where n is any specified integer number). In this computer the words ADVANCING and LINES are optional.
   In B-6700 if the ADVANCING option is not used, automatic advancing is provided to cause single spacing after writing (i.e., BEFORE ADVANCING 1 LINES). There is no maximum value specified for the number of lines that can be skipped at one time. Once ADVANCING is used, the subsequent WRITE statements are required to print the results on a different line. If the subsequent WRITE statements do not contain the ADVANCING option, the result will be overprinted on the previous line. In the case of a mnemonic-name, only channels 1 through 11 (inclusive) are valid. There must be at least one space between CHANNEL and the integer number while writing this in the SPECIAL-NAMES paragraph. Here besides the two optional words ADVANCING and LINES, TO can also be used. For example,

WRITE PRINT-REC AFTER ADVANCING TO 3 LINES.

   In DEC-10 if the ADVANCING option is not used and the recording mode is ASCII, BEFORE ADVANCING 1 LINES is assumed. There is no maximum value specified for the number of lines that can be skipped at one time. Identifier-1 and integer-1 can assume any value from 0 onwards. If it is zero, the paper is not advanced. In the case of a mnemonic-name, only channels 1 through 8 (inclusive) are valid. In this case the channel is written as CHANNEL (n). Here also the words ADVANCING and LINES are optional.

(h) ACCEPT and DISPLAY Statement

In B-6700, the FROM and UPON options are used for documentation purposes only. In DEC-10, when the mnemonic-name is used, the mnemonic-name must be equated to the console by the entry CONSOLE IS mnemonic-name in the SPECIAL-NAMES paragraph. In ICL-1900, the mnemonic-name should be associated to hardware names by the entry

hardware-name <u>IS</u> mnemonic-name

in the SPECIAL-NAMES paragraph. The manual may be consulted for valid hard-ware names. All the three compilers put restrictions on the maximum number of characters that can be received or displayed by a single ACCEPT or DISPLAY statement. We shall omit these details.

EXERCISES

1. Indicate which one of the following is not a valid delimiter in COBOL.
   (a) , (b) . (c) ; (d) space (e) -

2. Indicate which one gives the correct definition of "statement" and/or "sentence" in COBOL language.
   (a) All the statements of COBOL are also known as COBOL sentences.
   (b) A COBOL statement consists of a number of COBOL sentences, the last of which is terminated by a period.
   (c) A COBOL sentence consists of one or more than one statement, the last of which is terminated by a period.
   (d) There is no concept of statement and sentence in COBOL. Only English sentences can appear in comment lines.

3. Show what the following data names will contain when initialized as specified. Assume VALUE for VA.

77	A1	PIC	9(4)	VA	12.
77	A2	PIC	X(4)	VA	"12".
77	A3	PIC	X(5)	VA	ZEROES.
77	A4	PIC	X(8)	VA	ALL "456".
77	A5	PIC	X(5)	VA	ALL ZEROES.
77	A6	PIC	X(6)	VA	"SOME ERROR".
77	A7	PIC	X(7)	VA	"XYZ".
77	A8	PIC	9(4)V99	VA	12.5.

4. Write COBOL statements for the following:
   (i)   Add the value of BONUS to TOTAL-PAY.
   (ii) Subtract INCOME-TAX, PROVIDENT-FUND, CDS from the value of GROSS-PAY to get the NET-PAY.
   (iii) Calculate COMMISSION which is 5% of TOTAL-SALE.

(iv)   Make the value of data-name YOUR-AGE equal to 50.
(v)   Make the content of A be the characters THERE IS SOME ERROR.
(vi)   Make the content of AMOUNT equal to QUANTITY multiplied by RATE.

5.   A storage field FINAL-RESULT can contain twenty alphanumeric characters.
     What will be the content of FINAL-RESULT when the following data is
     moved to it?
     (i)   THERE IS NO ERROR
     (ii)   47892
     (iii) ASHOKE LAL JAIN
     (iv)   THIS TIME THERE MAY BE SOME TRUNCATION

6.   The following is PICTURE of TOTAL
     02   TOTAL   PIC 999V99.
     What will be the content of TOTAL when the following data is moved to
     it?
     (i)   ∧46
     (ii)   382 ∧ 2
     (iii) 23 ∧ 632
     (iv)   7892 ∧ 23
     (v)   490 ∧ 63
     where a caret (∧) indicates the position of the decimal point.

7.   Paragraph names are given in the following. Indicate whether they are
     valid or invalid.
     (i)   PARA-136   (v)   IF-AGE-GREATER-THAN-50
     (ii)   A678   (vi) STOP
     (iii) READ-AND-PRINT-PARA   (vii) PARA-STOP
     (iv)   PRINT/LINE   (viii) 24

8.   Indicate what will be the contents of A, B, C and D after the execution
     of each of the following instructions. In each instance, refer to the
     initial values of A, B, C and D and also place a cross (X) after any
     statement which is not valid. The caret (∧) implies a decimal point.

A	B	C	D
(PIC 99)	(PIC 99V9)	(PIC 99V9)	(PIC 99)
03	29 ∧ 4	03 ∧ 2	28

     (i)   ADD A TO C.
     (ii)   ADD A, D.
     (iii) SUBTRACT A, C FROM B.
     (iv)   DIVIDE A INTO D GIVING C REMAINDER D.
     (v)   DIVIDE A INTO 6.
     (vi)   MULTIPLY C BY 5.
     (vii) MULTIPLY A BY C GIVING D.
     (viii) SUBTRACT D, B FROM 80.
     (ix)   ADD B TO A GIVING D.
     (x)   MULTIPLY A BY C BY D.
     (xi)   MULTIPLY A TIMES C.
     (xii) ADD C, B GIVING D.
     (xiii) DIVIDE B BY A GIVING C.

9. In the following assume that the spacing and margin use are correct.
    Make corrections if there is any error.

(i)   OPEN TRANSACTION, FILE-A, FILE-B.

(ii) PROCEDURE DIVISION.
          OPEN INPUT TRANSACTION

          OUTPUT FILE-A.

      PARA-REPEAT.

          READ TRANS-REC AT END GO TO LAST-PARA.

          MOVE TRANS-REC TO FILE-A-REC.

          WRITE FILE-A AFTER ADVANCING 2 LINES.

          GO TO PARA-REPEAT.

      LAST-PARA.

          CLOSE INPUT TRANSACTION

              OUTPUT FILE-A.

(iii) PARA-READ-AGAIN.

          OPEN INPUT OLD-MASTER

              OUTPUT NEW-MASTER.

          READ OLD-MASTER AT END GO TO PARA-END.

          MOVE A TO B.

          WRITE NEW-MASTER-REC.

          GO TO PARA-READ-AGAIN.

      PARA-END.

(iv) PARA-BEGIN.

          OPEN INPUT FILE-A

              OUTPUT FILE-B.

      PARA-READ.

          READ FILE-B AT END GO TO PARA-END.

```
                    WRITE FILE-A-REC AFTER ADVANCING 2 LINES.

                    GO TO PARA-READ.

                    MOVE A TO B.

                PARA-END.
```

10. Assume the following DATA DIVISION entries.

```
        01  BILL.
            02   A       PIC 99.
            02   FILLER  PIC X(7).
```

Indicate whether the following statements in the PROCEDURE DIVISION
are correct or not.
   (i)   MOVE SPACES TO FILLER.
   (ii) MOVE "AB" TO A.
   (iii) MOVE SPACES TO A.
   (iv) MOVE ZEROS TO A.
   (v)   MOVE 23 TO A.
   (vi) MOVE "CORRECT" TO FILLER.

11. A deck of cards is being read as a file called RESULT. Each card
contains the information as follows:

Card Columns	Description
1-6	Roll No.
7-30	Name
31-33	Marks of English
34-36	Marks of Mathematics
37-39	Marks of Programming

Print all the information of a card and also the total marks of a
student in one line giving the proper spacing. Write DATA DIVISION
entries and PROCEDURE DIVISION statements for the above.

12. Consider another field in the output of Example 11 known as REMARK-IF-
ANY. If any student scores less than 40 in any subject, then print FAIL
in REMARK-IF-ANY, otherwise print the following:

Total Marks	REMARK-IF-ANY
$\geq$ 120 but < 150	THIRD
$\geq$ 150 but < 180	SECOND
$\geq$ 180	FIRST

Write DATA DIVISION entries and PROCEDURE DIVISION statements for the
above.

7

WRITING COMPLETE PROGRAMS

7.1 INTRODUCTION TO PROGRAM WRITING

We have now reached a stage when it should be possible for us to write at
least simple COBOL programs. To get started one must try to write the
IDENTIFICATION DIVISION and ENVIRONMENT DIVISION first. Although these divisions are mostly dependent to a great extent on the machine and compiler to
be used, they are mostly identical for different programs to be executed on
a particular computer. Thus once we can write these divisions for a program,
the same entries with trivial changes can be used for another program. A
major change can possibly be in the FILE-CONTROL paragraph of the INPUT-
OUTPUT Section in the ENVIRONMENT DIVISION. As mentioned earlier, all the
files to be handled in a program must be declared in this paragraph with
appropriate SELECT clauses. Since different programs will have different
files to be handled, the SELECT clauses must be written afresh for every
program. Thus to write the first two divisions of the program; the important
points that must be resolved by the programmer are:

    (i)   How many files the program must handle?
   (ii)   What are the names by which these files should be referred to in
           the data and the PROCEDURE DIVISION of the program?
  (iii)   What are the mediums used (or to be used) for file storage (e.g.,
           card, line-printer stationery, tape, disk, etc.)?

Once these questions have been answered properly there will be no problem
in completing the SELECT clauses.

    To illustrate the above idea, the following may be the IDENTIFICATION
DIVISION and ENVIRONMENT DIVISION of a sample program.

```
        IDENTIFICATION DIVISION.
        PROGRAM-ID.  SAMPLE.
        ENVIRONMENT    DIVISION.
        CONFIGURATION   SECTION.
        SOURCE-COMPUTER.   B-6700.
        OBJECT-COMPUTER.   B-6700.
        INPUT-OUTPUT   SECTION.
        FILE-CONTROL.
             SELECT    FILE-IN   ASSIGN    TO    READER.
             SELECT    FILE-OUT  ASSIGN    TO    PRINTER.
```

    In the case of another program, possibly a change in the program name
(SAMPLE in the above) and a change in the SELECT clauses will be quite

sufficient. In case the programmer wishes to assign suitable mnemonic names to the line printer channels, the SPECIAL-NAMES paragraph can be introduced after the OBJECT-COMPUTER paragraph. However, the point to be emphasized here is that a beginner must first of all prepare a sample of these two divisions keeping in mind the computer system to be used. This sample can be tailored to suit a particular program by incorporating the necessary changes. For this reason in our illustrations unless mentioned otherwise, we shall assume the IDENTIFICATION DIVISION and ENVIRONMENT DIVISION as shown above and the programs will be given starting from the place where the first change is necessary.

Having written the first two divisions, one should proceed to the FILE SECTION of the DATA DIVISION. For every file declared in the FILE-CONTROL paragraph, there should normally be a FD entry followed by the record description. The elementary and group items that form the record should be given suitable names and all elementary items must be defined with an appropriate PICTURE clause.

Once the FILE SECTION has been completed, it is desirable to proceed with the PROCEDURE DIVISION and working-storage section simultaneously. This point is very important for a beginner. It is extremely difficult to guess the required intermediate data items before writing the PROCEDURE DIVISION. On the other hand, it will be much easier to go ahead with the PROCEDURE DIVISION. As and when the space for a working data item is required, it may be immediately defined in the WORKING-STORAGE SECTION.

7.2 A SAMPLE PROGRAM

Let us now write a program for the flow chart illustrated in Fig.2.6. There are two files to be handled. The first one is an input file on card, each card of which contains the fields QUANTITY and UNIT-PRICE. To make the problem more realistic, we assume another field in the input record. This field named ITEM-NO is a code that identifies the particular material. We assume the following card layout for the input data.

Card Columns	Data Field	Data Type
1-6	ITEM-NO	Alphanumeric
7-14	QUANTITY	Numeric (including 2 decimal places)
15-22	UNIT-PRICE	Numeric (including 2 decimal places)

This input file is referred to in the program by the name CARD-FILE. The other file handled by the program is the output file containing the report to be generated. This file referred to in the program as REPORT-FILE is obviously a line-printer file and we assume the following layout for its records.

Print Positions	Data Fields	Data Type/Editing
5-10	R-ITEM-NO	Alphanumeric
15-23	R-QUANTITY	Numeric (Zero suppression, decimal point insertion)
30-38	R-UNIT-PRICE	Numeric (Zero suppression, decimal point insertion)
45-59	R-COST	Numeric (Zero suppression, decimal point insertion, 2 decimal places)

We can now write the program till the end of the FILE SECTION. This portion of the program is as follows:

.
.
.

```
FILE-CONTROL
    SELECT  CARD-FILE     ASSIGN  TO  READER.
    SELECT  REPORT-FILE   ASSIGN  TO  PRINTER.
DATA DIVISION.
FILE SECTION.
FD  CARD-FILE.
01  CARD-RECORD.
    02      ITEM-NO                 PIC     X(6).
    02      QUANTITY                PIC     9(6)V99.
    02      UNIT-PRICE              PIC     9(6)V99.
    02      FILLER                  PIC     X(58).

FD  REPORT-FILE.
01  REPORT-REC.
    02      FILLER                  PIC     X(4).
    02      R-ITEM-NO               PIC     X(6).
    02      FILLER                  PIC     X(4).
    02      R-QUANTITY              PIC     Z(5)9.99.
    02      FILLER                  PIC     X(6).
    02      R-UNIT-PRICE            PIC     Z(5)9.99.
    02      FILLER                  PIC     X(6).
    02      R-COST                  PIC     Z(11)9.99.
    02      FILLER                  PIC     X(73).
```

Having completed the FILE SECTION, we proceed to the PROCEDURE DIVISION. Each box in the flow chart should be converted into COBOL statements. For example, the START box in Fig. 2.5 indicates the necessary initialization operations consisting of opening the files and clearing (filling with spaces) the record area of the REPORT-FILE. The complete PROCEDURE DIVISION is shown below and the reader should try to understand the steps by comparing it with the flow chart (Fig. 2.6).

```
PROCEDURE DIVISION.
START-THE-PROCESS.
      OPEN    INPUT    CARD-FILE.
              OUTPUT   REPORT-FILE.
      MOVE    SPACES   TO   REPORT-REC.

READ-AND-PRINT.
      READ  CARD-FILE  AT END GO TO FINISH-THE-PROCESS.
      MULTIPLY QUANTITY BY UNIT-PRICE GIVING R-COST.
      MOVE ITEM-NO TO R-ITEM-NO.  MOVE QUANTITY TO
      R-QUANTITY. MOVE UNIT-PRICE TO R-UNIT-PRICE.
      WRITE REPORT-REC AFTER ADVANCING 2 LINES.
      GO  TO  READ-AND-PRINT.

FINISH-THE-PROCESS.
      CLOSE CARD-FILE REPORT-FILE.
      STOP  RUN.
```

It may be seen that no working storage is necessary in this program.

In the above we restricted ourselves to the flow chart of Fig. 2.6. Now, suppose that the total of the costs obtained for the individual items is to be printed at the end of the report. The modification is simple and the modified program is given in Fig. 3.1. The WORKING-STORAGE SECTION is required in this program.

None of the two versions of the program prints any heading in the report. However, everybody would like to have a heading on the top of every page of the report. Each page should also contain a page number at the top and a page total at the bottom. We shall now extend the program to incorporate these changes. The complete program and a portion of the sample report produced by the program is shown in Figs. 7.1 and 7.2 respectively. While the reader should independently go through this program in order to understand how the changes have been incorporated, the following points are included for guidance.

(i)   Since the REPORT-FILE contains more than one type of record (two heading lines, one detail line and two different types of total lines), REPORT-REC has been described with the picture X(132). The five different types of records have actually been defined in the WORKING-STORAGE SECTION. Whenever a particular record is required to be printed before the WRITE statement, a MOVE statement has been used to move the data from the record area in the working-storage to the REPORT-REC in the file section. This could also be accomplished by using FROM option in the WRITE statement. Also note that the records as defined in the WORKING-STORAGE SECTION have not been made equal to 132 characters by adding FILLER. This is because when we move these records to REPORT-REC, the unfilled positions on the right (of REPORT-REC) will be filled with spaces as per the rule of alphanumeric data movement.

(ii) The mnemonic name PAGE-TOP has been associated to the carriage control channel 1. Conventionally, channel 1 is used to indicate the top of the page through the carriage control tape.

(iii) It has been assumed that each page will contain a maximum of 45 detail lines.

```
IDENTIFICATION DIVISION
PROGRAM-ID. SAMPLE.
ENVIRONMENT DIVISION.
CONFIGURATION SECTION.
SOURCE-COMPUTER. B-6700.
OBJECT-COMPUTER. B-6700.
SPECIAL-NAMES.  CHANNEL 1  IS PAGE-TOP.
INPUT-OUTPUT SECTION.
FILE-CONTROL.
        SELECT CARD-FILE ASSIGN TO READER.
        SELECT REPORT-FILE ASSIGN TO PRINTER.
DATA DIVISION.
FILE SECTION.
FD  CARD-FILE.
    01   CARD-RECORD.
     02   ITEM-NO         PIC X(6).
     02   QUANTITY        PIC 9(6)V99.
     02   UNIT-PRICE      PIC 9(6)V99.
     02   FILLER          PIC X(58).
FD  REPORT-FILE.
01  REPORT-REC           PIC X(132).
WORKING-STORAGE SECTION.
77  PAGE-TOTAL           PIC 9(13)V99.
77  TOTAL-COST           PIC 9(14)V99 VALUE 0.
77  COST                 PIC 9(12)V99.
77  PAGE-COUNT           PIC 99 VALUE 0.
77  LINE-COUNT           PIC 99.
01  FIRST-HEADING.
     02   FILLER          PIC X(108) VALUE SPACES.
     02   FILLER          PIC X(4) VALUE "PAGE".
     02   PAGE-NO         PIC ZZZ9.
01  SECOND-HEADING.
     02   FILLER          PIC XX VALUE SPACES.
     02   FILLER          PIC X(8) VALUE "ITEM NO.".
     02   FILLER          PIC X(5) VALUE SPACES.
     02   FILLER          PIC X(8) VALUE "QUANTITY".
     02   FILLER          PIC X(5) VALUE SPACES.
     02   FILLER          PIC X(10) VALUE "UNIT PRICE".
     02   FILLER          PIC X(17) VALUE SPACES.
     02   FILLER          PIC X(4) VALUE "COST".
01  DETAIL-LINE.
     02   FILLER          PIC X(4) VALUE SPACES.
     02   R-ITEM-NO       PIC X(6).
     02   FILLER          PIC X(4) VALUE SPACES.
     02   R-QUANTITY      PIC Z(5)9.99.
     02   FILLER          PIC X(6) VALUE SPACES.
     02   R-UNIT-PRICE    PIC Z(5)9.99.
     02   FILLER          PIC X(6) VALUE SPACES.
     02   R-COST          PIC Z(11)9.99.
     02   FILLER          PIC X(73) VALUE SPACES.
```

FIG. 7.1. A Sample Program (contd.)

```
01  PAGE-TOTAL-LINE.
    02  FILLER          PIC X(50) VALUE SPACES.
    02  FILLER          PIC X(10) VALUE "PAGE TOTAL".
    02  PRINT-TOTAL     PIC Z(12)9.99.
01  GRAND-TOTAL-LINE.
    02  FILLER          PIC X(60) VALUE SPACES.
    02  FILLER          PIC X(11) VALUE "GRAND TOTAL".
    02  PRINT-GRAND-TOTAL   PIC  Z(13)9.99.
PROCEDURE DIVISION.
MAKE-A-START.
    OPEN INPUT CARD-FILE
         OUTPUT REPORT-FILE.
PRINT-THE-HEADINGS.
    ADD 1 TO PAGE-COUNT. MOVE PAGE-COUNT TO PAGE-NO.
    MOVE FIRST-HEADING TO REPORT-REC.
    WRITE REPORT-REC AFTER ADVANCING TO PAGE-TOP.
    MOVE SECOND-HEADING TO REPORT-REC.
    WRITE REPORT-REC AFTER ADVANCING 3 LINES.
    MOVE SPACES TO REPORT-REC.
    WRITE REPORT-REC AFTER ADVANCING 1 LINES.
    MOVE ZEROES TO LINE-COUNT, PAGE-TOTAL.

PRINT-THE-DETAIL-LINES.
    READ CARD-FILE AT END GO TO PRINT-THE-GRAND-TOTAL.
    MULTIPLY UNIT-PRICE BY QUANTITY GIVING COST, R-COST.
    ADD COST TO PAGE-TOTAL, TOTAL-COST.
    MOVE ITEM-NO TO R-ITEM-NO. MOVE QUANTITY TO R-QUANTITY.
    MOVE UNIT-PRICE TO R-UNIT-PRICE.
    MOVE DETAIL-LINE TO REPORT-REC.
    WRITE REPORT-REC AFTER ADVANCING 1 LINES.
    ADD 1 TO LINE-COUNT.
    IF LINE-COUNT IS LESS THAN 45 GO TO PRINT-THE-DETAIL-LINES.
    MOVE PAGE-TOTAL TO PRINT-TOTAL.
    MOVE PAGE-TOTAL-LINE TO REPORT-REC.
    WRITE REPORT-REC AFTER ADVANCING 2 LINES.
    GO TO PRINT-THE-HEADINGS.
PRINT-THE-GRAND-TOTAL.
    IF LINE-COUNT IS GREATER THAN 0
    MOVE PAGE-TOTAL TO PRINT-TOTAL
    MOVE PAGE-TOTAL-LINE TO REPORT-REC

    WRITE REPORT-REC AFTER ADVANCING 2 LINES.
    MOVE TOTAL-COST TO PRINT-GRAND-TOTAL.
    MOVE GRAND-TOTAL-LINE TO REPORT-REC.
    WRITE REPORT-REC AFTER ADVANCING 3 LINES.
    CLOSE CARD-FILE, REPORT-FILE.
    STOP RUN.
```

FIG. 7.1. A Sample Program

ITEM NO.	QUANTITY	UNIT PRICE	COST
ABC111	4000.00	20.50	82000.00
ABC112	2000.00	10.25	20500.00
ABC115	1500.00	15.00	22500.00
ABC116	200.50	10.00	2005.00
ABC121	4000.00	20.00	80000.00
ABC140	5000.00	20.50	102500.00

PAGE TOTAL 309505.00

GRAND TOTAL   309505.00

FIG. 7.2. Output of the Sample Programs of Fig. 7.1.

7.3 HOW TO RUN A COBOL PROGRAM

In order to run a COBOL program, it has to be compiled and linked to obtain the load module. Finally, the load module is to be executed. For all these, it is necessary to communicate with the operating system using statements/ commands of job control language. Since the job control language and the functioning of operating system in one computer are different from those in another computer, a general discussion on the subject is difficult. A beginner, therefore, should seek the guidance of an experienced programmer of the   installation. Later in this book (in Sec. 21.6), we have discussed the steps required for running a COBOL program on a personal computer.

Moreover, some of the programs illustrated in this book may require a few minor modifications. This is due to the fact that in many problems, we have assumed card file as the basic input file and line printer as the basic output file. We have done this and shall continue to do this, in order to have simplicity in the matter of file handling in the initial part of this book. However, the fact remains that today there are many installations where a card reader does not exist. Again, dot-matrix printers are extensively used in place of line printers. Let us therefore, explain the modifications required for the absence of a card reader and for the use of a dot-matrix printer instead of a line printer.

Suppose we wish to run the program in Fig. 7.1 on a computer that does not have a card reader. One alternative may be to create card-image file on a floppy disk or on some other varieties of disks. Each record of this card-image file is nothing but a replica of the card. Such a file can be easily created through the keyboard with the help of a software known as text-editor. A text editor called EDLIN is described in Ch.21. Many other text editors are also available. Thus creation of a card-image file is no problem.

Almost in every computer system, a card-image file (or any file created by a text editor) can be read through a COBOL program by specifying its organization as LINE SEQUENTIAL. Therefore, the SELECT clause (for the card file) which has been shown as

             SELECT CARD-FILE ASSIGN TO READER

in Fig. 7.1, should be changed to

             SELECT CARD-FILE ASSIGN TO DISK

                ORGANIZATION IS LINE SEQUENTIAL.

The FD entry for this file should also be changed.

Instead of

        FD CARD-FILE.

it should now be

        FD CARD-FILE LABEL RECORDS ARE STANDARD

              VALUE OF FILE-ID "file-title".

The file-title is actually a string of characters representing the name
under which the card-image file has been created by the text editor.   The
meanings of LABEL RECORDS and VALUE OF clauses are explained fully in
Ch.13.   In some computers, the word FILE-ID is required to be changed to
ID or IDENTIFICATION.
     We would like to observe further that the capabilities of text editors
are not limited to the card-image files where every record should consist
of 80 characters.   In fact, a text editor can be used to create files with
records of any length within certain limits.   In addition, the records can
also be of variable lengths.   A file created by a text editor is called a
text file and card-image file is just one kind of text file.   Therefore,
so far as the program in Fig. 7.1 is concerned, it is just sufficient to
create a text file having records of 22 characters each.   In that case, the
entry

             02   FILLER   PIC   X(58)

within the group named CARD-RECORD should be deleted.

     It may not be out of place to mention that records in text files, are
delimited by a special character or a group of characters.   Thus a record
of size 22 will actually be followed by one or two delimiter characters.
The actual delimiter characters are machine-dependent.   However these
delimiter characters are used by the supporting IOCS software and they are
of no importance to the programmer.
     It was stated earlier that in some computers, the LABEL RECORDS clause
is essential for all files.   Therefore, it may also be necessary to change
the FD entry for the printer file to

        FD REPORT-FILE LABEL RECORDS ARE OMITTED.

In case a dot-matrix printer is used, further changes are necessary because there is no concept of carriage control channels. In order to skip to the top of the page, the ADVANCING PAGE phrase is sufficient (see Sec. 13.7.1). Therefore, in the program of Fig. 7.1, the paragraph

> SPECIAL-NAMES.   CHANNEL   1   IS   PAGE-TOP

should be deleted and the third statement in the PRINT-THE-HEADINGS paragraph namely

> WRITE   REPORT-REC   AFTER   ADVANCING   PAGE-TOP

should be changed to

> WRITE   REPORT-REC   AFTER   ADVANCING   PAGE.

7.4 PROGRAM TESTING

Even an experienced programmer cannot guarantee that a program written by him does not contain any error. Therefore, the program has to be tested. When a program is compiled, the compiler checks for syntax errors and detects them. For example, ADD A TO B GIVING C is a syntactically wrong COBOL statement. If this statement appears in a COBOL program, the compiler will detect this as an error. Normally, the compiler provides a listing (printed copy) of the program along with appropriate error messages against the wrong statements. It is relatively simple to correct the syntax errors as the compiler locates them. When the program has been made free of syntax errors, the compiler will generate the object program. During the execution of the object program further errors known as execution errors are detected. For example, the statement DIVIDE A BY B GIVING C will result in an execution error, if at the time of division, the value of B is found to be equal to zero. In such cases the operating system will terminate the execution indicating the error. In order to fix these errors, the programmer must go through the program to find out why this has happened. Once the cause of the error has been located, the error can be corrected. When the program has been made free from syntax as well as execution errors, the results produced by the program may still be erroneous. This is because the program can contain logical errors. To detect such errors, the programmer should run the program with some test data, the results for which are precalculated manually. Any difference between these precalculated results and those obtained from the computer indicates the existence of logical errors in the program, provided the manual computations are done correctly. In the case of logical errors the programmer should read the program and follow its logic to locate the possible logical errors. To ensure that the program is free of logical errors, the test data set must be properly chosen so that all cases of the input data are covered by it. The above procedure for testing a program is known as debugging. It may, however, be noted that execution errors are also logical errors detected by the operating system.

7.5   PROGRAMMING STYLE

We know that there can be many different programs for solving a particular problem, all producing the same results. This shows that there exists enough scope for a programmer to apply his own style of programming. A good programmer should exploit this facility to develop better programs. This observation brings us to the question: What are the qualities of a ''good'' program? As an answer to this question we can list the following as the qualities of a program:

    (i)   Correctness
    (ii) Readability
   (iii) Portability.

    It is obvious that correctness is the most important of the qualities. A program that fails to produce correct results is not worth the name. The next important quality is the readability in the program. This means that the program should be written in such a way that if a person wants to read and understand the program, it should be possible for him to do so without much difficulty. This is an important consideration since the requirement of reading and understanding a program arises (i) when we want to make the program error-free at the time of testing it and (ii) when we want to incorporate subsequent modifications into the program. An application program will need modifications whenever there is a change in the factors that affect the program. For example, if there is any change in the pay structure of an organization, the payroll program will need immediate modification. In such cases a programmer must read and understand the program before incorporating the changes. Moreover, the program should be designed in such a way that future modifications can be incorporated easily. If a program is structured to meet this latter requirement, it is often found that the readability increases. Thus the adoptability of future modifications is not considered as a separate quality. Instead, it is linked with readability. In fact, readability of a program is an essential requirement for program maintenance and is the primary objective of what is known as structured programming. However, these points will be taken up in greater detail in Chapter 12. As regards the third quality, a portable program is the one that can be executed on different computers (with different compilers) without any change. However, in reality, it may not be possible to write a perfectly portable program. As such the programs that require only minor changes with a change in the computer are also considered to be portable programs.

    While developing a program, one must be careful about the points mentioned above. As we progress with the subsequent chapters we shall also make recommendations that can help a programmer to write readable and portable programs. For the time being, the only suggestion that we make here is that while giving names to data items, files, paragraphs or sections, one must choose meaningful names. Obviously, this increases the readability of the program. For example, a paragraph name called CALCULATE-THE-INTEREST is much more meaningful than the name PARA-13. Such a name gives an idea of the work being done in the said paragraph. In this connection we may recall that a paragraph name is required only if it is to be referred to in a statement such as GO TO. A paragraph name is also required in the beginning of PROCEDURE DIVISION or that of a section. Though not mandatory, additional meaningful paragraph names can be used to indicate the operations being done in the paragraph. Another suggestion for increasing the readability is to include comments in the programs. Comments should explicitly state the intentions of the programmer at various places of the program.

As regards the portability, we recommend that the reader should carefully note the implementation differences that are included at the end of different chapters. It is desirable to restrict to the subset of the language that can be acceptable to most compilers.

EXERCISES

1. The formula to convert a temperature from Fahrenheit to Celsius is $C = 5/9 (F - 32)$. Draw a flow chart and write a COBOL program that will read a deck of cards each containing a temperature in Fahrenheit in columns 1-4 and will then print the corresponding temperature in Celsius.

2. Each card of a deck contains the following input data
    (i)   item number
    (ii) cost
    (iii) scrap value and
    (iv) years of life.
    You are to calculate the yearly depreciation according to the following formula.

    $$\text{Yearly depreciation} = \frac{\text{Cost} - \text{Scrap value}}{\text{Years of life}}$$

    The fields yearly depreciation, cost and scrap value must have two places after the assumed decimal point. Design suitable card and report layouts, draw a flow chart and write a COBOL program for the problem.

3. Calculate and print total commissions and total sales for each salesman. The input consists of the salesman number and the amount of sales punched on cards. There is more than one card for each salesman but all cards relating to a particular salesman are grouped together. Moreover, to mark the end of the input data for a salesman, an additional card with the amount of sales as zero is provided after all the cards for each salesman. The commission should be calculated at the rate of 10%. The sample output should be as follows:

SALESMAN-NO	AMOUNT-OF-SALE	COMMISSION
1	233	23.30
	572	57.20
	298	29.80
TOTAL SALE : 1103	TOTAL COMMISSION : 110.30	
2	200	20.00
	250	25.00
.	.	.
.	.	.
.	.	.

    Draw a flow chart and write a program for the problem.

4. Had there been no zero sales card as the last card for each salesman, the problem would have become slightly difficult. Try to draw a flow chart and write a COBOL program for this modified problem.

8

MORE ABOUT DATA DIVISION

Important data-description clauses, such as PICTURE and VALUE have been described earlier. However, a DATA DIVISION entry can have other clauses as well. Some of these clauses can be effectively used to achieve improvements in the object program; others can be used for convenience in programming. These data-description clauses are the subject matter of this chapter. All the clauses described below are optional. They can appear in the data-description entry in any order except that the REDEFINES clause, if specified, must appear immediately after the data name being defined.

It is suggested that during the first reading, details of the various clauses may be skipped. Most of these clauses are required only by an experienced programmer.

8.1 USAGE CLAUSE

Normally, a computer can store data in more than one internal form. In COBOL, a programmer is allowed to specify the internal form of the data item so as to facilitate the use of the data item more efficiently. Broadly, there are only two general forms of internal representation — computational and display. Only numeric data items can be specified as computational, and as the name suggests, an item specified as computational can take part in arithmetic operations more efficiently. On the other hand, any data item can be specified as display. This form is suitable for input-output and character manipulations. Whether a data item is computational or display, it can be specified with a USAGE clause in addition to the PICTURE clause. The syntax of the USAGE clause is as follows:

$$\underline{\text{USAGE}} \text{ IS} \quad \left\{ \begin{array}{l} \text{COMPUTATIONAL} \\ \underline{\text{COMP}} \\ \underline{\text{DISPLAY}} \end{array} \right\} \quad [\text{ - integer }]$$

The usages COMP and COMPUTATIONAL mean the same thing. However, each of COMPUTATIONAL and DISPLAY can have several different forms. To distinguish among the various forms the integer should be specified. For example, a usage can be only COMP or it can be COMP-1. Both may be suitable for computational purposes, but they are represented internally in different forms. Besides DISPLAY and COMPUTATIONAL, the usage of an item may be INDEX (this will be discussed later).

The internal forms are obviously dependent on the architecture of the object computer and the various usages and their meanings are different on different computers. Consequently, a general description of the subject is not possible. For the purpose of illustration, a typical set (similar to that in IBM 370) of usages is described below.

A word in the object computer is assumed to be of 32 bits which is divided into four 8-bit bytes. A byte can hold a character represented in EBCDIC. There are five different forms of usage — DISPLAY, COMP, COMP-1, COMP-2, COMP-3.

DISPLAY Usage

This is the most common form of internal data. Each character of the data is represented in one byte and a data-item is stored in a couple of contiguous bytes. The number of bytes required is equal to the size of the data item.

One can specify the usage as DISPLAY. However, it is also the default. This means that if no usage is specified, it will be taken as DISPLAY.

COMPUTATIONAL (COMP) Usage

When usage is specified as COMP, the numeric data item is represented in pure binary. The item must be an integer (no assumed decimal point is allowed). Such data items are often used as subscripts (see Chapter 11 for the meaning of subscript).

Depending on the size of the data item, it can be stored either in a half-word or in full-word (32 bits). Only integral numbers in the range −32,768 to +32,767 can be accommodated in half-word. A full-word can store any integral number in the range −2,147,483,648 to 2,147,483,647. The PICTURE of a COMP item should not contain any character other than 9, S.

COMPUTATIONAL-1 (COMP-1) Usage

If the usage of a numeric data item is specified as COMP-1, it will be represented in one word in the floating-point form. The number is actually represented in hexadecimal (base 16). Such representation is suitable for arithmetic operations. The PICTURE clause cannot be specified for COMP-1 items.

COMPUTATIONAL-2 (COMP-2) Usage

This usage is the same as COMP-1 except that the data is represented internally in two words. The advantage is that this increases the precision of the data which means that more significant digits can be available for the item. The PICTURE clause cannot be specified for COMP-2 items.

COMPUTATIONAL-3 (COMP-3) Usage

In this form of internal representation the numeric data is represented in the decimal form, but one digit takes half-a-byte. The sign is stored separately as the rightmost half-a-byte regardless of whether S is specified in the PICTURE or not. The hexadecimal number C or F denotes a positive sign and the hexadecimal number D denotes a negative sign. In order that data fields can start and end on byte boundaries, numbers with an even number of digits are stored with an extra half-byte of zeroes on the left-hand side. Thus an item with

PICTURE S9(5)V9(3) USAGE IS COMPUTATIONAL-3

will require 5 bytes to be stored internally. Only the characters 9, S, V and P can be used in the PICTURE of a COMP-3 item.

The advantage of this usage is two-fold. Compared to the DISPLAY items it requires less space to be stored and the object computer can also directly operate on such numbers.

The following points may be noted in connection with the USAGE clause.

(i)   When an elementary data item is moved to another elementary data item, their usages need not be the same. Conversion of the data item will take place automatically if they differ. This arrangement is made by the COBOL compiler. The same is true for arithmetic operations where it is not necessary that the operands or the result field should be of the same usage.

(ii) The USAGE clause can be specified at any level. If usage is specified for a group item, it applies to all elementary items in the group. The USAGE clause of an elementary item cannot contradict the USAGE clause of a group item to which the item belongs.

(iii) If a group item is delcared to be COMP, COMP-1, COMP-2 or COMP-3, then all the elementary items within the group will have the respective usages. However, the group item itself is not COMP or any form of it and cannot take part in an arithmetic operation.

(iv) The data items to be read from or written to an I-O medium which essentially stores data in the character form (such as cards or line-printer stationery) should not be specified to be COMPUTATIONAL.

Example

Let us consider the following declaration in the WORKING-STORAGE SECTION.

77   I   PIC   9(3)   VALUE   IS   374.

Since the USAGE clause has not been specified, DISPLAY will be assumed. The value 374 will be stored internally in three consecutive bytes. According to our assumption, characters in the object computer are stored in EBCDIC. As such the said value as represented inside the computer storage will be as follows (consult Table 1.2 for the internal representations of the digits 3, 7 and 4 in EBCDIC):

1111   0011   1111   0111   1111   0100

Now, suppose the above declaration is changed to

77   I   PIC   9(3)   COMP   VALUE   IS   374

The value will be stored internally in pure binary in half word (16 bits — equivalent to 2 bytes). The value 374 is 101110110 in binary. As such the data when represented internally in 16 bits will be as follows:

0000   0001   0111   0110

In the above declaration if COMP-3 is specified instead of COMP, the internal representation will be as follows:

0011   0111   0100   1111

The three-digited field requires that 2 bytes be stored. The rightmost 4 bits of the second byte, namely, 1111 (F in hexadecimal) denotes positive sign.

It is important to note that in the three cases the value being represented is 374 and the program will produce the same output in each case. The difference is in the execution time and the storage space required by the object program. An appropriate use of the USAGE clause can increase the efficiency of the object program.

8.2 SYNCHRONIZED CLAUSE

The COBOL compiler normally allocates contiguous storage spaces. Thus a data item specified as COMP-1 will be allocated 4 contiguous bytes which is equivalent to one word. However, the first byte starts immediately after the byte which was allocated for the previous data item. As such the data item may not start from a word boundary. To exploit the full advantages of COMP-1, COMP-2 and COMP items, they must start on a word boundary. Moreover, COMP-2 items must have its first word on an even address. These difficulties can be solved by specifying the SYNCHRONIZED clause which has the following syntax:

{ SYNCHRONIZED

  SYNC }

It may be noted that the COMP items requiring a half-word will be aligned to a half-word boundary. COMP and COMP-1 items are aligned on a full-word boundary. COMP-2 items will be aligned to a double-word boundary. It may be noted that a few bytes may be left unused in the process of storage allocation with SYNCHRONIZED items. These are called slack bytes.

Let us consider the following declaration in WORKING-STORAGE SECTION:

```
01     MY-DATA.
       02     DATA-ONE      PIC     X(10) .
       02     DATA-TWO      PIC     9(6)      COMP  SYNC.
       02     DATA-THREE    PIC     S9(4)V99  COMP-3.
```

Let us see how many bytes will be required for MY-DATA assuming that it starts from a word boundary. DATA-ONE will require 10 bytes which means two and a half-words, since DATA-TWO, which is a 6-digited field and has been specified as SYNCHRONIZED, cannot be accommodated in a half-word. Therefore, 2 bytes will be treated as slack bytes and the next word will be allocated for DATA-TWO. DATA-THREE will require 4 bytes. Thus MY-DATA will require a total of 20 bytes of which two are slack bytes.

8.3 JUSTIFIED CLAUSE

In the case of alphanumeric or alphabetic data movement, the receiving field usually receives data starting from the left-hand side. If the sending field is of larger size than the receiving field, the extra characters at the right-hand side are truncated. On the other hand, if the source data is smaller in length, the remaining positions in the receiving field are space-filled. This standard left-hand alignment of alphanumeric or alphabetic data can be reversed by using the JUSTIFIED clause which has the form

$$\left\{ \begin{array}{l} \text{JUSTIFIED} \\ \text{JUST} \end{array} \right\} \qquad \text{RIGHT}$$

JUSTIFIED and JUST mean the same thing. If this clause is used, the data will be aligned at the rightmost character position. Truncation or space-fill, if necessary, takes place on the left-hand side.

It may be noted that the JUSTIFIED clause is rarely used and needs to be specified for the receiving data items only. It has no effect on internal-storage allocation and merely affects the data movement. Neither numeric nor numeric edited data items can have the JUSTIFIED clause. The reason for this is that numeric data are always aligned by the decimal point (explicitly or implicitly specified). This clause cannot be specified for an item whose size is variable or for group items.

8.4 REDEFINES CLAUSE

Sometimes it may be found that two or more storage areas defined in the DATA DIVISION are not in use simultaneously. In such cases only one storage area can serve the purpose of two or more areas if the area is redefined. The REDEFINES clause used for the purpose allows the said area to be referred to by more than one data name with different sizes and pictures. Let us consider the following example.

```
01    SALES-RECORD.
      02    SALES-TYPE          PIC
      02    SALES-BY-UNIT.
            03    QTY           PIC         9(4).
            03    UNIT-PRICE    PIC         9(8)V99.
      02    TOTAL-SALES         REDEFINES   SALES-BY-UNIT.
            03    AMOUNT        PIC         9(10)V99.
            03    FILLER        PIC         X(2).
```

This example describes a sales record which may either contain the total amount of sale (AMOUNT) or the quantity (QTY) and UNIT-PRICE. The purpose of such description may be to have two types of records and their types may be determined from the data item named SALES-TYPE. Depending on some predetermined values of SALES-TYPE the record will be interpreted in one of the two forms. Note that SALES-BY-UNIT and TOTAL-SALES refer to the same storage space. They really represent two different mappings of the same storage area.

The REDEFINES clause as illustrated above are quite common in use. However, the clause may be simply used for the purpose of conservation of storage space possibly in the working-storage section. In such cases two records having no meaningful connection between them can also be used to share same storage space provided both of them are not used in the program simultaneously. The syntax of the REDEFINES clause is as follows:

level-number data-name-1   <u>REDEFINES</u>   data-name-2

The following rules govern the use of the REDEFINES clause:

(i)   The level-number of data-name-1 and data-name-2 must be identical.

(ii)   Except when the REDEFINES clause is used to 01 level, data-name-1 and data-name-2 must be of same size. In the case of 01 level, the size of data-name-1 must not exceed that of data-name-2 (originally defined area).

(iii) Multiple redefinition is allowed. The entries giving the new descriptions must immediately follow the REDEFINES entry. In the case of multiple redefinitions the data-name-2 must be the data-name of the entry that originally defined the area.

(iv)   The REDEFINES clause must immediately follow data-name-1.

(v)   Entries giving new descriptions cannot have VALUE clauses (except in the case of condition-names, i.e., 88-level (see Chapter 10)). This means that data-name-1 or any of its subordinates must not have any VALUE clause.

(vi)   The REDEFINES clause must not be used for records (01 level) described in the FILE SECTION. The appearance of multiple 01 entries in the record description is implicitly assumed to be the redefinition of the first 01-level record.

(vii) This clause must not be used for level-number 66 or 88 items. (66-level items are described in the following section and 88-level items will be described in Chapter 10).

8.5 RENAMES CLAUSE

Sometimes a re-grouping of elementary data items in a record may be necessary so that they can belong to the original as well as to the new group. This is possible in COBOL by the use of the RENAMES clause. The following example illustrates the use of the RENAMES clause.

```
01   PAY-REC.
     03   FIXED-PAY.
          05   BASIC-PAY              PIC    9(6)V99.
          05   DEARNESS-ALLOWANCE     PIC    9(6)V99.
     03   ADDITIONAL-PAY.
          05   HOUSE-RENT             PIC    9(4)V99.
          05   MTHLY-INCENTIVE        PIC    9(3)V99.
     03   DEDUCTIONS.
          05   PF-DEDUCT              PIC    9(3)V99.
          05   IT-DEDUCT              PIC    9(4)V99.
          05   OTHER-DEDUCT           PIC    9(3)V99.

66   PAY-OTHER-THAN-BASIC RENAMES DEARNESS-ALLOWANCE THRU MTHLY-INCENTIVE
66   IT-AND-PF-DEDUCTIONS RENAMES PF-DEDUCT THRU IT-DEDUCT.
```

In the example, PAY-OTHER-THAN-BASIC will become a new group consisting of
DEARNESS-ALLOWANCE, HOUSE-RENT and MTHLY-INCENTIVE. Note that the new group
overlaps on two original groups, namely, part of FIXED-PAY and the entire
ADDITIONAL-PAY. Such overlapping is allowed provided the elementary items are
all contiguous. In a similar way IT-AN-PF-DEDUCTIONS has two elementary items
PF-DEDUCT and IT-DEDUCT. This new group is formed out of the original group
DEDUCTIONS. Alternatively, the same thing can also be done in the original
description itself by placing the IT-AND-PF-DEDUCTIONS at level 04 under
DEDUCTIONS. The exact syntax of the RENAMES clause is as follows:

```
66   data-name-1 RENAMES data-name-2 THRU data-name-3.
```

The following rules must be observed while using the RENAMES clause:
   (i)   All RENAMES entries must be written only after the last record
          description entry.
   (ii)   The RENAMES clause must be used only with the special level number
          66. The level number begins in margin A or any position after it.
          Data-name-1 must begin from margin B or any position after it.
          There must be at least one space between the level number and data-
          name-1.
   (iii) Data-name-2 and data-name-3 can be the names of elementary items
          or group items. They, however, cannot be items of levels 01,
          66, 77 or 88.
   (iv)   Data-name-1 may not be used as a qualifier. It can only be quali-
          fied by the name of the record within which it is defined.
   (v)   Neither data-name-2 nor data-name-3 can have an OCCURS (see
          Chapter 11) clause in its description entry, nor can they be
          subordinate to an item that has an OCCURS clause in its data
          description entry.
   (vi)   Data-name-3, if mentioned, must follow data-name-2, in the record
          and must not be one of its subfields.

8.6 QUALIFICATION OF DATA NAMES

The data names within a COBOL program need not be unique. When duplicate
data names are used, each time such a data name is referred to in the

PROCEDURE DIVISION, the programmer must qualify the data name to make it unique. A qualified data name is a data name followed by the words IN or OF which again is followed by a qualifier. A qualifier for a data name should normally be another data name whose level number is lower (i.e., of a higher hierarchical level) than that of the qualified data name. For example, let MY-REC be described in the DATA DIVISION in the following manner.

```
01    MY-REC.
      05    SALES-CODE              PIC      X(4).
      05    SALES-DATA.
            10    QUANTITY          PIC      9(4)V99.
            10    ITEM-CODE         PIC      XX.
```

Suppose, the data name QUANTITY has also been defined elsewhere in the DATA DIVISION and is therefore not unique. In order to refer to this data name we must qualify it by a qualifier. The qualifier in this case can be either SALES-DATA or MY-REC, each of which has level numbers lower than that of QUANTITY. The qualified name can be QUANTITY OF SALES-DATA or QUANTITY OF MY-REC. A qualifier can again be qualified. For example, QUANTITY can also be qualified as QUANTITY OF SALES-DATA OF MY-REC. The latter qualification can be used in spite of the fact that SALES-DATA is a unique name in the program. It may be noted in this connection that the qualification of a data name is allowed regardless of whether it is unique or not as it can provide for better documentation. However, a long qualification should be avoided.

General formats for the qualification of data names is as follows:

Format 1

$$\text{data-name-1} \left\{ \begin{array}{c} \underline{OF} \\ \underline{IN} \end{array} \right\} \text{data-name-2} \left[\left\{ \begin{array}{c} \underline{OF} \\ \underline{IN} \end{array} \right\} \text{data-name-3} \right] \dots$$

Format 2

$$\text{data-name-4} \left\{ \begin{array}{c} \underline{OF} \\ \underline{IN} \end{array} \right\} \text{file-name}$$

The following are the additional rules for specifying qualifications.

(i) A data name or record name in the FILE SECTION can also be qualified by a file name.

(ii) The file name and 01 level data names (i.e., records names) are the highest level qualifiers available for data names defined in the FILE SECTION and WORKING-STORAGE SECTION respectively. Consequently, the file names in the FILE SECTION and 01 level data names in the WORKING-STORAGE SECTION must be unique. Note that the 77-level data names must also be unique.

(iii) The same data name cannot appear at different levels in a hierarchy. Thus the qualification of a data name by itself is not possible.

(iv) The qualification is normally required in the PROCEDURE DIVISION. When a REDEFINES clause refers to a data name (which is a duplicate data name), the said data name need not be qualified.

(v) A qualifier must not be an index name or a subscripted data name (for index name and subscripted data name, see Chapter 11).

(vi) The complete set of qualifiers for a data name must not be the same as any partial set of qualifiers for another data name.

(vii) According to ANSI 74 standard, at least five qualifiers must be permitted by every implementor.

8.7 SIGN CLAUSE

A numeric data item when described with S in its picture character string indicates a signed field. The sign is stored in the zone part of the units positions (when the usage is DISPLAY). However, this causes certain difficulties. For example, suppose the record description associated with a card file is as follows:

05   SIGNED-FIELD   PIC   S9(3)

If a value —135 is to be read at SIGNED-FIELD, the corresponding card columns must contain 13N (5 with a negative zone is equivalent to N). Obviously, this is not convenient. To remove such difficulties, a SIGN clause has been introduced in ANSI 74 COBOL. The position of SIGN within the internal representation of data can be specified through this clause. The format is as follows:

$$\underline{SIGN} \quad IS \quad \left\{ \begin{array}{c} \underline{LEADING} \\ \underline{TRAILING} \end{array} \right\} \quad [\ \underline{SEPARATE} \quad CHARACTER \ ]$$

The SEPARATE phrase if used indicates that the sign is to be stored separately and not in the zone part. The TRAILING phrase indicates that the sign is to be stored in the trailing position either as a separate character or as a zone-sign in the units position depending on whether or not the SEPARATE phrase is specified. The phrase LEADING indicates that the sign is to be stored in the leading position either separately or as a zone-sign. The following example shows the internal representations in the four possible cases.

Example 1

77   XYZ   PICTURE S9(3) SIGN TRAILING SEPARATE VALUE —135.

The value is stored internally in four characters as

1	3	5	-

Example 2

77   XYZ   PICTURE S9(3) SIGN LEADING SEPARATE VALUE —135.

The value is stored internally in four characters as

-	1	3	5

Example 3

77   XYZ   PICTURE S9(3) SIGN TRAILING VALUE —135.

The value is stored internally in three characters as

1	3	5̄

Example 4

77   XYZ   PICTURE S9(3) SIGN LEADING VALUE —135.

The value is stored internally in three characters as

1̄	3	5

    The SIGN clause is meaningful and is permitted to be used when the data description entry is defined with
    (i)   a picture string containing an S and
    (ii) usage is DISPLAY.
    The default is, obviously, TRAILING without SEPARATE. This clause being a new feature introduced in ANSI 74 COBOL may not yet be available in many compilers.

8.8 IMPLEMENTATION DIFFERENCES

(a) USAGE

The meanings of various usage specifications are highly machine-dependent. Separate discussions for the three systems chosen for showing implementation differences are given below.

ICL 1900

Each word of ICL 1900 consists of 24 bits. A word can contain four characters, each represented by a six-bit 1900 character code. A word can also contain numeric data represented in binary. The following usages are available in 1900 COBOL: DISPLAY, DISPLAY-3, COMPUTATIONAL and COMPUTATIONAL-1.
    DISPLAY indicates that the data is to be stored internally in the six-bit character form. The sign of a negative numeric data is stored as zone bits in the leftmost character position. It may be noted that this is a departure from the normal practice. Usually in other systems the sign is stored as zone bits in the rightmost character position. DISPLAY-3 is identical to DISPLAY with just one exception. If a DISPLAY-3 field contains an operational sign indicated by S in PICTURE, the sign is stored as an additional 1900 character preceding the digits in the field. It may be noted that in 1900, S in PICTURE can represent a character position depending on whether the usage is DISPLAY or DISPLAY-3.
    COMPUTATIONAL can be specified only for numeric data. When COMPUTATIONAL or COMP is specified, the data is stored as a binary whole number. Scaling to take care of the assumed decimal point is done whenever necessary. The number of bits required to represent the data depends on the number of 9's specified in PICTURE. When $m(\leq18)$ digits are specified in the picture, n,

the number of bits required to represent the data is given by

$$n = \left(\frac{m}{\log_{10} 2} + \omega \right) \text{ Integer part}$$

An extra bit is required if S is specified in PICTURE. When the SYNCHRONIZED clause is also used, the data is represented in full words. If m = number of 9's in PICTURE, the following table gives w, the number of words required.

$$1 \leq m \leq 6 \quad w = 1$$

$$7 \leq m \leq 13 \quad w = 2$$

$$14 \leq m \leq 18 \quad w = 3$$

It may be noted that although COMPUTATIONAL specifies binary representation, the arithmetic on such fields is effectively decimal and no binary truncation error takes place.

In ICL 1900 COBOL, the picture of a computational item is specified by 1 to indicate that it is a binary data item. COMPUTATIONAL-1 can only be specified for such data items. Since this is a unique feature of the 1900 system, we shall skip its discussion. Interested readers should consult the relevant manual.

In 1900, the default usage is DISPLAY except when PICTURE contains a 1. In the latter case the default usage is COMPUTATIONAL-1 or COMP-1.

DEC-10

Each word in DEC-10 consists of 36 bits. Characters can be stored in DEC-10 SIXBIT form or in 7-bit ASCII or in 8-bit EBCDIC. Numeric data can be stored in binary or in the form of a string of packed decimal digits. The usage can be of the following forms: DISPLAY-6, DISPLAY-7, DISPLAY-9, COMP, COMP-1 and COMP-3. In the computational usages COMP can also be replaced by COMPUTATIONAL.

DISPLAY-6 specifies that the characters would be stored in the SIXBIT form with 6 characters per word. DISPLAY-7 specifies that the internal representation is in 7-bit ASCII code. SYNCHRONIZED RIGHT in the case of DISPLAY-7 items would mean that the data must end in the last (rightmost) but one bit of the word. DISPLAY-9 specifies 8-bit EBCDIC code. One word can accommodate only 4 characters. The word is assumed to be divided into 4 bytes of 9-bits each. The leftmost bit in each byte is unused.

An item declared as COMP means that its value is represented in binary with an assumed decimal point. If the PICTURE clause contains 10 or fewer 9's, it will be represented in one full word. Otherwise two are required. COMP-1 usage indicates that the numeric item should be stored in one word floating-point form. No PICTURE clause should be specified for COMP-1 items. COMP-3 items have the same meaning as COMP-3 items described in the text. The only difference is that the bytes are of 9 bits. The leftmost bit is unused and remaining 8 bits are used to represent two decimal digits.

In DEC-10, the usage can also be DISPLAY and this is also the default usage. DISPLAY is equivalent to either DISPLAY-6 or DISPLAY-9 depending on the setting of a compiler option (/X Switch). This means that the user has an option to choose either DISPLAY-6 or DISPLAY-9 as the default usage.

B-6700

In B-6700 a word consists of 48 bits. Characters can be represented in EBCDIC, ASCII or Burroughs 6-bit BCL code. Data can also be stored in the binary form. B-6700 has the following usage specifications: DISPLAY, DISPLAY-1, ASCII, COMP, COMP-1, COMP-2, COMP-4 and COMP-5.

In the DISPLAY usage data is stored in the 8-bit EBCDIC code with six characters per word. DISPLAY-1 specifies the representation of the 6-bit BCL code with eight characters per word. The ASCII specification indicates that the characters in the 7-bit ASCII code would be stored in 8-bits; the leftmost bit of the 8-bit is filled with zero. Thus the ASCII specification also indicates that only 6 characters can be stored in a word.

COMP can only be specified for numeric integral items. The PICTURE for a COMP item in B-6700 must not contain anything other than 9, S, V or P. Internally, the data is stored in the binary form. The leftmost bit represents the sign. If the number of 9's in the PICTURE is less than or equal to 11, one word is used for the data. Otherwise, two words are used. COMP-1 items are identical to COMP items so far as internal representation is concerned. COMP-1 items are stored on the stack. Because of the stack-based architecture of B-6700, access to items on the stack is efficient. Thus for increased efficiency, computational items in the WORKING-STORAGE may be declared as COMP-1 rather than COMP. However, COMP-1 can be specified only on level 77 and 01. COMP-2 items are internally represented as a string of 4-bit hexadecimal digits.

Regardless of the sign specification in the PICTURE, if the leftmost 4-bit contains a value greater than 9, these four bits are treated as a sign. Thus a positive value having a hex digit greater than 9 as its leftmost digit, will require extra 4-bits on its left. For example, with PIC 99 and usage COMP-2 any data between 00 and 9F can be represented in two 4-bit digits, whereas any data between A0 and AF will require three 4-bit digits. COMP-4 and COMP-5 items are respectively similar to COMP-2 and COMP-3 items of the text. The only exception is that a word in this case means 48 bits.

Remarks

The above description of the various usage clauses is applicable only to the elementary items. Usage can also be specified for group items. In general, the usage specified for a group also applies to the elementary items. However, there are exceptions and in some cases, a conflict in usage between an elementary item and the group containing it is also allowed. For such details the relevant manuals should be consulted.

Most of these computers also allow machine-dependent usages other than DISPLAY, COMPUTATIONAL and INDEX. These are beyond our scope and are not discussed here.

(b) SYNCHRONIZED

In all the three systems the SYNCHRONIZED clause has the following form

$$\left\{ \begin{array}{l} \underline{SYNCHRONIZED} \\ \underline{SYNC} \end{array} \right\} \quad \left[\begin{array}{l} \underline{RIGHT} \\ \underline{LEFT} \end{array} \right]$$

The use of the word RIGHT indicates that the elementary item will terminate on a word boundary. On the other hand, LEFT means that the elementary item will begin from a word boundary. LEFT or RIGHT must be specified in a SYNCHRONIZED clause for ICL-1900 and DEC-10.

In B-6700, LEFT or RIGHT may be omitted. In that case RIGHT is assumed.

(c) JUSTIFIED

Only in DEC-10, JUSTIFIED LEFT is also allowed. In this case, however, the data movement will be as per standard rules. It may be noted that JUSTIFIED LEFT can be specified for any item other then numeric items. Therefore, in DEC-10 the words LEFT or RIGHT must be specified with the JUSTIFIED clause. In ICL-1900 the word RIGHT is not optional and must appear with this clause.

(d) REDEFINES

Data items with level 77 cannot be redefined in ICL-1900.

EXERCISES

1. Find the number of bytes described by the following:

```
(a)  01    MY-RECORD.
         02  FIRST-GROUP.
             03  A1         PIC        X(4).
             03  A2         PIC        99.
         02  SECOND-GROUP   REDEFINES FIRST-GROUP.
             03  A3         PIC        9(3).
             03  A4         PIC        XX.
             03  A5         PIC        9.
         02  THIRD-GROUP.
             03  A6         PIC        X(16).
             03  A7         PIC        9(6).

(b)  01    RECORD-ONE.
         05  A.
             10  A1         PIC        S9(8)V99 USAGE IS COMP-3.
             10  A2         PIC        XXX.
             10  A3         PIC        999.
         05  B      REDEFINES    A.
             10  B1         PIC        X(4).
             10  B2         PIC        S9(4)V99 COMP-3.
             10  B3         PIC        9(6) COMP SYNC.
```

(Assume USAGE clauses as described in the text.)

(c) 01   THIS-REC.
        02   DATA-A   PIC   X(5).
        02   DATA-B   PIC   9(5).
        02   DATA-C.
            03   C-ONE   PIC   XX.
            03   C-TWO   PIC   9(4).
        02   DATA-F   PIC   XX.
        02   DATA-G   PIC   S9(6)V99.
    66   DATA-D   RENAMES   DATA-B   THRU   C-ONE.
    66   DATA-E   RENAMES   DATA-B   THRU   DATA-C.

2. Examine whether the following statements are correct or not.
   (a) The REDEFINES clause cannot be used to redefine an elementary item.
   (b) A 77-level item which takes part in a large number of arithmetic
       operations should be described as COMP rather than as a DISPLAY
       item.
   (c) A group containing only alphabetic fields cannot be redefined by a
       group that contains numeric fields.
   (d) The appropriate use of the USAGE clause can reduce the execution
       time of a program.
   (e) The USAGE clause cannot be used in FILE SECTION.
   (f) The RENAMES clause can affect the internal storage requirement.
   (g) If no usage is specified, numeric fields are taken as COMPUTATIONAL,
       whereas the alphanumeric and alphabetic fields are taken as DISPLAY.

3. Find what is wrong in the following:

   (a) 01   A-RECORD.
           02   A1   PIC   XX.
           02   A2   PIC   9(5).
           02   A3   PIC   A(7).
           02   A4   PIC   9(7)V99.
       66   B-REC   RENAMES   A3   THRU   A4.
       66   C-REC   RENAMES   A2   THRU   B-REC.

   (b) 01   DATA-REC.
           02   FIRST-DATA   PIC   9(6).
           02   SECOND-DATA   PIC   X(3).
           02   THIRD-DATA   PIC   9(5).

       01   VALUE-REC   REDEFINES   DATA-REC.
           02   FILLER   PIC   9(6) VALUE IS 37.
           02   FILLER   PIC   X(8) VALUE IS "NEW56732".

4. Consider the following DATA DIVISION entries.

   01   ABCD.
       05   A   PICTURE IS X(6).
       05   B   PICTURE IS X(6) JUSTIFIED RIGHT.
       05   C   PICTURE IS X(12).
       05   D   PICTURE IS X(12) JUSTIFIED RIGHT.

   Find the contents of these fields after the execution of the following
   statement.
           MOVE   "NO-ERROR"   TO   A   B   C   D.

5. A deck of cards contain only two types of cards. Card-type = 1 indicates that it is a salesman card. The layout is as follows:

Card Columns	Fields
1-6	Salesman-number
7	Card-type
8-40	Salesman-name
41-42	Age
43	Sex
44-45	Years-in-sales

Each salesman card is followed by the customer cards (card-type = 2). There is one card for each of the customers served by the salesman. The layout of this card is as follows:

Card Columns	Fields
1-6	Salesman-number
7	Card-type
8-30	Customer-name
31-70	Customer-address
71-80	Maximum-credit (in Rupees)

Describe these records in FILE SECTION according to the following instructions:

(a) Describe the record for a card of type 1 and then redefine the entire record to describe the card of type 2.
(b) Describe just one record and redefine only the portions that are not common in the two types of cards.

Suppose in the first case you use the names CARD-TYPE-1 and CARD-TYPE-2 to define the card-type in the two descriptions. Now, in the PROCEDURE DIVISION if after reading a card you want to find out its type (note that you do not have any prior knowledge of the type of the card that will be read), which of the two names will you use to test whether the card type is equal to 1 or 2?

6. Write a COBOL program to read the card file of the above problem and to print a report. The report consists of one line for each salesman containing all the data given on a salesman card except the card-type. This line is followed by the customer information. There is one line for each of the customers served by the salesman. All customer data except the card-type and salesman-number must be printed. Use any suitable report layout.

9

MORE ABOUT DATA MOVEMENT VERB AND ARITHMETIC VERBS

The verbs MOVE, ADD, SUBTRACT, MULTIPLY and DIVIDE have been discussed earlier in simplified forms. This chapter contains a detailed description of the additional features of these verbs. The arithmetic verb COMPUTER which was left out earlier, is now introduced here for the first time.

9.1 ELEMENTARY AND GROUP MOVES

The receiving or sending field of a MOVE statement can be either an elementary item or a group item. When both the fields are elementary items, the data movement is known as an <u>elementary move</u>. When at least one of the fields is a group item, it is called a <u>group move</u>. Let us first consider the elementary move.

The elementary move can be used for three different purposes: to transfer data, to edit data or to convert data. We are already familiar with the first two uses of the MOVE statement. The conversion of data takes place when the class and/or usage of the receiving field is different from those of the sending field. For example, let FIELD-1 and FIELD-2 be defined as

```
77      FIELD-1      PIC      9(5)   COMP.
77      FIELD-2      PIC      9(5).
```

Now, the execution of the statement MOVE FIELD-2 TO FIELD-1 will cause the conversion of the DISPLAY data in FIELD-2 to the binary form before being moved to FIELD-1.

Some moves in which the category and usage of the sending field is different from those of the receiving field are not legal. Before discussing the rules in this matter, let us recall that elementary data, literals and figurative constants can belong to any of the five categories (see Sec. 5.7) — alphabetic, alphanumeric, alphanumeric edited, numeric and numeric edited. For the purpose of the rules in respect of the MOVE statement, a data belonging to the numeric category is again subdivided as integer and noninteger. The following table shows the legality of the movement between different categories of data.

Categories of Sending Data Item/Literal/ Figurative Constant	Category of Receiving Data Item		
	Alphabetic	Alphanumeric, Alphanumeric Edited	Numeric, Numeric Edited
Alphabetic	AN	AN	Illegal
Alphanumeric	AN	AN	N
Alphanumeric Edited	AN	AN	Illegal
Numeric Integer	Illegal	AN	N
Numeric Non-integer	Illegal	Illegal	N
Numeric Edited	Illegal	AN	Illegal

In the above table AN indicates alphanumeric data transfer (see Sec. 6.2) and N indicates numeric data transfer (see Sec. 6.2). The following rules may be noted for those moves which are legal.

(i)   Alphanumeric data transfer is normally left justified. However, if JUSTIFIED RIGHT is specified for the receiving field, the movement is right justified.

(ii) If the receiving field is a signed numeric, the sign of the sending data is moved to the receiving field with any required sign conversion. (Note that the sign may be a zone sign or a separate character at the leading or trailing end.) If the sending item is unsigned, a positive sign is generated for the receiving item.

(iii) If the receiving field is an unsigned numeric, then only the absolute value of the sending field is moved; no operational sign is moved.

(iv) When the receiving field is alphanumeric or alphanumeric edited and the sending item is a signed numeric, the operational sign is not moved. In this case, if the sign is separate, the size of the sending field is considered one less than its actual size.

(v)   If the sending field is alphanumeric and the receiving field is numeric or numeric edited, the data is moved as if the sending field were described as an unsigned numeric integer field. Care should be taken to ensure that the alphanumeric field does not contain any character other than digits. Otherwise, the result is unpredictable.

(vi) When the sending field is alphanumeric or alphanumeric edited and the receiving field is alphabetic, care should be taken to ensure that the alphanumeric field does not contain any character other than letters or space. Otherwise, the result is unpredictable.

Examples

The following examples illustrate the various rules mentioned above.

Sending Field		Receiving Field Picture	Value of the Receiving Field After the Move
Picture	Value		
S9(3)	12̄3	9(3)	123
S9(3) LEADING SEPARATE	−123	S9(3)	12̄3
X(3)	12̄3	9(4)	0123
9(4)	2579	X(3)	257
S9(3) LEADING SEPARATE	−325	X(4)	325ƀ
X(4)	ABCD	A(5)	ABCDƀ
9(4)	0325	S9(4) TRAILING SEPARATE	0325+

As regards usages of the operands in a MOVE statement in general, a receiving or sending field can have any usage which is valid for its class. However, usages being largely implementor-defined, one must consult the relevant manual for the rules in this connection.

While an elementary move can be used for several purposes, a group move is used for data transfer only. Group moves are considered to be alphanumeric moves regardless of the class of elementary items contained in the groups. It may be noted that if any editing is specified for the receiving fields, it may not be performed. Let us consider the following illustrative example. Suppose that the records REC-1 and REC-2 are described in the DATA DIVISION in the following manner.

```
01      REC-1.
        02    GR-1.
              04     A1          PIC     9999.
              04     A2          PIC     99V9.
              04     A3          PIC     XXXX.
              04     A4          PIC     999.

        02    GR-2.
              04     B1          PIC     XXXX.
              04     B2          PIC     999.

01      REC-2.
              04     C1          PIC     ZZZZ.
              04     C2          PIC     99.9.
              04     C3          PIC     XXBXX.
              04     C4          PIC     ZZZ.
```

Let the current contents of REC-1 and REC-2 be as follows:

REC-1																			
GR-1														GR-2					
A1				A2			A3				A4			B1				B2	
0	3	4	5	6	7	1	A	B	2	3	4	5	6	2	3	C	D	4	2	3

REC-2														
C1				C2				C3				C4		
2	0	7	8	4	6	.	7	3	8		4	6	8	9	2

After the execution of the statement

    MOVE   GR-1   TO   REC-2

the contents of GR-1 will retain their original values whereas REC-2 will become as follows:

REC-2															
C1				C2				C3						C4	
0	3	4	5	6	7	1	A	B	2	3	4	5	6		

It may be noted that no editing has been performed. Moreover, GR-1 being shorter than REC-2 in terms of size, as per the rules for alphanumeric data movement, the extra portions in the right-hand side of REC-2 are filled with spaces.

9.2   CORRESPONDING OPTION

9.2.1   MOVE CORRESPONDING

Quite often it is required to move some of the data items of one group to some other data items in another group. If the names of the corresponding data items of the two groups are distinct, then for each data item, a separate MOVE verb should be used. However, if the corresponding data items of both the records have identical names, then instead of using separate MOVE statements, just one MOVE statement with the CORRESPONDING option can be used. The following example illustrates the use of the MOVE verb with the CORRESPONDING option.

Example

Consider the following DATA DIVISION entries.

```
01      PAY-REC.
        02      ID-NUMBER       PIC     9(5).
        02      NAME            PIC     X(25).
        02      DEPARTMENT      PIC     X(20).
        02      BASIC-PAY       PIC     9999V99.
        02      FILLER          PIC     X(24).
01      PRINT-REC.
        02      FILLER          PIC     X(5).
        02      ID-NUMBER       PIC     Z(5).
        02      FILLER          PIC     X(5).
        02      NAME            PIC     X(25).
        02      FILLER          PIC     X(5).
        02      DEPARTMENT      PIC     X(20).
        02      FILLER          PIC     X(5).
        02      BASIC-PAY       PIC     ZZZZ.99.
        02      FILLER          PIC     X(5).
        02      DEDUCTIONS      PIC     ZZZZ.99.
        02      FILLER          PIC     X(5).
        02      ALLOWANCES      PIC     ZZZZ.99.
        02      FILLER          PIC     X(5).
        02      NET-PAY         PIC     ZZZZ.99.
```

Suppose it is required that the data stored in the four fields of PAY-REC should be moved to those fields of PRINT-REC that are given the same data names. The following four MOVE statements can serve the purpose.

```
MOVE ID-NUMBER OF PAY-REC TO ID-NUMBER OF PRINT-REC.
MOVE NAME OF PAY-REC TO NAME OF PRINT-REC.
MOVE DEPARTMENT OF PAY-REC TO DEPARTMENT OF PRINT-REC.
MOVE BASIC-PAY OF PAY-REC TO BASIC-PAY OF PRINT-REC.
```

However, since both the records have same names for the concerned data items, the following statement

```
MOVE  CORRESPONDING  PAY-REC  TO  PRINT-REC.
```

will have the same effect. It is not necessary that the corresponding data names in the two records should appear in the same order. The general format of the MOVE CORRESPONDING statement is

$$\underline{MOVE} \left\{ \begin{array}{l} \underline{CORRESPONDING} \\ \underline{CORR} \end{array} \right\} \quad \text{identifier-1} \quad \underline{TO} \quad \text{identifier-2}$$

where identifier-1 and identifier-2 should be group names. Note that MOVE CORRESPONDING is not a group move, it is merely a means for specifying a number of elementary moves through a single MOVE statement. As such any editing, if specified, will be performed. Source and destination groups can include data names that are not common. Only those fields having identical names in the two records will take part in the data movement. The remaining data items in the destination group will remain unchanged.

9.2.2 ADD and SUBTRACT CORRESPONDING

The CORRESPONDING option can also be used with the ADD and SUBTRACT verbs. The following are the formats of these verbs with the CORRESPONDING option.

$$\underline{ADD} \left\{ \begin{array}{l} \underline{CORRESPONDING} \\ \underline{CORR} \end{array} \right\} \quad \text{identifier-1} \quad \underline{TO} \quad \text{identifier-2}$$

$$\underline{SUBTRACT} \left\{ \begin{array}{l} \underline{CORRESPONDING} \\ \underline{CORR} \end{array} \right\} \quad \text{identifier-1} \quad \underline{FROM} \quad \text{identifier-2}$$

In the case of the ADD statement numeric elementary items in the group referred to by identifier-1 are added to and stored in the corresponding elementary items of the group named in identifier-2. In the case of the SUBTRACT statement, the corresponding numeric elementary items of the group referred to by identifier-1 are subtracted from and are stored in the corresponding numeric elementary items of the group referred to by identi-fier-2.

9.2.3 General Rules Concerning CORRESPONDING Option

The following rules should be observed when the CORRESPONDING option is used.

(i) Identifier-1 and identifier-2 in all cases must refer to group items i.e., these identifiers must not be data items with level numbers 66, 77 or 88 (for level number 88, see Sec. 10.1.4).

(ii) Data items in identifier-1 and identifier-2 take part in the specified operation (MOVE, ADD or SUBTRACT) only when they have the same data name and same qualifiers up to but not including identifier-1 and identifier-2.

(iii) In the case of ADD or SUBTRACT CORRESPONDING only numeric data items are considered for addition or subtraction respectively. This means that data items other than numeric are not considered for the arithmetic operations even though they may have identical names in the two groups named in identifier-1 and identifier-2.

(iv) All data items subordinate to identifier-1 and identifier-2 with level numbers 66 or 88 or containing a REDEFINES or OCCURS (see Chapter 11) clause, are ignored for the purpose of the operation. Identifier-1 and identifier-2 may, however, have a REDEFINES or OCCURS clause or may be subordinate to data items having a REDEFINES or OCCURS clause.

(v) FILLER data items are ignored.

(vi) CORRESPONDING items can have different locations within the group and the field sizes can also be different.

Examples

Let us consider the following DATA DIVISION entries.

```
01      OLD-REC.
        02      FIRST-PART.
                03      ITEM-1          PIC         999.
                03      ITEM-2          PIC         999.
                03      ITEM-3          PIC         9(5).

        02      SECOND-PART.
                03      SEC-1           PIC         9(4).
                03      SEC-2.
                        04      SEC-21  PIC         X(5).

        02      THIRD-PART.
                03      THIRD-1         PIC         XXX.
                03      THIRD-2         PIC         999.
```

```
01      NEW-REC.
        02      FIRST-PART.
                03      ITEM-1          PIC     9999.
                03      ITEM-2          PIC     9(3).
                03      ITEM-3          PIC     X(5).
                03      ITEM-4          PIC     X(21).

        02      SECOND-PART.
                03      SEC-1           PIC     X(4).
                03      SEC-21          PIC     X(5).

        02      FOURTH-PART.
                03      THIRD-1         PIC     XXX.
                03      THIRD-2         PIC     999.
```

Now, let us see which data items will be moved if the PROCEDURE DIVISION contains the statement MOVE CORRESPONDING OLD-REC TO NEW-REC. The said data items are ITEM-1, ITEM-2, ITEM-3 and SEC-1. Note that SEC-21, THIRD-1 and THIRD-2 cannot take part in the operation. This is because although those names are common to both the groups, their qualifiers are different. If, on the other hand, the PROCEDURE DIVISION statement is ADD CORRESPONDING OLD-REC TO NEW-REC, only ITEM-1 and ITEM-2 will take part in the add operation. This is because ITEM-3 and SEC-1 in NEW-REC are not numeric data items.

9.3 ROUNDED OPTION

Let us consider the following DATA DIVISION entries.

```
77      A       PIC     99V999      VALUE   IS    23.412.
77      B       PIC     99V999      VALUE   IS    35.273.
77      C       PIC     99V9        VALUE   IS    41.5.
```

Now, after the execution of the statement ADD A B GIVING C, C will contain 58.6 instead of 58.685 as C can retain only one digit after the decimal point. Instead of this usual truncation, rounding can be specified through the ROUNDED option. The ROUNDED option can be specified as follows:

        ADD   A   B   GIVING   C   ROUNDED

Now, the content of C will be 58.7 instead of 58.6.

It may be noted from the above example that whenever an arithmetic operation is executed, if the number of places in the fractional part of the result happens to be greater than the number of places provided for the fractional part in the receiving field, truncation will occur. However, if the ROUNDED option is specified, 1 is added to the last digit whenever the most significant digit being thrown out is greater than or equal to 5. In the example shown here the most significant digit of the excess is 8 which is greater than 5. Therefore, 1 has been added to 6 which is the last digit

of the receiving field. On the other hand, if A and B contains 23.412 and
35.213 respectively, both the statements

$$\text{ADD} \qquad \text{A} \qquad \text{B} \qquad \text{GIVING} \qquad \text{C}$$

and

$$\text{ADD} \qquad \text{A} \qquad \text{B} \qquad \text{GIVING} \qquad \text{C} \qquad \text{ROUNDED}$$

will give the same result and in both the cases C will have the value
58.6.

The ROUNDED option can be specified in the case of any arithmetic verb
by writing the word ROUNDED after the identifier, denoting the field that
receives the result of the operation. The ROUNDED phrase cannot be specified
for the identifier that receives the remainder in the DIVIDE operation.

9.4 ON SIZE ERROR OPTION

If after an arithmetic operation, the result exceeds the largest value that
can be accommodated in the result field, the error is called a size error.
To take an example, let A and B be two elementary items with pictures 99 and
999 respectively. Suppose also that the current values of the two fields are
35 and 980 respectively. Now, the execution of the statement ADD A TO B
causes a size error. This is because the result field B is not large
enough to hold the result of the addition, namely, 1015.

When a size error occurs, the contents of the result field after the
operation is unpredictable. However, the processing is not terminated and
the computer will proceed with the execution of the next statement regardless of the fact that a size error occurred. Therefore, it is the responsibility of the programmer to monitor the arithmetic operation by specifying
the ON SIZE ERROR phrase at the end of the arithmetic statement. This
optional phrase can be used with any arithmetic verb and has the following
syntax:

$$;\quad \text{ON} \quad \underline{\text{SIZE}} \quad \underline{\text{ERROR}} \quad \text{imperative - statement}$$

When this phrase is specified the imperative statement gets executed, if
an ON SIZE ERROR occurs. Thus a statement

$$\text{ADD} \text{A} \text{TO} \text{B} \text{ON} \text{SIZE} \text{ERROR} \text{GO} \text{TO} \text{ERROR-PARA.}$$

will cause the control to be transferred to ERROR-PARA in the case of a
size error. Otherwise, the effect will be the same as that of ADD A TO B.
When the ON SIZE ERROR phrase is specified, the arithmetic statement must be
terminated by a period.

The ON SIZE ERROR phrase enables a programmer to take measures in case
a size-error condition arises. However, specifying the ON SIZE ERROR phrase
with each and every arithmetic operation can increase the execution time of
the program. Thus when the programmer is sure that there is no possibility
of a size error, the phrase may not be specified. In this connection it is
recommended that the programmer should give the result fields enough room so
that size error does not occur.

It may be worthwhile to note the differences between the ROUNDED and SIZE ERROR options. The ROUNDED option is concerned with the case when a loss of digits occurs at the right end. This loss merely makes the result approximate, but the result is not altogether wrong. The ROUNDED option only affects the nature of approximation. If specified, the result is approximated by rounding. Otherwise, it is approximated by truncation. On the other hand, SIZE ERROR is concerned with the case when a loss of digits occurs in the most significant part (left end). The result in such a case is totally wrong.

9.5 COMPUTE VERB

So far we have discussed only four arithmetic verbs, namely, ADD, SUBTRACT, MULTIPLY and DIVIDE. In COBOL there is another arithmetic verb called COMPUTE. This verb is so powerful that all the computations performed by the other four verbs can also be done by using only the COMPUTE verb. Its general format is

COMPUTE   identifier-1   [ROUNDED]   [, identifier-2 ROUNDED] ...

= arithmetic-expression [; ON SIZE ERROR imperative-statement]

The COMPUTE statement has the following meaning. During execution the arithmetic expression on the right of the equal sign is evaluated and the value is then moved to the identifier(s) on the left-hand side. If any identifier on the left of the equal sign is a numeric-edited item, editing takes place when the value of the expression is moved to the said identifier. The identifiers on the left of the equal sign (=) must be numeric or numeric-edited elementary items. The right-hand side must be an arithmetic expression. An arithmetic expression can be an identifier (numeric elementary items only), a numeric literal or can specify a computation involving two or more such identifiers and/or literals. An arithmetic expression has always a numeric value. The following are the rules for constructing arithmetic expressions.

(i) When an arithmetic expression specifies a computation, it may consist of two or more numeric literals and/or data names joined by arithmetic operators. The following table lists the operators and their meanings.

Operator	Meaning
**	Exponentiation
/	Division
*	Multiplication
—	Subtraction
+	Addition

There must be at least one space preceding and following the operator in an arithmetic expression. No two arithmetic operators can appear together in an expression. In this respect ** is considered to be a single operator.

(ii) Parentheses may be used to specify the order of operations in an arithmetic expression. Where parentheses are absent, the order is taken to be left to right as follows:

**	Exponentiation
/ *	Division and multiplication
— +	Subtraction and addition

When parentheses are used, the portion of the expression enclosed within parentheses is evaluated first. When parentheses are used within parentheses, the evaluation proceeds from the least inclusive pair of parentheses to the most inclusive pair.

(iii) An arithmetic expression may be preceded by a + or — sign. Such operators are called unary + or unary — operators.

Examples of valid arithmetic expressions are

```
3   *   I
RATE   *   QUANTITY   —   DISCOUNT
A   +   (   B   -   C   )   *   D   **   2
— B
```

The first example indicates a multiplication of 3 and the value of I. Thus if the current value of I is 5, the value of this expression is 15. The value of the second expression is evaluated by multiplying RATE by QUANTITY and then subtracting DISCOUNT from the product. Note that multiplication will be done first because it has a higher-order operation than subtraction. The third example illustrates the use of parentheses and has the following meaning:

$$A + (B - C) \times D^2$$

The — sign in the fourth example is a unary minus sign and if the current value of B is, say 47, then the value of the expression is —47. The following are examples of invalid arithmetic expressions.

```
A   +   —   B
4   (   K   —   1   )
```

The first one is invalid because the operators + and — cannot appear side by side. The second one is invalid as an arithmetic expression because no operator has been specified between the literal 4 and the expression K-1 enclosed in parentheses.

The COMPUTE statement specifies a series of arithmetic operations. During the execution it may be necessary to store the intermediate results internally before the final result can be computed. These intermediate results are stored in some locations in the memory. The compiler takes care of these locations and the programmer is not concerned with them.

Note that when the right-hand side of a COMPUTE verbs is a single identifier or literal, the effect is that of a MOVE statement.

Example 1

                COMPUTE   A = B + C

has the same effect as that-of ADD   B   C   GIVING   A.

Example 2

                COMPUTE   F = 1.8 * C + 32

The value of the expression on the right-hand side is evaluated and this
value is then moved to F. Suppose C and F are defined with pictures 99 and
ZZ9.9 respectively and the current value of C is 3. Then after the execution of the statement, F will have the value 37.4.

9.6 IMPLEMENTATION DIFFERENCES

(a) Elementary Move

It is not possible to discuss here all the rules for determining the results
of MOVEs among the various types of data fields. In real applications it may
be hardly required to make a use of the MOVE verb where the source and
receiving fields differ widely in terms of class or usage. However, in such
rare cases the reader is advised to consult the manual. The following are
only a few selected cases which may be of interest.

When the receiving field is numeric or numeric-edited and the source
field contains a nonnumeric character, the following result will take place
in the three systems. In DEC-10 the result is unpredictable. In B-6700 the
zone bits of the nonnumeric character is stripped off. In ICL-1900 the nonnumeric character is ignored and not moved. In all the three machines an
alphanumeric data item is allowed to be moved to a numeric or numeric-edited
item subject to the abovestated rules. In B-6700 and DEC-10 such moves are
treated as numeric moves while in ICL-1900 the value is transferred left
justified with truncation or zero fill on the right. Moreover, different
result can take place in ICL-1900, if in the above case, the usage of the
receiving field is not DISPLAY.

(b) Group Move

Group moves on B-6700 and DEC-10 are as described in the text. In ICL-1900
if one field is elementary and other a group, the group is treated as an
elementary alphanumeric field and the rules of the elementary move are
followed. Note that in this case, if the receiving field is elementary,
editing, if any, will take place. However, when both the fields are group
items, the usual group move takes place.

(c) CORRESPONDING Option

In B-6700 more than one receiving fields can be specified even when the
CORRESPONDING option is used with the MOVE verb.

(d)   COMPUTE Verb

In B-6700 more than one identifier can be specified on the left-hand side of the equal sign. If used, the value of the arithmetic expression on the right-hand side will be stored in each of the fields denoted by these identifiers.

In B-6700 the words FROM or EQUALS may be used instead of the equal sign. In DEC-10, EQUALS or EQUAL TO may be used in lieu of equal sign.

In DEC-10 the symbol ↑ can be used instead of ** in an arithmetic expression. In B-6700 two additional operators MOD and DIV are also available. MOD gives the remainder of a division and DIV gives the integer part of the quotient after a division.

In B-6700, left or right parentheses or operators in an arithmetic expression need not be preceded or followed by a space. The only exception is in the case of the minus sign. Unless a minus sign is not used as a unary minus sign, it must be preceded and followed by at least one space. In ICL-1900, a left parenthesis must be preceded by at least one space but need not be followed by a space on the right. The reverse of this is true for the right parenthesis.

EXERCISES

1. Four data names A, B, C and D have the following data descriptions.

77	A	PIC	99V999	VALUE	88.156.
77	B	PIC	9(4)V999	VALUE	9902.852.
77	C	PIC	9(4)V99	VALUE	10.5.
77	D	PIC	999	VALUE	200.

    Indicate what will be the contents of A, B, C and D after the execution of each of the following statements. In each case assume that before the execution of the statement, the fields A, B, C and D contain the initial values indicated by the VALUE clause.

    (a)   ADD A, B GIVING C ROUNDED ON SIZE ERROR MOVE ZERO TO C.
    (b)   ADD B, D GIVING C ROUNDED ON SIZE ERROR MOVE ZERO TO C.
    (c)   DIVIDE C INTO D GIVING C ROUNDED.
    (d)   MULTIPLY B BY C ON SIZE ERROR MOVE 1 TO C.
    (e)   SUBTRACT A FROM B GIVING C ROUNDED.
    (f)   MULTIPLY A BY 300.2 GIVING B ROUNDED ON SIZE ERROR MOVE 0 TO B.

2. Indicate which one of the following is not a valid statement.
    (a)   MOVE CORRESPONDING OLD-REC TO NEW-REC.
    (b)   MULTIPLY CORRESPONDING OLD-REC BY NEW-REC.
    (c)   ADD CORRESPONDING OLD-REC TO NEW-REC.
    (d)   SUBTRACT CORRESPONDING OLD-REC FROM NEW-REC.

3. For each of the following algebraic expressions, write the equivalent arithmetic expression.

(a) $\dfrac{1}{\pi^2} \cdot \dfrac{(b+c)^{4.5}}{a+d}$ (b) $a + (\dfrac{b-c}{d+e})^2$

(c) $p \cdot (1+\pi)^n$ (d) $\dfrac{(b^2 - 4.a.c)^{\frac{1}{2}}}{2.a}$

4. Rewrite the statements (a) to (e) in Exercise 1 by using the COMPUTE verb.

5. Let the pictures for the data names X and Y be 9(3)V9(5) and 9(4)V9(3). Write a COBOL statement to move the value of X to Y. The loss of extra digits in the fractional part should be taken care of by rounding.

6. Assume that the following data items are described in the WORKING-STORAGE SECTION.

         77   A   PIC   S9(3).
         77   B   PIC   9(4)V99.
         77   C   PIC   S9(4).

    Show the results of the following statements.

    (a) COMPUTE   A   =   2.6.
    (b) COMPUTE   A ROUNDED = 2.6.
    (c) COMPUTE   B   =   8112.682 / 1.2 + 95.2 / 2.1 * 405.5
         ON SIZE ERROR MOVE 0 TO B.
    (d) MOVE 2.8 TO B.
         COMPUTE   C ROUNDED = B / 3 + 2.4 * 1.5 / 2.6 - 7.8.
    (e) COMPUTE   A   =   (4.2 + .6) / 3.
    (f) COMPUTE   C = 4.2 / 3. + .6.

7. A worker is paid for overtime hours at a rate which is twice the normal rate. The hours worked in excess of 48 hours in a week is considered to be the overtime hours. Write COBOL statements to compute the total wages of a worker assuming that the fields RATE and WEEKLY-HOURS respectively contain the normal rate and total hours worked in a week. The wages should be ROUNDED.

8. The data names FACE-VALUE and RATE contain the face value of equity shares and the **rate** of dividend respectively. Write COBOL statement(s) to calculate the gross dividend using the formula:

$$\text{Gross dividend} = \frac{\text{Face value} \times \text{Rate}}{100}$$

10

CONDITIONAL AND SEQUENCE CONTROL VERBS

The elementary form of the conditional verb IF and sequence control verbs, such as GO TO and STOP have been discussed in Chapter 6. We shall now take up the detailed study of the IF verb. In addition, sequence control verbs, such as GO TO with DEPENDING phrase, ALTER and PERFORM will also be discussed in this chapter.

10.1 CONDITION

A condition is an entity that at one point of time can have only one of the two values — true or false. As already pointed out, the IF verb makes use of conditions. We shall also see in the next chapter that some forms of the PERFORM and SEARCH verbs also make use of the conditions. In COBOL a condition can be any one of the following:

   (i)   Relational condition
  (ii)   Sign condition
 (iii)   Class condition
  (iv)   Condition-name condition
   (v)   Negated simple condition and
  (vi)   Compound condition.

10.1.1 Relational Condition

The relational condition has been briefly discussed earlier. We know that a relational condition indicates a comparison between two operands and has the form

        Operand-1   relational-operator   operand-2

where the relational-operator can be any one of the following:

IS	[NOT]	GREATER	THAN
IS	[NOT]	>	
IS	[NOT]	LESS	THAN
IS	[NOT]	<	
IS	[NOT]	EQUAL	TO
IS	[NOT]	=	

It was stated earlier that the operands can be an identifier or a literal. However, either operand can also be an arithmetic expression but must contain at least one reference to an identifier. Sometimes, operand-1 and operand-2 are respectively referred to as the <u>subject</u> and <u>object</u> of the relational condition.

Comparison of Numeric Operands

We are familiar with the kind of relational conditions where both the operands are numeric. The comparison in this case is algebraic and the two operands can be compared regardless of the size and USAGE of the fields.

Comparison of Nonnumeric Operands

A nonnumeric operand (identifier/literal other than numeric) can be compared to another nonnumeric operand according to the following rules.

(i) Fields of Equal Sizes

Characters in the corresponding positions are compared to determine the value of the relational condition. Comparison starts with the leftmost character in both the fields and proceeds in a left to right manner. If the two characters being compared are found to be unequal at any stage, the field containing the greater (according to the collating sequence of the computer (NATIVE) or that specified by the PROGRAM COLLATING SEQUENCE clause in the OBJECT-COMPUTER paragraph) character is considered to be greater. Only when the characters are found to be identical does the comparison proceed to the next position on the right. Two fields are taken to be equal only when all such pairs of characters have been found to be identical and the rightmost end has been reached.

(ii) Fields of Unequal Sizes

If the two operands are not of equal size, the shorter field is considered to be extended on the right by spaces to make its size equal to the longer field and the rules for comparing fields of equal sizes are used.

Comparison of a Numeric Operand with a Nonnumeric Operand

A numeric operand can be compared to a nonnumeric operand subject to the following restrictions.
  (i) The numeric operand must be an integer data item or integer literal.
  (ii) Both the operands must have the same USAGE (DISPLAY or some form of DISPLAY).

At the time of comparison, the numeric operand is treated as if its value were moved to an alphanumeric field of the same size and the contents of this alphanumeric item were then compared to the nonnumeric field.

Group Item as an Operand in Relational Condition

When an operand of a relational condition is a group item, the said item is considered to be an alphanumeric field.

   The following examples illustrate the results of different comparisons. Usage DISPLAY is assumed in all cases.

A (Operand-1)		B (Operand-2)		Result of Comparison
Picture	Value	Picture	Value	
X(3)	001	X(4)	0001	A > B
X(4)	3254	X(3)	325	A > B
X(3)	BOY	X(4)	GIRL	A < B
X(3)	BOY	X(4)	BIRD	A > B
X(3)	BOY	X(4)	BOYⱭ	A = B
9(3)	354	X(2)	46	A < B
S9(2) LEADING SEPARATE	−46	X(2)	46	A = B (see Rule (iv) of Sec. 9.1)
9(3)	354	9(2)	46	A > B

10.1.2 Sign Condition

The sign condition determines whether or not the algebraic value of an operand is positive, negative or zero. The operand can be either a numeric identifier or an arithmetic expression. The format of this condition is as follows:

$$\left\{\begin{array}{c} \text{identifier} \\ \text{arithmetic-expression} \end{array}\right\} \quad \text{IS} \quad [\ \underline{\text{NOT}}\ ] \left\{\begin{array}{c} \text{POSITIVE} \\ \text{NEGATIVE} \\ \underline{\text{ZERO}} \end{array}\right\}$$

When arithmetic expression is used, it must contain at least one identifier. The POSITIVE option determines the value of the condition to be true only if the value of the operand is strictly positive. This means that the value zero is not treated as positive.

   The following examples illustrate the use of the sign condition.

Example 1

```
77    BALANCE      PIC        S9(6)V99.
              .
              .
              .
IF    BALANCE  IS  ZERO  GO  TO  NIL-BALANCE.
```

It may be noted that the above IF statement is equivalent to the following statement that makes use of a relational condition

```
IF  BALANCE  =  0  GO  TO  NIL-BALANCE.
```

Example 2

```
02    DEPOSIT      PIC        9(4)V99.
02    WITHDRAWAL   PIC        9(4)V99.
              .
              .
              .
IF    DEPOSIT  —  WITHDRAWAL  IS  POSITIVE  GO  TO  CALCULATION.
```

The control is transferred to the paragraph named CALCULATION if the current value of DEPOSIT is greater than that of WITHDRAWAL.

In general, any sign condition can be replaced by an equivalent relational condition. The use of the sign condition may perhaps be convenient in certain cases and its use may also increase the readability of the statement that uses it.

10.1.3 Class Condition

The class condition determines whether or not the value of an operand is numeric or alphabetic. An operand is numeric if it contains only the digits 0 to 9 with or without an operational sign. An operand is alphabetic if it contains only the letters A to Z and space. The format of the class condition is as follows:

$$\text{identifier}\quad\text{IS}\quad [\ \underline{\text{NOT}}\ ]\ \left\{\begin{array}{c}\underline{\text{NUMERIC}}\\[4pt]\underline{\text{ALPHABETIC}}\end{array}\right\}$$

The following rules apply in the case of a class condition.

(i)   The usage of the identifier must be DISPLAY or some forms of DISPLAY.

(ii) For the NUMERIC option the identifier must be either numeric or alphanumeric. If the data item is defined with an operational sign (picture contains S or a SIGN clause has been specified), then the appearance of sign (zoned in the unit's position or a leading or trailing sign, as the case may be) is considered to be normal.

(iii) For the ALPHABETIC option, the identifier must be either alphabetic or alphanumeric.

(iv) The identifier may be a group item. However, for the NUMERIC option, the group item must not contain elementary items described with an operational sign.

The class condition is very useful for the validation of the input data. In COBOL, the data is read into the record area in the same form as recorded on the external medium regardless of the specified class of the individual fields in the record. For example, if we are reading the value of a numeric field from a card and the corresponding positions in the card contains non-numeric characters, the system will not detect it to be an error. Instead, the nonnumeric characters will be stored in the character positions of the numeric field. This error may even pass unnoticed because during any subsequent numeric operation (such as numeric MOVE or arithmetic operation), only the numeric part of the characters in the field (except for the positions that may indicate an operational sign) will be used. Thus a possible punching mistake in the data card can go undetected unless proper care is taken. One may avoid some of these blunders (though not all) through the use of class conditions.

Let BASIC-PAY be a data name in a card record defined with picture 9(5)V99. Having read the card, we can test the value of BASIC-PAY to ensure that the data on the card is actually numeric. This can be done as follows:

        IF BASIC-PAY IS NOT NUMERIC GO TO PARA-ERROR.

If the data contains any character other than digits, control will be transferred to PARA-ERROR. Otherwise, control will go to the next sentence in sequence. It may be noted that the data must be punched with leading zeros, if any,, and not with leading spaces. The space character is considered to be an alphabetic character.

10.1.4 Condition-Name Condition

A condition name is an entity which itself is a condition and as such can have either a true or false value. However, a condition name cannot be defined independently. It must always be associated to a data name called the conditional variable. The condition name may be defined in any section of the DATA DIVISION and must be placed immediately after the entry that defines the conditional variable. There can be more than one condition names associated to a conditional variable. In that case all the condition name entries must follow the entry defining the conditional variable.

A condition name entry specifies either a single value or a set of values and/or a range of values for the conditional variable. The condition name becomes true whenever the conditional variable assumes any of these values. Otherwise, the condition name is set to false. It must be noted that it is not possible to set the value of a condition name explicitly. The value of a condition name is always set implicitly depending on the current value of the conditional variable. The format of a condition name entry is given below.

$$
88 \quad \text{condition-name} \quad
\left\{
\begin{array}{ll}
\underline{VALUE} & \underline{IS} \\
\underline{VALUES} & \underline{ARE}
\end{array}
\right\}
\text{literal-1}
\left[
\left\{
\begin{array}{l}
\underline{THRU} \\
\underline{THROUGH}
\end{array}
\right\}
\text{literal-2}
\right]
$$

$$
\left[
, \text{literal-3}
\left[
\left\{
\begin{array}{l}
\underline{THRU} \\
\underline{THROUGH}
\end{array}
\right\}
\text{literal-4}
\right]
\right] \quad \ldots .
$$

The following rules apply for a condition name:

(i)   Condition names must be described at level 88. The level number
       begins in margin A or any position after it. The condition name
       must begin from margin B or any position after it. There must be
       at least one space between the level number and condition name.

(ii)   The normal rules for naming a data item also apply in the case of
       a condition name.

(iii) If the same condition name is used in more than one place, the
       condition name must be qualified by the name of its conditional
       variable.

(iv)   The name of the conditional variable can be used as a qualifier
       for any of its condition names. If the reference to a conditional
       variable requires qualification or subscripting (this will be
       discussed in the next chapter), the same combination of qualifi-
       cation or subscripting must also be used for the associated
       condition name.

(v)   The values specified through the VALUE clause in the condition
       name entry must not conflict with the data description of the
       conditional variable. A literal in the VALUE clause can be either
       a numeric literal, nonnumeric literal or figurative constant.

(vi)   When the THRU/THROUGH phrase is used, literal-1 must be less than
       literal-2 and literal-3 must be less than literal-4.

(vii) A conditional variable can be an elementary item or a group item.
       However, it cannot be another condition name, or a 66-level item
       (RENAMES clause) or a group containing the JUSTIFIED clause, or
       the SYNCHRONIZED clause or the USAGE clause other than DISPLAY.

The following is an example of the use of condition names.

```
77  MARITAL-STATUS          PIC   9.
88  SINGLE        VALUE  IS   ZERO.
88  MARRIED       VALUE  IS   1.
88  WIDOWED       VALUE  IS   2.
88  DIVORCED      VALUE  IS   3.
88  ONCE-MARRIED  VALUES ARE  1, 2, 3.
88  VALID-STATUS  VALUES ARE  0 THRU  3.
```

It may be noted that six condition names have been defined here. All of them
are associated with the conditional variable MARITAL-STATUS. If at a point
of time, MARITAL-STATUS gets a value of 2 then the condition names WIDOWED,
ONCE-MARRIED and VALID-STATUS will become true and others will become false.

The condition names can be used as conditions. Thus in PROCEDURE DIVI-SION we may have statements, such as:

(a) IF SINGLE SUBTRACT 125 FROM DEDUCTIONS.
(b) IF ONCE-MARRIED ADD 30 TO SPECIAL-PAY.
(c) IF NOT VALID-STATUS GO TO ERROR-IN-STATUS.

In (a) above the statement SUBTRACT 125 FROM DEDUCTIONS will be executed if MARITAL-STATUS is equal to zero. Similarly, in (b) the ADD statement will be executed only when MARITAL-STATUS is equal to 1, 2 or 3 and in (c) the control goes to the procedure ERROR-IN-STATUS only when MARITAL-STATUS has a value other than 0, 1, 2 or 3. As in (c), a condition name can be preceded by NOT to indicate the negation of the condition.

The format for a condition-name condition is

[NOT]   condition-name

It is important to note the usefulness of a condition name. When a condition name specifies a single value for the conditional variable, the condition name is equivalent to a relational condition. For example, in (a) above the condition name SINGLE is equivalent to the relational condition MARITAL-STATUS = 0. Even when the condition name specifies more than one value for the conditional variable, the condition name can be replaced by an equivalent compound condition (to be discussed later). Thus it may not be absolutely necessary to make use of the condition names. The main advantage of a condition name is that it increases the readability of the statement that uses it. Certainly, the use of the condition name WIDOWED conveys more information to a reader of the program than the use of the relational condition MARITAL-STATUS = 2. Precisely for this reason, it is recommended that whenever possible, meaningful condition names should be used in a program.

10.1.5 Negated Simple Condition

Any of the simple conditions described above can be preceded by the logical operator NOT. The effect of placing the operator NOT before a simple condition is to reverse the value of the condition. It may be seen that the operator NOT can be used in two ways. In simple conditions it can be used as a part of the condition. It can also be used to precede a simple condition to make it a negated simple condition. An example of the first use may be DEPOSIT NOT LESS THAN 500.00 while an example of the second use is NOT DEPOSIT LESS THAN 500.00. Of course, in this case, both the conditions mean the same thing and can be used in either form. What matters is the role of the operator NOT. In the former case NOT is a part of a relational operator and in the latter case it is a logical operator. However, NOT must not precede a simple condition that includes NOT as a part of it.

10.1.6 Compound Condition

Two simple conditions can be connected by the logical operators AND or OR to form a compound condition (also known as combined condition). When two conditions are combined by AND, the compound condition becomes true only when both the constituent conditions are true. In all other cases the compound condition is false. On the other hand, if OR is used to combine two conditions, the compound condition is true if either or both the constituent conditions are true. It is false only when both the conditions are false.

For example, the compound condition AMOUNT GREATER THAN 499 AND AMOUNT LESS THAN 1000 is a compound condition which will be true only when the value of AMOUNT is in the range 500 to 999 (inclusive of both). This is because both the simple conditions are true for these values of AMOUNT. For other values of AMOUNT, only one of them is true. Similarly, the compound condition AMOUNT LESS THAN 500 OR AMOUNT GREATER THAN 999 will be false only when the value of AMOUNT is in the range 500 to 999.

A compound condition can consist of any number of simple or negated simple conditions joined either by AND or OR. Compound conditions in such cases are resolved as follows. Negated simple conditions are evaluated first. This is followed by the evaluation of pairs of resulting conditions around each AND in a left-to-right order. After this the resulting conditions around each OR are evaluated in a left-to-right manner. If required, parentheses can be used in compound conditions. In such cases all the conditions within the parentheses are evaluated first in accordance with the above rules. When parentheses are used within parentheses, evaluation proceeds from the least inclusive pair of the parentheses to the most inclusive pair.

In general, a compound condition has the following form:

$$\text{condition-1} \quad \left\{ \begin{array}{c} \text{AND} \\ \text{OR} \end{array} \right\} \quad \text{condition-2} \qquad \ldots$$

where condition-1 and condition-2 can be any one of the following:
- a simple condition
- a negated simple condition
- a compound condition optionally enclosed in parentheses
- a negated compound condition where a compound condition enclosed in parentheses is preceded by NOT.

It may be noted that no two logical operators can appear side by side except that the operators AND and OR may be immediately followed by NOT.

Using the abovementioned rules, fairly complicated compound conditions can be constructed. However, in actual practice, the need for a complicated compound condition hardly arises. For the sake of readability, it is recommended that the use of complex compound conditions should be avoided.

The following is an example of the use of a compound condition. Consider the sentence

```
        IF AGE IS LESS THAN 30 AND (HIGHLY-EDUCATED OR
        HIGHLY-EXPERIENCED) MOVE 3 TO BONUS-CODE.
```

Here, HIGHLY-EDUCATED and HIGHLY-EXPERIENCED are condition names. If either of them is true and if AGE is less than 30, 3 will be moved to BONUS-CODE. Notice the importance of parentheses. If these are removed, the compound condition can become true if HIGHLY-EXPERIENCED is true regardless of the value of AGE and that of the condition name HIGHLY-EDUCATED.

Abbreviation

Consecutive relational conditions in a compound condition can be abbreviated in certain cases as follows:

(i)   When the subjects in the consecutive relational conditions are identical, the subject may be omitted from all the conditions except from the one where it appears first.

(ii) When the subjects and relational operators in the consecutive relational conditions are identical, the subject as well as the relational condition may be omitted from all the conditions except from the one where they appear first.

Some examples of abbreviation are given below.

Example 1

The compound condition

> AMOUNT GREATER THAN 499 AND AMOUNT LESS THAN 1000

can be abbreviated to

> AMOUNT GREATER THAN 499 AND LESS THAN 1000

Here, the second appearance of the common subject AMOUNT has been omitted.

Example 2

The compound condition

> CARD-CODE = 3 OR CARD-CODE = 5 OR CARD-CODE = 7

may be abbreviated to

> CARD-CODE = 3 OR 5 OR 7

Here, the subjects as well as the relational conditions in the given compound condition are identical. Consequently, the second and third appearances of the subject and the relational condition have been omitted.

The consecutive relational conditions that are being considered for abbreviation may also contain the word NOT. In this case the interpretation of the abbreviated condition can become ambiguous. To resolve the ambiguity the following rule has been recommended in the ANSI standard. The word NOT preceding a relational operator in an abbreviated condition is considered part of the relational operator. Otherwise, NOT is considered to be a logical operator negating the condition preceded by it. The following examples can help to understand this rule.

Example 3

The condition

> AGE LESS THAN 30 AND NOT LESS THAN 20 OR 40

is interpreted to be an abbreviation of the compound condition

AGE LESS THAN 30 AND AGE NOT LESS THAN 20 OR AGE NOT LESS THAN 40.

This is because NOT precedes the relational operator LESS THAN in the abbreviated condition and as such it is interpreted to be a part of the relational operator NOT LESS THAN.

Example 4

The condition

NOT AGE LESS THAN 20 AND 30

will be interpreted to be an abbreviation of

NOT AGE LESS THAN 20 AND AGE LESS THAN 30.

Here, NOT precedes the data name AGE. It is therefore not considered to be part of the relational operator LESS THAN which has been abbreviated.

10.2 IF STATEMENT

We are already familiar with the simple form of the IF statement. The general form of the IF statement is as follows:

$$ \text{IF} \quad \text{condition} \quad ; \quad \begin{Bmatrix} \text{statement-1} \\ \text{NEXT SENTENCE} \end{Bmatrix} \quad \left[; \underline{\text{ELSE}} \quad \begin{Bmatrix} \text{statement-2} \\ \text{NEXT SENTENCE} \end{Bmatrix} \right] $$

The condition can be any one of the conditions discussed above. Each of statement-1 and statement-2 represents one or more COBOL statement. When more than one statement is specified, they must be separated by one or more spaces or by an optional semicolon (;) or comma (,). During execution, if the condition is found to be true, the statements represented by statement-1 are executed. On the other hand, if the condition is found to be false, the statements represented by statement-2 are executed. For ease of reference, we shall call the statements represented by statement-1 and statement-2 as then part and else part respectively. It may be noted that either the then part or else part is executed depending on the value of the specified condition. After that the control implicitly goes to the statement that immediately follows the IF sentence.

Normally, an IF statement should be terminated by a period (.) followed by a blank (see next section for exceptions). For this reason an IF statement is often referred to as an IF sentence. Sometimes, we encounter situations where no action needs to be specified if the condition is true, but some actions are necessary if the condition is false. In that case, the NEXT SENTENCE phrase can be used for the then part and the else part can be written to indicate the actions required. Similarly, the NEXT SENTENCE phrase can replace the else part if no action is required when the condition is false. The NEXT SENTENCE phrase indicates that the control should pass to the statement that follows the IF sentence. Note that if no action needs to be specified for the else part, the phrase ELSE NEXT SENTENCE can be omitted but in that case a terminating period is essential. It is in this form that we have used the IF statement so far. However, the phrase ELSE NEXT SENTENCE may not be omitted in certain cases and this point will be discussed later (see Example 2 in Sec. 10.2.1). For the time being, let us assume that ELSE NEXT SENTENCE may be omitted provided it precedes the terminal period of the IF sentence.

The following examples illustrate the use of the IF statement.

Example 1

```
IF  QUANTITY IS NUMERIC AND QUANTITY IS POSITIVE
      MOVE ZERO TO ERROR-CODE.COMPUTE SALES-VALUE = QUANTITY * RATE
ELSE MOVE 1 TO ERROR-CODE
      MOVE ZERO TO SALES-VALUE.
```

The specified condition tests whether or not the current value of the data name QUANTITY is numeric as well as positive. If the condition is true, ERROR-CODE is set to zero and SALES-VALUE is computed by multiplying QUANTITY by RATE. On the other hand, if the condition is FALSE, ERROR-CODE is set to 1 and SALES-VALUE is set to zero. In either case the control goes implicitly to the next statement after this IF sentence. The above sentence is equivalent to the following flow chart.

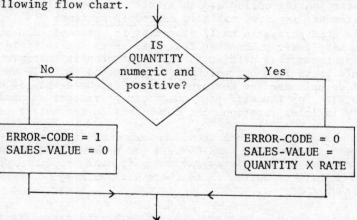

Example 2

IF OK-BALANCE NEXT SENTENCE ELSE MOVE 2 TO BALANCE-CODE.

Here, OK-BALANCE is a condition name. No action is specified if this condition is true. If the condition is false, BALANCE-CODE should be set to 2. The sentence is equivalent to the following flow chart.

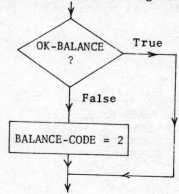

It may be noted that any IF sentence can be alternatively written by just negating the condition. In order to retain the meaning of the original sentence, the then and else parts are to be interchanged. Thus the following sentence has the same meaning as the one illustrated above.

IF NOT OK-BALANCE MOVE 2 TO BALANCE-CODE ELSE NEXT-SENTENCE.

If desired, the ELSE NEXT SENTENCE phrase may be dropped to get the following equivalent form.

IF NOT OK-BALANCE MOVE 2 TO BALANCE-CODE.

10.2.1 Nested IF Sentence

The then and else parts of an IF statement can contain other IF statements. The included IF statements in their turn may also contain other IF statements. Such inclusion of one or more IF statements within the scope of an IF statement is called nesting. Note that the most inclusive IF statement must have a terminating period and thus this statement along with all the included statements is often called a nested IF sentence.

Since the ELSE phrase in an IF statement is optional, a nested IF sentence may have fewer ELSEs than IFs. This makes the interpretation of a nested IF sentence rather difficult. The first step in interpreting such a sentence would be to find out which ELSE belongs to which IF and which are the IFs that do not have the corresponding ELSEs. Once this is done, the actions specified for the different cases can be recognised easily. To avoid any ambiguity in interpretation, the COBOL rule in the matter is as follows:

The nested IF sentence should be examined in a left-to-right manner to encounter each ELSE in the order of its appearance. As soon as an ELSE is encountered, it must be paired with the immediately preceding IF that has not yet been paired with another ELSE.

Note that the above rule also helps in detecting those IFs for which the ELSE phrase may be absent.

The above rule states how the COBOL compiler will interpret a nested IF sentence. Therefore, while writing such a sentence this rule must be applied to verify that the interpretation of the compiler will not be different from what is intended. The following are examples to show how the meaning of a nested IF sentence can be obtained by applying the above rule.

Example 1

Consider the following sentence

```
IF    ACCOUNT-CODE   IS EQUAL TO OLD-CODE
②    ADD TRANS-VALUE  TO TRANS-TOTAL
      IF    TRANS-VALUE  > 1000
      ①    ADD  1  TO  HIGH-COUNT
      ELSE  ADD  1  TO  LOW-COUNT.
      ①
```

This nested IF sentence contains two IFs and one ELSE. The IF-ELSE pair has been marked by the number 1 within a circle. The IF marked with 2 within a circle is a lone IF without any ELSE. Now it can be easily seen that the above sentence is equivalent to the following flow chart.

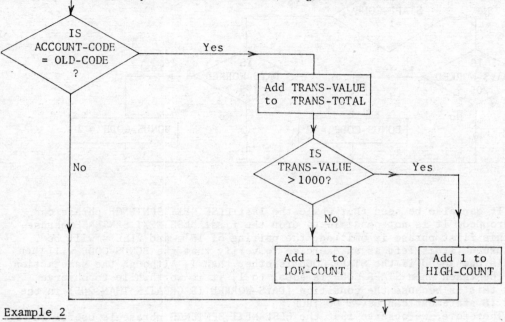

Example 2

Consider the following nested sentence:

```
IF STAFF-CODE  =  1
  ②   IF DAYS-WORKED IS GREATER THAN 175
      ①   MOVE 1 TO BONUS-CODE
      ELSE NEXT SENTENCE
      ①
  ELSE  IF  DAYS-WORKED IS GREATER THAN 205
  ②     ③   MOVE 2 TO BONUS-CODE
        ELSE NEXT SENTENCE.
        ③
```

The IF-ELSE pairs in this sentence can be detected by applying the rule stated above. We indicate the IF-ELSE associations by marking each pair with identical numbers within circles. The sentence can now be easily recognised as an implementation of the following flow chart.

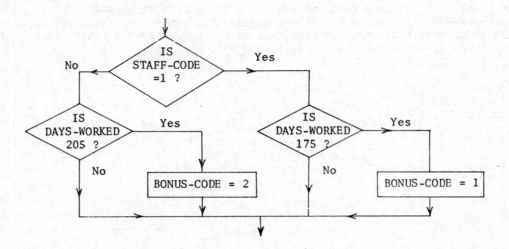

It can also be seen that while the last ELSE NEXT SENTENCE phrase can be dropped, it is not possible to drop the first ELSE NEXT SENTENCE phrase. If this first phrase is omitted, the pairing of IF's and ELSE's will be disturbed. It is left as an exercise to verify that the BONUS-CODE will then remain unchanged if the STAFF-CODE is other than 1. Although the same action will be taken when STAFF-CODE is equal to 1, it is worthwhile to observe that this is because the condition (DAYS-WORKED IS GREATER THAN 205) in the last IF statement can never be TRUE.

Therefore, we observe that the ELSE NEXT SENTENCE phrase is useful in certain cases. The phrase also increases the readability. Therefore, the use of NEXT SENTENCE either in the then or else parts of an IF statement is recommended. The only exception can be when the ELSE NEXT SENTENCE phrase is immediately followed by the terminating period of the IF sentence. This is because in this case the said ELSE must apply to the IF of the most inclusive IF statement of the nesting. Therefore, the control will be transferred to the next sentence regardless of whether or not the ELSE NEXT SENTENCE phrase is explicitly included.

Remarks

A limitation in COBOL is that no statement group representing the then or else parts of any IF statement in a nested IF sentence, can be terminated by a period unless the said group shares the terminating period with the IF sentence. Thus a very common source of error is to misplace a period in a nested IF sentence.

10.2.2 Coding Style for IF Sentences

In order to increase the readability of a program an IF sentence can be coded in such a way that from its appearance the structure of the IF sentence can be understood. The following guidelines may be used.

(i) Write the verb IF and the condition in one coding line.

(ii)   Write the then part in the subsequent coding lines with a shift of a few columns towards the right. Note that the statements in the PROCEDURE DIVISION can be coded from margin B or any column after it. Such shifting of the code towards the right is called <u>indentation</u>.

(iii) If the else part is used, write the statements in the subsequent coding lines with indentation but place the word ELSE immediately below the word IF.

(iv)   If the then or else parts contain IF statements, repeat the same for these as well.

For illustration, the two examples of the previous section may be consulted. Note that the IF-ELSE pairs and the then and else parts are revealed from the appearance of the statements themselves.

The above recommendations should be followed only for readability considerations. It should be clearly understood that the coding style can never have any effect on the compiler. Writing an ELSE immediately below an IF cannot establish any kind of link between them. Moreover, strict adherence to the above recommendations is also not necessary. Any coding style that reveals the structure of the IF sentence is good enough.

10.2.3 Decision Tables and IF Statements

The logic of computation represented by a decision table can be programmed by using the IF statements. A few methods for converting a decision table into COBOL statements are discussed below.

The first method that is discussed here is a simple, mechanical technique. In this method each rule in a decision table should be converted into a compound condition by combining the individual conditions (representing the entries for the said rule) by means of the logical operator, AND. Each such compound condition should specify the required actions. There should not be any else parts for the individual statements. To illustrate the method let us convert the last decision table discussed in Sec. 2.8.   The COBOL statements are as follows:

```
IF PRODUCT-TYPE  =  1   AND  CUSTOMER-CATEGORY = 1
          MOVE  10   TO COMMISSION, GO TO END-OF-TEST.
IF PRODUCT-TYPE  =  1   AND  CUSTOMER-CATEGORY = 2
          MOVE  8    TO COMMISSION, GO TO END-OF-TEST.
IF PRODUCT-TYPE  =  2   AND  CUSTOMER-CATEGORY = 1
          MOVE  = 12   TO COMMISSION, GO TO END-OF-TEST.
IF PRODUCT-TYPE  =  2   AND  CUSTOMER-CATEGORY = 2
          MOVE  = 8    TO COMMISSION, GO TO END-OF-TEST.
IF PRODUCT-TYPE  =  3   AND CUSTOMER-CATEGORY = 1
          MOVE  10   TO COMMISSION, GO TO END-OF-TEST.
IF PRODUCT-TYPE  =  3   AND CUSTOMER-CATEGORY = 2
          MOVE  10   TO COMMISSION, GO TO END-OF-TEST.
MOVE ZERO TO COMMISSION.

END-OF-TEST.
          .
          .    other statements
```

Note that the GO TO statements are required as the decision table is complete only by default, i.e., by means of the ELSE rule. For this specific decision table, however, the action to be taken in the case of the ELSE rule is similar to the actions needed for the other cases. Therefore, if the statement MOVE ZERO TO COMMISSION is placed in the beginning, the GO TO statements can be omitted. The idea is that we start with the COMMISSION as zero. If any of the conditions specified by the IF sentences is found to be TRUE, it will be overwritten by the appropriate value; otherwise, it will remain unchanged and the action specified by the ELSE rule will be met. When the decision table is complete, the GO TO statements are not necessary as the rules in the decision table must be mutually exclusive in that case. It may be further noted that the omission of the GO TO statements can make the object program less efficient. This is because even when a condition has been found to be true and the action has been taken, the remaining IF sentence will also be unnecessarily tried.

The second method is only a variation of the first. Here, we shall use a lesser number of IF sentences by using more complex conditions. The idea is to use just one compound condition for all rules that require identical actions. The conditions representing the decision rules that require identical conditions should be combined by the logical operator OR. For example, the first and last two (excluding the ELSE rule) rules of the said decision table require same action. The action is to set the value of the COMMISSION to 10. We can make use of the following IF sentence for these three rules.

```
IF   PRODUCT-TYPE  =  1  AND  CUSTOMER-CATEGORY  =  1  OR
     PRODUCT-TYPE  =  3  AND  (CUSTOMER-CATEGORY  =  1  OR  2)

     MOVE  10  TO  COMMISSION,  GO TO END-OF-TEST.
```

It may be noted that the three conditions that represent the said three rules have been combined by the logical operator OR. This compound condition has then been shortened by the use of parentheses and the abbreviation. In a similar way, the rules for which COMMISSION should be set to 8 can also be taken care of by means of a single IF sentence. This is left as an exercise.

The second method is as mechanical as the first and can be easily applied. The difference between the two is appreciable only when the decision table specifies identical actions for a number of decision rules.

The third method of converting a decision table is to represent it in the form of a nested IF sentence. We illustrate this by writing the nested IF statements for the same decision table.

```
MOVE  ZERO  TO  COMMISSION.
IF  PRODUCT-TYPE  =  1
    IF  CUSTOMER-CATEGORY = 1
        MOVE 10 TO COMMISSION
    ELSE IF CUSTOMER-CATEGORY = 2
            MOVE 8 TO COMMISSION
        ELSE NEXT SENTENCE
```

```
ELSE  IF  PRODUCT-TYPE = 2
          IF CUSTOMER-CATEGORY = 1
             MOVE 12 TO COMMISSION
          ELSE IF CUSTOMER-CATEGORY = 2
                  MOVE 8 TO COMMISSION
               ELSE NEXT SENTENCE
ELSE  IF  PRODUCT-TYPE = 3
          IF CUSTOMER-CATEGORY = 1 OR 2
             MOVE 10 TO COMMISSION.
```

The conversion of decision tables to nested IF sentences is not trivial. The chances of committing errors are quite high. Therefore, it is recommended that a beginner should avoid coding nested IF sentences.

10.3 GO TO WITH DEPENDING PHRASE

The GO TO statement with a DEPENDING phrase has the following form

GO TO procedure-name-1 [, procedure-name-2] ...,

procedure-name-n DEPENDING ON identifier

The statement transfers control to one of the procedures named in the statement depending on the value of the identifier. Depending on whether the value of the identifier is 1,2,...,n, the control is transferred to procedure-name-1, procedure-name-2,..., procedure-name-n respectively. If the value of the identifier is anything other than 1,2,...,n the said GO TO statement is ineffective and the control is transferred to the next statement in sequence. The identifier specified in the statement must be a numeric, integral elementary item. The following is an example of the statement.

GO TO O-B-PROCEDURE, RECEIPT-PROCEDURE, ISSUE-PROCEDURE
          DEPENDING ON TYPE-OF-TRANSACTION.

The names O-B-PROCEDURE, RECEIPT-PROCEDURE and ISSUE-PROCEDURE are either paragraph names or section names. The above statement is equivalent to the following three IF statements.

```
IF TYPE-OF-TRANSACTION = 1    GO TO O-B-PROCEDURE.
IF TYPE-OF-TRANSACTION = 2    GO TO RECEIPT-PROCEDURE.
IF TYPE-OF-TRANSACTION = 3    GO TO ISSUE-PROCEDURE.
```

10.4 ALTER STATEMENT

The ALTER statement can be used to modify the targets of GO TO statements written elsewhere in the PROCEDURE DIVISION. The syntax of the statement is as follows:

ALTER   procedure-name-1   TO [PROCEED TO] procedure-name-2

   [, procedure-name-3 TO [PROCEED TO] procedure-name-4]

Each of procedure-name-1, procedure-name-3, etc. is the name of a paragraph that contains only one sentence. This sentence must consist of a
single GO TO statement without the DEPENDING clause. During execution, the
ALTER statement replaces the objects of the GO TO statements in procedure-
name-1, procedure-name-3, etc. by procedure-name-2, procedure-name-4, etc.
respectively. The following examples illustrate the use of the ALTER statement.

Example 1

Consider the following GO TO sentence in the paragraph named MODIFIED-TRANSFER.

        MODIFIED-TRANSFER.   GO TO FIRST-TIME.

Suppose this GO TO sentence is to be modified after its first execution
so that the subsequent execution of the sentence transfers control to the
procedure named OTHER-TIMES. The required modification can be accomplished
by the execution of the following ALTER statement.

    ALTER MODIFIED-TRANSFER TO PROCEED TO OTHER-TIMES.

After the execution of this ALTER statement, the GO TO sentence in the
MODIFIED-TRANSFER becomes

    MODIFIED-TRANSFER.   GO TO OTHER-TIMES.

Example 2

Consider the following statements

    IF   TCODE = 1
        ALTER CHOOSE-THE-PATH TO PROCEED TO NEW-ACCOUNT
    ELSE
        ALTER CHOOSE-THE-PATH TO PROCEED TO OLD-ACCOUNT.
CHOOSE-THE-PATH.
    GO TO NEW-ACCOUNT.

The above statements transfer the control to one of the procedure names
OLD-ACCOUNT and NEW-ACCOUNT depending on whether or not the value of TCODE
is equal to 1. The above statements are equivalent to

    GO TO NEW-ACCOUNT, OLD-ACCOUNT DEPENDING ON TCODE.
    GO TO OLD-ACCOUNT.

Remarks:

The use of the ALTER statement should be avoided. This is because an ALTER
statement hides the actual structure of the flow of control, thereby reducing the readability of a program.

10.5 PERFORM STATEMENT

The PERFORM statement can be used to execute a group of consecutive statements written elsewhere in the program. We shall refer to this group of statements as the <u>range</u> of the PERFORM statement. During execution, when a PERFORM statement is encountered, a temporary departure from the normal sequential execution takes place and the statements contained in the specified range are executed. Upon execution of the said statements, the control implicitly returns to the next statement following the PERFORM statement. It is also possible to get the statements in the said range executed repetitively for a specified number of times or until a condition is satisfied. PERFORM is a powerful COBOL verb and has five different forms. In this chapter we shall discuss only the most elementary form of this verb. The others will be considered in the next chapter.

The format of a simple PERFORM statement is as follows:

$$\underline{\text{PERFORM}} \quad \text{procedure-name-1} \quad \left[\left\{ \begin{array}{l} \underline{\text{THRU}} \\ \underline{\text{THROUGH}} \end{array} \right\} \text{procedure-name-2} \right]$$

The statement group beginning with the first statement of the procedure named in procedure-name-1 and ending with the last statement of the procedure named in procedure-name-2, constitutes the range of the PERFORM statements. When the THRU phrase is omitted, the range consists of the statements contained in the procedure referred to by procedure-name-1. When the simple PERFORM statement is executed, this range is executed only once.

Some examples of the PERFORM statement are given below.

Example 1

       PERFORM   CALCULATE-TAX.

In this example, CALCULATE-TAX is either a section name or paragraph name. Suppose it is a section name. All the statements contained in this section will be executed as a result of the execution of the PERFORM statement and after the execution of these statements, the control will come back to the statement following the PERFORM statement.

Example 2

       PERFORM BEGIN-CALCULATION THRU END-CALCULATION.

Suppose, BEGIN-CALCULATION and END-CALCULATION are paragraph names. The execution of the above PERFORM statement will cause the execution of the group of the statements starting with the first statement of BEGIN-CALCULATION and ending with the last statement of END-CALCULATION. It may be noted that there may be other paragraphs in between these two paragraphs. All these paragraphs are also included in the range. Upon the execution of the range, the control returns to the statement following the PERFORM statement.

It may be noted that the return of control after the execution of the statements in the specified range takes place implicitly. This means that at the end of the range, the programmer should not put any statement (such as GO TO) to transfer the control explicitly to the statement following the PERFORM statement. The compiler establishes a <u>return mechanism</u> at the end of the range and it is this mechanism which is responsible for the return of the control.

The following points may be noted in connection with the range of a PERFORM statement.

(i) A GO TO statement is allowed within the range of a PERFORM statement. However, it is the responsibility of the programmer to ensure that the control ultimately reaches the last statement of the range.

(ii) There is no restriction as to what can be the last statement of a range except that it cannot be a GO TO statement. When an IF sentence is used at the end of a range, the next sentence (specified implicitly or explicitly) for that IF sentence refers to the return mechanism.

(iii) The use of a PERFORM statement within the range of another PERFORM statement is allowed. Some compilers allow unrestricted use of such nesting of PERFORM statements (except that there may be limitations on the depth of nesting depending on the operating system and hardware capabilities). Some compilers require that the range of the included PERFORM statement must be either completely within or completely outside the range of the invoking PERFORM statement. In other words, the sequence of ranges specified in the nested PERFORM statements should neither overlap nor share the same terminal statement. It is better to observe these restrictions for the sake of portability.

(iv) The range of statements that should be performed gets linked up with the PERFORM statement only when the latter is executed. If the control reaches the first statement of the range through normal sequence or through explicit transfer of the control, then also the range gets executed in the normal way. After the execution of the last statement of the range, the control falls through the next statement following the range.

10.6 EXIT STATEMENT

The EXIT verb indicates a no operation, and when executed, no action takes place. The syntax is

<u>EXIT</u>

and this must be the only statement in the paragraph in which it is used. The real use of an EXIT paragraph is in the last paragraph in a PERFORM range so that all routes leading to the return mechanism may be gathered here. For example, when within the range of a PERFORM statement is is desired to transfer the control to the end of the range, the EXIT paragraph provides a convenient place to branch. The following is an example of the use of the EXIT verb.

TAX-CALC.

```
      <Statements to calculate
              TAXABLE-INCOME>
      IF TAXABLE-INCOME NOT GREATER THAN 10000
          MOVE ZERO TO TAX GO TO EXIT-PARA.
      <Statements to calculate TAX when
          TAXABLE-INCOME is greater than 10000>

EXIT-PARA.

      EXIT.
```

The paragraphs may be referred to by the following PERFORM statement.

```
    PERFORM TAX-CALC THRU EXIT-PARA.
```

Note that we have two routes to the return mechanism. When TAXABLE-INCOME is more than 10000, EXIT-PARA is reached through the normal sequential execution. When TAXABLE-INCOME is less than or equal to 10000, EXIT-PARA is reached through the GO TO statement. In this connection note that in ANSI-74 COBOL, a paragraph may be empty. Therefore, the EXIT statement in EXIT-PARA can be omitted without causing any change.

10.7 A SAMPLE VALIDATION PROGRAM

We will now write a complete program using the statements discussed in this chapter. The particular program is a representative of the usual validation programs. The validation of the input data that are to be read from punched cards is very important. A deck of cards which has been punched by a key-punch operator is likely to contain errors and the task of a validation program is to detect these errors as far as possible. To achieve this objective, a validation program keeps some programming controls on the input data. The following are some of the commonly used input controls.

Check-digit Check

This type of control is usually kept on account numbers. For this purpose, a check digit is appended at the end of each account number. The check digit is computed by applying some arithmetic on the other digits of the account number so that each time an account number is read, the check digit can be verified comparing the check digit read with the check digit calculated. A common algorithm for the calculation of the check digit is known as the modulus-11 method. The algorithm is described below.

Suppose each account number consists of six digits and the last digit is a check digit. Let d_1, d_2, d_3, d_4 and d_5 be the first five consecutive digits of an account number and d_6 be the check digit. Then the algorithm for computing d_6 from d_1, d_2, ..., d_5 is as follows:

1. Compute $X = 2d_1 + 3d_2 + 4d_3 + 5d_4 + 6d_5$.

2. Divide X by 11 and let Y be the remainder of the division.

3. Compute $Z = 11-y$.

4. Take $d_6 = Z$ if Z is not equal to 10 or 11.
    When $Z = 10$, take $d_6 = 1$ and when $Z = 11$, take $d_6 = 2$.

Many variations of the above algorithm are possible. For example, instead of

    2, 3, 4, 5, ...

The following weights can also be used.

    (odd numbers) 3, 5, 7, 9, ...
    (prime numbers) 3, 5, 7, 11, ...

Sometimes, the account numbers for which Z becomes equal to 10 or 11 are rejected.
   The check-digit method is easily applicable for numeric account numbers. The method can also be used if the account number contains letters. In that case, the letters must be replaced by some values before applying the algorithm. For example, A may be replaced by 1, B by 2, and so on.
   An important consideration in this connection is that account numbers are to be allocated with the check digits. As such, normally, a program is written to generate a list of account numbers with check digits, and whenever necessary, a new account number is allocated from this list.

Limit or Reasonableness Check

This is another important control on the input data. It is used to identify whether an input data is greater or less than a predetermined limit. For example, if it is known that no worker is allowed to work more than 60 hours in a week, the value of hours worked can be checked to see whether it is within the limit or not.

Class Check

Each field that should contain numeric or alphabetic data can be checked to see whether the data read in the field belong to the expected class or not.

Batch Total Check

The input data can be assembled into batches of convenient sizes. For each batch one or more control totals can be manually calculated from the data in the batch. During data preparation the manually-prepared control totals are also included at the end of a batch. At the time of reading each batch of data, these control totals can be compared to the control totals generated by the computer for that batch. This input control is known as batch total check.
   The abovementioned input controls in a validation program enables the detection of input records that contain an error (note that a validation can never be 100% successful). The program then prints a check list containing a listing of those cards which contain errors along with appropriate error codes or error messages. In addition to this, the validation program also stores the data on the valid cards onto a magnetic tape or disk file.

Let us now concentrate on the particular validation program in which we are interested. Since table handling and file handling have not yet been covered, it will be difficult to implement the batch total check at this stage. Moreover, we will also omit the creation of a tape or disk file that contains the valid data. Consider the following card format.

Card Columns	Field
1-6/41-46	Account Number (numeric)
7-31/47-71	Name (alphanumeric)
32-37/72-77	Instalment amount (numeric with 2 places after the assumed decimal point)
38-39/78-79	Number of unpaid instalments (numeric)

It may be noted that two records are punched on cards. However, some cards may contain only one record. In that case, the columns 41-79 are left blank. The following validation checking is required.

(i)   Check digit check on account number.
(ii)   Numeric check on all numeric fields.
(iii)   Limit check on the number of unpaid instalments.
Its valid range is 1 to 24.

After the said validation, if the record is found to contain any error, the record should be listed along with the following error codes.

Error	Code
Class check failure (any field)	1
Check digit failure	2
Limit check failure	4

If a record contains more than one type of error, the codes are to be added. If the class check fails on the account number field, the check digit check need not be performed. In a similar way if the class check fails on the number of unpaid instalments, the limit check need not be performed.

A COBOL program for this problem is given in Fig. 10.1.

The processing of a record is done in the PROCESSING paragraph which takes help of another paragraph, namely, CHECK-DIGIT-CHECK. Note how the second record on a card is processed. After the processing of the first record, the contents of the second record is moved to the area of the first record and the PERFORM statement is used to perform the processing of this record. This could as well be done by means of the GO TO (with DEPENDING phrase) or ALTER statements. It is left as an exercise to modify the program accordingly.

```
FILE-CONTROL.

    SELECT CARD-FILE ASSIGN TO READER.
    SELECT CHECK-LIST ASSIGN TO PRINTER.

DATA DIVISION.
FILE SECTION.
FD  CARD-FILE.
01  CARD-REC.
    02  FIRST-REC.
    88  NO-RECORD VALUE SPACES.
        03  ACCOUNT-NO.
                04  D1                  PIC     9.
                04  D2                  PIC     9.
                04  D3                  PIC     9.
                04  D4                  PIC     9.
                04  D5                  PIC     9.
                04  D6                  PIC     9.
        03  NAME                        PIC     X(25).
        03  INSTL-AMT                   PIC     9(4)V99.
        03  NO-OF-UNPAID                PIC     99.
        88  VALID-RANGE                 VALUES  ARE  1  THRU  24.
    02  FILLER                          PIC     X.
    02  SECOND-REC                      PIC     X(39).
    02  FILLER                          PIC     X.

FD  CHECK-LIST.
01  CHECK-LIST-REC.
    02  FILLER                          PIC     X(15).
    02  RECORD-COPY                     PIC     X(39).
    02  FILLER                          PIC     X(10).
    02  ERROR-CODE                      PIC     9.
    88  NO-ERROR                        VALUE   ZERO.
    02  FILLER                          PIC     X(67).

WORKING-STORAGE SECTION.
77  CLASS-ERROR                         PIC     9.
77  CHECK-DIGIT-ERROR                   PIC     9.
77  LIMIT-ERROR                         PIC     9.
77  X                                   PIC     999.
77  Y                                   PIC     99.
77  Z                                   PIC     99.
77  CHECK-DIGIT                         PIC     9.

PROCEDURE DIVISION.
MAKE-A-START.
        OPEN   INPUT   CARD-FILE
               OUTPUT  CHECK-LIST.
        MOVE  SPACES   TO  CHECK-LIST-REC.
READ-A-CARD.
        READ   CARD-FILE  RECORD
            AT END GO TO LET-US-FINISH.
```

(contd.)

```
PROCESSING.
      MOVE  ZEROS  TO  CLASS-ERROR
                      CHECK-DIGIT-ERROR
                      LIMIT-ERROR.
      IF  ACCOUNT-NO  IS  NOT  NUMERIC
          MOVE  1  TO  CLASS-ERROR
      ELSE
          PERFORM CHECK-DIGIT-CHECK.
      IF INSTL-AMT  IS  NOT NUMERIC
          MOVE  1  TO CLASS-ERROR.
      IF  NO-OF-UNPAID  IS NOT  NUMERIC
          MOVE 1 TO CLASS-ERROR
      ELSE IF NOT VALID-RANGE
          MOVE 4 TO LIMIT-ERROR.
      ADD CLASS-ERROR CHECK-DIGIT-ERROR
          LIMIT-ERROR GIVING ERROR-CODE.
      IF NO-ERROR NEXT SENTENCE
      ELSE MOVE FIRST-REC TO RECORD-COPY
          WRITE CHECK-LIST-REC
                BEFORE ADVANCING 2 LINES.

PROCESSING-OF-NEXT-REC.
      MOVE SECOND-REC TO FIRST-REC
      IF NO-RECORD NEXT SENTENCE
      ELSE PERFORM PROCESSING.
      GO TO READ-A-CARD.

CHECK-DIGIT-CHECK.
      COMPUTE
          X = 2 * D1 + 3 * D2 + 4 * D3
                + 5 * D4 + 6 * D5.

      DIVIDE 11 INTO X
          GIVING X REMAINDER Y.
      SUBTRACT  Y  FROM 11 GIVING  Z.
      IF Z IS EQUAL TO 10
          MOVE 1 TO CHECK-DIGIT
      ELSE IF Z IS EQUAL TO 11
          MOVE 2 TO CHECK-DIGIT
        ELSE MOVE Z TO CHECK-DIGIT.
      IF D6 IS NOT EQUAL TO CHECK-DIGIT
          MOVE 2 TO CHECK-DIGIT-ERROR.

LET-US-FINISH.
      CLOSE CARD-FILE
            CHECK-LIST.
      STOP RUN.
```

FIG. 10.1.   A Sample Validation Program

10.8 IMPLEMENTATION DIFFERENCES

(a) Relational Operator

The following additional relational operators are available in B-6700.

$$\text{IS} \left\{ \begin{array}{c} \underline{\text{UNEQUAL}} \\ \underline{\text{EQUALS}} \\ \underline{\text{EXCEEDS}} \end{array} \right\} \text{TO}$$

    The meaning of these operators is apparent from their names. Of these, the operator EQUALS is also available in ICL-1900 and DEC-10.

(b) Nonnumeric Comparison

When one operand is nonnumeric, the following class/usage conflicts are allowed in the individual systems. The comparison in every case is alphanumeric.

  (i) B-6700: Any kind of conflict is allowed. However, a comparison is made having translated the values of both the operands to EBCDIC code. No translation takes place only in the following cases:
      o When the usage of each operand is ASCII.
      o When the usage is same and the relational operator is [NOT] = or any of its equivalent forms.

  (ii) ICL-1900: Usage conflict between DISPLAY and DISPLAY-3 is allowed. With the exception that alphabetic field can only be compared with an alphabetic or alphanumeric field, class conflicts (when the usages are DISPLAY or DISPLAY-3) are allowed.

  (iii) DEC-10: A comparison of the two fields are permitted if each is DISPLAY-6, DISPLAY-7 or DISPLAY-9 with the following exceptions. A numeric field may not be compared with a numeric edited field. A numeric field may be compared with an alphanumeric field provided the latter field contains only numeric digits.

(c) Abbreviation of Logical Operator

If the subject, relational operator and logical operator are identical in consecutive relational conditions of a compound condition, then in B-6700, the logical operator can also be dropped. The rule in this regard is as follows:

    Having omitted the subject and relational operator (as stated in the text), all logical operators except the rightmost one may be dropped.

Example

The compound condition

    TAX-CODE = 5 OR TAX-CODE = 7 OR TAX-CODE = 8

can be abbreviated as

        TAX-CODE = 5 7 OR 8

(d) Interpretation of NOT in Abbreviated Conditions

For the systems considered here, NOT in an abbreviated condition is interpreted as a logical operator rather than as a part of the relational operator. The ANSI 74 feature described in the text is available in B-6700
provided the ANSI 74 compiler option is set.

(e) Optional THEN in IF Statements

Many compilers allow the use of an optional THEN between the condition and
the then part of an IF statement. Of the three systems considered here, only
ICL-1900 allows this. This being a nonstandard feature may not be used.

(f) Range of Nested PERFORM Statements

In B-6700 and DEC-10, a PERFORM statement within the range of another
PERFORM statement is not restricted in the range of the procedure names it
may include. In ICL-1900, no overlapping of the ranges of nested PERFORM
statements is allowed. They cannot have common terminal statements.

(g) Certain Limitations

Sometimes, the individual manual for a system mentions certain limitations
regarding the depth of nesting for an IF sentence or the number of procedure
names that can be used in a GO TO statement with the DEPENDING phrase, etc.
For such limitations the reader may consult the appropriate manuals. However,
the limitations obtained from the manuals of the three systems under consideration are listed below to show the nature of differences that can be
expected.

  (i) Lengths of Compared Items: When the compared items happen to be
       groups, they can be very long. In DEC-10, the size of the compared
       items is limited to 2047 characters. In ICL-1900 this size must
       not exceed 120 characters.

  (ii) Depth of Nested IF Sentences: In DEC-10, a nested IF sentence can
        be at most 12 level deep. This means that starting from the most
        inclusive IF, in any of the paths we may have at most 12 IF's. In
        ICL-1900, within a complete sentence, there cannot be more than
        4 IF's with ELSE's and it can at most include 20 statements.

  (iii) Number of Procedure Names in a GO TO with DEPENDING Phrase: Only
         ICL-1900 puts a limit of 22 procedure names in some specific
         situations. See the manual for details.

(h) Restrictions for Segmentation

Certain restrictions on the ALTER and PERFORM statements are normally
imposed when a program contains sections with different segment numbers.
For a detailed discussion on this feature see Chapter 20.

EXERCISES

1. Find the errors in the following statements and correct them.

    (i)   IF VALUE-OF-MATERIALS IS MORE THAN 1300.50
              MOVE 3 TO MATERIALS-CODE.

    (ii) IF DATA-A IS NOT ALPHANUMERIC
              ADD 130 TO DATA-A.

    (iii) IF X IS GREATER THAN OR EQUAL TO 30
              DISPLAY "X IS GREATER THAN OR EQUAL TO 30".

    (iv) IF X IS EQUAL TO 30 40 OR 50
              GO TO NEXT SENTENCE
          ELSE MOVE 75 TO Y.

    (v)   ALTER CHANGE-THE-PATH TO GO TO CORRECT-PATH.

2. Consider the following nested IF sentence:

    IF SALARY-CODE = "X" IF BASIC-PAY IS GREATER THAN 1000 MOVE 180
    TO H-R-A ELSE IF BASIC-PAY IS GREATER THAN 945 COMPUTE H-R-A = 125 +
    BASIC-PAY - 945 ELSE MOVE 125 TO H-R-A ELSE IF BASIC-PAY IS GREATER
    THAN 800 MOVE 150 TO H-R-A ELSE IF BASIC-PAY IS GREATER THAN 750 COMPUTE
    H-R-A = 100 + BASIC-PAY - 750 ELSE MOVE 100 TO H-R-A.

    Find the resulting value of H-R-A if the above sentence is executed with
    (i) BASIC-PAY = 777,   SALARY-CODE = ''Y''   and H-R-A = 157
    (ii) BASIC-PAY = 888,   SALARY-CODE = ''X''   and H-R-A = 160.

3. Rewrite the following using the GO TO statement with the DEPENDING ON
    phrase.

    (a) IF ACCOUNT-CODE = 3 GO TO NEW-ACCOUNTS
         ELSE IF ACCOUNT-CODE = 4 GO TO DEAD-ACCOUNTS
             ELSE IF ACCOUNT-CODE = 5
                             GO TO ACTIVE-ACCOUNTS.

    (b) IF CARD-CODE = 1 ALTER PROCESS-PATH TO PROCEED TO
                                 ISSUE-CARD
         ELSE ALTER PROCESS-PATH TO PROCEED TO
                                 RECEIPT-CARD.

4. Rewrite the following nested IF sentence by using suitable condition
    names. Also indicate how the condition names are to be defined in the
    DATA DIVISION.

```
    IF MARKS > 80  OR = 30  MOVE  "A"  TO GRADE
  ELSE  IF MARKS > 60  OR = 60 MOVE  "B"  TO GRADE
      ELSE IF MARKS > 50  OR = 50  MOVE   "C"  TO GRADE
          ELSE IF MARKS NOT > 40
                      MOVE    "E"   TO GRADE
          ELSE  MOVE    "D"  TO GRADE.
```

Draw a flow chart for the above IF sentence.

5. Each card of a card file contains the following information.

Card Columns	Description
1-20	Name
21	Sex (Male = 0, Female = 1)
22-23	Age
24-26	Height
27-29	Weight

A paragraph named PROCESS-DATA is to be performed only if the data relates to a male candidate whose age is between 25 and 30 years (inclusive of both) and height exceeds 160 cm but is less than or equal to 175 cm and weight is over 65 kg.

Write the necessary IF statement using suitable condition names. Also show the record description for the said card file.

6. Write a decision table for the following IF sentence.

```
    IF (A = 1  AND NOT  B = 1  AND  C = 1)
      OR NOT (A = 1  OR  B = 1  OR  C = 1)
              PERFORM  ACTION-X
    ELSE IF (A = 1 AND B = 1 AND C = 1)
      OR (NOT A = 1  AND C = 1)
              PERFORM ACTION-Y
        ELSE PERFORM ACTION-Z.
```

7. Consider the following outline of PROCEDURE DIVISION. The numbers on the left indicate line numbers. Write the sequence of line numbers indicating the order in which the statements are executed.

```
100   PROCEDURE DIVISION.
110   PARA-START.    < statement >
120       < statement >
130       < statement >
140     PERFORM PARA-PROCESS-A THRU PARA-PROCESS-B.
150   PARA-PROCESS-A.    < statement >
160       < statement >
170       < statement >
180     PERFORM PARA-PROCESS-B.
190       < statement >
```

```
200    PARA-PROCESS-B.    < statement >
210          < statement >
220          < statement >
230    PARA-END.
240          < statement >
250          STOP RUN.
```

Assume that the statements mentioned here are not sequence control
statements.

8.   Assume the following descriptions in DATA DIVISION.

```
01     X-A              PIC   XX.
01     X-N    REDEFINES X-A     PIC  99.
88     A-TEST  VALUES  ARE  10  THRU  20.
```

Find what will be displayed as a result of the execution of the following statements.

```
MOVE   "AB"         TO      X-A.
IF     X-N    IS    EQUAL    TO  12
                    DISPLAY  "ERROR-ONE".
IF     X-N   - 12  IS   ZERO
                 DISPLAY   "ERROR-TWO".
IF     X-N  >  10  AND
       X-N  <  20
                 DISPLAY   "ERROR-THREE".
IF     A-TEST  DISPLAY  "ERROR-FOUR".
```

(Hint. Here numeric tests are being performed on data that contains
       letters. Numeric tests being algebraic, most compilers will
       ignore the zone bits of the data. If EBCDIC representation is
       assumed for DISPLAY, the numeric parts of A and B are 1 and 2
       respectively. This is an example of obscure coding and such
       coding should be avoided.)

11

TABLE HANDLING

Sometimes, it becomes necessary to handle a group of data consisting of similar items. Such a group is called a table. For example, let us consider a price list. Suppose that each item in this list consists of three fields — product code, product name and unit price. Such a price list can be viewed as a table because it consists of similar items or elements, each of which corresponds to a particular product. An individual element is similar to another element in respect of the number of fields within the element as well as their descriptions. In other words, a table must consist of homogeneous elements. Moreover, the elements of a table must be ordered in a way such that there is a first element, a second element, a third element and so on. The kind of table described above is known as one-dimensional table. It is also possible to have higher dimensional tables where an element in turn may be another table. The handling of tables through COBOL programs is the subject of this chapter. Since PERFORM statement is frequently used in connection with tables, the various forms of the PERFORM statement are also introduced here.

11.1 OCCURS CLAUSE AND SUBSCRIPTING

Let us introduce tables with the help of an example. Suppose there are five different direct tax rates which are to be stored in the form of a table named DIRECT-TAX-RATE. In order to handle this table in a COBOL program, we must know how to describe the table in the DATA DIVISION, how to put the tax rates into the table and how to refer to the individual tax rates in the PROCEDURE DIVISION. Let us start with the method for describing the table in the DATA DIVISION. One way of describing the said table could be as follows:

```
01   DIRECT-TAX-RATE.

     02   TAX-RATE-1         PIC  99.
     02   TAX-RATE-2         PIC  99.
     02   TAX-RATE-3         PIC  99.
     02   TAX-RATE-4         PIC  99.
     02   TAX-RATE-5         PIC  99.
```

Since each element of this table has identical description (PIC 99), an alternative method for describing the table is to describe a typical element and then to specify that the description is to be repeated five times. This is accomplished by the OCCURS clause as illustrated below.

```
01    DIRECT-TAX-RATE.

      02  TAX-RATE        PIC  99  OCCURS  5  TIMES.
```

This latter description has some advantages over the former one. First of all, the description is shorter than the previous one (Imagine, if there were more tax rates!). Secondly, the elements in the latter case, can be referred to in the PROCEDURE DIVISION by means of a technique known as subscripting. For example, the first element is referred to as TAX-RATE (1), the second one as TAX-RATE (2) and so on. The value (1,2, etc.) enclosed within parenthesis is called a subscript and the name along with the subscript is known as subscripted data name. The main advantage of subscripting is due to the fact that if desired, a data name can also be used as a subscript. For example, TAX-RATE (I) is a valid subscripted data name which refers to an individual element depending on the value of the subscript I. For example,

MULTIPLY AMOUNT BY TAX-RATE(I) GIVING TEMP-TAX

will cause TAX-RATE (4) to take part in the multiplication if the current value of I is 4. Since the value of I can be changed, the same statement can involve different tax rates at different points of time. Note that this flexibility is not possible for the former description of the table.
    The format of OCCURS clause is as follows:

OCCURS   integer TIMES

The following rules apply for the OCCURS clause and the subscripts.

(i)   The integer in the OCCURS clause must be a positive integer.

(ii) The OCCURS clause can be specified for an elementary item or for a group item. The clause causes contiguous area holding the elements to be set up internally. The number of elements is equal to the integer in the OCCURS clause. Each element is considered to be a repetition of the data item to which the OCCURS clause has been specified. In the case of a group item, all data items belonging to the group take part in each repetition of the group item. The OCCURS clause cannot be specified for an item whose level number is 01, 66, 77 or 88.

(iii) When a data name is described with the OCCURS clause, the data name as well as any of its subordinate items cannot be referred to in the PROCEDURE DIVISION without a subscript. According to ANSI 74 standard, a subscript can be either a positive integer or a data name denoting a positive integral value. However, many compilers also allow an arithmetic expression as a subscript. Thus a subscripted data name like TAX-RATE (3 * J) may be allowed in some compilers. If J has a value of 1, this will mean the third element of the table.

(iv) The highest value that a subscript can take is the one specified by the integer in the OCCURS clause. The lowest value of a subscript is implicitly assumed to be 1. The lowest and the highest values define the range of values that a subscript can assume. In the above example, the range is 1 to 5. If during the execution of a program, the value of a subscript is found to be outside its range, the program is terminated by the system.

(v)   The subscript must be enclosed within a pair of parentheses. In general, there should be a space preceding the left parenthesis and following the right parenthesis. However, the requirement of a space preceding the left parenthesis is not mandatory in many compilers.

(vi)   A data name used as a subscript cannot be another subscripted data name. However, it can be qualified. Thus TAX-RATE (A OF NEW - GROUP) is valid but TAX-RATE (A(K)) is invalid.

(vii) If a data name with OCCURS clause requires any qualification, the subscript should be written after the last qualification. For example, if TAX-RATE should be qualified, it must appear as TAX-RATE OF DIRECT-TAX-RATE (I) and not as TAX-RATE (I) OF DIRECT-TAX-RATE.

(viii) When an entry is defined with OCCURS clause, the VALUE clause cannot be specified for the associated data name or any data name subordinate to it.

(ix)   The REDEFINES clause cannot appear in the same data description entry which contains an OCCURS clause. However, REDEFINES clause can appear for a group item whose subordinate items are defined with the OCCURS clause.

(x)   The OCCURS clause can appear in the data description entry in any position after the level number and the data name.

Example

Consider the following table:

```
02    AMOUNT-TABLE      OCCURS   20   TIMES.
      03   AMOUNT          PIC   9(6)V99.
      03   AMOUNT-CODE     PIC   X.
```

Suppose it is required to find the total of all the amounts of the table in the following manner. If the amount code is 1, the corresponding amount is to be considered positive, otherwise the corresponding amount should be considered negative. (Note that the amount fields being unsigned contain only absolute value.) The following statements will perform the said task. It is assumed that the field named TOTAL and I are suitably defined, say with picture S9(7)V99 and 99 respectively.

```
MOVE   ZERO   TO   TOTAL.   MOVE   1   TO   I.
```

```
PARA-LOOP.

    IF   AMOUNT-CODE (I)  IS  EQUAL  TO  "1"
         ADD   AMOUNT (I)   TO  TOTAL
    ELSE  SUBTRACT   AMOUNT  (I)  FROM  TOTAL.
    ADD   1   TO   I.
    IF   I   IS   NOT   GREATER   THAN   20
         GO   TO   PARA-LOOP
```

It may be noted how the use of the data name as a subscript helps to write
the above code. The reader may try to find the required total without using
data name as subscripts. In that case the loop cannot be designed and one
must use twenty IF sentences to do the job.

11.2 ASSIGNING VALUES TO TABLE ELEMENTS

There are two different ways for storing values in a table. The first
method is to store the values by writing necessary statements in the
PROCEDURE DIVISION. The values that are to be stored may be obtained from
a file or these may be the results of certain computations. As an example
of this, let us consider the following. Suppose we wish to store values in
the following table.

```
01   PRICE-LIST.

     05  LIST-ITEM  OCCURS  50  TIMES.

         10   PROD-CODE  PIC   X(5).
         10   PROD-PRICE PIC   9(6)V99.
```

The values are available in a file named PRICE-FILE whose FD entry and
record description are shown below.

```
FD   PRICE-FILE.

01   PRICE-REC.

     05  ITEM-CODE     PIC    X(5).
     05  ITEM-PRICE    PIC    9(6)V99.
```

The PROCEDURE DIVISION statements to store the values of table from the
said file may be written as follows:

```
            .
            .
            .

     MOVE  1  TO  I.
READ-PARA.
```

```
        READ PRICE-FILE AT END GO TO END-OF-STORING.
        MOVE ITEM-CODE   TO   PROD-CODE (I).
        MOVE ITEM-PRICE TO   PROD-PRICE (I).
        ADD  1  TO  I.
        IF  I  NOT > 50  GO  TO  READ-PARA.
   END-OF-STORING.
```

It is assumed that the data name I which has been used as subscript, is
described in the WORKING-STORAGE SECTION with PIC 9(2). The above code
stores the values of the table from the first 50 records of PRICE-FILE. In
case the file has fewer records, the values are stored for as many table
elements as there are records.

The second method for storing values in a table is to assign initial
values to table elements through DATA DIVISION entries. This method is
somewhat tricky because the VALUE and OCCURS clause cannot appear together
in a data description entry. To overcome the problem, the technique takes
advantage of the REDEFINES clause. It is illustrated through the following
example.

```
01   MONTH-TABLE.

     02   FILLER   PIC   X(9)   VALUE   IS   "JANUARYɃɃ".
     02   FILLER   PIC   X(9)   VALUE   IS   "FEBRUARYɃ".
     02   FILLER   PIC   X(9)   VALUE   IS   "MARCHɃɃɃɃ".
     02   FILLER   PIC   X(9)   VALUE   IS   "APRILɃɃɃɃ".
     02   FILLER   PIC   X(9)   VALUE   IS   "MAYɃɃɃɃɃɃ".
     02   FILLER   PIC   X(9)   VALUE   IS   "JUNEɃɃɃɃɃ".
     02   FILLER   PIC   X(9)   VALUE   IS   "JULYɃɃɃɃɃ".
     02   FILLER   PIC   X(9)   VALUE   IS   "AUGUSTɃɃɃ".
     02   FILLER   PIC   X(9)   VALUE   IS   "SEPTEMBER".
     02   FILLER   PIC   X(9)   VALUE   IS   "OCTOBERɃɃ".
     02   FILLER   PIC   X(9)   VALUE   IS   "NOVEMBERɃ".
     02   FILLER   PIC   X(9)   VALUE   IS   "DECEMBERɃ".

01   MONTH-NAME   REDEFINES   MONTH-TABLE.

     02   MONTH   PIC   X(9)   OCCURS   12   TIMES.
```

Because of the REDEFINES clause, the tables MONTH-NAME and MONTH-TABLE
share the same storage area internally. Obviously, the values defined for
fields in MONTH-TABLE become the values of the corresponding elements of
MONTH-NAME. Thus MONTH(1) is initialized by the value "JANUARYɃɃ",
MONTH (2) is initialized by the value "FEBRUARYɃ", and so on.

It may be seen that it is not possible to define the table MONTH-NAME first and then to redefine it by MONTH-TABLE. This is because the rules for the REDEFINES clause does not permit the use of the VALUE clause in the redefined data name or in its subfields.

11.3 MULTI-DIMENSIONAL TABLES

The kind of table that has been considered above is called a <u>one-dimensional table</u>. When a table is such that each of its elements in turn is a table of one dimension, it is called a two-dimensional table. The following is an example of a two-dimensional table.

```
01     SALES-TABLE.

   02    BRANCH-FIGURES OCCURS  18  TIMES.

      03  MONTHLY-SALES   PIC   9(6)  V 99   OCCURS  12  TIMES.
```

The table is assumed to store monthly sales figures for 12 months for each of the 18 branches of an organization. Note that this is a two-dimensional table because each of the 18 BRANCH-FIGURES is itself a table having 12 elements. It may be further noted that a reference to an element of a two-dimensional table requires two subscripts. We must specify the branch as well as the month so that the desired element is identified. Thus MONTHLY-SALES (3, 5) means the sales figure for the fifth month of the third branch. Because of the organization specified in the above description of the table, the first subscript implicitly refers to the branch and the second subscript to the month. The two-dimensional table has been divided first into 18 one-dimensional tables through the entry at level 02. Each of these tables have then been defined by the entry at level 03. This organization can be diagramatically shown as

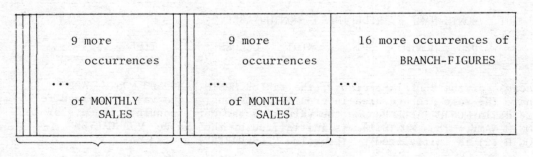

BRANCH-FIGURE (1)   BRANCH-FIGURE (2)

If required, the tables for the individual branches can be referred to by the name BRANCH-FIGURE with only one subscript indicating the branch. Thus BRANCH-FIGURE (4) will indicate the monthly sales table for the fourth branch.

The above notion of a two-dimensional table can be easily extended to tables having three or more dimensions. Handling of tables up to three dimensions are allowed by most compilers; some even allow more than three. The following rules may be noted in connection with multi-dimensional tables.

(i)   Multi-dimensional tables are to be defined as records with OCCURS clauses at various levels. As we go down the hierarchy, each lower level item with an OCCURS clause specifies an additional dimension. For example, consider the following table.

```
01   TABLE-EXAMPLE.

     02   A     PIC   9(5)   OCCURS   50   TIMES.
     02   B         OCCURS   20   TIMES.
          03   C     PIC   9(3).
          03   D   OCCURS   10   TIMES.
               04   E     OCCURS   15   TIMES   PIC   9(4) V 99.
               04   F   PIC      X(4).
```

A and C are one-dimensional, F is a two-dimensional table and E is a three-dimensional table. B and D are group items which can be referred to as one-dimensional and two-dimensional tables respectively.

(ii)   A table is stored in such a way that a subscript on the right of another subscript changes more rapidly than the latter.

The organization of the SALES-TABLE shown above illustrates this. The elements MONTHLY-SALES (1,1) to MONTHLY-SALES (1, 12) are stored first. The elements MONTHLY-SALES (2, 1) to MONTHLY-SALES (2, 12) are stored next, and so on. Note that the second subscript is changed more frequently than the first subscript. This fact should be taken into consideration while redefining a multi-dimensional table.

(iii)   Multiple subscripts should be separated from one another either by a comma or space.

11.4   PERFORM VERB AND TABLE HANDLING

The simple form of the PERFORM verb has been discussed earlier. Other forms of the PERFORM verbs are introduced here illustrating their suitability and use in table handling. In all these formats the range of statements to be performed is specified in the same manner as in the case of the simple PERFORM verb. The rules regarding the range of a PERFORM statement, as stated earlier, also remain valid in these cases.

11.4.1   PERFORM with TIMES Option

The format of the PERFORM statement with the TIMES option has the following syntax.

$$\underline{\text{PERFORM}}\quad \text{procedure-name-1}\quad \left[\left\{\begin{array}{c}\text{THRU}\\ \underline{\text{THROUGH}}\end{array}\right\}\quad \text{procedure-name-2}\right]$$

$$\left\{\begin{array}{c}\text{identifier}\\ \text{integer}\end{array}\right\}\quad \underline{\text{TIMES}}$$

The range is repetitively executed for the number of times specified through the identifier or the integer and after that the control goes to the next statement following the PERFORM statement. Thus the statement

PERFORM   PROCESS-TO-BE-PERFORMED   5   TIMES

means that the section or paragraph indicated by the name PROCESS-TO-BE-PERFORMED will be repetitively executed 5 times. Instead of the integer 5, we can also use an identifier, say N. In that case the number of times the said range is executed is equal to the current value of N. Obviously, the identifier should have a positive integral value. In case the value is negative or zero, the range is not executed at all and the control goes to the next statement in sequence. This fact can be gainfully used to specify the conditional execution of a PERFORM range. For example, consider the statement

PERFORM   EXECUTE-COMPUTATION   N   TIMES

If N has a value of zero, the procedure EXECUTE-COMPUTATION is not executed at all. On the other hand, if N has a value of 1, the procedure is executed only once. It may be noted that once the PERFORM statement has been initiated, any reference to the identifier will have no effect in respect of the number of times the range is executed.

The essential difference between the simple PERFORM and TIMES option is that in the first case the range gets executed only once, whereas in the latter case the execution of the range is repeated for the specified number of times. Naturally, it is meaningless to repeat the same set of statements unless the data items on which they operate do not change. It is therefore expected that the statements in the range would modify the data suitably. To take an example, the following PERFORM statement add the first 50 natural numbers in the data name SUM.

```
MOVE ZERO TO SUM, NUMB.
PERFORM ADD-PARA 50 TIMES.
    .
    .
    .
ADD-PARA.
    ADD 1 TO NUMB.
    ADD NUMB TO SUM.
```

Now, let us see how the PERFORM statement with the TIMES option can be used in table handling. Consider the example discussed at the end of the Sec. 11.1. The loop can be designed as follows:

```
MOVE ZERO TO TOTAL.  MOVE 1 TO I.
PERFORM PARA-LOOP  20  TIMES.
    .
    .
    .
PARA-LOOP.
    IF AMOUNT-CODE (I) IS EQUAL TO "1"
        ADD AMOUNT (I) TO TOTAL
    ELSE SUBTRACT AMOUNT (I) FROM TOTAL.
    ADD 1 TO I.
```

It may be noted that the test on I is no longer necessary as the PERFORM statement will arrange for the execution of the PARA-LOOP exactly 20 times.

11.4.2 PERFORM with UNTIL Option

The format of the PERFORM statement with the UNTIL option has the following syntax.

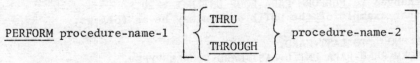

$$\underline{PERFORM} \text{ procedure-name-1} \left[\left\{ \begin{array}{c} \underline{THRU} \\ \underline{THROUGH} \end{array} \right\} \text{procedure-name-2} \right]$$

$$\underline{UNTIL} \text{ condition}$$

Like the TIMES option, the range is executed repetitively until the specified condition becomes true. Obviously, it is expected that the condition should be false in the beginning and as a result of the repeated execution of the range, the condition would become true at some stage. However, the PERFORM statement may not be terminated as soon as the condition becomes true. The range must be executed completely before the termination. In fact, the condition is tested only at the beginning of each repeated execution of the range, and if the condition is found to be true, the PERFORM statement is terminated and the control goes to the next statement following the PERFORM. Thus, if it so happens that the condition is true in the very beginning itself, the range is not executed at all and the control is transferred to the next statement. The operation of the UNTIL option is best illustrated through the following flow chart which shows the operations of the object code generated from the PERFORM statement.

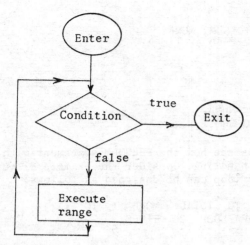

FIG. II.I   Flow Chart for PERFORM ... UNTIL

As examples, let us consider the last two examples discussed for the TIMES option. Of these, the first example can be written as follows:

```
    MOVE ZERO TO SUM, NUMB.
    PERFORM ADD-PARA UNTIL NUMB = 50.
ADD-PARA.
    ADD 1 TO NUMB, ADD NUMB TO SUM.
```

It may be noted that the only change here is in the PERFORM statement. The statement PERFORM ADD-PARA UNTIL NUMB = 50 has the same effect as that of PERFORM ADD-PARA 50 TIMES as the condition NUMB = 50 becomes true only when the procedure ADD-PARA has been executed for 50 times. In a similar way, in the second example, the statement PERFORM PARA-LOOP 20 TIMES may be changed to PERFORM PARA-LOOP UNTIL I > 20.

Another example of the UNTIL option may be as follows:

```
    MOVE "NO"  TO LAST-CARD.
    PERFORM READ-PARA UNTIL LAST-CARD EQUALS "YES".
```

Where READ-PARA is

```
READ-PARA.
    READ CARD-FILE AT END MOVE "YES" TO LAST-CARD.
    IF LAST-CARD EQUALS "NO" PERFORM PARA-PROCESS.
```

It is assumed that the LAST-CARD is a data-name defined in the working-storage section with picture X(3). Through the PERFORM statement, the READ-PARA is repeatedly executed until the end of the CARD-FILE is reached. It may be noted that the IF LAST-CARD EQUALS "NO", etc. is essential, otherwise, the PARA-PROCESS would be executed even after the end of file has been sensed.

11.4.3 PERFORM with VARYING Option

This option of the PERFORM statement has the following format:

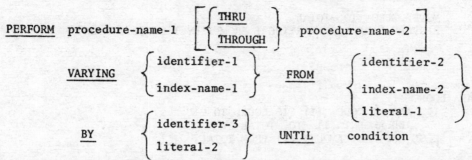

PERFORM procedure-name-1 $\left[\begin{Bmatrix} \text{THRU} \\ \text{THROUGH} \end{Bmatrix} \text{procedure-name-2} \right]$

VARYING $\begin{Bmatrix} \text{identifier-1} \\ \text{index-name-1} \end{Bmatrix}$ FROM $\begin{Bmatrix} \text{identifier-2} \\ \text{index-name-2} \\ \text{literal-1} \end{Bmatrix}$

BY $\begin{Bmatrix} \text{identifier-3} \\ \text{literal-2} \end{Bmatrix}$ UNTIL condition

This option is similar to the UNTIL option in the sense that the specified range is executed repetitively until the condition becomes true. In addition to this, identifier-1 is set to some initial value and it is incremented each time the range is executed. Identifier-1 must be a numeric data item and an index name can also be used instead of identifier-1. Index-names are discussed later in this chapter. For the time being, we shall not take index-names into consideration. The initial value to which identifier-1 is set at the beginning is specified through identifier-2 or index-name-2 or literal-1. The increment by which the value of identifier-1 is increased is specified through identifier-3 or literal-2 which appears after the word BY. The identifiers and literals in the FROM and BY phrases must be numeric and their values can be either positive or negative with or without fractional parts. The programmer may change the values of the identifiers in the VARYING, FROM and BY phrases through statements within the range, but this will affect the number of times the loop is executed (see Sec. 15.5). The function of the PERFORM with VARYING option is illustrated through the following flow chart (Fig. 11.2).

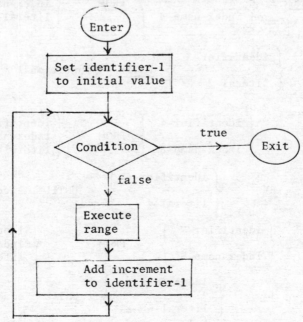

FIG. 11.2 Flow Chart for PERFORM ... VARYING

To illustrate the use of the varying option, let us consider the last example discussed for the TIMES option. The statements will now be as follows:

```
MOVE  ZERO  TO  TOTAL.
PERFORM PARA-LOOP VARYING I FROM 1 BY 1 UNTIL I > 20.
      .
      .
      .
      .
PARA-LOOP.
    IF  AMOUNT-CODE  (I)  IS EQUAL TO "1"
        ADD AMOUNT (I)  TO  TOTAL
    ELSE SUBTRACT AMOUNT (I) FROM TOTAL.
```

It may be noted that the initialization of I as well as its increment are taken care of by the PERFORM statement itself. The other example which adds the first fifty natural numbers can also be written using the VARYING option. This is left as an exercise.

11.4.4   PERFORM with the VARYING-AFTER Option

This option has the following format.

$$
\underline{\text{PERFORM}}\ \text{procedure-name-1}\ \left[\left\{ \begin{array}{l} \underline{\text{THROUGH}} \\ \underline{\text{THRU}} \end{array} \right\} \text{procedure-name-2} \right]
$$

$$
\underline{\text{VARYING}}\ \left\{ \begin{array}{l} \text{identifier-1} \\ \text{index-name-1} \end{array} \right\}\ \underline{\text{FROM}}\ \left\{ \begin{array}{l} \text{identifier-2} \\ \text{index-name-2} \\ \text{literal-1} \end{array} \right\}
$$

$$
\underline{\text{BY}}\ \left\{ \begin{array}{l} \text{identifier-3} \\ \text{literal-2} \end{array} \right\}\ \underline{\text{UNTIL}}\ \ \text{condition-1}
$$

$$
\left[\underline{\text{AFTER}}\ \left\{ \begin{array}{l} \text{identifier-4} \\ \text{index-name-3} \end{array} \right\}\ \underline{\text{FROM}}\ \left\{ \begin{array}{l} \text{identifier-5} \\ \text{index-name-4} \\ \text{literal-3} \end{array} \right\} \right.
$$

$$
\underline{\text{BY}}\ \left\{ \begin{array}{l} \text{identifier-6} \\ \text{literal-4} \end{array} \right\}\ \underline{\text{UNTIL}}\ \ \text{condition-2}
$$

$$
\left[\underline{\text{AFTER}}\ \left\{ \begin{array}{l} \text{identifier-7} \\ \text{index-name-5} \end{array} \right\}\ \underline{\text{FROM}}\ \left\{ \begin{array}{l} \text{identifier-8} \\ \text{index-name-6} \\ \text{literal-5} \end{array} \right\} \right.
$$

$$
\left. \left. \underline{\text{BY}}\ \left\{ \begin{array}{l} \text{identifier-9} \\ \text{literal-6} \end{array} \right\}\ \underline{\text{UNTIL}}\ \ \text{condition-3} \right] \right]
$$

This form is used when a nested repetition of the range is required while varying more than one identifier. For example, consider the following statement.

```
PERFORM    RANGE-TO-BE-EXECUTED
           VARYING   I   FROM   1   BY   1   UNTIL   I > 50
           AFTER     J   FROM   1   BY   1   UNTIL   J > 10.
```

The range RANGE-TO-BE-EXECUTED will be performed 500 times — first with I as 1 and J varying from 1 to 10 in step of 1, then I as 2 and again J varying from 1 to 10, and so on. Note that every time I changes value, J must vary from 1 to 10.

Moreover, each time the loop varying J is completed, J is initialized (by 1 in this case) before changing the value of I. Thus after the execution of this PERFORM statement, I will have a value of 51 but J will have a value of 1 and not 11. This fact will be revealed from the flowchart shown in Fig. 11.3. It shows the function of the PERFORM with the VARYING and one AFTER phrases.

Most compilers allow up to 3 levels of nesting which means that there can be one VARYING and two AFTER's. However, nesting of more than 3 levels are also allowed on some compilers. Every time the identifier or index name following a VARYING or AFTER phrase changes value, the identifier or index name following any subsequent AFTER phrase must vary through the complete range of values as specified in its FROM, BY and UNTIL combination.

As an example, let us consider the SALES-TABLE defined in Sec. 11.3. The table was defined as follows:

```
01     SALES-TABLE.
       02  BRANCH-FIGURES OCCURS  18  TIMES.
        03  MONTHLY-SALES PIC 9(6)V99 OCCURS 12 TIMES.
```

Now, suppose we wish to find the total of the 12 monthly sales for each branch and wish to store them in the following table.

```
01     SALES-TOTAL.
       02  BRANCH-TOTAL   PIC   9(7)V99 OCCURS 18 TIMES
```

In addition to this, the grand total of all the branch totals is to be computed and stored in the field having the name GRAND-TOTAL defined with PIC 9(8)V99. The COBOL statement to accomplish this may be as follows:

```
MOVE    ALL "0"   TO  SALES-TOTAL.
MOVE    ZERO       TO  GRAND-TOTAL.
PERFORM PARA-ADDITION
     VARYING   I   FROM   1   BY   1   UNTIL   I > 18.
     AFTER     J   FROM   1   BY   1   UNTIL   J > 12.
.
.
.
PARA-ADDITION.
     ADD MONTHLY-SALES (I,J)  TO  BRANCH-TOTAL (I), GRAND-TOTAL.
```

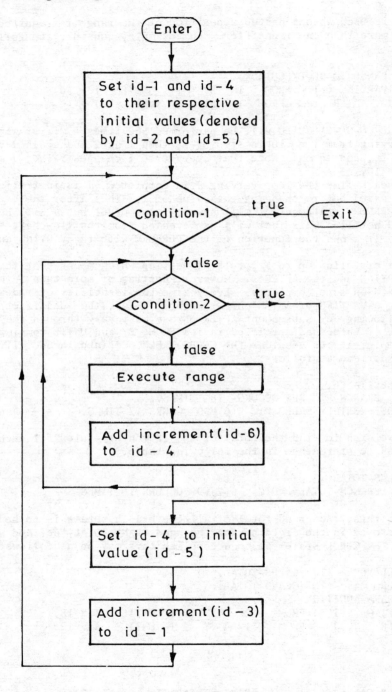

Fig. 11.3. Flowchart for PERFORM......VARYING.....AFTER

It may be noted that moving ALL "0" to the group name SALES-TOTAL fills
this table with zeros. This is merely a short cut for the initialization
of the SALES-TOTAL table. One can also initialize the table by moving zeros
to each element. This may be done as follows:

```
    PERFORM  INITIALIZE-TABLE
             VARYING  I  FROM  1  BY  1  UNTIL  I > 18.
    .
    .
    .
INITIALIZE-TABLE.
    MOVE  ZERO  TO  BRANCH-TOTAL (I).
```

11.5 INDEXED TABLES AND INDEXING

COBOL has an alternative to subscripting. This is known as indexing. An
index is a data item which is associated with a table or a particular dimension of a table through the use of INDEXED BY phrase of an OCCURS clause.
The following example illustrates table description with the INDEXED BY
phrase.

```
    01   ENROLL-TABLE.
         02 FACULTY  OCCURS  3  TIMES  INDEXED  BY  F1.
            03  DEPARTMENT  OCCURS  6  TIMES  INDEXED  BY  D1.
                04  YEAR  PIC  9(4)  OCCURS  5  TIMES  INDEXED  BY  Y1.
```

Here, F1, D1 and Y1 are index names associated with this table. These need
not be defined separately in the DATA DIVISION. An element of the table
can be referenced as YEAR (F1, D1, Y1) having set appropriate values to the
index names F1, D1 and Y1.
     Conceptually, an index is similar to a subscript but the internal value
of an index is quite different from that of a subscript. A subscript is
any integer data item and its value denotes the position or occurrence
number of the element within a table. On the other hand, the internal value
of an index is such that the element can be referenced in a more efficient
manner. Although the exact representation of an index is system dependent,
generally an index denotes a displacement of the element from the beginning
of the table. When we write

```
    04  YEAR  PIC  9(4)  OCCURS  5  TIMES  INDEXED  BY  Y1
```

the displacement for the first element is zero, that for the second element
is 4 (note that the size of each element is 4), that for the third element
is 8 and so on. The index Y1 assumes these values corresponding to the
occurrence numbers 1, 2, 3, etc. However, to a COBOL programmer, the knowledge of internal representation of an index is of no importance. The
programmer sets the value of an index by specifying the occurrence number
and not the internal value. Because of this, the value of an index can

only be set or altered by special statements like PERFORM, SET and SEARCH (discussed later) statements and not by statements like MOVE or ADD. All that the programmer should know is that the use of an index instead of a subscript, causes more efficient object code to be generated by the compiler.

The format of the OCCURS clause with INDEXED BY phrase is

<u>OCCURS</u>   integer TIMES

        [<u>INDEXED</u> BY index-name-1 [, index-name-2] ....]

The following rules apply when INDEXED BY phrase is used.

(i)   If indexing is done for any one level of a table, then indexing must be used for all levels. Thus it will be an error if in the above example the INDEXED BY phrase is used only for FACULTY and not for DEPARTMENT and YEAR.

(ii) Index names cannot be used in combination with subscripts. Thus a reference as YEAR (F1, S2, S3) will be treated as an error as F1 is an index name but S2 and S3 are data names. However, index names can be used in combination with numeric positive integral literals. Thus YEAR (F1, 2, 3) is valid because F1 is an index name, whereas 2 and 3 are numeric integral literals.

(iii) Indexes are valid only for the tables where they have been specified. Indexes for one table cannot be used for another table. Thus F1, D1 and Y1, being indexes for the table ENROLL-TABLE, cannot be used for other tables in the same program.

(iv) The index names must be unique. The same index name must not be used for different levels of a table.

(v)   The indexes must not appear anywhere in the DATA DIVISION except in the INDEXED BY phrase of the OCCURS clause. This means that the index names should be implicitly defined and should not be defined explicitly.

(vi) Indexes can be manipulated only by the SET, SEARCH (see sections 11.6 and 11.7) and PERFORM statements.

(vii) An index can be coded plus or minus an integer literal for the relative addressing of the table elements. For example, YEAR (F1 + 1, D1 - 2, Y1 - 1) is valid. If F1, D1 and Y1 assume the occurrence numbers 1, 3 and 4 respectively then this will refer to the third YEAR of the first DEPARTMENT of the second FACULTY.

(viii) There can be more than one index for each level. For example, the ENROLL-TABLE can also be defined as

```
01  FNROLL-TABLE.
    02  FACULTY OCCURS 3 TIMES INDEXED BY F1, F2, F3.
        03  DEPARTMENT OCCURS 6 TIMES INDEXED by D1, D2, D3.
            04  YEAR PIC 9(4) OCCURS 5 TIMES INDEXED BY
                                         Y1, Y2, Y3.
```

Index items defined through the INDEXED BY phrase of the OCCURS clause are one kind of indexes. There can be another kind of index items which are defined like data names in the DATA DIVISION with USAGE IS INDEX clause. Note that earlier we discussed only the DISPLAY and COMPUTATIONAL usages. INDEX is another type of usage. An index name defined with INDEX usage should not have any picture clause in the entry.

For example, the entry

    77   I   USAGE   IS   INDEX.

defines the index I.

An item defined with usage INDEX is called an index data item. The main use of an index data item arises when the value of an index needs to be preserved. The internal value of an index can be moved to an index data item (and vice-versa) without conversion (to occurrence number) with the help of a SET verb (discussed below).

11.6 SET VERB

The SET verb is used to set, increase or decrease the values of the indexes. For example, the statement

                SET   F1   TO   4

will set the value of the index F1 to 4.

There are several forms of the SET verb:

(i) To set one particular value to one or more index names we can use the following form.

    SET index-name-1 [, index-name-2] ... TO $\begin{cases} \text{identifier-1} \\ \text{integer-1} \\ \text{index-data-item} \\ \text{index-name-3} \end{cases}$

For example, SET F1, Y1 TO 3.

Only positive integral values can be set to an index.

(ii) To move the current value of an index to one or more identifiers, the following form of the SET verb can be used.

SET identifier-2 [, identifier-3] ... TO index-name-4

If A and B are data names and F1 is an index name, the statement

SET A, B TO F1

indicates that the current value of F1 will be stored in both the data names A and B.

(iii) When it becomes necessary to increment or decrement one or more indexes by a positive integer value, the following form may be applied.

$$\text{SET index-name-5 [, index-name-6] ...} \begin{Bmatrix} \underline{\text{UP}} \ \underline{\text{BY}} \\ \underline{\text{DOWN BY}} \end{Bmatrix} \begin{Bmatrix} \text{identifier-4} \\ \text{integer-2} \end{Bmatrix}$$

The phrase UP BY is used to increment the values of the indexes and the phrase DOWN BY is used to decrement their values.

Thus, to increment the current value of F1 and Y1 by 2, the following statement may be used.

SET F1, Y1 UP BY 2.

On the other hand, the statement

SET D1 DOWN BY A

indicates that the current value of the index D1 will be decremented by the current value of the data name A. If before the execution of the above statement, A and D1 contain 3 and 7 respectively, then after the execution of this statement, D1 will contain 4.

11.7 SEARCH VERB

The SEARCH verb is used to locate elements in one-dimensional tables. Let us consider the following problem. Suppose each element of a table consists of three fields, namely, the account number of a person, the name of that person and the amount that he has deposited. There are four hundred such elements in the table and we want to find out whether a particular name is present in the table or not. The desired name is given in the field called NAME and if this name appears in an element of the table, we would like to display the name as well as the corresponding account number and amount.

The DATA DIVISION entries for this problem are as follows:

DATA DIVISION.

- .
- .
- .

```
77   NAME              PIC      X(20).
01   SAVINGS-BANK-ACCOUNT.
     02   ACCOUNT-TABLE   OCCURS   400   TIMES
                          INDEXED  BY  A1.
          03   ACCOUNT-NUMBER     PIC      9(6).
          03   NAME-OF-THE-PERSON PIC      X(20).
          03   AMOUNT             PIC      9(6).99.
```

The following PROCEDURE DIVISION statements can be a solution to the above problem.

PROCEDURE DIVISION

- .
- .
- .

```
SET    A1    TO    1.
SEARCH    ACCOUNT-TABLE
          AT    END    DISPLAY    "NAME NOT FOUND"
WHEN    NAME  =  NAME-OF-THE-PERSON (A1)
        DISPLAY    ACCOUNT-NUMBER (A1), NAME
                   AMOUNT (A1).
```

In the above SEARCH statement, there are two parts — the AT END part and the WHEN part. If the condition NAME = NAME-OF-THE-PERSON (A1) is satisfied for some value of the index name A1, the statement DISPLAY ACCOUNT-NUMBER (A1), NAME, AMOUNT (A1) is executed. The AT END part is executed only when the entire table is searched and the condition is not satisfied for any value of A1. The increment of A1 is taken care of by the SEARCH verb.

To illustrate another use of the SEARCH verb, suppose we wish to search the same table to find the number of persons whose deposited amount is greater than 5000.00. For this we describe another data name NO-OF-PERSONS in the DATA DIVISION with the picture say 999. The following statements in the PROCEDURE DIVISION will perform the desired search.

```
            MOVE    ZEROS   TO  NO-OF-PERSONS.
            SET   A1   TO  1.
    PARA-REPEAT.
            SEARCH  ACCOUNT-TABLE
                AT END GO TO PARA-NEXT
            WHEN  AMOUNT  (A1)  IS GREATER  THAN 5000.00
                ADD   1   TO   NO-OF-PERSONS
                SET   A1   UP  BY  1
                GO   TO   PARA-REPEAT.
    PARA-NEXT.
            .
            .
            .
```

A loop has been designed here through the GO TO PARA-REPEAT
statement so that the entire table is searched. Note that
before the execution of the GO TO statement, the current value
of the index name A1 is incremented by 1 to point to the next
element of the table.

   We can extend the above problem to find the total number
of persons whose deposited amount is greater than 3000.00 and
also the total number of persons whose deposited amount is
greater than 5000.00. We assume that the date names TOTAL-NO-OF-
3000 and TOTAL-NO-OF-5000 have been defined in the DATA DIVISION
with the picture in each case as 999. The following statements
in the PROCEDURE DIVISION can fulfil the requirements.

```
        MOVE ZEROS TO TOTAL-NO-OF-3000, TOTAL-NO-OF-5000.
        SET A1 TO 1.
    PARA-AGAIN.
        SEARCH ACCOUNT-TABLE
            AT END GO TO PARA-NEXT
        WHEN AMOUNT (A1) > 5000.00
            ADD 1 TO TOTAL-NO-OF-5000, TOTAL-NO-OF-3000
        WHEN AMOUNT (A1) > 3000.00
            ADD 1 TO TOTAL-NO-OF-3000.
        SET A1 UP BY 1.
        GO TO PARA-AGAIN.
    PARA-NEXT.
            .
            .
            .
```

   In the above SEARCH statement there are two WHEN parts, and if any one
of the conditions is satisfied, the control will be transferred to the next
sentence. Due to the GO TO statement, the search will be performed with the
next value of A1 and this will be repeated till there is no element in the
table. When there is no element in the table, the AT END part will be
executed and the control will be transferred to the paragraph named PARA-
NEXT.

   The following is one of the forms of the SEARCH verb. This form of
SEARCH indicates a serial search.

$$\text{SEARCH} \quad \text{identifier-1} \quad \left[\text{VARYING} \left\{ \begin{array}{l} \text{identifier-2} \\ \text{index-name-1} \end{array} \right\} \right]$$

$$\left[; \text{ AT } \underline{\text{END}} \quad \text{imperative-statement-1} \right]$$

$$; \quad \underline{\text{WHEN}} \quad \text{Condition-1} \left\{ \begin{array}{l} \text{imperative-statement-2} \\ \underline{\text{NEXT}} \quad \underline{\text{SENTENCE}} \end{array} \right\}$$

$$\left[; \quad \underline{\text{WHEN}} \quad \text{Condition-2} \left\{ \begin{array}{l} \text{imperative-statement-3} \\ \underline{\text{NEXT}} \quad \underline{\text{SENTENCE}} \end{array} \right\} \right] \quad \dots$$

The following rules apply for the SEARCH verb.

(i) The SEARCH verb can only be applied to a table which has the OCCURS clause and INDEXED BY phrase. The identifier-1 indicates the table to be searched and it must not be indexed or subscripted.

(ii) Before the use of the SEARCH verb, the index must have some initial value. The initial value must not exceed the size of the table. If it exceeds, the search is terminated immediately. Then if the AT END clause is specified, statements after AT END will be executed, otherwise the control passes to the next sentence.

(iii) If the AT END condition is specified, as in the case of the first example, and if the element which is being searched is not found in the table, the statements after the AT END clause will be executed and the control will then be transferred to the next sentence if the statements after AT END do not transfer the control elsewhere in the program. On the other hand, if AT END is not used and the end of the table is reached, the control will be automatically transferred to the next sentence.

(iv) The SEARCH verb starts with the initial value of the index and tests whether the conditions stated in the WHEN clauses have been satisfied or not. If none of the conditions are satisfied the index is incremented automatically by 1. The process is continued until the index value exceeds the size of the table and the search is terminated. When one of the conditions is satisfied before the index value crosses the size of the table, the statements following the condition in the relevant WHEN clause are executed. If these statements do not transfer the control elsewhere, after their execution, it is transferred to the next sentence. The value of the index remains set at the point where the condition has been satisfied.

(v) Connected with the VARYING option, identifier-2 can be either a data, an integral elementary item or an index data item (described with USAGE AS INDEX clause). The purpose of specifying the VARYING clause is that identifier-2 is also incremented each time the index of the table is incremented.

However, it may be noted that the INDEXED BY phrase for a table can include more than one index names. In such cases the index named first is implicitly incremented by the SEARCH verb except when index-name-1 specifies an index of the table other than the first index. In the latter case, only the index name specified for index-name-1 is incremented. For example, let the table described earlier contain two indexes as shown below:

02 ACCOUNT-TABLE OCCURS 400 TIMES
INDEXED BY A1, A2.

Now, suppose that A2 is used as index-name-1. Then A2 is incremented instead of A1. However, if an index from another table or data name is used as index-name-1, then A1 is also incremented along with it.

(vi) When the SEARCH terminates without finding the particular element then the index of the table has no predictable value. This is also the case for identifier-2 when VARYING option is used.

The following is a flow chart showing the actions taken during the execution of a SEARCH statement with VARYING option and two WHEN clauses.

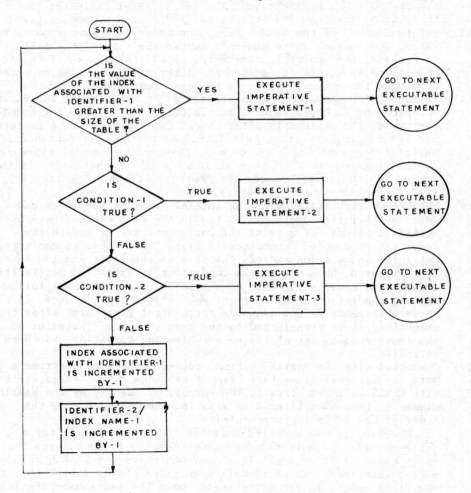

11.7.1 Sorted Tables and Binary Search

When the elements of a table are arranged among themselves in some specified order, the table is called a sorted table. For example, the SAVINGS-BANK-ACCOUNT table can be called a sorted table if the elements of the table are arranged, say in the ascending order of NAME-OF-THE-PERSON field. This field on which the table is sorted is usually called the key. There can be more than one key for ordering the elements. For example, consider the table

```
01    SALES-TABLE.
      02    SALES-DATA    OCCURS  500  TIMES.
            03  DIST-NO       PIC      99.
            03  ZONE-NO       PIC      9.
            03  SALESMAN-NO   PIC      9(3).
            03  SALES         PIC      9(5)V99.
```

The table may be sorted on the three keys — DIST-NO, ZONE-NO and SALESMAN-NO — in such a way that the elements are basically sorted on DIST-NO and then within each DIST-NO they are arranged on ZONE-NO and within each ZONE-NO they are arranged on SALESMAN-NO. DIST-NO in this case is called the major key, ZONE-NO is the next major key or the inter key and SALESMAN-NO is the minor key.

The SEARCH verb, as described in the previous section, can be applied to any table, whether it is sorted or not. The search begins with the element indicated by the starting value of the index and proceeds in a linear fashion. Such a search is called linear search. On the other hand, if the table is sorted on the data item for which the table is searched, a faster search is possible by specifying a different kind of search known as binary search. The format of the SEARCH verb indicating a binary search is different from the previous one. But before we discuss this format, it is necessary to introduce another form of the OCCURS clause. In this form along with the OCCURS clause it is also specified whether the table is sorted in ascending or descending order of the key. This form of the OCCURS clause is as follows:

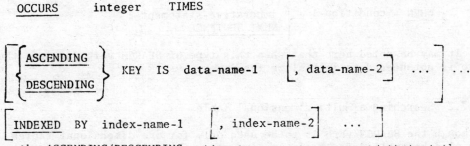

When the ASCENDING/DESCENDING option is used it is assumed that at the time of search the table is arranged either in ascending or in descending order, whichever is mentioned. If more than one data name is used, the first one is the major key, the second one is the next major key, and so on.

Let us now consider the same problem discussed in Sec. 11.7.1. with the difference that the table is now sorted on ACCOUNT-NUMBER in ascending order. The following will be the changes in the DATA DIVISION entries.

```
01   SAVINGS-BANK-ACCOUNT.
     02   ACCOUNT-TABLE OCCURS 400 TIMES
                        ASCENDING KEY IS ACCOUNT-NUMBER
                        INDEXED BY  A1.
     03   ACCOUNT-NUMBER      PIC  9(6).
     03   NAME-OF-THE-PERSON  PIC  X(20).
     03   AMOUNT              PIC  9(6).99.
```

It should be noted here that each key name must be the name of the data item belonging to the element of the table. There are some restrictions on the total number of keys depending on the compiler used.

To find whether the particular account number stored in the data name AC-NO is present in the table or not and to display the account number, name and the amount if it is present, the following PROCEDURE DIVISION statements may be used.

```
     SEARCH  ALL  ACCOUNT-TABLE
             AT  END  DISPLAY  " ACCOUNT NUMBER IS NOT THERE "
         WHEN  AC-NO  =  ACCOUNT-NUMBER (A1)
         DISPLAY  AC-NO, NAME-OF-THE-PERSON (A1),
                          AMOUNT (A1).
```

In this case it first splits the table into two halves and determines in which half the item being searched is present. Since the table is sorted, a single comparison of the given item, either with the last item of the first half or with the first item of the second half, can determine in which half the item is present. The half to which the desired item may belong is again divided into two halves and the previous procedure is followed. This continues until either the item is detected or the final division leads to a half consisting of a single item. Now, a single comparison with this item can establish either the presence or absence of the given item. This type of search is known as binary search and in this case the total number of comparisons is less than that of linear search.

In this case the SEARCH verb takes the following form.

SEARCH   ALL   identifier-1 $\left[\text{;AT END imperative-statement-1} \right]$

; WHEN   condition-1 $\left\{ \begin{array}{l} \text{imperative-statement-2} \\ \text{NEXT SENTENCE} \end{array} \right\}$

It may be noted here that when this type of SEARCH verb is used, the SET verb is not needed to initialize the index.

11.7.2 Searching a Multi-dimensional Table

Although the SEARCH verb is to be used only for one-dimensional tables, it can also be applied for a single dimension of a multi-dimensional table. The following is an example of such use of the SEARCH verb. Suppose, in a class there are 100 students and each student appears in 12 subjects. Each element of the table contains the registration number of a student, his name, the names of the subjects he has taken and the marks obtained in these subjects. the following are the DATA DIVISION entries for this problem.

```
01  STUDENT-RECORD.
    02  STUDENT-TABLE  OCCURS  100  TIMES
                   INDEXED BY STU.
        03  REGISTRATION-NO         PIC    9(8).
        03  STUDENT-NAME            PIC    X(20).
        03  SUBJECT-TABLE  OCCURS   12   TIMES
                       INDEXED  BY  SUB.
            04  SUBJECT-NAME        PIC    X(20).
            04  MARKS-OBTAINED      PIC    999.
```

Now our problem is to search the marks of all the 12 subjects of each
student. If it is less than 50, we want to display the registration number
of the student, his name, name of the subject and also the marks obtained
in that subject. To get the solution of the problem, we write the following
PROCEDURE DIVISION statements.

```
            PERFORM  MARKS-LESS-THAN-50  THRU  PARA-EXIT
                 VARYING P-STU  FROM   1  BY  1  UNTIL  P-STU > 100.

MARKS-LESS-THAN-50.
            SET     STU     TO P-STU.
            SET     SUB     TO 1.

PARA-SEARCH.
            SEARCH  SUBJECT-TABLE  AT  END  GO TO PARA-EXIT
                WHEN  MARKS-OBTAINED (STU, SUB) < 50
                DISPLAY REGISTRATION-NO  (STU),
                    STUDENT-NAME (STU), SUBJECT-NAME (STU, SUB),
                    MARKS-OBTAINED (STU, SUB)
                SET SUB UP  BY  1
                GO  TO  PARA-SEARCH.

PARA-EXIT.
            EXIT.
```

It may be noted that P-STU is a data name which can be defined in the
working-storage section or somewhere in the DATA DIVISION with its picture
as 999. The data name P-STU is used in the PERFORM statement instead of
index STU as some compiler does not allow the indexes to have a value more
than the size of the table. Here P-STU can have the value 101 which is more
than 100, the size of STUDENT-TABLE.

11.8 OCCURS DEPENDING CLAUSE

When a table of variable size is required, the OCCURS DEPENDING clause may
be used. The following is a simple example of this clause.

```
77    A1     PIC     99.
01    REC-1.
      02    P1    PIC    XX.
      02    P2    PIC 99   OCCURS 1 TO  90  TIMES
                        DEPENDING ON A1.
```

In the above example, depending on the value of the data name Al the size of P2 will be decided. It can be anything between 1 and 90.

The general form of this clause is as follows:

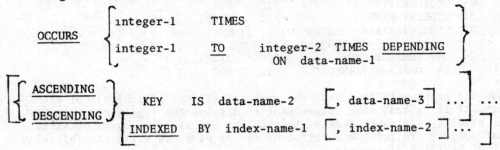

The following rules apply for the OCCURS DEPENDING clause.

(i)   Both integer-1 and integer-2 must be positive integers, and integer-1 must have a value less than integer-2. Integer-1 represents the minimum number of occurrences, and integer-2 represents the maximum number of occurrences.

(ii) Data-name-1 must be defined in DATA DIVISION. It can even appear in the same record with the data item having this clause, but it must not be subordinate to the entry whose description includes the DEPENDING clause. For example, the following is valid.

```
01    REC-1.
      02    Al    PIC    99.
      02    P1    PIC    XX.
      02    P2    PIC    99    OCCURS 1 TO 90 TIMES
                              DEPENDING ON Al.
```

However, the following is invalid.

```
01    REC-1.
      02    P1    PIC    XX.
      02    P2    PIC    99    OCCURS 1 TO 90 TIMES
                              DEPENDING ON Al.
            03 Al PIC    99.
```

(iii) When an entry in a table contains a DEPENDING clause, the said entry and any one or all its subordinate entries cannot be redefined. For example, the following is invalid.

```
01    REC-1.
      02    Al    PIC      99.
      02    P1    PIC      XX.
      02    P2    PIC      99    OCCURS 1 TO 90 TIMES
                                DEPENDING ON Al.
      02    P3    REDEFINES P2.
```

(iv) The value of data-name-1 is the count of the number of occurrences of the item described by the OCCURS clause, and its value must not exceed integer-2. In the above example the value of Al must not be greater than 90.

(v) If the table with the DEPENDING clause has indexes, the indexes must always correspond to the current value of the table size. The same rule also applies in case subscripts are used.

Let us consider the following DATA DIVISION entries.

```
01   REC-1.
     02   A1     PIC    99.
     02   P1     PIC    XX.
     02   P2     PIC    99   OCCURS  1   TO  90  TIMES
                 DEPENDING ON  A1   INDEXED BY  B1.
```

In PROCEDURE DIVISION if the value of A1 happens to be 60 then B1 will have to be set to 60 or less than 60. Similarly, if after some executions, A1 becomes 50, then B1 can assume any positive value up to 50.

(vi) Initial values cannot be assigned to items containing the DEPENDING phrase or items subordinate to them.

11.9 SORTING A TABLE

Sometimes, it becomes necessary to have the elements of a table sorted in the ascending or descending order of some key fields. For example, binary search cannot be applied unless the table is properly sorted. Unfortunately, COBOL does not provide any verb to sort a table. There is, of course, a SORT verb to sort the records of a file which we shall study afterwards. However, when it is required to sort a table, the programmer must write his own code for the purpose.

There are many algorithms that can be used to sort a table. In the following we discuss the sorting algorithm known as bubble sort. In the bubble sort, the consecutive elements of the table are compared, and if the keys of the two elements are not found in proper order, they are interchanged. The said comparisons start from the beginning of the table and continue till the end of the table. As a result of this, the element with the largest key will be pushed to the last element's position. After this the second pass is made. The second pass is exactly like the first one except that this time all the elements except the last are considered. After the second pass, the next largest element will be pushed down to the last but one element's position. The second pass is followed by a third and so on until either (n - 1) passes have been made or no interchange takes place in a pass. Here n is assumed to be the number of elements in the table. It may be noted that the nonoccurrence of any interchange in a pass ensures that the table is sorted. To show how this algorithm can be coded in COBOL, we will consider the SAVINGS-BANK-ACCOUNT table of Sec. 11.7. The COBOL code for the bubble-sort algorithm to sort this table is given below.

```
BUBBLE-SORT.
    PERFORM  BUBBLE-PASS
         VARYING  I  FROM  1  BY  1  UNTIL  I = N  OR
                             NO-EXCHANGE.
```

```
BUBBLE-PASS.
    MOVE  O  TO  EXCHANGE-FLAG.
    SUBTRACT  I  FROM  N  GIVING  K.
    PERFORM  ELEMENT-COMPARISON
        VARYING  J  FROM  1  BY  1  UNTIL  J > K.

ELEMENT-COMPARISON.
    SET   A1   TO   J.
    IF  ACCOUNT-NUMBER  (A1) > ACCOUNT-NUMBER  (A1 + 1)
        MOVE  ACCOUNT-NUMBER (A1)  TO  TEMP-ACC-NO
        MOVE  ACCOUNT-NUMBER (A1 + 1)  TO  ACCOUNT-NUMBER  (A1)
        MOVE  TEMP-ACC-NO  TO  ACCOUNT-NUMBER  (A1 + 1)
        MOVE  1  TO  EXCHANGE-FLAG.
```

The following WORKING STORAGE entries have been assumed for the above problem.

```
01  DATA-FOR-BUBBLE-SORT.
    02  I                PIC       9(3) COMP.
    02  J                PIC       9(3) COMP.
    02  K                PIC       9(3) COMP.
    02  N                PIC       9(3) COMP  VALUE  IS  400.
    02  EXCHANGE-FLAG    PIC       9(3) COMP  VALUE  IS  1.
    88  NO-EXCHANGE      VALUE     IS    ZERO.
    02  TEMP-ACC-NO      PIC       9(6)V99.
```

It may be noted that with the above statements in the PROCEDURE DIVISION, the table can be sorted by using the statement

                    PERFORM   BUBBLE-SORT.

However, it is important that at this point the data name EXCHANGE-FLAG must contain a nonzero value. In case its value is zero, no sorting takes place. It is precisely for this reason that EXCHANGE-FLAG has been initialized to 1. An alternative solution (and perhaps a better one) would be to code the BUBBLE-SORT paragraph as follows:

```
BUBBLE-SORT.
    MOVE  1  TO  EXCHANGE-FLAG.
    PERFORM  BUBBLE-PASS
        VARYING  I  FROM  1  BY  1  UNTIL
            I = N  OR  NO-EXCHANGE.
```

Another method which may be used to sort a table is shuttle sort. The shuttle sort is similar to the bubble sort. The table elements are compared and, if necessary, they are exchanged. However, in the first pass it considers only the first two elements of the table and sorts them. In the second pass it considers the third element of the table and sorts the first three elements. In general, in the ith pass, it assumes that the first i elements of the table is already sorted and proceeds to sort the first (i + 1) elements by comparing the (i + 1)th and ith element, then the ith element and (i - 1)th element, and so on, until either the top of the table is reacled or no exchange results from the comparison. The following is the algoritnm of the shuttle sort in COBOL.

```
SHUTTLE-SORT.
     PERFORM  SHUTTLE-PASS
           VARYING  I  FROM  2  BY  1  UNTIL  I > N.

SHUTTLE-PASS.
     MOVE  1  TO  EXCHANGE-FLAG.
     PERFORM  ELEMENT-COMPARISON
           VARYING  J  FROM  I  BY  -1  UNTIL  J < 2  OR
                                       NO-EXCHANGE.

ELEMENT-COMPARISON.
     SET  A1  TO  J.
     IF  ACCOUNT-NUMBER  (A1 - 1) > ACCOUNT-NUMBER (A1)
          MOVE   ACCOUNT-NUMBER  (A1 - 1)  TO  TEMP-ACC-NO
          MOVE   ACCOUNT-NUMBER  (A1) TO ACCOUNT-NUMBER (A1 - 1)
          MOVE   TEMP-ACC-NO TO ACCOUNT-NUMBER (A1)
     ELSE  MOVE  ZERO  TO  EXCHANGE-FLAG.
```

The same WORKING-STORAGE entries have been assumed here with the exception that K is no longer required.

It can be shown that the shuttle sort is better than the bubble sort if there are more than 12 elements in the table (Roy and Dastidar, 1976).

Remarks

If you do not understand these algorithms, try to follow the statements assuming some sample values for the account numbers.

11.10 INDEX DATA ITEM

This has been introduced earlier. An index data item is an elementary item which is defined in the DATA DIVISION with the USAGE IS INDEX clause. The format of this clause is

USAGE IS INDEX

The following rules apply when the clause is used.
   (i)   An index data item must not have a PICTURE.
   (ii) When the clause is specified for a group item, it applies to all elementary items contained in it. However, the group itself is not an index data item.
   (iii) An index data item can be part of a group item and such a group item may be referred to in a MOVE or input-output statement. It may be noted that an index data item within the group cannot be referred to by these statements. For example, consider the following descriptions.

```
01     DUMMY-INDEX.
       02 THE-INDEX USAGE  IS  INDEX.
01     SAVED-INDEX.
       02 INDEX-DATA  PIC   S9(6)  COMP.
```

Now,

```
      MOVE   THE-INDEX   TO   SAVED-INDEX
and   MOVE   THE-INDEX   TO   INDEX-DATA
```

are both invalid statements. However, the following statement is valid.

```
      MOVE  DUMMY-INDEX   TO   SAVED-INDEX.
```

Since, this is a group move, there will be no conversion of the index data stored in THE-INDEX and, for that matter, in DUMMY-INDEX. However, if we know that internally the index data items are implicitly treated as, say S 9(6) COMP items, then after the MOVE statement, the value of INDEX-DATA can be safely utilized.

The above example illustrates how the value of an index data item can be transferred to a numeric data item so that it can be used in arithmetic or other statements. However, the technique requires a knowledge of the internal representation of the index data items and as such, can adversely affect the portability.

11.11   USE OF INDEXES AND INDEX DATA ITEMS

Indexes and index data items can be directly referred to only in the SET, SEARCH and PERFORM statements. They can also be referred to in relational conditions. The use of indexes and index data items in the SET and SEARCH statements has been presented above. Index names can be used in the PERFORM statements in the VARYING, AFTER, FROM and BY phrases. To illustrate their use, the second example of Sec. 11.7 is rewritten using a PERFORM statement. The code may be as follows.

```
    MOVE   ZEROS  TO  NO-OF-PERSONS.
    PERFORM SEARCH-THE-TABLE
        VARYING  A1  FROM   1  BY  1  UNTIL  A1 > 400.
PARA-NEXT.
    where SEARCH-THE-TABLE is
SEARCH-THE-TABLE.
    IF AMOUNT (A1) IS GREATER THAN 5000.00
        ADD  1  TO  NO-OF-PERSONS.
```

Note that A1 is an index name. Therefore, the FROM and BY phrases have the same effect as the simple SET statement and the SET statement with the UP BY phrase respectively. In fact, the above PERFORM statement is equivalent to

```
            SET    A1   TO   1.
        PARA-REPEAT.
            IF  A1  NOT >-400
                PERFORM SEARCH-THE-TABLE
                SET  A1  UP  BY  1
                GO TO PARA-REPEAT.
```

In the above, the relational conditions A1 > 400 and A1 NOT > 400 have been used. Here again, the index name A1 appears. The COBOL rules for using index names in a relational condition are as follows:

(i)   When an index or index data item is compared with an identifier or literal, the occurrence number to which the index name corresponds is compared with the value of the identifier/literal. The identifier/literal must be numeric and the rule for numeric comparison applies.

(ii) When an index or index data item is compared with another index or index data item, their internal values are compared without conversion.

11.12   IMPLEMENTATION DIFFERENCES

(a)   OCCURS Clause

In ICL-1900 and DEC-10, tables cannot have more than three dimensions. There is no such restriction in B-6700. In ICL-1900 and DEC-10, the non-standard abbreviation OC is not available. In B-6700, OC can be used for OCCURS.

(b)   PERFORM Statement

In addition to what has been stated in the text, B-6700 allows the use of arithmetic expressions in the formats of the PERFORM statement at the following positions.

(i)   Before the word TIMES, to specify the number of times the range is to be performed.

(ii) In the FROM and BY phrases, immediately after the word FROM or BY. Thus,

PERFORM   THIS-PARA   N + 3   TIMES.

is a valid statement in B-6700.

(c)   Subscripting/Indexing

In ICL-1900, a subscript can be a positive integer or a data name containing a positive integer. Such a data name can be qualified but cannot be subscripted. In DEC-10, a subscript can be a positive integer or a data name containing a positive integer or a data name $\{ \overset{+}{-} \}$ integer. Thus, an element of table AREA may be referred to as AREA (N + 2) in DEC-10. As in the case of ICL-1900, a subscript cannot be subscripted. In B-6700, there is hardly any restriction on what a subscript can be. Any arithmetic expression can be a subscript provided its value is positive. If the value is not an integer, it is truncated to an integer.

In the case of indexing, all the three compilers allow relative indexing. This means that the format of indexing is as follows:

$$\left\{ \begin{array}{c} \text{index-name} \\ \text{integer} \end{array} \right\} \quad \left[\left\{ \begin{array}{c} + \\ - \end{array} \right\} \quad \text{integer} \right]$$

(d) Index/Index Data Item

An index or an index data item in DEC-10 is implicitly defined to be a COMP
item with S9(5) as the picture. DEC-10 does not make any distinction between
an index, index data item or a COMP data item defined with picture S9(5).
In B-6700, these items are assumed to be 9(11) COMP items. In ICL-1900,
three consecutive words are allocated for such items. The first is a word
address, the second is a character address and third is a bit address (in
ICL-1900 COBOL, bit items can also be defined), all relative to the start
of the table.

   In ICL-1900, there is a difference between an index and an index data
item. An index data item cannot be compared with the value of an integer or
that of a data name through a relational condition. However, this is possible
in the case of an index.

(e) SEARCH Verb

This verb is not available in ICL-1900. As such OCCURS clauses with ASCEND-
ING/DESCENDING phrase is also not available in ICL-1900.

(f) OCCURS with DEPENDING Clause

The syntax of this clause in ICL-1900 is as follows:

OCCURS integer TIMES [DEPENDING ON data-name-1]

[INDEXED BY index-name-1 [index-name-2] ...]

The integer indicates the maximum number of occurrences of the field.

EXERCISES

1. Which of the following statements cannot be supported?
   (a) Subscripting enables us to write a more compact code in the
        PROCEDURE DIVISION.
   (b) Subscripting enables us to refer to any element of a table by
        the same data name with the facility of identifying the parti-
        cular element through the value(s) of subscript(s).
   (c) Subscripting reduces the number of entries to be included in the
        DATA DIVISION.
   (d) Subscripting enables us to use loops in the PROCEDURE DIVISION.

2. What are the differences among a subscript, an index and an index data
   item?

3. Write DATA DIVISION entries to define a table having 12 elements and to
   initialize the table to contain the number of days in each of the 12
   months of an year (Assume 28 for February).

4. Consider the following WORKING-STORAGE SECTION entries:

   ```
   01  WEEK-DAY-NAMES    PIC    X(63)    VALUE  IS
   " MONDAYÞÞÞTUESDAYÞÞWEDNESDAYTHURSDAYÞFRIDAYÞÞÞSATURDAYÞSUNDAY " .
   01  WEEK-DAYS-NAME  REDEFINES  WEEK-DAY-NAMES.
      02  WEEK-DAY  PIC X(9)  OCCURS  7  TIMES.
   ```

   What will be the value of WEEK-DAY(4)?

5. A table contains the monthly sales data for the 12 months of a year and
   for the 4 sales zones where each zone has 8 districts. The table is
   defined in the WORKING-STORAGE SECTION in the following manner.

   ```
   01  SALES-TABLE.
      05  SALE-ZONE OCCURS 4 TIMES.
         10  SALE-DISTRICT OCCURS  8  TIMES.
            15  SALE-DATA PIC 9(5) OCCURS 12 TIMES.
   ```

   (a) How is the sale value for the third zone, seventh district and
        fourth month referred to in the PROCEDURE DIVISION?
   (b) What is the size of the SALES-TABLE (in number of bytes)?

6. Consider the table of the previous exercise. Write PROCEDURE DIVISION
   statements to find the total sale of each district within each zone and
   then find the total sale of each zone. Store these totals in two tables
   — one containing the district totals and the other containing the zone
   totals. Also, write DATA DIVISION entries to define these tables.

7. How many times will the procedure named PROCESS-ROUTINE be executed by
   the following PERFORM statements?
   ```
   (a)  PERFORM  PROCESS-ROUTINE  VARYING  A  FROM  1  BY  1
                                           UNTIL  A  =  15.
   (b)  PERFORM  PROCESS-ROUTINE  VARYING  A  FROM  1  BY  1
                                           UNTIL  A  >  15.
   (c)  PERFORM  PROCESS-ROUTINE  VARYING  A  FROM  1  BY  1
                                           UNTIL  A  <  15.
   (d)  PERFORM  PROCESS-ROUTINE  VARYING  A  FROM  1  BY  1
                                           UNTIL  A  =  B.
   ```

8. The following is a PROCEDURE DIVISION statement.
   ```
         PERFORM  PARA-AGAIN  VARYING  I  FROM  1  BY  1
                                       UNTIL  I  >  4
                AFTER  J  FROM  0  BY  -1  UNTIL  J  <  -2
                AFTER  K  FROM  1  BY  2   UNTIL  K  >  8
   ```
   (a) What combinations of values will I, J and K have in the loop?
   (b) How many times is the procedure named PARA-AGAIN executed?
   (c) Which data name varies least rapidly and which one most rapidly?

9. The following are DATA DIVISION entries.
   ```
         77   I          PIC    99.
         77   TOTAL      PIC    99.
         01   TABLE-1.
              02 FILLER    PIC   X(9) VALUE IS  "123456789".
         01   TABLE-2 REDEFINES  TABLE-1.
              02  A OCCURS 9 TIMES PIC 9.
   ```

Indicate how many elements of the array A would be added to TOTAL and what will be the final value of TOTAL when the control goes to PARA-2 in the following program segment?

```
            MOVE    ZERO    TO    TOTAL.
            PERFORM  PARA-1  VARYING  I  FROM  1  BY  2.
                                UNTIL  I  >  9.
            GO TO PARA-2.
PARA-1.
            ADD  A  (I)  TO  TOTAL.
PARA-2.
```

10. Consider the following DATA DIVISION entries.

```
01    SALES-TABLE.
      02  ZONE-SALES   OCCURS  4  TIMES.
          03  DISTRICT-SALES  OCCURS  5  TIMES.
              04  PRODUCT-SALE  OCCURS  3  TIMES
                                  PIC  9(5).
77    SOME-VALUE    PIC   9(4)  VALUE  0.
77    I             PIC   9.
77    J             PIC   9.
77    K             PIC   9.
```

What value will PRODUCT-SALE (3,2,2) get due to the following statements in the PROCEDURE DIVISION?

```
PERFORM  PARA-1
      VARYING  K  FROM  1  BY  1  UNTIL  K  GREATER  THAN  3
      AFTER    I  FROM  1  BY  1  UNTIL  I  GREATER  THAN  4
      AFTER    J  FROM  1  BY  1  UNTIL  J  GREATER  THAN  5.

PARA-1.
         ADD  1  TO  SOME-VALUE.
         MOVE  SOME-VALUE  TO  PRODUCT-SALE  (I,J,K).
```

11. The following table is described in the WORKING-STORAGE SECTION.

```
01    PERSONNEL-TABLE.
          02  PERSONNEL-INFORMATION  OCCURS  500  TIMES.
              03  PERSONNEL-NO    PIC  9(3).
              03  NAME
                  04  FIRST-NAME  PIC  X(20).
                  04  LAST-NAME   PIC  X(10).
              03  INCOME          PIC  9(5).
```

(a) What is the size of the PERSONNEL-TABLE (in number of bytes)?
(b) Write PROCEDURE DIVISION statements.
   (i) to find how many persons are there whose LAST-NAME is SHARMA.
   (ii) to find how many persons are there whose LAST-NAME is MITRA and whose INCOME is more than 18000.

12. Rewrite the following COBOL statements using the PERFORM with VARYING-AFTER options.

```
      SET   I   TO   1.
P1.   IF  NOT  I > 11  PERFORM  P2  THRU  P3
      SET   I   UP  BY  2  GO  TO  P1.
```

where P2 and P3 are consecutive paragraphs as follows:

```
P2.   SET  J  TO  25.
P3.   IF  NOT  J < 1  PERFORM  A-PARA
      SET  J  DOWN  BY  3  GO  TO  P3.
```

13. In each pass of the bubble-sort algorithm given in Sec. 11.9, the comparison of consecutive elements starts from the beginning of the table. However, the algorithm could also be applied on the table in the reverse direction. This means that in the ith pass, comparison starts with the nth and $(n-1)$th elements and ends when the $(i+1)$th and ith elements have been compared. With proper exchanges, the ith smallest element (smallest of those occupying ith to the nth positions at the beginning of the ith pass) is ''bubbled up'' to occupy the ith position. Write COBOL statements for this variation of the bubble sort.

14. Do you think the algorithms for the bubble and shuttle sort will work if two or more of the keys are identical?

12

STRUCTURED PROGRAMMING

The precise meaning of the term <u>structured programming</u> depends on the interpretation given to it by an individual. In general, it refers to a programming strategy that encompasses a number of methodologies to achieve certain
objectives. These objectives and methodologies are the points of discussion
in this chapter. In the initial part of this chapter the principles of
structured programming are discussed in general terms; the implementation
of these methodologies in COBOL programs is considered in the later part.

12.1 PROGRAM DESIGN

In the following we are primarily concerned with the logic of a program. The
term program is used in this chapter to mean only the PROCEDURE DIVISION of
a COBOL program. Moreover, another term, namely, <u>program design</u> will be
frequently used here. Therefore, before we proceed further let us explain
the meaning of program design. In the case of a conventional program, the
term program design means the activity of describing the program logic in
some nonprogramming language. For example, the preparation of a flow chart
before coding a program may be called the program design. In the case of
structured programming, we shall see that the program is progressively
decomposed into smaller partitions called <u>modules</u>. This decomposition of a
program into modules defines a structure in terms of interdependencies among
the various modules. The program design in this case, consists of describing
this structure in some nonprogramming language. In addition, the functions
and logic of the individual modules are also described during program design.
The general name of nonprogramming language that can be used for the abovementioned description is <u>pseudocode</u>. A pseudocode may or may not use any
graphic aid. Various types of pseudocodes are in use and none of them is
standard. At the end of this chapter we shall describe an extension of the
flowcharting technique which can be used as a pseudocode.

12.2 CURRENT TRENDS IN DATA PROCESSING

In order to appreciate the importance of structured programming, it is
necessary first to make a note of the current trends that influence the
program design objectives and methods. The recent past has seen a spectacular decrease in the hardware costs of computers. This trend is still
being maintained. As a result, the personnel costs relative to the hardware
costs are increasing at a faster rate. This calls for methods that can

increase personnel performance and thereby reduce the cost of program development.

Quite often, the purpose for which a program was developed gets changed. In such cases there are only two alternatives. Either the program should be declared obsolete and a new program should be developed in its place or the program should be modified incorporating the necessary changes. The personnel costs being on the increase, the question of discarding a program altogether does not arise. Instead the program is maintained by modifying it. This again calls for methods for program development so that the program is understood easily and modified easily. It may also be noted that rapidly changing business environment has increased the burden of program maintenance in recent times.

12.3 OBJECTIVES AND METHODOLOGIES OF STRUCTURED PROGRAMMING

The term structured programming was first used by E.W. Dijkstra (1972). Dijkstra and many other people have expanded the idea in subsequent works. The objective of structured programming is to provide methodologies so that (i) programs can be developed quickly and with fewer mistakes, (ii) programs can be read and understood easily and (iii) a portion of the program can be modified without upsetting the functions of other portions. In other words, the objective is to meet the challenge offered by the abovementioned trends in data processing.

The principles of structured programming are as follows:
  (i)   Structuring of control flow.
  (ii) Decomposing a program into ''partitions'' or ''modules''.
 (iii) Top-down approach towards program design.

These principles and the methodologies to implement them are outlined below.

12.3.1 Structuring of Control Flow

Except for the most trivial examples, programs are highly-complex systems of logic. The ability to design loop operations and to take alternative courses of actions depending on a condition can make a program very complex. This is because, quite often, loops are used within alternative paths or loops and alternative paths are used within loops or other alternative paths. The large size of a program and the interconnections between its various parts through the transfer of control also increase the program complexity. The idea behind the structuring of control flow is to keep this complexity under control so that the design and understanding of the program logic becomes easier.

Bohm and Jacopini (1966) and subsequently Mills demonstrated that programs can be structured by using a restricted set of control structures. These basic control structures are as follows:

a.	SEQUENCE	A sequence of two or more operations.
b.	IFTHENELSE	Execution of one of two operations depending on a condition.
c.	DOWHILE	The repetitive execution of an operation so long a condition is true.

SEQUENCE

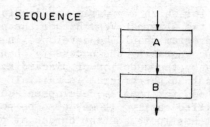

IFTHENELSE

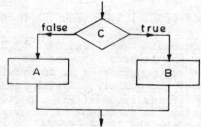

DOWHILE

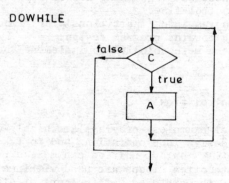

Fig. 12.1.   Three Basic Logical Structures

In the above description of these control structures, an operation means either an imperative statement or one of these three structures with the exception that the statement for the unconditional transfer of control (GO TO) is not to be considered as an imperative statement to represent an operation. The flow charts for the three structures are shown in Fig. 12.1.   In these flow charts each of A and B denotes an operation in the above sense of the term and C denotes a condition.

It may be seen that a concept of nesting is assumed in the above definition of an operation. Considering the imperative statements as the most elementary operations, they can be combined using the above structures to form larger and larger operations until the final program is realized as a single operation. On the other hand, such a pro ram can be dissected into progressively smaller operations.

What has been referred to as an operation in the above discussion is often called a proper program. The word program is a misnomer in this context because a proper program need not necessarily be a complete program. It can as well be used to indicate the components into which the complete program can be dissected and in turn to indicate any of the components of these components, and so on. It can be proved that any programming logic can be realized as a proper program.

An important property of a proper program is that it has only one entry and one exit. This is because proper programs are constructed using only the three basic control structures which themselves have this property (see the flow charts in Fig. 12.1). This property of one entry and one exit gives proper programs their main advantage. The advantage is that once the control enters the proper program, it executes the statements within the program until such time as it reaches the exit point. Thus, a proper program can be read in a topdown linear manner without having to divert the attention elsewhere in the program.

The abovementioned advantage of proper programs can be better understood if we make a comparison between a conventional program and a proper program. The structuring of proper programs using the restricted set of the said three control structures ensures complete elimination of GO TO statements which are frequently used in conventional programs. The disadvantage of a GO TO statement is that the program cannot be read by a programmer in a topdown linear fashion. The moment a GO TO statement is encountered, the human reader must leave the current area of the program and transfer his attention to some other part in order to understand the logic. The presence of many GO TOs in a program requires such transfer of attention every now and then and thereby may be sufficient to leave him totally confused, especially when he is a different programmer who must read and modify the program. In fact, the freedom of unconditional transfer of control to any place in the program as provided by the GO TO statement is more than needed. A careless use of this freedom can give the program a very complex structure of control flow. Thus the desirability of ''gotoless'' proper programs in preference to conventional programs is beyond doubt.

12.3.2 Modular Programming

Modular programming is a programming strategy where a program is decomposed into a number of identifiable partitions or modules. Thus, a module is a portion of a program that also fits the definition of a program. A module may be considered as decomposed into successively subordinate modules and conversely, a number of modules can be combined together to form a superior module. The important point in this case is that a superior module does not physically include the codes of its subordinate modules within itself. Instead, the subordinate modules are located elsewhere in the program and the superior module, whenever necessary, makes a reference to an immediate subordinate module and calls for its execution. This activity on the part of the superior module is known as the ''calling'' of a subordinate modules. Sometimes the subordinate module is referred to as the called module and the superior module as the calling module.

In order to support modular programming, the programming language must provide facilities for the definition and calling of modules. For example, the simple PERFORM statement in COBOL offers this facility. The range of the PERFORM statement is the called module, and calling is accomplished through the execution of the PERFORM statement itself. It may be noted that the PERFORM statement does transfer control to the called module but this transfer of control is unlike that of a GO TO statement. In the case of a PERFORM statement, upon the execution of the called module, the return of the control to the next sequential statement in the module is ensured. Thus a PERFORM statement has one entry and one exit. If the control enters a PERFORM statement, it also leaves the statement upon its execution. Although a PERFORM statement has been considered as an example, any statement that calls a module behaves in the same manner. We, therefore, observe that the statement which calls another module can be considered as an imperative statement and for that matter as an operation, in the sense of the term used in the definition of the three basic control structures.

The advantage of modular programming depends on how effectively the modules are designed. This point will be discussed in detail in the next section. For the time being it may be stated that each module must be designed to accomplish a distinct function. This gives the program a rather high modification potential. For example, in a payroll program there may be a module that calculates the dearness allowance from the basic pay using certain rules. If these rules get changed on a later date, the modification will be limited to the said module and/or to its subordinate modules, if any. It may be noted that it is easier to replace a module by a modified one than to make corrections in one particular part of a conventional program without upsetting the functions of the other parts.

12.3.3 Top-down Approach

The above description of modular programming presupposes a hierarchical structuring of modules. The process of designing a program as consisting of a hierarchical structure of modules can be viewed in two ways — top-down or bottom-up.

The top-down approach towards program design starts with the specification of the function to be performed by a program and then breaks it down into progressively subsidiary functions. The decomposition of the function progresses with an increasing levels of details. Each function at each level is ultimately realised in the form of a module. In the top-down approach the calling module is always designed before the called module. At the time of designing a module, the broad functions to be performed by its immediately subordinate modules are assumed. The details of how a subordinate module can perform the specified functions are not considered until the subordinate module is taken up for design. Thus the top-down approach represents a successive refinement of functions and this process of refinement is continued until the lowest level modules can be designed without further analysis.

The top-down structure can be viewed as a tree structure, a typical example of which is shown in Fig. 12.2. Each box in this figure is a module. The topmost module denoted by A represents the program. In future references we shall call this topmost module to be the main-line module. In this case, the main-line module is decomposed into three subordinate modules denoted by B, C and D. The modules B and D require further decomposition and in this

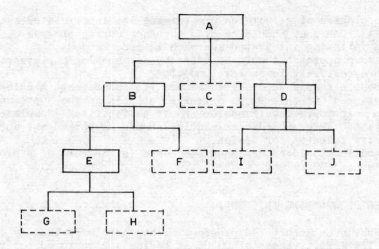

FIG. 12.2.   A Typical Top-down Structure

process the terminal modules are G, H, F, C, I and J. The functions of
these terminal modules are assumed to be simple enough to be easily programmed in the source language.

The bottom-up approach is the reverse of the top-down one. The process
starts with the identification of a set of modules which are either available or to be constructed. An attempt is made to combine the modules to form
modules of a higher level. This process of combining modules is continued
until the program is realized. The basic drawback of the bottom-up approach
is the assumption that the lowest level modules can be completely specified
beforehand, which in reality is seldom possible. Thus in the bottom-up
approach, quite often, it is found that the final program obtained by
combining the predetermined lowest level modules does not meet all the
requirements of the desired program.

A comparison of the advantages and disadvantages of the two approaches
is beyond the scope of the present discussion. It is sufficient to note
that the top-down approach towards program development is widely accepted
to be better than the bottom-up approach. The top-down approach has the
following advantages·

   (i)   It imitates the human tendency to solve a problem by outlining
         the broad concepts first and then subsequently going into the
         details.
  (ii)   The details of a module can be worked out with no or minimum
         change of the previously outlined concepts regarding its func-
         tions.
 (iii)   The programmer never loses sight of the assumptions made at the
         previous levels.
  (iv)   The development of modules can take place in parallel.

These advantages suggest that if the top-down approach is taken for
program design, the programs can be developed easily, quickly and without
committing a large number of errors.

12.3.4   Summing-Up

The three methodologies of structured programming are interrelated rather than distinct. As such they should be used together during program design and coding. The following integrated approach is recommended.

   (i)   A top-down approach should be taken by decomposing the program into progressively lower level modules.

  (ii)   Each module should be designed before its subordinate modules are designed. At this stage only the outlines of the functions of the next lower level modules should be finalized. Complete details of these subordinate modules should be worked out when those are taken up for design.

 (iii)   Each module should be designed and coded in the form of a proper program.

12.4   STRUCTURED PROGRAMMING IN COBOL

The above discussion on structured programming has been made largely in general terms. The effectiveness of COBOL in coding a structured program is now examined to show how the features of the language can be used to develop structured programs. The effectiveness of a programming language in this matter is determined by the ease and efficiency with which the three basic structures can be represented and the same with which a program can be modularized. These are discussed below.

12.4.1   Three Basic Structures

The three basic structures are immediately available in COBOL. The SEQUENCE structure refers to the sequential flow of control through imperative statements (other than GO TO) or statements that represent the other two structures. This structure is implicit in any programming language. The following example illustrates the sequence structure in COBOL.

```
PRINT-TOTALS.
        ADD  SALES-AMOUNT  TO  TOTAL-SALES.
        WRITE  PRINT-RECORD  FROM  TOTAL-RECORD
              AFTER  ADVANCING  2  LINES.
        MOVE  ZERO  TO  TOTAL-SALES.
```

The above paragraph consists of three imperative statements. Once the control enters the paragraph, the three statements are executed in the order of their appearance and the paragraph is exited after the execution of the third statement.

The IFTHENELSE structure is represented in COBOL through the IF statement. The statement

```
IF  WEIGHT  IS  GREATER  THAN  50
        MOVE  "A"  TO  TRANSPORT-CODE
ELSE  MOVE  "B"  TO  TRANSPORT-CODE.
```

is an example of the IFTHENELSE structure. A special case of the IFTHENELSE structure is when the else part of the IF statement is used. For example,

```
IF  ACCOUNT-NO  IS  EQUAL  TO  PREVIOUS-ACCOUNT-NO
          ADD  AMOUNT  TO  RUNNING-TOTAL.
```

The DOWHILE structure is represented in COBOL by the PERFORM statement with the UNTIL option. For example,

```
PERFORM    READ-AND-PRINT
              UNTIL  LAST-CARD.
```

The statement represents a loop. The range of the PERFORM statement indicated by the paragraph name READ-AND-PRINT constitutes the body of the loop. The loop body is repetitively executed until the value of the condition name LAST-CARD is true. It may be noted that the general DOWHILE structure as shown in Fig. 12.1 is slightly different from the PERFORM... UNTIL statement. In the DOWHILE structure the loop is repeated so long as the condition is true whereas in the PERFORM... UNTIL statement the range is performed so long as the condition is false. However, this does not indicate any structural difference between the two and therefore PERFORM... UNTIL is taken as the COBOL representation of the DOWHILE structure. In a similar way the PERFORM statement with the TIMES option is another representation of the DOWHILE structure. Here the condition is implicitly determined.

The three control structures being readily available, there should not be any problem in coding proper programs in COBOL. It may be noted that the GO TO and ALTER (always associated to a GO TO statement) statements do not have any place in such programs.

12.4.2 Modular Programming in COBOL

A program may be composed of a hierarchy of PERFORMED modules. Such modules take the form of a paragraph, section or number of consecutive paragraphs or sections in the PROCEDURE DIVISION and whenever required a module is called by means of a simple PERFORM statement

A module can also be coded in the form of what is known as <u>subroutines</u>. A COBOL subroutine is almost like a COBOL program having all the four divisions, but it cannot be executed independently. A subroutine may be 'called' in the calling modules by means of a CALL statement. The subroutine feature and CALL statement will be discussed in a later chapter (Chapter 19). For the time being, we consider only the PERFORMED modules. The following is an example illustrating the coding of such modules.

Suppose, a module to be designed prints a line of information from a record of 132 characters defined in the working-storage section with the name DETAIL-NAME. The record name for the line printer file is PRINT-RECORD. Every time this line is printed the contents of the data name LINE-COUNT should be increased by 1. Before printing this line it should be checked whether the contents of LINE-COUNT is less than or equal to 35. If it exceeds 35, a heading line from the record area named HEADING should be printed after skipping to the next page and the LINE-COUNT should be initialized to zero. This, of course, should be followed by the printing of DETAIL-LINE and the increment of LINE-COUNT.

A detail line should be printed after advancing the page by 2 lines. It may also be assumed that the channel 1 of the line printer is given the

mnemonic name PAGE-TOP in the SPECIAL-NAMES paragraph. The desired module
can now be defined in the form of a paragraph named PRINT-A-LINE which is
shown below.

```
    PRINT-A-LINE.
        IF  LINE-COUNT  IS  GREATER  THAN  35
            PERFORM  PRINT-HEADING.
        PERFORM  PRINT-DETAIL-LINE.
```

This module, however, is not self-complete; rather it assumes the existence
of the modules named PRINT-HEADING and PRINT-DETAIL-LINE. These modules can
again be written in the form of paragraphs as shown below.

```
    PRINT-HEADING.
        WRITE  PRINT-REC  FROM  HEADING
                        AFTER  ADVANCING  PAGE-TOP.
        MOVE  ZERO  TO  LINE-COUNT.
    PRINT-DETAIL-LINE.
        WRITE  PRINT-REC  FROM  DETAIL-LINE
                AFTER  ADVANCING  2  LINES.
        ADD  1  TO  LINE-COUNT.
```

It may be noted from this example that all the three modules are coded
as proper programs. The module named PRINT-A-LINE makes use of the IFTHENELSE
and SEQUENCE structures while the other two use only the SEQUENCE structures.
Another point that deserves mention is that the module named PRINT-A-LINE is
at a level higher than those of the modules named PRINT-HEADING or PRINT-
DETAIL-LINE. PRINT-A-LINE makes a reference and calls for the execution of
these latter modules through the simple PERFORM statements. It may also be
noted that the top-down approach requires the coding of the PRINT-A-LINE to
be completed before the other two are coded. At the time of writing the
codes for PRINT-A-LINE, it is sufficient to make assumptions about the broad
functions of these modules. For example, while writing the statement PERFORM
PRINT-HEADING, we simply assume that this paragraph which is to be coded
subsequently, will take care of the heading printing and other associated
operations. What these associated operations are and how the desired functions of PRINT-HEADING are to be specified are points to be taken into
consideration only when this paragraph is coded.

12.4.3 Combination of Basic Structures

COBOL has a large number of statements that represent a combination of the
basic structures. The use of these statements in a proper program is recommended.

The PERFORM statement with the VARYING or VARYING and AFTER options is
an example of such a statement. A little attention will show that this
statement represents a combination of the SEQUENCE and DOWHILE structures.

A special class of these statements consists of statements like READ
with the AT END clause or ADD with the SIZE ERROR option. In general, these
statements provide for an escape in some implicitly-specified cases and
they represent a combination of the SEQUENCE and IFTHENELSE structures. An
interesting point about these statements is that the use of GO TO statement

appears to be convenient to take care of the escape in the exceptional condition. Since a proper program must not contain any GO TO, it is important to learn how to avoid it in such situations. The technique is explained below with the help of two examples.

Example 1

Consider the following COBOL code.

```
MAIN-MODULE.
        MOVE ZERO TO END-OF-FILE.
        PERFORM READ-AND-PROCESS
                 UNTIL END-OF-FILE = 1.
    .
    .
    .
READ-AND-PROCESS.
        READ CARD-FILE RECORD
                 AT END MOVE 1 TO END-OF-FILE.
        IF END-OF-FILE = 0
                 PERFORM PROCESS-A-CARD.
```

It is assumed here that END-OF-FILE is defined in the WORKING-STORAGE SECTION as shown below.

```
77     END-OF-FILE         PIC      9.
```

To understand the above code, let us find out how the repetitive execution of the paragraph READ-AND-PROCESS is terminated. The UNTIL option in the PERFORM statement indicates that the loop is terminated when, at the beginning of a repetitive execution of READ-AND-PROCESS, it is found that END-OF-FILE contains the value 1. This is why the data name END-OF-FILE has been initialized to zero and when the end of file (for the CARD-FILE) is detected, 1 is moved to END-OF-FILE. However, notice the importance of the IF statement after the READ statement in the READ-AND-PROCESS paragraph. Since the statement after AT END is a MOVE statement and not a GO TO, the control after the execution of the MOVE statement reaches the statement following the READ statement. Thus the statement that follows the READ statement is executed when a card has been successfully read as well as when the end of file has been detected and thereby no card has been read. The IF statement helps to avoid the execution of the statement PERFORM PROCESS-A-CARD in the latter case.

Example 2

A table is to be searched to locate elements that meet a certain condition. There can be more than one such elements in the table. Each time such an element is located, a paragraph named FOUND-THE-ELEMENT is to be performed. However, if no such element is found in the table the paragraph named NOT-FOUND is to be performed. The code for this problem without using the GO TO statement may be as follows:

```
      MOVE  ZERO  TO  MATCH-COUNT  END-OF-TABLE.
      SET  TABLE-INDEX  TO  1.
      PERFORM  SEARCH-THE-TABLE
                  UNTIL  END-OF-TABLE = 1.
      IF  MATCH-COUNT = 0
          PERFORM  NOT-FOUND.
      .
      .
      .


SEARCH-THE-TABLE.
      SEARCH  STOCK-VALUE
        AT END MOVE 1 TO
                    END-OF-TABLE
      WHEN  STOCK-QUOTATION IS EQUAL TO
              STOCK-VALUE (TABLE-INDEX)
          PERFORM FOUND-THE-ELEMENT
          SET TABLE-INDEX UP BY 1
          ADD 1 TO MATCH-COUNT.
```

The following working-storage entries are assumed for this code.

```
      77   MATCH-COUNT          PIC      99
      77   END-OF-TABLE         PIC      9.
      01   STOCK-TABLE.
            02  STOCK-VALUE      PIC      9(4)V99
                    OCCURS  20  TIMES  INDEXED
                                  BY  TABLE-INDEX.
```

It may be seen that the data item END-OF-TABLE and the statement PERFORM SEARCH-THE-TABLE, etc. are required only to avoid the GO TO statement. It may also be worthwhile to compare this example with Example 1 to discover that the techniques for avoiding GO TO in the two cases are identical.

Another point that deserves mention here is that condition names can be used in both the examples. In example 1, a condition name, say LAST-CARD, can be associated to the data name END-OF-FILE in the following manner.

```
      77   END-OF-FILE         PIC      9.
      88   LAST-CARD           VALUE    IS   1.
```

In this case, the conditions END-OF-FILE = 1 and END-OF-FILE = 0 can be replaced by the condition names LAST-CARD and NOT LAST-CARD respectively. Such use of condition names obviously increases the readability which is an important objective of structured programming.

12.4.4 A Complete Structured Program

To illustrate how to write complete structured programs, let us consider a problem. Suppose there was an objective test consisting of 50 questions. Each question was provided with 5 alternative answers and the candidates were asked to tick off the correct answer. From the answer paper of each of the candidates a card has been punched in the following manner.

Columns	Fields
1 - 5	Roll Number
6 - 30	Name
31 - 80	Answers

The answer to question number 1 is punched in column 31, that of question 2 is punched in column 32, and so on. For example, if the candidate has ticked off answer number 4 for question 5, 4 is punched in column 35. If the candidates does not answer a question, 0 is punched in the respective column. We assume that the deck of cards containing the answers has been properly checked and does not contain any error. (This can be done by obtaining a listing of the cards and then verifying them manually or with the help of a validation program written for the purpose.) It is now required to print a list of the candidates with the marks obtained by them. In order to evaluate the answers, let us assume that the first card of the deck is a model answer card. No roll number or name appears in it. The correct answers are given in columns 31 to 80 in the manner stated earlier. The actual answer cards follow this card in the deck. Marks should be given according to the following rule. A candidate is entitled to 2 marks for each correct answer and 1 for each unattempted question. No marks should be given for a wrong answer. Figure 12.3 shows a structured program for the job.

```
IDENTIFICATION DIVISION.
PROGRAM-ID. A COMPETE STRUCTURED PROGRAM.

ENVIRONMENT DIVISION.
CONFIGURATION SECTION.
SOURCE-COMPUTER. B-6700.
OBJECT-COMPUTER. B-6700.
SPECIAL-NAMES. CHANNEL 1 IS TOP-OF-PAGE.
INPUT-OUTPUT SECTION.
FILE-CONTROL.
    SELECT ANSWER-FILE ASSIGN TO READER.
    SELECT OUTPUT-FILE ASSIGN TO PRINTER.

DATA DIVISION.
FILE SECTION.
FD ANSWER-FILE.
01  ANSWER-RECORD.
    02  ROLL-NO            PIC 9(5).
    02  NAME               PIC X(25).
    02  THE-ANSWERS.
        03   ANSWER   PIC 9 OCCURS 50 TIMES.

FD  OUTPUT-FILE.
01  OUTPUT-RECORD     PIC X(132).
```

(contd.)

```
WORKING-STORAGE SECTION.
77  LINE-COUNT             PIC 99 VALUE IS ZERO.
77  ANSWER-COUNT           PIC 99.
77  MARKS                  PIC 9(3).
77  END-OF-ANSWER          PIC X(3) VALUE IS "NO".
88  NO-MORE-ANSWER-CARD  VALUE IS "YES".
88  THERE-IS-ANSWER-CARD VALUE IS "NO".

01  THE-MODEL-ANSWERS.
    02  MODEL-ANSWER       PIC 9 OCCURS 50 TIMES.
01  HEADING-RECORD.
    02  FILLER             PIC X(10) VALUE SPACES.
    02  FILLER             PIC X(7)  VALUE "ROLL NO".
    02  FILLER             PIC X(25) VALUE SPACES.
    02  FILLER             PIC X(4)  VALUE "NAME".
    02  FILLER             PIC X(21) VALUE SPACES.
    02  FILLER             PIC X(5)  VALUE "MARKS".
    02  FILLER             PIC X(60) VALUE SPACES.

01  MARKS-RECORD.
    02  FILLER             PIC X(11) VALUE SPACES.
    02  ROLL-NO            PIC Z(5).
    02  FILLER             PIC X(16) VALUE SPACES.
    02  NAME               PIC X(25).
    02  FILLER             PIC X(12) VALUE SPACES.
    02  TOTAL-MARKS        PIC ZZ9.
    02  FILLER             PIC X(60) VALUE SPACES.

PROCEDURE DIVISION.
MAIN-LINE-PROGRAM.
    PERFORM GET-READY.
    PERFORM READ-AND-PROCESS-ANSWERS
            UNTIL NO-MORE-ANSWER-CARD.
    PERFORM PACK-UP.
    STOP RUN.

GET-READY.
    OPEN INPUT ANSWER-FILE
         OUTPUT OUTPUT-FILE.
    READ ANSWER-FILE RECORD
                AT END DISPLAY "NO CARDS" STOP RUN.
    MOVE THE-ANSWERS TO THE-MODEL-ANSWERS.
    PERFORM PRINT-THE-HEADING.
READ-AND-PROCESS-ANSWERS.
    READ ANSWER-FILE RECORD
                AT END MOVE "YES" TO END-OF-ANSWER.
    IF THERE-IS-ANSWER-CARD
                PERFORM EVALUATE-ANSWER-AND-PRINT.
```

(contd.)

```
EVALUATE-ANSWER-AND-PRINT.
    MOVE ZERO TO MARKS.
    PERFORM CHECK-EACH-ANSWER
                        VARYING ANSWER-COUNT FROM 1 BY 1
                    UNTIL ANSWER-COUNT IS GREATER THAN 50.
    PERFORM PRINT-MARKS-RECORD.

CHECK-EACH-ANSWER.
    IF ANSWER (ANSWER-COUNT) = MODEL-ANSWER (ANSWER-COUNT)
            ADD 2 TO MARKS
    ELSE IF ANSWER (ANSWER-COUNT) = ZERO ADD 1 TO MARKS
PRINT-MARKS-RECORD.
    IF LINE-COUNT IS GREATER THAN 35
                PERFORM PRINT-THE-HEADING.
    MOVE CORRESPONDING ANSWER-RECORD TO MARKS-RECORD.
    MOVE MARKS TO TOTAL-MARKS.
    WRITE OUTPUT-RECORD FROM MARKS-RECORD
        AFTER ADVANCING 2 LINES.
    ADD 1 TO LINE-COUNT.
PRINT-THE-HEADING.
    WRITE OUTPUT-RECORD FROM HEADING-RECORD
                AFTER ADVANCING TOP-OF-PAGE
                MOVE ZERO TO LINE-COUNT.

PACK-UP.
    CLOSE ANSWER-FILE  OUTPUT-FILE.
```

FIG. 12.3. A Complete Structured Program

The paragraph named MAIN-LINE-PROGRAM is the main module. The paragraphs GET-READY, READ-AND-PROCESS and PACK-UP are its subordinate modules. It is important to note that the main module should end with the STOP RUN statement.

12.5 WEAKNESSES OF COBOL AS A LANGUAGE FOR STRUCTURED PROGRAMMING

The merits of COBOL as a language for structured programming have been discussed in the previous section. Now, some of the weaknesses of this language will be pointed out. In order to be able to develop structured COBOL programs, it is extremely necessary to know about these weaknesses.

The first point in this respect is that the DOWHILE structure is not perfectly represented by the PERFORM with the UNTIL option. The section of the code (range of PERFORM) that is to be repeated by the PERFORM statement cannot be included within the statement itself, it has to be placed ''out-of-line''. Consider Example 2 of the previous section. The statements in the paragraph named SEARCH-THE-TABLE must appear physically at a different position from the PERFORM statement that repetitively executes these statements. Placing them immediately after the PERFORM statement would mean that these statements would be executed for an extra time and therefore cannot be done without making the code obscure Thus we find that each use of the DOWHILE structure, in COBOL, generates some out-of-line codes. The main objection against out-of-line codes is that when a human reader reaches a PERFORM statement in the process of his understanding the program, he should transfer his attention to the codes placed out-of-line. This allegation against PERFORM is similar to the allegation against the GO TO statement. However, there is a difference between PERFORM and GO TO statements. If the out-of-line range of the PERFORM statement has only one entry and one exit, it is ensured that the control after the execution of the PERFORM statement must reach the statement immediately following it. Thus, it may not be absolutely necessary for the human reader to transfer his attention to the out-of-line PERFORM range immediately. Instead, he can treat the code as a lower level module and continue the reading of the statements in-line with the PERFORM statement. Attention to the details of the coding in the PERFORM range can be given afterwards. Thus, the out-of-line coding requirement is not wholly in conflict with the principles of structured programming. What is unfortunate, in the matter, is that the number of modules in the program gets increased. Moreover, the design of modules is not always dictated by the requirements of the problem, it is also prompted by the requirements of the COBOL language. The implications of this drawback can be easily understood if we consider Example 2 of the previous section once again. The problem in this example is to search a table for elements satisfying certain condition. Every time an element is found to meet the condition, the paragraph FOUND-THE-ELEMENT is to be performed. On the other hand, if no such element can be located, the paragraph NOT-FOUND is to be performed. Thus, from the context of the problem, the search process should be decomposed into the two modules, namely, FOUND-THE-ELEMENT and NOT-FOUND and they must accordingly be modules of same level. An examination of the COBOL code for this problem will reveal that this has not been maintained.

Another weakness of COBOL is that there is no special terminator for the IF statements. Consequently, it becomes difficult to identify the scope of an IF statement within a nested IF sentence. Moreover, unless an IF statement within a nesting is terminated by an ELSE of the next inclusive IF statement, all IF statements in the nesting are terminated by the final terminating period. This causes some difficulty while writing proper programs. To illustrate this weakness let us consider the following example.

Example 1

Suppose we wish to code the flow chart of Fig. 12.4 in the form of a module. The flow chart uses only the basic control structures namely, IFTHENELSE and SEQUENCE. Therefore, there should not be apparently any difficulty in writing the COBOL code for this. However, an attempt in this respect will immediately reveal that the flow chart cannot be faithfully coded in COBOL. The most reasonable code for this flow chart is as follows. We assume the name TEST-MODULE for the said module.

```
TEST-MODULE.
    IF  A = B  PERFORM PARA-EQUAL
            ELSE PERFORM IF-UNEQUAL.
IF-UNEQUAL.
    IF  A > B
            PERFORM PARA-HIGH
    ELSE PERFORM PARA-LOW.
    PERFORM PARA-UNEQUAL.
```

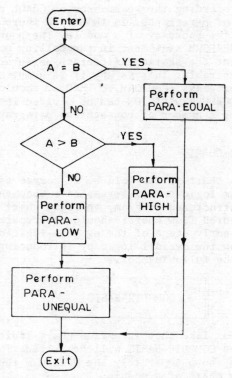

FIG. 12.4. A Flow Chart to be Coded as Proper Program

It may be seen that an extra module IF-UNEQUAL has been used. The need of
this module will be clear if we try to replace the PERFORM IF-UNEQUAL state-
ment by the statements in the IF-UNEQUAL paragraph. In that case the PARA-
UNEQUAL is performed always regardless of whether A is equal to B or not.
The problem can, however, be solved without introducing an extra module.
The best solution in that case would perhaps be as follows:

```
TEST-MODULE.
    IF  A = B  PERFORM  PARA-EQUAL
    ELSE  IF  A > B
                PERFORM PARA-HIGH
                PERFORM PARA-UNEQUAL
            ELSE
                PERFORM PARA-LOW
                PERFORM PARA-UNEQUAL
```

Obviously, the flow chart corresponding to this code is not the one shown
here. It must undergo a modification, although functionally the modified
flow chart and the given one are identical. It will be instructive to try
to understand that the cause of this difficulty is the practice in COBOL to
terminate all the otherwise unterminated IF statements (not terminated by
ELSE's) in a nesting by a single terminating period.

The third point regarding the weaknesses of COBOL arises when modules are coded as a range of paragraphs. In this case there is no facility in the language to indicate the boundary of a module. The boundary can only be determined from the PERFORM statement in the calling module. Moreover, the language cannot prevent the sharing of certain paragraphs by two or more modules which is undesirable. This is why it is sometimes recommended that in structured COBOL programs, PERFORM... THRU... should not be used. In this respect, the PROCEDURE DIVISION can be divided into a number of sections and a module requiring a number of consecutive paragraphs can be coded in the form of a section.

12.6   STRUCTURED FLOW CHARTS

The purpose of a flow chart is two-fold — it serves as an aid towards the development of program logic and it serves as a documentation aid. When the aim is to develop a structured program, the flow chart should also reflect it. Therefore, structured flow charts should be prepared in a top-down manner. Thus, at the early stage of the program-logic development, the flow chart should only show the overall logic by introducing modules. For this purpose we will use the following box.

COMPUTE-BASIC

The appearance of a box like this in a flow chart indicates that at this point the module named COMPUTE-BASIC will be called. The flow chart of the said module should be shown separately. We will use the following convention to draw the flow chart of a module.

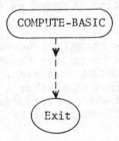

These additional boxes are enough to draw flow charts with modules in them. In addition to these, the interdependencies among the various modules can be shown by means of a module-dependencies diagram. A module-dependencies diagram is what has been shown in Fig. 12.2. Such a diagram very clearly reveals the hierarchical structure of the modules.

In order that the flow chart of any module can be easily implemented in the form of a proper program, the following recommendations are to be observed during flowcharting.

(i)   The flow chart for each module should have only one entry and one exit.

(ii) The flow chart should utilize only the SEQUENCE, IFTHENELSE and DOWHILE structures.

EXERCISES

1. For each of the following statements, indicate whether it is fully correct, partially correct or incorrect.
   (a) Less effort is required to code the DATA DIVISION as structured programming requires lesser data names to be defined.
   (b) Less effort is required to debug a structured program.
   (c) Less effort is required to modify a structured program.
   (d) Structured programming influences the coding of the PROCEDURE DIVISION rather than that of the DATA DIVISION.
   (e) If structured programming is used, the compiler generates a more efficient code.
   (f) The use of a GO TO statement is not desirable in a structured program.

2. Rewrite the following statements without using any GO TO.

```
        MOVE  50  TO  I.
P1.  IF  MY-TABLE (I)  IS  EQUAL  TO  250
           GO  TO  P2.
        SUBTRACT  1  FROM  I.
        IF  I  NOT  <  1  GO  TO  P1.
        MOVE  51  TO  IND.
        GO  TO  P3.
P2.  MOVE  I  TO  IND.
P3.
```

3. Convert the following into a ''gotoless'' code.

```
        READ-PARA.
           READ  A-FILE  RECORD
              AT  END  MOVE  HIGH-VALUES  TO  A-KEY
                     GO  TO  EXIT-PARA.
           IF  A-CODE  IS  EQUAL  TO  ZERO
                 GO  TO  READ-PARA.
        EXIT-PARA.  EXIT.
```

4. Suppose the values of the data names DAY and MONTH together represent a date. The value of DAY is the date of the month and the value of MONTH is a value between 1 and 12 where 1 stands for January, 2 for February, and so on. It is required to convert this date to a Julian date. A Julian date is a 3-digit date representing the number of days counted from the first of January. For example, the Julian date for 15th February is 46. Write a COBOL module (in the form of a proper program) that converts a given date (specified as the values of DAY and MONTH) to the Julian date and stores it in the data name JULIAN. The additional DATA DIVISION entries that may be required for the said module should be shown separately. Assume 28 days for February.

5. Suppose that the following restriction is placed on the use of STOP RUN statement. A STOP RUN statement can be used only as the last physical

statement in a program and the paragraph in which this STOP RUN statement appears cannot be executed through a PERFORM statement. Is it possible to write any structured COBOL program with the said restricted use of the STOP RUN statement?

6. Consider the problem discussed in Sec. 12.4.4. Write a structured program to print a list of the candidates in the descending order of the marks obtained by them. Where two or more candidates score the same marks, their name may appear in any order among themselves. Assume that the number of candidates is not more than 500.

   (Hint: Read a card, determine the marks obtained by the candidate and then store the name and marks in a table. When all the cards have been processed, sort the table by using the methods given in Sec. 11.9. Print the report from the table.)

13

SEQUENTIAL FILES

In respect of the file-handling capabilities of COBOL, so far our attention has been confined only to the files on card readers and line printers. We have now reached a stage when the magnetic-tape and magnetic-disk files can also be taken into consideration.

A data file is normally created on a tape or disk for the subsequent reading of the file either in the same program or in some other programs. Thus, sometimes, a tape file or disk file is an output file, and at other times, the same file is an input file. It may be noted that this is not true for card reader or line printer files. For example, a report file on a line printer is always an output file.

The objective in this chapter is to explain how to create and read a tape or disk file. However, for the time being, only the sequential files will be taken into consideration. A sequential file, as we already know, is a file whose records can be accessed in the order of their appearance in the file. This logic of accessing the records in a sequential manner is independent of the medium used to store a sequential file.

A magnetic tape file, such as a card or printer file, can only have a sequential organization. A disk file, on the other hand, can have different organizations including the sequential one. Disk files with organizations other than sequential, will be taken up later.

The COBOL features described here are applicable to tape files or disk files with sequential organization. However, as we proceed, we shall see that some of these features are also optionally available for card or printer files. In addition to all these, some features for line printer files are also discussed in this chapter as these were not introduced earlier.

13.1 FILE CHARACTERISTICS

The task of file handling is the responsibility of the system software known as IOCS (Input-Output Control System). Through the COBOL features, the programmer should only specify the various file characteristics or attributes to enable the IOCS to handle the file effectively. Therefore, before we go into the details of the COBOL features for file handling, we shall present a general discussion on the various file characteristics.

Record Size

We know that the records of a card file must consist of 80 characters and those for a file on the printer should consist of 132 characters (this can

vary with the model and make of the printer). The size of the records in a
tape or disk file, on the other hand, may be chosen by the programmer.
While preparing the record layout (see Sec. 2.2), the programmer should fix
suitable sizes for the individual fields in the record. The total of these
sizes is the record size. Although any suitable size can be fixed for the
records in a tape or disk file, the choice is subject to certain limitations
imposed by the computer system and its IOCS. To give an idea, typical limitations may be such that no record should exceed 2048 characters in length or
no record should be less than 2 characters in length.

A sequential tape or disk file can contain either fixed or variable-
length records. In most applications fixed-length records are used. However,
in certain cases it is required that records of different lengths should be
stored onto the file. In the case of such variable-length records the IOCS
normally stores the length of each record along with the data in the record.
Usually, the first four characters of a variable-length record represents
the length. Since the record size is not fixed, the maximum and minimum
record sizes are considered as the file attribute in this case.

Block Size

While handling a tape or disk file, normally a single record is not read or
written. Instead, the usual practice is to group a number of consecutive
records to form what is known as a block or physical record. For example, a
block can consist of 10 records. This means that the first 10 consecutive
records will form the first block of the file, the next 10 consecutive
records will form the second block of the file, and so on. The number of
records in a block is often called "blocking factor".

The actual handling of blocks is transparent to the programmer. The IOCS
takes care of the blocking. The programmer should only specify the number of
records that should be contained in a block. When a file is blocked, a physical read or write operation on the file is only applicable to the entire
block and not to the individual records in the block. However, the programmer
would like to read or write only one record at a time. This requirement of
the programmer is fulfilled by the IOCS in the following manner. The IOCS
reserves a memory space equal to the size of a block of the file. This memory
space is known as the buffer. When the programmer wants to read the first
record from the file, the IOCS reads the first block into the buffer but
releases only the first record to the program. The next time the programmer
wants to read a record, IOCS releases the second record from the buffer. In
this way only when all the records in the block has been released to the
program and the programmer wants to read the next record, the IOCS reads
another block. In this respect the function of the IOCS in the case of writing on a file is just the reverse of reading. However, it is important to
note that every read or write statement does not require the physical reading or writing of the file. Thus the read/write statements in the program
are logical operations; the physical reading or writing is done by the IOCS
at the block level. The records as defined in the program are sometimes
called logical records and the blocks which are records as stored on the
file medium are called physical records.

The advantage of blocking is two-fold. Firstly, blocking results
in saving in terms of input-output time required to handle a file.
For example, the aggregate of the time required to read ten
short records is much more than the time required to read a single record

which is ten times longer. The other advantage of blocking is that a substantial amount of storage space on the tape or disk can be saved. We know that in the case of tape files, an inter-record gap is generated between any two consecutive records. The total space occupied by these inter-record gaps is quite substantial. Blocking helps to get the number of such gaps reduced thereby decreasing the wastage of storage space on account of these gaps. In the case of disk files, the recording is done in terms of sectors. This means that if the record size is smaller than the sector size, the remaining space in the sector cannot be utilized for any useful purpose. Thus, for every record we stand to loose some amount of storage space in every sector. Even when a record is longer than the sector, the situation is no better. The sector that contains the last part of the record may not be full. Blocking in the case of disk files helps to reduce this wastage. It may be noted that the wastage can be completely eliminated if the block size is a multiple of the sector size.

Quite often, a programmer is faced with the problem of determining a suitable block size. In this respect it is suggested that the programmer should take into consideration the trade-offs. Having too large a block size would require a large buffer to be set up by the IOCS in the main memory of the computer. Having too small a block size would diminish the gains of blocking. Therefore, depending on the memory space available in the computer system and the number of files to be handled by the program, one must choose as large a block size as possible.

Files with fixed-length records have been implicitly assumed in the above discussion. However, blocking can also be used in the case of files with variable-length records. The difference in this case is that though a block still contains an integral number of logical records, the same number of records may not be present in every block. Most IOCS's require that the programmer should specify only the maximum block size and an IOCS tries to put as many records as may be accommodated in the block.

It may be noted that in most cases the size of the final block of the file will be shorter than the specified block size. This final block is often called a short block. The special treatment necessary for the short block is taken care of by the IOCS.

Buffers

Modern computers are capable of handling I-O operations independent of the CPU by means of the hardware known as data channel. This enables the overlapping of I-O operations with other CPU operations. To take advantage of the situation, the IOCS normally requires more than one buffer for a file. For example, if two buffers are allocated for an input file, the IOCS can fill-in one buffer while the program processes the records already read and available in another buffer.

The programmer may specify the number of buffers that the IOCS should use. While more overlapping is possible with more buffers, experience shows that the allocation of two buffers is very effective in most cases. However, sometimes the programmer may specify only one buffer for some of the files. This is when the block size is large and sufficient memory space is not available.

Label Records/Disk Directory

The blocks constituting a tape file is usually preceded and followed by records known as the header and trailer labels respectively. The header label normally contains information that helps the IOCS to identify the correct file. The most important of the information stored in the header label is what is known as the <u>file title</u>. The file title is the name assigned to the file and is used for the purpose of its identification. It may be noted that the file title is different from the file name used in a COBOL program. Within the boundary of the program, the file is referred to by the file name and not by its title. The title is the physical name that is used only by the IOCS to assign the correct file to the program. Thus the same file may be accessed in different programs, each using a different file name. However, all programs must specify the same title. We know how to specify the file name. The way to specify the file title in a COBOL program will be discussed later on. Besides the file title, the header label contains such information as the block size, record size, date of creation, etc. The trailer label usually contains the counts for the records and blocks in the file. These counts are stored by the IOCS during file creation and are verified during subsequent reading.

Normally, tape files should be created with standard header and trailer labels. However, the format of these labels can be different for different computers. Thus, when a file created on one computer is to be read on another computer, the files are normally created without the header and trailer labels. Such files are called <u>unlabelled files</u>.

In the case of magnetic-disk files the labels usually do not exist (there are many exceptions). Since, more than one file is stored on a disk pack, the IOCS also maintains a <u>disk directory</u> for all the files. This directory usually contains one entry for each of the files on the disk pack. The entry consists of the file title and the address of the starting sector. In some systems it also includes other header information, such as record size, block size, date of creation, etc. The concept of unlabelled files is meaningless when the medium is a disk.

Normally, two files with the same title cannot be retained on a disk pack. If a new file having a title identical with that of an existing file is created, the existing file is removed from the disk pack. In order to avoid this, in some systems, the concept of the <u>generation number</u> is used. This enables the user to have two files with the same title but different generation numbers.

13.2 FILE-CONTROL ENTRIES FOR SEQUENTIAL FILES

The characteristics of each of the files handled in a program are specified in the ENVIRONMENT DIVISION and DATA DIVISION. Those characteristics that depend primarily on the input-output device and the computer system are described in the ENVIRONMENT DIVISION, while characteristics that are of a general nature are described in the DATA DIVISION.

Most of the characteristics to be specified in the ENVIRONMENT DIVISION are described by means of the clauses in the SELECT entry of the FILE-CONTROL paragraph. The remaining specifications are placed in the I-O-CONTROL paragraph. The I-O-CONTROL paragraph is optional and the entries of this paragraph will be taken up for discussion subsequently. The general syntax of the SELECT entry for sequential files is as follows:

SELECT   [OPTIONAL]   file-name   ASSIGN TO hardware-name

[; RESERVE   integer-1 $\left\{ \begin{array}{l} AREA \\ AREAS \end{array} \right\}$]

[; ORGANIZATION IS SEQUENTIAL]

[; ACCESS MODE IS SEQUENTIAL]

[; FILE STATUS IS data-name-1]

We are already familiar with the simple form of this clause. It is known that there must be one SELECT entry for each file. The meanings of the OPTIONAL phrase and ASSIGN clause were discussed earlier (see Sec. 4.2.2.1). In this book the words TAPE and DISK will be used to specify the hardware names for the tape and disk files respectively. The remaining clauses are described below.

RESERVE Clause

This clause specifies the number of buffers to be used for the file. Integer-1 indicates this number. Thus, RESERVE 1 AREA means that only one buffer is to be used. The syntax of this clause can vary depending on the implementation. (See implementation differences for examples of such variations.) However, the clause is optional and, if it is not specified, two buffers are assumed in all systems.

ORGANIZATION/ACCESS Clauses

These two clauses indicate that the said file is organized as a sequential file and will be accessed sequentially. Both the clauses are optional and if omitted, sequential organization and sequential access mode is assumed. Therefore, for a sequential file, these clauses may only be used for documentation. These clauses are really important when direct-access files are used (see Chapter 15).

FILE STATUS Clause

This clause has been included in the above syntax for completeness. The meaning and use of this clause will be discussed later in this chapter (see Sec. 13.10).

The RESERVE, ORGANIZATION, ACCESS and STATUS clauses can be specified in any order. The clauses may be written starting from the B margin or any position after it.

13.3 FILE DESCRIPTION — FIXED-LENGTH RECORDS

The general characteristics of a file are described in the file description (FD) entry of the DATA DIVISION. The various clauses in the FD entry specify the said characteristics. For simplicity, only files with fixed-length records will be assumed in the beginning. The syntax of the FD entry for a tape or disk file with fixed-length records is as follows:

FD   file-name

$$
\left[\ ;\ \underline{\text{BLOCK}}\ \text{CONTAINS}\ \text{integer-1}\ \left\{ \begin{array}{l} \underline{\text{RECORDS}} \\ \text{CHARACTERS} \end{array} \right\} \right]
$$

$$
\left[\ ;\ \underline{\text{RECORD}}\ \text{CONTAINS}\ \text{integer-2}\ \ \text{CHARACTERS} \right]
$$

$$
\left[\ ;\ \underline{\text{LABEL}}\ \left\{ \begin{array}{l} \underline{\text{RECORD}}\ \ \text{IS} \\ \underline{\text{RECORDS}}\ \ \text{ARE} \end{array} \right\} \left\{ \begin{array}{l} \underline{\text{STANDARD}} \\ \underline{\text{OMITTED}} \end{array} \right\} \right]
$$

$$
\left[\ ;\ \underline{\text{VALUE}}\ \underline{\text{OF}}\ \text{implementor-name-1}\ \ \ \text{IS}\ \left\{ \begin{array}{l} \text{data-name-1} \\ \text{literal-1} \end{array} \right\} \right.
$$

$$
\left. \left[\ ,\ \text{implementor-name-2}\ \ \text{IS}\ \left\{ \begin{array}{l} \text{data-name-2} \\ \text{literal-2} \end{array} \right\} \right] \dots \right]
$$

$$
\left[\ ;\ \underline{\text{DATA}}\ \left\{ \begin{array}{l} \underline{\text{RECORD}}\ \ \text{IS} \\ \underline{\text{RECORDS}}\ \ \text{ARE} \end{array} \right\}\ \text{data-name-3}\ \left[\ ,\ \text{data-name-4} \right]\ \dots \right]
$$

$$
\left[\ ;\ \underline{\text{CODE-SET}}\ \text{is alphabet-name} \right]\ .
$$

We are already familiar with the FD indicator and the file-name part of this entry. The clauses are all optional and, if used, these can appear in any order. The clauses can be written starting from the B margin or any position after it. The meaning and use of each of these clauses are given below.

Before we go into the details of these clauses, let us note that the FD entry must be followed by one or more record description entries. There is nothing special about the record-description entries. The records are to be described in the usual manner.

13.3.1 BLOCK CONTAINS Clause

Integer-1 of the BLOCK CONTAINS clause specifies the block size either in terms of records or in terms of characters. For example, BLOCK CONTAINS 50 RECORDS means that there are 50 records in the block. If each of the record contains 150 characters, the said clause can as well be written as BLOCK CONTAINS 7500 CHARACTERS. When the block size is specified in CHARACTERS, care should be taken to ensure that the block size is a multiple of the record size. If the BLOCK CONTAINS clause is not used, one record per block is assumed.

13.3.2 RECORD CONTAINS Clause

This clause specifies the record size. Integer-2 specifies the number of characters in a record. Thus RECORD CONTAINS 65 CHARACTERS means that each record of this file consists of 65 characters. It may be noted that the record is described completely in the record-description entries that follow the FD entry. The compiler determines the size of the record from these descriptions. The RECORD CONTAINS clause is used for documentary purposes only. However, when used, care must be taken to ensure that the clause does not specify a record size contradictory to what can be determined from the record-description entries.

13.3.3 LABEL RECORD Clause

This clause specifies whether or not the standard header and trailer labels should be present in the magnetic-tape files. The word STANDARD indicates that the file should have standard header and trailer labels, while the word OMITTED specifies that the file is unlabelled. It may also be noted that the clause LABEL RECORDS ARE OMITTED provides the facility of reading the header and trailer labels as data records. One must, however, know the formats of these labels in that case.

The LABEL RECORD clause for disk files should be specified with the STANDARD option while in the case of card reader and printer files, the clause should use the OMITTED option. According to ANSI 74 standard, the clause must appear in the FD entry for any file. However, many compilers treat this clause as optional and if it is not specified STANDARD is assumed.

13.3.4 VALUE OF Clause

The VALUE OF clause is entirely implementation-dependent. In most compilers this clause is used to specify the file title. The clause in such cases has the form

```
VALUE OF { ID             } IS { data-name }
         { IDENTIFICATION }    { literal   }
```

Normally, every computer system uses certain conventions for the file title. As an example of a typical case, let us assume that the file title consists of 10 characters. The data name or literal specifies the title. If more than 10 characters are specified, only the first 10 characters are used and if less than 10 characters are specified, additional character positions on the right are space-filled. The following are examples of the VALUE OF clause.

```
VALUE    OF    IDENTIFICATION    IS    "FILEA"
VALUE    OF    ID    MY-FILE
```

In the first case, the actual file title that will be used is FILEA bbbbb. In the second case the value of the data name MY-FILE will be used as the title. For example, if MY-FILE is described as X(12) and contains the value PAYROLL-FILE at the time when the file is opened, the first 10 characters, namely, PAYROLL-FI will be used as a file title.

The abovementioned convention will be followed for the examples in this book.

Besides the title, the VALUE OF clause can also describe certain other items in the label records/disk directory associated with a file. Since these are implementation-dependent features no general discussion is possible. We shall, therefore, assume typical specifications which may vary with the implementation. A typical VALUE OF clause may be

$$\text{VALUE} \quad \text{OF} \quad \left\{ \begin{array}{l} \underline{\text{ID}} \\ \underline{\text{IDENTIFICATION}} \end{array} \right\} \quad \text{IS} \quad \left\{ \begin{array}{l} \text{data-name-1} \\ \text{literal-1} \end{array} \right\}$$

$$\left[\begin{array}{l} \underline{\text{SAVE-FACTOR}} \quad \text{IS} \quad \left\{ \begin{array}{l} \text{data-name-2} \\ \text{integer-1} \end{array} \right\} \end{array} \right]$$

The implementor name SAVE-FACTOR indicates the specification of the number of days for which an output file is to be saved. The number of days is actually specified by integer-1 or data-name-2. If the data-name option is used, the value of the data name when the file is opened is taken for the save factor. The save factor is stored in the tape label/disk directory entry for the said file. If required, before destroying a file, it may be checked whether the expiration date is over or not. (This is usually done with the help of system-utility routines.) However, the save factor does not provide any protection against the deliberate destruction of the file.

The VALUE OF clause should not be specified for unlabelled files.

13.3.5 DATA RECORD Clause

This clause documents the record names defined for the file. For example, DATA RECORDS ARE REC-1, REC-2, REC-3 means that there are three different record descriptions following the FD entry in which this DATA RECORDS clause is used. The record names used in these descriptions are REC-1, REC-2 and REC-3. The order of these names are not important. However, there should not be any conflict between the record names and their numbers specified in the DATA RECORDS clause and those determined from the record descriptions. The purpose of this clause is to provide for better documentation.

13.3.6 CODE-SET Clause

The CODE-SET clause is used to describe the code in which the data is recorded on the external medium. When the CODE-SET clause is specified, all the elementary items of the record must be explicitly or implicitly defined with the clause USAGE IS DISPLAY; signed items must be defined with the SIGN clause with the SEPARATE CHARACTER phrase. In case the external and internal codes are different, data translation takes place during the input-output operation.

The alphabet name must be specified in the SPECIAL-NAMES paragraph. The format is as follows:

alphabet-name   IS   implementor-name

The alphabet name is a user-defined word constructed in the same way as that of a data name. The implementor name is the name through which the external code can be identified in a particular compiler. The ANSI standard also specifies two key-words in place of the implementor name. These are STANDARD-1 and NATIVE. The key-word STANDARD-1 refers to the ASCII code and the key-word NATIVE refers to the native character set or the character set of the collat-ing sequence of the computer on which the program is compiled. In this text, we will assume the EBCDIC code for NATIVE. The ANSI standard has another format for the alphabet-name entry which is omitted here.

The following is an example of the use of the CODE-SET clause.

```
SPECIAL-NAMES.
        EXTERNAL-ALPHABET  IS  STANDARD-1.
FILE-CONTROL.  SELECT DATA-FILE ASSIGN TO TAPE.

FD DATA-FILE
      BLOCK CONTAINS 10 RECORDS
      LABEL RECORDS ARE OMITTED
      CODE-SET IS EXTERNAL-ALPHABET.

01  DATA-RECORD.
```

The above clauses suggest that the data is recorded on the unlabelled, magnetic-tape file in the ASCII code. At the time of reading the records, ASCII data will be translated into the internal code as specified in the record description (implicitly or explicitly by the USAGE clauses). If the CODE-SET clause is omitted, no translation takes place and the data on the external medium is assumed to be in the internal code.

The CODE-SET clause is usually used for reading magnetic-tape files created on the other computer systems which can perhaps record data on files in a specific code only. Similarly, the clause can also be used for creating a file to be read on a different system using a different code.

The CODE-SET clause is used to meet the requirements mentioned above. The said clause is an ANSI 74 feature and may not be available in some systems. However, in most systems the facility for code conversion is available, but only through special clauses used for the purpose.

13.3.7 Nonstandard Clauses

The different clauses described above are as per the ANSI standard. Most compilers also provide for additional nonstandard clauses to meet the specific requirements of the corresponding computer. The programmer should, therefore, consult the appropriate manual for descriptions of these clauses. However, examples of such nonstandard clauses are given in the implementation differences at the end of this chapter.

13.3.8 Examples of File-description Entries

Example 1

```
FD   FILE - A
     RECORD  CONTAINS  130  CHARACTERS
     BLOCK  CONTAINS  20  RECORDS
     DATA  RECORD  IS  FIRST-RECORD
     LABEL  RECORDS  ARE  STANDARD
     VALUE  OF  ID  IS  "MY-FILE".

01   FIRST-RECORD        PIC   X(130).
```

It may be noted that LABEL RECORD, RECORD CONTAINS and DATA RECORD clauses does not have any significant effect. This is because the STANDARD option is the default of the LABEL RECORD clause. RECORD CONTAINS and DATA RECORDS are for documentation only. The BLOCK CONTAINS clause specifies that 20 records per block should be used for the purpose of blocking. The title of the file is MY-FILE. If the file is an input file, this title will be used to identify the file. On the other hand, if the file is an output file, the title will be inserted in the label records/disk directory.

Example 2

```
FD   WORK-FILE   VALUE   OF   IDENTIFICATION
          IS    FILE-TITLE.

01   WORK-REC.
     02    A          PIC    X(15).
     02    B          PIC    9(7)V99.
     02    C          PIC    X(20).
     02    D          PIC    9(10).
```

The title of the file will be taken to be the value of the data name FILE-TITLE at the time the file is opened. The record size is 54 characters and the block size is also 54 characters since the BLOCK CONTAINS clause has not been specified.

13.4   STATEMENTS FOR SEQUENTIAL FILES

Basic operations on a file involve the reading and writing of its records. When the file is sequential, there are three verbs for the purpose. These are READ, WRITE and REWRITE. In addition, there are the OPEN and CLOSE verbs. We are already familiar with the functions of all these verbs except that of REWRITE. The REWRITE verb is a special form of the WRITE verb and is only applicable to the disk files.

The forms of these verbs as applicable to the sequential tape and disk files are discussed below. The READ statement, as already described for the card-reader files,is also valid for any sequential file regardless of the medium used. Consequently, the READ statement is not considered here for discussion. It may also be noted that only the simple forms of the OPEN and CLOSE verbs are described below. The other forms will be gradually introduced in this chapter.

13.4.1 OPEN Statement

We know that the processing of a file should begin with the execution of an
OPEN statement. A file can be opened in any one of the four open modes —
INPUT, OUTPUT, EXTEND and I-O.

When a file is opened in the INPUT mode, it becomes an input file. There
must be an existing file (unless the OPTIONAL phrase in the SELECT clause is
used) available on the specified medium. The records can be read sequentially
through subsequent executions of READ statements on the file.

When a file should be created for the first time, it must be opened in
the OUTPUT mode. Records can be placed onto the file through subsequent
executions of the WRITE statements. The EXTEND mode also opens a file for
output, but the file is positioned following the last record on the existing
file. The subsequent execution of the WRITE statements on the file add more
records to it. The EXTEND mode is useful when an existing file should be
appended by adding new records at its end.

While all the above three modes are valid for both tape as well as disk
files, the I-O mode is only available for disk files. When a file is opened
in the I-O mode, records can be read through the READ statements and can be
written on the file through the REWRITE statement. The WRITE statement cannot be used for files opened in the I-O mode.

The following is the syntax (simplified) of the OPEN statement.

$$\underline{\text{OPEN}} \quad \left\{ \begin{array}{l} \text{INPUT} \\ \underline{\text{OUTPUT}} \\ \underline{\text{EXTEND}} \\ \underline{\text{I-O}} \end{array} \right\} \quad \text{file-name-1} \quad \left[\, , \text{ file-name-2} \, \right] \quad \dots$$

$$\left[\left\{ \begin{array}{l} \text{INPUT} \\ \underline{\text{OUTPUT}} \\ \underline{\text{EXTEND}} \\ \underline{\text{I-O}} \end{array} \right\} \quad \text{file-name-3} \quad \left[\, , \text{ file-name-4} \, \right] \quad \dots \right] \quad \dots$$

As a result of the execution of the OPEN statement, the IOCS performs
certain tasks. These tasks include the testing of the availability of the
file, header-label processing, allocation of buffer areas, etc. However,
the OPEN statement does not read or write any record of the file.

13.4.2 CLOSE Statement

The following is the syntax (simplified) of the CLOSE statement.

$$\underline{\text{CLOSE}} \quad \text{file-name-1} \quad \left[\text{WITH } \underline{\text{LOCK}} \right]$$
$$\left[\, , \text{ file-name-2} \left[\text{WITH } \underline{\text{LOCK}} \right] \, \right] \dots$$

The CLOSE statement terminates the processing of the file. As a result
of the execution of the CLOSE statement, the IOCS performs the end of file
processing. This task includes the trailer-label processing for magnetic-

tape files and the processing of the disk directory for newly-created disk files.

When a CLOSE statement is executed, the file must be open. A simple CLOSE statement releases the file from the program. In the case of magnetic-tape files, the tape is rewound. If required, the file can be opened again in the same program by using an OPEN statement.

The function of the CLOSE statement with the LOCK option is exactly similar to the simple CLOSE statement except that the file cannot be opened in the same program.

For some systems, unless a disk file is finally closed with LOCK, the file is not retained on the disk. This means that if the last CLOSE statement executed on the file is not with LOCK, the file gets removed as soon as the program terminates.

13.4.3 WRITE Statement

The WRITE statement for tape and sequential-disk files has the following syntax.

WRITE record-name [FROM identifier]

As a result of the execution of the WRITE statement, the record is released from the record area and is written onto the file. The first execution of the WRITE statement writes the first record and subsequent executions write the records sequentially. The FROM option has the same meaning as in the case of line-printer files. It may be noted that once a record has been written, the record is no longer available in the area denoted by the record name. The file must be opened in the OUTPUT mode.

13.4.4 REWRITE Statement

The REWRITE statement is used to update an existing record in the disk file. The general format is as follows:

REWRITE record-name [FROM identifier]

It may be noted that the syntax is similar to that in the case of a WRITE statement and the FROM option has the same meaning.

The REWRITE statement can only be used if the file is opened in the I-0 mode and its execution must be preceded by the execution of a successful READ statement on the file. The REWRITE statement replaces the last record read. After the execution of the REWRITE statement, the record is no longer available.

13.5 EXAMPLES OF SEQUENTIAL FILE PROCESSING
(FIXED-LENGTH RECORDS)

Example 1

Given a deck of cards, the problem is to copy the card file onto a magnetic tape. The record size is obviously 80 characters. Let us assume that there

will be 18 records per block of the tape file. The title of the tape file to
be created is not fixed. It is assumed that the user of the program will
provide the title in the first 10 columns of the first card of the deck. This
first card which contains the title should not be copied onto the tape file.

The following program is a solution of the problem. The example shows
how to create a tape file whose title is provided during the execution as
data.

```
FILE-CONTROL.
SELECT KARD-FILE ASSIGN TO READER.
SELECT A-TAPE-FILE ASSIGN TO TAPE.

DATA DIVISION.
FILE SECTION.
FD  KARD-FILE.

01  KARD-REC.
    02  TITLE-OF-FILE               PIC     X(10).
    02  FILLER                      PIC     X(70).

FD  A-TAPE-FILE
    RECORD CONTAINS 80 CHARACTERS
    BLOCK CONTAINS 18 RECORDS
    VALUE OF IDENTIFICATION IS TITLE-OF-FILE
    LABEL RECORDS ARE STANDARD
    DATA RECORD IS TAPE-REC.

01  TAPE-REC                        PIC     X(80).

WORKING-STORAGE SECTION.
77  END-OF-KARD     PIC     9     VALUE   IS   0.
88  LAST-KARD       VALUE   IS   1.
PROCEDURE DIVISION.
MAIN-PROGRAM.
    PERFORM FILE-OPENING.
    PERFORM CARD-TO-TAPE  UNTIL  LAST-KARD.
    PERFORM END-OF-JOB.
    STOP RUN.

FILE-OPENING.
    OPEN INPUT KARD-FILE.
    READ KARD-FILE RECORD
            AT END DISPLAY  "NO DATA CARDS"
            STOP RUN.

    OPEN OUTPUT A-TAPE-FILE.

CARD-TO-TAPE.
    READ KARD-FILE RECORD AT END MOVE 1 TO END-OF-KARD.
    IF NOT LAST-KARD
        WRITE TAPE-REC FROM KARD-REC.

END-OF-JOB.
    CLOSE KARD-FILE
            A-TAPE-FILE  WITH LOCK.
```

The function of the FILE-OPENING paragraph may be seen in the above program. The KARD-FILE is opened first. Then the first card is read. This card is supposed to contain the file title in the first 10 columns. It may be noted that the AT END part of the READ statement can be executed only when no data card has been supplied. In this case a message to this effect is displayed and the program terminates. In the normal case (i.e., when data cards have been provided) the statement OPEN OUTPUT A-TAPE-FILE is executed next. It may be noted that when this statement is executed, TITLE-OF-FILE contains the given title. The functions of the paragraphs named CARD-TO-TAPE and END-OF-JOB are straightforward and need no explanation.

It may be noted that if the title of the tape file to be created is fixed and known at the time of program writing, the program becomes very simple. The VALUE OF IDENTIFICATION clause should now contain the actual title enclosed within quotes. The FILE-OPENING paragraph should consist of the following statement only.

```
          OPEN   INPUT   KARD-FILE   OUTPUT   A-TAPE-FILE.
```

Example 2

Suppose a disk file is to be modified in the following manner. LENGTH-CODE and LENGTH are two fields in the record. If LENGTH-CODE contains the value 1, the value of the LENGTH field should be replaced by multiplying itself by .3048. The LENGTH-CODE should also be changed to 9. In all other cases the record should remain unchanged.

The following shows the relevant portions of a program for the said task.

```
FILE-CONTROL.
    SELECT DISC-FILE   ASSIGN  TO DISK.
DATA   DIVISION.
FILE   SECTION.
FD   DISC-FILE
    RECORD   CONTAINS   100   CHARACTERS
    BLOCK   CONTAINS   30   RECORDS
    VALUE   OF   IDENTIFICATION   IS   "INV3025".

01   DISC-REC.
    02   FILLER            PIC        X(38).
    02   LENGTH-CODE       PIC        9.
    02   LENGTH            PIC        9(6)V99.
    02   FILLER            PIC        X(53).

WORKING-STORAGE SECTION.
77   END-OF-DISC          PIC        9   VALUE   IS   0.
88   LAST-RECORD          VALUE      IS   1.
PROCEDURE DIVISION.
THE-UPDATE-PROGRAM.
    OPEN   I-O   DISC-FILE.
    PERFORM   UPDATE-RECORDS   UNTIL   LAST-RECORD.
    CLOSE   DISC-FILE.   STOP RUN.
```

```
UPDATE-RECORDS.
     READ  DISC-FILE AT END MOVE 1 TO END-OF-DISC.
     IF NOT LAST-RECORD
          PERFORM CHECK-AND-REWRITE.
CHECK-AND-REWRITE.
     IF LENGTH-CODE IS EQUAL TO 1
          MOVE 9 TO LENGTH-CODE
          MULTIPLY .3048 BY LENGTH
          REWRITE DISC-REC.
```

Notice how the REWRITE statement has been used here. Everytime a record is read, it is not rewritten. Only when the LENGTH-CODE is found to be equal to 1, is the record modified and replaced by the REWRITE statement. This is possible because REWRITE replaces the record last read.

The problem can as well be solved without the use of the REWRITE statement. In that case we must have two disk files, one for input and the other for output. Both of them should have the same title so that once the output file is created and closed with the LOCK option, the old file is removed. In the PROCEDURE DIVISION, each record read must be written onto the output file (with or without the modification as the case may be) by means of the WRITE statement. It is left as an exercise to write the program without using the REWRITE statement.

13.6 SEQUENTIAL FILES WITH VARIABLE-LENGTH RECORDS

Magnetic-tape or disk files can contain variable-length records. In this case the file can have records with different fixed lengths or one or more records can contain variable number of table elements. In the latter case the table elements are defined with the OCCURS... DEPENDING clause.

Each record in a file with variable-length records carries a data item that contains the length of the record. For the purpose of reference this data item will be called the variable-length indicator or VLI The size and position of the VLI within the record varies from computer to computer. In most cases the VLI is determined through the logic generated by the compiler. Each time the WRITE statement associated to a file with variable-length records is executed, the said logic to determine the VLI is invoked. It may be noted that the size of the record whose name is specified in the WRITE statement gives the value of the VLI. However, the handling of the VLI is transparent to the programmer. In some computers, in addition to the automatic control of VLI, the programmer is also allowed to control the VLI. However, these features, being entirely implementation dependent, will not be discussed in this book.

The COBOL features for variable-length records are only limited to the file-description and record-description entries in the file section. The features are described below.

13.6.1 FD Entry for Variable-length Records

The RECORD CONTAINS and BLOCK CONTAINS clauses are quite different in the case of files with variable-length records. The syntax of these two clauses are as follows:

$$\underline{BLOCK} \quad CONTAINS \quad \left[integer\text{-}1 \quad \underline{TO} \right] \quad integer\text{-}2 \quad \left\{ \begin{array}{c} \underline{RECORDS} \\ CHARACTERS \end{array} \right\}$$

$$\underline{RECORD} \quad CONTAINS \quad \left[integer\text{-}3 \quad \underline{TO} \right] \quad integer\text{-}4 \quad CHARACTERS$$

The BLOCK CONTAINS clause indicates the size of the buffer to be set up for the file. Integer-2 specifies the said size. When CHARACTERS option is used the size is integer-2 characters. When the RECORDS option is used, the buffer will be sufficient to hold the integer-2 of the largest record. Integer-1 is mainly used for the purpose of documentation, and the compiler ignores this. What is actually done is that the buffer size is determined from integer-2 and then as many consecutive records as are possible to be accommodated in a buffer are considered as a block.

Integer-3 and integer-4 respectively denote the minimum and maximum sizes of the records in the file.

The above forms for the BLOCK CONTAINS and RECORD CONTAINS clauses are quite sufficient to indicate that the said file is a file with variable-length records. However, these clauses being optional in some computers, a nonstandard clause is also required. The clause is as follows:

$$\underline{RECORDING} \quad MODE \quad IS \quad \left\{ \begin{array}{c} \underline{F} \\ \underline{V} \end{array} \right\}$$

The option V indicates variable-length records while F indicates fixed-length records.

All other clauses described for fixed-length records are also available in the case of variable-length records.

13.6.2   Record Description for Variable-length Records

When the variable-length records consists of records of different lengths, each record type is to be described at level 01 following the FD entry for the file. There is nothing special as regards the record description. A variable-length record can also consist of a fixed number of characters followed by a variable number of contiguous table elements. The variable part is to be defined with the OCCURS... DEPENDING clause. The data item that specifies the number of contiguous table elements in the variable part must be defined in the fixed part. An example of such description of variable-length records is shown below. The example also includes the FD entry.

```
FD   VARIABLE-FILE
     RECORD CONTAINS 40 TO 92 CHARACTERS
     BLOCK CONTAINS 933 TO 1024 CHARACTERS
     LABEL RECORDS ARE STANDARD
     RECORDING MODE IS V
     VALUE OF IDENTIFICATION IS "VARFILE".
```

```
01   VARIABLE-RECORD.
     02   ACCOUNT-NUMBER      PIC      9(6).
     02   NAME                PIC      X(20).
     02   NO-OF-PAYMENTS      PIC      9.
     02   PAYMENTS OCCURS  1  TO  5  TIMES DEPENDING ON
               NO-OF-PAYMENTS  INDEXED BY TAB-INDEX.
          03   DATE-OF-PAYMENT            9(6).
          03   AMOUNT-OF-PAYMENT          9(5)V99.
```

It may be seen that the fixed part consists of 27 characters and the variable part can be either 13, 26, 39, 52 or 65 characters in length. The maximum block size has been chosen to be 1024 characters. The minimum block size of 933 has been arrived at by subtracting the maximum record size from the maximum block size and then adding 1 to it (933 = 1024 - 92 + 1). The reason for this is that once up to 933 characters of the buffer have been filled and the next record happens to be a record with maximum length, it cannot be accommodated in the same block. However, the figure 933 is for documentation only, the compiler does not make use of this figure at all.

13.6.3 Example of Sequential File Processing
(with Variable-length Records)

Suppose that survey data have been punched on the cards in the following format.

Field	Card Columns
General information	1-45
Property code	46
Property information	47-73

It is assumed that one card has been punched for each respondent. The general information is available for all. The property information is only available for those respondents who own some property. This is indicated by the property code which is 1 for property holders. If the property code is not equal to 1, columns 47 - 73 should be ignored.

The problem now is to create a magnetic-tape file for this survey data. Obviously, there can only be two types of records in this file. The shorter record will consist of the general information plus the property code whereas the longer record will contain all the three fields.

It may be noted that both the general and property information contains different fields. However, since in this problem we do not process these fields, it is sufficient for us to consider the general information and property information as elementary fields in the alphanumeric class.

The following is a sample COBOL program that creates the said file with variable-length records.

```
FILE-CONTROL
    SELECT SURVEY-FILE ASSIGN TO READER.
    SELECT VAR-TAPE-FILE ASSIGN TO TAPE.


DATA DIVISION.
FILE SECTION.
FD SURVEY-FILE.
01 SURVEY-REC.

    02  ACTUAL-DATA          PIC    X(73).
    02  FILLER               PIC    X(7).


FD  VAR-TAPE-FILE
    LABEL RECORDS ARE STANDARD
    VALUE OF IDENTIFICATION IS "SURVEYDATA"
    RECORDING MODE IS  V
    BLOCK CONTAINS 440 TO 512  CHARACTERS
    RECORD CONTAINS 46 TO 73  CHARACTERS.


01  LONG-RECORD.
    02  GENERAL-INFO         PIC    X(45).
    02  PROPERTY-CODE        PIC    9.
    02  PROPERTY-INFO        PIC    X(27).


01  SHORT-RECORD
    02  FILLER               PIC    X(46).

WORKING-STORAGE SECTION.
77  END-OF-CARD              PIC    X(3)   VALUE   IS  "NO".
88  LAST-CARD-DONE           VALUE  IS  "YES".


PROCEDURE  DIVISION.
MAIN-PROGRAM.
    OPEN    INPUT     SURVEY-FILE
            OUTPUT    VAR-TAPE-FILE.

    PERFORM  TAPE-FILE-CREATION
             UNTIL  LAST-CARD-DONE.

    CLOSE  SURVEY-FILE   VAR-TAPE-FILE.
    STOP  RUN.

TAPE-FILE-CREATION.
    READ    SURVEY-FILE   RECORD
                AT  END  MOVE  "YES"   TO  END-OF-CARD.

    IF  NOT  LAST-CARD-DONE
    MOVE ACTUAL-DATA TO LONG-RECORD
    IF PROPERTY-CODE  IS EQUAL TO 1
        WRITE  LONG-RECORD
    ELSE  WRITE  SHORT-RECORD.
```

It may be noted that for the variable-length records, a field within each record must indicate the type of the record. The PROPERTY-CODE in the above example is the said field. Unless this field is stored, it is difficult to use the file in a subsequent program. This is because the said field helps to identify the type of record that has been read.

13.7 FEATURES FOR UNIT-RECORD FILES

Some of the COBOL features described in the previous sections are also available for unit-record files, such as card-reader or line-printer files. So far as the file description is concerned, the RECORD CONTAINS and DATA RECORDS clauses can also be used for unit-record files. The CODE-SET clause is also available for the card-reader files. Usually, labels do not exist for the unit-record files and as such LABEL RECORDS ARE OMITTED can be specified for such files. In some computers it is mandatory for the programmer to specify LABEL RECORDS ARE OMITTED for the card-reader or line-printer files. In other computers the use of the LABEL RECORD clause for any file is optional and OMITTED is assumed for unit-record files. There are, however, computers such as B-6700 where the operating system normally also puts labels to the card-reader and line-printer files. In these computers the LABEL RECORD clause with the OMITTED option should not be normally specified for the card-reader or line-printer files. It is therefore recommended that the programmer should consult the appropriate manual regarding the use of the LABEL RECORD clause for the unit record files. For the purpose of this book, we will continue to omit the use of this clause for unit-record files.

In addition to the features stated above, there are some special features relating to page control for the line-printer file. These features are described below.

13.7.1 Special Features for Line-printer Files

The FD entry for a line-printer file may optionally contain the LINAGE clause having the following syntax.

$$
\underline{\text{LINAGE}} \text{ IS } \left\{ \begin{array}{l} \text{data-name-1} \\ \text{integer-1} \end{array} \right\} \text{ LINES } \left[, \text{ WITH } \underline{\text{FOOTING}} \text{ AT } \left\{ \begin{array}{l} \text{data-name-2} \\ \text{integer-2} \end{array} \right\} \right.
$$

$$
\left[, \text{ LINES AT } \underline{\text{TOP}} \left\{ \begin{array}{l} \text{data-name-3} \\ \text{integer-3} \end{array} \right\} \right] \left[, \text{ LINES AT } \underline{\text{BOTTOM}} \left\{ \begin{array}{l} \text{data-name-4} \\ \text{integer-4} \end{array} \right\} \right]
$$

The linage clause defines the size of a logical page (ideally, means the same as the physical page of continuous stationery but see Sec. 18.1 for details) released to the line printer through the executions of the WRITE statement. A logical page is divided into the following three parts:
- top margin
- page body
- bottom margin

The number lines that can be written and/or spaced within the logical page is called the page body. Nothing can be written in the top or bottom margins. The total number of lines in these three parts determines the size of a logical page.

A number of lines towards the bottom of a page body may be defined to be the footing area. The footing area is normally used to print subtotals or totals.

The integer-1/data-name-1 in the LINAGE clause specifies the number of lines in the page body. Similarly, integer-3/data-name-3 and integer-4/data-name-4 specify the number of lines in the top and bottom margins respectively. The integer-2/data-name-2 indicates the logical line number within the page body where the footing should begin. For this purpose, the first line in the page body has the logical line number 1.

All data-names used in a LINAGE clause must be unsigned, numeric integer data items. If any of the TOP, BOTTOM or FOOTING phrases is omitted, the relevant area is assumed to consist of zero lines.

The advantage of the LINAGE clause is that the programmer need not keep any line count for the purpose of page control. The line count is maintained in a special register called LINAGE-COUNTER which is generated by the compiler. At any point of time the LINAGE-COUNTER holds the logical line number at which the line printer is positioned within the page body. The value of the LINAGE-COUNTER·is appropriately updated by the execution of the WRITE statement on the file. The OPEN statement presents the LINAGE-COUNTER to 1. The LINAGE-COUNTER is also reset to 1 whenever the line printer is repositioned to the first line of the page body.

The LINAGE-COUNTER can be referred to in the PROCEDURE DIVISION, but the programmer should not modify its value. The LINAGE-COUNTER can be qualified by the file name. This is helpful when the system allows and the program uses more than one line-printer file in the same program and it is required to refer to the LINAGE-COUNTER.

When the LINAGE clause is used in the FD entry, a few additional features are available in the WRITE statement. The general syntax of the WRITE statement for a line printer is as follows:

```
WRITE    record-name    [ FROM  identifier-1 ]

[  { BEFORE }                { identifier-2 }   [ LINE  ]   ]
   { AFTER  } ADVANCING      { integer      }   [ LINES ]
                             { mnemonic-name }
                             { PAGE          }

[ ;  AT  { END-OF-PAGE }   imperative-statement ]
         { EOP         }
```

It may be noted that most of the options have already been introduced. The BEFORE ADVANCING PAGE or AFTER ADVANCING PAGE phrase can be used when the LINAGE clause has been specified. As a result, the device is positioned at the first line of the page body of the next logical page. If LINAGE clause is not specified, the drives is positioned at the line corresponding to channel 1.

Depending on whether BEFORE or AFTER has been specified, this positioning takes place before or after the printing of the said line.

The END-OF-PAGE phrase can be specified only when the LINAGE clause has been used. Whenever the WRITE statement causes printing or spacing within the footing area, the <u>end of page</u> condition occurs. In the event of the end-of-page condition, the control is transferred to the imperative statement following END-OF-PAGE. But this transfer of control takes place only after the said line with the specified spacing has been printed. If the printing spacing caused by the WRITE statement (with or without END-OF-PAGE) cannot be fully accommodated within the page body, an <u>automatic page overflow</u> condition arises and the following actions take place.

- If the BEFORE ADVANCING phrase is specified, the line is printed in the current position and the device is repositioned at the first line of the page body of the next logical page.
- If the AFTER ADVANCING phrase is specified, the line is printed on the first line of the page body of the next logical page.
- If the END-OF-FILE phrase is also specified, control is transferred to the imperative statement after the line has been printed.

The EOP and END-OF-PAGE have the same meaning.

The following example illustrates the use of the LINAGE clause and the associated WRITE statement.

Suppose the file and record description for a line printer file is as follows:

```
FD  LP-FILE
    LINAGE IS 50 WITH FOOTING AT 48
    LINES AT TOP 5 LINES AT BOTTOM IS 4
    RECORD CONTAINS 132 CHARACTERS.
01  LP-RECORD       PIC   X(132).
```

Now, consider the following WRITE statements in the PROCEDURE DIVISION.

```
(i)     WRITE  LP-RECORD  FROM  DETAIL-LINE
             AFTER ADVANCING  2  LINES.

(ii)    WRITE   LP-RECORD FROM HEADING-LINE
             AFTER ADVANCING PAGE.

(iii)   WRITE   LP-RECORD FROM DETAIL-LINE
             AFTER ADVANCING 2 LINES
             AT END-OF-PAGE GO TO PRINT-TOTALS.
```

The first statement is an ordinary WRITE statement. Suppose the paper is positioned at the 30th line of the page body. Then this statement will cause the paper to be advanced by 2 lines, i.e., to the 32nd line and the record will be printed on the 32nd line. If on the other hand, the paper is positioned at the 49th or 50th line, the WRITE statement will cause the printing of the record in the first line of the next page. In the former case LINAGE-COUNTER is increased by 2 and in the latter case it is set to 1.

The second WRITE statement causes the record to be printed on the first line of the next page regardless of the current position of the paper. The LINAGE-COUNTER is set to 1.

In the case of the third WRITE statement, the effect is identical to that of the first WRITE statement except that the control is transferred to PRINT-TOTALS in the following cases.

- If the value of LINAGE-COUNTER is greater than or equal to 48 after the printing.
- If page skipping takes place during the printing caused by this WRITE statement.

The LINAGE clause and the associated features are an ANSI 74 feature and therefore may not yet be available in many compilers.

13.8 SPECIAL FEATURES FOR MAGNETIC-TAPE FILES

A single reel of a magnetic tape is often called a volume. When the files are small, more than one file can be accommodated in the same reel. In this case, the volume is called a multifile volume. On the other hand, a file may occupy more than one tape reel. Such a file is called a multivolume file. The handling of a multivolume file does not normally require any special COBOL feature. When the end of one volume is reached, the volume is closed and the next volume is opened by the IOCS. Thus, the processing of volumes in the proper sequence is taken care of by the IOCS and the programmer need not take any special care. However, in the case of a multivolume file, the programmer may like to have some control. For example, the programmer may like to close a volume before the end of the volume has been reached. Such facilities are available in COBOL. COBOL also offers facilities for handling multifile volumes.

Besides the abovementioned features, COBOL also provides the facility of reading a tape file in the reverse direction. However, this facility can be used only when the tape drives are equipped with the hardware features for reading a tape in the reverse direction.

Most of the special features for tape files are available in COBOL through the OPEN and CLOSE statements. The features are therefore introduced here through a simultaneous discussion on these two statements. The general syntax for the OPEN and CLOSE statements are as follows:

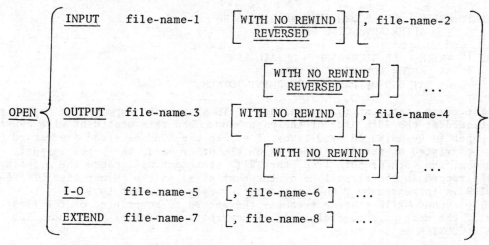

$$
\text{CLOSE} \quad \text{file-name-9} \quad
\left[
\begin{cases} \underline{\text{REEL}} \\ \underline{\text{UNIT}} \end{cases}
\begin{bmatrix} \text{WITH} \\ \text{FOR} \end{bmatrix}
\begin{array}{l} \underline{\text{NO}} \ \underline{\text{REWIND}} \\ \underline{\text{REMOVAL}} \end{array}
\right]
$$

$$
\text{WITH} \quad \begin{cases} \underline{\text{NO}} \ \underline{\text{REWIND}} \\ \underline{\text{LOCK}} \end{cases}
$$

$$
\left[\text{file-name-10} \quad
\left[
\begin{cases} \underline{\text{REEL}} \\ \underline{\text{UNIT}} \end{cases}
\begin{bmatrix} \text{WITH} \\ \text{FOR} \end{bmatrix}
\begin{array}{l} \underline{\text{NO}} \ \underline{\text{REWIND}} \\ \underline{\text{REMOVAL}} \end{array}
\right]
\right.
$$

$$
\left. \text{WITH} \quad \begin{cases} \underline{\text{NO}} \ \underline{\text{REWIND}} \\ \underline{\text{LOCK}} \end{cases}
\right] \ \ldots
$$

Normally, after the opening of a tape file, the file is positioned at its beginning. However, the REVERSED phrase within an OPEN statement positions the file at its end and the file is opened for access in the reverse direction. The NO REWIND phrase within an OPEN statement indicates that the file is already positioned and no repositioning is required.

After the closing of a tape file, the tape is normally rewound. The NO REWIND phrase within a CLOSE statement specifies that the tape should be left in the current position.

The words REEL and UNIT are synonymous in COBOL. CLOSE statement with the REEL/UNIT option allows the current volume to be closed before the end of volume has been reached. Having closed the current volume, the IOCS opens the next volume. Thus the file is still open at this point and the programmer should not explicitly open the file. The option is useful when the programmer wants to skip the remaining records in the current input volume.

The NO REWIND option used in conjunction with the REEL/UNIT option is not very useful and is not allowed in many systems. Where allowed, the current volume is left in its current position.

The FOR REMOVAL phrase, which is an ANSI 74 feature, causes the current reel unit to be rewound and the reel/unit is logically removed from the program. However, the volume may be accessed once again in the same program provided a CLOSE statement without the REEL/UNIT option is finally executed on the file and the file is opened by a new OPEN statement.

The following examples illustrate the use of the various options.

Example 1

Suppose TAPE-A is the file name for a temporary tape file. Having created the tape file, we wish to read the file in the reverse direction. This can be achieved by using the CLOSE and OPEN statements in the following sequence.

```
OPEN      OUTPUT     TAPE-A.

    < Statements for the creation of TAPE-A >

CLOSE     TAPE-A     WITH     NO     REWIND.
OPEN      INPUT      TAPE-A   REVERSED.

    < Statements for the reading of TAPE-A >
CLOSE     TAPE-A.
```

Example 2

The file MY-FILE is a multivolume file stored on two reels. The records of
this file should be processed sequentially. However, having processed the
first 500 records of the first reel, the remaining records in the reel
should be ignored. Then the processing should continue with the records in
the second reel. The relevant statements of the PROCEDURE DIVISION are shown
below.

```
PROCEDURE DIVISION.
START-PARA.
    OPEN     INPUT    MY-FILE.
    MOVE  ZERO  TO  RECORD-COUNT.  MOVE  1  TO  REEL-COUNT.

READ-PARA.
    READ   MY-FILE   RECORD
                  AT  END  GO  TO  END-OF-JOB.

    IF    REEL-COUNT  =   1
          ADD     1    TO   RECORD-COUNT
          IF  RECORD-COUNT  IS  GREATER  THAN  500
              CLOSE  MY-FILE  REEL
              MOVE   2   TO   REEL-COUNT
              GO  TO  READ-PARA.
        < The record is processed here >
    GO  TO  READ-PARA.

END-OF-JOB.
    CLOSE    MY-FILE.
    STOP  RUN.
```

Example 3

Suppose that TAPE-1, TAPE-2 and TAPE-3 are three output-tape files. These
being small files, are to be stored on a single-tape reel. The OPEN and
CLOSE statements for the creation of this multifile volume should appear in
the following sequence.

```
    OPEN     OUTPUT   TAPE-1.
      .
      .
      .
    CLOSE    TAPE-1  WITH  NO   REWIND.
    OPEN     OUTPUT   TAPE-2  WITH  NO  REWIND.
      .
      .
      .
    CLOSE    TAPE-2  WITH  NO   REWIND.
    OPEN     OUTPUT   TAPE-3  WITH  NO  REWIND.
      .
      .
      .
    CLOSE    TAPE-3.
```

It may be noted that TAPE-1, TAPE-2 and TAPE-3 cannot be opened simultaneously.

The creation of a multifile volume, as illustrated in the Example 3 above also requires a MULTIPLE TAPE clause in the I-O-CONTROL paragraph in the INPUT-OUTPUT SECTION of the ENVIRONMENT DIVISION. Thus, for the first time, we introduce the I-O-CONTROL paragraph. The paragraph may contain several clauses. The MULTIPLE TAPE clause is one of them. The syntax of the MULTIPLE TAPE clause is as follows:

MULTIPLE   FILE   TAPE   CONTAINS

    file-name-1   [POSITION   integer-1] [, file-name-2

                 [POSITION   integer-2]]   ...

It is not necessary to mention all the files in the multifile volume. Only those files that are used in the program should be mentioned. The POSITION phrase is not required if the consecutive files starting from the first are used in the program.

Thus the MULTIPLE TAPE clause for the files in Example 3 should be

MULTIPLE FILE TAPE CONTAINS TAPE-1, TAPE-2, TAPE-3.

The following is another example of the MULTIPLE TAPE clause with the POSITION phrase.

MULTIPLE FILE TAPE CONTAINS
        GOOD-FILE POSITION 3
        BAD-FILE POSITION   5.

This means that the third and the fifth files are used in the current program.

Remarks

The EXTEND option in the OPEN statement is only available when the file is stored in single reel.

13.9 I-O-CONTROL PARAGRAPH

Besides the MULTIPLE TAPE clause, the I-O-CONTROL paragraph of the INPUT-OUTPUT SECTION may contain a few other clauses. Some of these clauses are very useful in file handling. The complete syntax of the I-O-CONTROL paragraph is as follows:

I-O-CONTROL.

  [; RERUN [ON implementor-name] EVERY   integer-1 RECORDS

                    OF   file-name-1]   ...

```
  ┌                           ┐
  │        ┌ RECORD     ┐     │                      ┌              ┐
  │ ; SAME │ SORT       │ AREA FOR file-name-2 ┌ , file-name-3 ┐ ... │ ...
  │        │ SORT-MERGE │                      └              ┘      │
  └        └            ┘     ┘

  ┌                                                      ┌                     ┐
  │ ; MULTIPLE FILE TAPE CONTAINS file-name-4 │ POSITION integer-2 │
  └                                                      └                     ┘

        ┌                  ┌                    ┐ ┐          ┐
        │ , file-name-5 │ POSITION integer-3 │ │ ...    │ ...
        └                  └                    ┘ ┘          ┘
```

The entire paragraph is optional. Any combination of these clauses may be used. The first clause of the paragraph must not contain the preceding semi-colon (;). All integers in the above format must be unsigned, numeric, integer fields.

The MULTIPLE TAPE clause has been described in the preceding section. The functions of the RERUN and SAME AREA clauses are explained below.

When a program must handle a large-volume data, it is desirable to specify points at which the program may be restarted in the case of machine malfunction, power failure, operator errors, etc. The advantage of specifying such rerun points is obvious. Instead of restarting from the very beginning, the restart will take place from the last rerun point.

The RERUN clause (shown above in a simplified form) enables the programmer to specify that the rerun information should be periodically written onto a file (called the rescue file). Every time the specified number (integer-1) of records of the specified file (file-name-1) are processed, the dumping of the rerun information on the rescue file takes place. File-name-2 must be either an input or an output file defined in the program. Although several files can be processed by the program, it is sufficient to specify rerun points on any one of them. Thus a program can have only one RERUN clause.

The rescue file is specified through the implementor name which can be different for different computers. As an example, we will assume the implementor name to be RESCUE. The appearance of RESCUE in the RERUN clause indicates that a rescue file is required for the program. The entire operation of the rescue file is controlled by the operating system. The title, medium and other attributes of the rescue file can be specified outside the COBOL program through the job-control language. The rescue file should therefore not be defined in the COBOL program. The actual restart of the program using the rescue file is also controlled through the job-control language.

The following is an example of the RERUN clause.

    RERUN ON RESCUE EVERY 500 RECORDS OF STOCK-FILE.

The clause will cause the rerun information to be dumped on a rescue file on the completion of the processing of every 500 records of STOCK-FILE. Thus if the machine starts malfunctioning, say when the 1623rd record of STOCK-FILE was being processed, the program can be restarted from the processing of the 1501st record.

It may be noted that the reprocessing of a few records cannot be avoided during the restart. If the program opens any file in the I-O mode and modifies some of the records of this file during execution, the reprocessing can

have a disastrous effect. Therefore, while using the RERUN clause, care must
be taken to ensure that some amount of reprocessing will not cause any
damage.

The SAME AREA clause enables the programmer to specify the same area for
the buffers of two or more files. The clause is very useful when the program
must work with a limited memory space. The RESERVE clause in the FILE-CONTROL
paragraph provides a part of the solution as the buffer space can be reduced
by specifying only one buffer for the file. The SAME AREA clause enables
more than one file to share the same buffer area.

The shared area includes all storage areas assigned to the files. Only
one of the files specified in the SAME AREA clause should be open at a time.

On some computers, the sharing of areas between unit-record files on the
one hand, and the magnetic-tape or disk files on the other, is not allowed.
However, files specified in the SAME AREA clause need not have the same
organization or access. There can be more than one SAME AREA clause in a
program but a file name must not appear in two or more SAME AREA clauses.

A variation of the SAME AREA clause is the SAME RECORD AREA clause. In
this case only the record area is shared by the specified files. However,
all or some of the files may be open at the same time.

The memory area shared by all the files in the SAME RECORD AREA clause
is called the same record area. This area is considered as the record area
for all output files and that of the most recently-read input file. Therefore, care must be taken in the program while filling in the record area
of an output file. This may destroy the record read most recently.

Also note the difference between the SAME AREA and SAME RECORD AREA
clauses. The SAME AREA clause allows sharing of all the areas assigned to
the file (this area includes the buffer as well as the record area) while
the SAME RECORD AREA clause allows the sharing of record areas only. In the
former case only one of the files may be open at a time, while in the latter
case, all the files may be open at the same time.

The SORT and SORT-MERGE options of the SAME AREA clause will be described in the next chapter.

13.10 DECLARATIVES AND THE FILE STATUS CLAUSE

Input-output operations specified through OPEN, CLOSE, READ, WRITE or
REWRITE statements can either result in successful completion of the opera-
tion or can lead to some exception conditions. Examples of exception condi-
tions may be:
- AT END condition for a READ statement
- Record size error (the specified record size does not match with
  the actual record size)
- Parity error (parity checking on the data to be transferred,
  fails)
- Logic error (e.g., REWRITE does not follow a READ), etc.

Normally, when an exception condition arises during an input-output
operation, the program is discontinued. However, a premature termination of
the program just because of some error in the case of a few records may not
be desirable. The programmer may like the program to proceed with the records
for which the exception conditions do not arise.

There are two ways in which the discontinuation of the program in the
event of an exception condition may be avoided. However, the programmer must

take control of the situation in such cases. The first method is to take
control by specifying certain clauses of the input-output statements. For
example, the AT END clause of a READ statement allows the programmer to
take control when the AT END exception condition arises. While considering
direct-access files, we will see that an INVALID KEY clause is available
with READ, WRITE and other input-output statements. The INVALID KEY clause
also allows the programmer to take action in the event of some exception
conditions.

The above method of handling exception cases has only a limited application. This is because clauses, such as AT END or INVALID KEY do not cover
all exception conditions. The second method which we will describe now can
be applied to handle all exception conditions. The method consists of specifying the FILE STATUS clause and USE procedure.

The syntax of the FILE STATUS clause is as follows:

FILE   STATUS   IS   data-name

This clause, which must be specified in the FILE-CONTROL paragraph, was
introduced earlier without any explanation. When this clause is specified,
a value is moved into the data name by the operating system. The value is
moved every time an input-output statement is executed. The data name should
be defined in the DATA DIVISION as a two-character alphanumeric field. The
value that is moved in the data name indicates whether the current input-
output statement is successfully completed or an exception condition arises
during the operation. The values representing the various conditions are
obviously different for different computers. According to the ANSI standard,
the data name will have the following values in the case of sequential
files.

Value	Status of Input/Output Operation
00	Successful completion
10	AT END condition
30	Permanent error condition
34	Boundary violation

Examples of permanent errors may be parity error or the error when fixed-
length records have been specified but variable-length records are found,
or an attempt is made to read an unopened file, or a file opened for
output, etc. Boundry violation can arise when an attempt is made to write
a record beyond the specified boundary of the file. It may be noted that
according to the ANSI 74 standard, the file boundary is specified outside
the COBOL language, through the job-control language. (See the FILE-LIMITS
clause under implementation differences of this chapter for further details.)

Apart from the values given above, the ANSI standard leaves scope for
implementor-defined values. All these values should begin with the digit 9.

The FILE STATUS clause simply enables the programmer to get the status
of an input-output statement stored in a data field. The action to be taken
in the case of an exception condition is specified through a use procedure.
The use procedure consists of a section. The section header must be followed
by a USE statement. The USE statement is again followed by one or more
procedural paragraphs that should be executed in case an exception condition
is satisfied. The USE statement has the following syntax.

USE AFTER STANDARD $\left\{\begin{array}{l}\underline{\text{EXCEPTION}} \\ \underline{\text{ERROR}}\end{array}\right\}$ PROCEDURE ON $\left\{\begin{array}{l}\text{file-name-1 [, file-name-2]} \\ \underline{\text{INPUT}} \\ \underline{\text{OUTPUT}} \\ \underline{\text{I-O}} \\ \underline{\text{EXTEND}}\end{array}\right\}$

The USE statement itself is not executed. The procedural paragraphs that follow a USE statement are executed whenever an input-output error is detected. The words ERROR and EXCEPTION are synonymous and any one of them may be used. When INPUT or OUTPUT or I-O or EXTEND option is used, the use procedures are executed whenever an exception condition exists on any file opened in the said mode. The use of the file name option indicates that the associated procedures are executed on the exception conditions existing for the said files. The USE statement is a sentence and must be followed by a period and blank.

The USE statement, the associated procedures along with the section header for the USE statement constitute what is known as a declarative section. There can be more than one declarative section in a program. All declarative sections must be placed within the key words DECLARATIVES and END DECLARATIVES. The general format of the declaratives is as follows:

DECLARATIVES

    [section-name   SECTION   [segment-number].   declarative-sentence

    [paragraph-name.   [sentence]   ...]   ...   ...

END DECLARATIVES

The DECLARATIVES are optional, and if used, these must be placed immediately following the PROCEDURE DIVISION header. DECLARATIVES must be followed by a section name. The optional segment number will be discussed later. The declarative sentence is a sentence containing one USE statement. As we proceed we will encounter various other forms of the declarative sentence.

The procedures written in a declarative section must not refer to any nondeclarative procedure written after the END DECLARATIVES. Similarly, any nondeclarative procedure should also not refer to the declarative procedures. In some computers, however, a PERFORM statement in a nondeclarative procedure is allowed to refer to the paragraph name or section name within the declaratives.

Upon the execution of a use procedure, the control is implicitly returned to the input-output statement that caused its execution. The control then progresses in the usual sequence.

Example

In a program let MY-FILE be the file name for an input tape file. We wish to take control of all exception conditions. In the case of an AT END condition the job is terminated. In all other exception cases an error message is displayed. The relevant portions of the program are shown below.

```
FILE-CONTROL.
    SELECT MY-FILE ASSIGN TO TAPE
        FILE STATUS IS ERROR-CODE.

DATA DIVISION.
FILE SECTION.
FD  MY-FILE
        BLOCK CONTAINS  10  RECORDS
        VALUE OF IDENTIFICATION IS "INPUTTAPE"
        LABEL RECORDS ARE STANDARD.

01  FILE-REC.
    02  RECORD-ID                PIC         9(6).
        .
        .
        .

WORKING-STORAGE SECTION.
77  ERROR-CODE                   PIC         X(2).
77  PREVIOUS-RECORD-ID           PIC         9(6) VALUE IS ZERO.
77  END-OF-TAPE                  PIC         9 VALUE IS ZERO.



PROCEDURE DIVISION.
DECLARATIVES.
USE-PROCEDURE SECTION.
    USE AFTER EXCEPTION PROCEDURE ON MY-FILE.
ERROR-SERVICING.
    IF ERROR-CODE =  "10"
                   MOVE  1  TO  END-OF-TAPE
    ELSE DISPLAY  "ERRORbINbTHEbRECORDbTHATbFOLLOWSb",
                                      PREVIOUS-RECORD-ID,
                                      "STATUSbISb" , ERROR-CODE.
END DECLARATIVES.
NON-DECLARATIVE SECTION.
MAIN-PARA.
    PERFORM  OPEN-PARA.
    PERFORM  READ-A-RECORD UNTIL END-OF-TAPE = 1.
    PERFORM  CLOSE-PARA.
    STOP RUN.

READ-A-RECORD.
    READ MY-FILE.
    IF END-OF-TAPE EQUALS ZERO
            PERFORM PROCESS-A-RECORD
            MOVE RECORD-ID TO PREVIOUS-RECORD-ID.

PROCESS-A-RECORD.
```

OPEN-PARA.
                    .
                    .
                    .

CLOSE-PARA.
                    .
                    .
                    .

In the above example, notice the READ statement in the READ-A-RECORD paragraph. The statement does not require the AT END clause. The value ''10'' for the status code represents the AT END condition.

13.11 IMPLEMENTATION DIFFERENCES

In almost every implementation of the file-handling modules of COBOL, certain implementor-dependent features are included. This is also unavoidable as the ANSI standard leaves many things to be defined by the implementor. Among the three implementations considered in this book, there exist many differences, and it is not possible to include here a complete list of all these differences. Only the important points are discussed below.

(a) FILE-CONTROL Paragraph

(i)   RESERVE Clause: The ANSI 68 syntax for this clause was RESERVE integer ALTERNATE AREAS which has been replaced by RESERVE integer AREA(S) in ANSI 74. The RESERVE clause with ALTERNATE phrase is available in B-6700 and DEC-10. This clause, if specified, allocates integer +1 and integer +2 buffers for B-6700 and DEC-10 respectively. Therefore, to specify 1 buffer, NO and -1 should be used for the integer in B-6700 and DEC-10 respectively. NO can also be specified in DEC-10 in which case 2 buffers are allocated. The default is 2 buffers for both the compilers. In ICL-1900 the clause should be used without the ALTERNATE phrase. The integer can only be 1. If the clause is omitted, a standard number of buffers is allocated. If 1 AREA(S) is specified, more buffers are allocated.

(ii) ORGANIZATION/ACCESS Clauses: Since these clauses are used for documentation in the case of sequential files, their implementation differences are not discussed.

(iii) FILE-LIMIT Clause: The B-6700 and DEC-10 allow the boundaries of a disk file to be specified through a FILE-LIMIT clause. For example, the clause

                  FILE-LIMIT   IS   1   THRU   5000

in the SELECT entry means that the disk file has 5000 records. This clause is an ANSI 68 feature and has been deleted in the 1974 version. It has been assumed that its function is to be handled outside of the COBOL language.

(b)   FD Entry

Most of the clauses as described in the text will work in the three compilers.
The exceptions are discussed below. However, the additional features available in the three implementations are not considered.

(i)   BLOCK CONTAINS/RECORD CONTAINS Clauses: Most compilers put restrictions on the maximum and minimum record and block sizes. In B-6700 the minimum block size for tape files is 30 characters. This means that even when the block size which is specified is more than 30 characters and the record size is less than 30 characters, there can be problems. This is because the last block may be a short block.

(ii)   VALUE OF Clause: This clause is available in all the three compilers in the following form

$$\underline{\text{VALUE OF}} \quad \left\{ \begin{array}{l} \underline{\text{ID}} \\ \underline{\text{IDENTIFICATION}} \end{array} \right\} \quad \text{IS} \quad \left\{ \begin{array}{l} \text{data-name} \\ \text{literal} \end{array} \right\}$$

The file title is to be specified through the data-name/literal. In ICL-1900, a file title is a nonnumeric data which must not exceed 12 characters in length. In DEC-10, a file title is nonnumeric and 9 characters in length. The first 6 characters are taken to be the file title and the next 3 characters as its extension. In B-6700, a file title can consist of 1 to 14 levels and in each level the name can consist of 1 to 17 characters. A name is separated from its next lower level name by the character / (virgule). For example, LAXMI/VISHNU is a valid title in B-6700 which consist of 2 levels. When a data name is used, the field should contain the title followed by a period (.). When a literal is used, any virgule (/) in the title must be enclosed within quotes. For example,

VALUE   OF   ID   IS   "LAXMI"/"VISHNU".

In B-6700, SAVE-FACTOR is available as a separate clause. In ICL-1900, a separate clause having the following format is available.

$$\underline{\text{ACTIVE-TIME}} \quad \text{IS} \quad \left\{ \begin{array}{l} \text{data-name} \\ \text{literal} \end{array} \right\}$$

The meaning of this clause is the same as that of the SAVE-FACTOR clause discussed in the text. In DEC-10, the VALUE OF clause can include other clauses. One such clause is as follows:

$$\underline{\text{DATE-WRITTEN}} \quad \text{IS} \quad \left\{ \begin{array}{l} \text{data-name} \\ \text{literal-2} \end{array} \right\}$$

This clause specifies the date on which the file was written.

(iii)   CODE-SET Clause: This clause is an ANSI 74 feature and is available in B-6700 if appropriate compiler option is set.

The alphabet name clause in B-6700 is as follows:

$$\text{alphabet-name} \quad \text{IS} \quad \left\{ \begin{array}{l} \underline{\text{STANDARD-1}} \\ \underline{\text{NATIVE}} \\ \text{BCL} \end{array} \right\}$$

The keywords STANDARD-1, NATIVE and BCL respectively refers to the ASCII, EBCDIC and BCL (6-bit character code for Burroughs systems) character sets respectively.

(iv)   <u>LABEL RECORDS Clause</u>: In ICL-1900, the clause must be specified with the STANDARD option for disk and magnetic-tape files. In DEC-10 and B-6700, this clause is optional.

(v)   <u>RECORDING MODE Clause and Variable-length Records</u>: This nonstandard clause is very useful in ICL-1900. The format is as follows:

$$\underline{\text{RECORDING}} \quad \text{MODE} \quad \text{IS} \quad \left\{ \begin{array}{l} \text{F} \\ \text{V} \\ 2 \end{array} \right\}$$

RECORDING MODE F specifies that the file contains fixed-length records. RECORDING MODE V specifies that the file contains variable-length records. The option 2 is used for reading the binary-image cards. We will omit the discussion of this option. If this clause is omitted for magnetic-tape or disk files, the compiler will assume that the first word of the record contains the record size (in words). This is true regardless of whether the file contains fixed-length or variable-length records. If the said clauses are used, the compiler makes arrangement for the handling of this count word which is allocated space in the beginning of the record.

In DEC-10, an optional RECORDING MODE clause with many options (including V and F) is available. This clause should be specified in the SELECT entry. Files whose recording mode is F or V are implicitly considered to be files recorded on the medium in terms of EBCDIC characters. When RECORDING MOVE V is specified, the block size can also be variable. The blocking factor is determined from the integer-2 of the BLOCK CONTAINS clause. If the file is on a magnetic tape and RECORDING MODE V or F is used, the LABEL RECORDS OMITTED clause must be specified.

An optional RECORDING MODE clause is also available in B-6700. However, its purpose is different and will not be discussed here. While using variable-length records in B-6700, the RECORD CONTAINS clause is important. If this clause is absent, the maximum record size is determined from the first record description appearing after the FD entry. Subsequent record descriptions cannot be larger. If the clause is specified, the maximum record size is taken from it. The records can be described in any order provided that none of the record descriptions indicates a size greater than this record size. For variable-length records, the first four characters are implicitly assumed to contain the record length. Alternatively, any other field can also contain the record length provided a SIZE DEPENDING ON clause is specified in the following manner.

```
01 VARIABLE-RECORD SIZE 72 TO 96 DEPENDING ON
                COUNT-WORD.
```

The data name COUNT-WORD (or any other data name that is used in its place) must be defined within the description of this record. The SIZE DEPENDING clause must be specified for 01-level record names. If a SIZE DEPENDING clause is specified for one record description, it must also be specified for every record description that follows an FD entry.

(c)   OPEN/CLOSE Statements and MULTIPLE TAPE Entry

The handling of multivolume files and that of multifile volumes, are highly implementation-dependent. Accordingly, the various options of the OPEN and CLOSE statements vary widely from one system to another. The implementation differences in this respect, are so many that it is almost impossible to discuss them here. The interested reader is advised to consult the relevant manuals. However, it may be stated that in respect of the simple forms of the OPEN and CLOSE statements (Sec. 13.3.1 and 13.4.2), there is no difference. The FOR REMOVAL option is not available in the three systems under consideration. The EXTEND option in the OPEN statement is not available in ICL-1900 and DEC-10.

(d)   WRITE and REWRITE Statement

In B-6700, when the WRITE statement is used for a disk file, it has the following format:

```
WRITE   record-name  [ FROM  identifier ]

            [ ;  INVALID  KEY  imperative-statement ]
```

The imperative statement is executed when an attempt is made to the write beyond the file boundary. In the case of the REWRITE statement also, the INVALID KEY clause is to be specified in a similar manner. The imperative statement of the INVALID KEY clause is executed if the REWRITE is not preceded by the execution of a successful READ statement on the file.

In DEC-10, there is no REWRITE statement for sequential files. However, if the previous input-output statement on the file is a READ and if the file is opened in the I-O mode, the WRITE statement behaves like a REWRITE statement.

In ICL-1900, these statements are as described in the text. However, in ICL-1900, the WRITE statement is allowed even when a file is opened in the I-O mode. We shall not discuss the effect of this nonstandard feature.

(e)   Special Features for Line-printer Files

This ANSI 74 feature has been implemented in B-6700 and can be used if an appropriate compiler option is set.

(f) I-O-CONTROL Paragraph

The format of the RERUN clause, as given in the text, is implemented in all
the three compilers under consideration. In B-6700, the implementor name
can be DISK or DISKPACK. The dump is written on a diskfile which is defined
by the system. In ICL-1900, either TAPE - * or EDS-* may be specified. The
former indicates a dump to be taken on a tape file while the latter indicates a diskfile for the dump In DEC-10, no implementor-name is to be specified. The dump is taken on an implicitly-defined diskfile. For further
details see the relevant manual.
    The SAME [RECORD] AREA clause is available in all the three compilers.
In ICL-1900, when the RECORD option is used, all the files must have the
same RECORDING MODE. Moreover, SAME AREA should not be specified when one
is a unit record file and the other a magnetic-tape or magnetic-disk file.
In B-6700, the RECORD option can be used when the files have a common maximum record size. The SAME AREA clause in B-6700 is implemented for compatibility with the standard COBOL and has no effect.

(g) Declaratives and the FILE STATUS Clause

These features are not implemented in ICL-1900. The FILE STATUS clause is
available in DEC-10 as well as in B-6700. For the different values of the
data name of this clause, the relevant manuals should be consulted. In
general, the standard values given in the text are available with the exception that the boundary violation is not implemented in B-6700 (the value
''34''). In DEC-10, the syntax of the clause is slightly different. The word
FILE is not optional and, if desired, a hyphen (-) may be used to connect
the words FILE and STATUS. In DEC-10 the data name should be defined with
picture 9(2). Alternatively, seven more data names can be specified. If
specified, these words will contain additional information regarding the
status of the input-output operation on this file.
    The USE statement as shown in the text is available in both B-6700 and
DEC-10 compilers. The only difference is that the EXTEND option is not available in DEC-10.
    In DEC-10, a PERFORM statement in a nondeclarative procedure can refer
to a USE section or to procedures contained within such sections. However,
this facility may not be used for the sake of portability.

(h) AT END Clause in READ Statement

According to ANSI 68 COBOL, the use of the AT END phrase in a READ statement
(for sequential files) is mandatory. According to ANSI 74 COBOL, the AT END
phrase need not be specified if an applicable USE procedure is specified.
This modification has been implemented in B-6700 and can be used by specifying the ANSI 74 compiler option.

EXERCISES

1. There are several ways to reduce the memory space required by a program. Indicate which of the following cannot help us to get the memory requirement reduced.
     (i)   RESERVE clause
     (ii) RERUN clause
    (iii) REDEFINES clause
     (iv) SAME RECORD AREA clause

2. COBOL provides options to set up special procedures for handling input-output errors. Indicate which of the following does not provide the said facility.
     (i)   INVALID KEY clause
     (ii) AT END clause
    (iii) CLOSE statement with the LOCK option
     (iv) USE procedure

3. Write down the important points that indicate the advantages and disadvantages of blocking.

4. Write the FD entry for a file of the following specifications.
     (i)   Title in MYFILE
     (ii) The file is to be referred to in the program by the name INFILE
    (iii) The file is to be retained for 100 days
     (iv) Each record of the file consists of 120 characters
      (v) The blocking factor is 15

5. Each record of a disk file to be created is of 270 characters. Each sector of the diskpack on which the file is being created can contain 180 characters. Write an appropriate BLOCK CONTAINS clause.

6. Indicate which of the following clauses for an input file can specify a characteristic different from the corresponding characteristic that was specified during the file creation.
     (i)   BLOCK CONTAINS clause
     (ii) SELECT file-name part of the SELECT clause
    (iii) LABEL RECORDS clause
     (iv) DATA RECORD clause
      (v) VALUE OF ID clause
     (vi) RESERVE clause.

7. Each record of a tape file contains the following information.

Position	Field
1- 7	Prescription number (numeric)
8-11	Doctor's code (alphanumeric)
12-13	Patient's age
14	Patient's sex code (numeric)
15-16	Drug count

Position	Field
17-96	Repeating groups which may occur 1 to 10 times. Each group consists of the following·

    (i)   Drug code   -   5 alphanumeric characters

    (ii)   Quantity prescribed   -   2 numeric characters

    (iii) Unit of measure   -   1 digit code

Obviously, the records are of variable lengths. The field called drug count indicates the actual number of drugs that have been prescribed. The file is blocked. Each block can contain at the most 1024 characters. The file title is PATIENTFL.

You are to read this file to create a diskfile with a fixed length records having the following format:

Position	Field
1-7	Prescription number
8-9	Patient's age
10	Patient's sex
11-15	Drug code
16-17	Quantity prescribed
18	Unit of measure

It may be noted that each record of the previous file will contribute to generate as many records of this file as are indicated by the value of the drug count. Choose a suitable title and blocking factor.

8. Introduce a batch total check in the validation program of Sec. 10.7. Assume that a batch consists of 20 or fewer cards and each batch is followed by a batch total card which is designated by the punching of X in column 80. The batch total cards contains the manually-calculated total of the instalment amounts of the records contained in the batch. Assume a suitable field for this total on the batch total card. In addition to the printing of the check list (which must now include batch errors), your program should also create a sequential tape file containing the valid records.

(Hint: You will require a table capable of holding 20 records.)

14

SORTING AND MERGING OF FILES

Often, during the processing of sequential files, it is required that the records in a file appear in some predetermined sequence. The process of sequencing the records in some desired manner is known as sorting.

Sorting is done upon some key data item in the record. For example, consider the case of a payroll file where each record contains all the necessary information of an employee, such as his identification number, name, address, department number, basic pay, allowances, deductions, etc. In this record we can think of any one of the fields say, name as the key for sorting and can get a new file in the sorted order from the original file. The sorting is done either in the ascending order or descending order of the key. If the file is sorted on the name field in the ascending order, the record of the employee whose name is greater than that of another employee will appear later in the sorted file. It is possible to sort a file on more than one key. For example, if we want to sort the said payroll file according to the department number and within each department according to the identification number, then two keys are involved — department number and identification number. In this case, the department number is the major key and the identification number the minor key.

It will not be out of place to compare the sorting of a table (one-dimensional) with that of a file. When a table is sorted, all its elements are in the memory of the computer and the sorting process has the advantage of having an access to the elements of the table in any manner by specifying the appropriate subscripts or indexes. However, when a sequential file is to be sorted, its records reside on the file medium and can be accessed to only serially. The sorting of sequential files, therefore, requires special procedures.

In COBOL, there is no specific feature for the sorting of a table. However, it provides a SORT verb that can be used to sort a sequential file. The sorting of a table has been discussed in Sec. 11.9. In this chapter, the SORT verb will be discussed. In addition to the SORT verb, the MERGE verb will also be discussed here. The MERGE verb can be used to merge several sorted files to create a new file containing the records of these files in the sorting order.

14.1 THE SIMPLE SORT VERB

The SORT verb like many other COBOL verbs, can have different forms. In the beginning, let us consider the simple form of the SORT verb. This form is to

be used when it is required to sort a given input file. The input file is
not disturbed; instead, a new output file containing the records in a sorted
order is created. Besides the input and output files, the SORT verb also
requires a work file. The work file is used during the process of sorting.
Thus the simple SORT verb requires the naming of three files — the unsorted
input file, the sorted output file and the work file. The format of the
simple SORT verb is as follows:

$$\underline{\text{SORT}} \quad \text{file-name-1} \quad \text{ON} \begin{Bmatrix} \underline{\text{ASCENDING}} \\ \underline{\text{DESCENDING}} \end{Bmatrix} \text{KEY} \quad \text{data-name-1} \begin{bmatrix} , \text{ data-name-2} \end{bmatrix} \ldots$$

$$\begin{bmatrix} \text{ON} \begin{Bmatrix} \underline{\text{ASCENDING}} \\ \underline{\text{DESCENDING}} \end{Bmatrix} \text{KEY} \quad \text{data-name-3} \begin{bmatrix} , \text{ data-name-4} \end{bmatrix} \ldots \end{bmatrix} \ldots$$

$$\underline{\text{USING}} \quad \text{file-name-2} \quad \underline{\text{GIVING}} \quad \text{file-name-3}.$$

File-name-1 is the name of the work file, whereas the names of the
input and output files are to be specified in file-name-2 and file-name-3
respectively. File-name-2 and file-name-3 should be described in the usual
manner by means of an FD entry. The work file is to be defined by a sort
description entry (SD entry). The format of the SD entry is as follows:

$$\underline{\text{SD}} \quad \text{file-name}$$

$$\begin{bmatrix} ; \underline{\text{RECORD}} \text{ CONTAINS} \begin{bmatrix} \text{integer-1} \underline{\text{TO}} \end{bmatrix} \text{integer-2 CHARACTERS} \end{bmatrix}$$

$$\begin{bmatrix} ; \underline{\text{DATA}} \begin{Bmatrix} \underline{\text{RECORD}} \text{ IS} \\ \underline{\text{RECORDS}} \text{ ARE} \end{Bmatrix} \text{data-name-1} \begin{bmatrix} , \text{ data-name-2} \end{bmatrix} \ldots \end{bmatrix}$$

The clauses have the same meanings as in the case of FD entry (see Sec. 5.4).
The record description of the work file should be done in the usual manner.

The following rules should be taken into consideration while specifying
the SORT verb.

(i)   The input, output as well as the work file are opened by the SORT
      statement before the sorting begins and are closed by the SORT
      statement itself after the sorting is over. Obviously, none of
      these files should remain open when the SORT statement is speci-
      fied.

(ii) There can be any number of SORT statements in a program.

(iii) The sorting can be done on any number of keys. Data-name-1 is the
      most major key. If there are other keys, they must follow data-
      name-1 in the decreasing order of significance. For a particular
      key, either the word ASCENDING or the word DESCENDING is used
      depending on the requirement. In one SORT statement both the words
      ASCENDING and DESCENDING can be used if there is more than one key.
      If all the keys are in ASCENDING (or DESCENDING) order, the word
      ASCENDING (or DESCENDING) need be mentioned only once before the
      most major key.

(iv) All the keys on which the sorting is done, must appear with their descriptions in the record descriptions of file-name-1. These keys need not be described either in file-name-2 or in file-name-3. The order of appearance of the keys in the SORT statement has no relevance to their positions within the record.

(v)   Keys in the SORT statement do not require any qualification even when they are identical to data names defined elsewhere.

(vi) When two or more records in the input file have identical keys, their relative order within the input file may not be retained in the output file.

(vii) The file-name-2 and file-name-3 must be sequential files.

(viii) The SELECT clause for the work file file-name-1 is SELECT file-name-1 ASSIGN TO hardware-name.

The hardware-name for the work file can vary with the computer being used. For the purpose of this book, we shall assume the names SORT-TAPE and SORT-DISK to be the hardware names for work files on the tape and disk respectively.

Example

Assume that we have a card file with the following records description in the DATA DIVISION.

```
FD   KARD-FILE.
01   INPUT-RECORD.
     02    ID-NUMBER      PIC    .9(6).
     02    NAME           PIC    X(24).
     02    DEPARTMENT     PIC    X(10).
     02    BASIC-PAY      PIC    9(5)V99.
     02    ALLOWANCE      PIC    9(4)V99.
     02    DEDUCTION      PIC    9(4)V99.
```

Suppose we wish to sort this KARD-FILE first on DEPARTMENT in ascending sequence and then within each department in the descending sequence of BASIC-PAY, i.e., all records having the same value for DEPARTMENT are to be arranged from the highest to the lowest values of BASIC-PAY. To sort this file we require one work file and one output file. Let the names of the work file and output file be SORT-FILE and OUTPUT-FILE respectively. The DATA DIVISION entries for these two files are as follows:

```
SD   SORT-FILE.
01   SORT-RECORD.
     02    FILLER         PIC    X(30).
     02    DEPARTMENT     PIC    X(10).
     02    BASIC-PAY      PIC    9(5)V99.
     02    FILLER         PIC    X(12).

FD   OUT-FILE.
01   OUTPUT-RECORD        PIC    X(59).
```

It may be noted that since the KARD-FILE is to be sorted on two keys — DEPARTMENT and BASIC-PAY — only these two keys need be described in the work file called SORT-FILE. It may also be noted that an overall description

of the output record is sufficient. In fact, for the purpose of sorting,
individual fields of both input and output files need not be described.
However, they may need detailed descriptions if the fields are to be
referred to in other part of the program. The following statement will sort
the input file and will create the sorted output file.

```
SORT    SORT-FILE ON ASCENDING KEY DEPARTMENT
        DESCENDING KEY BASIC-PAY
        USING KARD-FILE GIVING OUTPUT-FILE.
```

14.2 FILE UPDATION

The active lifetime of a file is usually short. Very soon the information
stored on a file becomes old and it becomes necessary to modify the file
with current information. This process of modifying an old file with current
information is known as file updation. File updation is an important task
and one comes across file-updation programs in almost all applications.

Before presenting the procedure for file updation, it is necessary to
introduce the terms master file and transaction file. A master file is a
file that is used as an authority in a given job. It may contain somewhat
permanent, historical, statistical or identification type of data. A transaction file, on the other hand, is a file that contains new records or changes
to old records which are used to update the master file. The problem of file
updation can be defined as follows. Given an old master file and a transaction file, the problem is to create an updated new master file. The process
of updation may include

- Insertion of new records
- Modification of some existing records
- Deletion of obsolete records
- Copy of those records which are neither obsolete nor require any
  modification.

For the solution of the problem, let us consider an example. Suppose
the master file contains information regarding the subscribers of a magazine.
Each record contains the following fields: subscriber number, name and
address. The transaction records contain the following fields: subscriber
number, transaction code, name and address. The transaction code indicates
the type of transaction. If the code is 1, it is assumed to be the record
of a new subscriber. A transaction code equal to 2 indicates that the subscriber has not renewed the subscription and the record is to be deleted.
Transaction code 3 indicates that there has been a change of address for the
subscriber and the record is to be modified. In the case of transaction code
3, the name field and in the case of transaction code 2, the name as well as
the address fields, are not required. However, for simplicity we assume that
all records of the transaction file have the same structure and those fields
where data are not required contain blanks.

For the purpose of identifying the records, the subscriber number in
both the files are used as the keys. It is also assumed that both the files
are sorted in the ascending order of their respective keys. Let M-SUBSCRIBER-
NO and T-SUBSCRIBER-NO be the data names for the key fields in the records
of the master file and transaction file respectively. The logic of updation
requires that in the beginning one record from each file is to be read. The
keys are then compared. If the keys are unequal, the record having the lower

key is to be copied to the new master file. This record can be a transaction record (new subscriber) or a master record (one of those subscribers for which no change is required). In either case a new record from the said file (the file whose record has been copied) is to be read and the process is to be repeated by comparing the master key and transaction key. If the two keys match, it can either be a case of modification or deletion. Therefore, the transaction code is to be checked and depending on the situation, either the modified record is to be written on the new master file or the writing on the new master file is to be skipped. Whatever be the case, the next record from the master file and the transaction file is to be read now and the process is to be repeated. This logic will work until either the master file or transaction file is exhausted. Note that either of these files can be exhausted earlier. In this case the remaining records of the other file are to be copied onto the new master file. This can be accomplished through the abovementioned logic, provided that when the files are exhausted, a fictitious record with a high-value key is forced to be treated as the record just read. The program now terminates when both the keys are found to be equal to high values. The flow chart and a structured program for this problem, are shown in Figs. 14.1 and 14.2 respectively.

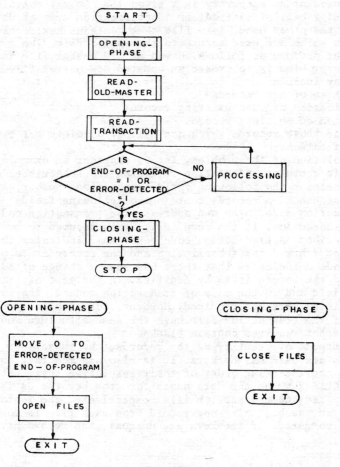

(contd.)

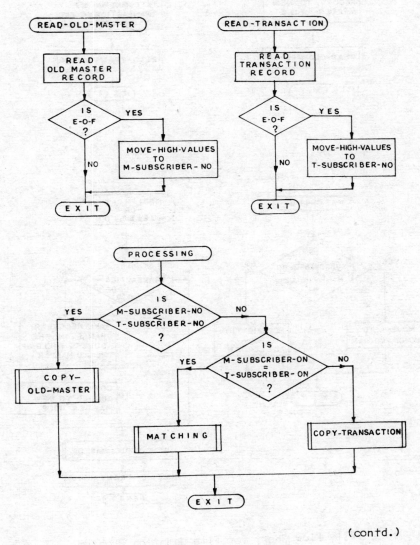

(contd.)

(contd.)

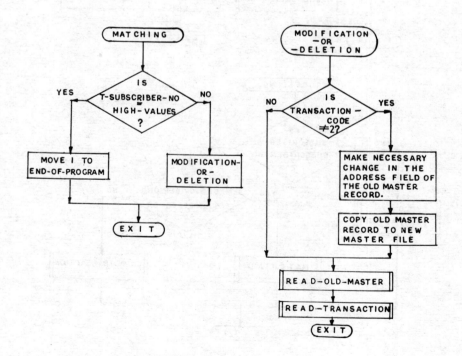

FIG. 14.1   Flow Chart for File Updation Problem

```
PROCEDURE DIVISION.
PARA-START.
     PERFORM  OPENING-PHASE.
     PERFORM  READ-OLD-MASTER.
     PERFORM  READ-TRANSACTION.
     PERFORM  PROCESSING  UNTIL  END-OF-PROGRAM = 1,
                              OR ERROR-DETECTED = 1.
     PERFORM  CLOSING-PHASE.
     STOP  RUN.

OPENING-PHASE.
     MOVE  O  TO  END-OF-PROGRAM, ERROR-DETECTED.
     OPEN  INPUT  OLD-MASTER, TRANSACTION
           OUTPUT  NEW-MASTER.

READ-OLD-MASTER.
     READ  OLD-MASTER  AT  END  MOVE  HIGH-VALUES  TO
                           M-SUBSCRIBER-NO.

READ-TRANSACTION.
     READ  TRANSACTION  AT  END  MOVE  HIGH-VALUES  TO
                           T-SUBSCRIBER-NO.

PROCESSING.
     IF  M-SUBSCRIBER-NO  IS  LESS  THAN T-SUBSCRIBER-NO
         PERFORM  COPY-OLD-MASTER
     ELSE IF  M-SUBSCRIBER-NO  IS  EQUAL  TO  T-SUBSCRIBER-NO
             PERFORM  MATCHING
             ELSE PERFORM  COPY-TRANSACTION.

COPY-OLD-MASTER.
     WRITE  NEW-MASTER-RECORD  FROM  OLD-MASTER-RECORD
            INVALID  KEY  MOVE  1  TO  ERROR-DETECTED.
     PERFORM  READ-OLD-MASTER.

COPY-TRANSACTION.
     MOVE  T-SUBSCRIBER-NO   TO  NEW-SUBSCRIBER-NO.
     MOVE  T-NAME  TO  NEW-NAME.
     MOVE  T-ADDRESS  TO  NEW-ADDRESS.
     WRITE NEW-MASTER-RECORD  INVALID KEY
           MOVE  1  TO  ERROR-DETECTED.
     PERFORM  READ-TRANSACTION.

MATCHING.
     IF  T-SUBSCRIBER-NO  IS  EQUAL  TO  HIGH-VALUES
         MOVE  1  TO  END-OF-PROGRAM
     ELSE  PERFORM  MODIFICATION-OR-DELETION.
```

(contd.)

```
MODIFICATION-OR-DELETION.
    IF  TRANSACTION-CODE  IS  NOT EQUAL TO  2
        MOVE  T-ADDRESS  TO  OLD-ADDRESS
        WRITE  NEW-MASTER-RECORD  FROM  OLD-MASTER-RECORD.
            INVALID KEY MOVE  1  TO  ERROR-DETECTED.
    PERFORM  READ-OLD-MASTER.
    PERFORM  READ-TRANSACTION.

CLOSING-PHASE.
    CLOSE  OLD-MASTER, NEW-MASTER, TRANSACTION.
PARA-END
    EXIT.
```

FIG. 14.2. Procedure Division Statements for File
            Updation Problem

14.3 VARIATIONS OF UPDATION

There are various forms of the updation problem. Some of them are discussed below.

14.3.1 Updation Without Insertion and More than One Transaction Record for a Master Record

Let us consider a problem where all the transaction records have corresponding master records. However, corresponding to a master record, there may be no transaction record or there may be one or more transaction records. Suppose the old master file contains information regarding the sale of a company. Each record contains the following fields: salesman number, name, total sale of the salesman up to the last day of the previous month from the first day of the year (referred to as year-to-date-sale) and the commission rate applicable to the particular salesman. The transaction record contains the following fields: salesman number, name, amount of sale and date of sale. There can be more than one record for a particular salesman in the transaction file. If a salesman is on leave in the current month, his information will not be in the transaction file. It is assumed that both the files are sorted on the salesman number which are denoted by M-SALESMAN-NO and T-SALESMAN-NO in the old master record and transaction record respectively. Now, to update the old master file we can use the previous flow chart with some modifications in the PROCESSING and MATCHING module as shown in Fig. 14.3.

In this case, when the two keys are equal, the corresponding field is updated and the record is read only from the transaction file. The master-file record is not read because there can be more than one record in the transaction file with the same salesman number. Also, in the PROCESSING module, when T-SALESMAN-NO becomes less than M-SALESMAN-NO, we move 1 to the field named ERROR-DETECTED instead of copying the transaction record

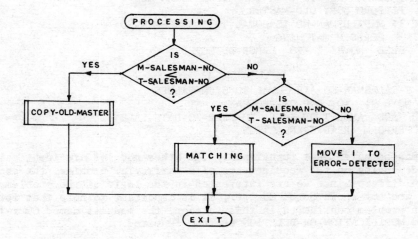

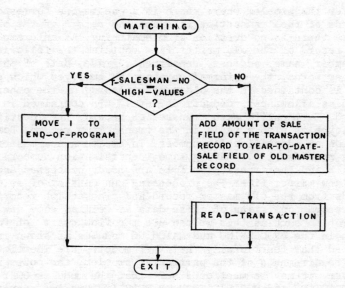

FIG. 14.3.   Partial Flow Chart for File Updation Without
Insertion and More Than One Transaction Record

in the new master file as in the previous case. This is because it has been
assumed that all the transaction records muat have corresponding master
records. The following are the two modules coded in COBOL.

PROCESSING.
```
    IF M-SALESMAN-NO  IS LESS THAN T-SALESMAN-NO
        PERFORM COPY-OLD-MASTER
    ELSE IF M-SALESMAN-NO IS EQUAL TO T-SALESMAN-NO
            PERFORM MATCHING
        ELSE  MOVE  1  TO  ERROR-DETECTED.
```

MATCHING.
```
    IF  T-SALESMAN-NO  IS EQUAL TO HIGH-VALUES
        MOVE  1  TO  END-OF-PROGRAM
    ELSE  ADD  AMOUNT-OF-SALE  TO YEAR-TO-DATE-SALE
        PERFORM  READ-TRANSACTION.
```

It may be noted that functionally the other modules are identical, though depending on the requirements of a particular problem, the codes in them can differ. Since we are interested in the logic of the problem, these modules are not shown here. However, it is important to note that for the updation problem considered in this section, the modules named COPY-TRANSAC-TION and MODIFICATION-OR-DELETION are not required.

14.3.2 File Matching

Let us now consider the problem where there is a one-to-one correspondence between the records of the transaction file and the record of the old master file. In this case there is no question of mismatching. As an example we assume that each record of the old master file contains the following fields: identification number, name, address, department, grade, date of joining and basic pay. In other words, the information about an employee which does not vary every month is contained in the old master record. On the other hand, information, such as allowances, deductions, etc., are contained in the transaction record. To identify each transaction record, the identification number of an employee is also a field in the transaction record. Both the files are sorted on an identification number. To create a new master file, the corresponding records (i.e., having same identification number) from both the old master file and the transaction file are read, processed and then written onto the new master file. The processing can consist of selecting appropriate fields from the old master record and transaction record and to construct a new record consisting of these data as well as some new computed results. For a problem such as this we can use the flow chart of Fig. 14.4. with some changes in the PROCESSING and MATCHING modules as shown in Fig. 14.4
It may be noted that functionally the other modules are identical, though depending on the requirements of the particular problem, the codes in them may differ. However, it may be mentioned here that the modules COPY-OLD-MASTER, COPY-TRANSACTION and MODIFICATION-OR-DELETION are not required for this problem. It is assumed that the MATCHING module refers to another module named PROCESSING-OF-RECORDS which takes care of the relevant processing of the old master record and transaction record and files in the record area of the new master file with the appropriate results and then finally writes the record onto the new master file.

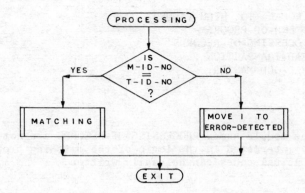

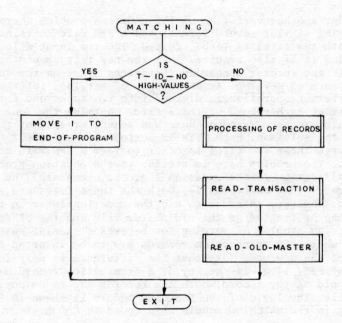

FIG. 14.4. Partial Flow Chart for File Matching

The following are the two modules coded in COBOL.

```
PROCESSING.
    IF  M-ID-NO  IS  EQUAL  TO  T-ID-NO
        PERFORM MATCHING
    ELSE MOVE  1  TO  ERROR-DETECTED.
```

```
MATCHING.
      IF  T-ID-NO  IS  EQUAL  TO  HIGH-VALUES
            MOVE  1  TO  END-OF-PROGRAM
      ELSE  PERFORM  PROCESSING-OF-RECORDS
            PERFORM  READ-TRANSACTION
            PERFORM  READ-OLD-MASTER.

PROCESSING-OF-RECORDS.
```

The details of the module named PROCESSING-OF-RECORDS are not shown here as we are mainly interested in the logic of the matching problem; in a specific case, the actual codes can be easily written.

14.3.3 File Merging

Let us now consider another variation of the updation problem where there are two files having similar record formats and a new file containing all the records of both the files is to be created. The two input files are sorted on a key and it is also required that the new file should be created in such a way that the records appear in the sorted order on the same key. This problem is known as merging. As an example of merging, let there be a company whose marketing operation is divided into two zones and for each zone there is a file. Each record of these files contains the zone name, district name, salesman name, product name and amount of sale of the particular product by the salesman. Each file is sorted on the product name. It is required to merge these two files together to form a new file containing all sales records. The problem here is similar to the updation problem and only a slight modification in the updation logic is necessary. The first point to note here is that conceptually, both the input files are really transaction files. However, in order to use the updation logic in this case, any one of them can be treated as the old master file and the other as the transaction file. The problem of merging now becomes a special case of the updation problem where all transaction records are to be inserted in the old master file to get the new one. Note that the difference is only in the MATCHING module of Sec. 14.2. If the key of a transaction record matches with that of the old master record, both the records are to be copied onto the new master file. The logic of the MATCHING module is shown in Fig. 14.5.
The following is the MATCHING module when coded in COBOL.

```
MATCHING.
      IF  T-PRODUCT-NAME  IS  EQUAL  TO  HIGH-VALUES
            MOVE  1  TO  END-OF-PROGRAM
    ELSE  PERFORM  COPY-TRANSACTION
            PERFORM  COPY-OLD-MASTER
            PERFORM  READ-TRANSACTION
            PERFORM  READ-OLD-MASTER.
```

It may be noted that functionally the other modules are identical, though depending on the requirements of the particular problem, the code in them may differ. However, it may be mentioned here that for the problem

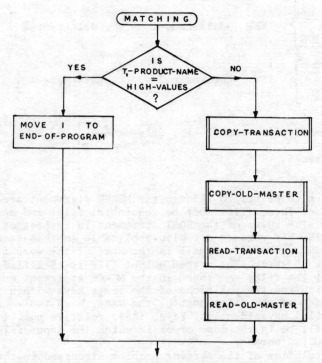

FIG. 14.5.   Partial Flow Chart for File Merging

considered in this section, the module name MODIFICATION-OR-DELETION is not required.

An extension of the above problem is when it is required to merge more than two input files to create a single, merged file. As an example, let us consider that the said company operates in more than two zones and for each zone there is a file. This problem may be solved by the repeated execution of the program that merges two files.

14.4   SIMPLE MERGE VERB

Like sorting, the merging of files is frequently required in various commercial applications. In the previous section we have seen how two sorted files can be merged. The merging of the files can also be done in COBOL with the help of the MERGE verb. It is possible to merge two or more files with one MERGE statement. The format of the simple MERGE verb is as follows:

MERGE   file-name-1

ON $\left\{\begin{array}{l}\underline{\text{ASCENDING}} \\ \text{DESCENDING}\end{array}\right\}$ KEY   data-name-1 $\left[\,,\text{ data-name-2}\right]$ ...

$\left[\text{ON} \left\{\begin{array}{l}\underline{\text{ASCENDING}} \\ \text{DESCENDING}\end{array}\right\} \text{ KEY data-name-3 } \left[\,,\text{ data-name-4}\right] \dots \right]$ ...

USING file-name-2, file-name-3 $\left[\,,\text{ file-name-4}\right]$ ...

GIVING file-name-5.

The input files to be merged through the MERGE statement are specified
in the USING phrase. These files must be sequential files and must be sorted
on the merge keys. The rules of the SORT statement in respect of the
ASCENDING/DESCENDING KEY phrases are also applicable in this case. As in
the case of the SORT verb, file-name-1 is the name of the work file and must
be described in an SD entry. The merged output file is specified in the
GIVING phrase. All the files mentioned in the MERGE statement must have
records of same size and the positions of the merge keys within the record
descriptions of each of the files must be the same. When two records from
different input files have identical keys, their relative positions within
the merged file will be in the same order in which the input file names are
specified in the USING phrase.

The complete solution of the merging problem discussed in the previous
section is given here using the MERGE verb. It is assumed that there are
three zones and as such three sales files are to be merged. These files are
named as ZONE-FILE-1, ZONE-FILE-2 and ZONE-FILE-3.

```
FILE CONTROL.
        SELECT    ZONE-FILE-1    ASSIGN  TO  TAPE.
        SELECT    ZONE-FILE-2    ASSIGN  TO  TAPE.
        SELECT    ZONE-FILE-3    ASSIGN  TO  TAPE.
        SELECT    WORK-FILE      ASSIGN  TO  MERGE-DISK.
        SELECT    MERGED-FILE    ASSIGN  TO  TAPE.

DATA DIVISION.
FILE SECTION.
FD   ZONE-FILE-1
     BLOCK  CONTAINS  20  RECORDS
     VALUE  OF  ID  "ZONEFILE1".
01   FILE-1-RECORD  PIC      X(90).

FD   ZONE-FILE-2
     BLOCK  CONTAINS  15  RECORDS
     VALUE  OF  ID  "ZONEFILE2".
01   FILE-2-RECORD  PIC      X(90).
```

```
FD   ZONE-FILE-3
     BLOCK  CONTAINS  10  RECORDS
     VALUE  OF  ID  "ZONEFILE3".
01   FILE-3-RECORD    PIC    X(90).


FD   MERGED-FILE
     BLOCK  CONTAINS  20  RECORDS
     VALUE  OF  ID   "MERGEDFILE".
01   MERGED-RECORD    PIC    X(90).


SD   WORK-FILE.
01   WORK-RECORD.
     02  FILLER        PIC    X(50).
     02  PRODUCT-NAME  PIC    X(20).
     02  FILLER        PIC    X(20).

PROCEDURE DIVISION.
MERGING-PARA.
        MERGE  WORK-FILE  ON  ASCENDING  KEY  PRODUCT-NAME
        USING  ZONE-FILE-1,  ZONE-FILE-2,  ZONE-FILE-3
        GIVING  MERGED-FILE.
        STOP  RUN.
```

It has been assumed that all the three input files and the final merged
file named as MERGED-FILE are tape files. As in the case of the SORT verb,
in this case also the file name defined as SD entry requires a special hardware name in the SELECT clause depending on the system where the program is
to be run. Here we assume the hardware name to be MERGE-DISK. It may also
be mentioned that all the three input files can be blocked differently or
can have the same records per block.

14.5 INPUT AND OUTPUT PROCEDURE IN SORT STATEMENT

The SORT verb that we have discussed so far simply sorts all the records of
an input file on a key or a number of keys in a specified manner and gives
a sorted output file. The output file contains all the records of the original input file, but the relative position of the records are different. The
records of the work file, input file and output file must all have the same
character size and the position of the keys within the record must be the
same for all the three files. In certain applications some editing of the
input records before the sorting operation is required. Sometimes, editing
of the sorted records before they are placed on the output file is also
necessary. Editing in this context can mean the selection of appropriate
records for sorting. For example, it may not be necessary to sort all the
records of a file. Instead, only those records which meet certain conditions
are to be selected for sorting and the output file should get only these
selected records in the sorted order. Editing can also mean that a part or
whole of the input/output record or all or some of the input or output
records are to be edited. For example, a file with variable-length records
will require padding with some characters to make them records of fixed
length for the purpose of sorting. Similar editing will be necessary after
the sorting to bring the records to their original forms. Files having

multiple-record formats with the sort key placed at different positions in different records need modification so that all the records after modification will have sort keys in the same position within each record. The SORT verb allows the user to specify input and output procedures which can be suitably coded to take care of the required editing. The procedures are nothing but sections of the code placed outside the SORT statement. Thus when an input procedure is specified, the sorting process does not get the input records from a file. Instead, the SORT statement before the start of the sorting operation implicitly performs the specified input procedure. This procedure, which is to be written by the programmer, must read the input records from the input file, perform the required editing on them and then release the records to the sorting operation by means of a RELEASE statement. Normally, the input procedure includes a loop which is terminated when all the records to be sorted have been released. After this the procedure is exited. The output procedure is designed almost in the same manner as in the case of an input procedure. The difference in this case is that the output procedure is implicitly performed by the SORT statement after the completion of the sorting operation. The output procedure can get the records from the sorting operation in the sorted order by means of a RETURN statement. These two procedures are like normal procedures although they must be designed as consisting of one or more sections. The general format of the SORT statement can now be written as follows:

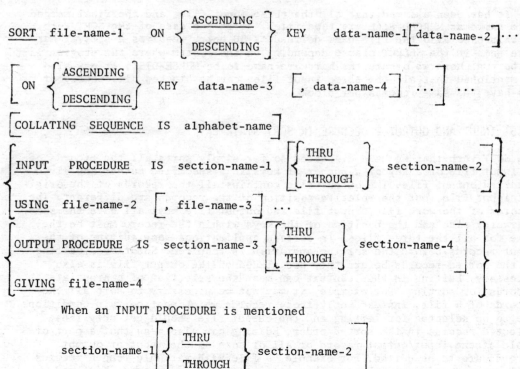

When an INPUT PROCEDURE is mentioned

$$\text{section-name-1} \left[\left\{ \begin{array}{l} \underline{\text{THRU}} \\ \underline{\text{THROUGH}} \end{array} \right\} \text{section-name-2} \right]$$

specifies the range of statements in the procedure. Before the start of the sorting, the control is passed to the input procedure to obtain the records

to be sorted. The statements in this procedure should read or otherwise
generate the records, edit them and release each of them to the sorting
operation by means of a RELEASE statement. As such there must be at least
one RELEASE statement within the procedure. The format of the RELEASE statement is as follows:

RELEASE   record-name   [FROM   identifier]

The record-name must be the name of the record specified in the work file
(i.e., file-name-1 which is defined as a sort-description entry). The FROM
phrase has the same meaning as in the case of the WRITE statement.

When an output procedure is specified, the control is passed to it after
the sorting operation. Here also

$$\text{section-name-3} \begin{bmatrix} \begin{Bmatrix} \text{THRU} \\ \text{THROUGH} \end{Bmatrix} \text{section-name-4} \end{bmatrix}$$

mentioned after the output procedure specifies the range of statements in
the procedure. This procedure again allows the selection and/or modification
of the sorted records and writing them onto an output file. Obviously, there
must be at least one RETURN statement to make available the sorted records
for editing. The format of the RETURN statement is as follows:

RETURN   file-name   RECORD   [INTO   identifier]

; AT   END   imperative statement .

In this case the file-name must be the name of the work file. The INTO
phrase has the same meaning as in the case of the READ statement.

When the USING option is used, note that more than one file name may be
specified. If this is done, all records from these files are transferred to
the sorting operation. However, most compilers allow only one file name to
be specified after USING.

The optional COLLATING-SEQUENCE clause is an ANSI 74 feature. It allows
the programmer to specify a collating sequence other than the NATIVE collating sequence. The way to specify an alphabet name has been discussed in
connection with the CODE-SET clause (see Sec. 13.3.6).

The following are the restrictions when these procedures are used.
  (i)   Procedures must not contain any SORT/MERGE statement.
  (ii) An explicit transfer of control outside the procedures (through
        ALTER, GO TO, PERFORM, etc.) is not allowed.
  (iii) The control must not be passed to any part of these procedures
        from elsewhere in the program. In other words, the control must
        reach the statements only through associated SORT statements.
  (iv) Procedures must consist of one or more sections and they must
        appear contiguously in the body of the program.
  (v)   The input and output procedures must not share any section or
        any part between them.

14.6 AN EXAMPLE OF SORT STATEMENT WITH INPUT/OUTPUT PROCEDURES

Suppose, each record of a file to be sorted contains the following fields besides others — account-status, amount and account-number. The account-number is the key on which the records are to be sorted. The following kinds of editing are required.

    (i)   If the account-status of a record in the input file is equal to zero, the record is to be ignored and should not be selected for sorting.

    (ii) If the amount is found to be equal to zero, the record should not be ignored but an appropriate message along with the corresponding account-number is to be displayed.

Figure 14.6 shows the PROCEDURE DIVISION of the required program. The first editing has been implemented in the input procedure named CHECK-STATUS. The output procedure named CHECK-AMOUNT is designed to perform the second editing. It may be worthwhile to note the reason for having both output and input procedures for this problem. If we wish to have only an output procedure to take care of both kinds of editing, the program will become less efficient. This is because the records are ignored only after they have taken part in the sorting operation. If we wish to have only an input procedure to take care of both kinds of editing, the displays will not appear in the sorted sequence of the account numbers. In the code of Fig. 14.6 the following names have been assumed.

Name	Description
IN-FILE	Input file
OUT-FILE	Output file
WORK-FILE	Work file
SORT-REC	Record name of work file
IN-REC	Record name of input file
OUT-REC	Record name of output file
ACCOUNT-STATUS	Account-status in input file
AMOUNT	Amount in output file
ACCOUNT-NUMBER	Account-number both in work file and output file

```
PROCEDURE DIVISION.
SORTING  SECTION.
PARA-BEGIN.
      SORT  WORK-FILE  ON  ASCENDING KEY ACCOUNT-NUMBER
            INPUT  PROCEDURE  IS  CHECK-STATUS
            OUTPUT  PROCEDURE  IS  CHECK-AMOUNT.
      STOP RUN.

CHECK-STATUS  SECTION.
PARA-OPEN-INPUT.
         OPEN  INPUT  IN-FILE.
PARA-READ.
```

(contd.)

```
            READ  IN-FILE  AT END  GO TO END-OF-INPUT
            IF  ACCOUNT-STATUS  IS  EQUAL  TO  ZERO
                  NEXT  SENTENCE
            ELSE  RELEASE SORT-REC  FROM  IN-REC.
            GO  TO  PARA-READ.
      END-OF-INPUT.
            CLOSE  IN-FILE.
      PARA-EXIT-INPUT.
            EXIT.
      CHECK-AMOUNT  SECTION.
      PARA-OPEN-OUTPUT.
            OPEN  OUTPUT  OUT-FILE.
      RETURN-AND-CHECK.
            RETURN  WORK-FILE  RECORD  INTO  OUT-REC
                    AT END  GO  TO  END-OF-OUTPUT.
            IF  AMOUNT  IS  EQUAL  TO  ZERO
                DISPLAY  "ZERO  BALANCE IN",  ACCOUNT-NUMBER
                  OF  OUT-REC.
            WRITE  OUT-REC.
            GO  TO  RETURN-AND-CHECK.
      END-OF-OUTPUT
            CLOSE  OUT-FILE.
      PARA-EXIT-OUTPUT.
            EXIT.
```

FIG. 14.6. A Sample Program with INPUT/OUTPUT
Procedures

14.7 MERGE VERB WITH OUTPUT PROCEDURE

Like the SORT verb, the MERGE verb can also have an output procedure.
However, no input procedure can be specified for the MERGE verb. The syntax of the MERGE verb is given below.

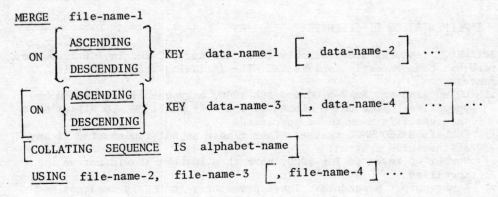

```
MERGE    file-name-1

        ┌ ASCENDING  ┐
  ON    │            │  KEY  data-name-1  [ , data-name-2 ]  ...
        └ DESCENDING ┘

  ┌        ┌ ASCENDING  ┐                                        ┐
  │  ON    │            │  KEY  data-name-3  [ , data-name-4 ]  ... │  ...
  └        └ DESCENDING ┘                                        ┘

  [ COLLATING  SEQUENCE  IS  alphabet-name ]

    USING  file-name-2,  file-name-3  [ , file-name-4 ]  ...
```

$$\begin{bmatrix} \underline{OUTPUT} \quad \underline{PROCEDURE} \quad IS \quad section\text{-}name\text{-}1 \begin{bmatrix} \begin{Bmatrix} \underline{THRU} \\ \underline{THROUGH} \end{Bmatrix} \quad section\text{-}name\text{-}2 \end{bmatrix} \\ \underline{GIVING} \quad file\text{-}name\text{-}5 \end{bmatrix}$$

The rules for specifying and coding the output procedure is identical to those in the case of the SORT verb.

14.8 SAME SORT AREA CLAUSE

Like the SAME AREA clause (see Sec. 13.9), this clause can also be specified in the I-O-CONTROL paragraph to have two or more files to share same memory area during execution. The clause has the following format.

$$\underline{SAME} \begin{Bmatrix} \underline{SORT} \\ \underline{SORT\text{-}MERGE} \end{Bmatrix} \quad AREA \quad FOR \quad file\text{-}name\text{-}2 \quad [\ , \ file\text{-}name\text{-}3 \ ] \ ...$$

At least one of the files quoted in this clause must be defined with SD. The SAME SORT AREA clause enables two or more sort/merge work files to use same area. However, in many systems, the areas required by a file is allocated only when a file is opened and deallocated when the file is closed. In such systems, the SAME SORT AREA clause may not be useful, because only one sort/merge file can be open at a time. The words SORT and SORT-MERGE mean the same thing.

14.9 MEMORY SIZE CLAUSE

The MEMORY SIZE clause (see Sec. 4.2.1) of the OBJECT-COMPUTER paragraph can be specified to indicate the maximum amount of memory space that can be used by the sorting operation. This clause is optional and, if omitted, a standard memory size is assumed.

14.10 IMPLEMENTATION DIFFERENCES

The SORT/MERGE features are available in B-6700 and DEC-10. In ICL-1900 the SORT verb has been recently implemented. The following are the notable differences.
  (i)   USING clause: In B-6700 and ICL-1900, only one file name can be specified in the USING clause of the SORT verb. DEC-10 allows more than one file name to be specified.
 (ii)   COLLATING SEQUENCE clause: This clause is not implemented in any of the three systems.
(iii)   Number of keys: In ICL-1900, more than 10 keys should not be specified.
 (iv)   Input-output procedures: These procedures in DEC-10 need not be sections. A consecutive paragraph may be coded as input or output procedure. However, the input and output procedures must not over-lap.

(v)   MERGE statement: In B-6700 a maximum of 8 files can be merged by a
       single MERGE statement.

(vi)   SAME SORT AREA clause: This clause is available in all the three
        compilers for compatibility reasons and has no effect.

(vii)   Some additional restrictions: The compilers under consideration
         put certain restrictions on the class, usage and size of the keys
         as well as on the record size. These are minor restrictions in
         the sense that they do not pose any serious problem in most appli-
         cations. We shall therefore not discuss them.

(viii)   MEMORY-SIZE clause: The MEMORY SIZE clause is not optional in
          ICL-1900 and as such must be used. The memory size specified must
          not be less than 5000 words.

EXERCISES

1. The following is a COBOL statement using the SORT verb:

    SORT FILE-IN ON ASCENDING KEY DEPARTMENT
          BASIC-PAY USING FILE-A GIVING FILE-B.

    (a) Which is the major key field?
    (b) Which is the minor key field?
    (c) Which file should have an SD entry and what data names must
         appear in the record description of this file?
    (d) If we wish to sort the minor key in descending order, what will
         be the SORT statement?
    (e) What is the name of the final sorted file?
    (f) On how many keys is the file sorted and what are the names of
         the keys?

2. The following is a MERGE statement:

    MERGE WORK-FILE ON ASCENDING KEY PERSONAL-NUMBER
       USING PERSONAL-FILE, SALARY-FILE, TAX-FILE,
             ADVANCE-FILE
       GIVING COMPANY-FILE

    (a) Which file should have an SD entry?
    (b) What are the files which are to be merged?
    (c) What is the name of the merged file?
    (d) On how many keys does the merging take place?

3. Fill up the blanks in the following:
    (a) The work file to be referred to in SORT or MERGE statements is
         identified by the......level indicator in the DATA DIVISION.
    (b) The RELEASE verb may be considered to be a special form of the
         ......verb.
    (c) An input procedure in a SORT verb must have a statement begin-
         ning with the verb.......
    (d) The MERGE verb cannot have an......PROCEDURE.

4. Consider the problem considered in Sec. 14.3.1. Write the complete program for this problem. Assume suitable field descriptions for the purpose.

5. Write a structured program for the problem in Sec. 14.4 without using the MERGE verb.

6. Write a program that will sort a magnetic-tape file into the trans-code within the account-number order.

Positions	Fields
1-8	Account-number (alphanumeric)
9-15	Not used
16-17	Trans-code (numeric integer)
18-60	Not used

7. Consider Problem 6 given above. Sort the file with the following editing:
   (i) Any trans-code greater than 50 should be changed to zero before sorting.
   (ii) Two sorted output files are to be created. The first one contain all records in the sorted order and the second one should contain only those records whose trans-code is equal to zero. The second file must be in the account-number order.

8. Consider the following card formats:

Card Type 1

Card Column	Field
1- 8	Supplier's code
9-30	Supplier's name
31-79	Supplier's address
80	Card type (1 digit code)

Card Type 2

Card Column	Field
1- 8	Supplier's code
9-16	Part number
17-43	Part description
44-51	Part number
52-78	Part description
79	Not used
80	Card type (1 digit code)

Note that card type 2 can contain one or two part numbers with corresponding descriptions. In case there is one part number the second part number and its description are blank fields. Except where specified otherwise, consider all fields to be alphanumeric.

Write a program to read these cards and to copy them onto a disk file. Sort this disk file on the supplier code and within it on a card type. Read this sorted file to generate a check list which must contain the following.
   (i) All type 1 cards for which there is no corresponding type 2 card.
   (ii) All type 2 cards for which there is no corresponding type 1 card.
   (iii) All cards containing card type other than 1 or 2.

15

MORE ABOUT STRUCTURED PROGRAMMING

The proponents of structured programming appear to be divided on the question of using the GO TO statements in structured programs. While some recommend the total avoidance of GO TO's in structured programs, others favour a constrained use of the statement. Without entering into this controversy, it may be stated that the GO TO statements need not be avoided just for the sake of avoiding them. Only when their use requires a compromise with the readability of the program, must they be eliminated.

How to avoid GO TO's in a program was discussed earlier. When to use them is the point to be discussed in this chapter. In the latter part of this chapter an example is presented to show how certain programming difficulties are eliminated if structured programming is used.

15.1 CONSTRAINED USE OF GO TO

Some general rules for the constrained use of GO TO's in COBOL programs have been provided by Armstrong (1973). The rules are given below. It may be noted that each rule is more restrictive than the preceding one.
  (i)   Use GO TO to transfer the control within a module without crossing its boundaries. In other words, a short-range GO TO statement whose object is either the name of the paragraph in which it appears or the name of any other paragraph in a series of paragraphs that constitutes the module is allowed according to this rule.
  (ii) Use GO TO to transfer the control in the forward direction within a module. This rule is more restrictive than the previous one as it does not allow the use of the GO TO statement to transfer the control in the backward direction.
  (iii) Use GO TO to transfer the control to the exit paragraph of the series of paragraphs constituting the module.
  It is worthwhile to note that these rules ensure a localized flow of control so that the readability of the module is not likely to be seriously affected. Moreover, the module as a whole can still be viewed to have a single entry and single exit.

Let us now consider some programming situations where the GO TO statement can be conveniently used obeying the abovementioned rules.

15.2 GO TO STATEMENT AND SORT-MERGE FEATURE

We know that an input procedure can be specified in a SORT statement and an output procedure can be specified in a SORT or MERGE statement. It is extremely difficult to code these input and output procedures without using the GO TO statement. For example, consider the input procedure of the example in Sec. 14.3 and let us try to code it without using the GO TO statements. A possible solution may be

```
CHECK-STATUS  SECTION.
PARA-MAIN.

      MOVE  ZERO  TO  END-FLAG.
      PERFORM  READ-PARA
             UNTIL END-FLAG IS EQUAL TO  1.
      CLOSE  IN-FILE.

READ-PARA.

      IF  END-FLAG  =  ZERO
          READ IN-FILE AT END MOVE 1 TO END-FLAG.
      IF END-FLAG  =  ZERO
          IF ACCOUNT-STATUS IS NOT EQUAL TO ZERO
             RELEASE SORT-REC FROM IN-REC.

PARA-EXIT.  EXIT.
```

Note the difficulty in this case. The PARA-MAIN is similar to a main-line paragraph of a structured program in the sense that it controls the other paragraphs in the input procedure. The main-line module of a structured program usually ends with a STOP RUN statement so that the other modules controlled by it are never executed by having the control falling through them. However, the PARA-MAIN cannot have a STOP RUN statement after the CLOSE statement for obvious reasons. Thus, having executed the CLOSE statement, the control falls through the paragraph named READ-PARA. In order to prevent the execution of the READ statement in this case, the first IF statement is required. The second IF statement also serves the same purpose, though it is also necessary to avoid GO TO in the AT END clause. Although it has been possible to avoid GO TO, it cannot be denied that with these IF statements the code has become somewhat obscure. Moreover, each introduction of IF statements (note that had there been more paragraphs in this input procedure, more IF statements would have been necessary) which are executed every time the loop is executed, can generate a terribly inefficient code. A GO TO PARA-EXIT statement after the CLOSE statement would have solved much of the difficulties. Thus it is better not to write obscure codes by avoiding GO TO just for the sake of avoiding it.

15.3 GO TO WITH DEPENDING ON IN STRUCTURED PROGRAMS

Consider the following code.

```
PROCESS-AN-ACCOUNT.

        GO TO   CASE-ONE
                CASE-TWO
                CASE-THREE
                CASE-FOUR
                DEPENDING  ON  ACCOUNT-TYPE.

        < process invalid accounts >

        GO  TO  END-OF-PROCESS.

CASE-ONE.

        < process  ACCOUNT-TYPE = 1 >

        GO TO   END-OF-PROCESS.

CASE-TWO.

        < process  ACCOUNT-TYPE = 2 >

        GO TO   END-OF-PROCESS.

CASE-THREE

        < process ACCOUNT-TYPE = 3 >

        GO TO   END-OF-PROCESS.

CASE-FOUR

        < process ACCOUNT-TYPE = 4 >

END-OF-PROCESS. EXIT.
```

   The above code represents a structure which is known as the CASE structure. A CASE structure is very useful when the programmer wants to specify
different actions for the different values of a transaction code. In the
above example, the paragraphs named CASE-ONE, CASE-TWO, CASE-THREE and CASE-
FOUR contain statements that are to be executed when the value of ACCOUNT-
TYPE is 1, 2, 3 and 4 respectively. The statements that are to be executed
for any other (invalid) value of ACCOUNT-TYPE are written immediately after
the GO TO DEPENDING ON statement. It may be noted that the GO TO statement
in each case brings the control to the exit para (named END-OF-PROCESS).
Thus the range of paragraphs PROCESS-AN-ACCOUNT THRU END-OF-PROCESS has
only one entry and one exit. The flow chart of a general CASE structure is
shown in Fig. 15.1.
   Since the CASE structure has only one entry and one exit, it is often
considered to be a basic structure for structured programming. In some
programming languages, a CASE statement is available that directly implements the structure. There is no CASE statement in COBOL. The COBOL statement which is closest to a CASE statement is GO TO with the DEPENDING phrase.

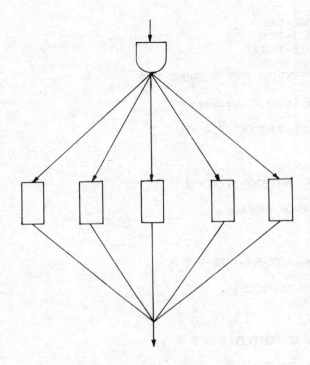

FIG. 15.1.   CASE Structure

However, the implementation of the CASE structure through this statement requires the use of GO TO statements as shown in the above example. Moreover, GO TO with the DEPENDING phrase has the same drawbacks as those of a GO TO statement.

An alternative implementation for a CASE structure in COBOL is possible through IF statements. For this purpose the IF statements can be used in two ways — either in the form of a nested IF sentence or in the form of a sequence of IF sentence, each representing a case condition. However, when a large number of cases are to be handled, the code with IF statements can become obscure. The representation of the CASE structure through the GO TO DEPENDING ON statement is more convenient.

15.4   SUMMING-UP

To conclude this discussion on the use of GO TO statements, we would like to recommend the following.

Avoid GO TO if it can be done without too much effort. When a GO TO statement is to be used, try to use it only to transfer the control in the forward direction, preferably to the exit paragraph of a module.

15.5   DISCIPLINED USE OF COBOL STATEMENTS

Merely a disciplined use of GO TO statement is not all. A disciplined use of other COBOL statements is also necessary. There are many instances where a COBOL statement can be written in an <u>ambiguous</u> way. The word ambiguity in this context mean uncertainty of how a COBOL compiler may interpret the concerned statement. For example, there were many ambiguities in the ANSI 68 standard and different implementors interpreted them in different ways. Some of these have been resolved in ANSI 74, but there are still many ANSI 68 compilers. In the following, we include some instances of the ambiguous COBOL statements and advise the readers not to use them in programs. Such discipline increases the readability as well as portability of a program.

(a)   MOVE Statement

An ambiguous use of a MOVE statement may be as follows:

        MOVE   A(I)   TO   I   B   C.

It is not clear what will be moved to B and C since the value of I is being changed. According to ANSI 74 interpretation, the value of A(I) as indicated by the old value of I, will be moved to B and C. However, how a compiler will behave in this case is doubtful.

This kind of ambiguous use is also possible in the case of those arithmetic verbs where more than one receiving field can be specified.

(b)   FROM in VARYING or VARYING-AFTER Clauses

Consider the statement

        PERFORM   THIS-PARA
            VARYING   I   FROM   J   BY   1   UNTIL   I > J + 10.

Now, suppose the paragraph THIS-PARA contains the statement

        SUBTRACT   1   FROM   J.

which is executed each time the paragraph is performed. Now, the question is: How many times is the loop executed?

According to ANSI 68 standard, the answer is 10 times. However, according to ANSI 74 standard, the answer is 6 times. This is because, according to ANSI 74, any change to FROM, BY and VARYING variables (identifiers/index-names) affects the operation of the PERFORM statement while according to ANSI 68, any change to FROM variable has no effect on the operation of the PERFORM statement. However, in respect of the variables in the VARYING and BY phrases there is no difference between the two standards. Obviously, the kind of use shown above should be avoided.

(c)   WRITE and REWRITE Statements

When a WRITE statement or a REWRITE statement is successfully executed on a file, the record area is not supposed to retain the information. However, in some compilers, the record area still contains the information, particularly when blocking is not used. As a result, some programmers make use of the data from this area in the subsequent part of the program. Obviously, this is not a healthy practice and should not be used. In order to avoid this practice, we would recommend that whenever necessary, the programmer should use the WRITE and REWRITE statements with the FROM option. Obviously, there is no ambiguity of the COBOL language in this matter.

Some similar instances, such as the interpretation of NOT in the abbreviated conditions, have already been discussed in appropriate places.

15.6   CONTROL BREAKS AND STRUCTURED PROGRAMMING

The problem of control breaks arises frequently during the processing of sorted sequential files. Let us illustrate the problem with the help of an example. Suppose, the following is the record format of a sequential disk file.

Position	Field
1	Zone Number (numeric)
2 - 3	District Number (numeric)
4 - 5	Salesman Number (numeric)
6 - 11	Amount of Sale (numeric with 2 digits after assumed decimal point)
12 - 60	Not used for this problem.

Each record pertains to the sale of a product made by the salesman of the company. The file is sorted. The keys in the order of significance are zone number, district number and salesman number. Obviously, all records relating to a particular salesman appear together in the file, because it is sorted on salesman number as the minor key. Similarly, all records that relates to a particular district also appear together in the file, and so on. The problem is to print a report containing the following:

   (i)   For each sale, a detail line containing the information regarding the sale.

  (ii)   For each salesman, a line containing the total sales made by him.

 (iii)   For each district, a line containing the total sales of the district.

 (iv)   For each zone, a line containing the total sales of the zone.

  (v)   A final line containing the total sales of all the zones.

It may be noted that these total lines will appear in between the detail lines. Thus, at the end of the last detail line for a salesman, his total line will appear in the report. In case he happens to be the last salesman of a district, this total line should be followed by the district total line otherwise, it should be followed by the first detail line of the next salesman, and so on. A sample portion of the desired report is shown in Fig. 15.3.

To tackle a problem like this, it is important to recognize the following situations.

   (i)   <u>Minor Break</u>: The salesman number of a record differs from the salesman number of the previous record but the zone numbers and district numbers in the two records are identical.

(ii) <u>Intermediate Break</u>: The district number of a record differs from the district number of the previous record but the zone numbers in the two are identical. Note that an intermediate break also indicates a minor break.

(iii) <u>Major Break</u>: The zone number of a record differs from the zone number of the previous record. Note that a major break also indicates intermediate and minor breaks.

In this example there are only three levels of control break as because, there are three levels of keys. In general, there may be one or more levels of breaks.

The processing of records should consist of appropriate actions in the case of the abovementioned breaks as well as when there is no break. However, the logic mentioned above has enough scope for pitfalls about which the reader should be aware. The following points may be noted:

(i)   A higher level control break also indicates all lower level control breaks. Therefore, the test for a control break should start from the highest level key field and proceed to the lowest level key field.

(ii) To ensure that there is no break, the programmer must check all the key fields for equality. The fact that there is no minor break, does not necessarily ensure that there cannot be a break at higher levels.

(iii) The checking of a control break is only done after reading a new record from the file. Appropriate action on the control break should be followed by the processing of this record. The programmer must not read a new record before the processing of this record is over. This is a common mistake and is known as the problem of ''vanishing records''.

(iv) The first record should be processed separately.

(v)   When the end of the input file is reached, the situation is considered as a final break. All actions of a major break plus some additional steps (the printing of the grand total in the above problem) should be taken in this case.

These pitfalls can be easily avoided if the top-down approach is taken to write a structured program for such a problem. Figure 15.2 shows a structured program for the abovementioned example. Since this is a structured program, the reader should be able to follow it without further explanation. Note that CR-ZONE, CR-DISTRICT and CR-SALESMAN stand for zone number, district number and salesman number respectively in the input file record.

For simplicity and for printing the report decently, it has been assumed that there are only 4 zones, 12 districts and 20 salesmen. It has also been assumed that the zone numbers, district numbers and salesman numbers are allocated continuously, starting from 1. Thus the salesman number can be any number from 1 to 20 and district number can be any number from 1 to 12 and zone numbers can be any number from 1 to 4. Three tables have been defined to contain the actual names corresponding to these codes. In a real-life application, these tables may be of larger sizes and consequently, some direct access files (discussed in the next chapter) may have to be used.

```
        IDENTIFICATION DIVISION.
        PROGRAM-ID. AN EXAMPLE OF CONTROL BREAK.
        AUTHOR. AUTHORS OF THIS BOOK.
        INSTALLATION. COMPUTER CENTRE.
        DATE-WRITTEN. 5TH MARCH, 1981.
        SECURITY. READER OF THIS BOOK.

        ENVIRONMENT DIVISION.
        CONFIGURATION SECTION.
        SOURCE-COMPUTER. B-6700.
        OBJECT-COMPUTER. B-6700.
        INPUT-OUTPUT SECTION.
        FILE-CONTROL.
            SELECT DISK-FILE ASSIGN TO DISK.
            SELECT REPORT-FILE ASSIGN TO PRINTER.

        DATA DIVISION.
        FILE SECTION.
        FD  DISK-FILE.
        01  DISK-REC.
            02  CURRENT-ZONE-LEVEL.
                03  CR-ZONE           PIC 9.
                03  CURRENT-DISTRICT-LEVEL.
                    04  CR-DISTRICT    PIC 99.
                    04  CR-SALESMAN    PIC 99.
            02  AMT            PIC 9(4)V99.
            02  FILLER         PIC X(69).
        FD  REPORT-FILE LINAGE IS 59.
        01  REPORT-LINE     PIC X(132).

        WORKING-STORAGE SECTION.
        77  FLAG                  PIC 9.
        77  SALESMAN-SUM          PIC 9(5)V99.
        77  DISTRICT-SUM          PIC 9(7)V99.
        77  ZONE-SUM              PIC 9(9)V99.
        77  COMPANY-SUM           PIC 9(10)V99.
        77  PAGE-NO               PIC 99.
        77  END-OF-PROGRAM        PIC X.

        01  SALESMAN-11
            02  SALES-MAN.
                03  FILLER  PIC X(18) VALUE IS "ANIL KUMAR SAHA    ".
                03  FILLER  PIC X(18) VALUE IS "ARUMOY KULKARNI    ".
                03  FILLER  PIC X(18) VALUE IS "BIMAL MOHANTI      ".
                03  FILLER  PIC X(18) VALUE IS "CHANDAN CHOWDHURY ".
                03  FILLER  PIC X(18) VALUE IS "DANIEL MATHEWS     ".
                03  FILLER  PIC X(18) VALUE IS "DHURJATI BANERJEE ".
                03  FILLER  PIC X(18) VALUE IS "E.A.S. PRASANNA    ".
                03  FILLER  PIC X(18) VALUE IS "FAROOQ AHMED       ".
                03  FILLER  PIC X(18) VALUE IS "GOPAL BANERJEE     ".
```

(contd.)

```
          03  FILLER  PIC X(18) VALUE IS "GULAM SIDHIQUE     ".
          03  FILLER  PIC X(18) VALUE IS "MANARANJAN HAZRA   ".
          03  FILLER  PIC X(18) VALUE IS "NILADRI BOSE       ".
          03  FILLER  PIC X(18) VALUE IS "PIJUS KANTI DAS    ".
          03  FILLER  PIC X(18) VALUE IS "PRADIP CHANDA      ".
          03  FILLER  PIC X(18) VALUE IS "PRIYOTOSH GOSWAMI ".
          03  FILLER  PIC X(18) VALUE IS "RAJSEKHAR NANDI    ".
          03  FILLER  PIC X(18) VALUE IS "RAMESH SAXENA      ".
          03  FILLER  PIC X(18) VALUE IS "SHILBADRA GHOSH    ".
          03  FILLER  PIC X(18) VALUE IS "SRIMANTA DALUI     ".
          03  FILLER  PIC X(18) VALUE IS "UTPAL CHATTERJEE   ".
      02  SALESMAN-1 REDEFINES SALES-MAN.
          03  SALESMAN-NAME PIC X(18) OCCURS 20 TIMES.

  01  DISTRICT-11 VALUE IS "DARJEELINGJALPAIGURICOOCHBI
  -     "HARMALDA    RAIGANGE BARASAT  BASIRHAT  BANGAON    MIDNAPU
  -     "R BURDWAN   DURGAPUR ASSANSOL ".
      02 DISTRICT-NAME PIC X(10) OCCURS 12 TIMES.
  01  ZONE-11 VALUE "NORTHEAST SOUTHWEST ".
      02 ZONE-NAME PIC X(5) OCCURS  4 TIMES.
  01  PREVIOUS-ZONE-LEVEL.
      02  PR-ZONE             PIC 9.
      02  PREVIOUS-DISTRICT-LEVEL.
          03  PR-DISTRICT     PIC 99.
          03  PR-SALESMAN     PIC 99.


  01  SALESMAN-LINE-1.
      02  FILLER              PIC X(41) VALUE SPACES.
      02  FILLER              PIC X(47) VALUE ALL "-".
      02  FILLER              PIC X(44) VALUE SPACES.


  01  DETAIL-LINE.
      02  FILLER              PIC X(14) VALUE SPACES.
      02  A                   PIC 9.
      02  FILLER              PIC X(18) VALUE SPACES.
      02  B                   PIC Z9.
      02  FILLER              PIC X(16) VALUE SPACES.
      02  C                   PIC Z9.
      02  FILLER              PIC X(19) VALUE SPACES.
      02  D                   PIC ZZZZ.99.


  01  SALESMAN-LINE-2.
      02  FILLER              PIC X(41) VALUE SPACES.
      02  FILLER              PIC X(16) VALUE "TOTAL SALE OF    ".
      02  SALESMAN            PIC X(20).
      02  SALESMAN-AMOUNT     PIC Z(5).99.


  01  DISTRICT-LINE-1.
      02  FILLER              PIC X(29) VALUE SPACES.
      02  FILLER              PIC X(71) VALUE ALL "*".
```

(contd.)

```
01   DISTRICT-LINE-2.
     02   FILLER              PIC X(29) VALUE SPACES.
     02   FILLER              PIC X(16) VALUE "TOTAL SALE OF   ".
     02   DISTRICT            PIC X(44).
     02   DISTRICT-AMOUNT     PIC Z(7).99.

01   ZONE-LINE-1.
     02   FILLER              PIC X(13) VALUE SPACES.
     02   FILLER              PIC X(98) VALUE ALL "-".
01   ZONE-LINE-2.
     02   FILLER              PIC X(13) VALUE SPACES.
     02   FILLER              PIC X(16) VALUE "TOTAL SALE OF   ".
     02   ZONE                PIC X(70).
     02   ZONE-AMOUNT         PIC Z(9).99.

01   PAGE-NO-PRINTING.
     02   FILLER              PIC X(109) VALUE SPACES.
     02   FILLER              PIC X(8) VALUE "PAGE NO ".
     02   P-NO                PIC Z9.
01   HEADING-LINE.
     02   FILLER              PIC X(13) VALUE SPACES.
     02   FILLER              PIC X(16) VALUE "ZONE".
     02   FILLER              PIC X(20) VALUE "DISTRICT".
     02   FILLER              PIC X(24) VALUE "SALESMAN".
     02   FILLER              PIC X(6)  VALUE "AMOUNT".

01   REPORT-LINE-1.
     02   FILLER              PIC X(39) VALUE SPACES.
     02   FILLER              PIC X(45) VALUE "SALES REPORT OF XYZ
-    "COMPANY FOR THE YEAR 1981".

01   LAST-PAGE-LINE-1.
     02   FILLER              PIC X(45) VALUE SPACES.
     02   FILLER              PIC X(75) VALUE ALL "*".
01   LAST-PAGE-LINE-2.
     02   FILLER              PIC X(45) VALUE SPACES.
     02   FILLER              PIC X(44) VALUE "TOTAL SALE OF XYZ CO

-    "MPANY FOR THE YEAR 1981".
     02   COMPANY-AMOUNT      PIC Z(10).99.

PROCEDURE DIVISION.
MAIN-PARA.
     PERFORM INITIALIZE-PARA.
     PERFORM REPORT-HEADING.
     PERFORM PAGE-HEADING.
     PERFORM READ-PARA.
     PERFORM COMPARE-PARA UNTIL END-OF-PROGRAM = "Y".
     PERFORM CONTROL-BREAK-1.
     PERFORM REPORT-FOOTING.
     PERFORM CLOSING-PHASE.
     STOP RUN.
```

(contd.)

```
INITIALIZE-PARA.
    OPEN INPUT DISK-FILE OUTPUT REPORT-FILE.
    MOVE ZEROES TO SALESMAN-SUM, DISTRICT-SUM, ZONE-SUM,
            FLAG, COMPANY-SUM, PAGE-NO
    MOVE "N" TO END-OF-PROGRAM.
    READ DISK-FILE AT END MOVE "Y" TO END-OF-PROGRAM.
    MOVE CURRENT-ZONE-LEVEL TO PREVIOUS-ZONE-LEVEL.
    ADD AMT TO SALESMAN-SUM.

READ-PARA.
    READ DISK-FILE AT END MOVE HIGH-VALUES TO CURRENT-ZONE-LEVEL,
                        MOVE "Y" TO END-OF-PROGRAM.

COMPARE-PARA.
    IF CURRENT-ZONE-LEVEL = PREVIOUS-ZONE-LEVEL
        ADD AMT TO SALESMAN-SUM
         PERFORM DETAIL-LINE-PRINTING
        PERFORM READ-PARA
    ELSE PERFORM CONTROL-BREAK-1.

CONTROL-BREAK-1.
    IF CR-ZONE = PR-ZONE PERFORM CONTROL-BREAK-2
        ELSE PERFORM BREAK-IN-ZONE-LEVEL.
CONTROL-BREAK-2.
    IF CR-DISTRICT = PR-DISTRICT PERFORM BREAK-IN-SALESMAN-LEVEL
    ELSE PERFORM BREAK-IN-DISTRICT-LEVEL.

BREAK-IN-ZONE-LEVEL.
    MOVE 1 TO FLAG.
    PERFORM PRINT-SALESMAN.
    ADD SALESMAN-SUM TO DISTRICT-SUM.
    PERFORM PRINT-DISTRICT.
    ADD DISTRICT-SUM TO ZONE-SUM.
    PERFORM PRINT-ZONE.
    MOVE 0 TO FLAG.
    ADD ZONE-SUM TO COMPANY-SUM.
    MOVE ZEROES TO SALESMAN-SUM, DISTRICT-SUM, ZONE-SUM.
    PERFORM PAGE-HEADING.
    MOVE CURRENT-ZONE-LEVEL TO PREVIOUS-ZONE-LEVEL.

BREAK-IN-DISTRICT-LEVEL.
    MOVE 1 TO FLAG.
    PERFORM PRINT-SALESMAN.
    ADD SALESMAN-SUM TO DISTRICT-SUM.
    PERFORM PRINT-DISTRICT.
    MOVE 0 TO FLAG.
    ADD DISTRICT-SUM TO ZONE-SUM.
    MOVE ZEROES TO SALESMAN-SUM, DISTRICT-SUM.
    MOVE CURRENT-DISTRICT-LEVEL TO PREVIOUS-DISTRICT-LEVEL.
```

(contd.)

```
BREAK-IN-SALESMAN-LEVEL.
    PERFORM PRINT-SALESMAN.
    ADD SALESMAN-SUM TO DISTRICT-SUM.
    MOVE ZEROES TO SALESMAN-SUM.
    MOVE CR-SALESMAN TO PR-SALESMAN.

PAGE-HEADING.
    ADD 1 TO PAGE-NO.
    MOVE PAGE-NO TO P-NO.
    MOVE SPACES TO REPORT-LINE.
    WRITE REPORT-LINE AFTER ADVANCING TO PAGE.
    WRITE REPORT-LINE FROM PAGE-NO-PRINTING AFTER ADVANCING
        2 LINES.
    IF FLAG = 0 AND END-OF-PROGRAM = "N"
    PERFORM HEADING-LINE-PRINTING.

HEADING-LINE-PRINTING.
    WRITE REPORT-LINE FROM HEADING-LINE AFTER ADVANCING 2 LINES.

PRINT-SALESMAN.
    WRITE REPORT-LINE FROM SALESMAN-LINE-1
        AFTER ADVANCING 2 LINES AT END-OF-PAGE
        PERFORM PAGE-HEADING.
    MOVE SALESMAN-NAME (PR-SALESMAN) TO SALESMAN.
    MOVE SALESMAN-SUM TO SALESMAN-AMOUNT
    WRITE REPORT-LINE FROM SALESMAN-LINE-2
        AFTER ADVANCING 1 LINE AT END-OF-PAGE
        PERFORM PAGE-HEADING.
    WRITE REPORT-LINE FROM SALESMAN-LINE-1
        AFTER ADVANCING 1 LINE AT END-OF-PAGE
        PERFORM PAGE-HEADING.

PRINT-DISTRICT.
    WRITE REPORT-LINE FROM DISTRICT-LINE-1
        AFTER ADVANCING 2 LINES AT END-OF-PAGE
        PERFORM PAGE-HEADING.
    MOVE DISTRICT-NAME (PR-DISTRICT) TO DISTRICT.
    MOVE DISTRICT-SUM TO DISTRICT-AMOUNT.
    WRITE REPORT-LINE FROM DISTRICT-LINE-2
        AFTER ADVANCING 1 LINE AT END-OF-PAGE
        PERFORM PAGE-HEADING.
    WRITE REPORT-LINE FROM DISTRICT-LINE-1
        AFTER ADVANCING 1 LINE AT END-OF-PAGE
        PERFORM PAGE-HEADING.
```

(contd.)

```
PRINT-ZONE.
    WRITE REPORT-LINE FROM ZONE-LINE-1
        AFTER ADVANCING 2 LINES AT END-OF-PAGE
        PERFORM PAGE-HEADING.
    MOVE ZONE-NAME (PR-ZONE) TO ZONE.
    MOVE ZONE-SUM TO ZONE-AMOUNT.
    WRITE REPORT-LINE FROM ZONE-LINE-2
        AFTER ADVANCING 1 LINE AT END-OF-PAGE
        PERFORM PAGE-HEADING.
    WRITE REPORT-LINE FROM ZONE-LINE-1
        AFTER ADVANCING 1 LINE AT END-OF-PAGE
        PERFORM PAGE-HEADING.

DETAIL-LINE-PRINTING.
        MOVE PR-ZONE TO A.
        MOVE PR-DISTRICT TO B.
    MOVE PR-SALESMAN TO C.
        MOVE AMT TO D.
        WRITE REPORT-LINE FROM DETAIL-LINE AFTER ADVANCING 1 LINE
            AT END-OF-PAGE PERFORM PAGE-HEADING.

REPORT-HEADING.
    WRITE REPORT-LINE FROM REPORT-LINE-1 AFTER ADVANCING 30 LINES
        AT END-OF-PAGE PERFORM PAGE-HEADING.
    ADD 1 TO PAGE-NO.

REPORT-FOOTING.
    MOVE COMPANY-SUM TO COMPANY-AMOUNT.
    WRITE REPORT-LINE FROM LAST-PAGE-LINE-1
        AFTER ADVANCING 30 LINES.
    WRITE REPORT-LINE FROM LAST-PAGE-LINE-2
        AFTER ADVANCING 1 LINE.
    WRITE REPORT-LINE FROM LAST-PAGE-LINE-1
        AFTER ADVANCING 1 LINE.

CLOSING-PHASE.
    CLOSE DISK-FILE, REPORT-FILE.
JOB-TERMINATION.
    EXIT.
```

FIG. 15.2. An Example of Control Break

ZONE	DISTRICT	SALESMAN	AMOUNT
2	4	6	800.50
2	4	6	3500.00
2	4	6	750.00
		TOTAL SALE OF DHURJATI BANERJEE	5050.50
2	4	19	2050.00
2	4	19	2000.25
		TOTAL SALE OF SRIMANTA DALUI	4050.25
	TOTAL SALE OF MALDA		9100.75
2	5	7	900.75
2	5	7	2000.50
2	5	7	1005.00
		TOTAL SALE OF E.A.S. PRASANNA	3906.25
2	5	9	2500.00
2	5	9	3000.50
2	5	9	4500.00
		TOTAL SALE OF GOPAL BANERJEE	10000.50
	TOTAL SALE OF RAIGANGE		13906.75
TOTAL SALE OF EAST			23007.50

FIG. 15.3.   A Sample Output of the Program in Fig. 15.2.

EXERCISES

1. Write a few points on the merits and demerits of the GO TO statement.

2. There is one COBOL statement (besides the GO TO) that can never be used in structured programs. What is that statement? What are the allegations against it?

3. Modify the program of Exercise 7 of Chapter 14 to include the case when there can be more than one type 2 card corresponding to a type 1 card.

4. The problem discussed in Sec. 2.7.2 is a problem of the control break. Write a program according to the conventional flow chart given in Fig. 2.8.

5. Write a structured program for the previous problem and make a note of the advantages of structured programming in this case.

6. Consider the file created in Exercise 7 of Chapter 13. Write a program to generate a frequency table in the following:

	Number of Patients			
	Male		Female	
Drug Code	below 12 years	above 12 years	below 12 years	above 12 years

Note that the drug code in this table must appear in the sorted order.

16

DIRECT ACCESS FILES

Files which are stored on a direct access storage medium such as a magnetic disk, are often called direct access files. Each record of such a file has a unique address and therefore can be accessed directly rather than sequentially. COBOL supports three different organizations for disk files — sequential, relative and indexed sequential. Sequential organization has been discussed previously. The COBOL features for handling the relative and indexed sequential files are introduced in this chapter. In addition, various points regarding the selection and use of these organizations are also discussed here.

16.1 RELATIVE FILES

A relative file is a magnetic-disk file organized in such a way that each record is identified by a relative record number. The relative record number specifies the position of the record from the beginning of the file. Thus the relative record number 1 identifies the first record, the relative record number 2 identifies the second record and so on.

A relative file can be accessed either sequentially or randomly. When the file is accessed sequentially, the records are accessed in the increasing order of their relative record numbers. When a file is accessed randomly, the programmer must specify the relative record number. The record is accessed directly regardless of the previous access of any other record in the file.

It may be noted that in the case of relative organization, the reading as well as the writing can be done randomly. Thus when a file is created by writing the records randomly, some of the record positions may remain empty. While these positions can be filled in subsequently, the programmer should avoid specifying these empty positions while reading such a relative file randomly. If a relative file is read in a sequential manner, such empty positions within it, if any, are ignored.

The handling of relative files requires some special codes in the FILE-CONTROL paragraph as well as in the PROCEDURE DIVISION. These are discussed below.

16.1.1 FILE-CONTROL Paragraph for Relative Files

The general format for the SELECT clause for a relative file is as follows:

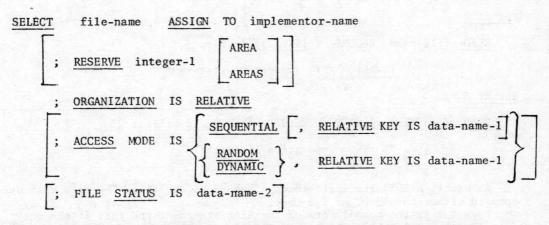

Except for the ORGANIZATION and ACCESS MODE clauses, all other clauses
have the same meaning as in the case of sequential files. The ORGANIZATION
clause specifies that the said file is a relative file. Whether the file
should be used sequentially or randomly, should be specified through the
word SEQUENTIAL or RANDOM in the ACCESS MODE clause. The clause ACCESS MODE
IS DYNAMIC indicates that the file is accessed sequentially and/or randomly
in the PROCEDURE DIVISION. The phrase RELATIVE KEY must be specified when
the access mode is RANDOM or DYNAMIC. The data-name-1 is called the relative key data item and it indicates the field that contains the relative
record number. The programmer must place an appropriate value in the relative key data item while using a record randomly. Data-name-1 must be an
unsigned integer and may be qualified. However, this data name must not be
part of the record description for the said relative file. If the ACCESS
MODE clause is not specified, SEQUENTIAL is assumed.

16.1.2 PROCEDURE DIVISION Statements for Relative Files

The statements OPEN, CLOSE, READ, WRITE and REWRITE which are available for
sequential files are all available for the relative files. In addition, two
other verbs, namely, DELETE and START are also available. As regards the
OPEN and CLOSE statements, there is no difference between a relative file
and sequential disk file.

READ Statement

The general formats for the READ statement are shown below.

Format 1

    READ file-name RECORD [INTO identifier]

            [; AT END imperative-statement]

Format 2

>   READ   file-name   RECORD   [INTO   identifier]
>
>   [;   INVALID   KEY   imperative-statement]

Format 3

>   READ   file-name   [NEXT]   RECORD   [INTO   identifier]
>
>   [;   AT   END   imperative-statement]

As usual, a READ statement reads a record of the file. The file must be open in either the INPUT or I-O mode.

Format 1 is the normal form of the READ statement and this is the only form that is applicable to sequential files. In the case of relative files, this format is used when the access mode is sequential. If the RELATIVE KEY phrase is also specified with the ACCESS MODE SEQUENTIAL clause, then upon the successful completion of the READ statement, the relative record number of the accessed record is placed in the relative key data item.

Format 2 is used when the access mode is either random or dynamic. The record to be read is identified from the contents of the relative key data item. For example, suppose REL-FILE and REL-KEY are the names for the relative file and relative key data item respectively. The following statements will read the fiftieth record from this file.

```
MOVE      50    TO    REL-KEY.
READ   REL-FILE   RECORD   INVALID-KEY   GO   TO   PARA-INVALID.
```

The imperative statement of the INVALID KEY phrase is executed when the read is unsuccessful. Reading is considered unsuccessful if attempt is made to read a record (i) from an empty record position of the relative file or (ii) from outside the externally defined boundaries* of the file.

Format 3 of the READ statement can be used when the access mode is dynamic and the records are to be read sequentially. As a result of the execution of this statement, the next record from the file is read. The next record is identified according to the following rules:

(i)   When the READ NEXT statement is the first statement to be executed after the OPEN statement on the file, the next record is the first record of the file.

(ii)   When the execution of the READ NEXT statement follows the execution of another READ statement on the same file (Format 2 or Format 3 above), the next record is the record following the one previously read.

(iii) When the execution of the READ NEXT statement follows the

---

*Note that previously, the boundaries of a file could be defined through FILE-LIMITS clause of the file-control entry. This clause has been deleted in the ANSI 74 standard. Now the file limits are to be specified outside the COBOL language, possibly through the job-control language.

execution of the START statement (discussed later in this chapter),
the next record is the record to which the file is logically positioned by the START statement.

Note that the above rules permit the switch from random to sequential
reading in the case of relative files with the dynamic access mode.

When format 1 or format 3 is used, empty record positions within the
relative file are ignored.

WRITE Statement

The WRITE statement for a relative file has the following format.

WRITE   record-name   [FROM   identifier]

[;   INVALID   KEY   imperative-statement]

. At the time of execution of the WRITE statement, the file must be open
either in the OUTPUT or I-O mode. Upon successful execution of the WRITE
statement, a record is released to the file and the record area associated
with the record name no longer contains the record. The FORM phrase has the
same meaning as in the case of a sequential file.

When the file is accessed randomly, the statement releases the record
to that relative record position on the file which is indicated by the
record number in the relative key data item. For example, suppose REL-OUTPUT
and REL-KEY are the record name and relative key data item name for a relative file opened in the I-O mode. Then, upon execution of the following
statements

MOVE   50   TO   REL-KEY.

WRITE   REL-OUTPUT   INVALID   KEY   GO TO   PARA-INVALID.

the record is written at the fiftieth record position on the file.

When the file is accessed sequentially, records are released to the
file in the sequential record positions. If the relative key data name is
specified with the ACCESS MODE IS SEQUENTIAL clause, the record number of
the record just released is written in the said data name.

The imperative statement of the INVALID KEY phrase is executed in the
following cases:

(i)   When an attempt is made to write beyond the externally-defined
boundaries of the file.

(ii) When an attempt is made to write in the record position which
already contains a valid record.

REWRITE Statement

The REWRITE statement has the following format for a relative file.

REWRITE   record-name   [FROM   identifier]

[;   INVALID   KEY   imperative-statement]

The REWRITE statement is used to replace an existing record by the
contents of the record specified in the record name. The file must be opened
in the I-O mode. The FROM phrase has the same meaning as in the case of the

WRITE statement. When the access mode is RANDOM or DYNAMIC, the record to be replaced is identified by the contents of the relative key data item. When the access mode is SEQUENTIAL, prior to the execution of the REWRITE statement, a READ statement on the file must be successfully executed, and there should not be any other input-output statement on the file in between the READ and REWRITE statements. In this case, the record read by this READ statement is replaced by the REWRITE statement. The INVALID KEY phrase should not be specified as the INVALID KEY phrase of the previously executed READ statement serves the purpose. The imperative statement after the INVALID KEY is executed when an attempt is made to replace a record position which is empty. An empty record position is that position where no record has been written earlier or the record position whose data has been deleted through a DELETE statement. Upon successful execution of the REWRITE statement, the record area does not contain the released data.

DELETE Statement

The format of the delete statement is as follows:

DELETE   file-name RECORD   [;   INVALID KEY

imperative-statement]

The DELETE statement deletes the data contained in the specified record position of a relative file. The said data is no longer available. The record position whose contents is to be deleted is identified in the same manner as in the case of the REWRITE statement. Thus, when the ACCESS MODE IS SEQUENTIAL the execution of the DELETE statement must be preceded by the execution of a READ statement on the file and the INVALID KEY phrase should not be specified. The INVALID KEY condition arises when an attempt is made to delete the record of an empty record position. In this case the statement after the INVALID KEY is executed. The file must be opened in the I-O mode. The execution of a DELETE statement does not affect the contents of the record area.

START Statement

The format of the START statement is given below.

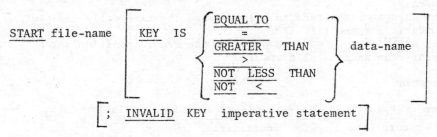

The START statement enables the programmer to position the relative file at some specified point so that subsequent sequential operations on the file can start from this point instead of the beginning. The KEY IS phrase indicates how the file is to be positioned. The data name in this phrase must be the data name in the RELATIVE KEY phrase of the SELECT clause. When the EQUAL TO or NOT LESS THAN condition is specified, the file is positioned at the point indicated by the relative key-data item. When the GREATER THAN condition is specified, the file is positioned at the next relative position of the position indicated by the relative key data item. Thus

```
START MY-FILE KEY IS GREATER THAN REL-KEY
        ; INVALID KEY GO TO INVALID-PARA.
```

will position the file at the fifty-first record position if the relative key data item REL-KEY contains 50.

The INVALID KEY condition arises if the specified record position is empty. In that case the imperative statement after the INVALID KEY phrase is executed.

The START statement requires that the file must be opened in the INPUT or I-O mode. The access mode can only be SEQUENTIAL or DYNAMIC.

16.1.3 Examples of Relative File Handling

Example 1

Suppose a relative file named HISTORY contains monthly sales data for the past years starting from January 1960. This means that the first record of HISTORY consists of sales data for January 1960, the second record consists of sales data for February 1960, and so on. Further, suppose that the SELECT clause for this file is as follows:

```
SELECT HISTORY ASSIGN TO DISK
        ORGANIZATION IS RELATIVE
        ACCESS MODE IS DYNAMIC
        RELATIVE KEY IS REL-POSITION.
```

where the RELATIVE KEY data item is defined in the WORKING-STORAGE section in the following manner.

```
77 REL-POSITION     PIC    9(3).
```

It is required to process 10 records of this file starting from the one corresponding to the month and year indicated by the contents of data names MTH and YEAR respectively. For example, if MTH contains 3 and YEAR contains 72, then 10 records starting from the one for March 1972 are to be processed. The said records may be accessed by the following statements.

```
MOVE 0 TO INDICATE-ERROR.
COMPUTE REL-POSITION = (YEAR - 60)*12 + MTH.
START HISTORY KEY IS EQUAL TO REL-POSITION
        INVALID KEY MOVE 1 TO INDICATE-ERROR.
IF INDICATE-ERROR = 1
        DISPLAY "STARTING RECORD ABSENT"
ELSE PERFORM READ-AND-PROCESS
        VARYING I FROM 1 BY 1 UNTIL I > 10 OR REL-POSITION = 0.
```

```
READ-AND-PROCESS.
    READ  HISTORY  NEXT  RECORD
        AT  END  MOVE  ZERO  TO .REL-POSITION.

    IF  REL-POSITION  IS  EQUAL  TO  ZERO
            DISPLAY  "THERE  ARE  LESS  THAN  10  RECORDS
                        FROM  THE  START  POSITION"
    ELSE  PERFORM  PROCESS-HISTORY-RECORD.
```

It may be noted that the formula on the right-hand side of the equality
sign in the COMPUTE statement gives the relative record position of the
starting record. The 10 records starting from this position are read. It
is assumed that a record is processed in the paragraph named PROCESS-
HISTORY-RECORD.

Example 2

Suppose we wish to modify a record of the HISTORY file in the above example.
The following statement may be used for the purpose.

```
    MOVE  0  TO  ERROR-INDICATOR.
    COMPUTE  REL-POSITION = (YEAR - 60)*12 + MTH.
    READ  HISTORY  RECORD
            INVALID  KEY  DISPLAY  "RECORD ABSENT"
            MOVE  1  TO  ERROR-INDICATOR.

    IF  ERROR-INDICATOR NOT EQUAL TO 1
        PERFORM MODIFY-HISTORY-REC
        REWRITE HISTORY-REC
            INVALID KEY DISPLAY "RECORD ABSENT".
```

Note that the INVALID KEY condition for the REWRITE statement will not
arise. Nevertheless, we must use the INVALID KEY phrase to meet the requirement of syntax. The INVALID KEY phrase may be omitted if a USE statement
for the file is given in the DECLARATIVES.

16.2 INDEXED SEQUENTIAL FILES

A record in a relative file can be accessed randomly by specifying the
relative position of the record in the file. However, in most applications
it may be difficult to specify the relative record position. For example,
we may wish to read the record corresponding to employee number say, 1372,
in the personnel file. If the file has a relative organization, a knowledge
of the employee number 1372 is not good enough to read the desired record.
We must also know the relative record number for this record (note that
this number may be different from 1372). In the case where we wish to have
access the records randomly and want to identify them by the values of the
key rather than the relative record numbers, the file may be organized to
be indexed sequential.
    In indexed sequential files (also referred to as indexed files), the
records are stored in the key sequence order (usually ascending order). In
addition, some index tables are also created and maintained with the file.

The purpose of the index tables is that they provide a means of identifying
the groups of records in the file. Thus in order to have access to a record,
first, the group to which a record belongs is identified with the help of
the index tables. Then the group is sequentially searched to locate the
record. To cite an analogy let us consider a thumb dictionary. To look up a
word, say ''river'', in the dictionary we first of all locate the first
page containing the words beginning with the letter ''r''. This we do with
the help of the thumb index. All that remains now is to locate the word
''river'' by sequentially going through the words in this page and the
subsequent pages. The dictionary here is analogous to an indexed file and
its thumb index is analogous to the index tables.

An indexed file in COBOL can be accessed either sequentially or randomly. However, while creating an indexed file the records can be written only
sequentially and in the ascending order of the key. When an indexed file is
accessed randomly, the sequence in which the records are accessed is controlled by the programmer by specifying the value of a data item called record
key.

Indexed files in a COBOL program can be handled through suitable special
codes in the FILE-CONTROL paragraph and in the PROCEDURE DIVISION. These are
described below.

16.2.1 FILE-CONTROL Paragraph for Indexed Files

The general format for the SELECT clause for an indexed file is as follows:

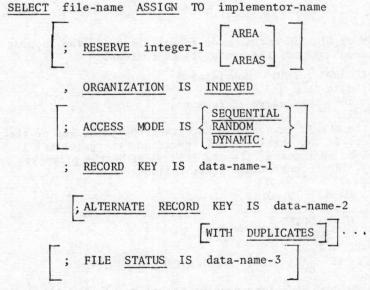

It may be noted that most of the clauses are also available for the
relative and sequential files and they have the same meaning as in those
cases. The ORGANIZATION clause indicates that the file is an indexed file.
The RECORD KEY clause specifies the record key data item on the basis of
which the file is sequenced. The data-name-1 must be an alphanumeric field

within the record description for the file. In case there are multiple
record descriptions, the key field from any of the descriptions can be
specified. The field which is specified in the RECORD KEY clause (data-
name-1) is also known as the prime key. While the file is sorted and stored
on the basis of the prime key, the records of an indexed file can be accessed either by specifying the prime key or an alternate key. In the latter
case the ALTERNATE RECORD KEY phrase is to be specified. The data-name-2
denotes the alternate key and must be defined within the record description.
Two or more records having the same value for the prime key are not allowed
in an indexed file. However, such duplicates are allowed for the alternate
key. If the file has to have records with a duplicate alternate key,
the WITH DUPLICATES phrase should be specified. An absence of this phrase
indicates that the alternate key values are unique. The option for alternate keys has not yet been implemented in many compilers. One should therefore consult the relevant manual before using the said facility.

16.2.2 PROCEDURE DIVISION Statements for Indexed Files

All the statements that are available for a relative file are also available for the indexed files. The syntax, function and use of these statements
are also identical to a great extent. Therefore, only the important points
and particularly those in respect of which there is a difference between a
statement for the indexed file and the corresponding statement for the relative file are discussed below. An obvious general difference is that the
record key should be considered in place of the relative key.

READ Statement

When either the RANDOM or DYNAMIC access mode is specified and the records
are to be read in a random manner, the syntax is as follows:

```
READ file-name RECORD [ INTO identifier ]
     [ ; KEY IS data-name ]
     [ ; INVALID KEY imperative-statement ]
```

The data name in the KEY IS phrase must be either the prime key or the
alternate key data item. If the phrase is not specified, the prime key is
assumed. Let PERSONNEL be an indexed file and let EMP-NO be the prime key and
NAME the alternate key. The select clause is as follows:

```
SELECT PERSONNEL ASSIGN TO DISK

       ORGANIZATION IS INDEXED
       ACCESS MODE IS RANDOM
       RECORD KEY IS EMP-NO
       ALTERNATE KEY IS NAME WITH DUPLICATES.
```

The data names EMP-NO and NAME representing the prime key and alternate
key respectively are fields defined within the record description for the
file PERSONNEL. Now, suppose we wish to read the record for, say the employee
number 1372. Then the following statements can be given.

```
MOVE "1372" TO EMP-NO.
READ PERSONNEL RECORD
     KEY IS EMP-NO INVALID KEY PERFORM NOT FOUND
```

The INVALID KEY condition arises if the record with the specified key is not found in the file. Then the statement PERFORM NOT-FOUND is executed. In a similar way, we can read a record by specifying the alternate key. For example, suppose we wish to read the record for the employee whose name is S.K. GHOSH. This can be done as follows:

```
MOVE    "S.K. GHOSH"  TO  NAME.
READ  PERSONNEL  RECORD
      KEY  IS  NAME
           INVALID  KEY  PERFORM  NOT-FOUND.
```

A difficulty arises if there are two employees having the same name S.K. GHOSH. In that case only one of the records will be read.

When the access mode is either SEQUENTIAL or DYNAMIC and records are accessed sequentially, the syntax of the READ statement is identical to that in the case of a relative file.

WRITE Statement

The records are written to the logical position as determined from the value of the record key. When the file is opened in the OUTPUT mode, the records must be released to the file in the ascending order of the record key values regardless of the access mode. Records can be released in any order only when the file is opened in the I-O mode and the RANDOM or DYNAMIC access mode is specified. The INVALID KEY condition arises in the following cases:

(i) When an attempt is made to write a record beyond the externally-defined boundaries of the file.

(ii) When the file is opened in the OUTPUT mode and the value of the record key is not greater than the value of the record key for the previous record written.

(iii) When the value of the record key is equal to the record key of a record already present in the file.

Except for the points stated above the statement is similar to that in the case of a relative file.

REWRITE Statement

As in the case of a relative file, the REWRITE statement requires that the file must be opened in the I-O mode, and if the SEQUENTIAL access mode is specified, the value of the record key of the record being replaced must be equal to that of the record last read from this file. The INVALID KEY condition arises in the following cases:

(i) When the record key does not match that of an existing record in the file.

(ii) For SEQUENTIAL access, when the value of the record key is not identical to that of the last record read from the file.

The INVALID KEY phrase should be used even when the SEQUENTIAL access mode is specified (see Sec. 13.10 for exceptions).

DELETE Statement

The file must be opened in the I-O mode. If the access mode is SEQUENTIAL, the INVALID KEY phrase should not be specified. Instead, the last input-output statement executed on the file must be a successful READ statement for the said record. When the DELETE statement is executed, the record read by the said last READ statement, is deleted. If the access mode is RANDOM or DYNAMIC then the record to be deleted is determined by the value of the record key. In this case the INVALID KEY phrase should be specified (see Sec. 13.10 for exceptions). The INVALID KEY condition arises if the file does not contain the said record.

START Statement

As in the case of a relative file, the START statement positions the file to the first logical record whose record key satisfies the condition specified by the KEY phrase. The access mode must be SEQUENTIAL or DYNAMIC and the file must be opened in the I-O or INPUT mode. The data name in the KEY phrase must be the record key, alternate key or any alphanumeric data item that must be the leftmost field in the record key. If the KEY phrase is omitted, the relational operator EQUAL with the data name equal to that of the record key is assumed. The INVALID KEY condition arises if the condition specified by the KEY phrase (either explicitly or implicitly) cannot be met. To take an example, let the SELECT clause for an indexed file be

```
SELECT   INDEXED-FILE   ASSIGN   TO   DISK
     ORGANIZATION   IS   INDEXED
     ACCESS   MODE   IS   SEQUENTIAL
     RECORD   KEY   IS   REC-KEY.
```

Let us further assume that the record description of the file describes the record key in the following way.

```
02    REC-KEY.
     03   FIRST-PART      PIC      X.
     03   FILLER          PIC      X(7).
```

Now, suppose we wish to position the file at the first record whose record key begins with the letter ''C''. This can be done as follows:

```
MOVE    "C"    TO    REC-KEY.
START   INDEXED-FILE
          KEY   IS   NOT   LESS   THAN   REC-KEY
          INVALID   KEY   PERFORM   ERROR-A.
```

The same can also be done as follows:

```
MOVE    "C"   TO   FIRST-PART.
START   INDEXED-FILE
          KEY   IS   EQUAL   TO   FIRST-PART
          INVALID   KEY   PERFORM   ERROR-B.
```

It may be noted that the size of the record key is greater than that of FIRST-PART, the data name in the KEY phrase. In such cases the comparison proceeds as in the case of an alphanumeric comparison with the exception that the longer field is considered to have been truncated on the right as if to make its size equal to that of the shorter field. Therefore, in the second example only the leftmost character of the record key of the records will be compared with the character C.

It may be further noted that the two examples shown above will serve the purpose provided the file contains at least one record whose record key begins with the letter ''C''. In case there is no such record in the file, the actions in the two cases will be different. In the first case the file will be positioned to the first record whose record key begins with a letter greater than ''C''. The INVALID KEY condition can arise if the file does not contain even such a record. In the second case the absence of any record with its record key beginning with ''C'' means that the INVALID KEY condition arises.

TABLE 16.1.   Permissible Input-Output Statements for Different File Organizations

		Open Mode									
		FILE ORGANIZATION									
		SEQUENTIAL				RELATIVE			INDEXED		
	Statement	I	O	I-O	E	I	O	I-O	I	O	I-O
FILE ACCESS — SEQUENTIAL	READ	x		x		x		x	x		x
	WRITE		x		x		x			x	
	REWRITE			x				x			x
	START					x		x	x		x
	DELETE							x			x
ACCESS — RANDOM	READ					x		x	x		x
	WRITE						x	x		x	x
	REWRITE							x			x
	START										
	DELETE							x			x
MODE — DYNAMIC	READ					x		x	x		x
	WRITE						x	x		x	x
	REWRITE							x			x
	START					x		x	x		x
	DELETE							x			x

16.2.3 Updation of Relative and Indexed Files

It has been stated earlier that sequential files are updated by creating a new master file from an existing old master file and a transaction file. Such an updation is known as updation by copy. This general technique of file updation is also applicable to relative or indexed files. However, direct access files can be updated by the technique known as updation by overlay. In this case no new file is created. Instead, the necessary changes are incorporated in the body of the file. In other words, the records that do not undergo any modification occupy the same position in the disk area allocated for the file. The COBOL language provides a limited facility for updating a sequential disk file by overlay. This is available through the REWRITE statement. An example of such updation has been discussed earlier. However, the complete facility of updation by overlay is available in the case of relative and indexed files through the WRITE, REWRITE and DELETE statements. During the updation, the WRITE, REWRITE and DELETE statements are respectively used to insert, modify and delete records.

The updation of relative or indexed files can be easily implemented in COBOL by suitably using the said statement. However, it may be instructive to know how a record is really inserted, modified or deleted in the case of these direct access files.

Let us consider the relative file first. Usually, each record in a relative file is preceded by a record header which contains various information relating to the record. The header is affixed and maintained by the input-output control system (IOCS) that supports the relative file organization. The record header normally contains an item called the status code. The status code indicates whether a record position is empty or whether it contains a data record. It may be noted that when a relative file is created, there can be record positions where no record is written. The IOCS takes care of setting the status codes to indicate that these are empty record positions. Thus, the record positions are reserved for future insertions. When a record is to be deleted, the record is not physically removed. Instead the status code is changed to indicate it to be an empty position. When a record is rewritten, the status code remains unchanged. Only the record contents are modified.

Only a typical internal organization for a relative file has been described above to provide an insight into the updation operations. Obviously, the internal organization can vary depending on the computer and its IOCS.

Let us now consider the indexed files. To understand how updation by overlay is done in the case of an indexed file, it is essential to know about the internal organization of the file. The internal organization is very much different in different systems. To give a general idea we shall present a simplified description of the indexed file organizations in the B-6700 system.

In the B-6700 implementation, an indexed file consists of three logical sections — prime data area, data overflow area and index tables. A prime data area is the occupied portion of the file. The prime data area is divided into a number of rows called prime-data rows. The data overflow area is that area of the file which is unoccupied by any data at the time of file creation. The records after file creation can only be added to the overflow area. There are two types of overflow area — the overflow space provided in each prime data row and the file overflow area. There are two levels of index tables — the fine table and coarse table. Each prime data row contains a fine table.

The fine-table entries consist of selected keys and the addresses of the corresponding records in the prime-data row. There is one coarse table for the complete file. This table also contains pairs of keys and addresses. Each pair of key and address refers to a fine table. The key is the first key in the fine table and the address is the address of the fine table. The coarse table is stored at the beginning of the file overflow area.

The coarse table provides the facility to locate a fine table which in turn serves to locate a data record. The data records are linked together in a logical sequence. Each record contains links to its logical predecessor and successor. In order to accommodate insertions and deletions, the records are not physically moved. Instead, links are modified. The fine table which corresponds to a prime data row also contains a link to the next available unoccupied space in the overflow area. During updation, whenever a record is inserted, it is placed in the overflow area indicated by the fine table and its logical position in the file is established by properly setting its links.

We do not wish to go into further details regarding the management of overflow areas and that of the links. The IOCS takes care of these management problems. However, it is important to note that when an indexed file has been updated for a number of times, its structure can become cumbersome with a large number of records crowded in the overflow areas. It is, therefore, recommended that an indexed file must be restructured periodically. This can be done by copying the indexed file in the form of a sequential file and then recreating it again from this sequential file.

16.2.4 An Example of Handling Indexed File

A sample program showing how to handle an indexed file is shown in Fig. 16.1. The program updates an existing indexed file (CITY-POP), each of whose records contains the name of a city (CITY) and its population (POP). The transaction file (TRANS) is a card file. The transaction code (T-CODE) is a one-digit code having the following meaning.

Transaction Code	Meaning
1	The transaction record is to be inserted
2	The corresponding master record is to be deleted
Other than 1 or 2	The master record is to be replaced by the transaction record

The record key of the indexed file is the field representing the name of a city (CITY). It is assumed that the transaction data do not contain any error. In the case of updation errors (e.g., the file already contains a record whose key is equal to the record being inserted) appropriate error messages are displayed.

```
     FILE-CONTROL.
          SELECT  TRANS  ASSIGN  TO  READER.
          SELECT  CITY-POP  ASSIGN  TO  DISK
              ORGANIZATION IS  INDEXED
              ACCESS  MODE  IS  RANDOM
              RECORD  KEY  IS  CITY.

     DATA DIVISION.
     FILE SECTION.
     FD  TRANS.
     01  TRANS-REC.
          02     T-CITY              PIC          X(20).
          02     T-POP               PIC          9(10).
          02     T-CODE              PIC          9.
     88  INSERTION                   VALUE        IS   1.
     88  DELETION                    VALUE        IS   2.
          02     FILLER              PIC          X(49).
     FD   CITY-POP
          LABEL  RECORDS  ARE  STANDARD
          RECORD  CONTAINS  30  CHARACTERS
          VALUE  OF  ID  IS    "POPULATION"

     01  POP-REC.
          02     CITY                PIC          X(20).
          02     POP                 PIC          9(10).

     WORKING-STORAGE SECTION.
     77  E-O-F                       PIC          9.
     88  LAST-CARD                   VALUE        IS   1.

     PROCEDURE DIVISION.
     MAIN-PROGRAM.
          PROGRAM     BEGINNING.
          PERFORM     PROCESSING
                      UNTIL  LAST-CARD.
          PERFORM     THE-END.
          STOP  RUN.

     BEGINNING.
          OPEN  INPUT  TRANS
                I-O   CITY-POP.
          MOVE ZERO  TO   E-O-F.
     PROCESSING.
          READ  TRANS  RECORD
                  AT  END  MOVE  1  TO  E-O-F.
          IF  NOT  LAST-CARD
                  PERFORM UPDATION.
```

(contd.)

```
UPDATION.
    MOVE  T-CITY  TO  CITY.
    IF  INSERTION
            PERFORM  INSERT-REC
    ELSE  IF  DELETION
            PERFORM  DELETE-REC
        ELSE  PERFORM  MODIFY-REC.

INSERT-REC.
    MOVE  T-POP  TO  POP.
    WRITE  POP-REC
            INVALID  KEY
                DISPLAY  "INSERTION¢ERROR¢",   CITY.

DELETE-REC.
    DELETE  POP-REC
            INVALID  KEY
                DISPLAY   "DELETE¢RECORD¢NOT¢FOUND¢",   CITY.

MODIFY-REC.
    MOVE  T-POP  TO  POP.
    REWRITE  POP-REC
            INVALID  KEY
                DISPLAY   "UPDATE¢RECORD¢NOT¢FOUND¢",  CITY.

THE  END.
    CLOSE  TRANS  CITY-POP.
```

FIG. 16.1.   A Sample Program Handling Indexed File

16.2.5 File Descriptions for Relative and Indexed Files

The FD entry for a relative or an indexed file is identical to that of a
sequential file. Therefore, the clauses as discussed in Sec. 13.3 and 13.6
are applicable in these cases. However, it may be noted that some compilers
do not allow variable-length records or the blocking of records in the case
of direct access files.

16.2.6 DECLARATIVES and FILE STATUS Clause

The input-output exception conditions in the case of a direct access file
can be handled by a declarative procedure in a manner similar to that of
sequential files. The material presented in Sec. 13.10 is therefore also
applicable for relative or indexed files. The syntax of the USE statement
is identical to that in Sec. 13.10 except that the EXTEND option is not
available.

Table 16.2 shows the contents of the file status data name after an
input-output statement has been executed. The said values for sequential
files are also shown.

TABLE 16.2. Contents of File Status Data Name After Execution
of Input-Output Statement

Content of file status data name	Status	READ	WRITE	REWRITE	DELETE	START	OPEN	CLOSE
0 0	Successful completion	S/R/I	S/R/I	S/R/I	S/R/I	S/R/I	S/R/I	S/R/I
0 2	Duplicate alternate key (Warning only)	I	I	I				
1 0	At end	S/R/I						
2 1	Invalid key due to sequence error		I	I				
2 2	Invalid key due to duplicate key		R/I					
2 3	Invalid key due to no record found	R/I		R/I	R/I	R/I		
2 4	Invalid key due to boundary violation		R/I					
3 0	Permanent error	S/R/I	S/R/I	S/R/I	R/I		S/R/I	S/R/I
3 4	Permanent error due to boundary violation		S					
9 n	Implementor defined							

S = SEQUENTIAL organization
R = RELATIVE   organization
I = INDEXED   organization

n = Implementor defined character

16.2.7 Direct Organization

Besides the relative or indexed organization, a direct access file can also
be designed to have what is known as <u>direct organization</u>. In this organization, data records are stored or "accessed" using a scheme of converting the
key of a record into the disk address to which the record is placed. Thus,
no index table as in the case of an indexed file is necessary; instead, an
efficient technique for transforming the key to the address is required. The
difficulty in having a direct organization is that in most cases it is
hardly possible to find a key transformation algorithm that converts each
key to a unique address. As such with most key transformation algorithms,
two or more keys are transformed into the same address, causing a conflict.
There are ways and means to tackle such situations; but these are beyond
the scope of the present book.

COBOL does not support direct organization. However, the programmer can
take help of the relative organization to implement it. If the key transformation algorithm converts the keys to relative addresses, this can be
easily achieved.

16.2.8 Selection of File Organization

While designing a file, the programmer must select a suitable organization
for a file. The order in which the choice is to be made is as follows:
sequential, relative, indexed and direct. In specifying this order we have
taken into consideration the following factors.

  (i)   Implementation difficulty.
  (ii) Software support required.
  (iii) Efficiency of processing.

There is no doubt that in each of these counts, the sequential organization is most preferable. It is simple to implement, requires very low software support and considering that the file is required to be accessed sequentially, the efficiency of processing is also good. However, all files cannot
be designed to be sequential files. For example, if the records of a sequential file are to be accessed randomly, then every time a record is "accessed",
the search must begin from the first record. The relative file organization
has also limited applicability in the sense that in order to access a record,
one must specify the relative record position rather than the key. The
indexed and direct organizations are very useful when a random access of
records (by specifying the key) is required. So far as the efficiency of
file processing is concerned, direct organization is better than indexed
organization provided that a good key-transformation algorithm is available.
However, it is extremely difficult to implement a direct organization particularly when the file size is large.

With the preferential order of the various organizations mentioned above,
we shall now consider three factors that can influence the choice of files —
file activity, file volatility and file interrogation.

File Activity

File activity is a measure of the proportion of records processed during an
update run. Thus we define the activity ratios as follows:

$$\text{Activity ratio} = \frac{m}{n}$$

where,   m = number of records to be inserted, modified or deleted, and
         n = number of records in the file.

Obviously, the activity ratio for each update run will be different. However, experience shows that normally, the ratio does not fluctuate widely. Moreover, it is sufficient to have only a fair estimate of the activity ratio.

   A file is called an active file if the ratio is high. For an active file (activity ratio greater than .4), it is expected that sequential organization will be economical as well as efficient.

File Volatility

File volatility relates to the number of times the updations of records are required during some time period. For example, where the records of a file are updated for a number of times during a working day, the file is said to have high volatility. It may be noted that it is not the volume of updation but the frequency of updation that determines volatility. A suitable direct access organization may be selected for a highly-volatile file.

File Interrogation

Some files contain reference data. These files are used mainly for the purpose of interrogation. Interrogation means a reference to a specific record for a specific response without changing the record in any manner. For example, price list can be a file which is to be constantly interrogated during a billing run. File interrogation can be efficiently handled if some kind of direct access organization is used.

16.3   IMPLEMENTATION DIFFERENCES

The ANSI 74 features for the handling of relative and indexed files have been described in the text. The features for indexed files are new additions and the features for relative files have been substantially revised. As such considerable implementation differences exist. A brief account of the essential differences are noted below.

(a)   Relative Files

   (i)   B-6700: There is no ORGANIZATION clause. The ACCESS MODE IS
         RANDOM clause specifies that the file is a relative file.
         SEQUENTIAL and DYNAMIC options of this clause are not available
         when the file is relative. Instead of the RELATIVE KEY clause,
         the ACTUAL KEY clause is to be specified. The format of this
         clause is

                    ACTUAL KEY IS   data-name

         and it has the same meaning as that of the RELATIVE KEY clause
         of the text. Thus the SELECT clause for the file in Example 1

of Sec. 16.1.3 should be

```
SELECT HISTORY ASSIGN TO DISK
ACCESS MODE IS RANDOM
ACTUAL KEY IS REL-POSITION
FILE-LIMITS ARE 1 THRU 500.
```

The FILE-LIMITS clause specifies that there can be at most 500 records in the file. Only READ (Format 1 and Format 2) WRITE and SEEK statements are available for relative files. The SEEK statement is functionally similar to the START statement and has the following format.

<u>SEEK</u> file-name RECORD

The SEEK statement positions the file at the record position indicated by the value of the actual key data name. However, the SEEK statement is implicitly executed by every READ or WRITE statement and it is therefore not necessary to specify it separately. If used, the SEEK statement will position the file while the processing of the subsequent statements will go on.

The format 2 of the READ statement is to be used for relative files in B-6700. The programmer must move the appropriate value to the actual key data field before the READ statement is executed. The WRITE statement can be used to write a new record or to rewrite an existing record. The record position is determined from the value of the actual key data name. The invalid key condition arises when the actual key specified is outside the boundary of the file.

In B-6700, the ACTUAL KEY clause can also be specified for files whose access mode is SEQUENTIAL. The SEEK statement can be used on such a file to position it at a desired record position. The program can resume sequential processing from this point. Moreover, the actual key data item is updated following each WRITE and before each READ except in the case of a READ statement that is logically preceded by a WRITE statement on the file.

(ii) DEC-10: The features are similar to these in the case of B-6700. The actual key data name must be numeric integers with COMP usage. The sequential reading of a relative file is possible by moving zero to the actual key data item. If the actual key is equal to zero, the next available record is read (empty record positions are ignored). The WRITE statement cannot be used to overwrite an existing record. However, a WRITE statement can be used to rewrite a record, provided: (a) the file is open in the I-O mode, (b) WRITE is logically preceded by a READ statement on the file and (c) the actual key data name contains a zero.

(iii) <u>ICL-1900</u>: Relative organization is not supported in ICL-1900. However, a more powerful file organization facility is provided. This is called DIRECT organization. In this organization, the records of a file are stored in buckets (file areas which may be of 512, 1024, 2048 or 4096 characters in size). The logical bucket numbers are determined from the keys by an address-generation procedure to be designed and written by the programmer. It may be noted that a bucket can hold more than one record. In fact, all records whose keys determine the same bucket number are placed in the said bucket. If a bucket is full, an overflow bucket can be opened. Up to two levels of overflow can be handled by the ICL house keeping routines that support the DIRECT organization. This organization is suitable for implementing the direct organization discussed in Sec. 16.2.7. For further information the reader may refer to the relevant manual.

(b) Indexed Files

(i) <u>B-6700</u>: ANSI 74 indexed I-O features have been implemented in B-6700 and can be used by specifying an appropriate compiler option. The ASSIGN TO clause is slightly different. It should be written as

ASSIGN TO integer-1 * integer-2 DISK

Integer-1 specifies the number of rows (see Sec. 16.2.3) and integer-2 specifies the size of each row.

The ALTERNATE KEY option has not been implemented. Therefore, the KEY IS option in the READ statement is only available for documentation. The VALUE OF clause can contain three optional-implementor defined phrases. These can be used to have an efficient organization. See the relevant manual for further details regarding these phrases.

(ii) <u>DEC-10</u>: There is no ORGANIZATION clause in the FILE-CONTROL paragraph. The ACCESS MODE clause is as follows:

ACCESS MODE IS INDEXED

The RECORD KEY clause is shown below:

$\left\{ \begin{array}{l} \underline{\text{SYMBOLIC}} \\ \underline{\text{NOMINAL}} \end{array} \right\}$ KEY data-name-1, <u>RECORD</u> KEY IS data-name-2

Data-name-1 must not appear in the record description while data-name-2 must appear in the record description. The RECORD KEY clause is only required to indicate the location of the key within the record. Before reading or writing a record, the programmer should move the key value only to data-name-1. Data-name-1 and data-name-2 must agree in respect of class, usage, size and point location.

READ, WRITE and DELETE statements are available. The START statement is not implemented and the SEEK statement is not available
for indexed files.

The READ statement with the INVALID KEY option can only be used
to read records from an indexed file. The NEXT option in the
READ statement is not available. The DELETE and REWRITE statements need not be logically preceded by a READ statement. The
file can be opened either in the OUTPUT mode or the I-O mode when
these statements are executed. In all cases the record is identified by the value stored in the symbolic (nominal) key data item.

An indexed file can be read sequentially by moving LOW-VALUES to
the symbolic key data item. If this data field contains LOW-
VALUES, the next record is read from the file.

(iii)   ICL-1900: The ORGANIZATION clause is as follows:

ORGANIZATION IS INDEXED [FIRST-LEVEL] [SECOND-LEVEL]

Like the DIRECT files (discussed above), the records of indexed
files are also stored in buckets. The FIRST-LEVEL or SECOND-LEVEL
option indicates the level up to which the overflow buckets are
to be allocated. The overhead of specifying an additional level
is that an extra word is required for the housekeeping software
in every bucket. The options need not be specified if only the
READ and DELETE statements are to be used on the file.

The RECORD KEY clause is to be specified as

SYMBOLIC KEY IS data-name

The data-name must be a character field but can belong to any
class.

The ACCESS MODE clause should be specified as

ACCESS MODE IS RANDOM.

There is no START statement. Instead, a SEEK statement which has
the following format, is available.

SEEK file-name RECORD

The SEEK statement positions the file at the record indicated
by the value of the symbolic key data name. A SEEK statement
must logically precede each READ, WRITE or DELETE statements
when the file is accessed randomly. DELETE statement can also
be logically preceded by a READ statement.

No INVALID KEY clause can be specified for the REWRITE statement.
The INVALID KEY clause can be omitted in the case of a DELETE
statement if it is preceded by the execution of a READ statement.

If after reading a specific record, it is required to have
access to the next record of an indexed file, a READ statement

not preceded by a SEEK will serve the purpose. For example,

```
SEEK  AN-INDEXED-FILE  RECORD.
READ  AN-INDEXED-FILE  INVALID KEY
                GO TO  PARA-ERROR.
READ  AN-INDEXED-FILE  AT END
                GO TO THE-END.
```

The second READ statement will read the next record. The NEXT option is not available in the READ statement.

EXERCISES

1. A magnetic-tape file contains fixed-length records having the following format.

```
01  PART-REC.
    02  PART-NO.
        03  PART-CODE        PIC        X(3).
        03  PART-SL-NO       PIC        9(3).
    02  DESCRIPTIONS.
        03  DESC             PIC        X(30).
        03  UNIT-CODE        PIC        9.
        03  UNIT-PRICE       PIC        9(4)V99.
```

Read this file to create the following two files:

(i) PARTREL: A relative file containing all the records of the tape file in the same format. In addition, the first record of this file should contain the record number of the last record written on the file in positions 1 to 6. The remaining positions of the first record should have blanks.

(ii) PARTDIR: A sequential disk file containing the value of PART-NO and the relative record number of the corresponding record in PARTREL.

2. Sort the PARTDIR file created in the previous problem in the ascending order of PART-NO and store the sorted records in the form of an indexed file named PARTINDEX.

3. Suppose you are given a magnetic-tape file containing transaction records which have the same format as the record of the tape file in Exercise 1, with the exception that the transaction record has one additional character to its right. This character contains a transaction code indicating the insertion for 1, deletion for 2 and modification in all other cases. Write a program to update the PARTREL and PARTINDEX files with this transaction file. Note that you must also update the first record of PARTREL.

4. Due to a number of updations, the overflow area of PARTINDEX file has become crowded. Write a program to clean the overflow area.

5. Suppose, transaction cards contain PART-NO in columns 11 to 16 along with other information which is not relevant to this problem.

   Write a program to read each card and to check whether PART-NO given on the card exists in the PARTINDEX file or not. Print an edit list containing the listing of all cards for which PART-NO was not found in the indexed file.

17
CHARACTER HANDLING

A string refers to a sequence of characters. Any field in COBOL having a
DISPLAY usage can be considered to be a string. String-manipulating operations include the comparison of two strings, concatenation (joining of two
or more strings to form a longer string), segmentation (reverse of concatenation), scanning (searching a string, say for locating the appearance of a
specified character or group of characters) and replacement (replacing a
specified character or group of characters in the string by another specified character or group of characters).

   This chapter deals with string-handling verbs, such as EXAMINE, INSPECT,
STRING and UNSTRING. The EXAMINE verb which was present in the earlier
versions of COBOL has now been replaced by the more powerful verb INSPECT
in the ANSI 74 COBOL. However, in view of the fact that most of the implementations still retain the EXAMINE verb, it is also discussed here.

17.1 EXAMINE VERB

This verb is used to scan a string to find the number of occurrences of a
given character in it. In addition, the verb can also be used to replace
some or all occurrences of the said character by another character. There
are three different options of this verb as given below:

Option 1

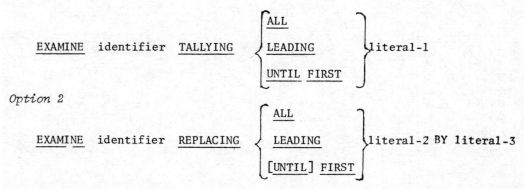

EXAMINE identifier TALLYING
$$\begin{Bmatrix} \text{ALL} \\ \text{LEADING} \\ \text{UNTIL FIRST} \end{Bmatrix}$$ literal-1

Option 2

EXAMINE identifier REPLACING
$$\begin{Bmatrix} \text{ALL} \\ \text{LEADING} \\ \text{[UNTIL] FIRST} \end{Bmatrix}$$ literal-2 BY literal-3

Option 3

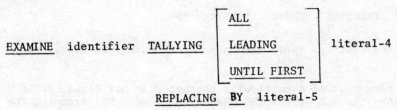

EXAMINE identifier TALLYING

ALL
LEADING
UNTIL FIRST

literal-4

REPLACING BY literal-5

The following rules govern the function of this verb.

(i) The identifier which indicates the string to be scanned/replaced must have DISPLAY usage.

(ii) Each literal is a single character and its class must be identical to that of the identifier. The literal can also be any figurative constant except ALL.

(iii) Examination of the identifier starts from the leftmost character and proceeds to the right. The identifier can be nonnumeric or numeric. In the case of a numeric data item, it must consist of numeric characters with or without an operation sign and each character is examined except the sign. Regardless of its position, the sign is completely ignored by the EXAMINE statement.

(iv) If the TALLYING option is used, then during the execution of the EXAMINE verb, a count is kept in a specified register called TALLY. This register is set to zero at the start of the execution.

(v) When option 1 is used, the meanings of ALL, LEADING and the UNTIL FIRST phrases are as follows. If the ALL phrase is used, the character specified by literal-1 is matched against the characters in the string, and for each match the TALLY register is increased by 1. If, on the other hand, the LEADING phrase is used, the contiguous occurrences of literal-1 starting from the leading position of the identifier are examined, and for each match, the TALLY register is increased and the search terminates as soon as no match occurs. In the case of UNTIL FIRST, the TALLY register is increased by 1 each time a character is tested and the increment as well as the search is terminated as soon as the character specified by literal-1 is encountered.

Example

Let us consider the following DATA DIVISION entry.

    77   A   PIC   X(5)   VALUE   IS   "EERIE".

Now the statement

    EXAMINE   A   TALLYING   ALL   "E"

will store 3 in the TALLY register as there are altogether three E's in the string. However, the statement

    EXAMINE   A   TALLYING   LEADING   "E"

will store 2 in TALLY since there are only two leading E's. The statement

    EXAMINE   A   TALLYING   UNTIL   FIRST   "I"

will store 3 in the TALLY as there are only three characters before the character I.

It may be noted here that if a particular character is not found, TALLY is set to zero when the ALL or LEADING phrase is used. For example, the statement

    EXAMINE   A   TALLYING   LEADING   "R"

will set TALLY to zero since the leading character is not R. If the UNTIL FIRST phrase is used and the specified character is not found the TALLY will contain the size of the string.

(vi)   In option 2 all the three phrases discussed above have the same meanings as in option 1 except that instead of increasing the TALLY register, the matched characters are replaced by the specified character mentioned in literal-3. When option 3 is used, the effect is a combination of option 1 and option 2, i.e., the TALLY register gets increased and at the same time the matched characters are replaced by the specified character mentioned in literal-4 For example, the statement

        EXAMINE   A   TALLYING   ALL   "E"   REPLACING   BY   "B"

with A defined as before, will store 3 in TALLY register and will change the content of A to "BBRIB".

(vii)   Note that the word UNTIL in option 2 is optional. If the UNTIL is dropped and FIRST alone is used, only the first appearance of the character specified by literal-2 will be replaced by the character specified by literal-3. On the other hand, if UNTIL FIRST is used, all characters up to the first appearance of the character specified by literal-2 will be replaced. Thus the statement

        EXAMINE   A   REPLACING   FIRST   "I"   BY   "P"

will change the content of A to   "EERPE",   whereas the statement

        EXAMINE   A   REPLACING   UNTIL   FIRST   "I"   BY   "P"

will change the content of A to "PPPIE". In each of the cases A is assumed to be defined as before.

17.2   INSPECT VERB

The INSPECT verb is similar to the EXAMINE verb. It enables the programmer
to tally and/or replace the occurrences of a single character or groups of
characters in a data field. As in the EXAMINE verb, in this case also there
are three options which are described below.

Option 1

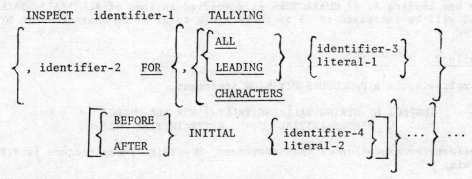

The following rules may be noted when this option is used.
   (i)   All identifiers must be elementary items with usage DISPLAY.
         Identifier-1 can, however, be a group item having its subordinate
         items with usage DISPLAY.
  (ii)   The contents of identifier-1 are scanned for the occurrence of the
         specified characters in a left-to-right manner.
 (iii)   Unlike the EXAMINE statement, there is no special register called
         TALLY. Identifier-2 is the field where the count will be stored.
  (iv)   In the case of the ALL phrase, the characters specified by identi-
         fier-3 or literal-1 are matched against the characters of identi-
         fier-1 and for each match the value of the identifier-2 is increas-
         ed by 1.
   (v)   In the case of the LEADING phrase, only the contiguous occurrence
         of identifier-3 or literal-1 starting from the leading position of
         identifier-1 are examined, and for each match, identifier-2 is
         increased by 1. The search terminates as soon as no match occurs.
  (vi)   If the CHARACTERS phrase is specified, identifier-2 is increased
         by 1 for each character in identifier-1.
 (vii)   The BEFORE or AFTER phrase only limits the length of identifier-1
         to be searched. BEFORE means that the leading portions of identi-
         fier-1 up to (but not including) the first occurrence of identi-
         fier-4 or literal-2 is searched. AFTER means that the trailing
         portions of identifier-1 after the first occurrence of literal-4
         or literal-2 is searched.

Example 1

Let us consider the following PROCEDURE DIVISION statement.

         INSPECT MY-STRING TALLYING TALLY-COUNT FOR ALL "A".

Let the picture of MY-STRING be X(20) and suppose its content before the execution of the above statement is as follows:

ANANTAɃKUMARɃMAITYɃɃ

If TALLY-COUNT (whose picture is say, 99) originally contains 08, then after the execution of the statement, TALLY-COUNT will contain 13 as there are a total of 5 A's in MY-STRING. On the other hand, if ALL in the statement is changed to LEADING, TALLY-COUNT will be increased to 09 as there is only one leading A. If CHARACTERS is specified instead of ALL ''A'', TALLY-COUNT will be increased to 28 as there are a total of 20 characters in MY-STRING.

Example 2

The following is a PROCEDURE DIVISION statement

        INSPECT MY-STRING TALLYING TALLY-1 FOR ALL "ABC"
              BEFORE INITIAL "."   AFTER INITIAL "Z"

If before the execution of this statement, MY-STRING whose picture is X(20) contains

                ɃɃBACDABCZPABCABCPQ.

and TALLY-1 whose picture is 99 contains 02, then after the execution of the statement TALLY-1 will contain 04. This is because the group ABC occurs twice after the first occurrence of Z in MY-STRING.

Example 3

Let us consider the following DATA DIVISION entries

        77   TALLY-1   PIC   9   VALUE IS ZERO.
        77   TALLY-2   PIC   9   VALUE IS ZERO.
        77   A   PIC   9(5).99.

    Now, to separately find how many zeros there are in A to the left and right of the decimal point, the following statement may be specified.

        INSPECT A TALLYING TALLY-1 FOR ALL   "0"
              BEFORE INITIAL   "." TALLY-2 FOR ALL   "0"
              AFTER INITIAL   "." .

Option 2

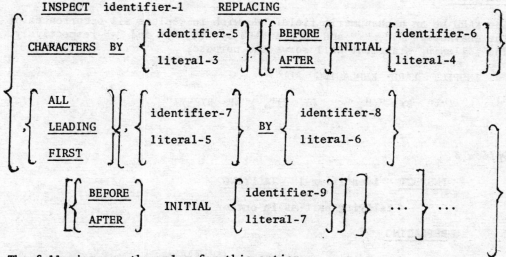

The following are the rules for this option.

(i) This option of the INSPECT verb allows the user to replace matched characters by the specified characters mentioned by the identifier or literal after the word BY.

(ii) If the CHARACTERS phrase is specified, identifier-5 or literal-3 must refer to a single character.

(iii) The ALL and LEADING phrases have the same meaning as in option 1 except that no count is increased. Instead, the matched characters are replaced by the specified characters.

(iv) When the FIRST phrase is used, the leftmost occurrence of identifier-7 or literal-5 matched within the contents of identifier-1 is replaced by identifier-8 or literal-6.

(v) The BEFORE and AFTER phrases have the same meaning as in option 1.

(vi) The size of identifier-7/literal-5 must be equal to that of identifier-8/literal-6. If literal-5 is a figurative constant, identifier-8/literal-6 must denote a single character. If literal-6 is a figurative constant, its size is considered equal to that of identifier-7/literal-5.

Example 4

Frequently, we need to replace the leading blanks in a field by zeros. For example, let AMOUNT described with picture 9(5), be a field in the record description for an input file. If the field contains leading blanks, its contents will be treated as non-numeric. In order to replace the leading blanks by zeros, we can use the statement

    INSPECT AMOUNT REPLACING LEADING "ƀ" BY "0".

Example 5

Let KARD be an alphanumeric field. We wish to replace all occurrences of the characters "%", "<" and "b̸" in KARD by "(", ")" and "+" respectively. The following statement will serve the purpose.

```
INSPECT  KARD  REPLACING  ALL

     "%"  BY  "(",  "<"  BY  ")",  "b̸"  BY  "+"
```

Option 3

```
INSPECT   identifier-1   TALLYING

     < tallying part as in option 1 >

REPLACING

     < replacing part as in option 2 >
```

This option is a combination of the previous two options.

Example 6

In Example 5, if we also want to find the total number of replaced characters, the following statement will serve the purpose.

```
INSPECT  KARD  TALLYING TALLY-COUNTER
               REPLACING  ALL   "%"  BY  "("
                                "<"  BY  ")"
                                "b̸"  BY  "+"
```

In this case TALLY-COUNTER will contain the total number of such replaced characters. For example, if there are 12 such characters, TALLY-COUNTER will contain 12 if its initial value was 0.

17.3 STRING AND UNSTRING VERBS

Two or more strings of characters can be combined to form one longer string with the help of the STRING statement, whereas the UNSTRING statement facilitates the splitting of one string to many substrings. These verbs can also be used to transfer characters from a string to another string starting at some particular character position either in the receiving field or in the sending field.

The general format of the STRING verb is as follows:

STRING $\begin{Bmatrix} \text{identifier-1} \\ \text{literal-1} \end{Bmatrix}$, $\begin{bmatrix} \text{identifier-2} \\ \text{literal-2} \end{bmatrix}$ ...

DELIMITED BY $\begin{Bmatrix} \text{identifier-3} \\ \text{literal-3} \\ \underline{\text{SIZE}} \end{Bmatrix}$

$\begin{bmatrix} , \begin{Bmatrix} \text{identifier-4} \\ \text{literal-4} \end{Bmatrix} \end{bmatrix}$ $\begin{bmatrix} , \begin{Bmatrix} \text{identifer-5} \\ \text{literal-5} \end{Bmatrix} \end{bmatrix}$ ...

DELIMITED BY $\begin{Bmatrix} \text{identifier-6} \\ \text{literal-6} \\ \underline{\text{SIZE}} \end{Bmatrix}$ ...

INTO identifier-7 $\begin{bmatrix} \text{WITH } \underline{\text{POINTER}} \text{ identifier-8} \end{bmatrix}$

$\begin{bmatrix} ; \text{ ON } \underline{\text{OVERFLOW}} \text{ imperative-statement} \end{bmatrix}$

The following rules should be followed when this verb is used.

(i) This statement is used to concatenate one or more strings into one by placing them side by side. The strings to be concatenated are the complete or partial contents of literals/identifiers-1,2,4,5, etc. referred to as sending fields. The concatenated string is placed in identifier-7 referred to as the receiving field.

(ii) Sending strings may be alphanumeric literals, figurative constants or identifiers with usage DISPLAY. Figurative constants are treated as single characters.

(iii) The receiving string, i.e., identifier-7 must also be with usage DISPLAY. If certain portions of the receiving string does not receive any character, these portions will retain the original characters.

(iv) If the DELIMITED BY SIZE phrase is used, the entire contents are transferred from left to right into identifier-7 until the rightmost character is transferred or identifier-7 is full. For example, consider the following DATA DIVISION entry.

```
        77    FIELD-1        PIC        X(4)      VALUE      "RAIN".
```

Now, the execution of the statement

```
        STRING    "MA"    DELIMITED SIZE    INTO    FIELD-1
```

will make the content of FIELD-1 to become "MAIN". It may be noted that the characters I, N in FIELD-1 remain unchanged.

(v) If the DELIMITED phrase without the SIZE option is used, the characters of the sending strings are transferred from left to right to identifier-7. The transfer of characters to identifier-7

will be terminated when any one of the following conditions takes place.
(a) The end of the sending strings are reached.
(b) The character specified in the DELIMITED phrase is encountered.
(c) Identifier-7 is full.
The character specified in the DELIMITED phrase (e.g., literals/ identifiers-3 and 6) is not transferred.

Example 1

Let us consider the following DATA DIVISION entries.

```
77   FIELD-1        PIC   X(4)   VALUE   "RAIN".
77   FIELD-2        PIC   X(4)   VALUE   SPACES.
```

Now the execution of the statement

```
STRING FIELD-1 DELIMITED BY  "I"  INTO FIELD-2
```

will store RAϾϾ in FIELD-2. It may be noted that in this case, the character "I" specified in the DELIMITED phrase, is encountered before reaching the end of FIELD-1. The character I is not transferred to FIELD-2.

Example 2

The following are the DATA DIVISION entries.

```
77   FIELD-1        PIC   X(4)    VALUE   "ABCD".
77   FIELD-2        PIC   X(6)    VALUE   "MAϾINϾ".
77   FIELD-3        PIC   X(9)    VALUE   "121,34,56"
77   FIELD-4        PIC   X(14)   VALUE   SPACES.
```

The statement

```
STRING FIELD-1, FIELD-2, FIELD-3 DELIMITED BY
              "Ͼ" , ","   INTO FIELD-4
```

will make the contents of FIELD-4 to be ABCDMA121ϾϾϾϾϾ. In this example, first, all the four characters of FIELD-1 are transferred to FIELD-4 as FIELD-1 does not contain any one of the delimiters. Next, only two characters of FIELD-2 are transferred to FIELD-4 as the third character of FIELD-2 is a delimiter. Lastly, three characters of FIELD-3 are transferred to FIELD-4 as the fourth characters of FIELD-3 is a delimiter. The remaining characters of FIELD-4 are spaces as originally FIELD-4 contains spaces.

   (vi) The delimiters (i.e., identifier-3/literal-3 and identifier-6/ literal-6) in the DELIMITED phrase can denote one or more characters. When identifier is used it must have DISPLAY usage. Figurative constants (except ALL) used for literals will be considered as single character fields.
   (vii) There can be several delimiters in a STRING statement. If any one of these delimiters is encountered, the transmission of characters will be terminated.

(viii)   The sending data items are transferred in the order of their appearance in the STRING statement. The rules of alphanumeric data transfer are applicable, except that no space filling will be provided.

(ix)   The purpose of the POINTER phrase is to specify the leftmost position within the receiving field (identifier-7) where the first transferred character will be stored. The said position is indicated by the contents of identifier-8 which must be an elementary numeric integer field. The absence of the POINTER phrase is considered as if the programmer has specified it with a value of 1 in identifier-8. If initially identifier-8 contains a value less than 1 or greater than the number of positions in identifier-7, then no character will be transferred.

As each character is transferred to the receiving field, the value of identifier-8 is increased by 1. For example, let FIELD-1, FIELD-2, FIELD-3 and FIELD-4 be described as before and let the statement be

```
STRING FIELD-1, FIELD-2, FIELD-3  DELIMITED
BY "b", ","  INTO  FIELD-4
WITH POINTER  CHARACTER-POSITION.
```

If we assume that CHARACTER-POSITION initially contains 03 then after the execution of the statement FIELD-4 and CHARACTER-POSITION will contain bbABCDMA121bbb and 12 respectively.

(x)   The STRING statement terminates when all data has been transferred or the end of the data item referred to by identifier-7 has been reached. In the latter case, if further characters cannot be transferred owing to the fact that end of identifier-7 has been reached, the statement following the OVERFLOW phrase will be executed, if specified. If the OVERFLOW phrase is not specified, the control is transferred to the next executable statement in sequence.

Example 3

Suppose there is a field called NAME defined as follows:

```
02    NAME.
      03    FIRST NAME        PIC        X(10).
      03    MIDDLE-NAME       PIC        X(6).
      03    SURNAME           PIC        X(20).
```

We assume that in each field the characters are stored as left justified. Now, while printing this name we want to print SURNAME first, then the FIRST-NAME and finally the MIDDLE-NAME by leaving only one space after each of these names. Only the set of non-blank characters from the left of the fields are to be considered.

Let the receiving field be defined as

```
      02        OUTPUT-REC              PIC        X(39).
```

We also define the following field.

```
      77        A                      PIC        X  VALUE SPACE.
```

The following statement is a solution of the above problem.

```
STRING   SURNAME  DELIMITED BY SPACES,
         A  DELIMITED  BY  SIZE,
         FIRST-NAME  DELIMITED  BY  SPACES,
         A  DELIMITED  BY  SIZE,
         MIDDLE-NAME  DELIMITED  BY SPACES
         INTO  OUTPUT-REC.
```

The general format of the UNSTRING verb is as follows:

UNSTRING   identifier-1

$$\left[\underline{\text{DELIMITED}} \text{ BY } \left[\underline{\text{ALL}}\right] \left\{ \begin{array}{l} \text{identifier-2} \\ \text{literal-1} \end{array} \right\} \left[\text{, } \underline{\text{OR}} \left[\underline{\text{ALL}}\right] \left\{ \begin{array}{l} \text{identifier-3} \\ \text{literal-2} \end{array} \right\} \right] \dots \right]$$

$$\underline{\text{INTO}} \quad \text{identifier-4} \left[\text{, } \underline{\text{DELIMITER}} \text{ IN identifier-5}\right]$$
$$\left[\text{, } \underline{\text{COUNT}} \text{ IN identifier-6}\right]$$

$$\left[\text{, identifier-7} \left[\text{, } \underline{\text{DELIMITER}} \text{ IN identifier-8}\right]\right.$$
$$\left.\left[\text{, } \underline{\text{COUNT}} \text{ IN identifier-9}\right]\right] \dots$$

$$\left[\underline{\text{WITH}} \underline{\text{POINTER}} \text{ identifier-10}\right]$$
$$\left[\underline{\text{TALLYING}} \text{ IN identifier-11}\right] \left[\text{; ON } \underline{\text{OVERFLOW}} \text{ imperative-statement}\right]$$

The following rules should be followed when the UNSTRING verb is used.

(i)   The data in identifier-1 is separated and placed in multiple-receiving fields, namely, identifier-4, identifier-7, etc.

(ii) The sending field, i.e., identifier-1 can only be an alphanumeric field with DISPLAY usage.

(iii) The receiving fields, i.e., identifier-4, identifier-7, etc., must also have DISPLAY usage. They can be described as alphabetic, alphanumeric or numeric fields.

(iv) All literals must be described as nonnumeric literals. If a literal is a figurative constant, it is treated as a single character.

(v)   Identifier-6, identifier-9, identifier-10 and identifier-11 must be elementary numeric integer data items.

(vi) If the DELIMITED BY phrase is not used, the characters in the sending field are transferred from left to right into the receiving fields until the rightmost character of the sending field is transferred or the receiving fields are full.

(vii)   If the DELIMITED BY phrase is used, the sending field is examined for the occurrence of the character or characters (known as delimiter) in the DELIMITED BY phrase. The examination terminates when the delimiter is found or the end of identifier-1 is reached. The characters examined (excluding the delimiting character) are then transferred to the current-receiving field according to the rules of the MOVE statement. If identifier-1 still contains some characters and there are more receiving fields, the above operation is repeated, starting from the first character to the right of the delimiter.

When two contiguous delimiters are encountered and the word ALL is not mentioned, the first delimiter terminates the transfer of data to the current-receiving field and the second delimiter causes the filling of the next receiving field either with spaces or with zeros depending on the description of the field. When ALL is specified, two or more contiguous occurrences of the delimiter are together considered as a single delimiter.

The word OR may be mentioned to enable the programmer to specify more than one delimiter. In that case the occurrence of any one of the delimiters will terminate the data transfer to the current-receiving field and the process will continue to fill other receiving fields until the end of identifier-1 is reached or there are no more receiving fields.

Example 4

Let us consider the following DATA DIVISION entries.

```
77      FIELD-1            PIC           X(10).
77      FIELD-2            PIC           X(10).
77      FIELD-3            PIC           X(15).
77      DATA-FIELD  PIC   X(38)  VALUE  IS  "A.K. KRISHNAMURTY."
```

Now, the execution of the statement

```
      UNSTRING  DATA-FIELD  DELIMITED  BY  "."
            INTO    FIELD-1,  FIELD-2,      FIELD-3
```

will store the character A followed by 9 blanks in FIELD-1, the character K followed by 9 blanks in FIELD-2 and KRISHNAMURTY followed by 3 blanks in FIELD-3. The first period (.) after A in DATA-FIELD terminates the transfer of characters from this sending field to the first receiving field FIELD-1. The second period after K again terminates the transfer of characters to the second receiving field FIELD-2 and ultimately the third period terminates the transfer of characters to FIELD-3.

Example 5

Let us consider the following DATA DIVISION entries.

```
77    FIELD-1      PIC      X(5).
77    FIELD-2      PIC      X(5).
77    FIELD-3      PIC      X(5).
77    DATA-FIELD   PIC      X(15)   VALUE IS  "ABCDEFGCCHIJKCL".
```

The statement

```
        UNSTRING  DATA-FIELD  DELIMITED  BY    "C"
              INTO  FIELD-1, FIELD-2, FIELD-3.
```

will store ABƀƀƀ in FIELD-1, DEFGƀ in FIELD-2 and ƀƀƀƀƀ in FIELD-3. Since there are two contiguous C's after the character G and the word ALL is not mentioned, the first of these two C's will terminate the transfer of characters to DEFG in FIELD-2 and the second C will cause the filling of the FIELD-3 with spaces as it is an alphanumeric field. On the other hand, the following statement in the PROCEDURE DIVISION

```
        UNSTRING DATA-FIELD DELIMITED BY ALL  "C"
              INTO FIELD-1, FIELD-2, FIELD-3
```

will store ABƀƀƀ in FIELD-1, DEFGƀ in FIELD-2 and HIJKƀ in FIELD-3. In this case the word ALL has been used. Hence the two contiguous C's after the character G will be treated as one delimiter.

Example 6

Let us consider the same DATA DIVISION entries as in Example 2 and let DATA-FIELD contain "A.KƀƀMAJUMDARƀƀ".
    The statement

```
        UNSTRING DATA-FIELD DELIMITED BY "."  OR ALL "ƀ"
              INTO FIELD-1, FIELD-2, FIELD-3
```

will store Aƀƀƀƀ in FIELD-1, Kƀƀƀƀ in FIELD-2 and MAJUM in FIELD-3. In this case the termination of the transfer of characters takes place if either the delimiter period (.) or spaces is encountered. The first termination takes place due to the delimiter period whereas the second and third terminations take place due to spaces.

(viii) The optional DELIMITER IN phrase or COUNT IN phrase can be specified only if the DELIMITED BY phrase is used. The delimiting character will be moved to the identifier specified in the DELIMITER IN phrase. If the delimiting character is not found within identifier-1, the said identifier will be space filled. When the COUNT IN phrase is specified, a value equal to the number of characters examined (except the delimiting character) is moved to the identifier specified in the COUNT IN phrase.

Example 7

The following are the DATA DIVISION entries.

```
77      FIELD-1      PIC      X(3).
77      FIELD-2      PIC      9(4).
77      FIELD-3      PIC      X(4).
77      COUNT-1      PIC      99    VALUE  IS   ZERO.
77      COUNT-2      PIC      99    VALUE  IS   ZERO.
77      COUNT-3      PIC      99    VALUE  IS   ZERO.
77      D1           PIC      X.
77      D2           PIC      X.
77      D3           PIC      X.
77      DATA-FIELD   PIC      X(12) VALUE IS   "12/345/678/9".
```

The statement

```
            UNSTRING  DATA-FIELD  DELIMITED  BY   "/"
            INTO  FIELD-1  DELIMITER IN D1 COUNT IN COUNT-1
                  FIELD-2  DELIMITER IN D2 COUNT IN COUNT-2
                  FIELD-3  DELIMITER IN D3 COUNT IN COUNT-3
```

will store the character ''/'' in D1, D2 and D3 since this is the only delimiter character considered here. The contents of the other fields are as follows:

FIELD-1	`1 2 `	As FIELD-1 is an alphanumeric field, the space is on the right
COUNT-1	`0 2`	As only two characters are moved from DATA-FIELD to FIELD-1
FIELD-2	`0 3 4 5`	As FIELD-2 is a numeric field, the zero-fill is on the left
COUNT-2	`0 3`	As only three characters are moved to FIELD-2
FIELD-3	`6 7 8 `	As FIELD-3 is an alphanumeric field
COUNT-3	`0 3`	As three characters are moved to FIELD-3

(ix) The POINTER phrase has the same meaning as in the STRING statement.

(x)   When the TALLYING phrase is specified, the value of identifier-11 after the operation will be equal to the initial value plus the number of receiving fields acted upon.

(xi) An OVERFLOW condition arises in the following cases:

    (a) All receiving areas that have been acted upon and the data item referred to by identifier-11 still contain characters that have not been examined.

    (b) The value of identifier-10 is less than 1 or greater than the size of the identifier-1.

The control is transferred to the statement included in the ON OVERFLOW phrase provided the overflow condition exists and the OVERFLOW phrase is specified. Otherwise, the control is transferred to the next sequential statement.

Example 8

Let the following be the DATA DIVISION entries.

```
77   FIELD-1                        PIC      X(6).
77   FIELD-2                        PIC      X(6).
77   FIELD-3                        PIC      X(6).
77   FIELD-4                        PIC      X(6).
77   D1                             PIC      X.
77   D2                             PIC      X.
77   D3                             PIC      X.
77   D4                             PIC      X.
77   C1                             PIC      9.
77   C2                             PIC      9.
77   C3                             PIC      9.
77   C4                             PIC      9.
77   T                              PIC      9.
77   DATA-FIELD PIC  X(26)  VALUE  IS   "THEREƀƀMAY-BE-SOMEƀƀERRORƀ".
```

Now, consider the following PROCEDURE DIVISION statement.

```
UNSTRING DATA-FIELD DELIMITED  "-"  OR  ALL  "ƀ"

INTO   FIELD-1    DELIMITER   D1   COUNT   C1
       FIELD-2    DELIMITER   D2   COUNT   C2
       FIELD-3    DELIMITER   D3   COUNT   C3
       FIELD-4    DELIMITER   D4   COUNT   C4

TALLYING    T
ON   OVERFLOW PERFORM ERROR-ROUTINE.
```

The execution will proceed as follows:

"THEREƀ" is stored in FIELD-2, "ƀ" is stored in D1 and 5 is stored in C1
"MAYƀƀƀ" is stored in FIELD-2 "-" is stored in D2 and 3 is stored in C2
"BEƀƀƀƀ" is stored in FIELD-3, "-" is stored in D3 and 2 is stored in C3
"SOMEƀƀ" is stored in FIELD-4, "ƀ" is stored in D4 and 4 is stored in C4.

T is set to 4 and since still there are some characters in DATA-FIELD, the procedure ERROR-ROUTINE will be performed.

Example 9

Let there be a field called FIELD-1 with picture X(40). This field is assumed to contain integers separated by commas. The last integer is followed by blank spaces only. The maximum integer is six-digited, the numbers are unsigned and there may be a maximum of six such numbers in FIELD-1. It is required to write the statements necessary to retrieve each number from the field and display its value.

Let us define the following fields in the DATA DIVISION.

```
77    I           PIC  9.
77    TALLY-COUNT  PIC  9.
01    TABLE-1.
02    T    OCCURS  6 TIMES PIC 9(6).
```

The following are the PROCEDURE DIVISION statements for the solution of the above problem.

```
UNSTRING FiELD-1 DELIMITED  "," OR  ALL SPACES
    INTO T(1), T(2), T(3), T(4), T(5), T(6)
    TALLYING TALLY-COUNT.

PERFORM PARA-DISPLAY  VARYING  I  FROM  1  BY  1
                    UNTIL  TALLY-COUNT = 0.

PARA-DISPLAY.
    DISPLAY   T(I)
    SUBTRACT   1   FROM  TALLY-COUNT.
```

17.4 IMPLEMENTATION DIFFERENCES

(a) EXAMINE Verb

This verb is implemented in all three compilers.

(b) INSPECT Verb

This verb is available in B-6700 as a part of the ANSI 74 implementation. Therefore, the ANSI 74 compiler option is to be used. This verb is not available in the other two compilers.

(c) STRING and UNSTRING Verbs

These verbs are implemented in B-6700 and DEC-10. If these verbs are to be used in B-6700, the ANSI 74 compiler option is to be set.

EXERCISES

1. Consider the statement

       EXAMINE A-STRING REPLACING LEADING "0" BY "*",

    Suppose A-STRING contains the eight characters 00034005 before the execution of this statement. What will be the total number of 0's replaced by the EXAMINE statement? Indicate what the picture of A-STRING should be. Rewrite the above statement using INSPECT.

2. A field named STRING-1 contains 80 characters. The character (/) or (,) is used to indicate the end of a word within these 80 characters. Write

a COBOL statement to find the number of words in STRING-1 and the lengths of the individual words.

3. A field named NAME contains 40 characters. Write a COBOL statement to change all instances of ''MR.'' by ''SRI'' and ''MRS'' by ''SMT''.

4. In our punching keyboard, the numeric characters appear as upper case. The lower case characters corresponding to the digits 0, 1, 2, 3, 4, 5, 6, 7, 8 and 9 are /, U, I, O, J, K, L, M, (,) and (.) respectively. Suppose, the data in card columns 1 to 10 should have contained numeric digits, but out of mistake they have been punched wrongly with the corresponding lower case characters. The remaining positions have been punched correctly. Can you write a COBOL program to create a sequential disk file containing the information punched on these cards? Your program should restore the wrongly-punched data.

5. Write the COBOL code in the form of a module that is to be performed. The module should convert a decimal integer stored at ARABIC (defined with picture 999) to its Roman equivalent and will store it at ROMAN (defined with picture X(10)). When the Roman string is less than 10 characters, the characters should be stored left justified with the remaining positions space-filled. Show also the DATA DIVISION entries for the tables that might be necessary for the conversion.

6. A disk file (LINE SEQUENTIAL) has been created with the help of a text editor. A record contains a name (upto 20 characters) followed by five 2-digited values. These fields in each record have been entered in free format. Sample records are shown below.

A. K. ROY	68	72	86	74	80	
S. SUBRAMANIUM	48	90	75	65	70	
D. K. PATRANABIS	68	70	85	88	65
R. SINHA	75	82	72	40	50	

Write a program to print a report containing the name and the average of the values that follow the name in the input data. Design a suitable report format.

18

REPORT WRITER

Reports play a very important role in commercial data processing. The reports are the finished products of a data-processing department and are meant for use by the management at various levels. Naturally, a programmer would like to make a report as impressive as possible and in this respect COBOL provides all the facilities that may be needed for the purpose. However, considering the need of frequent report generation, the ANSI COBOL includes the report-writer module. Using the features of a report writer, it is possible to generate reports from a sorted file very easily. The use of the report-writer feature can generally reduce the effort needed to code the PROCEDURE DIVISION. The relevant software that supports the report-writer feature can handle the printing of the report heading, page heading, skipping to a new page, testing for end of page, summation of amount fields, testing for control breaks, printing of totals for control breaks, printing of final totals, and so on. To take advantage of these facilities the programmer does not write any procedural statement. Instead, he includes a suitable report description in the program. There are, of course, three verbs — INITIATE, GENERATE and TERMINATE— available to the programmer to specify the opening, generation and closing of the report respectively.

18.1 GENERAL FORMAT OF A REPORT

Computer-generated reports are printed on a continuous stationery which contains horizontal perforations. The portion of the stationery contained within two consecutive perforations is called a physical page. However, for the report-writer feature, the programmer should define the logical page, each of which consists of a fixed number of printable lines. Thus a report is assumed to be printed on several logical pages. Ideally, each logical page should be of the same size as that of a physical page, though theoretically, the programmer has the liberty to define a logical page of any size.

A report can consist of all or some of the seven report groups which are described below. A group in this context means one or more lines printed together on a report.

(i)   Report heading: This group represents the title of the report and is printed only once in the very beginning.

(ii) Report footing: This group is also printed only once and at the very end of the report. This group usually includes a collection of totals.

   (iii) **Page heading:** This group is printed on the top of each logical page. This group can include the page number, usual column headings and brought-forward totals from the previous page.

   (iv) **Page footing:** This group is printed at the bottom of each page. The group can include carry-forward totals.

   (v) **Control footing:** An important function of the report-writer feature is that it takes care of control breaks in the input file from which the report is being generated. Whenever there is any change in a specified key field, the control break occurs and at that point the control-footing group is printed. This group can include sub-totals of some fields.

   (vi) **Control heading:** This group is also printed on a control break but only before the next detail group is printed (see below). For example, if a control break occurs on the salesman number, then we might like to get the name of the next salesman printed.

      In this connection it is important to note the order in which the control headings and control footings are printed. Suppose that in the input file, the district number is a major key and the salesman number the minor key. A break in the district number also means a break in the salesman number. Thus when a control break occurs on the district number, the control footings and headings will be printed in the following order.

      Control footing for salesman
      Control footing for district
      Control heading for district
      Control heading for salesman

  (vii) **Detail:** This group constitutes the main body of the report. The records of the input file can be listed in this group. A record may be printed in one or more lines.

Except for the detail group, all other groups are optional. It may be noted that only one each of the report heading, report-footing, page-heading and page-footing groups can be specified for a report. There can be as many control-heading and control-footing groups as there are control fields. But, several detail groups can be specified for a report.

Let us now look at the language features.

18.2 FILE SECTION — REPORT CLAUSE

Whenever the report-writer facility is used, a line-printer file is to be specified in the file section. This file holds the report. A normal SELECT clause in the FILE-CONTROL paragraph should also be coded for the file. The format of the FD entry for this file is as follows:

$$\text{FD}\quad \text{file-name}\quad \left\{ \begin{array}{l} \underline{\text{REPORT}}\ \ \text{IS} \\ \\ \underline{\text{REPORTS}}\ \ \text{ARE} \end{array} \right\}$$

$$\text{report-name-1}\ \ [\ ,\ \text{report-name-2}\ ]\ \ ...$$

No record description should follow this entry. The report names specified must be defined in the report section with the record description (RD) entry. Only one line-printer file is enough for all the reports to be generated in a program. The order of the report names in the FD entry has no significance.

18.3 OUTLINE OF REPORT SECTION

The report section is another section of the DATA DIVISION. This section must be coded when the report-writer feature is to be used. The report section must appear as the last section of the DATA DIVISION. Each report in the report section should be defined by means of the RD entry. The RD entry describes the following.

(i)   The data items on which the control breaks take place. We shall refer to these data items as control data items. Report writer also accepts the word FINAL as a control data item. The word FINAL implies the highest break in the control hierarchy and the FINAL break takes place at the beginning and at the end.

(ii) The size of the logical page.

(iii) The positions (line numbers) where the report groups are to appear on the page.
The RD entry is followed by the description of the various report groups for the report. Each report group is described by a 01 level entry, where among other things, the type of the report group is specified. The 01 level entry can have subordinate entries where the formats of the individual lines in the group are described. Besides the format, the subordinate entries also specify the source where the value of an item to be printed comes from.

Example

Let us consider the following report description.

```
RD    MY-REPORT
      CONTROLS ARE FINAL ACCOUNT-NO
      PAGE 60 LINES
      HEADING  2
      FIRST DETAIL 6 LAST DETAIL  52
      FOOTING  56.

01    TYPE PAGE HEADING.
      02   LINE NUMBER IS 2.
           03 COLUMN  50  PIC  X(13)
                         VALUE "WEEKLY REPORT".
           03 COLUMN  72  PIC  X(7)
                         VALUE "PAGE NO".
           03 COLUMN  80  PIC  ZZ9
                         SOURCE IS PAGE-COUNTER.

01    TYPE CONTROL FOOTING ACCOUNT-NO.
```

A little explanation will help to understand the above code. The name of the report is MY-REPORT. In the other part of the program the report may be referred to by this name. Two control data items, namely, the keyword FINAL and the data name ACCOUNT-NO has been specified for the report.

The data name ACCOUNT-NO must appear in the record description of the file from which the report file is generated. The PAGE clause indicates that each logical page consists of 60 lines. The other clauses, namely, HEADING, FIRST DETAIL, LAST DETAIL, and FOOTING specify the line number to indicate where the various report groups may appear on the logical page. The interpretations of these line numbers will be explained in the next section. The 01 entry following the RD entry describes the PAGE HEADING group. All the report groups that are to be specified for a report must now appear one after another (all as 01 level groups), but their order of appearance is not significant. Let us now look at the descriptions within the entry for the PAGE HEADING group. The LINE NUMBER clause at level 02 indicates that the first line of the group (as a matter of fact there is only one line in this group) is to be printed at line number 2. The elementary entries at level 03 describe the format of the line. The COLUMN clause indicates the print position where the field begins. The SOURCE and VALUE clauses indicate the value of the field. The PAGE-COUNTER is a special register of the report-writer feature which contains the page number. Thus, SOURCE IS PAGE-COUNTER means that the value to be printed is the value of PAGE-COUNTER moved to this field.

18.4   REPORT SECTION — REPORT-DESCRIPTION ENTRY

The report-description entry contains information of the overall format and structure of a report named in the file section. Each report name mentioned in the file section appears again in the report section with the level indicator RD. The following is the general format of the RD entry.

RD report-name

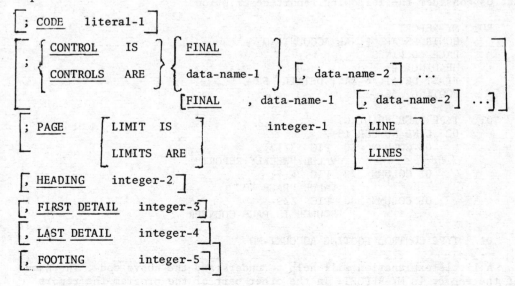

CODE

This clause is optional and is required to identify a particular report when more than one report is specified to the same printer file. The code can be a two-character nonnumeric literal. For example, CODE "01" will assign the code 01 to each line of this report so that the system software that handles this feature can distinguish a line belonging to one report from another.

CONTROL

This clause specifies the names of the control data items. The order in which the control data names appear in this clause determines their hierarchy. The keyword FINAL, if specified, should be the first control name. The other data names must appear in the record description of the file from which the report is generated.

PAGE

This clause specifies the size of the logical page. If it is omitted, HEADING, FIRST DETAIL, LAST DETAIL and FOOTING clauses must also be omitted.

HEADING, FIRST DETAIL, LAST DETAIL and FOOTING

The integers in these clauses divide the logical page into different regions. Only lines of a specific report group can appear in a particular region. Table 18.1 shows the boundaries of each region and the corresponding report groups

TABLE 18.1.   Different Regions of Logical Page and the
Corresponding Report Groups

Region		Report Groups
First Line	Last Line	
1	integer-2-1	No group
integer-2	integer-3-1	Report heading* and page heading
integer-3	integer-4	Detail, control heading and control footing
integer-4	integer-5	Control footing
integer-5+1	integer-1	Page footing and report footing*

*It is also possible to print the report-heading and report-footing groups on separate pages.

that may be printed in the region. The first line and last line columns of this table respectively indicate the uppermost and lowermost line numbers included within the regions. When the clauses are not specified, the defaults are as follows:

(i)   If HEADING is omitted, 1 is assumed
(ii) If FIRST DETAIL is omitted, integer-2 is assumed
(iii) If LAST DETAIL is omitted, integer-5 is assumed and
(iv) If FOOTING is omitted, integer-4 is assumed unless LAST DETAIL is also omitted, in which case integer-1 is assumed.

18.5 REPORT-GROUP DESCRIPTION

The RD entry should be followed by a number of report-group entries similar to the record entries following an FD entry. The entry with level indicator 01 should specify, among other things, the type of the report group. There are three different formats and these are given below.

Format 1

01   [data-name-1]

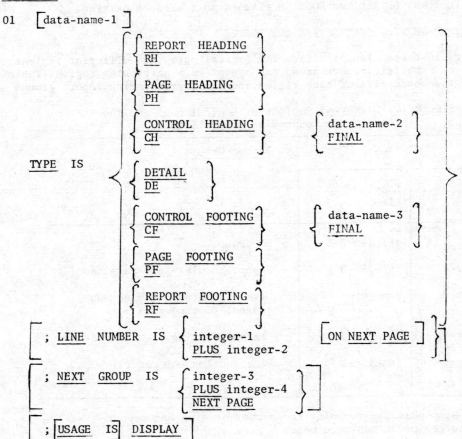

Format 2

level-number   [data-name-1]

    ⌈ ; LINE NUMBER IS { integer-1   [ON NEXT PAGE] } ⌉
    ⌊   { PLUS integer-2   } ⌋

    [; [USAGE IS] DISPLAY]

Format 3

level-number   [data-name-1]

    [; BLANK WHEN ZERO]
    [; COLUMN NUMBER IS integer-3]
    [; GROUP INDICATE]

    ⌈ ; { JUSTIFIED } RIGHT ⌉
    ⌊   { JUST   }   ⌋

    ⌈ ; LINE NUMBER IS { integer-1 [ON NEXT PAGE] } ⌉
    ⌊   { PLUS integer-2   } ⌋

    ; { PICTURE } IS character-string
      { PIC   }

    ⌈ ; SOURCE IS { TODAYS-DATE }   ⌉
    | { identifier-1 } |
    | ; { SUM identifier-2 [, identifier-3] ...   } ...|
    | {   [UPON data-name-2 [, data-name-3] ...] } |
    | {   [RESET ON { FINAL   }]   } |
    | {   { data-name-4 }   } |
    ⌊ ; VALUE IS literal-1   ⌋

    [; [USAGE IS] DISPLAY]

    The level numbers in Formats 2 and 3 can be any integers from 02 to
49. Format 2 represents a printable line within a report group and is

analogous to a group item within a record description. Format 3 represents fields within a printable line and is analogous to an elementary item. Data-name-1 is optional in all the three formats and need to be specified only when the item is to be referred to in a PROCEDURE DIVISION statement. The function of the other clauses are explained below.

TYPE

The TYPE clause is used to identify the various kinds of report groups. Of seven report groups, a report must contain at least one DETAIL report group. The report groups REPORT HEADING, PAGE HEADING, PAGE FOOTING and REPORT FOOTING can appear only once in the description of a report. The report groups CONTROL HEADING and CONTROL FOOTING can appear once for each of the control items including FINAL.

LINE

The LINE clause specifies a print line. This clause indicates the print line either by an absolute line number or by a relative line number. Let us consider the following example.

```
01   TYPE  REPORT  HEADING.
     02   LINE NUMBER IS 20.
          03  COLUMN 50 PIC  X(13)  VALUE "WEEKLY REPORT".
     02   LINE NUMBER IS PLUS  2.
          03  COLUMN  50  PIC  X(15)  VALUE "PREPARED BY ABC".
```

In the above example, the first 02 level entry indicates that the absolute-line number is 20 on which the 13 characters WEEKLY REPORT, including one space in between WEEKLY and REPORT will be printed starting from column number 50. The second 02 level entry specifies a relative-line number and therefore the 15 characters PREPARED BY ABC will be printed on the 22nd line.

The NEXT PAGE phrase in a LINE clause indicates that the print line of the report group is to be printed on a new page in the position indicated by the line number.

The following rules may be noted in connection with this clause.

 (i)   LINE clause must be used to establish the line number of every printed line of a report group.
 (ii)   The line numbers should not be specified in a way such that it contradicts the regions specified by PAGE and its associated clauses.
 (iii) Within a report group, once this clause is specified at some particular level, the subordinate entries should not contain this clause.
 (iv)   When LINE clauses with absolute and relative line numbers are mixed in a report-group description, the entries with relative-line numbers must not precede entries with absolute-line numbers.
 (v)   The NEXT PAGE phrase can be specified only once in a report group. If present, it must be in the first LINE clause in that report group.
 (vi)   The NEXT PAGE phrase can be specified only in the report-group entries for the CONTROL HEADING, DETAIL, CONTROL FOOTING and REPORT FOOTING groups.

NEXT GROUP

This clause specifies how many lines are to be skipped after the current-report group has been printed. This clause is effectively used in a CONTROL FOOTING report group to skip lines or to move to new page to print the information of the next detail group. The following is an example of this clause.

```
01    TYPE  CONTROL  FOOTING  ACCOUNT-NO
          LINE PLUS 3 NEXT GROUP NEXT PAGE.
    02    COLUMN  20  PIC X(17)  VALUE  "ACCOUNT NUMBER IS".
    02    COLUMN  40  PIC X(5)   SOURCE  ACCOUNT-NO.
```

The NEXT GROUP clause indicates that when the control break on ACCOUNT-NO occurs; then after the printing of the control-footing line (there is only one line in the group), a page skipping will take place.

The starting line position for the next group can be indicated by specifying either an absolute line number or a relative position as in the case of the LINE clause. This clause can be specified only in the case of REPORT HEADING, DETAIL and CONTROL FOOTING report groups. When specified in a CONTROL FOOTING report-group description, the clause is ignored when a higher-level control break occurs.

COLUMN

This clause specifies the starting column from which the printing will start. The number mentioned in the COLUMN clause must be a positive integer number and must not be greater than the maximum print position. If this is omitted, items are not printed.

GROUP

This clause indicates that the item is only to be printed on the first occurrence of the print lines after a control or page break. In subsequent occurrences of the print line, spaces appear in its place. The clause can only be coded in a DETAIL report group and at the elementary item level. If the RD entry does not contain either any control item or PAGE clause, the item with the GROUP INDICATE clause is printed only once at the first occurrence of the DETAIL report group. The following example shows the use of this clause.

```
01    DETAIL-LINE  TYPE  DETAIL  LINE  PLUS 1.
    02    COLUMN  10  GROUP  INDICATE  PIC 9(4)   SOURCE   YEAR.
    02    COLUMN  20  GROUP  INDICATE  PIC 99     SOURCE   MONTH.
    02    COLUMN  30  PIC 99 SOURCE  DAY.
    02    COLUMN  40  PIC X(6) SOURCE  PRODUCT-NO.
    02    COLUMN  50  PIC Z(4)9.99 SOURCE  SALE-AMOUNT.
```

In this example it is assumed that YEAR, MONTH and DAY are control data items. The following is the sample report lines for the above description.

1981	05	01	AA1000	500.00
		01	AA2000	1000.00
		01	AA2100	600.00
		01	AB0150	700.00
		01	AC1000	1200.25
1981	05	02	AA2000	1300.00
		02	AB0150	800.25

Note that due to the GROUP INDICATE clause the values of the first two items appear only when the line is printed after a control break. The value of the third printable item appear in all the detail lines because no GROUP clause has been specified.

SOURCE

Like the GROUP clause, the SOURCE clause should also be specified for an elementary printable item. This clause identifies the sending data item whose value is to be moved to the said printable item. Editing, if any, specified in the associated PICTURE clause of the printable item will be taken into account. The sending data item can be qualified, subscripted or indexed but must conform to the rules for the sending field in the MOVE statement. Identifier-1, which denotes the source field, can appear in any section of the DATA DIVISION, including the report section. If it is in the report section, it can be any one of the following:

    (i) PAGE-COUNTER
   (ii) LINE-COUNTER and
  (iii) A sum counter.

PAGE-COUNTER and LINE-COUNTER are two special registers maintained by the supporting software for the report-writer feature. LINE-COUNTER contains the line number of the last line printed or skipped. PAGE-COUNTER contains the current page number. The values of PAGE-COUNTER can also be changed by the programmer but this is not possible in the case of LINE-COUNTER. The names PAGE-COUNTER and LINE-COUNTER are implicitly defined and the programmer should not define them. If there are more than one reports in a program, these register names must be qualified by the corresponding report names, e.g., SOURCE IS LINE-COUNTER OF FIRST-REPORT. The sum counter will be described later.

When a control break occurs, the SOURCE items contain the current values. However, there is an exception. If the SOURCE item is a control item, then in the case of a CONTROL FOOTING report group, the value of the SOURCE item is the previous value rather than the current value.

Example 1

Consider the following:

```
01   TYPE  IS  CONTROL  FOOTING MONTH LINE  IS  PLUS  2.
    02  COLUMN  10  PIC  X(19)  VALUE  "TOTAL SALE OF MONTH".
    02  COLUMN  40  PIC  99  SOURCE MONTH.
    02  COLUMN  55  PIC  Z(4)9.99  SOURCE  TOTAL-SALES.
```

In this case, MONTH will have the old value instead of the new value. It may be noted that this is very handy because the value of TOTAL-SALES at this point should relate to the previous month rather than to the next month whose beginning has been detected.

Note:

At this point we would like to draw attention to a ''tricky'' situation. Consider the following.

```
01   TYPE IS  CONTROL  FOOTING MONTH LINE  IS  PLUS  2.
     02  COLUMN  10  PIC  X(19)  VALUE
                                ''TOTAL  SALE  OF  MONTH''.
     02  COLUMN  40  PIC  X(9)  SOURCE
                                MONTH-NAME (MONTH).
     02  COLUMN  55  PIC  Z(4)9.99  SOURCE
                                TOTAL-SALES.
```

This report-group description is similar to that in the above example except that in this case, instead of the 2-digit month code, the month name is to be printed. The month names are picked up from a table whose elements are referred to by the subscripted data name, MONTH-NAME. Now, the value of MONTH is our point of interest. The control data item MONTH has been used as a subscript and not directly as a source data item. Therefore, the compiler may not interpret it as a source data item and hence MONTH will have the current value.

The USE BEFORE REPORTING statement (discussed later in this chapter) can come in handy to overcome such a situation. The sample program given at the end of this chapter illustrates the technique.

SUM

It has been stated earlier that totals can be automatically generated through the report-writer feature. All that the programmer has to do is to specify a suitable SUM clause. The SUM clause defines a sum counter and names one or more identifiers whose values are to be summed. This clause can only appear in the CONTROL FOOTING report group. Identifier-1, identifier-2, etc. must be numeric items. When more than one identifier is specified, the values of all the identifiers are added to the sum counters.

The identifiers in the SUM clause can be defined in any section of the DATA DIVISION. They may be qualified, subscripted or indexed. When they are defined in the report section, they must be the name of other sum counters. The sum counters must be defined in the same report group or in a report group which are in a lower level of the control hierarchy.

Example 1

```
01   DETAIL-LINE  TYPE  DETAIL  LINE  PLUS  1.
     02  COLUMN  20  PIC  Z9  SOURCE  DISTRICT-NO.
     02  COLUMN  30  PIC  Z9  SOURCE  SALESMAN-NO.
     02  COLUMN  40  PIC  ZZZ9.9  SOURCE  SALE-AMOUNT.

01   TYPE  CONTROL  FOOTING  SALESMAN-NO  LINE  PLUS  2.
     02  SALESMAN-TOTAL  COLUMN  39  PIC  ZZZZ9.9
                                SUM  SALE-AMOUNT.
```

In the above example, SUM names an identifier SALE-AMOUNT which appears in the SOURCE clause in the DETAIL report group. The name of the sum counter is SALESMAN-TOTAL. The name needs to be specified only if this sum counter is to be referred to. It may be noted that SALESMAN-TOTAL contains editing characters, but the editing takes place only when the value of the sum counter is printed. Until it is printed, it retains its numeric character.

Example 2

Consider the following example.

```
01   TYPE  CONTROL  FOOTING  DISTRICT-NO  LINE  PLUS  2.
    02  COLUMN  38  PIC  Z(5)9.99  SUM  SALESMAN-TOTAL.
```

Here the SUM clause refers to the sum counter SALESMAN-TOTAL of the previous example.

Two or more DETAIL report groups can contain the same SOURCE item. If it is necessary to sum this SOURCE item only when one of the DETAIL lines is printed, the UPON phrase is used. Consider the following example.

Example 3

```
01   A1  TYPE  DETAIL  LINE  PLUS  1.
    02  LINE-1  COLUMN  40  PIC  ZZZ9.9  SOURCE  AMOUNT.

01   A2  TYPE  DETAIL  LINE  PLUS  1.
    02  LINE-2  COLUMN  50  PIC  ZZZ9.9  SOURCE  AMOUNT.

01   TYPE  CONTROL  FOOTING  LINE  PLUS  2.
    02  COLUMN  39  PIC  Z(4)9.9  SUM  AMOUNT
                                      UPON  LINE-2.
```

In this case AMOUNT is summed only when LINE-2 is printed. On the other hand, if the UPON phrase is not mentioned, AMOUNT will be added each time LINE-1 and LINE-2 are printed.

RESET

The sum counter is automatically reset to zero when the CONTROL FOOTING for the particular control item is printed. This implicit resetting of the sum counter can be changed by specifying the RESET clause. When the RESET clause is used, the sum counter is reset to zero only when a control break on data-name-4 (or FINAL) takes place. Obviously, data-name-4 must be a higher level control data item as compared to the one associated with the SUM clause. The RESET clause is primarily used to get the running totals.

13.6   PROCEDURE DIVISION STATEMENTS

INITIATE Statement

This statement initiates the processing of the report. It initializes the sum counters, LINE-COUNTER and PAGE-COUNTER to their initial values. All the

counters are initialized to zero except the PAGE-COUNTER which is initialized to 1. It does not open the printer file which is associated with the
report. The general format is

<u>INITIATE</u>   report-name-1   [, report-name-2] ...

GENERATE Statement

A GENERATE statement prints a detail report group of the report. In addition, it performs the following operations.
  (i)   It controls the PAGE-COUNTER and LINE-COUNTER registers and, when-
        ever necessary, takes care of the printing of the page-heading and
        page-footing report groups. The first GENERATE statement also
        produces the report heading if this report group is specified.
 (ii)   It handles the control breaks and, whenever necessary, arranges
        for the printing of the control-footing and control-heading report
        groups.
(iii)   It takes care of the summation at the sum counters and resets the
        sum counters to zeros when appropriate control breaks occur.
 (iv)   It also arranges for the execution of the USE procedures. (The
        USE statement is discussed below.)
The general format of the GENERATE statement is as follows:

$$\underline{\text{GENERATE}} \quad \left\{ \begin{array}{l} \text{data-name} \\ \text{report-name} \end{array} \right\}$$

    The data name must be the name of a TYPE DETAIL report group. When the
report name is specified, a summary report is generated. A summary report
is the one in which only the totals are printed and the detail groups are
omitted. However, when a summary report is specified, the report writer
behaves exactly like a GENERATE statement with the data name except that
the detail lines are not printed. According to the ANSI standard, when
GENERATE with the report name is to be used, there should not be more than
one detail group specified for the report.

TERMINATE Statement

The execution of this statement causes the completion of the processing of
a report. It produces the FINAL as well as all the lower level control
breaks. It takes care of the printing of all control footing, page footing
and report footing, if these are specified. The general format of this
statement is

<u>TERMINATE</u>   report-name-1   [, report-name-2] ...

    Once a report is terminated by a TERMINATE statement, it can be again
initiated through an INITIATE statement. The TERMINATE statement does not
close the line-printer file that holds the report.

USE BEFORE REPORTING Statement

The USE BEFORE REPORTING statement like the other USE statements should be
specified only in the DECLARATIVES (see Sec. 13.10). The statement is

normally used to gain control before the printing of a report group. The format of this statement and the associated coding is shown below.

```
    DECLARATIVES.

    Section-name  SECTION [segment-number].
             USE  BEFORE  REPORTING data-name.

    [paragraph-name. [sentence] ... ]

END DECLARATIVES.
```

The data name must be the name of a report group other than DETAIL. Only one USE statement may be specified for a report group. When specified, the procedural paragraphs that follow the USE statement are executed just before the printing of the report group, but after any summation is done. The INITIATE, TERMINATE and GENERATE statements cannot appear within the USE procedure.

Example 1

The following PROCEDURE DIVISION statements show the use of the INITIATE, GENERATE and TERMINATE statements. A USE procedure is also illustrated.

```
PROCEDURE DIVISION.

DECLARATIVES.

PAGE-HEADER SECTION.
    USE  BEFORE  REPORTING  PG-HEADING.

TEST-BEGIN-PARA.
    IF  MONTH  =  PREVIOUS-MONTH  MOVE  "(CONT.)"  TO
                                        REQUIRED-SPACE
    ELSE  MOVE  SPACES  TO  REQUIRED-SPACE
          MOVE  MONTH  TO  PREVIOUS-MONTH.

TEST-EXIT-PARA.
    EXIT.

END DECLARATIVES.

HOUSEKEEPING-PARA.
    OPEN  INPUT  PAYROLL-FILE  OUTPUT  REPORT-FILE.
    INITIATE  PAY-REPORT.

READ-AND-REPORT-PARA.
    READ  PAYROLL-FILE  AT  END  GO  TO  JOB-END-PARA.
    IF  BASIC-PAY  IS  GREATER  THAN  1000
            GENERATE  DETAIL-LINE-1
    ELSE  GENERATE  DETAIL-LINE-2.
    GO  TO  READ-AND-REPORT-PARA.
```

```
JOB-END-PARA.
      TERMINATE  PAY-REPORT.
      CLOSE  PAYROLL-FILE  REPORT-FILE.
      STOP  RUN.
```

The report is named PAY-REPORT. It is generated from a file named PAY-ROLL-FILE. REPORT-FILE is the name of the line printer file that holds the report. There are two detail groups —DETAIL-LINE-1 and DETAIL-LINE-2. The purpose of the USE procedure is to print the word (CONT.) within the page-heading group on the second and subsequent pages.

SUPPRESS Statement

One use of the USE procedure can be to suppress the printing of the group in certain cases. For this purpose, the SUPPRESS statement can be used. The general format of the SUPPRESS statement is

                    SUPPRESS   PRINTING.

The statement can only appear within the procedure for a USE BEFORE REPORT-ING statement.

Example 2

```
OMIT-ZERO-TOTAL SECTION.
            USE   BEFORE   REPORTING CTL-FOOTING.

SUPPRESS-PARA.
            IF  TOTAL-COUNT EQUALS ZERO OR 1
                     SUPPRESS.
            MOVE ZERO TO TOTAL-COUNT.
```

CTL-FOOTING is the name of a control footing report group. The example suppresses the printing of the control footing group when the value of the TOTAL-COUNT is equal to zero or 1.

18.7 SAMPLE PROGRAM

To illustrate the use of the report-writer feature, a sample program is shown in Fig. 18.1. The problem is identical to that considered in Sec.15.6 and as such the problem definition is not repeated here. The sample program has two differences with the previous program in terms of the report that is generated. In the current program, the heading lines appear after a control breaks and not on the top of each page. The GROUP INDICATE clause suppresses the printing of control items on appropriate lines. This was not done in the previous case. A sample output of the report is shown in Fig. 18.2.

18.8 IMPLEMENTATION DIFFERENCES

The report-writer feature is implemented on both the B-6700 and DEC-10 compilers. The SUPPRESS statement, however, is not available in both the cases.

```
      IDENTIFICATION DIVISION.
      PROGRAM-ID. AN EXAMPLE OF REPORT WRITING.
      AUTHOR. AUTHORS OF THIS BOOK.
      INSTALLATION. COMPUTER CENTRE.
      DATE-WRITTEN. 5TH MARCH, 1981.
      SECURITY. READER OF THIS BOOK.

      ENVIRONMENT DIVISION.
      CONFIGURATION SECTION.
      SOURCE-COMPUTER. B-6700.
      OBJECT-COMPUTER. B-6700.
      INPUT-OUTPUT SECTION.
      FILE-CONTROL.
          SELECT DISK-FILE ASSIGN TO DISK.
          SELECT REPORT-FILE ASSIGN TO PRINTER.

      DATA DIVISION.
      FILE SECTION.
      FD  DISK-FILE  VALUE OF ID IS "SALESFILE".
      01  DISK-REC.
          02  ZONE          PIC  9.
          02  DISTRICT      PIC  99.
          02  SALESMAN-NO   PIC  99.
          02  AMOUNT        PIC  9999V99.
          02  PRODUCT-NO    PIC  9(5).
          02  FILLER        PIC  X(64).
      FD  REPORT-FILE REPORT IS XYZ-REPORT.

      WORKING-STORAGE SECTION.
      77  PREVIOUS-SALESMAN  PIC  99.
      77  PREVIOUS-DIST      PIC  99.
      77  PREVIOUS-ZONE      PIC  9.

      01  SALESMAN-11.
          02  SALES-MAN.
              03 FILLER PIC X(18) VALUE IS "ANIL KUMAR SAHA    ".
              03 FILLER PIC X(18) VALUE IS "ARUMOY KULKARNI    ".
              03 FILLER PIC X(18) VALUE IS "BIMAL MOHANTI      ".
              03 FILLER PIC X(18) VALUE IS "CHANDAN CHOWDHURY ".
              03 FILLER PIC X(18) VALUE IS "DANIEL MATHEWS     ".
              03 FILLER PIC X(18) VALUE IS "DHURJATI BANERJEE ".
              03 FILLER PIC X(18) VALUE IS "E.A.S. PRASANNA    ".
              03 FILLER PIC X(18) VALUE IS "FAROOQ AHMED       ".
              03 FILLER PIC X(18) VALUE IS "GOPAL BANERJEE     ".
              03 FILLER PIC X(18) VALUE IS "GULAM SIDHIQUE     ".
              03 FILLER PIC X(18) VALUE IS "MANARANJAN HAZRA   ".
              03 FILLER PIC X(18) VALUE IS "NILADRI BOSE       ".
              03 FILLER PIC X(18) VALUE IS "PIJUS KANTI DAS    ".
              03 FILLER PIC X(18) VALUE IS "PRADIP CHANDA      ".
```

(contd.)

```
          03 FILLER  PIC  X(18)  VALUE  IS  "PRIYOTOSH GOSWAMI ".
          03 FILLER  PIC  X(18)  VALUE  IS  "RAJSEKHAR NANDI   ".
          03 FILLER  PIC  X(18)  VALUE  IS  "RAMESH SAXENA     ".
          03 FILLER  PIC  X(18)  VALUE  IS  "SHILBADRA GHOSH   ".
          03 FILLER  PIC  X(18)  VALUE  IS  "SRIMANTA DALUI    ".
          03 FILLER  PIC  X(18)  VALUE  IS  "UTPAL CHATTERJEE  ".
     02 SALESMAN-1 REDEFINES SALES-MAN.
          03 SALESMAN-NAME PIC X(18) OCCURS 20 TIMES.

 01  DISTRICT-11 "DARJEELINGJALPAIGURICOOCHBI
 -      "HARMALDA    RAIGANGE  BARASAT  BASIRHAT  BANGAON   MIDNAPU
 -      "R BURDWAN   DURGAPUR  ASSANSOL ".
     02 DISTRICT-NAME PIC X(10) OCCURS 12 TIMES.
 01  ZONE-11 VALUE "NORTHEAST SOUTHWEST ".
     02 ZONE-NAME PIC X(5) OCCURS  4 TIMES.


 REPORT SECTION.
 RD  XYZ-REPORT CONTROLS ARE FINAL, ZONE, DISTRICT, SALESMAN-NO,
     PAGE LIMIT IS 59 LINES HEADING 2 FOOTING 58.

 01  TYPE IS REPORT HEADING NEXT GROUP NEXT PAGE.
     02  LINE NUMBER 28 COLUMN NUMBER 40 PIC X(46) VA "SALES REPOR
 -      "T OF XYZ COMPANY FOR THE YEAR 1981".

 01  HD TYPE IS PAGE HEADING.
     02  LINE NUMBER 2.
          03 COLUMN NUMBER 110 PIC X(8) VA "PAGE NO ".
          03 COLUMN NUMBER 119 PIC ZZ9  SOURCE IS PAGE-COUNTER.

 01  ZONE-HEADING TYPE IS CONTROL HEADING ZONE.
     02  LINE NUMBER IS PLUS 1.
          03  COLUMN NUMBER IS 1 PIC X(132) VA SPACES.

 01  DISTRICT-HEADING TYPE IS CONTROL HEADING DISTRICT.
     02  LINE NUMBER IS PLUS 1.
          03  COLUMN NUMBER IS 1 PIC X(132) VA SPACES.

 01  SALES-HEADING TYPE IS CONTROL HEADING SALESMAN-NO.
     02  LINE NUMBER IS PLUS 1.
          03 COLUMN NUMBER 14 PIC X(4) VA "ZONE".
          03 COLUMN NUMBER 30 PIC X(8) VA "DISTRICT".
          03 COLUMN NUMBER 50 PIC X(11) VA "SALESMAN-NO".
          03 COLUMN NUMBER 74 PIC X(6) VA "AMOUNT".
     02  LINE NUMBER IS PLUS 1.
          03 COLUMN NUMBER 1 PIC X(132) VA SPACES.

 01  DETAIL-LINE TYPE IS DETAIL LINE NUMBER IS PLUS 1.
     02  COLUMN NUMBER 15 GROUP INDICATE PIC 9  SOURCE IS ZONE.
     02  COLUMN NUMBER 34 GROUP INDICATE PIC 99 SOURCE IS
          DISTRICT.
     02  COLUMN NUMBER 55 GROUP INDICATE  PIC 99 SOURCE IS
          SALESMAN-NO.
     02  COLUMN NUMBER 72 PIC Z(5).99 SOURCE IS AMOUNT.
```

(contd.)

```
01   S1   TYPE IS CONTROL FOOTING SALESMAN-NO.
     02 LINE NUMBER IS PLUS 2.
          03   COLUMN NUMBER 42 PIC X(47) VA ALL "-".
     02   LINE NUMBER IS PLUS 1.
          03   COLUMN NUMBER 42 PIC X(14) VA "TOTAL SALE OF ".
          03   COLUMN NUMBER 58 PIC X(18) SOURCE IS
               SALESMAN-NAME (PREVIOUS-SALESMAN).
          03   TOTAL-SUM COLUMN 79 PIC Z(6).99 SUM AMOUNT RESET ON
               SALESMAN-NO.
     02   LINE NUMBER IS PLUS 1.
          03 COLUMN NUMBER 42 PIC X(47) VA ALL "-".
     02   LINE NUMBER IS PLUS 1.
          03 COLUMN NUMBER 1 PIC X(132) VA SPACES.

01   D1   TYPE IS CONTROL FOOTING DISTRICT.
     02 LINE NUMBER IS PLUS 3.
          03 COLUMN NUMBER 30 PIC X(71) VA ALL "*".
     02   LINE NUMBER IS PLUS 1.
          03   COLUMN NUMBER 30 PIC X(14) VA "TOTAL SALE OF ".
          03   COLUMN NUMBER 49 PIC X(10) SOURCE IS
               DISTRICT-NAME(PREVIOUS-DIST).
          03   TOTAL-DIST-SUM COLUMN NUMBER 89 PIC Z(8).99 SUM
               TOTAL-SUM RESET ON DISTRICT.
     02   LINE NUMBER IS PLUS 1.
          03 COLUMN NUMBER 30 PIC X(71) VA ALL "*".
     02   LINE NUMBER IS PLUS 1.
          03 COLUMN NUMBER 1 PIC X(132) VA SPACES.

01   Z1   TYPE IS CONTROL FOOTING ZONE NEXT GROUP IS NEXT PAGE.
     02   LINE NUMBER IS PLUS 4.
          03 COLUMN NUMBER 14 PIC X(98)  VA ALL "-".
     02   LINE NUMBER IS PLUS 1.
          03   COLUMN NUMBER 14 PIC X(14) VA "TOTAL SALE OF ".
          03   COLUMN NUMBER 29 PIC X(5) SOURCE IS
               ZONE-NAME(PREVIOUS-ZONE).
          03   TOTAL-ZONE-SUM COLUMN NUMBER 99 PIC Z(10).99 SUM
               TOTAL-DIST-SUM RESET ON ZONE.
     02   LINE NUMBER IS PLUS 1.
          03 COLUMN NUMBER 14 PIC X(98) VA ALL "-".
     02   LINE NUMBER IS PLUS 1.
          03   COLUMN NUMBER 1 PIC X(132) VA SPACES.

01   TYPE CONTROL FOOTING FINAL.
     02 LINE NUMBER IS 30 ON NEXT PAGE.
          03 COLUMN NUMBER 46 PIC X(75) VA ALL "*".
     02 LINE NUMBER IS PLUS 1.
          03   COLUMN NUMBER IS 46 PIC X(44) VA "TOTAL SALE OF XYZ C
     -"OMPANY FOR THE YEAR 1981 ".
          03   COLUMN NUMBER 106 PIC Z(12).99 SUM TOTAL-ZONE-SUM.
     02 LINE NUMBER IS PLUS 1.
          03 COLUMN NUMBER 46 PIC X(75) VA ALL "*".
```

(contd.)

```
PROCEDURE DIVISION.
DECLARATIVES.
SALES-MAN-RTN SECTION.
    USE BEFORE REPORTING SALES-HEADING.
TEST-SALES-MAN.
    MOVE SALESMAN-NO TO PREVIOUS-SALESMAN.
DIST-RTN SECTION.
    USE BEFORE REPORTING DISTRICT-HEADING.
TEST-DIST.
    MOVE DISTRICT TO PREVIOUS-DIST.
ZONE-RTN-SN SECTION.
    USE BEFORE REPORTING ZONE-HEADING.
TEST-ZONE.
    MOVE ZONE TO PREVIOUS-ZONE.
END DECLARATIVES.
REPORTER SECTION.
INITIATION-OF-REPORT.
    OPEN INPUT DISK-FILE
         OUTPUT REPORT-FILE.
    INITIATE XYZ-REPORT.
MIDDLE-PORTION.
    READ DISK-FILE AT END GO TO LAST-PORTION.
    GENERATE DETAIL-LINE GO TO MIDDLE-PORTION.
LAST-PORTION.
    TERMINATE XYZ-REPORT.
    CLOSE DISK-FILE REPORT-FILE.
    STOP RUN.
```

FIG. 18.1.   An Example of Report Writer

```
ZONE    DISTRICT       SALESMAN-NO        AMOUNT

2        04              06              3500.00
                                          750.00
                                          800.50

        -------------------------------------------------
        TOTAL SALE OF   DHURJATI BANERJEE    5050.50
        -------------------------------------------------


ZONE    DISTRICT       SALESMAN-NO        AMOUNT

2        04              19              2000.25
                                         2050.00


        -------------------------------------------------
        TOTAL SALE OF    SRIMANTA DALUI      4050.25
        -------------------------------------------------



        *************************************************************
        TOTAL SALE OF   MALDA                            9100.75
        *************************************************************

ZONE    DISTRICT       SALESMAN-NO        AMOUNT

2        05              07               900.75
                                         1005.00
                                         2000.50

        -------------------------------------------------
        TOTAL SALE OF     E.A.S. PRASANNA     3906.25
        -------------------------------------------------


ZONE    DISTRICT       SALESMAN-NO        AMOUNT

2        05              09              3000.50
                                         2500.00
                                         4500.00

        -------------------------------------------------
        TOTAL SALE OF    GOPAL BANERJEE      10000.50
        -------------------------------------------------


        *************************************************************
        TOTAL SALE OF    RAIGANGE                        13906.75
        *************************************************************

-------------------------------------------------------------------
TOTAL SALE OF EAST                                       23007.50
-------------------------------------------------------------------
```

FIG. 18.2. A Sample Output of Report

EXERCISES

1. (a) Of the seven report groups, which one requires a data name in its description?
   (b) Why is the COLUMN NUMBER clause used in the description of an elementary item in a report group?
   (c) Does the data name LINE-COUNTER need to be defined in the DATA DIVISION?
   (d) How many times can CONTROL FOOTING FINAL appear in a report?
   (e) Is it possible to use more than one GENERATE statement in a COBOL program for any one report?

2. Explain how control break is related to the printing of report groups.

3. Explain the meaning of the following terms:
   (i) Page footing
   (ii) Control heading
   (iii) Report footing.

4. Normally, each execution of the GENERATE statement is to be logically preceded by the execution of another COBOL statement. Can you identify this verb?

5. Compare the role of the USE statement (i) when used in connection with input/output statements and (ii) when used in the report-writer feature.

6. Write a program for the problem discussed in Sec. 2.7.2 using the report-writer feature.

7. "The LINAGE clause in the FD entry of a line printer file is a poor man's Report Writer". Discuss.

19

COBOL SUBROUTINES

A basic requirement of modular programming is to divide a large program into
smaller and more manageable parts known as modules. A module in a COBOL
program can be realized in two ways——as a PERFORM module or as a separately
compiled subroutine The way to divide a program into a number of PERFORM
modules has been discussed earlier. In the following, we discuss how modules
in the form of subroutines can be designed and implemented.

The term subroutine is often used to denote any kind of module, but in
this chapter it is used to mean only those modules that are coded and compiled separately from the calling modules. Thus, unlike PERFORM modules, a
COBOL subroutine is similar to a COBOL program having all the four divisions.
A subroutine can be compiled separately but cannot be executed independently.
Before execution, the object code of the subroutine must be bound with the
object code of the program calling the subroutine to form what is known as
the run unit. A run unit is a set of one or more object programs which functions as a unit during execution. One member of this set must be a main
program which is not called by any other program in the run unit. The rest.
must be subroutines. A subroutine, if necessary, can call another subroutine.

It may be noted that subroutine is not a COBOL term. In COBOL terminology, the main program as well as the subroutines are called programs. A
program may be a source program or an object program depending on the context. The programs that constitute a run unit must be logically connected
together so that they can communicate between themselves. This facility of
communication among the programs in a run unit, in COBOL terminology, is
called inter-program communication. The inter-program communication facility
provides (i) the capability of transfer of control from one program to
another and (ii) the capability of accessing same data items by two or more
programs.

Since we are familiar with the PERFORM modules, it may be worthwhile
to note how these communications are available in the case of PERFORM modules. As regards the former facility, the PERFORM statement enables us to
transfer the control between the modules. The second facility is implicitly
available because all the PERFORM modules being included within the program
are entitled to make use of any data item defined in the DATA DIVISION.
However, in the case of subroutines, all the programs — be it a main program
or a subroutine ——must have their respective DATA DIVISION. Naturally, the
facility of establishing connections between two programs in respect of
certain data items, is very much necessary.

19.1 STRUCTURE OF A COBOL SUBROUTINE

A distinguishing feature that makes a COBOL subroutine different from a main program is the PROCEDURE DIVISION header. The PROCEDURE DIVISION header must have a USING phrase. The general format of a PROCEDURE DIVISION header is

PROCEDURE DIVISION [USING data-name-1 [, data-name-2] ...]

The operands data-name-1, data-name-2, etc., of the USING phrase are those data names which are to be connected with the corresponding data names in the program calling this subroutine. Further details regarding the said data connectivity will be given afterwards. For the time being, let us only note that the operands of the USING phrase must be either 01-level or 77-level data items. These must be defined in a section of the DATA DIVISION known as the linkage section.

Structurally, the linkage section is similar to the working-storage section and appears in the DATA DIVISION immediately after the working-storage section. In case the working-storage section is absent, it should follow the file section and if the file section is also absent, it should be the first section of the DATA DIVISION.

The linkage section appears in the called program (subroutine) and describes records or noncontiguous data items in respect of which connection should be established with the calling program (main program or another subroutine). The corresponding data items in the calling program may be defined in any section of the DATA DIVISION.

The following is the general format of the linkage section·

LINKAGE SECTION.

$$\left[\begin{array}{l} \text{77-level-data-description-entry} \\ \text{record-description-entry} \end{array} \right] \; ...$$

The data description entries are similar to those in the case of working-storage section except that the VALUE clause is not allowed to be specified for any entry in the linkage section. The VALUE clause may, however, be used for defining the condition names. As regards the allowable usages of the linkage section data items, substantial differences exist among the various compilers. In certain compilers, even 77-level alphabetic or alphanumeric data items are not allowed. In such cases an alphabetic or alphanumeric data item can be defined at level 01.

Besides the USING phrase in the PROCEDURE DIVISION header and linkage section, there is another significant feature that makes a subroutine different from the main program. In the case of a main program, the logical end of a program is indicated by a STOP RUN statement. However, a STOP RUN statement cannot be used for the same purpose in the case of a subroutine. This is because the STOP RUN statement always terminates a run unit regardless of whether it is used in a subroutine or in a main program. Normally, upon the execution of a subroutine it is required that the control must be returned to the calling program. For this purpose the EXIT PROGRAM statement is available in COBOL The format of this statement is as follows:

EXIT PROGRAM

The statement must be the only statement in a paragraph. In certain compilers, a nonstandard GOBACK statement is available which has the following
format.

GOBACK

Functionally, the GOBACK statement is identical to an EXIT PROGRAM statement. The GOBACK statement need not be the only statement in a paragraph.
     Among the abovementioned features of a COBOL subroutine, the presence
of an EXIT PROGRAM or GOBACK statement is indicative of a subroutine. The
USING phrase in the PROCEDURE DIVISION header and thereby the linkage section may be absent. It may be noted that in such a case there is no common
data item that can be shared by both the called and calling programs. The
only means of communication in this case is by means of files. The subroutine and the main program will refer to the same file by specifying the
same title. For example, the main program can create a file and then call
a subroutine that makes use of the file. However, the calling and called
programs are not allowed to open the same file simultaneously.

19.2 THE CALLING OF A SUBROUTINE

In order to be able to call a subroutine (for execution) from the main
program or from another subroutine in the run unit, the object code for
the said subroutine must be given a name. The PROGRAM-ID entry in the
subroutine can be used for the purpose. For example,

PROGRAM-ID. SUBNM.

indicates that the name of the subroutine is SUBNM.
     However, in most compilers, the object code of the called program is
assigned a suitable name during compilation. The name can be specified
externally through the job-control language of the relevant computer system.
     The calling program can call a subroutine by means of a CALL statement
which has the following format.

$$
\text{CALL} \left\{ \begin{array}{l} \text{identifier-1} \\ \text{literal-1} \end{array} \right\} \left[\underline{\text{USING}} \text{ data-name-1 } [\text{ , data-name-2 }] \dots \right]
$$

[; ON OVERFLOW imperative-statement]

     The execution of a CALL statement causes the transfer of the control to
the first statement in the PROCEDURE DIVISION of the called subroutine. In
other words, the execution of the subroutine is caused by a CALL statement
and the execution of the calling program remains suspended until the subroutine executes the EXIT PROGRAM statement and returns the control to the
calling program. The particular subroutine being called is specified by the
value of identifier-1 or literal-1. The identifier-1 must be an alphanumeric
data item. Literal-1 must be a nonnumeric literal.

The ON OVERFLOW clause in the CALL statement may be used to take care of an exceptional case. The exceptional case arises when the called program specified by identifier-1/literal-1 is not available in the run unit. In this exceptional case, if the ON OVERFLOW clause is specified, the imperative statement is executed; otherwise, the run unit is aborted.

A program in COBOL can call another program which in turn can call yet another program, and so on. However, a called program must not call itself or its calling program nor any program that this calling program is not allowed to call.

Data-name-1, data-name-2, etc., are the data names in respect of which the connection is to be established with the called program. These operands of the USING phrase in the CALL statement are often referred to as actual parameters. These parameters get connected with the data names specified in the USING phrase of the PROCEDURE DIVISION header of the called program. As opposed to the actual parameters, the data names in the USING phrase of the PROCEDURE DIVISION header are often called formal parameters. The number of the actual and formal parameters must be the same and the size, class and usage of the corresponding actual and formal parameters must be identical. Some compilers allow some limited class/usage conflicts between the formal and actual parameters. However, we shall not go into these points as it is not difficult to avoid such conflicts in actual applications. The correspondence between the actual and formal parameters are positional and not by name. Thus the corresponding actual and formal parameters may or may not have different names. For example, let the PROCEDURE DIVISION header of a subroutine named CALDA be

PROCEDURE DIVISION USING GROSS, DEARNESS .

The subroutine can be called in a calling program as shown below:

CALL "CALDA" USING GROSS-PAY, D-A.

Through this CALL statement, the actual parameter GROSS-PAY gets linked with the formal parameter GROSS and the actual parameter D-A linked with the formal parameter DEARNESS. Thus, when the called program is executed every reference to GROSS (or DEARNESS) is interpreted as if it were a reference to the GROSS-PAY (or D-A) of the main program. The process of establishing connections between the actual and formal parameters is called parameter passing.

In addition to what has been stated above, a few more rules govern the function of parameter passing. These are implementor-defined. The following are some of the typical rules.

(i)   An actual parameter must be a data name (subject to minor restrictions) in any section of the DATA DIVISION. In particular, they can also be data names in the linkage section, in which case it means that the calling program is also a called program. In this way a data item can be transferred from one program to another, in a chain.

(ii) In the list of actual parameters, some data names can appear more than once; but the same is not permitted for the list of formal parameters.

(iii) The formal parameters are not allocated a separate memory space. Instead, a formal parameter refers to the same memory location occupied by the corresponding actual parameter. Here again, there can be implementation differences with respect to certain data items. For example, in some compilers, a separate memory space is allocated for formal parameters which are index names. When the subroutine is called, the values of such actual parameters are copied onto the memory locations allocated for the corresponding formal parameters. In some compilers, the programmer is given the choice of specifying whether a parameter is to be ''called by reference'' (no separate location for the formal parameter) or whether it is to be ''called by value'' (separate locations for the actual and formal parameters). It may be noted that if a parameter is called by value and the subroutine in the course of its execution modifies the value of the said parameter, the change will not be reflected in the actual parameter. On the other hand, if a parameter is called by reference, the said change will be reflected in the actual parameter of the calling program.

19.3   STATE OF A SUBROUTINE AND CANCEL STATEMENT

Besides the parameters defined in the linkage section, a subroutine can use files and data items defined in the file section and in the working-storage sections. These files and data items together form the local environment of the subroutine. At a point of time, the values of the various attributes of the local files as well as the values of all the local data items constitute what is known as the state of the subroutine. When a subroutine is called for the first time, it is said to be in its initial state. However, when a subroutine is called next, it will be in its last-used state. To make things more clear, let us take an example. Suppose a subroutine is programmed in such a way that when it is entered for the first time, a file is opened, some records are read sequentially and the subroutine is exited without closing the file. Clearly, the initial state of the subroutine and its state when it is called next are different. In the former case the file is not even open, whereas in the latter case not only is the file open, but its records (starting from the one next to the record read last) are ready for reading. Although this facility of getting back the subroutine in its last-used state can be gainfully utilized in certain situations, in other situations this may be undesirable. It is precisely for this reason that the CANCEL statement has been provided in COBOL. If a subroutine is cancelled through the CANCEL statement and then called again, its execution will begin with the initial state rather than the last-used state. In other words, the CANCEL statement enables us to restore the initial stage of a subroutine. The general format of the CANCEL statement is as follows:

$$\underline{\text{CANCEL}} \quad \left\{ \begin{array}{l} \text{identifier-1} \\ \text{literal-1} \end{array} \right\} \quad \left[\begin{array}{l} \text{, identifier-2} \\ \text{, literal-2} \end{array} \right] \quad \ldots$$

The programs specified through the values of identifier-1/literal-1, identifier-2/literal-2, etc. are cancelled by the CANCEL statement. As a result, the said program ceases to have any logical relationship to the run unit. The memory space occupied by the program is released to the operating system after its cancellation.

The following rules can be noted in connection with the CANCEL statement.

(i) A program that has been called but has not yet executed its EXIT PROGRAM statement cannot be cancelled. In other words, a program cannot be cancelled by itself nor can it be cancelled by a subroutine which has been directly or indirectly called by it.

(ii) If the CANCEL statement specifies a program that has not yet been called or that has already been cancelled, no action takes place for that program.

19.4 AN EXAMPLE ILLUSTRATING USE OF SUBROUTINE

Figures 19.1 and 19.2 illustrate a subroutine and a main program calling the subroutine. The subroutine edits a name received through the formal parameter GIVEN-STRING and returns the edited name through the formal parameter EDITED-STRING. Both these parameters are of 80 characters in size. It is assumed that the name in the GIVEN-STRING can have a maximum of five words. The name can appear in a free format and two words are separated by one or more blanks. It is further assumed that each word in a name cannot have more than 25 characters. For simplicity, it has been assumed that GIVEN-STRING contains the name as expected and the exceptional cases cannot arise. The subroutine edits the name by moving the last word (considered to be the surname) first and by pushing the other words on its right without changing their order. The subroutine also edits the name to ensure that there remains just one blank between the words. The main program reads the names from a deck of cards. One card contains one name. Each name is passed to the subroutine and the edited name is obtained from it. The main program then prints the edited name. The processing is repeated on all the names in the deck.

```
IDENTIFICATION DIVISION.
PROGRAM-ID.  EDITNM.
ENVIRONMENT DIVISION.
CONFIGURATION SECTION.
SOURCE-COMPUTER.   B-6700.
OBJECT-COMPUTER.   B-6700.
INPUT-OUTPUT SECTION.
FILE-CONTROL.
DATA DIVISION.
WORKING-STORAGE SECTION.
77     FIELD-COUNT        PIC     99.
77     CTL-COUNT          PIC     99.
77     CTL-POINTER        PIC     99.
01     WORD-SPACE.
       02  STRING-WORD  PIC  X(25)  OCCURS  5  TIMES.
```

(contd.)

```
LINKAGE-SECTION.
01   GIVEN-STRING           PIC    X(80).
01   EDITED-STRING          PIC    X(80).

PROCEDURE DIVISION.
    USING GIVEN-STRING EDITED-STRING.
BEGIN-SUB-PROGRAM.
    MOVE  SPACES  TO  WORD-SPACE.
    MOVE 0 TO FIELD-COUNT.
    MOVE 1 TO CTL-COUNT.
    INSPECT GIVEN-STRING TALLYING CTL-COUNT
    FOR LEADING   "ƀ".
    UNSTRING GIVEN-STRING DELIMITED BY ALL  "ƀ"
         INTO STRING-WORD (1) STRING-WORD (2) STRING-WORD (3)
             STRING-WORD (4) STRING-WORD (5)
             WITH POINTER CTL-COUNT
             TALLYING IN FIELD-COUNT.
    SUBTRACT 1 FROM FIELD-COUNT GIVING CTL-COUNT.
    MOVE SPACES TO EDITED-STRING.
    MOVE 1 TO CTL-POINTER.
ADD-WORD.
    STRING STRING-WORD (FIELD-COUNT) DELIMITED BY SPACES
         INTO EDITED-STRING WITH POINTER CTL-POINTER.
    ADD 1 TO CTL-POINTER.
PARA-LAST.
   PERFORM ADD-WORD
 VARYING FIELD-COUNT FROM 1 BY 1 UNTIL FIELD-COUNT > CTL-COUNT.
PARA-EXIT.
    EXIT PROGRAM.
```

FIG. 19.1.   Subroutine EDITNM

```
  .
  .
  .
INPUT-OUTPUT SECTION.
FILE-CONTROL.
      SELECT FILE-CARD  ASSIGN  TO  READER.
      SELECT FILE-LINE  ASSIGN  TO  PRINTER.
DATA DIVISION.
FILE SECTION.
FD FILE-CARD.
01  CARD-REC                    PIC    X(80).
FD  FILE-LINE.
01  LINE-REC.
      02  FILLER                PIC    X(10).
      02  EDITED-REC            PIC    X(80).
      02  FILLER                PIC    X(42).
WORKING-STORAGE SECTION.
10  NAME-EDITED                 PIC    X(80).
PROCEDURE DIVISION.
PARA-OPEN.
      OPEN INPUT FILE-CARD
            OUTPUT FILE-LINE.
      MOVE SPACES TO LINE-REC.
PARA-READ.
      READ FILE-CARD RECORD AT END GO TO PARA-FINAL.
      CALL "EDITNM"  USING CARD-REC NAME-EDITED.
      MOVE NAME-EDITED TO EDITED-REC.
      WRITE LINE-REC AFTER ADVANCING 2 LINES.
      GO TO PARA-READ.
PARA-FINAL.
      CLOSE FILE-CARD FILE-LINE
      STOP RUN.
```

FIG. 19.2. Main Program Calling the Subroutine
EDITNM

19.5 ADVANTAGES AND DISADVANTAGES OF COBOL SUBROUTINES

The implementation of modules in the form of COBOL subroutines is not very popular with programmers. The reasons for this may be the following:

(i)   The facility of inter-program communication is a latter addition in COBOL as such many earlier COBOL compilers did not support any facility for coding the subroutines.

(ii) The implementation of modules as PERFORM module is so simple and natural in COBOL that the need for having separately compiled subroutines is hardly felt.

(iii) More effort is required to write a COBOL subroutine than in the case of other programming languages.

Because of the abovementioned disadvantages, a COBOL module is rarely implemented in the form of a subroutine. Only when the same module may be required in more than one application, it may be helpful to design it in the form of a separately compiled subroutine.

19.6   IMPLEMENTATION DIFFERENCES

Subroutine Name

In ICL-1900 and DEC-10 the subroutine name should be specified in the PROGRAM-ID paragraph. In ICL-1900 a subroutine name can have 11 or lesser number of characters. In DEC-10 the number of characters in a subroutine name can be 1 to 6. In B-6700, any entry in the PROGRAM-ID paragraph is considered to be a comment entry. A name can therefore be assigned to a subroutine (outside the COBOL language) only through the work-flow language (job-control language for B-6700).

Linkage Section

The linkage section is optional in B-6700. The formal parameters which are data names can be defined either in the working-storage section or in the linkage section.

Exiting a Subprogram

The EXIT PROGRAM statement is available in all the three compilers under consideration. In B-6700, EXIT PROCEDURE can also be written instead of EXIT PROGRAM. The GOBACK statement is available in DEC-10.

Calling a Subprogram

The CALL statement is available in all the three compilers under consideration. In B-6700, the called program name should not be specified in the CALL statement. Instead, a section name (discussed below) is to be specified. In ICL-1900, the called program name should appear in the CALL statement in place of identifier-1/literal-1. In DEC-10, the called program name or an entry name (see ENTRY statement below) can be specified in place of identifier-1/literal-1.

In B-6700, an actual parameter can be a 01-level or 77-level data name or a literal. In ICL-1900 and DEC-10, an actual parameter can be a record name or a data name defined in any section of the DATA DIVISION. However, the field corresponding to an actual parameter must be word-aligned. In other words, they must begin on a word boundary. Consequently, an appropriate SYNCHRONIZED clause can be used in the entries that define the said data names.

A subroutine can be called by means of an ENTER statement in all the three systems under consideration. Since the CALL statement serves the purpose, we shall not include any discussion on the ENTER statement.

CANCEL Statement

There is no CANCEL statement in ICL-1900 and B-6700.

ENTRY Statement

This statement is available in DEC-10. Its purpose is to provide an alternate entry point in a subroutine. If a subroutine contains an entry statement, it can be called either by the subroutine name or by the entry name.
If the CALL statement in the calling program contains an entry name, the
called program is entered at the ENTRY statement and the execution proceeds
from there. The format of the ENTRY statement is as follows:

> ENTRY entry-name [USING identifier-1 [, identifier-2] ...]

At run-time, except when a CALL statement refers to an entry name, the
ENTRY statements are ignored. This statement, though useful, is a nonstandard feature.

Calling Program in B-6700

The B-6700 COBOL requires a number of special declarations to be included
in the program that must call an externally compiled subroutine. The following declarations about the called subroutine are required in the calling
program.

   (i)   The called subroutine must be declared in the DECLARATIVES section
         of the PROCEDURE DIVISION of the calling program by means of a USE
         statement.
   (ii) The formal parameters of the subroutine appearing in the USE state-
         ment must be declared in a section of the DATA DIVISION called
         LOCAL-STORAGE SECTION. When file names are used as parameters,
         these formal files are to be described in the FILE SECTION in the
         usual manner.
   (iii) The USE statement does not make reference to the subroutine by
         its actual name, instead the subroutine is referred to either
         through a mnemonic-name or through a data-name. Therefore, there
         must be either a declaration or a statement to associate the
         actual subroutine name to the name used in the USE statement.

Before we introduce the USE statement, let us first see how the formal
parameters are declared in the LOCAL-STORAGE SECTION. In this section there
must be an LD entry for each subroutine to be called (provided parameters
other than files are to be passed). The syntax is as follows:

LOCAL-STORAGE SECTION.

[LD local-storage-name-1.

    [formal-parameters-for-subroutine-1] ...]

It may be noted that the local-storage-name must be unique.
As mentioned earlier, the USE statement must also refer to the subroutine to be called. One of the ways in which this reference can be made
is to associate a mnemonic name with the actual name of the subroutine and
then to use this mnemonic name in the USE statement. For example, the following declaration in the SPECIAL-NAMES paragraph

        "MYSUB"   IS   CALLED-ROUTINE.

would associate the mnemonic-named CALLED-ROUTINE with the actual name MYSUB.

The syntax of the use statement in the DECLARATIVES section is as follows:

DECLARATIVES.

section-name SECTION.

$$\text{USE EXTERNAL} \left\{ \begin{array}{l} \text{identifier} \\ \text{mnemonic-name} \end{array} \right\} \text{AS PROCEDURE}$$

$$\left[\text{; WITH} \left\{ \begin{array}{l} \text{file-name} \\ \text{local-storage-name} \end{array} \right\} \left[\text{,} \left\{ \begin{array}{l} \text{file-name} \\ \text{local-storage-name} \end{array} \right\} \right] \ldots \right.$$

$$\left. \text{; USING} \quad a_1, a_2, \ldots, a_n \right]$$

END DECLARATIVES.

The formal parameters a_1, a_2, ..., a_n are data names described in the LOCAL-STORAGE SECTION. The parameters must appear in the same order as in the PROCEDURE DIVISION header of the called subroutine although their names may be different from those used in the subroutine. The formal parameters in the calling program as well as in the called subroutine should be of a matching type.

The USE statement is merely a declaration and the subroutine is not invoked unless it is explicitly called. The CALL statement should specify the name of the section that contains the USE statement. The number, order, type, size and the level number of the items in the actual-parameter-list must be identical with those of the items in the formal-parameter-list of USING clauses in USE statement as well as in the PROCEDURE DIVISION header of the subroutine. Figure 19.3 shows the coding of the calling program of Fig. 19.2 for B-6700.

```
IDENTIFICATION DIVISION.
ENVIRONMENT DIVISION.
CONFIGURATION SECTION.
SPECIAL-NAMES.
                "EDITNM" IS SUB-ROUTINE.
INPUT-OUTPUT SECTION.
FILE-CONTROL.
    SELECT FILE-CARD ASSIGN TO READER.
    SELECT FILE-LINE ASSIGN TO PRINTER.
DATA DIVISION.
FILE SECTION.
FD FILE-CARD.
01  CARD-REC          PIC  X(80).
```

(contd.)

```
FD  FILE-LINE.
01  LINE-REC.
    02 FILLER              PIC  X(10).
    02 EDITED-REC          PIC  X(80).
    02 FILLER              PIC  X(42).
WORKING-STORAGE SECTION.
10  NAME-EDITED           PIC  X(80).
LOCAL-STORAGE SECTION.
LD FORMAL-PARAMETERS.
01 GIVEN-NAME             PIC  X(80)  REF.
01 EDITED-NAME            PIC  X(80)  REF.
PROCEDURE DIVISION.
DECLARATIVES.
S1 SECTION.
  USE EXTERNAL SUB-ROUTINE AS PROCEDURE
  WITH FORMAL-PARAMETERS
  USING GIVEN-NAME EDITED-NAME.
END DECLARATIVES.
MAIN-PROG SECTION.
PARA-OPEN.
  OPEN INPUT FILE-CARD.
          OUTPUT FILE-LINE.
  MOVE SPACES TO LINE-REC.
PARA-READ.
    READ FILE-CARD RECORD AT END GO TO PARA-FINAL
    CALL S1 USING CARD-REC NAME-EDITED.
    MOVE NAME-EDITED TO EDITED-REC.
    WRITE LINE-REC AFTER ADVANCING 1 LINES.
    GO TO PARA-READ.
PARA-FINAL.
    CLOSE FILE-CARD FILE-LINE
    STOP RUN.
```

FIG. 19.3. Main Program Calling the Subroutine
EDITNM (B-6700)

Parameters in B-6700

In B-6700 COBOL a formal parameter may be:
   (i)   77-level COMP, COMP-1, COMP-4 or COMP-5 items.
   (ii) 01-level COMP, COMP-2, DISPLAY and DISPLAY-1 items.
   From the above list the reader may note that the frequently used 77-level DISPLAY items of any type are not good enough as formal parameters and these should be declared at level 01 only.
   B-6700 COBOL allows parameters to be passed either ''by reference'' or ''by value''. Whether a parameter is to be received ''by value'' or ''by reference'' can be specified by the RECEIVED clause which can appear in the description of the formal parameter in the LINKAGE SECTION (or in WORKING-STORAGE SECTION if it contains formal parameters) and in the LOCAL-STORAGE SECTION. The syntax of the RECEIVED clause is as follows:

$$
\text{RECEIVED BY} \left\{ \begin{array}{l} \underline{\text{REFERENCE}} \\ \underline{\text{REF}} \\ \underline{\text{CONTENT}} \end{array} \right\}
$$

RECEIVED BY REFERENCE (or REF) means that any reference made to the parameter either in the calling program or in the subroutine will make reference to the same data area in the memory. This is what is known as call by reference. On the other hand, if CONTENT is specified, a copy of the current value of the actual parameter is assigned to the corresponding formal parameter. This is known as call by value. As a consequence, any subsequent change in the value of the formal parameter within the subroutine merely affects the ''copy'' and not the original actual parameter. Therefore, any formal parameter corresponding to an actual parameter that should change in value during the execution of the subroutine cannot be received by CONTENT.

The reader may note that to specify RECEIVED BY REFERENCE is safe. The advantage of receiving a parameter by CONTENT is that this results in a more efficient object program. However, only the 77-level items may be received by CONTENT. If the RECEIVED clause is not explicitly specified, 77-level COMP-1 items are taken to be RECEIVED BY CONTENT and other items are taken as RECEIVED BY REFERENCE.

Note:

The B-6700 subroutine feature offers a number of facilities in addition to what has been discussed above. Moreover, B-6700 COBOL supports invocation of the subroutine as a parallel task so that the calling program and called program can run together. A discussion on these nonstandard facilities is beyond our scope and is therefore omitted.

EXERCISES

1. For each of the following statements, indicate whether it is correct or incorrect.
   (a) The appearance of the EXIT PROGRAM statement in the PROCEDURE DIVISION conclusively indicates that the said program is a subroutine.
   (b) A CALL statement must not appear in a program containing a LINKAGE SECTION.
   (c) The CANCEL statement restores the initial state of a subroutine.
   (d) Among the programs whose object codes form the run unit, there must be at least one program that does not have a LINKAGE SECTION.
   (e) If a subroutine is cancelled by a CANCEL statement, it cannot be called again in the same program that cancels it.

2. Is it possible to open and close a file in the calling program and to read the records of the file in the called program?

3. A data name X is defined in the WORKING-STORAGE SECTION of both the calling and the called programs with the same PICTURE clause. However,

X is neither used in the CALL statement of the calling program nor in the PROCEDURE DIVISION header of the called program (note that the latter is not possible). State whether the two data fields are related or not.

4. The calling program contains the statement

    CALL   "SUBA"   USING   A, B, C.

    and the PROCEDURE DIVISION header of the called subroutine (named SUBA) is

    PROCEDURE   DIVISION   USING   C, B, A.

    Show how the actual and formal parameters will be connected.

5. Though PERFORM and CALL accomplish functions that are similar in nature, there are a few basic differences. Indicate which one of the following is not a correct statement of a difference between the two.
    (a) PERFORM does not allow parameters whereas CALL does.
    (b) PERFORM refers to the same program whereas CALL refers to a separately compiled subprogram.
    (c) PERFORM refers to only one paragraph whereas CALL refers to an entire subprogram consisting of any number of paragraphs.
    (d) PERFORM allows repeated invocations in the same statement whereas CALL invokes the subprogram only once.
                                                        [NSTPC, 1980]

6. Suppose each record of a transaction file on a magnetic tape consists of 120 characters in the following format.

Field	Position	Type
Transaction-key	1-6	Numeric
Transaction-data	7-120	Alphanumeric

Write a subroutine, that will read the next sequential record from the file and will return it to the calling program. When the subroutine is called for the first time, it must open the file and return the record. When the end of the file is reached, the subroutine must close the said file and should return a record with high-values in the transaction-key field and spaces in the transaction-data field.

20

SEGMENTATION AND LIBRARY FACILITY

20.1 SEGMENTATION

Normally, the entire object program resides in the memory of the computer
during execution. However, when the object program is so large that the
entire program cannot be accommodated in the memory, the segmentation
technique may be used. Segmentation causes the object code for the PROCEDURE
DIVISION to be physically subdivided into segments. A segment in the case
of a COBOL source program consists of one or more sections. It can be either
a permanent segment or an independent segment. A permanent segment resides
in the memory for all the time that the object program is executed. An
independent segment, on the other hand, is brought into the memory only
when it is needed. An independent segment can be overlayed by another
incoming independent segment. An independent segment is brought into the
memory when a GO TO or PERFORM statement that names a procedure located in
the segment is executed.

When segmentation is used, the PROCEDURE DIVISION must be written as
consisting of sections. Therefore, there must not be any paragraph which is
not within a section. Each section is assigned a segment number (also called
priority number) by writing the number in the section header. The format of
the section header with the segment number is shown below.

> section-name SECTION [segment-number].

The segment number can be any number having a value between 0 and 99
(both inclusive). If the segment number is omitted, 0 is assumed. There can
be more than one section having the same segment number. They together form
a segment. However, they need not appear in the PROCEDURE DIVISION as
contiguous sections. Sections in the declarative part of the PROCEDURE
DIVISION cannot be assigned a segment number greater than 49.

The segment number determines whether a segment is permanent or independent. Segments having segment numbers less than 50 are considered to be
permanent segments, while segments whose numbers are greater than or equal
to 50 are taken to be independent segments. However, the programmer can
reduce the segment numbers of the permanent segments by using the SEGMENT-
LIMIT clause in the OBJECT-COMPUTER paragraph. The format of this clause is
as follows:

> SEGMENT-LIMIT IS integer

The integer must have a value between 1 and 49 (both inclusive). When the SEGMENT-LIMIT clause is used, all segments whose segment number is less than the integer become permanent segments. The segments whose segment numbers are greater than or equal to the specified integer but not greater than 49 are called <u>quasi-permanent</u> segments (also called <u>overlayable-fixed segments</u>). A quasi-permanent segment can also be overlayed by another segment. Thus we find that there can be, in fact, three types of segments:
- permanent segments
- quasi-permanent segments
- independent segments.

The differences among the three are that permanent segments cannot be overlayed while quasi-permanent and independent segments can be overlayed. When a quasi-permanent segment is again brought into the memory, it is brought in the last-used state. It may be noted that if a GO TO statement in a quasi-permanent segment was altered by an ALTER statement (before it was overlayed), it would remain in the ALTERED state when the segment is brought again to the memory. Thus, logically, a quasi-permanent segment is like a permanent segment, although it is overlayed and called from time to time. On the other hand, whenever an independent segment is brought to the memory, it is made available in its initial state and not in its last-used state. However, an independent segment retains its last-used state in the following cases.

(i) If a PERFORM statement in an independent segment executes procedures in permanent segments, the control is returned to the said independent segment in its last-used state.

(ii) If a CALL statement is executed in an independent segment, then after the execution of the subroutine, the control returns to the said segment in its last-used state.

Example

Consider the following:

        OBJECT-COMPUTER. SEGMENT-LIMIT 31.

Now, a segment whose segment number is between 0 and 30 is a permanent segment. A segment whose segment number is between 31 and 49 is a quasi-permanent segment. Such a segment can be overlayed; but when it is brought again, it is made available in the last-used state. Any segment whose segment number is between 50 and 99 is an independent segment and whenever such a segment is brought into the memory it is in the initial state.

20.1.1 Segmentation Restrictions

Segmentation puts certain restrictions on the use of ALTER, PERFORM, SORT and MERGE verbs. These restrictions are as follows:

(i) A GO TO statement in an independent segment can be altered only by an ALTER statement located in the same segment.

(ii) A PERFORM statement which is located in a permanent segment is allowed to have within its range only one of the following:

(a) Procedures wholly included within one or more permanent or quasi-permanent segments.

(b) Procedures wholly included in a single independent segment.

     (iii) A PERFORM statement which is located in an independent or quasi-permanent segment, is allowed to have within its range only one of the following:

        (a) Procedures wholly included within one or more permanent segments.

        (b) Procedures wholly included within the same segment in which the PERFORM statement appears.

     (iv) The restrictions on the SORT/MERGE statements and the corresponding input/output procedures are identical to those in the case of the PERFORM statement and its range.

Example

Consider the following code:

```
EXAMPLE  SECTION  60.
FIRST-PARA.  MOVE 1 TO CONTROL-COUNT.
ALTER-PARA.
     IF  CONTROL-COUNT = 10
         ALTER GO-PARA TO PROCEED TO EXIT-PARA.
     PERFORM PROCEDURE-DO.
     ADD 1 TO CONTROL-COUNT.
GO-PARA.
     GO TO ALTER-PARA.
EXIT-PARA. EXIT.
```

According to item (iii) of the abovementioned segmentation restrictions, PROCEDURE-DO must appear in a segment having a segment number either equal to 60 or less than 50. It may be noted that if PROCEDURE-DO was contained in another independent segment and if the PERFORM statement was still allowed to perform it, then there would be an infinite loop. This is because such a freedom would normally require the segment containing EXAMPLE and that containing PROCEDURE-DO overlaying each other alternately (normally, at one point of time, only one independent segment resides in the memory). This means that each time the segment containing EXAMPLE is brought into the memory, it would be in its initial state, thereby nullifying the effect of the ALTER statement.

20.1.2 Planning for Segmentation

In order to make effective use of the segmentation facility, proper planning is necessary. The following are the general guidelines for such planning:

     (i) Segmentation should be done in such a way that the independent segments are brought into the memory as sparingly as possible. Ideally, each independent segment should be brought in (through a PERFORM or GO TO statement) only once. This reduces the overhead of bringing segments from the auxiliary memory to the main memory.

     (ii) There should be as few independent segments as possible. A reduction in the number of independent segments makes it easier to observe the segmentation restrictions.

(iii) Normally, the memory space that is allocated for the independent
segments is equal to the size of the largest independent segment.
Thus the programmer should attempt to have independent segments of
roughly equal sizes. This will enable him to have maximum utilization of the overlayable space.

The segmentation feature of COBOL may not be available on systems having
a virtual-memory environment. This is because the operating system and
compiler take care of segmentation automatically.

20.2 LIBRARY FACILITY

The library facility enables the programmer to include texts saved on a
library file into the program library. A library text in this context means
a portion of a COBOL source program. A library file can contain one or more
such library texts each of which can be identified by a suitable text name.
A programmer who wishes to include such a text can write an appropriate
COPY statement in the program. The effect would be identical to that of
writing the entire text in place of the COPY statement.

Before we go into the language features, let us explain the usefulness
of this facility. Quite often it is found that two or more COBOL programs
of a user contain identical codes in various portions. For example, when
two programs must handle the same master file, both can contain identical
FD entries and record descriptions (we assume that same file name, record
names, data names and level indicators are being used). Moreover, the file
may contain several types of records and as such the said descriptions may
require several coding lines. In a situation like this, the relevant portion
of the first program can be stored in a library file under a text name. In
the second program a copy statement can be used to include the said text.
The COPY statement also allows the programmer to get the text copied with
some limited modifications.

The procedure for creating a library file consisting of one or more
library texts will not be discussed here. This is because the library files
are normally created by using the manufacturer-supplied utility routines.

The format of the COPY statement is given below:

```
COPY     text-name  ┌ ┌OF ┐ library-name ┐
                    │ │IN │              │
                    └ └   ┘              ┘

         ┌                 ┌ == pseudo-text-1= = ┐        ┌ == pseudo-text-2= = ┐
         │ REPLACING       │ identifier-1        │   BY   │ identifier-2        │
         │                 │ literal-1           │        │ literal-2           │
         │                 └ word-1              ┘        └ word-2              ┘

         ┌                 ┌ == pseudo-text-3= = ┐        ┌ == pseudo-text-4= = ┐ ┐
         │       ,         │ identifier-3        │   BY   │ identifier-4        │ │ ...
         │                 │ literal-3           │        │ literal-4           │ │
         │                 └ word-3              ┘        └ word-4              ┘ ┘
```

The following rules should be observed while using the statement.

(i)   A COPY statement can appear in a COBOL source program wherever a separator or character string can appear. However, a COPY statement cannot occur within another COPY statement. The library text must not contain any COPY statement.

(ii) A COPY statement must be preceded by a space and must be terminated by a period. During compilation the entire copy statement including the terminating period is replaced by the named text.

(iii) When there is more than one COBOL library file, the text name should be qualified by the library name.

(iv) The pseudo text is a string of characters within a double equal signs (=).The double equal signs only delimit the pseudo text and is not part of it.

(v)   The word can be any COBOL word.

(vi) When the REPLACING option is used, each occurrence of pseudo-text-1, identifier-1, literal-1 or word-1 in the library text being copied is replaced by the corresponding pseudo-text-2, identifier-2, literal-2 or word-2.

(vii) The pseudo-text-1 must not be empty nor must it only consist of spaces or comment lines. However, pseudo-text-2 may be empty, i.e., = = = = .

(viii) Comment lines within the text is copied without any change.

(ix) Text names and library names are user-defined names such as data names and must contain at least one letter.

Example

Let TEXT1 be the name of the following text in the library file.

```
RECORD CONTAINS 130 CHARACTERS
BLOCK CONTAINS 10 RECORDS
LABEL RECORDS ARE STANDARD
VALUE OF ID IS "FILEA".
```

Now, the following code

```
FD  FILE-MASTER
    COPY TEXT1.
```

at the time of compilation will become

```
FD FILE-MASTER
    RECORD CONTAINS 130 CHARACTERS
    BLOCK CONTAINS 10 RECORDS
    LABEL RECORDS ARE STANDARD
    VALUE OF ID IS "FILEA".
```

On the other hand, consider the following code

```
FD FILE-MASTER
    COPY TEXT1 REPLACING = = 10 RECORDS = =
```

```
        BY = = 900 CHARACTERS = =
        130  BY  180  "FILEA"  BY  "FILEB"..
```

At the time of compilation the code becomes

```
    FD  FILE-MASTER
        RECORD  CONTAINS  180  CHARACTERS
        BLOCK   CONTAINS  900  CHARACTERS
        LABEL   RECORDS   ARE  STANDARD
        VALUE   OF  ID  IS  "FILEB".
```

Note:

The COPY verb has been substantially enhanced in ANSI 74. The pseudo text
is a new feature. Moreover, in ANSI 68 there were restrictions in respect
of the positions where a COPY statement could appear in the source program.
These restrictions have now been removed.

20.3 IMPLEMENTATION DIFFERENCES

(a) Segmentation

The segmentation facility is available in DEC-10 and ICL-1900. In B-6700 it
is neither available nor required. The SEGMENT-LIMIT clause in B-6700 has a
different meaning. Except for very minor differences in respect of restrictions on PERFORM, SORT and MERGE verbs, there are no implementation
differences.

(b) Library Facility

The COPY verb and associated facilities are available in all the three
compilers under consideration. We shall skip the implementation differences
as one must learn many other things about the individual system in order to
be able to make effective use of this facility.

EXERCISES

1. Suppose we divide our program into two segments — one permanent and
    the other independent. Will it serve any real purpose? Explain.

2. Segmentation in COBOL is allowed only on PROCEDURE DIVISION. Suppose it
    was also allowed on DATA DIVISION. Under that assumption state the
    advantages and disadvantages of having independent segments for some
    DATA DIVISION items.

3. Suppose the following text appears in the library file under the text
    name OCTXT.

            PIC 9(4) OCCURS 20 TIMES.

Indicate the entries that will be generated after the replacement of the text in the following cases.

(i)   05   FREQ   COPY   OCTXT   REPLACING

= = 9(4) = =   BY   = =   X(5) = =

20   BY   100.

(ii) 05   FREQ   COPY   OCTXT   REPLACING = =   OCCURS   20   TIMES = = BY = = = = .

4. Make a comparison between the REPLACING phrase used in a COPY statement and that used in an INSPECT statement.

5. Suppose you are writing a very long COBOL program. Once the source cards are punched, you detect a mistake. Due to oversight, in about 50% cases, you have written DATA-1 for DATA-ONE. Do you think the COPY verb can be helpful in this context? If so, explain how it can be helpful. You can assume that there is no other data item with the name DATA-1 in the said program.

21

COBOL FOR PERSONAL COMPUTERS

21.1 INTRODUCTION

In recent times personal computers have become immensely popular for their
low prices. These are IBM PC or PC-XT computers or their compatibles. The
disk operating system (MS-DOS or simply DOS) and the COBOL compiler (MS-
COBOL) for these personal computers are the copyright products of Microsoft
Corporation of USA. Because of the popularity of PC/PC-XT, we have devoted
this chapter on COBOL features for these computers. In order to make full
utilisation of the capabilities, one must also be familiar with the DOS and
associated softwares. As such, brief descriptions of essential features of
DOS and other softwares are also included here. However, for a complete
description one must consult the relevant manuals.

21.2 THE HARDWARE

The usual configuration for a PC is as follows:

CPU	:	Microprocessor based system using Intel 8088 (each word consists of 16 bits).
Co-processor	:	Intel 8087 microprocessor for high-speed computation. This is an optional feature.
ROM	:	8K read only memory.
Memory (RAM)	:	Minimum 128K bytes. Maximum 640K bytes.
Auxiliary Storage	:	Two floppy drives usually with 1.2M bytes storage capacity.
Visual Display Unit (VDU)	:	25 x 80 characters (25 lines each containing 80 characters) capable of generating 256 different characters. The VDU can optionally be with colour.

Dot Matrix Printer	:	Usually with 80/132 column positions and 150-160 characters/second.
Keyboard	:	Typewriter-like keyboard with 83 keys.

The essential difference between a PC and a PC-XT is that the latter has a fixed Winchester disk drive with 20/40 M bytes capacity in addition to the two floppy drives. Sometimes, a PC-XT is available with only one floppy drive and a Winchester drive. It may be pointed out that DOS refers to these drives with one letter codes namely, A, B and C. The codes A and B denote the two floppy drives while C denotes the Winchester drive. A more powerful version of PC namely PC-AT is also available. The following discussions apply equally to PC-AT as well.

21.3 THE KEYBOARD

The keyboard provides the means of entering data as well as programs and is the basic input device for PC. There are 83 keys in the keyboard which is internally controlled by the Intel 8048 microprocessor. The keys can be broadly classified into two groups — character keys and control keys. Character keys represent letters (capital as well as small), digits and special characters. The control keys are used for controlling the operations of the keyboard. Whenever a character key is pressed, the character is also displayed on the VDU screen at the current position of the cursor. The cursor then moves to the next position on the right and if the end of the line has been reached, it moves to the first position of the next line.
     With each of the 83 keys, there is an associated number in the range 1 to 83 known as the key scan code. When a key is pressed, the keyboard processor sends the scan code to the CPU and when the key is released, the processor again sends a code which is the scan code plus 128. For example, the scan code for A is 30. Therefore, when A is pressed, 30 is sent and when it is released 158 is sent. The CPU of the PC, finally converts the two scan codes into ASCII code (for example, ASCII code for A is 65). For simplicity, we shall take the simplified (and somewhat incorrect) view that whenever a key is pressed an ASCII code is transmitted. However we want to make it clear that the conversion of keystroke into ASCII code is done by software and therefore, the code for any key can be changed easily. Moreover, the interpretation of a keystroke depends on the program that accepts the input from the keyboard and this is why some of the control keys (like ESC) is found to behave differently under different software. Therefore, the general description of the functions of the control keys as given below should be taken as typical.
     The keyboard is divided into three main sections — the function keys on the left, the typewriter key area in the middle and the numeric keypad on the right (Fig. 21.1). In the function key section, there are ten multi-purpose functions keys labelled F1 to F10. These are "soft keys", in the sense that their functions depend on what are programmed into them by the

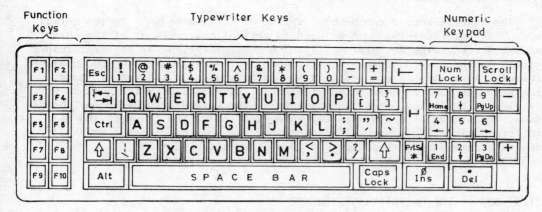

FIG. 21.1 Keyboard Keys

software currently being used. There are no universal functions attached
to them. We shall describe one use of F1 key in connection with EDLIN
Software. We shall also see how function keys can be used through COBOL
programs. The typewriter key area contains the character keys, space bar
and the shift keys (to shift from lower case to upper case or reverse). In
addition to these keys, the typewriter area contains a few control keys.
Some of these are described below:

Caps Lock   This is a toggle key. When pressed it puts the alphabetic
                 keys in the uppercase mode until this key is pressed again.
                 The next time the key is pressed the keyboard returns to
                 lowercase mode. It may be noted that this key does not
                 affect the digit keys on the first row nor the keys for
                 punctuation marks.

Backspace   This key (labelled as ←) is the rightmost key of the first
                 row of the typewriter area. It is used to erase the
                 character which is on the immediate left of the cursor. The
                 cursor also moves back in the position of the deleted
                 character.

Enter   This key (labelled as ↵) is the rightmost key of the second/
                 third row of the typewriter area. This key usually signals
                 the end of data being entered through the keyboard. The
                 cursor is moved to the first column position of the next
                 line.

ESC (Escape)   Like the enter key, this key is generally used as a termi-
                 nator key.

Ctrl (Control)   This key is used like the shift key. When pressed alone,
                 nothing happens. However, when pressed in combination with
                 another key, the scan code of the second key is altered in
                 some way. For example, A and Ctrl-A have different codes.

The numeric keypad can be used in one of the two modes. In the normal mode, the numeric keypad can be used to control the movement of the cursor on the screen. The keys for 8,2,4 and 6 control the cursor movement respectively in the upward, downward, left and right directions. When the numlock (numeric lock) key is pressed, the keypad is placed in the numeric mode. The keys can then be used to enter digits. Like capslock, the numlock key is also a toggle key. When pressed again, the keypad returns to the normal mode. The keypad also contains two keys labelled as Ins (Insert) and Del (Delete). These have special meanings for the screen editors. We shall describe some use of these keys in connection with EDLIN.

There are a few other keys which are not described here.

21.4 DOS — THE OPERATING SYSTEM FOR PC

As mentioned previously, the disk operating system for the PC is known as DOS. This software is loaded into the memory when the power is turned on. Whenever DOS is ready for any task from the user, it displays a prompt which can be any one of the following:

         A>   B>   C>

depending on the drive on which DOS is currently working (default drive). Initially, the default drive is either A   or   C depending on the drive from which DOS is loaded. In the case of a PC-XT, the initial loading usually takes place from the C drive (Winchester drive) and the prompt therefore is C>. In all examples, without any loss of generality, we shall assume that C is the default drive unless specifically mentioned.

Once DOS is ready, it can be used to display the directory of the files stored on the disk, to copy a file from one disk to another, to permit storage or removal of files and many other important operations. In order to use DOS, the user must specify a DOS command. A DOS command may be an internal command or an external command. Internal commands are built into DOS and can be executed immediately. An external command is required to be given when we wish to execute a program stored on disk in the form of an executable file. The external command consists of the file specification for the desired executable file.

21.4.1 File Specification

The file specification enables DOS to locate the file on one of the disks. A file specification has the following three parts:
    (i)   drive-specifier
    (ii) file-name
    (iii) extension

The drive specifier is the letter A, B or C denoting the drive containing the desired file. The drive specifier along with colon(:), can be omitted if the file is in the default drive. The file name is a name consisting of one to eight characters. The characters that can appear in a name can be a letter, a digit or some special character such as hyphen(-). The extension is, as the name suggests, an extension of the file name and is usually used to denote the type of file. It consists of one to three characters. This part of the file specification is optional and if omitted, the period(.) in the file specification should also be omitted. The following are examples of valid file specifications:

```
A:MYCOBOL.COB
DATA-A.DAT
C:NEW-PROG
```

.EXE is one of the extensions that tells DOS that the file under consideration is an executable program file. However, the file specification, when selected as an external command, need not quote the extension. For example, let the file MYPROG.EXE be an executable program file. In order to run this program the external command should be

```
    C > MYPROG      if the file is stored in C (default drive)
or  C > A:MYPROG     if the file is stored in A
or  C > B:MYPROG     if the file is stored in B.
```

The following conventions are generally allowed in the matter of extensions to file names (although it is possible to override them by any other extension):

File Type	Extension
COBOL Source File	. COB
Object file	. OBJ
Listing file	. LST
Library file	. LIB
Data file	. DAT

It may be noted that the object file is produced by the COBOL compiler from the COBOL source file. This file is used by the linker (LINK) program as input. The purpose of the linker is to combine separately compiled object modules and to define unresolved external references by searching library files (.LIB files). It finally produces the load module (.EXE file) which can be executed as a DOS external command. The COBOL compiler and/or linker can optionally produce listing files (.LST file) which contains formatted listing of the program along with error messages, if any.

21.4.2 Some Important Internal Commands

DOS has a large number of built-in internal commands. It is beyond the scope of the present book to discuss these commands as we are primarily interested in COBOL features. In the following, we discuss only some examples of the DOS commands to give an overview of the nature and power of these commands. Each command is to be terminated by pressing the enter key.

(i)   C > DIR/P

Since there can be several files residing on a disk, DOS maintains a
directory on each disk. The above command will display all the directory entries for the default drive onto the screen. The parameter P will
pause the display when the screen is full. To continue with further
display, any key can be pressed.

(ii)   C > A:

This command will change the default drive from C to A.

(iii)   C > TYPE B:MYFILE.TXT

This command will list the contents of the specified file (MYFILE.TXT
residing on the floppy in drive B) on the screen. The drive specifier
part may be dropped if the file is on the default drive.

(iv)   C > TYPE B:MYFILE.TXT > PRN

This command will print the contents of the specified file onto the
printer. Such command is useful to print the listing file produced by
the COBOL compiler.

(v)   C > COPY   MYFILE.ABC   A:

This command will copy MYFILE.ABC residing on the default drive (C here)
onto drive A with the same file name and extension.

(vi)   C > COPY   A: MYFILE.ABC

This command will copy the file MYFILE.ABC residing on the A drive onto
the default drive.

(vii) C > COPY   MY *.*   A:

All files having file names beginning with MY and having any extension
will be copied from the default drive to A drive.

(viii) C > COPY   A:MYFILE.ABC   NEWFILE.XYZ

This command will copy MYFILE.ABC residing on A drive onto the default
drive under the name NEWFILE and extension .XYZ. The opposite is also
possible in a similar manner.

(ix)   C > COPY   MYFILE.ABC   *.XYZ

This command will create a second copy of MYFILE.ABC residing on the
default drive onto the same drive having the same file name but extension changed to .XYZ.

(x)   C > ERASE   A:ANYFILE.XYZ

This command will remove the specified file from the disk directory.
The file will not be available again.

21.5 CREATION OF COBOL SOURCE/DATA FILE THROUGH EDLIN

EDLIN is a software which comes with DOS and can be used to create, modify and display source files or data files. EDLIN is a line editor and the files created by it consists of lines of variable lengths having a maximum of 253 characters per line. During the creation or editing process EDLIN generates and displays line numbers but these are not actually present in the file. We shall first describe how EDLIN can be used to create COBOL source files. As in the case of DOS commands, the EDLIN commands should also be terminated by pressing the enter key.

21.5.1 Creating a New Source File

To create a new source file, the following command should be given

      C > EDLIN   file-name.COB

The following message and prompt will be displayed by EDLIN:

New File

* - (- denotes the position of the cursor)

The EDLIN command I (insert) should be given now. EDLIN will respond by displaying

1 : *-

This means that EDLIN is ready for input. The first line of the COBOL source can be entered at this time. Having typed the line, the Enter Key is to be pressed. EDLIN will then display the prompt

2 : * -

The second line can be entered now. In this way, the entire text of the COBOL source program should be entered. Finally to come out of the insert mode, press

      ∧ C   (∧ denotes Ctrl key. Press Ctrl and C simultaneously)

EDLIN will prompt by displaying

      * -

At this point, to save the file and to exit from EDLIN press E.

The following is an example of EDLIN session for the creation of a new source file having 80 lines.

```
C > EDLIN            TEST.COB
New File
* I
   1:*            IDENTIFICATION DIVISION.
   2:*            PROGRAM-ID. PROG1.
      :
      :
  81:* ∧ C
   * E
   C >
```

21.5.2 Editing on Existing Source File

To edit an existing source file, use the command

    C > EDLIN   file-name.COB

The following message and prompt will be displayed by EDLIN:

End of input file
* -

The file is now ready for correction/display. The following EDLIN commands can be used to perform the necessary operations.

(i) L (List Lines) command

To list a range of lines from the source file, use the command

    * line-1,   line-2   L

Note that * is the prompt from EDLIN and need not be typed. For example,

    * 10, 15 L

will display the range of lines from 10 to 15. If the command

    * line L

is given, a total of 23 lines starting with the specified line will be displayed.

(ii) Edit Line command

To edit any particular line, use the command

    * line

For example, to edit line 20 enter the command

    * 20

EDLIN will display the contents of the line as shown below.

    20 :   05   FIELD-A   PIC   X(10)
    20 :

The entire line can be replaced by typing the new line followed by the pressing of the enter key. In the case of minor changes, the F1 function key can be pressed to copy characters from the existing line as and when necessary. Only the changed characters are to be typed. For example, if FIELD-A in line 20 is to be changed to FIELD-B, go on pressing the F1 key until the hyphen (-) has appeared on the screen. Now, type B and continue to press F1 until the end of the line is reached. Finally, press enter to replace the original line by the modified one. To insert or delete characters from the line being edited, help of the Ins or Del keys can

be taken. For example, to delete next two characters the del key
can be pressed twice. To insert one or more characters starting
from the current cursor position, press the Ins key and type the
additional characters. Subsequent pressing of F1 will terminate
insertion and start the copy of characters from the existing line.

(iii)   I (Insert lines) command

We have already seen this command in connection with the creation
of new source file. The same command can be used to insert one or
more lines before a particular line. The command is as follows:

* line   I

The following prompt will appear on the screen.

    line   :   *

Successive lines can be inserted now. Finally, press ⋀ C to come
out of the insertion mode. Note that the line numbers of the
existing lines following the inserted text will get increased by
the number of lines inserted. To insert new lines at the end of
the source file, use the line number of the last line plus one.

(iv)   D (Delete Lines) command

This command can be used to delete a single line or a range of
lines from the existing file. The formats of this command are as
follows:

* line   D
* line-1, line-2 D

Having deleted the line/range of lines, EDLIN will display * as
the prompt. All subsequent lines in the file will be renumbered.

(v)   E (End Edit) command

This command has also been discussed earlier. The format is

* E

The command can be used to terminate EDLIN and to save the edited
file by replacing the original one.

(vi)   Q (Quit Edit) command

The format of this command is

* Q

This command can be used to terminate EDLIN without saving the
edited file. The command is useful when the lines of a file have
been displayed and no editing has been done. When the command is

given, EDLIN displays the following:

Abort edit (Y/N) ?

Enter Y to terminate.

We feel the above commands are sufficient to work with EDLIN. However, we have not described the commands in all details and there are many other commands in EDLIN. Interested readers should consult the DOS manual for further information on EDLIN.

While entering COBOL source it should be remembered that the position following the * is the column position 1. Obviously, sufficient spaces should be given for the margins (7 to 10 spaces for area A entries and 11 or more for area B entries).

21.5.3 Creation and Editing of Data Files

Data files can also be created through EDLIN exactly in the same way as the source file. Only difference is that the extension in the file name may not be .COB. Usually, the extension .DAT is used for data files but, in fact, this extension can be anything. Even the extension part can be omitted.

Data files created by EDLIN (or any other text editor) are known as text files. In COBOL terminology such files are called LINE SEQUENTIAL files. In order to read data from text files, the SELECT clause in the COBOL program should be as follows:

SELECT   file-name   ASSIGN   TO   DISK
                      ORGANIZATION   IS   LINE   SEQUENTIAL.

This explains how data files containing primary input data can be created in the absence of a card reader. Another point that should be noted in this connection is that a line in the text file created by EDLIN can consist of as many as 253 characters. However, an actual line may consist of fewer characters. The record description in the COBOL program should contain the description of the actual data line. It is not necessary to use FILLER entries to make the description complete upto 253 characters. This is possible becasue each line in the text file is terminated by carriage return (ASCII value 13) and linefeed (ASCII value 10) characters.

21.6 COMPILATION AND LINKING OF COBOL PROGRAMS

Various compilation and linking options are possible. However, there is a simple way to compile and link a COBOL program. To compile a COBOL source stored in the file called program-name.COB the command is

C > COBOL   program-name;

For example, if the source program file is TEST.COB the command for compilation should be

        C >   COBOL   TEST ;

As a result of this, the program will be compiled and if there is no syntax
error in the program, the following message will be displayed

    No Errors or Warnings.

    This means that we can now proceed with linking. On the other hand, if
the program contains errors or anomalies, then error messages will be displayed on the screen. An error message consists of a four digit line number
(indicating the source line containing the error) followed by a colon (:)
and then followed by an explanation. If the explanation begins with an /F/
or a /W/, it means that it is a warning. In other cases, the error should
be considered as severe requiring correction in the program. If only warnings have been issued, the user may ignore them and can proceed with linking. However, one must take into consideration these warnings to see
whether there is really any error in the program or not.
    The simple way to link a program is to give the following command

    C > LINK   program-name;

After successful linking, to run the program, the command should be

    C > program-name

    In the above description, we have assumed that the COBOL compiler,
linker as well as the source file are on the default drive. The compiler
and the linker will produce the program-name.OBJ and program-name.EXE files
respectively on the same drive. The program-name in the preceding description always refers to the file-name part of the source file specification.
    The simple approach described above may not be sufficient. In many
cases, the user would desire a print-out of the program along with the
error messages, if any. To accomplish this, the command for compilation
should be

    C > COBOL   program-name

    In response to this, the compiler will issue two prompts requesting the
file names for object file and listing file. The prompts are as follows:

    Object file-name [program-name.OBJ]:
    Source listing [NUL.LST]:

The first prompt expects an object file name and states that in case this
is not given, program-name with the extension changed to .OBJ will be
assumed. In most cases this latter alternative will be acceptable and
therefore, our response should be to press the Enter key only. The second
prompt expects the listing file name and states that the default is no list
file (NUL). To have a listing file, our response should be to enter a
suitable name for it. As a result, the listing file with extension .LST
will be produced. Subsequently, this file can be printed by means of the
TYPE command (discussed earlier) of DOS.

The COBOL language for PC (MS-COBOL) provides facilities for COBOL sub-routines (discussed in Sec. 21.10). In case, we have a main program and several subroutines, each of the subroutines as well as the main program are to be separately compiled by the COBOL command discussed above. Let PROG1.OBJ be the name of the file containing the object code for the main program and let SUB1.OBJ and SUB2.OBJ be the files containing object codes for the subroutines. To link them together, the command should be

    C > LINK   PROG1 + SUB1 + SUB2;

The linker will produce the load module with the title PROG1.EXE. Therefore, to run the program, the command should be

    C > PROG1

21.7 MAJOR IMPLEMENTATION DIFFERENCES OF MS-COBOL FEATURES

The MS-COBOL follows greatly the guidelines of ANS1-74 standard of COBOL. As such, most of the COBOL features described in this book are available without any change. Important limitations and differences of MS-COBOL are described below. Items marked with asterisk (*) in this and subsequent sections, are not limitations for the recent enhanced versions of MS-COBOL. These apply only to old versions that may be in use.

(i)   Small and Capital Letters: MS-COBOL does not distinguish between small letters and capital letters except when the letters appear within a non-numeric literal.

(ii) PROGRAM-ID Paragraph: The paragraph is essential and must be specified. The program name appearing in this paragraph must begin with a letter and can consist of letters, digits and hyphen(-). Only the first six characters are retained by the compiler.

*(iii) Figurative Constants: Figurative constants ZERO, SPACE, LOW-VALUE, HIGH-VALUE and QUOTE including plural forms are available. In addition to these, ALL literal has also been implemented. However, the literal in this case, must be a single character non-numeric literal or a figurative constant. For example,

    01   STARS   PIC   X(10)   VALUE   IS   ALL "*"

is valid in MS-COBOL while

    01   HEADING-LINE-2   PIC   X(30)   VALUE   IS   ALL "*-*"

is not valid because the literal after ALL contains three charac-ters.

(iv) Non-numeric Literal: A non-numeric literal can be delimited either by quotation marks (") or apostrophes (') and may contain any combination of ASCII characters not exceeding 120 characters in length. Thus both

"BISHOP'S   CANDLESTICKS"   and   'BISHOP''S CANDLESTICKS'

are valid as non-numeric literals.

*(v)   Alphabet Name: The only alphabet name that is available is ASCII which is also the NATIVE as well as STANDARD-1 alphabet. As such any clause that uses alphabet name such as PROGRAM COLLATING SEQUENCE in OBJECT-COMPUTER, alphabet-name IS clause in SPECIAL-NAMES or CODE-SET clause in FD entry, must quote the alphabet name as ASCII. These are, therefore, used only for documentation purposes.

(vi)   Alphabetic Items: In general, alphabetic items are treated as alphanumeric items and no distinction is made between the two classes. However, the class condition test ALPHABETIC is available.

*(vii)   Condition Names: Condition names are supported. However, the 88-level entry must specify either a single value, a list of values or a range of values. Any combination of values and ranges or multiple ranges are not allowed. Consider the following example.

```
05   CENTRE-CODE          PIC    9(2).
88   CALCUTTA             VALUE IS  10.
88   EAST-ZONE            VALUES ARE 10 THRU 17.
88   MAJOR-CENTRE         VALUES ARE 10 20 21 30 40 43.
88   VALID-CENTRE         VALUES ARE 10 THRU 17  20 THRU
                          26 30 THRU 38  40 THRU 45.
```

The last one (VALID-CENTRE) is not permitted because it contains multiple ranges.

*(viii)   RENAMES Clause: This clause is not implemented.

*(ix)   OCCURS with DEPENDING Clause: While OCCURS is available, OCCURS with DEPENDING ON option is not supported.

(x)   USAGE Clause: Only one form of DISPLAY usage is available. USAGE IS DISPLAY means that data should be stored internally in ASCII format. This is also the default usage. There are three forms of COMPUTATIONAL specification - COMPUTATIONAL (or COMP), COMPUTA-TIONAL-0 (or COMP-0) and COMPUTATIONAL-3 (or COMP-3). USAGE IS COMP denotes that the item is capable of taking part in computation and compiler checks to ensure that it is a numeric item. However, internally the data is stored in decimal form as if it were defined with DISPLAY. COMP-0 defines a 16-bit binary integer field. It is also assumed to be a signed field regardless of whether sign (S in PIC) is specified or not. With a COMP-0 item, PIC 9, PIC 9(2)...., PIC 9(5) can be specified but they are all equivalent to PIC 9(5). A COMP-3 data item is stored in packed decimal form. It is similar to COMP-3 item described in the text (see Sec. 8.1).

*(xi)   Arithmetic Verbs: All the arithmetic verbs namely, ADD, SUBTRACT, MULTIPLY, DIVIDE and COMPUTE are supported. However, multiple destinations are not allowed. For example, all the following statements

```
SUBTRACT        5    FROM        A    B
ADD        A   B   C   GIVING        D    E
MULTIPLY        A   BY        B        GIVING        C    D
```

will be treated as invalid because they use multiple result fields. The REMAINDER phrase in DIVIDE statement is not supported.

*(xii)   CORRESPONDING Option: MOVE, ADD and SUBTRACT statements with CORRESPONDING option are not available.

*(xiii)   ALTER Statement: An ALTER statement can modify only one paragraph. Thus the statement

```
ALTER     MODIFIED-TRANSFER      TO    PROCEED    TO    OTHER-TIMES
          NEW-TRANSFER     TO    PROCEED    TO    NEW-GATE
```

is not valid. Two ALTER statements should be used.

*(xiv)   INSPECT Statement: A field can be inspected for comparison/ replacement by only single character field. Therefore,

```
INSPECT     MY-FIELD      REPLACING      ALL    "XY"    BY    "AB"
```

is not valid.

Moreover, series of specifications in TALLYING as well as REPLACING options are not permitted. For example, the following statements will not be accepted.

```
INSPECT     FIELD-A        REPLACING      ALL    "X"    BY    "A",
            "Y"    BY        "B",  "Z"    BY        "C".
```

This should be done by three INSPECT statements.

(xv)   Report-Writer: This module is not implemented.

*(xvi)   COPY Statements: Only a very simplified form of COPY statement is available. The format is

```
COPY        file-name
```

where the file-name denotes a disk file containing the text to be copied. This file should be a text file and can be created by EDLIN or any other text editor. The statement must be the last statement of the line in which it appears. It can be used anywhere in the ENVIRONMENT, DATA or PROCEDURE divisions.

21.8   FILE HANDLING

In a PC, a file can be either a PRINTER or a DISK file. Therefore, the
ASSIGN clause has the following form

$$ \underline{ASSIGN} \qquad TO \qquad \left\{ \begin{array}{c} \underline{DISK} \\ \underline{PRINTER} \end{array} \right\} $$

We shall consider PRINTER files first.

21.8.1   PRINTER File

The SELECT clause as usual may optionally contain RESERVE clause, ORGANIZA-
TION IS SEQUENTIAL clause, ACCESS MODE IS SEQUENTIAL clause and FILE STATUS
clause in addition to ASSIGN clause. Except for ASSIGN and FILE STATUS,
the others are not important because RESERVE clause is not functional (this
is also true for DISK files) and the other two (ORGANIZATION and ACCESS
MODE clauses) in the said form are the default.

The FD entry in the FILE SECTION must contain LABEL RECORD clause with
OMITTED option. Fully functional LINAGE clause is available for PRINTER
files (see Sec. 13.7.1). RECORD CONTAINS, DATA RECORDS and CODE-SET
clauses may be included for documentation purposes.

Since a PC supports only dot matrix printers and not line printers,
CHANNEL-n/mnemonic-name cannot be specified with ADVANCING phrase in WRITE
statement. The ADVANCING phrase can specify either PAGE or a number of
LINE/LINES. The number specified should have a value between 0 to 120.
The 0 value means no spacing, 1 means single line spacing and so on. Thus

        WRITE   PRINT-REC   AFTER   ADVANCING   0 LINE

will over-print the line on the previous line printed.

21.8.2   DISK File

A disk file can have any one of the following four organizations:

        LINE SEQUENTIAL
        SEQUENTIAL
        RELATIVE
        INDEXED

The ORGANIZATION clause within the SELECT clause should select an appropriate organization for the file.

Records are accessed sequentially in both LINE SEQUENTIAL and SEQUENTIAL
files. A record in a LINE SEQUENTIAL file is terminated by carriage return
and line feed delimiters. COMP-0 or COMP-3 items should not be written onto
LINE SEQUENTIAL file because data value may have the same binary code as
those of carriage return and line feed characters. A record in a SEQUENTIAL
file is preceded by a 2-byte record length. Thus internally LINE SEQUENTIAL

and SEQUENTIAL files have different formats. As mentioned earlier, LINE SEQUENTIAL files are generally created by non-COBOL programs such as text editors (like EDLIN). However, such files can also be created by COBOL programs, if required.

A RELATIVE file or an INDEXED file can be accessed sequentially, randomly or dynamically as specified through the ACCESS MODE clause. Records in a RELATIVE file are fixed length records; the length is equal to that of the largest record described for the file. An INDEXED file internally consists of two files — a key file and a data file. The file title provided in the VALUE OF clause (discussed afterwards) specifies the data file which contains the records. The key file has the same file name as the data file but its extension is .KEY. The user need not do anything for this file. The file is created automatically by the system software. The key file holds the key values, pointers to keys and pointers to data. It has a rather complicated structure known as prefix B + tree (see Comer, 1979). However, compared to usual structure (see Sec. 16.2) it provides faster access to records. Moreover, the structure does not get degraded as a result of subsequent insertions.

As regards the COBOL features, there is not much change from what have been described for disk files in this book. Statements that are available for SEQUENTIAL files also apply for LINE SEQUENTIAL files. Important implementation limitations and differences are listed below.

   (i)   RESERVE clause: This clause is available but is not functional. Only syntax checking is done.

 *(ii)   RERUN clause: The RERUN clause in the I-O-CONTROL paragraph is not implemented.

(iii)   BLOCK CONTAINS clause: This clause is also available for syntax checking and is not functional.

 (iv)   LABEL RECORDS clause: This clause with the STANDARD option must be specified in the FD entry for any disk file.

  (v)   VALUE OF clause: This clause specifies the file title. The format is

$$\text{\underline{VALUE}} \quad \text{\underline{OF}} \quad \text{\underline{FILE-ID}} \quad \text{IS} \quad \left\{ \begin{array}{l} \text{data-name-1} \\ \text{literal-1} \end{array} \right\}$$

The literal-1 must be a non-numeric literal containing the file title of the form drive-code: file-name. extension. The drive-code part and/or extension part may be omitted. Some examples are given below.

```
VALUE   OF   FILE-ID      "A:TRANS1.DAT"
VALUE   OF   FILE-ID      "PRODUCT.JAN"
VALUE   OF   FILE-ID      "TOOLS"
```

When data-name-1 is used, the data name should contain the file title terminated with a space character. For example, the VALUE OF clause may be

        VALUE   OF   FILE-ID   FILE-TITLE

where FILE-TITLE is a data-name defined in the WORKING-STORAGE SECTION as follows

        01   FILE-TITLE   PIC X(12)   VALUE   "PRODUCT.JAN".

Because the field length is 12, there will be a space after the name.

(vi)   START statement for INDEXED file: The data name in the KEY phrase of the START statement for an INDEXED file must only be the record key. It cannot be an alphanumeric data item representing leftmost part of the record key (see START statement in Sec. 16.2.2).

*(vii) ALTERNATE RECORD KEY for INDEXED file: The ALTERNATE RECORD KEY option is not implemented.

(viii) DECLARATIVES and FILE STATUS clause: In general, the user should either specify the AT END/INVALID KEY phrases with the input-output statements or should specify DECLARATIVES with appropriate USE statement (see Sec. 13.10). This is required for the handling of error/exception conditions. If this is not done, error messages are given (at compile time or at run time depending on the computer/compiler). In MS-COBOL, FILE STATUS clause has been given a superior role. If this clause is used, both DECLARATIVES as well as AT END/INVALID KEY phrase can be dropped. The program (Fig. 21.7) presented at the end of this chapter illustrates this with several input-output statement. Also note that DECLARATIVES and USE statement are available only for SEQUENTIAL files.

21.9 SORT/MERGE FEATURES

The SORT/MERGE facility may not be available in all versions of MS-COBOL. When available, the features are fully implemented. The following points may be noted. The SELECT clause for the work file is

        SELECT   file-name   ASSIGN   TO   DISK

            SORT STATUS   IS   data-name-1

The SORT STATUS clause is similar to the FILE status clause and data-name-1 must be a two-character alphanumeric field. After successful completion, the value "00" is stored in data-name-1. In the case of a SORT/MERGE error, an appropriate error code is stored in this field.

    The SD entry in the DATA DIVISION may have only the RECORD CONTAINS, DATA RECORDS and VALUE OF FILE-ID clauses. Each of these clause is optional.

21.10 INTER-PROGRAM COMMUNICATION

The Inter-Program communication features which support subroutine facilities as described in chapter 19 of this book, are available with the following exceptions:

*(i) The CANCEL statement is not implemented.

*(ii) The CALL statement is supported in the following simplified form:

>   CALL literal-1 [USING data-name-1 [data-name-2] ...]

>   Note that identifier in place of literal-1 and ON OVERFLOW phrase are not supported. The literal-1 must quote the name that appears in the PROGRAM-ID paragraph of the called program (subroutine). Only the first six characters of the name which must begin with a letter, is used by the compiler.

In addition to the above facilities, there is a CHAIN statement which can be used to call separately linked program. The format of the CHAIN statement is as follows:

$$\text{CHAIN} \quad \begin{Bmatrix} \text{literal-1} \\ \text{identifier-1} \end{Bmatrix} \quad [\ \underline{\text{USING}}\ \{\text{identifier-2}\}\ ...\ ]$$

The literal-1/identifier-1 must specify the program being chained. When identifier-1 is used the chained program name must be its value and there must be a terminating space following the name.

Let us consider the following example. Suppose we have two programs PROG1 and PROG2. Let the last statement to be executed in PROG1 be

>   CHAIN   "PROG2.EXE".

instead of a STOP RUN. Suppose that both the programs have been separately compiled and linked and the executable run units (load modules) are stored on disk under the names PROG1.EXE and PROG2.EXE. If we now execute PROG1, the program will run as usual until the CHAIN statement is encountered. At this point PROG2 will be loaded and control will be transferred to PROG2 so as to enable it to run. Note that PROG1 including all its data areas will be destroyed from the memory.

The USING option of the CHAIN statement can be used to transfer data from the chaining program to chained program. In this case, the PROCEDURE DIVISION header of the chained program should be as follows:

>   PROCEDURE DIVISION [CHAINING {data-name-1}...]

The parameters in the CHAIN statement and that in the PROCEDURE DIVISION header should match with each other in terms of description. The data-name-1 should be described in the WORKING-STORAGE SECTION.

It should be noted that CHAIN statement is quite different from the CALL statement. The CALL statement transfers control to a program within

the same run unit whereas the CHAIN statement transfers control to a
different run unit. In the case of a CALL statement control returns to the
calling program after the completion of the called program. This question
does not arise in the case of a CHAIN statement because the chaining program is destroyed. However, a chained program can chain another program
including the one that chained it. However, at one point of time only one
program will remain in the memory. The main use of the CHAIN statement is
to split a large program into smaller programs and to run them in a chain.

21.11 DEBUG AND COMMUNICATION MODULES

ANSI-74 COBOL provides guidelines for two modules called debug and communication modules. The debug module is useful for program testing and the
communication module enables one to communicate with other computers by
sending and receiving messages. We have not discussed these features in
this book because these are rarely implemented. These modules are also not
available in MS-COBOL. However, MS-COBOL provides powerful but non-standard
debugging features. These being beyond the scope of the present book are
not included here.

21.12 SCREEN AND ACCEPT/DISPLAY VERBS

The screen and keyboard of a PC/PC-XT provide a powerful means for direct
interaction between the user and the computer. The screen may be used
interactively to display messages that interrogate and the keyboard may be
used to receive responses from the user. Normally, the response also gets
displayed on the screen.

An interactive program establishes a dialogue with the user. In most
cases, the dialogue is passive in the sense that the program opens the
dialogue and the user simply responds to it through the keyboard. A dialogue can be designed in the following manner:

- Interrogation
- Menu Selection
- Form Filling.

Interrogation means that the program asks for certain data by displaying
suitable message or question. The user responds by entering the requested
data. In the case of menu selection, the program presents a number of
alternatives to the user by displaying these appropriately and the user is
asked to choose one of the alternatives by entering a suitable code. For
example, a program may display the following menu:

Menu (colour)

1. BLACK
2. BLUE
3. GREEN
4. RED
5. YELLOW

ENTER CHOICE :

If the user responds by entering 3, the program will know that he has chosen GREEN and will act accordingly. Form Filling means that the program will display a form on the screen and will expect the user to enter data at various positions on the form. A simple form filling example is discussed later in this section.

In order to enable the programmer to write interactive programs for the kind of dialogues described above, the ACCEPT and DISPLAY verbs in MS-COBOL have been substantially enhanced. Though these are MS-COBOL enhancements, similar facilities are also available in many other modern COBOL compilers. As such, we discuss these enhancements in the following. It is needless to mention that apart from dialogue design, the enhanced DISPLAY verb can also be used to display results in suitable format. One can even display graphical figures by putting suitable characters at various positions on the screen.

21.12.1 Scrolling and Non-scrolling Modes

The screen of PC/PC-XT can be operated in any one of the two modes — scrolling and non-scrolling. When operated in the scrolling mode, after each ACCEPT or DISPLAY, all the lines on the screen move up by one line each. When the screen operates in the non-scrolling mode, the screen becomes fixed. The screen has 25 lines and each of these lines consists of 80 character positions known as columns. Thus in the non-scrolling mode there are altogether 25 × 80 = 2000 positions each of which can be referenced by a pair of numbers. For example, (5, 10) denotes tenth column position on the fifth line.

21.12.2 Simple ACCEPT/DISPLAY Verbs

The simple forms of the ACCEPT and DISPLAY verbs are similar to those described in the text (see Secs 6.5.5 and 6.5.6). When these forms are used, the screen is assumed to be in the scrolling mode. In the case of ACCEPT, no prompt is displayed but the cursor remains stationary awaiting input. Data keyed in from the keyboard is to be terminated by pressing the enter key. Data can also be accepted from system by specifying DATE, DAY or TIME. In the case of DISPLAY, if PRINTER is specified for mnemonic-name then display takes place on the printer. If the UPON phrase is omitted, display takes place on the screen.

21.12.3 ACCEPT/DISPLAY Verbs with Position Specification

The enhanced ACCEPT/DISPLAY verbs can accept or display data starting from a specified position of the screen. The screen is assumed to be in the non-scrolling mode. Some examples are given below.

Example 1

          ACCEPT (5, 15) A.

The value of A will be accepted beginning from position (5, 15) that is, from the 15th column position of the 5th line. The cursor will move to this position and the program will wait for user's response. When the value of A has been entered and the Enter key has been pressed, the value will move from screen to A.

Example 2

          DISPLAY (10, 20) "MESSAGE"

The word MESSAGE will appear on the screen beginning from column position 20 of line number 10.

Example 3

          DISPLAY (5, 1)   "WHAT IS YOUR NAME ?"
          ACCEPT   (5, 25)   NAME.

The sentence WHAT IS YOUR NAME? will be displayed on the fifth line beginning from the first column position. After that the cursor will move to column position 25 of the same line and the program will wait for user's response. This example shows how interrogation type of dialogues can be implemented.

     The complete format of these verbs with position specification are shown below

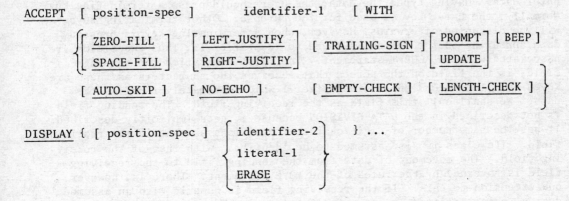

ACCEPT [position-spec]   identifier-1   [WITH

$$\left\{ \begin{bmatrix} \text{ZERO-FILL} \\ \text{SPACE-FILL} \end{bmatrix} \begin{bmatrix} \text{LEFT-JUSTIFY} \\ \text{RIGHT-JUSTIFY} \end{bmatrix} [\text{ TRAILING-SIGN }] \begin{bmatrix} \text{PROMPT} \\ \text{UPDATE} \end{bmatrix} [\text{ BEEP }] \right.$$

[AUTO-SKIP]   [NO-ECHO]   [EMPTY-CHECK]   [LENGTH-CHECK] }

DISPLAY { [position-spec] $\left\{ \begin{array}{l} \text{identifier-2} \\ \text{literal-1} \\ \text{ERASE} \end{array} \right\}$ } ...

where position-spec has the following format:

$$\left(\left[\begin{array}{l} \underline{\text{LIN}} \ [\ \{\pm\} \quad \text{integer-1} \ ] \\ \text{integer-2} \end{array} \right] \quad \left[\begin{array}{l} , \ \underline{\text{COL}} \ [\ \{\pm\} \quad \text{integer-3} \ ] \\ , \ \text{integer-4} \end{array} \right] \right)$$

The following rules may be noted.

(i) The position-spec part specifies the line position and column position. A comma separates them. There must be a blank space after the comma. LIN and COL are special registers in MS-COBOL which behave like numeric data fields defined with COMP-0 usage. User program can use these as data names without describing them in DATA DIVISION.

        MOVE   10 TO LIN.   MOVE   15   TO   COL.

        DISPLAY   (LIN, COL - 3)   FIELD-A

will have the same effect as

        DISPLAY   (10, 12) FIELD-A

The line position part or the column position part can be omitted. In that case, current line or current column will be assumed. For example,

        ACCEPT   (, 10)   A

will mean that data for A will be accepted from column position 10 of the current line.

(ii) Identifier-1 which is used with ACCEPT statement should be either alphanumeric or numeric. ACCEPT also allows input to edited fields (alphanumeric or numeric), but we do not discuss it here because this is not very useful.

(iii) When an ACCEPT statement is executed, the user is expected to enter data. Having typed the data, the user should press a terminating key. Normally, the Enter key is used for the purpose. Other terminating keys will be discussed afterwards. However, when a terminating key is pressed, data appearing on the screen is moved to identifier-1. Thus two fields are associated with an ACCEPT statement. The first one called the sending field, is the field on the screen that receives the characters as these are keyed in. The second one is identifier-1 which ultimately receives the data. We shall call this field as the receiving field. The sending field is not described in the DATA DIVISION because it gets implicitly described. It has the same number of digit/character positions as that in the receiving field. Its class is also assumed to be identical with that of the receiving field. The movement of data from the sending field to the receiving field is governed by the rules of the MOVE statement. There is, however, one exception to this. If the receiving field is numeric with an assumed decimal point position, a decimal point (.) must be entered in the sending field in place of the assumed position. Of course, this decimal point will

not be moved into the receiving field. For example, suppose that identi-
fier-1 is described with PIC 9(4)v99 and we have entered 34.2 in the sending
field then the data loaded in identifier-1 will be 003420. Also note that
it is not necessary to key-in digits/characters for all the positions of the
sending field. The unkeyed positions will be filled with zeros or spaces as
described below.

    (iv) The WITH phrase in the ACCEPT statement can have several options.
Some of these namely, LEFT-JUSTIFY, RIGHT-JUSTIFY, TRAILING-SIGN, ZERO-FILL,
SPACE-FILL and NO-ECHO are concerned with the format in which the sending
field data should appear on the screen after the ACCEPT statement has been
executed. The others are concerned with the key-in operation in response
to the ACCEPT statement.
    LEFT-JUSTIFY or RIGHT-JUSTIFY can be specified only for alphanumeric
fields. Data will appear on the screen left justified or right justified
depending on the option chosen. The default is LEFT-JUSTIFY. The TRAILING-
SIGN should be specified only for numeric fields. When the option is specified, operational sign character (+ or -), if any, will appear after the
rightmost digit position. If omitted, the sign character, if any, will
appear on the left of the leftmost digit position. ZERO-FILL or SPACE-FILL
can be specified to state that unkeyed positions should be filled with zeros
or spaces respectively. The default is ZERO-FILL for numeric fields and
SPACE-FILL for alphanumeric fields. If SPACE-FILL is specified for a
numeric field, space filling takes place only at the leading unkeyed positions. Moreover, any leading operational sign appears on the immediate left
of the most significant digit. NO-ECHO means that the data typed for the
sending field will appear on the screen as asterisks (*) but it will be
moved to the receiving field as usual. This is helpful for security purposes.
    To avoid any confusion, let us make it clear once again that the above
mentioned options apply only to the appearance of input data on the screen
and not to the receiving field. Thus RIGHT-JUSTIFY will not place the data
in identifier-1 in right justified manner. If this is required, JUSTIFIED
RIGHT clause should be specified for identifier-1. Similarly, when identi-
fier-1 is numeric, digit positions corresponding to the unkeyed positions
of the sending field, will have zeros regardless of whether ZERO-FILL or
SPACE-FILL is specified.
    LENGTH-CHECK ensures that all digit/character positions are keyed-in.
Therefore, terminating keys will be ignored until all the positions are
full. EMPTY-CHECK ensures that at least one digit/character position is
keyed-in. No terminating key will be accepted until this requirement is
satisfied. AUTO-SKIP means that data will be accepted as soon as characters
for all the positions have been typed. It will not wait for any terminating
key to be pressed. Moreover, if any terminating key is pressed before all
the positions are filled-in, it will have its usual effect. PROMPT is a
very useful option. If PROMPT is specified, each of the input positions on
the screen will display a prompt which is either a period (.) or a zero
depending on whether identifier-1 is alphanumeric or numeric respectively.
In the case of numeric fields, the positions of decimal point and sign, if
any, are prompted with a period (.) and a space respectively. The prompt

provides the user with a visual idea about the length and class of the expected input data. If UPDATE option is specified, the current contents of identifier-1 are displayed on the screen. If Enter key is now pressed without pressing any character key, the same value is accepted as if the characters were keyed-in by the user. However, if some characters are also typed before pressing the Enter key, the action depends on the class of expected input. In case of alphanumeric data, the unkeyed characters remain unchanged and in case of numeric data, the old value of identifier-1 is completely changed by the new value typed. The BEEP option causes an audible alarm to be sounded when the program is ready for CCEPT. This may be useful to draw user's attention at the time of input through ACCEPT.

(v) The DISPLAY statement causes the value of identifier-2/literal-1 to be displayed beginning from the specified position. In order to obtain the display in edited form, identifier-2 should preferably be an edited field. When the ERASE option is used, the portion of the screen beginning from the specified position to the end of the screen is cleared. Thus

          DISPLAY (1, 1)   ERASE

has the effect of clearing the entire screen.

Example of ACCEPT with some of the above mentioned options are shown below.

Example 4

Suppose NUMB-A is described with PIC S9(4)V9 and its current value is 0032∧7.   Let us note the effect of the following ACCEPT statement.

ACCEPT (10, 20) NUMB-A WITH PROMPT TRAILING-SIGN.

At the beginning the following prompt will appear on the screen starting from position (10, 20)

     0000.0∦

The space (∦) is the effect of TRAILING-SIGN. If this were not specified, space would appear at the leftmost position. Note the position of the cursor (denoted by -). Now suppose that the user types the characters 1, 2, 3, ., 4 and - successively. The changes on the screen are shown below.

     0001.0∦   0012.0∦   0123.0∦   0123.0∦   0123.4∦   0123.4 $\bar{}$

If the Enter key is pressed now, the value at NUMB-A will be

     0123∧$\bar{4}$

Example 5

Suppose DATA-A is described with PIC X(5). Let us consider the following statement

          ACCEPT (1, 1) DATA-A WITH RIGHT-JUSTIFY PROMPT.

At the start of the ACCEPT statement the prompt will be as follows:

Suppose that the user types the character A,B,C successively. The changes on the screen are shown below.

          A . . . .   A B . . .   A B C . .

If the Enter key is pressed now, the display on the screen will be ∅∅ABC but the value stored at DATA-A will be ABC∅∅. Note that RIGHT-JUSTIFY will cause the appearance of ABC on the screen to be right justified but will not have any effect on the input to DATA-A.

21.12.3.1 TERMINATING KEYS

The entry of the data to be accepted by an ACCEPT statement is normally terminated by pressing the Enter key. However, the entry can also be terminated by pressing the Function keys (F1 to F10) and Escape key (Esc) besides some other keys (see manual for these). It is also possible to determine which key has been pressed for terminating the input. There is a special form of ACCEPT statement for this purpose. The format is

          ACCEPT   identifier-3   FROM ESCAPE KEY

Identifier-3 should be a two-digit integer field. Upon execution of this statement, identifier-3 will have a value that will indicate the key that terminated the most recently executed ACCEPT statement. The values are shown below.

KEY	VALUE
Enter key	00
Escape key	01
F1 - F10	02-11

Example 6

Consider the following statement

```
ACCEPT      (15, 1)    A.
ACCEPT   ESC-VALUE    FROM    ESCAPE   KEY.
IF   ESC-VALUE = 2    GO    TO    PARA-F1.
```

In this case, control will be transferred to PARA-F1 if the entry for A is terminated by pressing the F1 key.

This is a powerful facility which can enable us to make the function keys operational by the program.

21.12.4 Two Programs Showing the use of ACCEPT/
DISPLAY with Position Specification

We shall now present two programs. The first program creates a LINE SEQUENTIAL file by accepting data from the screen. Each record of the file created by the program has only two fields — NAME (described with X(20)) and AGE (described with 9(3)). To provide ease for data entry, the program displays the form shown in Fig. 21.2. The user responds by entering data against NAME and AGE. Note that cursor is placed in appropriate positions by the program itself. To terminate the program, the function key F1 is to be pressed when the data for NAME is requested. The program is shown in Fig. 21.3.

```
------------------------------------------
                  FILL THE FORM
------------------------------------------

     NAME :  ............................

     AGE :

------------------------------------------
```

FIG. 21.2 A Form for Data Entry

The second program illustrates how graphical figures can be displayed. The program given in Fig. 21.4 asks for an integer. The value entered is taken as the number of lines to be displayed. The program then displays lines consisting of asterisks (*). The first line contains one asterisk,

```
            IDENTIFICATION DIVISION.
            PROGRAM-ID.  TEST.
            ENVIRONMENT DIVISION.
            CONFIGURATION SECTION.
            INPUT-OUTPUT SECTION.
            FILE-CONTROL.
                SELECT OUT-FILE ASSIGN TO DISK
                     ORGANIZATION IS LINE SEQUENTIAL.
            DATA DIVISION.
            FILE SECTION.
            FD OUT-FILE
                LABEL RECORDS ARE STANDARD
                VALUE OF FILE-ID  "MYFILE.DAT".
            01   OUT-REC.
                 05   NAME        PIC X(20).
                 05   AGE         PIC 9(3).
            WORKING-STORAGE SECTION.
            01   ALL-HYPHEN       PIC X(30) VALUE ALL "-".
            01   ESC-CODE         PIC 99.
            PROCEDURE DIVISION.
            DISPLAY-FORM.
                    OPEN OUTPUT OUT-FILE.
                    DISPLAY (1, 1) ERASE.
                    DISPLAY (1, 1) ALL-HYPHEN.
                    DISPLAY (2, 10) "FILL THE FORM".
                    DISPLAY (3, 1) ALL-HYPHEN.
                    DISPLAY (5, 1) "NAME :".
                    DISPLAY (6, 1) "AGE :".
                    DISPLAY (8, 1) ALL-HYPHEN.
            FILL-THE-FORM.
                    ACCEPT (5, 10) NAME WITH PROMPT.
                    ACCEPT ESC-CODE FROM ESCAPE KEY.
                    IF ESC-CODE = 2 GO TO FINISH-ENTRY.
                    ACCEPT (6, 10) AGE WITH PROMPT.
                    WRITE OUT-REC. GO TO FILL-THE-FORM.
            FINISH-ENTRY.
                    CLOSE OUT-FILE WITH LOCK.
                    STOP RUN.
```

FIG. 21.3. A Form Filling Program.

```
IDENTIFICATION DIVISION.
PROGRAM-ID. TEST.
ENVIRONMENT DIVISION.
DATA DIVISION.
WORKING-STORAGE SECTION.
01  I       PIC  9(2)  COMP-0.
01  J       PIC  9(2)  COMP-0.
01  M       PIC  9(2)  COMP-0.
01  T-CH    PIC  X.
01  N       PIC  9(2).
PROCEDURE DIVISION.
1.
    DISPLAY  (1, 1) ERASE.
    DISPLAY  (4, 1) "HOW MANY LINES?".
    ACCEPT (4, 20) N WITH    PROMPT.
2.
    PERFORM 3 VARYING I
        FROM 1 BY 1 UNTIL 1 > N.
    DISPLAY (25, 1)  "PRESS ANY KEY TO TERMINATE".
    ACCEPT  (25, 30) T-CH  WITH  PROMPT.
    STOP RUN.
3.
    SUBTRACT 1 FROM I GIVING J.
    MULTIPLY J BY 2 GIVING M.
    ADD 1 TO M.
    SUBTRACT J FROM 40  GIVING COL.
    ADD 8 I GIVING LIN.
    PERFORM 4 VARYING J
        FROM 1 BY 1 UNTIL J > M.
4.
    DISPLAY (LIN, COL)  "*".
    ADD 1 TO COL.
```

FIG. 21.4.   A Program to Display a Triangular
             Figure of Asterisks.

the second three asterisks, the third five asterisks and so on. The figure
looks like a triangle of asterisks and is shown in Fig. 21.5.   The program
illustrates the use of LIN and COL.

21.13 ACCEPT/DISPLAY VERBS WITH SCREEN SECTION

MS-COBOL offers more powerful forms of ACCEPT and DISPLAY verbs such that
a single ACCEPT/DISPLAY statement can accept/display data for several fields

HOW MANY LINES?   07

```
                                          *
                                         ***
                                        *****
                                       *******
                                      *********
                                     **********
                                    *************
```

PRESS ANY KEY TO TERMINATE

FIG. 21.5.   Triangle of Asterisks Displayed by
             Program in Fig. 21.4.

on the screen. However, these fields need to be described in an exclusive
section of the DATA DIVISION known as SCREEN SECTION. The SCREEN SECTION
is a non-ANSI feature of MS-COBOL and if used, should appear as the last
section of DATA DIVISION. The format of this section is shown below.

SCREEN SECTION.

      screen-description-entry.

The screen description entry can be either a group item or an elementary item that should be involved during ACCEPT, DISPLAY or both. An
elementary item describes an individual field on the screen. A group item
describes a group of items that may be involved by a single ACCEPT/DISPLAY
statement. A group item or an elementary item begins with a level number
similar to that in the other sections. The level numbers must be in the
range 01 to 49. The level number in the screen description entry, is
followed optionally by a screen name which is a user defined name like a
data name. The purpose of the screen name is to use it in the ACCEPT or
DISPLAY statement. The screen name is followed by several clauses meant
for a complete description of the said entry. However, before we go into
these clauses, let us present the general formats of the ACCEPT and DISPLAY
statements.

ACCEPT   screen-name   [ON ESCAPE   imperative-statement]

DISPLAY   screen-name

The ON ESCAPE phrase in the ACCEPT statement may be specified to gain
control when a terminating key other than the Enter key, is pressed. Note
that the ACCEPT statement is expected to receive values for several fields.
However, during its execution, if any terminating key other than the Enter
key is pressed the entire ACCEPT is terminated, an appropriate ESCAPE KEY
value is set and the imperative statement in the ON ESCAPE phrase, if

specified, is executed. The value set for the ESCAPE KEY and the manner in which this value can be interrogated, is identical to what has been described in the previous section in connection with the terminating keys.

The screen name appearing in the ACCEPT/DISPLAY statement is obviously a name described in the SCREEN SECTION. An elementary item described under a screen name, is distinguished as an input field, an output field or an input-output field depending on how it has been described. Note that the same screen name can be used in ACCEPT as well as in DISPLAY statement However, only the values for input and input-output fields will be accepted by an ACCEPT. Similarly, the contents of output and input-output fields are the only things that will be displayed by a DISPLAY statement.

Let us now see how a screen item may be described. We consider the elementary item first. A screen description entry for an elementary item in the simple form is shown below.

     level-number [screen-name] [location-specification] field-specification.

The location specification indicates the starting position on the screen wherefrom the desired item should be accepted/displayed. The format for the location specification is as follows:

[LINE NUMBER IS [PLUS] integer-1] [COLUMN NUMBER IS [PLUS] integer-2]

The LINE clause denotes the line number on the screen and COLUMN clause denotes the column position on the line. When PLUS is used, it means that current line number (line number of last item prescribed) or the current column number (column position of the last item described) plus the value of integer-1 or integer-2 respectively. When a 01 level screen item is encountered, the current line number as well as the current column number is assumed. If both clauses are omitted, current position is assumed. When LINE is specified but COLUMN is omitted, column position 1 of the said line is assumed.

The field specification describes how the field should appear on the screen after DISPLAY or ACCEPT statement. However, it also indicates the receiving field to which the data should be moved during an ACCEPT or the source field from which the data should be brought to the screen during a DISPLAY. The general format for field specification is given below.

$$\left\{ \begin{array}{l} [[\text{ VALUE }] \quad \text{IS} \quad \text{literal-1}] \\[2mm] [\left\{ \begin{array}{l} \underline{\text{PICTURE}} \\ \underline{\text{PIC}} \end{array} \right\} \text{IS} \quad \text{character-string} \left\{ \begin{array}{l} [\underline{\text{FROM}} \left\{ \begin{array}{l} \text{literal-2} \\ \text{identifier-1} \end{array} \right\}] \; [\underline{\text{TO}} \text{ identifier-2}] \\[3mm] [\underline{\text{USING}} \text{ identifier-3 }] \end{array} \right\}] \end{array} \right\}$$

The PICTURE clause describes the screen item in the usual way through the character string. Any valid picture character (including editing characters) can appear in the character string. When TO clause is used, the screen item becomes an input item and is used only during an ACCEPT. It has no effect during a DISPLAY. When the VALUE or FROM clause is used, the screen item becomes an output item and is used only during a DISPLAY. It has no effect during an ACCEPT. Identifier-2 indicates the receiving field to which the accepted data should be moved from the screen. Similarly literal-1, literal-2 or identifier-1 indicates the source of the data to be displayed. Note that both FROM and TO can be used for the same screen item. In that case, the field becomes an input-output item and is used during DISPLAY as well as ACCEPT. USING has the combined effect of TO and FROM. Thus USING identifier-3 is equivalent to FROM identifier-3 TO identifier-3. Identifiers in the field specification may be qualified but cannot be subscripted.

The group item in the simplest form consists of level number and the screen name.

Let us consider a few examples of screen description entries.

Example 1

05 LINE 10 COLUMN 15 PIC X(10) FROM ORDER-NO.

This elementary item is an output item and will be involved only during a DISPLAY that quotes the screen name of the group to which it belongs. The source field is ORDER-NO which is described elsewhere in the DATA DIVISION. The value of ORDER-NO will be displayed in 10 positions starting from the position (10, 15) on the screen. The DISPLAY statement will move the value of ORDER-NO to this screen field with PIC X(10) and usual rules for the MOVE statement will apply.

Example 2

05 COLUMN 20 VALUE IS "What is your name?"

This is also an output item and during a DISPLAY involving this screen item, the value of the literal will be displayed starting from column position 20 of the current line.

Example 3

10 LINE 5 COLUMN PLUS 2 PIC 9(5)V99 TO ACC-NO.

This is an input field and will be involved only during an ACCEPT associated to this field. The value will be accepted from line number 5 starting from a position which is given by the current column number plus 2. When the value has been entered on the screen, ACCEPT will move it to ACC-NO which is the receiving field described elsewhere in the DATA DIVISION. The usual rules of the MOVE statement (with the exceptions mentioned for ACCEPT with position specification) will apply.

Example 4

```
01 MY-SCREEN.
    05  LINE  2  COLUMN  5  VALUE  "ENTER DATE".
    05  COLUMN  15  PIC  X(6)  USING  TRANS-DATE.
    05  LINE  5  COLUMN  5  VALUE  "ORDER NUMBER".
    05  COLUMN  15  PIC  X(7)  TO  ORDER-NO.
```

In the case of DISPLAY MY-SCREEN, all the elementary screen items except
the last one (being a input item) will be displayed. In the case of ACCEPT
MY-SCREEN, only the second and the last screen items will be involved.
Because of the USING clause in the second item, the current value of TRANS-
DATE will be displayed during ACCEPT. The date can be changed by reentering
a new date. If Enter key is pressed without typing any character, the same
value will be accepted (it is similar to UPDATE option described in the
previous section). As regards the last item, a prompt consisting of seven
consecutive periods (.) will appear on the screen starting from the position
(5, 15). When the value has been entered, it will be moved to ORDER-NO. In
this connection note that for all fields described with TO clause, ACCEPT
displays a prompt as in the case of PROMPT option described in the previous
section. A screen description entry may have many more optional clauses in
addition to what has been described above. The general format for an
elementary item is as follows:

        level-number   [screen-name]

    [BLANK SCREEN] [location - specification] [BLANK LINE] [BELL]

    ⎧ ⎡ UNDERLINE   ⎤ ⎫
    ⎪ ⎢   ⎥ ⎪
    ⎨ ⎢ REVERSE-VIDEO   ⎥ ⎬ field-specification [BLANK WHEN ZERO]
    ⎪ ⎢ HIGHLIGHT   ⎥ ⎪   ⎡ ⎧ JUSTIFIED ⎫   ⎤
    ⎩ ⎣ BLINK   ⎦ ⎭   ⎢ ⎨ JUST   ⎬ RIGHT   ⎥
                                         ⎣ ⎩   ⎭   ⎦

    [AUTO] [SECURE] [REQUIRED] [FULL]
```

When BLANK SCREEN is specified, the entire screen is erased and the cursor
is placed in the home position (1, 1).  On the other hand, BLANK LINE erases
the part of the current line starting from the current position to the end
of the line.  When BELL is used, an audible alarm is sounded when the said
screen field is to be accepted.  UNDERLINE means that the characters in the
said screen field should be displayed with underline.  Similarly, REVERSE-
VIDEO means that character will appear in black on white background instead
of the usual white on black background.  Note that REVERSE-VIDEO when speci-
fied, applies only to characters in the said field and not to any other
```

part of the screen. HIGHLIGHT means that the characters will appear in bold form. BLINK means that the characters will be flashed and erased alternately when displayed on the screen. BLANK WHEN ZERO and JUSTIFIED RIGHT have the usual meanings but apply to the screen item only and not to the source or receiving fields. AUTO, SECURE, REQUIRED and FULL respectively correspond to AUTO-SKIP, NO-ECHO, EMPTY-CHECK, LENGTH-CHECK described in connection with ACCEPT verb with position specification (see previous section). Except for the change of name there is no other change in respect of these options.

The clauses mentioned above can be specified in any order. However, during execution the actions will take place in the following order:

    BLANK SCREEN
    LINE/COLUMN positioning
    BLANK LINE
    ACCEPT/DISPLAY of data

It may be noted that ACCEPT/DISPLAY with SCREEN SECTION is an alternative facility for ACCEPT/DISPLAY with position specification. Either of these forms can be used to do the same thing. Of course, ACCEPT/DISPLAY with SCREEN SECTION has a few additional facilities like UNDERLINE, REVERSE-VIDEO, HIGHLIGHT and BLINK. Both the forms work on the screen in non-scrolling mode.

A group item in the SCREEN SECTION has the following general format

    level-number [screen-name]

    [AUTO] [SECURE] [REQUIRED] [FULL]

These clauses have the same meanings as in the case of elementary items except that when these are specified at the group level, they apply to all the elementary items in the group.

21.13.1 Program with SCREEN SECTION

A complete program with SCREEN SECTION is shown in Fig. 21.6. This is an alternative version of the program given in Fig. 21.3 of Section 21.12.1. The use of HIGHLIGHT clause makes the displayed form slightly different. The program can be terminated during any ACCEPT by pressing the Esc key.

21.14 A CASE-STUDY IN INTERACTIVE PROGRAMMING

As a final example, we present a program that updates an indexed sequential file interactively. It can also be used for the first-time creation of the file and to enquire the contents of any record stored in the file. Each record of this file consists of three fields namely, ACC-NO, BALANCE and LAST-DATE representing respectively account number, current balance and the last date of transaction. The key field is ACC-NO. At the start of the execution, the program asks for the current date. When the date has been

```
IDENTIFICATION DIVISION
PROGRAM-ID. TEST.
ENVIRONMENT DIVISION.
CONFIGURATION SECTION.
INPUT-OUTPUT SECTION.
FILE-CONTROL.
    SELECT OUT-FILE ASSIGN TO DISK
        ORGANIZATION IS LINE SEQUENTIAL.
DATA DIVISION.
FILE SECTION.
FD OUT-FILE
    LABEL RECORDS ARE STANDARD
    VALUE OF FILE-ID  "MYFILE.DAT".
01  OUT-REC.
    05  NAME        PIC X(20).
    05  AGE         PIC 9(3).
SCREEN SECTION.
01  CLEAN-SLATE.
    05  BLANK SCREEN.
01  FORM-FORMAT.
    05 LINE 1 COLUMN 1  PIC X(30) FROM ALL "-".
    05 LINE 2 COLUMN 10 VALUE "FILL THE FORM"  HIGHLIGHT.
    05 LINE 3 COLUMN 1  PIC  X(30) FROM ALL "-".
    05 ENTRY-PART.
       10 LINE 5.
           10  COLUMN 1 VALUE  "NAME:".
           10  COLUMN 10 PIC X(20)  TO NAME.
       10 LINE 6.
           10  COLUMN 1 VALUE  "AGE:".
           10  COLUMN 10 PIC 9(3)  TO AGE.
    05 LINE PLUS 2 PIC X(30) FROM ALL "-".
PROCEDURE DIVISION.
DISPLAY-FORM.
    OPEN OUTPUT OUT-FILE.
    DISPLAY CLEAN-SLATE.
    DISPLAY FORM-FORMAT.
FILL-THE-FORM.
    ACCEPT FORM-FORMAT
            ON ESCAPE GO TO FINISH-ENTRY.
    WRITE OUT-REC.
    GO TO FILL-THE-FORM.
FINISH-ENTRY.
    CLOSE OUT-FILE WITH LOCK.
    STOP RUN.
```

FIG. 21.6. A Form Filling Program with Screen Section.

entered, the program wants to know whether the indexed file (title is assumed to be SAMPLE   for the data file and SAMPLE.KEY for the associated key file) exists or not. If the user enters N (capital or small), an empty file is created just by opening and closing the file. This enables the user to create the file through subsequent insertions. If the user enters any character other than N, an existing file is assumed. Once these initializations are over, the program displays the main menu in the following form and waits for the user to respond by entering his choice (1, 2 or 3).

    Enter Choice
    1. To Enquire
    2. To Update
    3. To Terminate

If the response is 1, the program asks for the account number and having accepted it, displays the contents of BALANCE and LAST-DATE (see ENQUIRE and associated paragraphs in the program). If the response is 3, the program terminates. When 2 is chosen, the program displays a second menu which is shown below

    Enter Choice
    1. To Insert
    2. To Delete
    3. To Modify

If 1 is chosen, the value for account number, balance and date are asked one after another. In the case of date, the program displays the current date. If only Enter is pressed, current date is taken. However, user may also enter any other date by typing the same. Having obtained the values of the three fields, the program inserts the record in the file and after successful insertion displays OK (see INSERT-RECORD and associated paragraphs).

    If 2 is chosen, the program asks the account number and having accepted it, deletes the record from the file. After successful deletion, OK is displayed (see DELETE-RECORD and associated paragraphs).

    If 3 is chosen, the program displays a third menu which is as follows.

    Enter Choice
    1. Deposit
    2. Withdrawal
    3. Correction

Whatever be the choice, the program successively asks the account number, amount of transaction and date. In the case of a deposit, amount is added with the existing balance. In the case of a withdrawal, the amount is subtracted from the balance (no checking has been provided for negative balance, to keep the program simple). In the case of a correction, amount replaces the balance. In all cases, the date is updated by the date that has been entered. As in the case of an enquiry, here also current date is accepted, if Enter key is pressed without typing any date (see MODIFY-RECORD and associated paragraphs).

Having completed a transaction or an enquiry, the program returns to the main menu. Whenever the user enters a wrong choice (other than 1, 2 and 3), the program returns to the main menu. In the case of an error (for example, modification of a non-existing record, insertion of a record having the same key as that of an existing record, etc.) the program displays an appropriate message asks the user to press the Enter key to return to the main menu (see GIVE-A-MESSAGE paragraph). The program is shown in Fig.21.7. We invite the reader, to go through the program and to discover for himself, how these interactive features have been implemented.

```
            IDENTIFICATION DIVISION.
            PROGRAM-ID. TEST.
            ENVIRONMENT DIVISION.
            INPUT-OUTPUT SECTION.
            FILE-CONTROL.
                SELECT INDEXED-FILE ASSIGN TO DISK
                    ORGANIZATION IS INDEXED ACCESS MODE
                    IS RANDOM RECORD KEY IS ACC-NO
                    FILE STATUS IS STATUS-OF-FILE.
            DATA DIVISION.
            FILE SECTION.
            FD INDEXED-FILE
                LABEL RECORDS ARE STANDARD
                VALUE OF FILE-ID IS "SAMPLE".
            01   INDEX-REC.
                02   ACC-NO  PIC   X(7).
                02   BALANCE      PIC   9(7)V99.
                02   LAST-DATE    PIC   9(6).
            WORKING-STORAGE SECTION.
            01   STATUS-OF-FILE   PIC   X(2).
            88   DUPLICATE-KEY    VALUE IS   "22".
            88   MISSING-KEY      VALUE IS   "23".
            88   NO-ERROR         VALUE IS   "00".
            01   INPUT-DATE.
                02   I-DAY        PIC   9(2).
                02   FILLER       PIC   X.
                02   I-MTH        PIC   9(2).
                02   FILLER       PIC   X.
                02   I-YEAR       PIC   9(2).
            01   NUMERIC-DATE.
                02   N-DAY        PIC   9(2).
                02   N-MTH        PIC   9(2).
                02   N-YEAR       PIC   9(2).
            01   THIS-DATE        PIC   X(8).
```

(contd.)

```
        01   CHOICE          PIC  9.
        01   UPDATE-CODE     PIC  9.
        01   FLAG            PIC  X.
        01   ACCOUNT-NO      PIC  9(7).
        01   AMOUNT          PIC  9(7)V99.
        01   EDIT-AMOUNT     PIC  Z(6)9.99.
        01   EDIT-DATE       PIC  99/99/99.
        PROCEDURE DIVISION.
        MAKE-A-START.
            DISPLAY  (1, 1) ERASE.
            DISPLAY  (5, 20) "Enter Date (DD/MM/YY)"
            ACCEPT   (7, 20) INPUT-DATE WITH PROMPT.
            MOVE INPUT-DATE TO THIS-DATE.
            DISPLAY (10, 20) "Do you have an existing file (Y/N)?"
            ACCEPT (11, 20) FLAG.
            IF FLAG = "N" OR "n"
                    OPEN OUTPUT INDEXED-FILE CLOSE INDEXED-FILE.
            OPEN I-O INDEXED-FILE.
        DISPLAY-MENU.
            DISPLAY  (1, 1) ERASE.
            DISPLAY  (5, 1) "Enter Choice".
            DISPLAY  (7, 1) "1  To Enquire".
            DISPLAY  (8, 1) "2  To Update".
            DISPLAY  (9, 1) "3  To Terminate".
            ACCEPT   (11, 1) CHOICE.
            IF CHOICE = 3
                CLOSE INDEXED-FILE WITH LOCK  STOP RUN.
            IF CHOICE = 2
                PERFORM UPDATE-RECORD
            ELSE IF CHOICE = 1
                    PERFORM ENQUIRE.
            GO TO DISPLAY-MENU.
        UPDATE-RECORD.
            DISPLAY (7, 1) ERASE.
            DISPLAY (7, 1) "1  To Insert".
            DISPLAY (8, 1) "2  To Delete".
            DISPLAY (9, 1) "3  To Modify".
            ACCEPT (11, 1) UPDATE-CODE.
            IF UPDATE-CODE = 1 PERFORM INSERT-RECORD
            ELSE  IF  UPDATE-CODE = 2
                        PERFORM  DELETE-RECORD
                  ELSE  IF  UPDATE-CODE = 3
                            PERFORM MODIFY-RECORD.
        INSERT-RECORD.
            PERFORM  GET-ACCOUNT-NO.
            DISPLAY (8, 1) "Balance"
```

(contd.)

```
        ACCEPT (8, 10) BALANCE WITH PROMPT.
        PERFORM GET-DATE.
        WRITE INDEX-REC.
        PERFORM GIVE-A-MESSAGE.
    GET-ACCOUNT-NO.
        DISPLAY (1, 1) ERASE.
        DISPLAY  (6, 1) "Account Number".
        ACCEPT (6, 17) ACCOUNT-NO WITH PROMPT.
        MOVE ACCOUNT-NO TO ACC-NO.
    GET-DATE.
        DISPLAY (10, 1) "Date (DD-MM-YY)".
        MOVE THIS-DATE TO INPUT-DATE.
        ACCEPT (10, 30) INPUT-DATE WITH UPDATE.
        PERFORM DATE-CONVERSION.
        MOVE NUMERIC-DATE TO LAST-DATE.
    GIVE-A-MESSAGE.
        IF NO-ERROR
        DISPLAY (14, 5)  "Ok".
        IF DUPLICATE-KEY
           DISPLAY (14, 5)  "Sorry, Record Already Exists".
        IF MISSING-KEY
           DISPLAY  (14, 5) "Sorry, Record Is Missing".
        IF NOT ( DUPLICATE-KEY OR MISSING-KEY OR NO-ERROR)
        DISPLAY (14, 5)  "Unknown Error".
        DISPLAY  (20, 1) "Press RETURN to go to Main Menu".
        ACCEPT FLAG.
    DELETE-RECORD.
        PERFORM  GET-ACCOUNT-NO.
        DELETE INDEXED-FILE.
        PERFORM GIVE-A-MESSAGE.
    MODIFY-RECORD.
        DISPLAY (7, 1) ERASE.
        DISPLAY (7, 1) "1  Deposit".
        DISPLAY (8, 1) "2  Withdrawal".
        DISPLAY (9, 1) "3  Correction".
        ACCEPT (11, 1) CHOICE.
        IF CHOICE = 1 OR 2 OR 3
                PERFORM MODIFY.
    MODIFY.
        PERFORM GET-ACCOUNT-NO.
        READ INDEXED-FILE INVALID KEY PERFORM GIVE-A-MESSAGE.
        IF NO-ERROR PERFORM MODIFY-IT.
    MODIFY-IT.
        DISPLAY (8, 1) "Amount".
        ACCEPT (8, 10) AMOUNT WITH PROMPT.
        IF CHOICE = 1
            ADD  AMOUNT TO BALANCE
```

(contd.)

```
                    ELSE IF CHOICE = 2
                            SUBTRACT AMOUNT FROM BALANCE
                    ELSE MOVE AMOUNT TO BALANCE.
              PERFORM GET-DATE.
              REWRITE INDEX-REC.
              PERFORM GIVE-A-MESSAGE.
        DATE-CONVERSION.
              MOVE I-DAY TO N-DAY.
              MOVE I-MTH TO N-MTH.
              MOVE I-YEAR TO N-YEAR.
        ENQUIRE.
              PERFORM GET-ACCOUNT-NO.
              READ INDEXED-FILE INVALID KEY
                    PERFORM  GIVE-A-MESSAGE.
              IF STATUS-OF-FILE = "00"
                  DISPLAY (1, 1) ERASE
                  DISPLAY (5, 10) "Account Number : ", ACC-NO
                  MOVE BALANCE TO EDIT-AMOUNT
                  DISPLAY (7, 10) "Balance : ", EDIT-AMOUNT
                  MOVE LAST-DATE TO EDIT-DATE
                  DISPLAY (9, 10) "Last Transaction On : ", EDIT-DATE
                  DISPLAY (20, 1) "Press RETURN to go to Main Menu"
              ACCEPT FLAG.
```

FIG. 21.7. An Interactive Updation Program.

21.15 REMARKS ON MS-COBOL

The MS-COBOL compiler, like any other software, is updated from time to
time. Naturally, several versions of MS-COBOL compiler are in use today.
A new version generally provides improved facilities in addition to the
existing ones. As such, a COBOL program written according to the features
described above, is expected to run satisfactorily under any version of MS-
COBOL compiler. However, at the same time one should remember that some of
the limitations mentioned herein may not be present in later versions. For
example, with release 2.1 onwards features for indexed sequential file
handling has been greatly enhanced. ALTERNATE KEY phrase is now available.
Another important change that has taken place with this release is that
COBOL compiler generates the compiled program in an intermediate code (with
extension .INT). No linking is necessary; the program can be executed
directly with the help of the RUNCOB command. Thus the commands for running
a simple COBOL program should be

```
    C > COBOL       program-name;
    C > RUNCOB      program-name
```

where program-name .COB is the name of the source file containing the COBOL
program.

EXERCISES

1. The command and responses to the prompts given during the compilation of a COBOL program are shown below

    C > COBOL   NEWCOB ↵
    Object file-name [NEWCOB.OBJ]: ↵
    Source listing [NUL.LST] : NEWCOB ↵

Where ↵ denotes the pressing of Enter key.

Write the DOS command to print the source listing produced by the compiler.

2. With reference to MS-COBOL, identify each of the following statement as true or false.

    (a) 'Microsoft Cobol' is a valid non-numeric literal

    (b) The data field described in the following will occupy 5 bytes in the memroy

        01   X   PIC   9(2)   COMP-O.

    (c) LABEL RECORDS clause is essential for a PRINTER file but can be omitted for disk files.

    (d) ACCEPT-DISPLAY verbs with position specification sets the screen in scrolling mode.

    (e) ACCEPT-DISPLAY verbs with SCREEN SECTION sets the screen in non-scrolling mode.

    (f) RENAMES and REDEFINES clauses are not allowed.

    (g) SCREEN SECTION when used, must appear in between FILE SECTION and WORKING-STORAGE SECTION.

3. The following program segments/statements may not be accepted by MS-COBOL compiler. Rewrite these so that they may become acceptable.

    (a) Description and use of a condition name are as follows:

    05   TRANS-CODE   PIC X.
    88   VALID-CODE   VALUES ARE 'A' THRU 'D' 'J' THRU 'M'.
    IF NOT VALID-CODE   GO TO 30.

    (b) INSPECT CHARACTER-STRING TALLYING

    TALLY-A FOR ALL "A" AFTER INITIAL ".".
    TALLY-B FOR LEADING "*".

    (c) SUBTRACT A B C FROM D E.

4. The following statements show the differences between a CALL and a CHAIN. One of these is wrong. Identify it.

    (a) CALL statement refers to the called program by the name that appears in the PROGRAM-ID paragraph (of called program) while

CHAIN statement refers to the chained program by the name of the load module (.EXE).

(b) The PROCEDURE DIVISION header for a called program may optionally have a USING phrase while that for a chained program may optionally have a CHAINING phrase.

(c) If necessary, a chained program can chain its chaining program. Similarly, a called program can call its calling program.

(d) The formal parameters in a **called** program must be described in the LINKAGE section while the parameter in a chained program should be described in the WORKING-STORAGE SECTION.

5. When ACCEPT statement is used with position specification several optional phrases are available. The corresponding facilities are also available through specifications in SCREEN SECTION. Some of the correspondences shown below are wrong. Identify these.

```
  (i)   SECURE and NO-ECHO
 (ii)   HIGHLIGHT and BEEP
(iii)   USING and UPDATE
 (iv)   FULL and EMPTY-CHECK
  (v)   JUSTIFIED RIGHT and RIGHT-JUSTIFY
```

6. Write a COBOL program that will ask for a name and will then display the initials. For example, if the name is given as GEORGE BERNARD SHAW, the program should display G.B.S. Assume that the individual names are separated by one or more spaces.

7. Write a COBOL program that will display the following menu:

```
1  Circle
2  Square
3  Triangle
4  Rectangle
Choose one shape
```

Depending on the choice, the program will display the shape filed with asterisks (*). You can assume suitable sizes for these shapes.

8. A LINE SEQUENTIAL file with the following record layout is to be created.

Field	Picture
Order Number	9(6)
Customer Number	9(5)
Salesman Number	9(4)
Date	9(6)
Number of items	9
Item groups (1 to 5 occurrences)	each consisting of
Product Code	X(6)
Quantity	9(5)V99

Write a COBOL program that will create this file and will enable data entry through form-filling. Assume a suitable form layout for this purpose.

9. Write COBOL statement(s) that will check whether the last ACCEPT (with position specification) was terminated by pressing F2 key or not. If F2 key was used as the terminating key, transfer control to the paragraph known as FUNC-TWO.

10. Recode the program given in Fig. 21.6 using SCREEN SECTION.

22

FEATURES OF COBOL - 85

22.1 INTRODUCTION

COBOL-85 is the new standard approved by American National Standards
Institute (ANSI) in 1985. This new standard is a substantial revision of
COBOL-74 (ANSI 74 COBOL). Several new statements and language features
have been included in COBOL-85 in addition to modifications to some of the
existing features. A few of the existing features of COBOL-74 have been
deleted or declared as obsolete. Since COBOL-85 is the first official
standard after the widespread acceptance of structured programming concepts,
the objective of a majority of the changes is to facilitate the writing of
structured programs in COBOL. Others are meant for general improvements in
the capabilities of the language.
    Most of the COBOL compilers in use today are, of course, based on
COBOL-74 standard and compilers fully implementing COBOL-85 features are
yet to come. However, compilers incorporating selected features of COBOL-
85 have already made their appearances. Gradually, more and more features
will be incorporated. As such, it is in the fitness of things that we
describe the important features of COBOL-85 in this chapter. In doing this,
we shall cover most of the new features and only the important amendments.
We shall not generally discuss the deletions because manufacturers are
expected to retain these features as their own extensions for the purpose
of compatibility with the earlier versions of their COBOL compilers.

22.2 COBOL-85 FEATURES FOR GENERAL
IMPROVEMENT OF THE LANGUAGE

For the purpose of discussion, the changes and enhancements incorporated in
COBOL-85 are classified here into two groups. The first group contains the
various features meant for the general improvement of the COBOL language.
The other group consists of the features specifically meant for structured
programming. In this section, we are going to present the elements of the
first group. The changes and enhancements in the language are introduced
in comparison with the existing features of COBOL-74 and earlier versions.

Therefore, a knowledge of the topics presented in the previous chapters is assumed to be the prerequisite. It may also be mentioned that no specific order is followed while presenting the individual features.

22.2.1 Program Structure

Every COBOL program begins with the IDENTIFICATION DIVISION header and ends with the last physical statement in the PROCEDURE DIVISION. According to the new standard, an optional END PROGRAM terminator can be used to mark the physical end of the program. The format is

> <u>END</u>   <u>PROGRAM</u>   program-name.

The program name is the name given in PROGRAM-ID paragraph. The complete programs given later in this chapter illustrate the use of this feature.

The END PROGRAM terminator as such, is not a great facility. Its introduction became necessary because in COBOL-85, it is possible to physically include one program within the scope of another program. The included program can in turn include yet another program within its scope and in this way one can have a "nesting" of programs. An included program is really a subroutine which is called by the including program. The structure of a COBOL program is shown below.

<u>IDENTIFICATION</u> <u>DIVISION</u>.

<u>PROGRAM-ID</u>.   program-name-1.

other-paragraphs-of-identification-division.

[<u>ENVIRONMENT</u> <u>DIVISION</u>.

environment-division-contents.]

[<u>DATA</u> <u>DIVISION</u>

data-division-contents.]

<u>PROCEDURE</u> <u>DIVISION</u>.

procedure-division-contents.

[nested-source-program] ...

<u>END</u>   <u>PROGRAM</u>   program-name-1.

The first point to note from the above is that the included program (indicated as nested-source-program) should be placed after the last physical statement of the PROCEDURE DIVISION of the including program. The included program should also have the above structure. The other point that should be noted is that the ENVIRONMENT DIVISION as well as the DATA DIVISION are now optional. Thus if a program does not require any file to be selected the entire ENVIRONMENT DIVISION can be omitted. The occasion for omitting DATA DIVISION arises only in the case of nested source programs, because these programs can reference the data described in their including programs and as such may not require any data to be described locally.

In the remaining part of this section, we shall deal with the nesting of programs and if desired, this part can be omitted during first reading. Let us consider the outline of a sample nesting of programs shown in Fig. 22.1 where each individual program is shown within a rectangle.

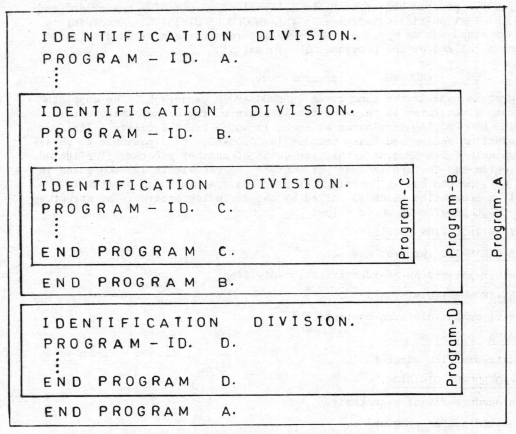

FIG. 22.1.   Outline Showing a Sample Nesting of Programs.

In this nesting, A is the outermost program. It directly includes B and D. The program C is directly included within B and indirectly included within A (because B is included in A). All the programs together determines the run unit.

One important feature of nesting is that any data name, file name, record name, condition name, index name or report name defined in an including program can be referenced by a directly or indirectly included program, provided the said name has been declared to be a global name by the use of GLOBAL clause. For example, suppose program A in Fig. 22.1 contains the following description.

```
01   DATA-X       PIC      9(5)      IS    GLOBAL.
```

Then as a result, DATA-X becomes a global name and can be referenced in the included programs (B, C or D). The format for the global clause is

IS <u>GLOBAL</u>

and the clause can be used only in 01 level entries, FD entries and RD entries. When the GLOBAL clause is used at a group level, it applies to all subordinate items. Any condition name or index name associated with a global data name is automatically treated as a global item.

It is just possible that an included program describes a name which is identical to a global name described in an including program. For example, in the program outlined in Fig. 22.1, let DATA-X be described as global in A. Let DATA-X be also described in C without the GLOBAL clause. Now, any reference to DATA-X in C, will mean the local DATA-X (i.e., the DATA-X described in C). However, any reference to DATA-X in B will mean the global DATA-X. The rule in this matter is as follows.

A name referenced in a program is taken to be the name described within the program itself. If no description for the name is found in the referencing program, the name in the program that most directly contains the referencing program is taken. For example, let DATA-X be separately described as global in A as well as in B. Then any reference to DATA-X in A or D will mean the item described in A. Note that reference to DATA-X in C will mean the global item in B and not the global item in A because B contains C more directly.

An item described in an included program is not normally available to its including program or any program outside its scope. However, if an item is described with the EXTERNAL clause, it can be referenced by any program in the run unit. The format of this clause is

IS <u>EXTERNAL</u>

and can be used just like the GLOBAL clause. However, the clause should not be used with REDEFINES clause. Moreover, the VALUE clause should not be specified for an external item. An external item is not treated as part of the program which contains its description. In fact, all external items are placed together in an area common to all the programs in the run unit.

To accommodate nesting of programs the syntax of the <u>PROGRAM-ID</u> paragraph has been extended. The format of this paragraph is

<u>PROGRAM-ID</u>. program-name [IS $\left\{\begin{matrix} \underline{COMMON} \\ \underline{INITIAL} \end{matrix}\right\}$ PROGRAM.]

The two vertical lines including COMMON and INITIAL indicate that either of these or both can be used. A nested program without the COMMON clause can be called only from the program that contains it. If the nested program contains the COMMON clause, it can be called from the containing program or any program contained within the containing program. In Fig. 22.1, if B is declared as common through the use of COMMON clause then it can be called from A as well as from D. It cannot be called from D unless B is declared as common. The COMMON clause should be used only for the nested programs. The INITIAL clause indicates that whenever the program is called, it will be available in the initial state rather than the last-used state (see Sec. 19.3). Thus a program having the INITIAL clause gets implicitly cancelled after every call.

At the end of this chapter we shall illustrate the use of nesting of programs through an example.

22.2.2 Nameless Data Description Entry

A data description entry may not use any data name. For example,

```
05      PIC   9(6)      VALUE   ZERO.
```

is now a valid data description entry. The compiler will treat it as a FILLER entry. Thus the above description is equivalent to

```
05      FILLER    PIC       9(6)      VALUE   ZERO.
```

Moreover, the word FILLER is now allowed even at the group level. For example,

```
01   FILLER.
     02      DATA - 1    PIC   X(3).
     02      DATA - 2    PIC   9(4)V99.
```

is quite valid.

22.2.3 De - Editing

COBOL-85 allows the movement of numeric edited data item to a numeric data item through the MOVE verb. This will result in the de-editing of the value. For example, consider the following data description entries:

```
02      EDITED-FIELD        PIC   ZZZ9.99.
02      UNEDITED-FIELD      PIC   9(4)V99.
```

Now, after the execution of the following MOVE statements

```
MOVE   245.5   TO    EDITED-FIELD
MOVE      EDITED-FIELD    TO     UNEDITED-FIELD.
```

EDITED-FIELD and UNEDITED-FIELD will contain ƀ245.50 and 0245 ⋀ 50 respectively. Note that such move was not allowed in COBOL-74.

22.2.4 ADD with GIVING Phrase

An optional word TO has been added in the syntax for the ADD statement with the GIVING option. In the simplified case (that is, without the SIZE ERROR and ROUNDED phrases) the format is

$$\underline{ADD} \left\{ \begin{array}{l} \text{identifier-1} \\ \text{literal-1} \end{array} \right\} \dots \text{TO} \left\{ \begin{array}{l} \text{identifier-2} \\ \text{literal-2} \end{array} \right\} \underline{GIVING} \text{ identifier-3}$$

Thus ADD A TO B GIVING C is now valid. This is equivalent to ADD A B GIVING C.

22.2.5 Relational Condition

The following relational operators have been added to the existing list of relational operators. These have the usual meanings.

        IS GREATER THAN OR EQUAL TO
        > =

        IS LESS THAN OR EQUAL TO
        < =

Thus

       (i)   IF BASIC-PAY NOT < 500 MOVE 1 TO SALARY-CODE
      (ii)   IF BASIC-PAY > 500 OR = 500 MOVE 1 TO SALARY-CODE
     (iii)   IF BASIC-PAY > = 500   MOVE 1 TO SALARY-CODE

are equivalent. Note that (iii) is not allowed in COBOL-74. Further, note that unlike the other relational operators, NOT cannot be used with these new relational operators. Thus BASIC-PAY NOT > = 500 (to mean BASIC-PAY < 500) is incorrect.

22.2.6 Class Condition

An alphabetic data may consist of uppercase letters, lowercase letters and the space character. To test the contents of an alphabetic or alphanumeric field, three class tests have been provided in COBOL-85. These are

     IS [NOT] ALPHABETIC

     IS [NOT] ALPHABETIC-UPPER

     IS [NOT] ALPHABETIC-LOWER

The ALPHABETIC test checks for uppercase letters, lowercase letters and space. The ALPHABETIC-UPPER checks for uppercase letters and space. Similarly, the ALPHABETIC-LOWER checks for lowercase letters and space. The last two are new additions. There is no change in respect of NUMERIC test. Consider the following statement as an example of the new test.

     IF   FIELD-A IS NOT ALPHABETIC-UPPER
              MOVE   9   TO   CLASS-CODE.

The value 9 will be moved to CLASS-CODE if FIELD-A contains any character other than uppercase letters and space.

In COBOL-85, there is also provision for user defined class as well as the corresponding class test. This is not a very important feature and we shall not discuss it here.

22.2.7 REDEFINES Clause

According to COBOL-85 a redefined data item can be equal or smaller in size than that of the data item it redefines. Note that in COBOL-74, the two must be equal (see Sec. 8.4). For example,

```
02   DATA-A          PIC     X(12).
02   DATA-B          REDEFINES DATA-A.
     03   FIELD-A     PIC     9(3)V99.
     03   FIELD-B     PIC     99.
```

is now allowed.

22.2.8 Table Handling

There are a number of changes related to OCCURS clause and the associated language elements. These are listed below.

(i)   A table may have upto 7 dimensions. In COBOL-74, a table was limited to only 3 dimensions.

(ii) VALUE clause can appear with the OCCURS clause. In that case, all elements of the table are set to the same value. For example,

```
01   MY-TABLE.
     02   TABLE-DATA     OCCURS   10   TIMES   PIC 9(4)  VALUE 1.
```

is now allowed. All elements namely, TABLE-DATA(1) .... TABLE-DATA(10) will be initialized to 1. (See also INITIALIZE verb described afterwards.) This was not permitted in COBOL-74.

(iii) The minimum number of occurrences that can be specified through OCCURS with DEPENDING phrase is zero. In COBOL-74, this was 1. For example, now the following description is allowed.

```
01   REC-1.
     02   A1     PIC   99.
     02   P1     PIC   XX.
     02   P2     PIC   99.
          OCCURS  0 TO 90 TIMES DEPENDINC ON A1.
```

(iv) According to COBOL-74 standard, a subscript could be either a literal or any identifier denoting a positive integral value. In COBOL-85, relative subscripting is also allowed. This means that expression like I+1 or J+3 are now permitted as subscripts. Note that relative indexing was permitted even in COBOL-74.

22.2.9 INITIALIZE Verb

A new INITIALIZE verb has been introduced. The syntax is

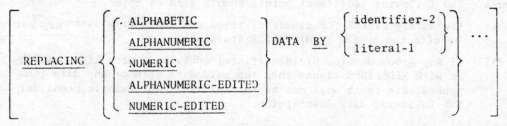

The purpose of this verb is to initialize identifier-1 which can be either
a group item or an elementary item. When identifier-1 specifies a group
item, only those items that belong to the category denoted by the REPLACING
phrase will be initialized by the value denoted by identifier-2/literal-1.
For example, let us consider the following data description in the WORKING-
STORAGE SECTION.

```
01  A.
    02  A1    PIC    9(5).
    02  A2    PIC    X(4).
    02  A3    PIC    9(3).
    02  A4    PIC    Z(3)9.99.
```

Now, the statement

```
INITIALIZE  A  REPLACING  NUMERIC  DATA  BY  50
```

will initialize only A1 and A3 by the specified value because these are the
only numeric fields within A. However, the following statement

```
INITIALIZE A
    REPLACING   NUMERIC  DATA  BY  50
    REPLACING   ALPHANUMERIC  DATA  BY  "A"
    REPLACING   NUMERIC-EDITED  DATA  BY  54.2
```

will initialize all the fields within A.

   The initialization process is equivalent to the execution of a sequence
of implicit MOVE statements where the sending field is identifier-2/literal-1
and the receiving field is the elementary items of identifier-1 picked up
for initialization. The fields are initialized in the sequence they appear
within the group denoted by identifier-1. Thus the already mentioned second
INITIALIZE statement will initialize A1,A2,A3 and A4 to 00050, Aℬℬℬ, 050 and
ℬℬ54.20 respectively.

   When identifier-1 is an elementary item then the initialization takes
place only if the category mentioned in the REPLACING phrase matches with
that of identifier-1. Note that the REPLACING phrase is optional. If it is

omitted, all numeric fields are initialized to zero and all other fields are initialized to spaces. Thus

INITIALIZE   A

will initialize A1 and A3 to zero values. A2 and A4 will be filled with spaces. The following additional points should also be noted.

(i)   Elementary FILLER (or nameless) items and index data items may not be affected by the INITIALIZE statement.

(ii) If any group denoted by identifier-1 contains a data item describ- ed with REDEFINES clause then the said data item or any data item subordinate to it will not be initialized. For example, consider the following data description.

```
01   A.
     02  A1              PIC  9(5).
     02  A2              PIC  X(10).
     02  B  REDEFINES   A2.
         03  B1          PIC  9(4).
         03  B2          PIC  9(4)V99.
```

Now, if we write INITIALIZE A, then A1 will be filled with zeros and A2 will be filled with spaces. It will be wrong to assume that A2 will be filled with zeros because B1 and B2 are not initialized. However, identi- fier-1 can contain a REDEFINES clause or may be subordinate to an item containing REDEFINES clause. For example,

INITIALIZE   B

will place zeros in all positions of A2 because B1 and B2 will be initializ- ed to zero values.

Identifier-1 or any item subordinate to it may also contain OCCURS clause. In that case all occurrences will be initialized. For example, let a table be defined as

```
01   A.
     02  B         PIC   9(5)   OCCURS   20   TIMES.
```

Now, INITIALIZE A will set all elements of the table to zero. The INITIA- LIZE verb is functionally similar to the MOVE verb when the latter is used for initialization. However, a single INITIALIZE statement can be equiva- lent to several MOVE statements. The function of INITIALIZE verb is also similar to the VALUE clause. The difference is that initialization through VALUE clause takes place only once at the beginning of program execution whereas the INITIALIZE statement can be used as and when necessary.

22.2.10 SET Verb with TRUE Phrase

In COBOL-74 and in earlier versions, there was no way to set a condition name to TRUE or FALSE except by having a suitable value assigned to the

conditional variable. For example, suppose a condition name is described
as follows

```
01  TAX-CODE     PIC  9.
88  EXEMPTED     VALUE  IS  ZERO.
```

Now, to set EXEMPTED to TRUE, we must move (explicitly or implicitly) a
zero value to the conditional variable TAX-CODE. While, this indirect way
of assigning TRUE value to a condition name still remains valid, COBOL-85
has a direct alternative. We can use the statement

```
SET    EXEMPTED    TO    TRUE
```

for the said purpose. This will not only set EXEMPTED to TRUE it will also
move a zero value to TAX-CODE. The syntax of this SET verb is

```
SET    { condition-name }  ...      TO  TRUE
```

Note that the condition name can be set to TRUE (and not to FALSE) by this
SET statement. When a list of values is specified in the condition name
description entry, the first listed value will be moved to the conditional
variable. For example, consider the following

```
05  PROD-CODE      PIC  99.
88  SOFTWARE       VALUES  ARE  10  THRU  19.
```

Now, SET SOFTWARE TO TRUE will cause 10 to be moved to PROD-CODE. Note that
this form of the SET verb is a new addition. There is no change in respect
of the existing SET verb that operates on index names and index data items.

22.2.11 Reference Modification

In COBOL-85, it is possible to reference part of a data field by specifying
the leftmost character position and length. For example, let us consider
the following data description entry

```
05  DATA-FIELD   PIC  X(11)   VALUE   "MATHEMATICS".
```

Now, the statement

```
MOVE   DATA-FIELD   (4: 2)  TO   OLD-FIELD
```

will move the value "HE" to OLD-FIELD. Here DATA-FIELD (4: 2) is a reference modification denoting two consecutive bytes starting from the fourth
byte position (from left) within DATA-FIELD. The syntax for reference
modification is

```
data-name  (leftmost-character-position :  [length] )
```

Note that length specification is optional and if omitted, all the remaining
bytes of the data field will be referenced. For example, MOVE DATA-FIELD
(3:) TO OLD-FIELD will move the value "THEMATICS" to OLD-FIELD.
There must be a space after the delimiter colon (:). The leftmost
character position as well as the length can be a literal, an identifier or
an arithmetic expression denoting a positive integral value.

The data name whose reference is modified can be of any class and category, but it should have DISPLAY usage. When a reference modification is used, the data item denoted by the data name is treated as if it were an alphanumeric data item. The data item created by reference modification is considered to be an elementary item and can be used anywhere an elementary alphanumeric data item is allowed. However, it should not be used for the sending field in an UNSTRING statement or for the receiving field in a STRING statement.

The introduction of reference modification has caused two changes in the COBOL language. First of all, colon (:) was not present in the COBOL character set; it had to be included. Secondly, the definition of an identifier had to be extended so as to treat a reference modification as an identifier.

The facility provided through reference modification is also available through appropriate use of REDEFINES and RENAMES clauses. Essentially, it enables us to create and reference a subordinate field without explicitly defining it in the DATA DIVISION. As such, it may save some coding effort required in the DATA DIVISION (see Ex. 6 at the end of this chapter). However, such saving in terms of coding effort goes against the spirit of COBOL where a major emphasis is on self documentation of programs.

22.2.12 INSPECT Verb with CONVERTING Option

Three forms of this verb were introduced in COBOL-74 (see Sec. 17.2). Now, the fourth form of this verb has been provided. The syntax of this new INSPECT verb with CONVERTING option is shown below.

$$\underline{\text{INSPECT}}\ \text{identifier-1}\ \underline{\text{CONVERTING}}\ \begin{Bmatrix} \text{identifier-2} \\ \text{literal-1} \end{Bmatrix}\ \underline{\text{TO}}\ \begin{Bmatrix} \text{identifier-3} \\ \text{literal-2} \end{Bmatrix}$$

$$\begin{bmatrix} \begin{Bmatrix} \underline{\text{BEFORE}} \\ \underline{\text{AFTER}} \end{Bmatrix}\ \text{INITIAL}\ \begin{Bmatrix} \text{identifier-4} \\ \text{literal-3} \end{Bmatrix} \end{bmatrix}\ \ldots$$

Like INSPECT with REPLACING option, this option can also be used to replace matched characters in identifier-1 by certain other characters. Identifier-2/literal-1 and identifier-3/literal-2 provide the basis for matching and replacement. We shall refer to these fields as subject field and object field respectively. These two fields must be of identical size so that corresponding to each character in the subject field, there be a character in the object field. A character in identifier-1 is selected for replacement only if the said character is also found in the subject field. It is then replaced by the corresponding character in the object field. For example, let us consider the statement

INSPECT FIELD-A CONVERTING "ABCDE" BY "EDCBA".

Now, if FIELD-A contains "ABBREVIATE" before the execution, it will contain

"EDDRAVIETA" after the execution of the said INSPECT statement. In general,

    INSPECT   A   CONVERTING   B   TO   C

is equivalent to

    INSPECT   A   REPLACING   ALL   B(1: 1)   BY   C   (1: 1)
                                                B(2: 1)   BY   C   (2: 1)
                                                ....
                                                $B(n: 1)$ BY   C $(n: 1)$

where n is a literal denoting the size of B as well as C. However, INSPECT with CONVERTING option is more convenient. An actual use of this option is illustrated in the first example of Sec. 22.4.

    The BEFORE and AFTER phrases have the same meanings as in the case of other options. All identifiers must have DISPLAY usage explicitly or implicitly.

22.2.13   CONTINUE Verb

The CONTINUE statement is yet another addition in COBOL-85. It indicates no operation. The format is

<u>CONTINUE</u>

It can be used anywhere a conditional statement or an imperative statement may be used. For example,

    READ   FILE-A   RECORD   AT   END   CONTINUE.

is used when we are sure that the end of file condition will not arise during the execution of this READ statement.

    The CONTINUE statement is functionally similar to the EXIT statement but their objectives are different. While EXIT should be used to have a common end point for a sequence of paragraphs, CONTINUE can be used anywhere when a null path is required. It can also be used in IF statements in place of NEXT SENTENCE phrase.

22.2.14   File Handling

Several changes most of which are of minor nature have been made in the features concerning file handling. We do not wish to discuss all these minor changes because file handling is largely dependent on the operating system of a particular computer and deviations from the standard are quite common. Therefore, we restrict only to the important changes.

    (i)   ASSIGN clause: The syntax of the ASSIGN clause has been modified to

$$\underline{ASSIGN} \quad TO \quad \left\{ \begin{array}{l} \text{implementor-name} \\ \text{literal} \end{array} \right\}$$

The literal is a new addition and is expected to denote file specification. For example,

SELECT MY-FILE ASSIGN TO "SALARY".

will select the sequential file named SALARY on the user's disk. This form of the ASSIGN clause eliminates the need for using VALUE OF clause in FD entry which has now been made obsolete (that is, VALUE OF may be deleted from COBOL in future revision).

(ii) FD entry: All clauses in FD entry including the LABEL RECORDS clause are optional. A new form of RECORD clause specifically meant for files with variable length records, has been added. The format of this clause is shown below.

RECORD IS VARYING IN SIZE [[FROM integer-1] [TO integer-2]

CHARACTERS] [DEPENDING ON data-name-1]

This clause is in addition to the existing RECORD CONTAINS clause for fixed length records. Let the clause be specified in the following manner:

RECORD IS VARYING IN SIZE FROM 72 TO 96 CHARACTERS

DEPENDING ON COUNT-WORD.

The actual size of the record (which must be between 72 and 96) is determined by the value of COUNT-WORD. When the DEPENDING phrase is omitted, the length is determined from the record description which may contain a variable part defined through the OCCURS with DEPENDING phrase (see Sec. 13.6.2 for an example of such a description).

(iii) File status codes: File status codes have been discussed earlier (see Sec. 13.10 and Table 16.2). Many of the codes were either undefined or left for the implementor to define. In COBOL-85, 25 new file status codes have been defined. For example, the code 04 means that the length of the record that has been read, is inconsistent with the record description. We would advise the reader to consult the manual for the actual codes implemented on the system to be used.

(iv) SORT and MERGE statements: The input and output procedures for the SORT statement and the output procedure for the MERGE statement need not be coded as one or more consecutive sections. They can be coded as consecutive paragraphs because the INPUT PROCEDURE and OUTPUT PROCEDURE phrases can now refer to paragraph names also. A new optional phrase with the syntax

WITH DUPLICATES   IN ORDER

has been added within the SORT verb. When used, it will mean that among the records with identical keys, the original relative order should be maintained (compare with (vi) in Sec. 14.1). The following example shows how to use the phrase.

```
SORT  WORK-FILE  ON  ASCENDING  KEY  DEPARTMENT
      DESCENDING  KEY  BASIC-PAY
      WITH  DUPLICATES  IN  ORDER
      USING  IN-FILE  GIVING  OUT-FILE.
```

Moreover, in COBOL-85, multiple file names can be given in the GIVING phrase of the SORT and MERGE verbs to have multiple output files. The files named in the USING and GIVING phrases of MERGE statement can have sequential, relative or indexed organization.

(v)   START statement: To have parity with the newly introduced relational operators, the START statement has been enhanced. The statement will now accept the following additional forms of the KEY phrase (see Secs. 16.1.2 and 16.2.2).

$$\underline{\text{KEY}} \text{ IS} \left\{ \begin{array}{l} \underline{\text{GREATER}} \text{ THAN OR } \underline{\text{EQUAL}} \text{ TO} \\ \underline{>\ =} \end{array} \right\} \text{data-name}$$

These have the same meaning as the KEY IS phrase with NOT LESS THAN or NOT < option.

22.2.15 USAGE Clause

Two more usages have been specified in the standard. These are BINARY and PACKED-DECIMAL. The exact internal representation will obviously depend on the computer system and compiler. In most cases, BINARY will be same as COMP and PACKED-DECIMAL will be identical to what has been described as COMP-3 in this book (see Sec. 8.1).

22.2.16 COBOL Subroutines

In COBOL-85, parameters can be passed to a subroutine either by reference or by content. If a parameter is passed by reference, the calling program as well as the called program refer to the same storage area for the value of the parameter. Thus if the called program changes the value of the formal parameter, it will be reflected in the value of the actual parameter. On the other hand, if a parameter is passed by content, the formal and actual parameters do not share the same storage area. At the time of calling, a copy of the current value of the actual parameter is passed to the formal parameter. Therefore, if the called program changes the value of the formal parameter, the change will not be reflected in the value of the actual parameter. In order to accommodate these two types of parameter passing, the

USING phrase in the CALL verb has been augmented. The format of this phrase is

$$\underline{\text{USING}} \quad \left\{ \begin{array}{ll} [\ \text{BY} \quad \underline{\text{REFERENCE}}\ ] & \text{identifier} \quad \dots \\ \quad \text{BY} \quad \underline{\text{CONTENT}} & \text{identifier} \quad \dots \end{array} \right\} \quad \dots$$

Note that BY REFERENCE is optional. Therefore, if neither CONTENT nor REFERENCE is specified, REFERENCE is assumed. Each specification of REFERENCE or CONTENT applies to all the succeeding identifiers until a different phrase (REFERENCE/CONTENT) is specified. Let us now consider an example of the CALL statement.

          CALL "NEW-SUB" USING   BY   CONTENT   DATA-X
               DATA-Y   BY   REFERENCE   DATA-Z.

Let the PROCEDURE DIVISION header for the subroutine (whose PROGRAM-ID specifies the name NEW-SUB) be

          PROCEDURE DIVISION USING DATA-A DATA-B DATA-C.

Obviously, the actual parameters DATA-X, DATA-Y and DATA-Z correspond to the respective formal parameters DATA-A, DATA-B and DATA-C. Here, DATA-X and DATA-Y are passed by content while DATA-Z is passed by reference. This means that DATA-Z and DATA-C share the same storage area. Therefore, if the subroutine changes the value of DATA-C, the value of DATA-Z will get changed. However, the same is not true either for DATA-X and DATA-A or for DATA-Y and DATA-B. When the CALL statement is executed the values of DATA-X and DATA-Y are moved respectively to DATA-A and DATA-B. Thereafter the relation between the formal and actual parameters ceases.

The important question that we face now is when to pass a parameter by reference and when to pass it by content. As a general rule, if we see that the subroutine should calculate the value of a parameter and return the value to the calling program, the parameter must be passed by reference. On the other hand, if the subroutine should only use the value of a parameter and must not alter the original value of the actual parameter, it should be passed by content (see Sec. 22.4.3 for further details).

Another change in the inter-program communication (subroutine) facility relates to the EXIT PROGRAM statement. In COBOL-74, this statement had to be coded as the only statement in a paragraph. This restriction has been relaxed. The EXIT PROGRAM statement can now be the last statement of any paragraph within a subroutine.

22.2.17 DISPLAY Verb

The syntax of the DISPLAY verb has been extended in COBOL-85. It is as follows:

$$\text{DISPLAY} \quad \begin{Bmatrix} \text{literal-1} \\ \text{identifier-1} \end{Bmatrix} \quad \ldots \quad [\; \underline{\text{UPON}} \quad \text{mnemonic-name} \;]$$

$$[\; \text{WITH} \quad \underline{\text{NO}} \quad \underline{\text{ADVANCING}} \;]$$

The WITH NO ADVANCING phrase to be used with interactive terminals, is a new addition in COBOL-85. Generally, after the execution of a DISPLAY statement, the cursor moves to the first position of the next line on the screen. When WITH NO ADVANCING phrase is used, the cursor is positioned after the last character displayed. Therefore, a subsequent ACCEPT statement will read data from the next character position on the same line.

This facility is rather poor for good interactive programming. As such, many compilers provide powerful extensions of ACCEPT and DISPLAY verbs. The features of MS-COBOL discussed in the previous chapter is an example of such extension.

22.3 COBOL-85 FEATURES FOR STRUCTURED PROGRAMMING

The new features of COBOL-85 incorporated mainly to facilitate structured programming are most interesting. We shall now proceed to describe these features one by one.

22.3.1 IF Verb

The IF verb has been substantially enhanced in COBOL-85. The syntax is shown below.

$$\underline{\text{IF}} \quad \text{condition} \quad \text{THEN} \quad \begin{Bmatrix} \{ \text{statement-1} \} \ldots \\ \underline{\text{NEXT SENTENCE}} \end{Bmatrix}$$

$$\begin{Bmatrix} \underline{\text{ELSE}} \quad \{ \text{statement-2} \} \ldots \quad \underline{\text{END-IF}} \\ \underline{\text{ELSE}} \quad \underline{\text{NEXT}} \quad \underline{\text{SENTENCE}} \\ \underline{\text{END-IF}} \end{Bmatrix}$$

As in COBOL-74, the ELSE NEXT SENTENCE phrase can be omitted if the statement is terminated by a period(.). Thus any IF statement written according to the syntax of COBOL-74 is still valid. The statement has now been augmented by the introduction of the optional word THEN and the scope terminator END-IF. The purpose of THEN is to provide better documentation of the statement and has no functional effect. The use of the scope terminator END-IF enables us to write nested IF sentences more easily. The following are some examples of the new forms.

Example 1

```
IF  PRICE  IS  GREATER  THAN  OR  EQUAL  TO  500.00
    THEN  MOVE  1  TO  PRICE-CODE
    ELSE  MOVE  2  TO  PRICE-CODE  END-IF
ADD  AMOUNT  TO  TOTAL.
```

The meaning of the above code is obvious. If the specified condition is true, 1 is moved to PRICE-CODE   otherwise 2 is moved. The statement ADD AMOUNT TO TOTAL is executed in either case. Notice that the IF statement has been terminated by the scope terminator END-IF and not by a period(.). If END-IF is omitted, a period must be used in its place otherwise the meaning of the code will get changed.

Example 2

```
    IF   STAFF-CODE = 1
         THEN  IF  DAYS-WORKED  IS  GREATER  THAN  175
                   THEN  MOVE  1  TO  BONUS-CODE  END-IF
         ELSE  IF  DAYS-WORKED  IS  GREATER  THAN  205
                   THEN  MOVE  2  TO  BONUS-CODE  END-IF
    END-IF.
```

If STAFF-CODE = 1 and DAYS-WORKED > 175, BONUS-CODE is set to 1. If STAFF-CODE is not equal to 1 and DAYS-WORKED > 205, BONUS-CODE is set to 2. In all other cases, BONUS-CODE is not changed. It is worthwhile to observe how the use of END-IF terminators reveals the structure of the nested IF sentence. See example 2 of Sec. 10.2.1 for an equivalent code written in COBOL-74.

Example 3

In earlier versions of COBOL, the scope of an IF statement could be terminated either by a period(.) or by the ELSE of an inclusive IF. As such, within a nested IF sentence, the scopes of all IF statements that could not be terminated by ELSE's had to be terminated by a final terminating period. This limitation in the matter of forced sharing of terminating period by several IF statements within a nesting, had been a major difficulty in program writing and had invited a lot of criticisms against COBOL. These points have already been highlighted in Sec. 12.5 with the help of an example. With the introduction of END-IF terminator, all these criticisms cease to exist. To illustrate this power of END-IF terminator, consider the flowchart given in Fig. 12.4.   The code for this flowchart can now be written as follows:

```
    TEST-MODULE.
         IF  A  =  B  THEN  PERFORM  PARA-EQUAL
         ELSE  IF  A > B
                   THEN  PERFORM  PARA-HIGH
                   ELSE  PERFORM  PARA-LOW
              END-IF
              PERFORM   PARA-UNEQUAL
         END-IF.
```

Because of the END-IF terminator, it has been possible to terminate the scope of the included IF statement just in front of PERFORM PARA-UNEQUAL.

The difficulties mentioned in Sec. 12.5 were due to the absence of this facility. Now, neither an extra module like IF-UNEQUAL nor the duplication of PERFORM PARA-UNEQUAL is necessary.

22.3.2 Enhancements for Conditional Verbs

COBOL has a large number of verbs that implicitly test certain conditions. READ with AT END or INVALID KEY phrase, ADD with ON SIZE ERROR phrase are examples of such conditional statements (see Sec. 6.7 for a list). In COBOL-85, two types of enhancements have been incorporated for these conditional statements. Firstly, optional END-verb scope terminator have been included for each of these verbs. Examples of END-verb scope terminators are END-READ, END-ADD, END-WRITE, etc. Secondly, corresponding to each phrase that tests an implicit condition, a matching optional phrase has been provided within the scope of such statements. The matching phrase tests the opposite condition. NOT AT END, NOT INVALID KEY are examples of such matching phrase. The following examples illustrate these two features.

Example 1

```
    DIVIDE  PRICE  BY  QTY  GIVING  RATE
         ON  SIZE  ERROR  MOVE  ZERO  TO  NEW-RATE
         NOT  ON  SIZE  ERROR  ADD  1  RATE  GIVING  NEW-RATE
    END-DIVIDE.
```

There should not be any difficulty in understanding the meaning of the above statement. NEW-RATE is calculated by the formula 1 + PRICE/QTY. In the case of an overflow during the division of PRICE by QTY, NEW-RATE is set to zero. What is to be noticed from the example is how the scope terminator END-DIVIDE and the matching phrase NOT ON SIZE ERROR have been used.

Example 2

```
    READ  IN-FILE  RECORD
         AT  END  SET  NO-MORE-RECORD  TO  TRUE
         NOT  AT  END
                 MOVE  IN-REC  TO  OUT-REC
                 WRITE  OUT-REC
    END-READ.
```

Whenever a record of IN-FILE is successfully read by the above READ statement, the imperative statements in the matching NOT AT END phrase are executed. In case the end of file is reached, the condition name NO-MORE-RECORD is set to true.

Note the usefulness of NOT AT END phrase. If we do not use this phrase, an additional IF statement is required. The equivalent code without this phrase is shown below.

```
READ  IN-FILE  RECORD
    AT  END  SET  NO-MORE-RECORD  TO  TRUE  END-READ.
IF  NOT  NO-MORE-RECORD
    MOVE  IN-REC  TO  OUT-REC  WRITE  OUT-REC  END-IF.
```

Conditional Phrase	Matching Phrase	Verb
AT END	NOT AT END	READ , RETURN
AT {END-OF-PAGE / EOP}	NOT AT {END-OF-PAGE / EOP}	WRITE
INVALID KEY	NOT INVALID KEY	READ, WRITE, REWRITE, DELETE, START
ON SIZE ERROR	NOT ON SIZE ERROR	ADD, SUBTRACT, MULTIPLY, DIVIDE, COMPUTE
ON OVERFLOW	NOT ON OVERFLOW	STRING UNSTRING
ON OVERFLOW	—	CALL
WHEN	—	SEARCH

TABLE 22.1.   Verbs Having Conditional and Matching
Conditional Phrases

Table 22.1 shows the verbs and the relevant conditional and matching phrases. The matching phrase, if used, should be written after the conditional phrase. Like the conditional phrase, the matching phrase should include only imperative statements within itself.

Each of the verbs mentioned in Table 22.1 can have the explicit END-verb scope terminator. When a conditional statement is ended with an explicit END-verb scope terminator, the statement can be called a delimited scope statement. A delimited scope statement is treated as an imperative statement and can be used anywhere an imperative statement is used. However, we have seen COBOL compilers (incorporating COBOL-85 features) which do not treat a delimited scope statement at par with an imperative statement. Therefore, before using a delimited scope statement as an imperative statement, one should ensure that the facility is available in the relevant compiler.

22.3.3 EVALUATE Verb

EVALUATE is a new statement in COBOL-85. It implements the "CASE" structure discussed in Sec. 15.3. In order to make the statement powerful, many options have been provided in this statement. The general format of the EVALUATE statement is shown below.

```
EVALUATE   subject-1 [ ALSO   subject-2 ]  ...
    {{WHEN   object-1    [ ALSO   object-2 ] ...}...} imperative-
                                                statement-1}...
    [ WHEN  OTHER  imperative-statement-2 ] [ END-EVALUATE ]
```

where a subject is

$$\left\{ \begin{array}{l} \text{identifier} \\ \text{literal} \\ \text{expression} \\ \text{TRUE} \\ \text{FALSE} \end{array} \right\}$$

and an object is

$$\left\{ \begin{array}{l} \text{ANY} \\ \text{condition} \\ \text{TRUE} \\ \text{FALSE} \\ [\text{ NOT }] \left\{ \begin{array}{l} \text{identifier-1} \\ \text{literal-1} \\ \text{arithmetic-expression-1} \end{array} \right\} \left\{ \begin{array}{l} \text{THROUGH} \\ \text{THRU} \end{array} \right\} \left\{ \begin{array}{l} \text{identifier-2} \\ \text{literal-2} \\ \text{arithmetic-} \\ \text{expression-2} \end{array} \right\} \end{array} \right\}$$

The meaning of the statement is explained by the following rules:

(i)   Associated with an EVALUATE statement there is a list of subjects and several lists of objects.

(ii) The list of subjects is specified between the word EVALUATE and the first appearance of WHEN. A subject can be an identifier or literal. It can also be an arithmetic/conditional expression or the keywords TRUE/FALSE. Thus when evaluated, a subject will have either a numeric value, a non-numeric value or a conditional value (denoted by TRUE, FALSE or conditional expression). Let us consider a few examples of subject specification.

Examples

(a)   TRUE

The list of subject consists of only one element which will evaluate to the conditional value TRUE.

(b)   TRANS-CODE

We assume that TRANS-CODE is an identifier. Here also the list of subjects consists of only one element which will evaluate to the value of TRANS-CODE.

(c) TRANS-CODE ALSO DATE-OF-TRANS ALSO CUSTOMER-CODE

Here the list of subjects consists of three elements. These are the values of TRANS-CODE, DATE-OF-TRANS and CUSTOMER-CODE. Note that the values of the subjects need not be of the same class. For example, TRANS-CODE may be numeric while CUSTOMER-CODE may be alphanumeric.

When a list of subjects contains more than one subject, the position of a subject within the list is important. We shall refer to this position as ordinal position.

(iii) Each WHEN phrase specifies a list of objects. The value of an object can be one of the following: a numeric/non-numeric value, a range of numeric/non-numeric values, a conditional value, or any value. Identifier-1/literal-1/arithmetic expression-1 denotes the single valued numeric/non-numeric object when THROUGH/THRU phrase is omitted. When THROUGH/THRU phrase is specified, a range of numeric/non-numeric values are indicated. Condition-1/TRUE/FALSE denotes a conditional value for the concerned object. The reserved word ANY denotes any value for the object. The ALSO phrase provides the means to specify a list of multiple objects. Some examples of object list specification is shown below.

Examples

(a) 3

The object list consists of only one element which evaluates to 3.

(b) 3 THRU 10

Here also the object list consists of one element but the element evaluates to a range of values.

(c) VAL-1 THRU VAL-2 ALSO ANY ALSO AMOUNT > 500

The list of object consists of three elements. The first one evaluates to a range of values, the second one evaluates to any value and the third one evaluates to a conditional value TRUE or FALSE depending on the value of AMOUNT.

As in the case of a list of subjects, the ordinal position of an object within the list of objects is important.

(iv) During the execution of an EVALUATE statement, the values denoted by the list of subjects are compared with the values denoted by the list of objects in a WHEN phrase to establish a "match" between the two. The comparison process is as follows:

- The value of a subject is compared with the value/range of values of the object in the corresponding ordinal position.

- In the case of a single valued (numeric/non-numeric) object, the subject-object comparison is made in the usual way.
- When a range of values is specified for the object, the subject-object comparison results in TRUE, if the value of the subject falls within the range.
- In the case of conditional values, the subject-object comparison results in TRUE, if both evaluate to the same value (i.e., both are TRUE or both are FALSE).
- If ANY is specified for an object, the subject-object comparison always results in TRUE.
- The list of subjects is said to "match" with the list of object, if all the corresponding subject-object comparisons result in TRUE.

(v) Note that each WHEN phrase specifies a list of objects. The WHEN phrases are taken up for a "match" in the order they appear within the EVALUATE statement. Whenever a "match" results, the first imperative statement following the said WHEN phrase is selected for execution and the EVALUATE statement is exited. The WHEN OTHER phrase, if specified, is selected only if none of the previous WHEN phrases is selected.

(vi) It is needless to mention that a subject and the corresponding object must be such that they are comparable. There should be as many objects as there are subjects in the list of subjects.

The EVALUATE statement without the ALSO phrases becomes greatly simplified because in that case we have only one subject and one object (for each WHEN). This form of EVALUATE statement is useful in implementing "CASE" structure without the use of GO TO ...... DEPENDING ON statement. The real use of ALSO phrases is in the case of converting a decision table to a program. The following examples illustrate the use of EVALUATE statement.

Example 1

Let each of MONTH and NO-OF-DAYS be two-digited numeric integer fields. The values 1,2,3, etc. for MONTH denote respectively, January, February, March, etc. Depending on the value of MONTH, we wish to move 30,31 or 28 to NO-OF-DAYS. For example, if the value of MONTH is 1, we shall move 31; if it is 2, we shall move 28 and so on. The EVALUATE statement for the purpose is as follows:

```
EVALUATE   TRUE
    WHEN  MONTH = 4  OR 6  OR 9  OR 11
          MOVE  30  TO  NO-OF-DAYS
    WHEN  MONTH  =  2
          MOVE  28  TO  NO-OF-DAYS
    WHEN  OTHER  MOVE  31  TO  NO-OF-DAYS
END-EVALUATE.
```

In this case, we have assumed that MONTH has a correct value.

Example 2

Suppose MARKS contains the marks obtained by a student. GRADE is an one-character alphanumeric field. We wish to calculate GRADE according to the following rules:

MARKS	GRADE
80-100	A
60-79	B
45-59	C
30-44	D
0-29	E

The EVALUATE statement for the purpose is shown below.

```
EVALUATE MARKS
    WHEN  80  THRU  100  MOVE  "A"  TO  GRADE
    WHEN  60  THRU  79 MOVE  "B"  TO  GRADE
    WHEN  45  THRU  59 MOVE  "C"  TO  GRADE
    WHEN  30  THRU  44 MOVE  "D"  TO  GRADE
    WHEN  ZERO  THRU  29 MOVE  "E"  TO  GRADE
    WHEN  OTHER  MOVE  "W"  TO  GRADE
END-EVALUATE.
```

The literal "W" is moved to GRADE in the case of wrong marks.

Example 3

Let us consider the last decision table of Sec. 2.8. This was coded with IF statement in Sec. 10.2.3. Let us code it with the help of the EVALUATE statement.

```
EVALUATE PRODUCT-TYPE  ALSO   CUSTOMER- CATEGORY
    WHEN  1  ALSO  1  MOVE  10  TO  COMMISSION
    WHEN  1  ALSO  2  MOVE  8   TO  COMMISSION
    WHEN  2  ALSO  1  MOVE  12  TO  COMMISSION
    WHEN  2  ALSO  2  MOVE  8   TO  COMMISSION
    WHEN  3  ALSO  1  THRU  2  MOVE  10 TO  COMMISSION
    WHEN  OTHER  MOVE  ZERO  TO  COMMISSION
END-EVALUATE.
```

Notice how elegantly the decision table has been coded.

Example 4

The EVALUATE statement in example 3 can also be written as follows.

```
EVALUATE   PRODUCT-TYPE  ALSO   CUSTOMER-TYPE
    WHEN   1   ALSO  1
    WHEN   3   ALSO  1   THRU  2
                 MOVE  10   TO   COMMISSION
    WHEN   1   ALSO  2
    WHEN   2   ALSO  2
                 MOVE  8   TO   COMMISSION
    WHEN   2   ALSO  1
                 MOVE  12   TO   COMMISSION
    WHEN  OTHER  MOVE  ZERO  TO  COMMISSION
END-EVALUATE.
```

Note that where a WHEN phrase does not contain an imperative statement, the
next available imperative statement is executed. Thus if PRODUCT-TYPE = 1
and CUSTOMER-TYPE = 1, 10 will be moved to COMMISSION.

22.3.4 PERFORM Verb

In COBOL-85, the PERFORM statement has been subjected to two major, enhancements. In order to explain these two revisions, we consider PERFORM with
UNTIL option as a typical representative of the PERFORM statements. The new
format of PERFORM with UNTIL option is shown below.

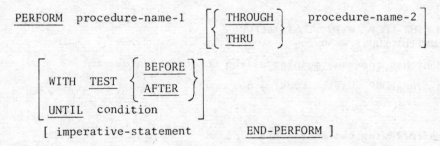

The TEST phrase is a new addition. If TEST BEFORE is specified, the condition is tested at the beginning of each repeated execution of the specified
PERFORM range. On the other hand, if TEST AFTER is specified, the condition
is tested at the end of each repeated execution of the PERFORM range. Thus
if the condition is true at the very beginning, the range is not executed at
all when TEST BEFORE is specified and it is executed once when TEST AFTER is
specified. Note that in earlier versions of COBOL, the PERFORM statement
with UNTIL option, behaves as in the case of TEST BEFORE phrase. As such,
the TEST BEFORE is the default. The functioning of the statement with TEST
AFTER phrase is best illustrated through the flowchart shown in Fig. 22.2.

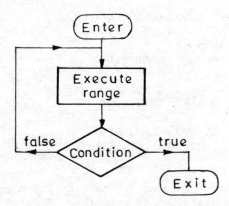

FIG. 22.2. Flowchart for PERFORM ... UNTIL with TEST AFTER

The TEST phrase is also available for PERFORM with VARYING option as well as PERFORM with VARYING ..... AFTER option. However, TEST phrase is not available for PERFORM with TIMES option although it is also meant for loops. There is no question of TEST phrase in the case of simple PERFORM. The following examples illustrate the use of the TEST phrase.

Example 1

    PERFORM THE-LOOP WITH TEST BEFORE
        UNTIL KOUNT > 30

This statement has the same meaning as the COBOL-74 statement

    PERFORM THE-LOOP UNTIL KOUNT > 30.

Example 2

Consider the following two statements

    PERFORM THE-LOOP WITH TEST BEFORE
        VARYING KOUNT FROM 1 BY 1 UNTIL KOUNT > 30.

and

    PERFORM THE-LOOP WITH TEST AFTER
        VARYING KOUNT FROM 1 BY 1 UNTIL KOUNT > 30.

The essential difference between the two is that in the first case the loop is executed 30 times with 1,2,3 ...., 30 as the value of KOUNT. In the second case, the loop is executed 31 times with 1,2,3,......,31 as the value of KOUNT. In this connection note that when TEST AFTER is specified, the condition is tested immediately after the execution of the range (denoted by the paragraph THE-LOOP) and before augmenting the value of the controlling identifier (KOUNT in this case).

Example 3

Suppose we have a sequential file denoted by TEST-FILE in the program.
Further suppose that the record description for this file has an integer
field named TAG. We wish to skip the records of this file until a record
with the value of TAG as 9 has been read. The code for this is shown with
PERFORM statements having TEST BEFORE and TEST AFTER phrases.

```
    PERFORM  READ-A-RECORD  WITH  TEST  AFTER
  .          UNTIL  TAG  IS  EQUAL  TO  9.
  .
READ-A-RECORD.
    READ  TEST-FILE  AT  END  DISPLAY  "NO SUCH RECORD"  STOP  RUN.
```

The above code is quite valid because TAG is tested only after the execution
of READ-A-RECORD. However, if we change the TEST phrase to TEST BEFORE, TAG
will be tested before reading any record. This is wrong because TAG is
undefined in that case. Therefore, to code the same thing with TEST BEFORE
phrase we must proceed as follows.

```
    PERFORM  READ-A-RECORD.
    PERFORM  READ-A-RECORD  WITH  TEST  BEFORE
          UNTIL  TAG  IS  EQUAL  TO  9.
```

The paragraph READ-A-RECORD remains as before.

This example illustrates a situation where TEST AFTER should be preferred to TEST BEFORE. In fact, the structure of PERFORM.....UNTIL with TEST
AFTER shown in Fig. 22.2 is known as "DOUNTIL" structure as opposed to the
"DOWHILE" structure (see Sec. 12.3.1). DOUNTIL structure is often considered as a basic structure for structured programming.

Apart from the TEST phrase, the other major revision of the PERFORM
statement is the introduction of "in-line" PERFORM. A major weakness of the
PERFORM statement had been that the section of code (range) that is to be
executed, could not be included within the statement itself. It had to be
placed "out-of-line". The introduction of "in-line" PERFORM causes this
criticism to vanish. With all forms of the PERFORM statement, imperative
statement(s) can be included within the scope of the statement which is
finally ended by the END-PERFORM scope delimiter. The following examples
illustrate the use of "in-line" PERFORM.

Example 4

```
    PERFORM  UNTIL  I > 30
       ADD  TABLE-A(I)  TO  TOTAL
       ADD  1  TO  I
    END-PERFORM.
```

The range of the PERFORM statement consists of the two ADD statements which
are included within the scope of the PERFORM itself.

Example 5

```
PERFORM  30  TIMES
    ADD  TABLE-A (I)  TO  TOTAL
    ADD  1  TO  I
END-PERFORM.
```

This example illustrates in-line PERFORM with TIMES option. The meaning is same as the corresponding out-of-line code where two ADD statements must be in a separate paragraph referenced by the PERFORM statement.

Example 6

```
PERFORM  VARYING  I  FROM  1  BY  1  UNTIL  I > 30
    ADD  TABLE-A  (I)  TO  TOTAL
END-PERFORM.
```

This is an in-line PERFORM statement with VARYING option.

Example 7

```
PERFORM
    MOVE  IN-REC  TO  OUT-REC
    WRITE  OUT-REC
END-PERFORM.
```

This is an illustration of the in-line simple PERFORM statement. Although this type of coding is allowed, the PERFORM statement is ineffective here. The PERFORM and END-PERFORM pair simply provides a kind of "bracket" to the included imperative statements. The bracket has no effect on the execution.

The following points should be noted in connection with the enhanced PERFORM statement.

(i) When procedure name (with or without the THROUGH/THRU phrase) is specified, the PERFORM statement is considered to be the usual out-of-line PERFORM. The imperative statement and the delimiter END-PERFORM must not be specified in that case.

(ii) When procedure name is omitted, the PERFORM statement is assumed to be in-line PERFORM. The imperative statement and the scope delimiter END-PERFORM should be specified in that case.

(iii) An in-line PERFORM statement functions exactly like an otherwise identical out-of-line PERFORM statement with the exception that the imperative statements contained within the scope are executed instead of the out-of-line range.

Over and above the two major enhancements mentioned above, the PERFORM statement with VARYING ... AFTER option can now have an unlimited number of AFTER phrases. In COBOL-74, the number of AFTER phrases was limited to two.

22.4   SAMPLE PROGRAMS

We conclude this chapter by presenting three complete programs which use many of the COBOL-85 features described in the preceding sections.   In order to make these programs a little more interesting, we use the extended forms of the ACCEPT and DISPLAY verbs as in the case of Microsoft COBOL.   These forms though non-standard, are available in many COBOL compilers.   In the sample programs, these non-standard statements are shown in lowercase letters.   In the first two programs we also assume files to have LINE SEQUENTIAL organization as in MS-COBOL.

22.4.1   File Encription

The first program uses two sequential files — IN-FILE and OUT-FILE.   Each record read from the IN-FILE is first enciphered and then written on the OUT-FILE.   The program terminates when all the records of IN-FILE have been processed and OUT-FILE has been created.   The encipherment involves substitution of letters from a standard alphabet by the corresponding letters from a cipher alphabet.   For example, let the standard and cipher alphabets be

        ABCDEFGHIJKLMNOPQRSTUVWXYZ   and
        ZYXWVUTSRQPONMLKJIHGFEDCBA

respectively.   This means that any "A" appearing in a record of IN-FILE is substituted by "Z", any "B" by "Y" and so on.   In order that the user may have his own way of defining the standard and cipher alphabets, the program allows the user to provide the said alphabets from the terminal.   Each alphabet is assumed to be a string of 26 alphanumeric characters and the values of standard and cipher alphabets are assigned to S-STRING and T-STRING respectively.   To have more flexibility, the program allows the user to enter the actual file titles from the terminal before entering the alphabets.

        Such a file encryption program is useful for security purposes. However, our objective here is to illustrate effective use of COBOL-85 elements like INSPECT verb with CONVERTING phrase, INITIALIZE verb and NOT AT END phrase with the READ verb.

22.4.2   File Updation

The second program is an updation program for sequential files.   The problem and the updation logic have been discussed in Sec. 14.2.   Here, the şame logic is used in a different way.   First of all, we represent the updation logic in the form of a decision table shown in Fig. 22.4.   The logic is based on the comparison of master (MASTER-KEY) with transaction key (TRANS-KEY) and the decision table shows the required actions in various situations. We leave it for the reader to satisfy himself that the logic shown in Fig. 22.4 is correct.   The purpose of using a decision table is that it can be

```
IDENTIFICATION DIVISION.
PROGRAM-ID. ENCRYPTION.
ENVIRONMENT DIVISION.
INPUT-OUTPUT SECTION.
FILE-CONTROL.
    SELECT IN-FILE ASSIGN TO DISK
        organization is line sequential.
    SELECT OUT-FILE ASSIGN TO DISK
        organization is line sequential.
DATA DIVISION.
FILE SECTION.
FD  IN-FILE LABEL RECORDS ARE STANDARD
    VALUE OF file-id IS IN-TITLE.
01  IN-REC       PIC   X(80).
FD  OUT-FILE LABEL RECORDS ARE STANDARD
    VALUE OF file-id IS OUT-TITLE.
01  OUT-REC      PIC   X(80).
WORKING-STORAGE SECTION.
01  IN-TITLE     PIC   X(14).
01  OUT-TITLE    PIC   X(14).
01  S-STRING     PIC   X(26).
01  C-STRING     PIC   X(26).
01  IN-FILE-STATUS PIC 9.
    88 FILE-HAS-NO-RECORD  VALUE  IS  1.
PROCEDURE DIVISION.
BEGIN-PROGRAM.
    display (1, 1) erase.
    display (5, 10) "Input File:". accept (5, 25) IN-TITLE.
    display (7, 10) "Output File:". accept (7, 25) OUT-TITLE.
    OPEN INPUT IN-FILE OUTPUT OUT-FILE.
    display (10, 10) "Standard Alphabet:".
    accept (10, 25) S-STRING.
    display (12, 10) "Cipher   Alphabet:".
    accept (12, 25) C-STRING.
    INITIALIZE IN-FILE-STATUS.
    PERFORM PROCESS-A-RECORD UNTIL FILE-HAS-NO-RECORD.
    STOP RUN.
PROCESS-A-RECORD.
    READ IN-FILE RECORD
        AT END SET FILE-HAS-NO-RECORD TO TRUE
        NOT AT END
            INSPECT IN-REC CONVERTING S-STRING TO C-STRING
        WRITE OUT-REC FROM IN-REC.
END PROGRAM ENCRYPTION.
```

FIG. 22.3. A File Encryption Program.

RULES

	1	2	3	4	5	6	7	8
MASTER-KEY < TRANS-KEY	N	N	N	Y				E
MASTER-KEY > TRANS-KEY	Y	N	N	N				
MASTER-KEY = TRANS-KEY	N	Y	Y	N				L
MASTER-HAS-MORE-RECORDS	Y	Y	Y	Y	Y	N	N	
TRANS.-HAS-MORE-RECORDS	Y	Y	Y	Y	N	Y	N	S
INSERTION (TRANS-CODE=1)	Y	N	N			Y		
DELETION (TRANS-CODE=2)	N	Y	N			N		E
MODIFICATION (TRANS-CODE=3)	N	N	Y			N		
WRITE FROM MASTER-REC				X				
WRITE FROM TRANS-REC	X							
WRITE MODIFIED RECORD FROM MASTER-REC/TRANS-REC				X				
COPY REMAINING RECORDS OF MASTER-FILE								
COPY REMAINING RECORDS OF TRANS-FILE					X			
READ MASTER-FILE RECORD		X	X	X		X		
READ TRANS-FILE RECORD	X	X	X					
TERMINATE							X	X
REPORT ERROR								X

FIG. 22.4. Updation Logic

mechanically translated into a program with the help of the EVALUATE statement. This is exactly what has been done in the updation program shown in Fig. 22.5. However, there is some difference between the EVALUATE statement and the said decision table. The first line of the decision table which deals with the condition MASTER-KEY < TRANS-KEY has not been implemented because this is superfluous when the other two conditions (MASTER-KEY > TRANS-KEY and MASTER-KEY = TRANS-KEY) are used. Again, the last three conditions namely, INSERTION, DELETION and MODIFICATION are combined into one because at one point of time only one of these conditions can be true. With these explanations, we now invite the reader to go through the program in Fig. 22.5 to appreciate how a single EVALUATE statement has been used to take care of somewhat complicated logic of file updation. We do not claim that the program is elegant. However, what we want to point out is the simplicity in program writing achieved through the EVALUATE statement.

```
IDENTIFICATION DIVISION.
PROGRAM-ID. UPDATE-MASTER.
ENVIRONMENT DIVISION.
INPUT-OUTPUT SECTION.
FILE-CONTROL.
      SELECT MASTER-FILE ASSIGN TO DISK
            organization is line sequential.
      SELECT TRANS-FILE ASSIGN TO DISK
            organization is line sequential.
      SELECT NEW-MASTER ASSIGN TO DISK
            organization is line sequential.
DATA DIVISION.
FILE SECTION.
FD    MASTER-FILE LABEL RECORDS ARE STANDARD
      VALUE OF file-id IS "MASTER".
01    MASTER-REC.
      05 MASTER-KEY         PIC  X(5).
      05                    PIC  X(45).
FD    TRANS-FILE LABEL RECORDS ARE STANDARD
      VALUE OF file-id IS "TRANS".
01    TRANS-REC.
      05 TRANS-CODE         PIC  9.
       88 INSERTION      VALUE IS 1.
       88 DELETION       VALUE IS 2.
       88 MODIFICATION   VALUE IS 3.
      05 TRANS-DATA.
         10 TRANS-KEY        PIC  X(5).
         10                  PIC  X(45).
FD    NEW-MASTER LABEL RECORDS ARE STANDARD
      VALUE OF file-id IS "NEWMAST".
01    NEW-REC               PIC  X(50).
WORKING-STORAGE SECTION.
01    CONDITION-NAMES.
      02 END-OF-MASTER       PIC  X(5).
         88 MASTER-HAS-MORE-RECORDS VALUE IS "FALSE".
         88 MASTER-HAS-NO-RECORD     VALUE IS "TRUE".
      02 END-OF-TRANS        PIC  X(5).
         88 TRANS-HAS-MORE-RECORDS  VALUE IS "FALSE".
         88 TRANS-HAS-NO-RECORD      VALUE IS "TRUE".
      02 END-OF-BOTH         PIC  X(5).
         88 TERMINATION    VALUE IS "TRUE"
01 FLAG                      PIC  X.
PROCEDURE DIVISION.
MAIN-PROGRAM.
      OPEN INPUT MASTER-FILE TRANS-FILE
           OUTPUT NEW-MASTER.
      INITIALIZE CONDITION-NAMES REPLACING
           ALPHANUMERIC DATA BY "FALSE".
      display (1, 1) erase.
      PERFORM READ-MASTER. PERFORM READ-TRANS.
      PERFORM UPDATION UNTIL TERMINATION.
      CLOSE MASTER-FILE TRANS-FILE NEW-MASTER WITH LOCK.
      STOP RUN.
```

(contd.)

```
UPDATION.
    EVALUATE
        MASTER-KEY > TRANS-KEY
          ALSO MASTER-KEY = TRANS-KEY
            ALSO MASTER-HAS-MORE-RECORDS
            ALSO TRANS-HAS-MORE-RECORDS
             ALSO TRUE
        WHEN TRUE ALSO FALSE ALSO TRUE ALSO TRUE ALSO INSERTION
             WRITE NEW-REC FROM TRANS-DATA PERFORM READ-TRANS
        WHEN FALSE ALSO TRUE ALSO TRUE ALSO TRUE ALSO DELETION
             PERFORM READ-MASTER PERFORM READ-TRANS
        WHEN FALSE ALSO TRUE ALSO TRUE ALSO TRUE ALSO MODIFICATION
             WRITE NEW-REC FROM TRANS-DATA
             PERFORM READ-MASTER PERFORM READ-TRANS
        WHEN FALSE ALSO FALSE ALSO TRUE ALSO TRUE ALSO ANY
             WRITE NEW-REC FROM MASTER-REC PERFORM READ-MASTER
        WHEN ANY ALSO ANY ALSO TRUE ALSO FALSE ALSO ANY
             PERFORM COPY-REST-OF-MASTER
        WHEN ANY ALSO ANY ALSO FALSE ALSO TRUE ALSO INSERTION
             PERFORM COPY-REST-OF-TRANS
        WHEN ANY ALSO ANY ALSO FALSE ALSO FALSE ALSO ANY
             SET TERMINATION TO TRUE
        WHEN OTHER
             PERFORM ERROR-ACTION
    END-EVALUATE.
READ-MASTER.
    READ MASTER-FILE RECORD
         AT END SET MASTER-HAS-NO-RECORD TO TRUE.
READ-TRANS.
    READ TRANS-FILE RECORD
         AT END SET TRANS-HAS-NO-RECORD TO TRUE.
COPY-REST-OF-MASTER.
    PERFORM  UNTIL MASTER-HAS-NO-RECORD
        WRITE NEW-REC FROM MASTER-REC
        PERFORM READ-MASTER
    END-PERFORM.
COPY-REST-OF-TRANS.
    PERFORM  UNTIL TRANS-HAS-NO-RECORD
        WRITE NEW-REC FROM TRANS-DATA
        PERFORM READ-TRANS-WITH-TEST
    END-PERFORM.
READ-TRANS-WITH-TEST.
    PERFORM READ-TRANS.
    PERFORM ERROR-ACTION WITH TEST BEFORE
        UNTIL TRANS-HAS-NO-RECORD OR INSERTION.
ERROR-ACTION.
    display (10, 10) "Error occurs when transaction is: ", trans-key
    display (11, 10) "Transaction ignored.".
    display (14, 10) "Press Enter key to continue".
    accept (14, 40) flag.
    PERFORM READ-TRANS.
END PROGRAM UPDATE-MASTER.
```

FIG. 22.5.   An Updation Program

22.4.3 Sample Nesting of Programs

The third program shown in Fig. 22.6 illustrates program nesting. The program reads the value of N from terminal and then reads N integers again from the terminal and stores them in a table. It then sorts the integers using shuttle sort technique and displays them in ascending order.

The program under consideration uses a nesting of three programs — MAIN-PROGRAM, SHUTTLE-SORT and INSERT. MAIN-PROGRAM includes SHUTTLE-SORT which in turn includes INSERT. The input of integers and their display after sorting are taken care of by MAIN-PROGRAM. Sorting of the N integers in A(1), A(2), ..., A(N) is done by calling SHUTTLE-SORT. The shuttle sort technique was discussed earlier (see Sec. 11.9). It requires (N-1) passes. The comparisons and exchanges required in each pass are done in INSERT. Note that SHUTTLE-SORT calls INSERT for (N-1) times providing successively 2,3,...,N as the value of the parameter. Here, I is the actual parameter and J is the formal parameter and the parameter is passed by reference.

At the beginning of each pass, INSERT assumes that the first (J-1) elements namely, A(1), A(2), ..., A(J-1) are already sorted. It inserts A(J) in proper position through repeated comparisons and exchanges so that at the end of the pass the first J elements namely, A(1), A(2), ..., A(J) are sorted. The assumption that (J-1) elements are sorted at the beginning of the pass, is obviously valid for J=2 and remains valid for any J because in each pass one element is progressively included in the sorted part. Thus when INSERT has been called for J=N, the sorting is complete.

The insertion process in a pass starts with a comparison of A(J) and A(J-1) and if they are not in the correct order, they are exchanged. The process is then repeated on A(J-1) and A(J-2) and so on. However, if at any stage of insertion process, the adjacent elements are found to be in the correct order there is no need to proceed further.

Note that the INSERT program does not directly work with the parameter J. Instead, it moves J to K and then proceeds with K. This is essential because the parameter passing is by reference. If we change the value of J in INSERT, the value of I in SHUTTLE-SORT will get changed. Since we do not wish to disturb I, possible change in J had to be avoided by working with K. Had the parameter been passed by content, we could work with J directly. Therefore, this is an occasion when parameter passing by content is desirable. In that case, the CALL statement in SHUTTLE-SORT should be changed to

        CALL "INSERT" USING BY CONTENT J END-CALL

and all references of K within INSERT should be changed to those of J. Moreover, the description of K in the WORKING-STORAGE SECTION and the statement MOVE J TO K should be deleted from INSERT.

The MAIN-PROGRAM also illustrates an use of DISPLAY verb with NO ADVANCING phrase.

```
IDENTIFICATION DIVISION.
PROGRAM-ID. MAIN-PROGRAM.
DATA DIVISION.
WORKING-STORAGE SECTION.
01  N       PIC 999.
01  THE-LIST IS GLOBAL.
    05  A   PIC 9(4) OCCURS 100 TIMES.
01  I       PIC 999.
PROCEDURE DIVISION.
BEGIN-PROGRAM.
    DISPLAY "What is N" WITH NO ADVANCING. ACCEPT N.
    PERFORM VARYING I FROM 1 BY 1 UNTIL I > N
        ACCEPT A ( I )
    END-PERFORM.
    CALL "SHUTTLE-SORT" USING N END-CALL.
    PERFORM VARYING I FROM 1 BY 1 UNTIL I > N
        DISPLAY A ( I )
    END-PERFORM.
    STOP RUN.
IDENTIFICATION DIVISION.
PROGRAM-ID. SHUTTLE-SORT.
DATA DIVISION.
WORKING-STORAGE SECTION.
01  I       PIC 999.
LINKAGE SECTION.
01  N       PIC 999.
PROCEDURE DIVISION USING N.
BEGIN-SHUTTLE-SORT.
    IF N > 1 THEN
        PERFORM VARYING I FROM 2 BY 1 UNTIL I > N
            CALL "INSERT" USING I END-CALL
        END-PERFORM
    END-IF.
    EXIT PROGRAM.
```

(contd.)

```
IDENTIFICATION DIVISION.
PROGRAM-ID. INSERT.
DATA DIVISION.
WORKING-STORAGE SECTION.
01   TEMP   PIC 9(4).
01   K      PIC 999.
LINKAGE SECTION.
01   J      PIC 999.
PROCEDURE DIVISION USING J.
BEGIN-INSERT.
     MOVE J TO K.
     PERFORM UNTIL K <= 1
       IF A ( K ) < A ( K - 1 )
          THEN MOVE A ( K ) TO TEMP
               MOVE A ( K - 1 ) TO A ( K )
               MOVE TEMP TO A ( K - 1 )
               SUBTRACT 1 FROM K
          ELSE MOVE 1 TO K
       END-IF
     END-PERFORM.
     EXIT PROGRAM.
END PROGRAM INSERT.
END PROGRAM SHUTTLE-SORT.
END PROGRAM MAIN-PROGRAM.
```

FIG. 22.6.   A Sample Program showing Program Nesting

EXERCISES

1. Indicate whether or not the following are correct according to COBOL-74
    and then according to COBOL-85 standard.

    (a)   01   A.
              02   PIC   X(9)   VALUE   "MONDAY...".
              02   PIC   X(9)   VALUE   "TUESDAY..".
              02   PIC   X(9)   VALUE   "WEDNESDAY".

    (b)   01   B.
              02   B1   PIC   X(8).
              02   B2   OCCURS 5 TIMES PIC 999 VALUE   0.

    (c)   02   A   PIC   X(8).
          02   B   REDEFINES   A.
              03   B1   PIC   X(4).
              03   B2   PIC   999.

    (d)   MOVE   DATA-A   TO   DATA-B

          where DATA-A and DATA-B are described as

              01   DATA-A   PIC   Z(5)99.
              01   DATA-B   PIC   9(5)V99.

(e)   ADD   1   TO   I   GIVING J.

(f)   IF   A < B   THEN   CONTINUE   ELSE   MOVE   10   TO   B.

(g)   IF   SELF-AMOUNT = 1000   THEN   MOVE   ZEROES   TO   COMMISSION.

(h)   IF   A   IS   NOT   ALPHANUMERIC-UPPER   GO   TO   P1.

(i)   MOVE   A(3)   TO   B.

(j)   MOVE   A(3:)   TO   B.

2. The following are DATA DIVISION entries

```
01   B.
     02   B1      PIC      X(8).
     02   B2      PIC      X(4).
     02   B3      PIC      Z(3)9.99.
     02   C       OCCURS   5   TIMES   PIC   999.
```

Indicate what will be the contents of B1, B2, B3 and C after the execution of the following statements.

(a)   INITIALIZE   B
             REPLACING   NUMERIC   DATA   BY   ZEROES
             REPLACING   NUMERIC-EDITED   DATA   BY   1.0
             REPLACING   ALPHANUMERIC   DATA   BY   SPACES.

(b)   INITIALIZE   B
             REPLACING   NUMERIC-EDITED   DATA   BY   1.0.

3. The following are DATA DIVISION entries.

```
     77   A   PIC   ZZ9.99.
     77   B   PIC   999V99.
```

What will be the contents of B after the execution of the following statements?

```
     MOVE   25.25   TO   A.
     MOVE   A   TO   B.
```

4. The following are DATA DIVISION entries.

```
01   FIRST-PART
     02   A1      PIC      X(4).
     02   A2      PIC      9(4).
```

```
02   A3      PIC    X(5).
02   B       REDEFINES   A3.
     03   B1    PIC   9(3)
     03   B2    PIC   XX.
```

Indicate what will be the contents of A1, A2, A3, B1 and B3 after the execution of the following two statements.

```
INITIALIZE   FIRST-PART.
INITIALIZE   B.
```

5. Rewrite the following COBOL-85 statements using only COBOL-74 features.

(a)   05   CLASS-TEST   PIC   9.
      88   NEW-CLASS   VALUE   IS   1.
Now, SET   NEW-CLASS   TO   TRUE.

(b)   PERFORM   UNTIL   FLAG-X
          MULTIPLY   I   BY   PROD-X   END-MULTIPLY
          ADD   1   TO   I   END-ADD
      END-PERFORM.

(c)   EVALUATE   K
      WHEN   1
      WHEN   2   MOVE   1   TO   K
      WHEN   3
      WHEN   4   MOVE   3   TO   K
      WHEN   5
      WHEN   6   MOVE   5   TO   K
      END-EVALUATE.

(d)   IF   NEW-SWITCH
          THEN   READ   NEW-FILE
                    AT   END   CONTINUE   END-READ
              MOVE   NEW-REC   TO   THE-REC
          ELSE   READ   OLD-FILE
                    AT   END   CONTINUE   END-READ
              MOVE   OLD-REC   TO   THE-REC
      END-IF.

6. The record description for a PRINTER file is as follows:

```
01   PRINT-REC
     02   FILLER          PIC   X(5).
     02   ACCOUNT-NO      PIC   9(6).
     02   FILLER          PIC   X(5).
     02   NAME            PIC   X(30).
     02   FILLER          PIC   X(5).
     02   AMOUNT          PIC   Z(6)9.99.
     02   FILLER          PIC   X(71).
```

The above description is used to print a detail line of a desired report. Write procedure division statements to print an appropriate heading for the said report. You must not describe any other record for the purpose.

[Hint: use reference modification.]

7. A hexadecimal digit is any one of the following: 0 to 9, A,B,C,D,E and F. The letters denote the values 10,11,12,13,14 and 15 respectively. If HEX-CODE (described with PIC X) contains a valid hexadecimal digit, move its numeric value to HEX-VALUE (described with PIC 99); otherwise, display a suitable error message. Write the necessary COBOL statements for the purpose by using

(a) a single nested IF sentence
(b) an EVALUATE statement

8. Let the CALL statement within MAIN-PROGRAM in Fig. 22.6 be changed as follows:

    CALL "SHUTTLE-SORT" USING BY CONTENT N END-CALL

Will it effectively change the operation of the run unit? Give reasons in your support.

9. Suppose that neither GLOBAL nor EXTERNAL clause is available in COBOL-85. Recode the program in Fig. 22.6 under the said constraint. [Hint: The table should also be passed as parameter.]

10. In Fig. 22.6, MAIN-PROGRAM includes SHUTTLE-SORT which in turn includes INSERT. Suppose we wish to modify the nesting so that MAIN-PROGRAM directly includes SHUTTLE-SORT as well as INSERT. This will require the END PROGRAM SHUTTLE-SORT terminator to be shifted and placed before the IDENTIFICATION DIVISION header of INSERT. What additional change(s) will be necessary? [Hint: Consider PROGRAM-ID paragraph.]

Appendix A

BIBLIOGRAPHY

BOOKS

1. Armstrong, R.M., *Modular Programming in COBOL*, John Wiley and Sons, New York, 1973.

2. Bleazard,G.B., *Program Design Methods*, National Computing Centre, Manchester, 1976.

3. Brown, Gary D., *Advanced ANS COBOL with Structured Programming*, John Wiley and Sons, New York, 1977.

4. Cohn, Lawrence S., *Effective Use of ANS COBOL Computer Programming Language*, John Wiley and Sons, New York, 1975.

5. Farina, Mario V., *COBOL Simplified*, Prentice-Hall, Englewood Cliffs, 1968.

6. Grauer, Robert T., *Structured Methods through COBOL*, Prentice-Hall Inc., 1983.

7. Lim, Pacifico A., *A Guide to Structured COBOL with Efficiency Techniques and Special Algorithms*, Van Nostrand Reinhold Company, New York, 1980.

8. McCraken, Daniel D., *A Simplified Guide to Structured COBOL Programming*, John Wiley and Sons, New York, 1976.

9. Nickerson, Robert C., *COBOL Programming*, Winthrop Publishers, Cambridge, Massachusetts, 1977.

10. Philipakis, Andreas S. and Leonard J. Kazmir, *Information Systems through COBOL*, McGraw-Hill Kogakusha, Tokyo, 1978.

11. Philippakis, A.S. and Leonard J. Kazmier, *Advanced COBOL*, McGraw-Hill Book Company, Singapore, 1987.

12. Robinson, P.B., *Advanced COBOL ANS 74*, Macdonalds and Jane's/American Elsevier, London/New York, 1976.

13. Roy Mohit K. and Debabrata Ghosh Dastidar, *Computer Sorting Techniques*, Roy and Chowdhury, Calcutta, 1976.

14. Saxon James A. and William R. Englander, *ANS COBOL Programming*, Prentice-Hall, Englewood Cliffs, 1977.

15. Stern, Nancy B. and Robert A. Stern, *COBOL Programming*, John Wiley and Sons, New York, 1975.

16. Worth, Thomas, *COBOL for Beginners*, Prentice-Hall, Englewood Cliffs, 1977.

PAPERS

1. Bohm C. and G. Jacopani, "Flow diagrams, Turing machines and languages with only two formation rules", *Comm. ACM*, vol.9, no.5, May 1966.

2. Comer, Douglas, "The Ubiquitous B-Tree", *ACM Computing Survey*, vol.II, no.2 (June, 1979), pp. 121-137.

3. Dijkstra, E.W., "Notes on structured programming", Dahl, Dijkstra and Hoare, Academic Press, New York, 1972.

4. Ledgard, Henry C., and W.C. Cave, "COBOL under control", *Comm. ACM*, vol. 9, no.5, no.11, Nov. 1976.

5. Mills, H.D., "Mathematical foundations for structured programming", IBM Federal Systems Division, FSC-72-6012, Feb. 1972.

MANUALS

1. *B 7000/B 6000 Series COBOL Reference Manual*, Burroughs Corporation, 1003-2, 9-5001464, 1977.

2. *Dec System 10 COBOL Programmer's Reference Manual*, Digital Equipment Corporation - DEC-10-LCPRA-B-DNI, 1977.

3. *Horizon III COBOL Reference Manual*, Hindustan Computers Ltd., June, 1987.

4. *ICL 1900 Series COBOL Technical Manual*, International Computers Ltd., 4427, 1976.

5. *Microsoft COBOL Reference Manual*, Microsoft Corporation, 1984.

6. *NCR VRX COBOL Students Text*, NCR, 1978.

7. *NOS/VE COBOL Reference Manual*, Control Data Corporation, 1987.

Appendix B

RESERVED WORD LIST

The following is a list of COBOL reserved words. The list contains all
reserved words of American National Standard COBOL, 1974 (COBOL-74).
Additional reserved words introduced in COBOL-85 are also included in the
list. Each of these COBOL-85 reserved words is preceded by a plus sign
(+). A question mark (?) preceding a word indicates that the word is
treated an additional reserved word in one or more of the compilers
considered here (B-6700, ICL-1900, DEC-10, MS-COBOL). The plus sign or
the question mark is used as an indicator and is not a part of the reserved
word.

?ABORT-TRANSACTION	?APPLY	BOTTOM
?ABOUT	?ARCTAN	BY
?ABS	ARE	?BZ
ACCEPT	AREA	
ACCESS	AREAS	CALL
?ACTIVE-TIME	?AS	CANCEL
?ACTUAL	ASCENDING	?CARD-PUNCH
ADD	?ASCII	?CARD-READER
?ADDRESS	ASSIGN	?CARD-READERS
ADVANCING	AT	?CASSETTE
AFTER	?ATTACH	?CASSETTES
ALL	AUTHOR	?CAUSE
?ALLOW	?AUTO-SKIP	CD
?ALLOWING	?AUXILIARY	CF
+ALPHABET	?AWAIT	CH
ALPHABETIC		?CHANGE
+ALPHABETIC-LOWER	?BACKUP	?CHANNEL
+ALPHABETIC-UPPER	?BEEP	?CHANNEL-n (n=1 to 7)
+ALPHANUMERIC	BEFORE	CHARACTER
+ALPHANUMERIC-EDITED	?BEGIN-TRANSACTION	CHARACTERS
ALSO	?BINARY	?CHECK
ALTER	?BIT-nn (nn=00 to 23)	?CHECKPOINT
ALTERNATE	?BITS	?CHEQUE
AND	BLANK	?CLASS
+ANY	BLOCK	?CLEAR
		CLOCK-UNITS

CLOSE
?CMP
?CMP-1
COBOL
CODE
CODE-SET
?COL
COLLATING
COLUMN
COMMA
?COMMON
COMMUNICATION
COMP
?COMP-0
?COMP-1
?COMP-2
?COMP-3
?COMP-4
?COMP-5
?COMPILE
?COMPILETIME
COMPUTATIONAL
?COMPUTATIONAL-0
?COMPUTATIONAL-1
?COMPUTATIONAL-2
?COMPUTATIONAL-3
?COMPUTATIONAL-4
?COMPUTATIONAL-5
COMPUTE
CONFIGURATION
?CONSOLE
?CONSTANT
CONTAINS
+CONTENT
+CONTINUE
CONTROL
?CONTROL-POINT
CONTROLS
+CONVERSION
+CONVERTING
COPY
?CORE-EDS
?CORE-MT
CORR
CORRESPONDING
?COS
COUNT
?CP

?CREATE
?CRUNCH
CURRENCY
?CURRENT
?CURRENT-DATE
?CYLINDER

DATA
?DATA-BASE
?DATA-BASE-KEY
?DATA-BASE-RESTART
DATE
DATE-COMPILED
DATE-WRITTEN
DAY
+DAY-OF-WEEK
?DB
?DB-KEY
DE
?DEALLOCATE
DEBUG-CONTENTS
DEBUG-ITEM
+DEBUG-LENGTH
DEBUG-LINE
DEBUG-NAME
+DEBUG-NUMERIC CONTENTS
+DEBUG-SIZE
+DEBUG-START
+DEBUG-SUB
DEBUG-SUB-1
DEBUG-SUB-2
DEBUG-SUB-3
+DEBUG-SUB-ITEM
+DEBUG-SUB-N
+DEBUG-SUB-NUM
DEBUGGING
?DEC
DECIMAL-POINT
DECLARATIVES
?DECSYSTEM-10
?DECSYSTEM-20
?DECSYSTEM-30
?DEFERRED
DELETE
DELIMITED
DELIMITER
?DENSITY

DEPENDING
?DEPTH
DESCENDING
DESTINATION
?DETACH
DETAIL
?DIGITS
?DIRECT
DISABLE
?DISALLOW
?DISC
?DISK
?DISKPACK
?DISKPACKS
DISPLAY
?DISPLAY-1
?DISPLAY-2
?DISPLAY-3
?DISPLAY-4
?DISPLAY-5
?DISPLAY-6
?DISPLAY-7
?DISPLAY-9
?DISPLAY-UNIT
?DIV
DIVIDE
?DIVIDED
DIVISION
DOWN
?DUMP
?DUP
?DUPLICATE
DUPLICATES
DYNAMIC

?ECHO
?EDS
?EDS-*
EGI
ELSE
EMI
?EMPTY
ENABLE
END
+END-ADD
+END-CALL
+END-COMPUTE

+END-DELETE
+END-DIVIDE
+END-EVALUATE
+END-IF
+END-MULTIPLY
END-OF-PAGE
+END-PERFORM
+END-READ
+END-RECEIVE
+END-RETURN
+END-REWRITE
+END-SEARCH
+END-START
+END-STRING
+END-SUBTRACT
?END-TRANSACTION
+END-UNSTRING
+END-WRITE
?ENDING
ENTER
?ENTRY
ENVIRONMENT
EOP
?EPI
EQUAL
?EQUALS
?ERASE
ERROR
ESI
+EVALUATE
?EVEN
?EVENT
EVERY
?EXAMINE
?EXCEEDS
EXCEPTION
?EXCHANGE
?EXCL
?EXCLUSIVE
?EXECUTE
?EXHIBIT
EXIT
?EXP
?EXPONENTIATED
EXTEND
+EXTERNAL

+FALSE

FD
?FDS
?FDS-*
FILE
FILE-CONTROL
?FILE-ID
?FILE-LIMIT
?FILE-LIMITS
?FILE-MESSAGES
?FILE-STATUS
FILLER
FINAL
?FIND
FIRST
?FIRST-LEVEL
?FIRSTONE
?FLOAT
FOOTING
FOR
?FORTRAN
?FORTRAN-IV
?FREE
?FREED
FROM

GENERATE
?GENERATION-NO
?GET
GIVING
+GLOBAL
GO
?GOBACK
GREATER
GROUP

?HANDY-KEYS
HEADING
?HERE
HIGH-VALUE
HIGH-VALUES

I-O
I-O-CONTROL
?ID
IDENTIFICATION
IF
IN
INDEX
?INDEX-BUFFER

INDEXED
INDICATE
INITIAL
+INITIALIZE
INITIATE
INPUT
INPUT-OUTPUT
?INQUIRY
?INSERT
INSPECT
INSTALLATION
?INTERCHANGE
?INTERRUPT
INTO
INVALID
?INVOKE
IS

?JOURNAL
JUST
JUSTIFIED

KEY
?KEYBOARD
?KEYS
LABEL
LAST
?LD
LEADING
?LEAVING
LEFT
?LEFT-JUSTIFY
LENGTH
?LENGTH-CHECK
LESS
?LIBRARY
?LIKE
LIMIT
LIMITS
?LIN
LINAGE
LINAGE-COUNTER
LINE
LINE-COUNTER
LINES
LINKAGE
?LN
?LOCAL
?LOCAL-STORAGE

?LOCATION
 LOCK
?LOCKED
 LOW-VALUE
 LOW-VALUES
?LOWER-BOUND
?LOWER-BOUNDS

?MACRO
?MAX
?MCF
?MCF-*
?MEMBER
 MEMORY
 MERGE
 MESSAGE
?MESSAGE-PRINTER
?MIN
?MOD
 MODE
?MODIFIED
?MODIFY
 MODULES
?MONITOR
 MOVE
 MULTIPLE
?MULTIPLE-I-O
?MULTIPLIED
 MULTIPLY
?MYSELF

 NATIVE
 NEGATIVE
 NEXT
 NO
?NOMINAL
?NON-STANDARD
?NONE
 NOT
?NOTE
?NULL
 NUMBER
 NUMERIC
+NUMERIC-EDITED

 OBJECT-COMPUTER
?OBJECT-PROGRAM
?OC
 OCCURS

?ODD
 OF
 OFF
 OMITTED
 ON
?ONES
?ONLY
 OPEN
?OPT
 OPTIONAL
 OR
+ORDER
?ORGANISATION
 ORGANIZATION
+OTHER
?OTHERS
?OTHERWISE
 OUTPUT
 OVERFLOW
?OWN
?OWNER

+PADDING
 PAGE
 PAGE-COUNTER
?PAPER-PUNCH
?PAPER-READER
?PAPER-TAPE-PUNCH
?PAPER-TAPE-READER
?PARITY
?PDP-10
 PERFORM
?PETAPE
 PF
 PH
 PIC
 PICTURE
?PLACES
 PLUS
?POINT
 POINTER
 POSITION
?POSITIONING
 POSITIVE
?PREPARED
?PRINTER
?PRINTERS
 PRINTING
?PRIOR

?PRIORITY
?PRIVACY
 PROCEDURE
 PROCEDURES
 PROCEED
?PROCESS
?PROCESSING
 PROGRAM
 PROGRAM-ID
?PROMPT
?PROT
?PROTECT
?PROTECTED
?PUNCH
+PURGE

 QUEUE
 QUOTE
 QUOTES

 RANDOM
?RANGE
 RD
 READ
?READ-REWRITE
?READ-WRITE
?READER
?READERS
?READY
 RECEIVE
?RECEIVED
 RECORD
?RECORDING
 RECORDS
?RECREATE
 REDEFINES
 REEL
?REEL-NUMBER
?REF
+REFERENCE
+REFERENCE-MODIFIER
 REFERENCES
 RELATIVE
 RELEASE
 REMAINDER
?REMARKS
?REMOTE
 REMOVAL
?REMOVE

RENAMES
+REPLACE
REPLACING
REPORT
REPORTING
REPORTS
RERUN
RESERVE
RESET
?RESTART
?RETAIN
?RETAINED
?RETR
?RETRIEVAL
RETURN
REVERSED
REWIND
REWRITE
RF
RH
RIGHT
?RIGHT-JUSTIFY
ROUNDED
RUN
?RUN-UNIT

SAME
?SAVE-FACTOR
?SCHEMA
SD
SEARCH
?SECOND-LEVEL
SECTION
SECURITY
?SEEK
SEGMENT
SEGMENT-LIMIT
SELECT
?SELECTIVE
SEND
SENTENCE
?SENTINEL-PROCESSING
SEPARATE
SEQUENCE
?SEQUENCED
SEQUENTIAL
SET
?SETS

SIGN
?SIGNED
?SIN
?SINGLE
?SIXBIT
SIZE
?SN
SORT
?SORT-*
SORT-MERGE
SOURCE
SOURCE-COMPUTER
SPACE
?SPACE-FILL
SPACES
SPECIAL-NAMES
?SPO
?SQRT
STANDARD
STANDARD-1
+STANDARD-2
?STANDARD-ASCII
START
STATUS
STOP
?STORE
STRING
SUB-QUEUE-1
SUB-QUEUE-2
SUB-QUEUE-3
?SUB-SCHEMA
SUBTRACT
SUM
?SUPERVISOR
SUPPRESS
?SUSPEND
?SWITCH
SYMBOLIC
SYNC
?SYNCHRONISED
SYNCHRONIZED
?SYSTEM
?SZ

TABLE
?TALLY
TALLYING
TAPE

?TAPE-*
?TAPE7
?TAPE9
?TAPES
TERMINAL
TERMINATE
+TEST
TEXT
THAN
+THEN
THROUGH
THRU
TIME
TIMES
TO
?TODAY
?TODAYS-DATE
TOP
?TRACE
?TRAILING-SIGN
TRAILLING
?TRANSFER-REPLY
+TRUE
TYPE
?TYPEWRITER

?UNAVAILABLE
?UNEQUAL
UNIT
?UNLOCK
UNSTRING
UNTIL
UP
?UPDATE
?UPDATES
UPON
?UPPER-BOUND
?UPPER-BOUNDS
USAGE
?USAGE-MODE
USE
?USER-NUMBER
?USER-SENTINEL
USING

?VA
VALUE
VALUES

VARYING
?VERB

?WAIT
WHEN

WITH
?WITHIN
WORDS
WORKING-STORAGE
WRITE

ZERO
?ZERO-FILL
ZEROES
ZEROS

Appendix C

DATA DIVISION FORMATS

Features of DATA DIVISION have been described in the various chapters of this book. As such there was no scope to include the general format of DATA DIVISION within the text. The COBOL-74 general format (except Communication Section which is not discussed in this book) is shown below. Additional clauses introduced in COBOL-85 have also been included. These appear in boldface characters.

General Format for DATA DIVISION:

```
DATA DIVISION.
[ FILE SECTION.
[ FD  file-name  [ IS EXTERNAL ]  [ IS GLOBAL ]
    ┌                                              ⎧ RECORDS    ⎫ ┐
    │ ; BLOCK CONTAINS [ integer-1 TO ] integer-2  ⎨            ⎬ │
    └                                              ⎩ CHARACTERS ⎭ ┘

    ┌             ⎧ IS VARYING IN SIZE [[ FROM integer-3 ] [ TO integer-4]  ⎫ ┐
    │             ⎪ CHARACTERS ] [ DEPENDING ON data-name-1 ]               ⎪ │
    │ ; RECORD    ⎨                                                          ⎬ │
    │             ⎪                                                          ⎪ │
    └             ⎩ CONTAINS [ integer-5 TO ] integer-6 CHARACTERS          ⎭ ┘

    ┌          ⎧ RECORD IS   ⎫ ⎧ STANDARD ⎫ ┐
    │ ; LABEL  ⎨             ⎬ ⎨          ⎬ │
    └          ⎩ RECORDS ARE ⎭ ⎩ OMITTED  ⎭ ┘

    ┌                                         ⎧ data-name-2 ⎫ ┐
    │ ; VALUE OF implementor-name-1   IS      ⎨             ⎬ │
    └                                         ⎩ literal-1   ⎭ ┘

        ┌                               ⎧ data-name-3 ⎫ ┐
        │ , implementor-name-2 IS       ⎨             ⎬ │   ...
        └                               ⎩ literal-2   ⎭ ┘
```

```
[ ; DATA { RECORD IS    } data-name-4  [ , data-name-5 ] ... ]
         { RECORDS ARE  }

[ ; LINAGE IS { data-name-6 } LINES [ , WITH FOOTING AT { data-name-7 } ] ]
              { integer-7   }                           { integer-8  }

[ , LINES AT TOP { data-name-8 }  , LINES AT BOTTOM { data-name-9  } ]
                 { integer-9  }                     { integer-10 }
```

[; CODE-SET IS alphabet-name]

```
[ ; { REPORT  IS  } report-name-1  [ , report-name-2 ] ... ]
    { REPORTS ARE }
```

[record-description-entry] ...] ...

```
[ SD  file-name

  [             { IS VARYING IN SIZE [ [ FROM integer-1 ] [ TO integer-2 ]  } ]
  [ ; RECORD    {    CHARACTERS ] [ DEPENDING ON data-name-1 ]               } ]
  [             { CONTAINS [ integer-3 TO ] integer-4 CHARACTERS             } ]

  [ ; DATA { RECORD  IS  } data-name-2  [ , data-name-3 ] ... ]
           { RECORDS ARE }
```

{ record-description-entry } ...] ...

[WORKING-STORAGE SECTION.

```
[ 77-level-description-entry  ]  ... ]
[ record-description-entry    ]
```

[LINKAGE SECTION.

```
[ 77-level-description-entry  ]  ... ]
[ record-description-entry    ]
```

[REPORT SECTION.

[RD report-name [IS GLOBAL]

    [; CODE literal-1]

$$\left[\; ; \left\{ \begin{array}{l} \underline{\text{CONTROL}} \text{ IS} \\ \underline{\text{CONTROLS}} \text{ ARE} \end{array} \right\} \left\{ \begin{array}{l} \text{data-name-1} \quad [\; , \; \text{data-name-2} \;] \; ... \\ \underline{\text{FINAL}} \quad [\; , \; \text{data-name-1} \;] \; ... \end{array} \right\} \right]$$

$$\left[\; , \; \underline{\text{PAGE}} \left[\begin{array}{l} \text{LIMIT IS} \\ \text{LIMITS ARE} \end{array} \right] \text{integer-1} \left[\begin{array}{l} \text{LINE} \\ \text{LINES} \end{array} \right] [\; , \; \underline{\text{HEADING}} \text{ integer-2}] \right.$$

$$[\; , \; \underline{\text{FIRST}} \; \underline{\text{DETAIL}} \text{ integer-3}] \quad [\; , \; \underline{\text{LAST}} \; \underline{\text{DETAIL}} \text{ integer-4}]$$

$$\left. [\; , \; \underline{\text{FOOTING}} \text{ integer-5}] \right]$$

$$\{ \text{ report-group-description-entry } \} \; ... \;] \; ... \;]$$

DATA DIVISION

General Format for Data Description Entry

FORMAT-1:

$$\text{level-number} \left[\left\{ \begin{array}{l} \text{data-name-1} \\ \underline{\text{FILLER}} \end{array} \right\} \right]$$

$$[\; ; \; \underline{\text{REDEFINES}} \text{ data-name-2}] \; [\text{ IS } \underline{\text{EXTERNAL}}] \; [\text{ IS } \underline{\text{GLOBAL}}]$$

$$\left[\; ; \left\{ \begin{array}{l} \underline{\text{PICTURE}} \\ \underline{\text{PIC}} \end{array} \right\} \text{ IS character-string} \right]$$

$$\left[\; ; \; \underline{\text{USAGE}} \text{ IS} \left\{ \begin{array}{l} \underline{\text{BINARY}} \\ \underline{\text{COMPUTATIONAL}} \\ \underline{\text{COMP}} \\ \underline{\text{DISPLAY}} \\ \underline{\text{INDEX}} \\ \textbf{PACKED-DECIMAL} \end{array} \right\} \right]$$

$$\left[\; ; \; \underline{\text{SIGN}} \text{ IS} \left\{ \begin{array}{l} \underline{\text{LEADING}} \\ \underline{\text{TRAILING}} \end{array} \right\} [\; \underline{\text{SEPARATE}} \text{ CHARACTER}] \right]$$

$$[\; ; \; \underline{\text{OCCURS}}$$

$$\left\{ \begin{array}{l} \text{integer-1 TIMES} \\ \text{integer-1 } \underline{\text{TO}} \text{ integer-2 TIMES } \underline{\text{DEPENDING}} \text{ ON data-name-3} \end{array} \right\}$$

$$\left[\left\{\begin{array}{l}\underline{ASCENDING}\\ \underline{DESCENDING}\end{array}\right\} \quad \underline{KEY} \quad IS \quad data\text{-}name\text{-}4 \quad [\ ,\ data\text{-}name\text{-}5\ ] \ \ldots \right] \ \ldots$$

$$[\ \underline{INDEXED}\ BY\ index\text{-}name\text{-}1\ [\ ,\ index\text{-}name\text{-}2\ ]\ \ldots\ ]\ ]$$

$$\left[\ ;\ \left\{\begin{array}{l}\underline{SYNCHRONIZED}\\ \underline{SYNC}\end{array}\right\} \quad \left[\begin{array}{l}\underline{LEFT}\\ \underline{RIGHT}\end{array}\right]\ \right]\ ]$$

$$\left[\ ;\ \left\{\begin{array}{l}\underline{JUSTIFIED}\\ \underline{JUST}\end{array}\right\} \quad \underline{RIGHT}\ \right]$$

[; $\underline{BLANK}$ WHEN $\underline{ZERO}$]

[; $\underline{VALUE}$ IS literal] .

FORMAT 2:

66 data-name-1 $\underline{RENAMES}$ data-name-2 $\left[\left\{\begin{array}{l}\underline{THROUGH}\\ \underline{THRU}\end{array}\right\} \quad data\text{-}name\text{-}3\right]$

FORMAT 3:

88 condition-name; $\left\{\begin{array}{l}\underline{VALUE}\ IS\\ \underline{VALUES}\ ARE\end{array}\right\}$ literal-1 $\left[\left\{\begin{array}{l}\underline{THROUGH}\\ \underline{THRU}\end{array}\right\}literal1\text{-}2\right]$

[, literal-3 $\left[\left\{\begin{array}{l}\underline{THROUGH}\\ \underline{THRU}\end{array}\right\} \quad literal\text{-}4\right]$ ...]

General Format for Report Group Entry

This is given in Sec. 18.5.

Appendix D

COBOL-85 FORMATS FOR PERFORM VERB

The PERFORM verb has been substantially enhanced in COBOL-85. These
enhancements are fully explained in Chapter 22 considering the general
format for PERFORM with UNTIL option as a typical case. For the sake of
completeness all general formats of the PERFORM verb are given below.

FORMAT 1:

PERFORM [procedure-name-1 [{ THROUGH / THRU } procedure-name-2]]

    [imperative-statement-1 END-PERFORM]

FORMAT 2:

PERFORM [procedure-name-1 [{ THROUGH / THRU } procedure-name-2]]

{ identifier-1 / integer-1 } TIMES [imperative-statement-1 END-PERFORM]

FORMAT 3:

PERFORM [procedure-name-1 [{ THROUGH / THRU } procedure-name-2]]

[WITH TEST { BEFORE / AFTER }] UNTIL condition-1

[imperative-statement-1 END-PERFORM]

FORMAT 4:

```
PERFORM  [ procedure-name-1  [ { THROUGH }      procedure-name-2 ] ]
                               { THRU    }

         [ WITH  TEST  { BEFORE } ]
                       { AFTER  }

           VARYING  { identifier-1 }      FROM   { identifier-2 }
                    { index-name-1 }             { index-name-2 }
                                                 { literal-1    }

              BY  { identifer-3 }     UNTIL   condition
                  { literal-2  }

         [ AFTER  { identifier-4 }      FROM   { identifier-5 }
                  { index-name-3 }             { index-name-4 }
                                               { literal-3    }

              BY  { identifier-6 }    UNTIL   condition-2 ]  ...
                  { literal-4   }

         [ imperative-statement-1  END-PERFORM ]
```

INDEX

496   COBOL programming